To the Battles of
Franklin and Nashville
and Beyond

To the Battles of Franklin and Nashville and Beyond

Stabilization and Reconstruction in Tennessee and Kentucky, 1864–1866

Benjamin Franklin Cooling

The University of Tennessee Press / Knoxville

Copyright © 2011 by The University of Tennessee Press / Knoxville.
All Rights Reserved. Manufactured in the United States of America.
Cloth: 1st printing, 2011.
Paper: 1st printing, 2024.

Published in cooperation with the Tennessee Civil War National Heritage
Area, which is a partnership of the National Park Service.

Library of Congress Cataloging-in-Publication Data

Cooling, B. Franklin.
To the battles of Franklin and Nashville and beyond: stabilization and re-
construction in Tennessee and Kentucky, 1864–1866 / Benjamin Franklin
Cooling. — 1st ed.
    p. cm.
Includes bibliographical references and index.
ISBN-13: 978-1-57233-751-0 (hardcover)
ISBN-10: 1-57233-751-6 (hardcover)

1. Tennessee—History—Civil War, 1861–1865—Campaigns.
2. Kentucky—History—Civil War, 1861–1865—Campaigns.
3. United States—History—Civil War, 1861-1865—Campaigns.
4. Franklin, Battle of, Franklin, Tenn., 1864.
5. Nashville, Battle of, Nashville, Tenn., 1864.
I. Title.

E470.5.C83 2011
976.8'63—dc22
2011001890

In Memory of
David Monroe Beers
(1934–1986)

We "soldiered" together
at Fort Jackson, South Carolina,
Spring/Summer 1957

Contents

Illustrations

Figures

Maps

Preface

On July 21, 1862, a year to the day after the disastrous battle of First Bull Run, Rutland, Vermont, quarry owner and operator William Young Ripley prophetically wrote to his son serving with the First Vermont Volunteers in the eastern Union army. "This war is a war of the *people*," said the elder Ripley, "and the men at Washington—will find that they are only agents of the matter—if they go ahead and lead, with vigor, the people will follow & support them." But if they falter, he declared, then another Cromwell or Napoleon would appear "and tell them to make room for more competent men." Two years later, many people, both North and South, reckoned that they each had a homegrown tyrant on their hands—either Abraham Lincoln or Jefferson Davis. Both presidents led their causes vigorously, but the people on both sides were war weary, those in Tennessee and Kentucky especially so.[1]

The upper heartland of the river valleys—Ohio, Tennessee, Cumberland, and Mississippi—remained in disarray by the third year of war. This could be seen when Colonel Benjamin Harrison of the Seventieth Indiana (and a future U.S. president) went home on leave to campaign for President Abraham Lincoln's reelection. The Hoosier warrior thought that "after witnessing the scenes of desolation and decay in the track of a great army, the sight of the busy streets and peaceful residences of Indianapolis was like a gleam of paradise." But that had not been the case for his passage northward from the war zone. In fact, he found unsettled conditions all the way from north Georgia to the Ohio River. Even steamboat passage on that stream proved risky. It was common, attested Colonel W. T. Richie, purveyor of army supplies and one of Harrison's fellow passengers, "for guerillas to lie in wait in convenient ambuscades along the river for the purpose of killing what people they could in the boats, and at various times . . . to capture and destroy

. . . vessels." Harrison experienced such an encounter on his trip home. Apparently, he responded like a true combat veteran. Still, the incident signified an untamed twilight zone stretching behind the contending armies. This zone of the interior, as the military later defined it, was neither pacified nor reconstructed. It embraced both occupied and only nominally loyal Tennessee and Kentucky.[2]

The war was really no closer to conclusion by 1864 than it had been at the moment of Ripley's letter. Grand strategies of both sides always remained works in progress, with Tennessee and Kentucky often at the cusp of that work. Moreover, these upper South states served as laboratories for evolving such work. The Confederacy stood with its back increasingly to the wall, to be sure. But the Union faced an unfinished task—with a national election year impending. Survival, the fundamental principal of the nation, had not been assured. Military offensives and counteroffensives had not achieved final victory. Part of the story involved the great contest for Atlanta. But matching this in intensity and immensity were the "book-end" sagas in the heartland—James Longstreet's operation to redeem East Tennessee at the beginning and Sam Hood's tragic last hurrah to liberate Middle Tennessee and perhaps Kentucky at the end. Moreover, cavalry raids against enemy logistical systems supporting those armies seemed incessant and achieved only marginal or short-term gains while providing collateral damage to civilian infrastructure.[3]

Equally destabilizing were the ever-present shadow warriors—term them insurgents, partisans, guerrillas, or freedom fighters. Under the Confederate Partisan Ranger Act of 1862, these warriors supposedly functioned (1) in organizations assigned to specified territory and (2) as irregular or independent soldiers operating under a designated leader and unit. When the latter elements were lost, raids failed and unit cohesion disappeared. In the words of veteran general Theodore Ayrault Dodge, "War is supposed to be conducted only by organized bodies of troops under recognized leaders, for organization alone can control the actions of the individual soldiers." Such was not the case, as by 1864 lawlessness took over vast portions of the countryside, while the tyranny of Federal occupation supervised cities and towns. Such tyranny, in truth, traversed the spectrum from acquiescence to summary execution and often defied the newly codified rules set out by Francis Lieber, Columbia College professor and adviser to the Lincoln War Department.[4]

War weariness, civil dissidence, economic and political upheaval, and most certainly sociocultural revolution unsettled the upper heartland and signified redirection of the conflict for both North and South. Events there influenced the larger scope of the war yet remained remote and detached from policy makers in both Washington and Richmond. "We were where the waves advanced and retreated," recalled Clarksville, Tennessee, lawyer Joseph B. Killebrew, "overlapped first by one side and then the other, after each change we had to govern ourselves accordingly." So, in the heartland lay the success or failure of the sequence— secession, war stabilization, reconstruction—leading to either reunion or disunion. This story of the final year and a half of conflict and first throes of reconstruction and national unification may not have been appreciated at the time. But events of our own time shape our view of history.[5]

Had this book been completed before the millennium, it would have focused more traditionally upon the final stages of the Civil War in the upper heartland. John Bell Hood's last Confederate hurrah—the counteroffensive of 1864—would have overwhelmed the story as part of such traditional military history. The pattern of my two previous volumes, war in the context of armies, battles, and commanders, would have seen a sequel to the opening events of Forts Henry and Donelson (*Forts Henry and Donelson: The Key to the Confederate Heartland*) and interim contests and tribulations for war and society (*Fort Donelson's Legacy: War and Society in Kentucky and Tennessee, 1862–1863*) before turning to the culminating and conclusive episodes at Franklin and Nashville. A more opaque backdrop would have portrayed the unsettled continuation of raids and partisan warfare upon the people.

National security experts early in the twenty-first century have introduced a new term that fairly begs for historical perspectives. In "hybrid" or "compound war," as they term it, catastrophic terrorism and disruptive lawlessness mix with traditional combat and irregular operations to form a new kind of warfare. Today's military interventionism as witnessed in Iraq and Afghanistan further illustrates an integration theme of counterinsurgency, stabilization, reconstruction, and nation-building, further laying claim for historical analysis. Perhaps just as policymakers and practitioners need to study and apply history, however, Civil War historians should better prepare them by a more holistic explanation of causation, conflict, stabilization, reconstruction, and reconciliation. It is in this context that the present volume seeks to explain ending the Civil War in the upper heartland.[6]

Key to the Heartland introduced the capture of Forts Henry and Donelson as opening the upper South to Federal invasion, occupation, and Reconstruction but not as ending the conflict. Even one of the primary lessons, that of joint army-navy cooperation on the inland rivers, could not quickly accomplish the Union's anaconda strategy. Perhaps even geography—that of long distances causing slow travel—had its role despite the use of steam-motive technology on land and water. However, rapid and large-scale exploitation leading to possible war termination lay beyond Union capabilities at this point. The Confederacy would try to recover, to counterattack with an unceasing goal of placing its northern frontier on the Ohio River. The war continued from victory to defeat, from combat to occupation, stabilization, and pacification, and ultimately to widening Union occupation, early Reconstruction, and the attempted restoration of national authority. Still peace did not return. The unfinished quest to reopen the Mississippi Valley and the great rail access to Chattanooga and Atlanta etched new names like Shiloh and Corinth, Perryville and Stones River, Tullahoma and Chickamauga and Chattanooga on unfurled banners before the Great River flowed unvexed to the sea by mid-1863—covered in my second volume, *Fort Donelson's Legacy*. General Grant and his team were part of that continuing story's second phase, as were Bedford Forrest and other veterans of the Henry-Donelson affair.

The *Legacy* volume introduced additional themes to the midwar story in the upper heartland. It focused on the relationship of war and society. That unhappy relationship included military occupation and the substitution of military government for civil rule in Tennessee. Loyalty oaths, persecution and intimidation, the formation of both Union and Confederate fighting units in both Kentucky and Tennessee ensued. Instability and discomfort for civilians and the distinctive rise of partisan warfare alongside periodic invasions and cavalry raids formed a pattern. By the close of 1863, the war had ended only for the dead, the dying, and the cheerless living, of whom there were many all over Tennessee and Kentucky. Resolution of the issues causing the war in the first place and arising from its passage lay in the future. Which leads to the present and culminating part of the story, told in *To the Battles of Franklin and Nashville, and Beyond*.

Two years after Henry-Donelson, the great crusade for either Confederate independence or Union survival led to the dark and bloody but hallowed ground of Franklin and then Nashville. This final lurch of Confederate counterhopes for nation building was matched in a way by final Union redemption of East Tennessee earlier in 1864 as well as a final solution to the occupancy problem for the rest of the region. Rebel cavalry raids as well as Union counter-operations preceded these final climatic wartime moments. Inside the calendar of events lay relent-less brutality and bloodshed at military and civilian levels. Guerrillaism, license to plunder and persecute, and harsh war and punitive Recon-struction policies mixed boisterously and relentlessly in Volunteer and Bluegrass history in that time frame. Opposition to national dictates hounded a unionist government in both states. Moreover, Black Flag warfare, summary executions of combatants and noncombatants alike, and blatant banditry became the norm, defying the historiography that places such conflict mainly west of the Mississippi in Missouri and Kan-sas. Fort Pillow symbolized far more about the war's harsh turning than anything Forrest, Wheeler, or Morgan accomplished as regular Con-federate wizards of the saddle. In that sense, Franklin and Nashville hardly put an end to the uncivil Civil War in the heartland. The pivotal, concluding period from 1864 to 1865 provided only the beginning of a transition from war to peace and Reconstruction.

An apocryphal, surely facetious vignette on the front page of the April 21, 1865, edition of the *83rd Illinoisan* published in Clarksville, Tennessee, provided an appropriate, lighter touchstone. Purporting to be a letter "captured among the effects of Hood's army [after the di-sastrous fall campaign], so the story goes," and having "a good deal of music" therein, thought the editors, a Nashville belle named "Marie" wrote to her brother "Tom" in the rebel army on January 29, 1865. Each succeeding paragraph told Tom how "you will be astonished to hear that your friends of the female denomination are dropping off ev-ery day" to the blandishments of young Yankee officers. First, "Mollie, the unconquerable, who used to parade that large Beauregard breast-pin, and who used to sing *'Maryland my Maryland'* with so much pa-thos," was married four months before to "a Federal with but one bar on his shoulder." Then there was Sallie, "who used to sleep with the *'Bonnie Blue Flag'* under her pillows, who looked daggers and pistols at the invaders, who would not speak to her schoolmates . . . because they received and treated Federal officers with due politeness, she too is gone—yes, married to a Federal officer with two bars!" And, alas, poor Tom, even his old sweetheart Anna, "the one whom you dedicated your sweet verses, and whose melodious voice so often mingled with yours in days of yore," who had defied Yankee generals and whole army corps, who had been sent across the lines to the South and then North in exile, "she too has hauled down the stars and bars, and is about to surrender at discretion." Passing her house "the other night with a gentleman, who protects us during your absence," to ascertain "the state of her political sentiments from her musical programme," Marie had "heard very distinctly the words of *'Rally Round the Flag'* and the *'Union Forever.'"*[7]

So Marie advised her brother to come home and "look to your interests in that quarter" and "tell the boys down in Dixie, if they do not return soon they will not find a single girl or widow below 'conscript age' in these parts," as "marry who you can" seemed to be the watchword. Her principles had not changed, Marie proclaimed, and despite having a captain boarding with her family *"merely* by way of protection," who sometimes cast a sly glance at her during dinner, "I am as true to the South as ever." At this point in her letter, Marie began adding postscripts. First, she asked Tom if he thought it "would be a violation of my Southern principles to take an occasional ride, for my health, with the Captain." He had such a nice horse and buggy. Then, in a second addition to the letter, she noted "that impertinent fellow actually squeezed my hand as he helped me out of the buggy this evening" after a delightful ride. She wanted Tom to come home and protect her, "as I don't like to live this way much longer." Her third postscript sounded more resolute: "If ever I should marry a Yankee (but you know my principles too well for that) I would do it merely as the humble instrument to avenge the wrongs of my poor oppressed country." Little peace should said Yankee husband find day or night, thorns should be planted in his couch, "his dreams should be of Holofernous [one of Nebuchadnezzar's generals who led an Assyrian army against Israel and was beheaded in his sleep by Judith], and my dry goods bill as long as the Internal Revenue Law."

Finally, fair Marie could not help but end her missive with "P.S. IV": "Come home brother Tom, and take the amnesty oath for two months or thereabout." She then let him in on a secret. "On due consideration I have come to the determination to make a martyr of myself!" Yes, brother Tom, she wrote, "I am going to marry the captain on patriotic principles."

The ten chapters plus postscript of *To the Battles of Franklin and Nashville, and Beyond* carry the story from Forts Henry and Donelson's wartime legacy to the upper heartland's final rite of passage from war to peace. "Marie" and "Tom" were there in numbers, as were Grant and Forrest, but so were new characters from governors to generals, bandits, and civilians, as well as men in the ranks. Perhaps their story did not end even then. They themselves suggest the need for perhaps a fourth volume treating reconstruction and reconciliation—a story that continues to trouble America today. In that case, the three volumes themselves merely provide a beginning.

Acknowledgments

I am indebted to the following: Stuart Cruikshank of Nashville, Tennessee; Lon Carter Barton, Mayfield, Kentucky; William C. Laybourn, Grand Junction, Colorado; Edward Gleeson, Oak Lawn, Illinois; Skip Doscher, Brentwood, Tennessee; Maj. Arthur Edinger, USMC (Ret.), Shelbyville, Kentucky; Jim Jobe and Susan Hawkins, Fort Donelson National Military Park, Dover, Tennessee; Hunter Whitesell, South Fulton, Tennessee; Hunter Haycock, Buchanan, Tennessee; Ursula Beach, Clarksville, Tennessee; Walter T. Durham, Gallatin, Tennessee; and Richard P. Gildrie, Austin Peay State University, Clarksville, Tennessee. I also wish to thank the archival staffs at Duke University; University of North Carolina, Chapel Hill; University of Tennessee, Knoxville; the Huntington Library; the State Historical Society of Iowa; Murray State University; Western Kentucky University; Kentucky Historical Society; the Filson Club; the Clarksville-Montgomery County Museum (Tennessee); and the Indiana Historical Society. University of Tennessee Press director Scot Danforth and his editors, Gene Adair, Thomas Wells, and Karin Kaufman, have been wonderful to work with on this volume. Bill Nelson and Steve Stanley provided superb maps.

CHAPTER 1

~~~

The Henry-Donelson Legacy

The news struck southerners in different ways. Young Lexington, Kentucky, unionist Frances Peters recorded in her diary for February 18, 1862, that a forty-gun salute was fired that evening upon word that Nashville had been taken. It was as simple as that. Eighteen-year-old Gallatin, Tennessee, resident Laura Williams wrote her brother (serving with the Second Tennessee in Virginia) how after "our defeat at Fort Donelson everybody seems deranged" while "huddled around the streets looking every minute for [the Yankees] to come" to her little Middle Tennessee town. South Carolina plantation matron and widow Ada W. Bacot, volunteering her services as a nurse in a Charlottesville, Virginia, hospital, showed even more alarm in her own diary entry for Monday night, February 24. She could not believe the newspaper accounts about a surrender of twelve to thirteen thousand "of our troops to the Yankees" downriver from the Tennessee capital and hoped it would not prove true. Her superior, Dr. Edward J. Rembert, head surgeon and director of all South Carolina–sponsored hospitals there in the Piedmont, was "indignant to think that Southern men would commit such folly [and] so am I," she pronounced irritatedly. There had to have been some very good reason for the surrender or "the men would never have allowed themselves to be given up to so contemptible a foe," she decided.[1]

One thing was abundantly clear. Disaster had suddenly befallen an aspiring Confederate nation. Within a fortnight, the loss of two key river forts in northwestern Tennessee—Forts Henry and Donelson—had imperiled the experiment. The dramatic army-navy victory of Brigadier

General Ulysses S. Grant and Flag Officer Andrew Hull Foote shattered the rebel defense line in the West. A corps-sized force of prime fighting men plus their arms and equipment, artillery, and supplies fell into Union hands. The supreme Confederate commander in the theater, General Albert Sidney Johnston, hastily withdrew his main army from forward positions in southern Kentucky at Bowling Green and Columbus on the Mississippi River. Soon he had evacuated most of the state of Tennessee west of the Cumberland Plateau in a move that proved disastrous to the spirits of southern patriots everywhere. At one blow, the North had seemingly eliminated both the Bluegrass State and Volunteer State from rebel control. With the fall of the twin rivers forts, Union gunboats could range all the way up the Tennessee River to Muscle Shoals, Alabama—and did so in the weeks following the victory. Similarly, the path lay open on the Cumberland River to Nashville and the fertile Middle Tennessee breadbasket, also exploited in the weeks ahead by both the army and navy. Vital ironworks and rolling mills were lost to the Confederate war effort. Precious croplands and breeding grounds for invaluable horses and mules, as well as transportation arteries, were snatched from rebel hands. Most especially, after nearly a year of stinging rebuffs in the East, Federal armies had achieved their first singular victories and gained a rising new hero in Ulysses S. Grant.[2]

Confusion reigned at first in the wake of Confederate retreat. The sister and brother-in-law of Confederate congressman James McCallum wrote him on March 19, 1862, "Our country is in such a condition that we know not what calculations to make for any future time, but we would fair hope that things may take a favourable turn." They were most worried about their sons, who had surrendered and now appeared in a Yankee prison camp where "they are in a very cold climate and not only among strangers, but enemies, and God only knows what their fate is to be. They are in the hands of God and we must trust his providence for their protection." Diarist Louisa Brown Pearl, wife of Nashville's first school superintendent (who had exiled himself to the North with three of their children (a fourth serving with the Confederate First Tennessee at Cumberland Gap), recorded the perplexity. "It is supposed that Fort Donelson has fallen," she wrote from Nashville, where she had remained to protect their house and property and to provide solace to that fourth son. Later, "we learn that it is not so, but that a terrible battle is still raging," followed by "conflicting reports make me undecided what to do." "I will stay where I am," she concluded finally, "if the army make no resistance." And no resistance had resulted when

Johnston surprised everyone by quickly transiting the city en route to rallying points in northern Alabama and Mississippi. George Eagleton of the Forty-Fourth Tennessee "shed many a tear for our unfortunate soldiers, for our Country, our families, and our homes!" "Everywhere we are whipped," he declared dejectedly, as "the people through the country seemed to be in a great panic." Nashvillians would style this the "Great Panic," fleeing their cherished "Athens of the South" in every conveyance that might be begged, borrowed, or seized.[3]

"Every nerve must be strained to sustain ourselves as the Cause is ruined," bemoaned Alabama state legislator and planter Augustus Benners from his rural hamlet of Greensboro. Indeed, Nashville's loss was more than merely psychological. The city, with its seventeen thousand prewar population, provided the region's political and cultural hub. It had become a major Confederate logistical base, supporting Johnston's forward positions. Quantities of munitions, food, medical supplies, and other war material had been prepared and stored here. Saving them now became as problematical as saving Johnston's army. The latter was accomplished; the former was not. Second Alabama private Hiram Talbert Holt wrote his wife from distant Fort Gaines near Mobile, Alabama, that the surrender made him feel "so sad." Tennessee cavalryman Thomas Black Wilson noted that coming so soon after the initial "terrible blow" in late January at Fishing Creek or Mill Springs in southeastern Kentucky, the loss of Forts Henry and Donelson "capped the climax of our woes." After the war, he declared, "I look on Fort Donelson as one of the most important battles of the war."[4]

On the Union side, Sergeant Major William Swanzey of the Forty-Sixth Illinois (a participant at Fort Donelson) wrote his wife from Fort Henry on March 2, "I think the war will not last long." Camp rumor held that Tennessee and Kentucky had returned to the Union. If so, he proclaimed, "I should not be much surprised if the war would be over in a few months if we gain a few more battles like the last[;] they may as well give it up." A young officer with the Twenty-third Indiana, B. F. Welker, wrote his sister from Fort Heiman (just across the Tennessee River from Fort Henry) on February 27, "I think the time not far distant when our grand army will march in solid phalanx through all the rebellious states and replant the stars and stripes over every capital from when[ce] [it] has been torn by traitor hands." Then everyone could return home to await the rebellion of the abolitionists, as there were as many members of the U.S. Congress who "entertain principles just as obnoxious to the Constitution as does old Jeff Davis or any of his crew." To Welker, and others in Union ranks, "I stand on the old land-marks of Democracy and they alone will save the Union if ever saved at all." Events would not turn out that way, however.[5]

Assessing Victory and Defeat

The North went wild with news of the victories, just as a dark cloud of foreboding passed across the sun of the Confederacy. Editors, politicians, and soldiers vied with one another in heaping praise or blame, principally upon the leaders in the Tennessee battles. It was easy to see how Grant's initials equated with the "unconditional surrender" terms that he imposed at Fort Donelson. Here might be the savior of the Union, perhaps even on his way to the White House. His colleague, Flag Officer Andrew Foote, enjoyed slightly less renown for his part in the victory, and like Grant's venerable second-in-command, fellow brigadier Charles Ferguson Smith, he would die before his time, robbing both men of the full measure of their success. But other Yankee heroes emerged from this affair—John McClernand, Lewis "Lew" Wallace, John Logan, and James Birdseye McPherson, to name a few. Even Missouri Department chief Henry Halleck (under whose overall direction the operation had succeeded), grabbed his share of fame for masterminding and managing the campaign. He would go soon to Washington as general-in-chief. Of course, at the bottom were the foot soldiers and gunboat sailors who really had effected the result.

By comparison, only blame and shame attached to the senior Confederate leadership in the West. Despite personal shielding by his friend and president, Jefferson Davis, and subsequent determination to redeem himself in battle, Sidney Johnston's reputation was forever sullied (his redemption snuffed out, perhaps, by a Federal bullet at Shiloh on April 6). Johnston at no time displayed the talent befitting Davis's early declaration that his friend was the greatest soldier then living. Yet given a very difficult assignment stretching back six long months, to mobilize, train, equip, and prepare an inadequate Confederate defense in the entire Western theater, many would contend that Johnston had prepared the best he could under the circumstances. A winter of great sickness and suffering in rebel camps in Kentucky with little (beyond moral) support from Richmond had proven frustrating to the proud soldier. Yet his only response to the Grant/Foote breakthrough at Forts Henry and Donelson had been precipitous retreat. He had not gone in person to the point of greatest danger, the twin rivers (and, in fact, he never inspected that critical weak point at any time during his entire assignment).

Johnston delegated to equally overrated subordinates the task of stopping the blue juggernaut on the rivers. They had failed miserably. He retained ultimate responsibility, of course, even while understandably trying to save surviving components of his army. The Davis administration blunted the clamor of distraught political foes and baying newspaper editors seeking Johnston's scalp. In truth, neither strategic brilliance nor keen grasp of the operational situation on the twin rivers attended Johnston's leadership. He personally shepherded a forlorn Army of Central Kentucky south through Nashville and on to Alabama and Mississippi, leaving Leonidus Polk to withdraw from the Mississippi bastion at Columbus and the hapless Fort Donelson brigadiers to get out of their predicament. Johnston hardly proved the Confederate Napoleon that many had expected. Yet what of the quintet of brigadiers in whom he had placed so much confidence—and responsibility?[6]

The trail of more immediate culpability led directly to Brigadier General Lloyd Tilghman at Fort Henry and to the unlikely quadripartite command of John B. Floyd, Gideon J. Pillow, Simon B. Buckner, and Bushrod R. Johnson at Fort Donelson. They paid the price of defeat with varying degrees of punishment. Only Kentuckians Tilghman and Buckner actually accompanied their legions to Union prison for nearly six months, thereby gaining subsequent Lost Cause peerage. Buckner had been among the faint of heart advocating capitulation at the pivotal moment on the Cumberland. Even then, neither he nor Tilghman shared the prisoner-of-war hardships of junior officers and enlisted men since they and their immediate subordinates enjoyed special favor at Fort Warren in Boston Harbor. Buckner, Tilghman, and Bushrod Johnson (the fifth, innocuous brigadier involved in events on the twin rivers who escaped capture altogether) all eventually regained command responsibilities and served honorably. Floyd and Pillow received justifiable censure and exile to backwater assignments for the duration of the war.

The Fort Warren prisoners initiated the perception that Pillow was the real cause of the fiasco, ably perpetuated by Third Tennessee major Nathan Cheairs, who personally endured the degradation of what he termed "the most disgraceful, unnecessary and uncalled for Surrender that occurred during the four years of the war." Thousands of good and true men were "the *victims* of his *utter worthlessness* as a *General*," railed Cheairs. If Pillow had been at home *tied* to his *wife's apron's strings*" instead of commanding at Fort Donelson, claimed Cheairs, "that gallant little army who fought so bravely on that bloody field, would now be in *Dixie land* instead of *Northern prisons*." Such sentiments became a litany echoing through the years until the last veteran of the experience reached his grave. But cavalryman Tom Wilson may have come closest to the simple truth when he suggested that "by a most inexcusable blunder Gens Pillow and Buckner[,] two men who hated each other and could agree on nothing and who had a most contemptible opinion of each other's military ability were sent there. There was no consent of action between them and hence the disaster."[7]

Wilson's later reflections had an additional take on the importance of Fort Donelson. He thought that the northern states had gained very little military renown during the early American Republic since successful leaders like Andrew Jackson, William Henry Harrison, and Winfield Scott had been southerners. The esprit of the southern army at the outset of the rebellion was similarly much the better of the contenders, he claimed, and the battle of First Bull Run added to the self-confidence of that army while proving the opposite to their opponents. If only Fort Donelson had perpetuated that spirit with a victory, he contended, "and it might have been done by having more men and a capable leader there," thereby going far "towards ending the war." He like others advanced that Johnston ought to have personally gone to the endangered spot with all of Polk's corps from Columbus, Kentucky (little appreciating the operational and logistical difficulties of doing so). "We were confident of gaining the battle but instead of that to have our army surrendered after it had beaten the enemy in the fighting was too bad," Wilson suggested. It was disheartening "to the last degree" and resulted in the loss of a great many men to the southern army "who left ranks to visit their homes and did not return while large numbers in Kentucky and Tennessee who would have joined us stayed at home or went against us." Ironically, one officer emerged from the ashes of enmity and disaster with promise. A lowly Tennessee cavalry commander, Nathan Bedford Forrest, would make his mark and, together with a phoenix-like rebirth of what ultimately became an "Army of Tennessee," denied Illinois Sergeant Major Swanzey's prediction of the early demise of the young Confederacy.

Few southerners realized the potential from Forrest's escape at Fort Donelson, if they even knew of it at the time. And Johnston's bedraggled evacuees offered little solace to Kentucky and Tennessee citizens left behind the retreating army. Money and food packages from home succored the rebel captives, and eventually, by late summer and fall, prisoner exchange brought most of them back to the South. At least some of these veterans re-formed their units and returned to the fighting by year's end. Others drifted home to possibly avoid further unsavory battlefield experiences or to join newly forming "partisan ranger" contingents for local protection of their neighborhoods. Historian Daniel Sutherland suggests the protean beginnings of guerrilla warfare even earlier in the upper heartland. By the end of the summer of 1862, he advances, "guerrillas had shaped the war on the border" every bit as much as they had done in the Trans-Mississippi. Then, too, both Kentucky and Tennessee witnessed the return of major fighting as the region became the cockpit of war in the Western theater. "The whole South has now waked up," as erstwhile Kentucky Confederate governor George W. Johnson had confidently predicted to his wife on February 15, the very day that gray-clad soldiery broke through Grant's encirclement at Donelson prior to surrender. The politician felt if overcoming the early defeats led to a negotiated peace, independence, and reciprocal free trade, then "our disaster will be valuable to us." The resultant Confederate resurgence did not finish the war in the West, however. The South awakened, the North hardened, and for both sides the next two years in the upper heartland meant a seesawing presence of armies eating out the countryside, periodic slaughter between those armies, and all the disquieting, unsettling conditions of a war zone fraught with cavalry raids and partisan depredations, divided citizenry, and stern military rule. Economic stagnation, military occupation, and slow political renewal paralleled a general breakdown in law and order. Peace was not just around the corner after Henry-Donelson. Rather, in modern military parlance, it became a phase in conflict resolution and stabilization, pointing toward but not effecting reconstruction.[8]

Seasons of Lost Opportunities

"My opinion was and still is," wrote Grant in his 1885 memoirs, "that immediately after the fall of Fort Donelson the way was opened to the National forces all over the South-west without much resistance." If one general, responsible for everything west of the Alleghenies, had taken the initiative, he "could have marched to Chattanooga, Corinth, Memphis and Vicksburg," and there would have been ample troops to that end, he continued. Instead, petty jealousies over the victories, timidity about over-extension and a reactive foe, plus divided theater command plagued the Union side. Speed of movement and unity of command eluded the northern cause in the West. Grant further contended that rapid movements and acquisition of rebellious territory not only would have stimulated northern volunteering but there were "tens of thousands of strong able-boded young men still at their homes in the south-western states, who had not gone into the Confederate army in February 1862 and who had no particular desire to go." He added, "If our lines had been extended to protect their homes, many of them never would have gone." Alas, he continued, Providence had ruled otherwise. The enemy gained time to collect armies and fortify new positions so that "twice afterwards," during the war, "he came near forcing his north-western front up to the Ohio River."[9]

Grant alluded to Braxton Bragg's fall campaign of 1862, as well as that of John B. Hood two years later. More importantly, he referred to the six- or seven-week period between Fort Donelson and Shiloh as having been a window for sweeping opportunities. After Shiloh, the Confederacy enacted conscription and partisan ranger legislation that opened other dimensions of southern resistance. The subsequent creeping Federal advance to the Mississippi and Alabama lines, the over-extension of Federal operational and logistical lines subject to Confederate cavalry raiders like Forrest, John Hunt Morgan, and Joseph Wheeler, and divided Union operational command secured time for the Confederacy to regroup and reconstitute its forces in the West. Shiloh, rather than Henry-Donelson, may well have set the mark in this regard with its 20 percent casualties for approximately 109,000 combatants engaged. Grant himself told a major of the Sixteenth U.S. Regular Battalion that by comparison, Fort Donelson "was as a morning dew to a heavy rain." A chap in the Second Iowa who fought in both actions felt Donelson "was completely cast in the shade by the cool courage and bull-dog obstinacy with which either side contested every inch of ground [at Shiloh]." One impressionable Alabamian transiting Corinth, Mississippi (to which Confederate casualties passed from Shiloh), wrote his wife that "look what every way you chose you saw a world of men, thousands of them wounded and groaning and dying." You could hardly stomach the place it smelled so badly, he thought. Thus Henry Holt, soon to be promoted to first sergeant, may have been "looking momentarily for the greatest battle that has been fought in modern times, a battle fought with deep interest to all the world," but neither Union nor Confederacy could abide such a slaughter-pen, however martyred the patriots who fought such a battle.[10]

Momentum slowed as both armies bound up their wounds. The great Mississippi River commercial city of Memphis fell to the Federals on June 6, 1862. The surge of Union power dissipated due to geographical distances that plagued logistics. Irresolute generalship took over and a groundswell of irregular warfare and civil resistance emerged. Federal commanders found that occupation of conquered territory required garrisons and counterguerrilla operations that siphoned resources from the main offensives. By late summer and early fall a great Confederate renaissance had advanced northward out of Mississippi and Tennessee headed for the Ohio. Alabamian Holt wrote glowingly of "great and glorious victories everywhere," with Kentucky and Tennessee "nearly liberated." "We will conquer a peace soon," he believed. Then these drives receded like waves on the beach. No subsequent bloody battle from Perryville to Chattanooga by the end of 1863 had provided a Civil War Austerlitz or Waterloo—a decisive encounter to end the war. Both Union and Confederacy used rivers and railroads to move reinforcements from distant theaters seeking that event, but to no avail. The great campaigns ebbed once more in the froth of human blood and gore. A patchwork of military, political, and economic happenstance paralleled the battles in a struggle for stabilization and reconstruction. Much of upper East Tennessee remained in Confederate hands, and scores of small and midlevel encounters raged across the war-torn landscape from the Ohio and Mississippi to the mountains. The upper heartland, a staging ground during the first year of war, now became an inconclusive dark and bloody ground.[11]

More than the armies themselves, raiding expeditions and localized (if expanding) pockets of partisan resistance and occupation counter reaction kept alive the dreams of southern resurgence in this sector. The upper South, in fact, became infested with bandits and terrorists in patriot guise who did relatively little to help the main armies but wreaked havoc on the fringe. In combination but not in coordination, these elements restrained the Federal juggernaut in 1862 and 1863. Yet always Confederate efforts remained incapable of forcing that juggernaut back to the Ohio. Historians James D. Brewer, Dan Sutherland, and Robert R. Mackey have captured the tenor of Confederate irregular operations with Mackey, in particular, contending that the Confederacy tried to fight such a conflict in conjunction with conventional war, "doing so within the limits of nineteenth century concepts of guerrilla, partisan, and raiding warfare." His "triad" of people's war (guerrilla), partisan operations, and conventional cavalry raiding was a "powerful tool" against which the Union military had to develop an extensive and effective counterforce. Such development matured by the end of 1863, but it tied down garrisons, special forces, and naval elements and

promoted the enlistment of unionist Home Guards. Sutherland, however, suggests the Confederate government saw its Partisan Ranger Act
(and subsequent June amendment prohibiting conscripts from jumping
to that alternative form of service) as an "attempt to regulate" guerrilla
warfare, to control the unbridled independent actions since, as Secretary
of War George Randolph explained to one Virginia colonel, to have two
independent armies conducting two independent systems of warfare in
the same sector "would lead to inevitable confusion and disaster." In
retrospect, both "systems" of warfare effectively prolonged combat in
the West and the Upper South's agony.[12]

There were moments when Confederate resurgence seemed promising. The late summer and fall of 1862 was one, with Braxton Bragg and
Joseph Kirby Smith attempting to redeem the upper heartland. A similar
but stillborn move by Sterling Price and Earl Van Dorn never departed
northern Mississippi. By this point, moreover, the partisan upsurge
and vulnerability of such places as Nashville alerted Union authorities.
The magnificent Fort Negley and other forts were begun to protect
Nashville, for instance, with gangs of free and enslaved blacks (male
and female, up to three thousand in number) working with poor shel-

Sketch by a private from Company D, First Ohio Cavalry, as he passed Fort
Donelson on the steamer *Maregno*, March 4, 1862. Author's collection.

INTERIOR OF FORT DONELSON.

INTERIOR OF THE LOWER WATER BATTERY AT FORT DONELSON.—Sketched by Mr. Alexander Simplot—[See Page 101.]

Top: Confederate camps within Fort Donelson. *Bottom:* Interior of Fort Donelson's water battery. From *Harper's Pictorial History of the Great Rebellion.*

ter and inadequate food to ensure protection to their liberators. Then came the so-called siege of Nashville, from September 7 to November 7, when Confederate generals John C. Breckinridge at Murfreesboro and Nathan Bedford Forrest and John Hunt Morgan operating directly against the state capital panicked the occupants. Particularly galling were the partisans, who effectively closed off resupply and forced Yankee foragers into the countryside, "made to yield of its abundance," in the words of one *North American and United States Gazette* reporter. He damned "the guerrilla system of warfare [as] the most destructive to public morals and private interests that could be invented" while praising the fort on St. Cloud's Hill and its ancillary works as having "saved [Nashville] from any serious attack."[13]

In one sense, the decisive event of the period occurred beyond the upper heartland. Robert E. Lee's disrupting but equally unsuccessful Maryland foray (corresponding with Confederate advances in the West) and the ever-lengthening casualty *lists* for both sides, and the Union's pyrrhic victory at Antietam on September 17 gave President Abraham Lincoln an opportunity for advancing preliminary emancipation for all slaves in the rebellious states. Slaveholding Tennessee and Kentucky remained exempt, yet the move effectively pointed the way for black freedom beyond the already ersatz or de facto emancipation that accompanied advancing Union forces on land and water. Decidedly unfavorable opinions of the war's course (as well as emancipation) disenchanted northerners and affected state and congressional elections that autumn. Still, the Confederacy garnered neither foreign intervention nor a chance to winter on the banks of the Ohio. In fact, cold weather descended upon combatants, citizens, and slaves all over a heartland that faced the uncertainties, privations, and interventions of stalemated war.

Little improvement emerged the following year, either, as Federal armies slowly drove southward into Mississippi and East Tennessee, consolidating their authority. Grumbling northern soldiers like two Illinois deserters at a rebel outpost in Bedford County, Tennessee, in March proclaimed that "they are not fighting for what they volunteered to fight for" and would "not fight any longer to free the Negroes." Yet in truth, Lincoln's Emancipation Proclamation undermined Confederate infrastructure as much as any advance of Union arms across the upper heartland. According to the 1860 census, notes African American historian Armstead L. Robinson, over a million slaves populated Tennessee, Alabama, and Mississippi (to which might be added Kentucky's one-quarter of a million more). Perhaps one hundred thousand of them lived within a hundred miles of Nashville. In a sense, the vast preponderance were now lost to Confederate use—as hewers of wood, drawers of water, and labor substitutes for the yeomen whites who went off to fight for the South's peculiar institution.[14]

Both Knoxville and Chattanooga eventually passed to Union control in the final half of 1863. Formal Confederate presence receded to the northeast corner counties of Tennessee on the rail link with Virginia. Here Confederate Lieutenant General James Longstreet's corps from the Army of Northern Virginia (which had helped Braxton Bragg secure singular victory at Chickamauga in September) took tenuous hold while Grant's victorious host and Bragg's army, shattered after the November disasters at Missionary Ridge and Lookout Mountain, went into winter encampments in northern Georgia astride the route to Atlanta and the deeper South. Those battles had been almost a fluke, implied participant Major General William F. "Baldy" Smith, writing nearly a quarter-century later. "The order to assault the rifle pits was an absurd one," he commented, retrieved "from disgrace and defeat because the soldiers went in & did the necessary thing." But, then, that was almost always the way for either side.[15]

Even advantages accruing to partisan rangers seemed muffled to Richmond authorities. A new secretary of war, James A. Seddon, told Confederate president Jefferson Davis in his annual report that these independent but government-authorized bands had only accrued "license, depredations, [and] grave mischiefs" for the cause. Operating under inefficient officers and even within claimed Confederate territory, much less territory lost to the Federals, they had "come to be regarded as more formidable and destructive to our own people than to the enemy," he claimed. Appearing as freebooters in many respects, poorly disciplined while denying much-needed manpower to the regular forces in the eyes of army generals, these fighters operated beyond proper supervision. In a sense, their activities and the passive rebellion of slaves only added to the general dislocation and instability of the heartland. Perhaps of utmost importance, the prewar granaries of hogs, hominy, and other farm and commercial products of the region, as well as manufactories, infrastructure, and productive civilian populace, more directly benefited occupying Yankees than hope-driven rebels. The interrelationships between sections of the great Mississippi Valley and the interdependencies of Deep and upper South had been interrupted conclusively.[16]

Tennessee Stabilization and Early Reconstruction

Historian James Patton asserted years later that the duration of Confederate administration in Tennessee was not lengthy and "it ended with the surrender of Fort Donelson on February 16, 1862." Not strictly true, since much of East Tennessee remained under Richmond's control until at least September 1863, if not longer. Governor Isham G. Harris and his government had fled the capital, with the legislature adjourning indefinitely on February 20 and the executive eventually electing to travel with Johnston's recovering army. Within two weeks, Lincoln had installed former Tennessee senator, two-term governor, and staunch East Tennessee unionist Andrew Johnson as his military governor at Nashville with the rank of brigadier general. This controversial move rippled across the upper southland. Johnson had kept his seat in the Senate and denounced secessionists generally as rebels and traitors, vowing that "treason must be punished" when dispatched to Nashville. Heretofore without precedent, the Federal government sent him with imprecise instructions. But he quickly stripped Nashville mayor Richard B. Cheatham and the city council of office and appointed replacements. The new council likewise removed other officials, including schoolteachers,

Sketch of Nashville, Tennessee, 1862. From *Harper's Pictorial History of the Great Rebellion.*

while Johnson further suppressed editors and clergymen, many of whom were openly hostile to the new regime. Confederate authorities ironically meted out similar treatment elsewhere where their authority still held sway, like East Tennessee. Meanwhile, Grant declared martial law in West Tennessee while the state overall remained unconducive to reconstruction.[17]

Johnson's problem proved twofold from the beginning. An anathema to the Middle and West Tennessee planter oligarchy, he was disliked as a rough-hewn East Tennessee commoner, famed more for contests with prewar nemesis William G. Brownlow than political finesse. His fellow Tennesseans now perceived him as the henchman of Washington, a proconsul alien to American tradition, and traitor to his state and region. Moreover, Johnson's range of control remained limited to Nashville and depended mostly upon Federal arms. His continued identification with the Democratic party rendered him suspect among northern Radical Republicans as well as some in the Lincoln administration itself. However, he and the president were as one in thought, and Lincoln and his military governor both viewed Johnson's role as wooing loyal Tennesseans (although possibly overestimating their num-

Railroad bridge across the Cumberland at Nashville. From *Harper's Pictorial History of the Great Rebellion.*

bers and influence). In due course, threats and plots to his person and administration would surface from guerrilla bands and unsympathetic citizenry in Tennessee. Even Bragg would sanction his kidnapping by force. Moreover, Johnson's unclear relationship with Union military authorities in combatant commands promised difficulty. Military commanders resented his presence and interference, while the general populace soon rued his heavy-handed puppetry from a central government.[18]

Johnson might arrive with "powers, duties and functions," but nobody knew precisely what that meant. His powers certainly included the charge to establish required offices and tribunals and even suspend the writ of habeas corpus. The new administrator ultimately intended restoration of loyal civil government. He permitted local officials from the Confederate period to continue their work until new elections, provided they took a loyalty oath. He tried to alleviate fears among all Tennesseans by proclaiming that the United States government would fulfill "its high constitutional obligation to guarantee to every state in this Union a republican form of government." He spoke with a mixture of firmness and conciliation in the spirit of Lincoln's own professed intent of "full and complete amnesty for all past acts and declarations" for those promising future loyalty. The fact was that the false Lorelei of southern unionism had lured Johnson and Lincoln both. East Tennessee and Appalachia (with random pockets elsewhere along the Tennessee River) might be so inclined. The majority of Tennesseans defied both the new military governor and Washington.

Thus Johnson encountered a predictable postcombat tinderbox. While moving to reopen controlled trading and economic patterns in occupied territory (Nashville began to rejuvenate itself in that regard by late spring, while Memphis did so during the summer), his efforts to restore authority met with rebuffs from old officials, who simply refused to take what soon became "the hated oath" of Union fealty. Judiciary, clergy, newspaper editors, and elected officials—the necessary influential and respected vertebrae of societal structure—generally defied him. So Johnson purged opposition to his policies. In many cases this meant incarceration or exile of offenders, to the howls of irate secessionists and their aggrieved followers. There may well have been three categories of Tennessee citizenry present by this time: secessionists, unionists, and neutralists (free and slave African Americans and women having no say in the proceedings though obviously a stake in the result). Far too few citizens and officials still fit the second category to satisfy the Union administration.

Minority unionists and those wavering in sentiment sought signs that Johnson and the Federal military could protect them, that harsh or illegal acts would not threaten their well-being or interfere with the rights or institutions to which all citizens had been devoted. As historian Patton observed, "To adjust all of these unique complications, the utmost firmness, tact, and courage were requisite." Possessing neither the temperament nor the patience, Johnson quickly found himself hamstrung even by regular Union military commanders bent upon prosecution of the war untrammeled by a politically appointed brigadier demanding protection for his civil restoration effort. Rejuvenation of Confederate military fortunes offset Union military operations as well as efforts to secure the countryside, protect logistical lifelines, and underwrite Johnson's governance. Expulsion of a Confederate presence from the state, a prerequisite for the governor's success, proved far more difficult than first promised by the Forts Henry and Donelson victories. Resolution of Confederate suppression in East Tennessee, moreover, awaited pacification in other sections of the state. Johnson had arrived with high hopes and very little prior planning as to actual stabilization and reconstruction.[19]

Attempts to organize unionist mass meetings of support for Johnson seemed promising at first. Yet his May attempt to secure a favorable circuit judge for the Nashville district foundered badly. While telling Lincoln that once the state had been freed of Confederates, "Tennessee will be for the Union by 70,000" votes, he could do little to deliver on that promise. The president badly wanted some indicator, as it "would be worth more to us than a battle gained." Johnson's faith hinged on freeing East Tennessee. That project, as well as real progress anywhere else, languished while the Union army battled main-force Confederates, attempted to clear intimidating partisans, and prove to the populace that the Confederate revolution had failed. Since even Johnson came to understand the precedence of military over civil affairs, he and his subordinates, like Attorney General Horace Maynard and Secretary of State Edward H. East, were locked in constant battle with Union military authorities, from the Army of the Cumberland generals to the lowliest provost marshal.

It was difficult to determine who was more imperious and prickly, Johnson or the generals. Lincoln stroked both sides, permitting Johnson increasing power to cope with continuing disloyalty while organizing home defense forces from Tennessee unionists. His famous turnabout in attitude could be seen in a July 26 statement to the president: "We have all come to the conclusion here that treason must be made odious and traitors punished and impoverished." "I am doing the best I can," he added, as "hard war" universally supplanted rose-water and kid-glove policies. The more southerners resisted, the more Union officials pushed back. In turn, the cycle of escalating and unrelenting civil disobedience and unrest led to ceaseless confrontation and conflict, imprisonment and exile, intimidation and persecution. Johnson clashed with everyone, it seemed, producing resentment, arbitrariness, and a vindictive spirit. Assistant Secretary of War Thomas A. Scott told his chief Edwin M. Stanton in July 1862 that he had feared such might happen given the Tennessean's prewar and secession stances. Now Johnson's demeanor prevented cooperation for Union restoration. Still, Lincoln retained his difficult proconsul, possibly because of Johnson's antislave and antipatrician positions.[20]

Lincoln and Johnson tried again to hold a wartime plebiscite in the late fall of 1862. The president needed some sign of political regeneration for accommodating border state concerns when he announced his preliminary Emancipation Proclamation. Neither Kentucky nor Tennessee citizenry warmed to his idea of compensated emancipation, but commissioners sent from Washington to Tennessee in October tried to stir favorable popular sentiment for congressional and state elections. A less-than-optimistic Johnson vowed help since two districts (the Ninth and Tenth) in West Tennessee had been reclaimed by Union troops and their residents petitioned the military governor to hold regular congressional elections. The result failed once more. For one thing, a mass meeting to choose candidates produced vehement anti-emancipation resolutions (hardly surprising considering West Tennessee depended heavily upon slave economics). Then Confederate cavalryman Nathan Bedford Forrest rampaged through the area in his famous December raid, bent as much on disrupting the elections as on recruiting men and material. The polls never opened. Johnson could find small comfort that the New Year's battle of Stones River conveniently fueled Lincoln's faith. The next six months slowly vindicated such faith. Early summer witnessed Major General William Rosecrans's unsung but virtually bloodless Tullahoma campaign, which freed Chattanooga and paved the way for Major General Ambrose Burnside to liberate East Tennessee in September. Johnson stumped the North for Union and emancipation, and began recruiting United States Colored Troops as well as Tennessee state black units. Events slackened the governor's feud with military authorities.

Johnson and Rosecrans actually enjoyed better relations than had been the case with Don Carlos Buell, "Old Rosy's" predecessor. Rosecrans was "hard war"; Buell had been a conciliator of the conservative George B. McClellan stripe. Still, Johnson presided over a disturbed landscape, if, indeed, his influence extended little beyond Nashville and the army's reach. Two years of seesaw war contributed to "the devastation of the Heartland." In June 1863, Confederate governor-in-exile Harris cast a forlorn attempt to adhere to the state constitutional provision for holding August gubernatorial and congressional elections. "We must exhibit to the enemy an unalterable firmness of purpose and determination to preserve and perpetuate our free institutions," he proclaimed from behind Confederate lines. William Brimmage Bate of Castallian Springs announced for governor, but he was serving in the Confederate army at the time and deferred to Judge Robert L. Caruthers of Lebanon. Johnson's military-governor status overawed a unionist convention in July at Nashville, and that body eventually demurred from putting forth a civil candidate. On the appointed election day, a competing Union or anti-administration faction in West Tennessee submitted a candidate, William B. Campbell, whereby the election in Bedford and Shelby Counties named him the popularly elected governor. Counterpart elections held in rebel army camps on August 4 proclaimed the elderly Caruthers the victor and returned a Tennessee delegation to the Confederate Congress. Of course, Caruthers made no attempt to take office, nor could he have breached Federal bayonets at Nashville to oust Johnson. All told, the August 1863 election cycle proved a farce, confirming that Tennessee remained unready to return to the Union.[21]

Bragg effectively defeated Rosecrans at Chickamauga in September 1863, besieging the defeated Federals in Chattanooga. Meanwhile, Johnson had already responded to a September presidential enjoinder to begin the reorganization of the loyal state government under Article 4 or the guarantee clause of the Constitution. Let the reconstruction work be accomplished only by loyalists, urged Lincoln; all others should be excluded so that Johnson might "trust that your government so organized will be recognized here as being the one republican form to be guaranteed to the state, and to be protected against invasion and domestic violence." In reply, Johnson rambled about the "many humble men, the peasantry and yeomanry of the South," who had been decoyed or perhaps driven to rebellion and who might now look forward to amnesty. He added how the intelligent and influential leaders must suffer—or poetically, "the tall poppies must be struck down." He then set about organizing his policy. Mass meetings were again held to rally support, and Bragg's moment of glory evaporated when Grant lifted Chattanooga's siege in November. Lincoln issued his presidential amnesty proclamation on December 8 (with its promise of full pardon and restoration of property other than slaves upon taking an oath of future loyalty, as well as the 10 percent voter idea for restoring government). By now Bragg had sent a force under James B. Longstreet to retake Knoxville. He failed, and the Confederate presence receded to the state's extreme northeastern corner. "Perhaps at last restoration was at hand," thought loyalists.[22]

Kentucky Adjustments

Kentucky political scientist Penny Miller has observed that Kentucky was both "a physical battleground between North and South" and "an internal battleground for its own soul—and politics." Unlike Tennessee, slaveholding and borderland Kentucky did not secede yet witnessed its professed neutrality violated and then rendered untenable by both sides.

It ended up aligning with the national cause (although periodically courted by rival Confederate state regimes and distinctly uncomfortable with Washington's dictated policies). Escalating internal division over loyalty oaths, opposition to national emancipation and conscription, as well as military persecution of dissidence, produced turmoil rivaling that in Tennessee. Additionally, Kentucky too had a strong representation in rebel army ranks offset by native sons both white and black in Union blue. While spared a large number of battles compared to Virginia and Tennessee, the Bluegrass State experienced its own destructive cavalry raids, bloody disruption of the Smith-Bragg invasion of 1862 at Munfordville, Richmond, and Perryville, and a virulent homegrown guerrilla or partisan warfare. Zealously retaining a states' rights determination, Kentucky could not escape tumultuous civil-military relations in the political arena. Secession-leaning governor Beriah Magoffin, and his successor, moderate conservative James F. Robinson, battled Lincoln administration pressures, expressed through military officials seemingly unmindful of delicate Bluegrass sensibilities. Kentucky historian E. Merton Coulter later wrote, "One year of federal occupation made Kentucky a hot-bed of discontent and aroused in her a suspicion of almost every act of the National administration." Such friction rather than confrontation between armies unsettled wartime politics in both Tennessee and Kentucky.[23]

Frankly, Kentucky's loyalty to the Union always remained mottled. Magoffin had tried to negotiate the tricky shoals of neutrality in 1861 and then found himself buffeted by extremists wanting other direction. Kentuckians sought a promise that they could continue to "receive the fullest protection of the government in the enjoyment of their lives, their liberties, and their property." They wanted the war not to oppress or subjugate or overthrow established institutions of the states and their residents. However, if Kentucky avoided becoming a killing ground for the most part, what transpired reconfirmed the unpredictability of warfare as part of a political process. Both Tennesseans and Kentuckians experienced the tyranny of governance occasioned by the frustration of oppressive Union military presence. Authorities trod a fine line between allowing traditional Kentucky political disputation but within limitations on civil liberties due to civil war. Enforcers such as the Home Guards and provost marshals repeatedly trampled state and national declarations of respect for lives, liberty, and property. So the process of disintegrating relations began—fanned, for instance, by unauthorized liberation of slave property by northern volunteers

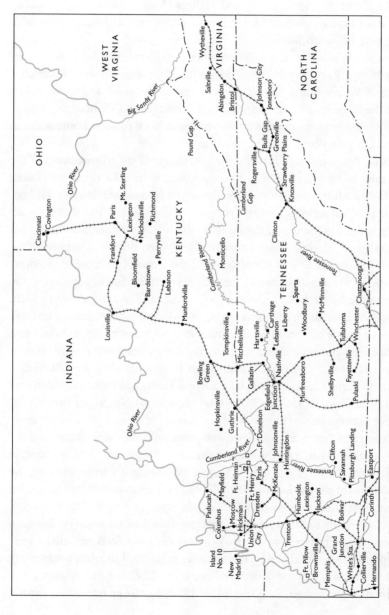

Western border states. Map by Bill Nelson.

traversing the state en route to the battlefields farther south. All too often Kentuckians, regardless of political persuasion, were treated as "secesh" by troops from north of the Ohio. Arrests, often indiscriminately
applied because of whim or perception rather than proof, counterbal-
anced good intentions of protection under the law avowed by generals
like Grant, Sherman, Buell, and Halleck. Violations became especially
blatant under passionate local commanders such as Brigadier General
Jeremiah Tilford Boyle.

Boyle was one of a galaxy of energetic Kentucky Union field commanders, like Speed Fry, Theophilus Garrard, Thomas Bramlette,
Frank Wolford, and Steven Gano Burbridge, who flocked to the colors
at the beginning of the war. Boyle, Burbridge, and Wolford in particular would become controversial when sent back to their home state, as
Secretary of War Edwin M. Stanton told Boyle specifically on May 27,
1862, "on account of his intimate knowledge of the requirements of the
service in his State." Wolford would gain notoriety for openly opposing
Lincoln administration policies. Boyle and Burbridge allowed their hostile political feelings toward disloyalty to dictate their interference with
elections, assessment of damages by guerrillas, and eradication of that
pestilence. Matters escalated particularly when Boyle's arbitrariness toward anyone aiding or seeming to aid the secessionist cause led to overt
persecution when Confederate military activity further inflamed the
situation by mid-1862. Accusation, arrest, and the expulsion of men,
women, and children suspected of not following the unionist line followed in due course. Federal military interference with the judiciary and
state elections under the pretext of countering disloyalty evoked strident
protests, but to little avail. Even Lincoln thought they were "having a
stampede in Kentucky" when he advised Halleck to look into the matter
in July. Unionist George Robertson thought by November that his fellow Kentuckians were ripe for "popular uprising against military usur-
pation and defiance of our laws, our peace, and the cause of the Union."
By the new year, a fellow spirit contended, "fully one-third of the state
of Kentucky" was disloyal. Lincoln's longstanding contention that the
Bluegrass held the key to maintaining the Union notwithstanding, his
overly zealous minions risked losing the state.[24]

Some of Kentucky's most egregious difficulties with Washington
centered on the issue of slavery. Whether rumors of compensated emancipation that circulated in the summer of 1862, Lincoln's preliminary
emancipation announcement of September 22 or the full-fledged proclamation's effect on New Year's Day 1863, Kentucky unionists plunged

to "the sloughs of despondency." Confederate sympathizers were glee-
ful. A wave of conservatism manifested itself in Kentucky legislative resolutions in March 1863 voicing various grievances against the Lincoln
administration but centering upon abolition. The embers of secession
lay ready to ignite once more, with Major General Horatio G. Wright,
commanding Federal troops in the Department of the Ohio, poised to
pounce on disloyal legislators. A new law, passed on March 2, forbade
any black, "claiming or pretending to be free," from entering the state
under the proclamation provisions, and those proclaiming such were to
be considered runaways. All of this came seemingly six months too late
for Confederate hopes. In historian Coulter's colorful words, when the
fall Confederate counter-offensive to Kentucky failed, "the old order
returned, and the people settled down again into the conditions of the
hated and vexatious military regime, having experienced a month of
rare excitement." With 1863 a gubernatorial election year, the comity
of Federal-state relations remained sorely tested. When the so-called
States Rights party (old Democrats) met at Frankfort on February 18,
the gauntlet was thrown down before Governor Robinson. To quote
one Kentucky newspaper, "This odiousness of the radical acts of the
administration had prepared, or was rapidly preparing the Kentucky
mind for revolt against the Union."[25]

The States Rights party may or may not have actually aimed at
secession. It did, however, seek to rally opposition to heavy-handed
unionist control. When one ill-advised Ohio colonel tried to suppress
a States Rights party meeting, thinking men took notice across the
Commonwealth. The Union Democracy (as the party in power chose
to call itself) met subsequently in the spring, eventually nominating
former Union officer Thomas E. Bramlette to head the ticket. Yet few
were truly appeased. The candidate's perceived radicalism soon split the
Union Democracy into war and peace factions. An announced opposition candidate to Robinson appeared in Charles A. Wickliffe, a former
delegate to the failed Washington Peace Conference in 1861. The ensuing campaign between the Union Democrats and the Peace Democracy
(as the competing parties termed themselves) was heated and exciting.
Union Democracy became tainted by association with the Lincoln administration, and the States Righters became tainted with secession, as
rebellion and even traitorism resulted in unceasing name calling.

Confederate cavalryman John Hunt Morgan's famous Ohio raid
that summer, traversing the Bluegrass unimpeded by Boyle's soldiery,
truly inflamed matters. On July 10, Robinson announced that all

individuals expatriated according to war legislation were disfranchised. The Federal army then intervened to enforce such injunctions to the detriment of free elections. The new Department of the Ohio commander, Ambrose E. Burnside, overreacted by declaring martial law at the end of the month (ostensibly to preserve free elections and prevent disloyal persons from voting), while ever-troublesome Boyle (still in charge of military affairs in western Kentucky) let it be known that voting for Wickliffe would be proof of disloyalty. Stringent oath taking and proof of loyalty dictated the ballot. Wickliffe's name was stricken from the ballot in many places, the whole ticket was suppressed elsewhere, and at least one local office seeker was thrown into jail.[26]

Little wonder, then, that Bramlette outscored Wickliffe by 68,422 to 17,503 votes in the August election and both branches of the legislature went for the Union Democrats. Burnside had departed by this time on his campaign to free East Tennessee. But Boyle and other hard-line soldiers remained in place and the election farce placated little of the profound discontent among Kentuckians. As Coulter concluded, active military interference only exacerbated Kentucky's grievances against Washington. He dismissed the notion that Wickliffe's election would have led to secession, "that the state would have ceased to support the war seems much more likely." Bramlette began his term with a message to the new legislature in December that Kentucky had "no cause of complaint against the Federal government." Preservation of the Union remained uppermost (something of the old line conservative, preemancipation stance), while "neither the preservation nor the destruction of slavery is essential to our State or National Existence." As with Andrew Johnson, Bramlette set about consolidating prosecution of the war and restoration of the Union as his priorities. Both leaders faced a sullen if acquiescent populace, increasingly weary of wartime political strife as well as all that it had spawned by way of violence, destruction, hatred, and uniformed presence. Neither man necessarily enjoyed political control or power aside from that wielded at the point of the bayonet. Social and economic dislocation confounded the situation still further in both Kentucky and Tennessee.[27]

Upper Heartland War, Society, and Economics

Possibly the greatest contrast between the two upper heartland states at war could be found with respect to society and the economy. Both might consider themselves a war zone at one time or another and Kentuckians could bewail "military occupation" as readily as suffering Tennesseans. Yet the travail of actual conflict affected each of them in different ways. True, the passing of armies and raiders periodically created excitement and localized destruction more damaging than omnipresent partisans. But the continuing presence of Federal occupation forces and the more widespread pressure of those partisans (guerrillas, insurgents, patriots) after the spring of 1862 wrought greater havoc and dislocation in Tennessee. Kentucky's civilian experience came at a lower threshold of violence and more with regard to suppression of civil liberties, perhaps. In either case, historian Coulter's phrase that in supplying the Union army of occupation as well as both sides' armies, and in carrying out the necessary military operations in the state, "much property was bought, seized, and destroyed" and so "interfered with the people's peace of mind," applied to both the Bluegrass State and Volunteer State.[28]

None of the great cities in those states sustained battle damage, although countless commentators proclaimed the degradation of quality of life and physical presence due to army presence. Until Atlanta in the fall of 1864, no southern city suffered Carthaginian treatment at all. Vicksburg incurred bombardment scars from battle yet survived to wear such wounds proudly. Certainly from Louisville and Lexington to Nashville, Memphis, Chattanooga, and Knoxville no upper South city experienced the physical damage of twentieth-century warfare. Rather, they became treasured trophies, used by invader and occupier to reestablish military, political, and commercial power for stabilizing and reconstructing conquered provinces. Smaller towns often became strategic hamlets in similar fashion while the individual farms, plantations, mills, and infrastructure so vital to internal commerce and existence, if not military support, became targets of both sides. Alternative uses for public and private structures indubitably felt the sting of "military necessity"—appropriation, confiscation, or destruction. When building forts, using facilities and infrastructure, or demanding services for war purposes, neither side seemed reluctant to alter the normal pattern of life and commerce. Since Americans had not experienced military occupation or war in the homeland since the conflicts with Great Britain, it was natural that citizen and soldier comments then and reminiscences later (in fact a century or more of Lost Cause complaint) would bemoan the seeming barbarism of "vandal invasion" (as southerners chose to call it).

Mills, warehouses, and manufacturing establishments provided legitimate military targets, as did crops, livestock, and the whole southern labor system built upon human bondage. If caught trafficking with the enemy, property owners could expect punishment. Bridges, railroads, and river transport in the upper heartland also experienced heavy wartime use and even destruction on occasion. Traffic on the Ohio River, depressed during the secession year, revived following the winter and spring victories of the Federals in 1862, only to slump again with the Confederate invasion of the fall. Such cyclical wartime patterns simply compressed the normal peacetime business cycles of prosperity and depression, one might say. But from early 1863 onward, war business boomed, fortunes were made at inflated prices, and trade by profiteering and shrewd combinations of acumen and loyalty prospered. Gunboats patrolled the rivers to ensure unimpeded passage. Northern Kentucky, at least, enjoyed prosperity. Of course, prosperity and survival depended greatly on matters of political affinities, loyalty, and location. Rural areas suffered more than urban sectors in that regard.

In retrospect, Federal occupation aimed mostly at the hearts and minds of the people. Hated loyalty oaths and other persecution and

State and Confederate officials converted prewar Tennessee factories to war production, making them Federal military targets. Courtesy of Douglas Sexton and Skip Doscher.

intimidation related to political postures and actions. It was here that provost marshals, counterguerrilla operatives, or line army units, as well unionist state Home Guards laid greater ills upon the land and its populace. As Coulter suggested, "War speaks disorganization and destruction economically and socially; it also speaks artificial prosperity and new relationships." For the agrarian economy of the upper South, this transformation may have been as psychologically upsetting as physically dislocating in terms of prewar North-South patterns between upper and lower portions of the heartland. Then, too, continuing dislocation through annual life cycles of planting and harvest meant a lowering of economic standards to subsistence levels in many places—not helped by predators in blue and gray. In southern minds this disruption attending northern invasion equated with barbarism and incivility. Lost labor and productivity came with marauding and billeting soldiery and partisans.

By the end of 1863, as soldiers of both sides ravaged the countryside, civilians increasingly expressed sentiments of "pox on both houses." Professor Bob Womack recounted the story of one Middle Tennessean, Monroe Bearden, who had lost a son at Stones River or Murfreesboro at the beginning of the year. He frequently made a pilgrimage to the spot his son fell in battle. On one such occasion that summer following the fight, Bearden reflected how "this is a sad place for me, still I like to linger near it." He then drove his cotton-laden wagon to Nashville—to sell to the Yankee enemy. Survival and accommodation overcame grief at midwar in the upper heartland.[29]

Rural Kentucky and Tennessee undoubtedly suffered most from the migrations of the armies, raiders, and guerrillas. Croplands were renewable, but haystacks, grain bins, and animal pens, once visited by the soldiery and guerillas, confiscated or otherwise regulated by higher authority to benefit the military effort directly, left the owner bereft not only of his or her own salvation but also of access to the marketplace. There might be truth in a northern journalist's point two years later that "in our occupation of cities along the Mississippi, the Rebels found a ready supply from our markets," since Union occupation "chastised the Rebels with one hand, while we fed and clothed them with the other." Occupation forces and logistical centers for the passing armies, more than those armies themselves, provided the wherewithal, legal or illegal, moral or immoral, for supplying the needs of the populace. But accompanying such wartime upheaval came the departure of livestock and crops (either for food or other utilization by the armies), slave labor (via confiscation, ersatz emancipation, transfer to wage compensation from military utilization or vagabond freedom), and financial deprecia-tion (since money and property value declined accordingly). Privation produced animosity toward oppressors (seen and unseen). Coulter was undoubtedly correct in asserting that an army of occupation, whatever its intentions, quickly grows unpopular.

And so it was at the Civil War's midpoint. Notwithstanding res-toration of a modicum of Federally supervised commerce in cities and larger towns, Yankee traders and speculators exchanged war supplies (excepting munitions) and manufactured goods for desperately sought cotton, and even a healthy clandestine trade north and south flourished, particularly through unreconstructed western Kentucky of the Jackson Purchase (between Paducah and the Tennessee line). Of course, liquor and prostitution added to commercial transaction. Trade was never as fulsome or predictable as in peacetime, and the value of such commerce remained unquantifiable absent the regular tools of civil government. Trade policies of the Federal and Confederate governments writ large (thanks to military and treasury authority) wreaked havoc with both states to the detriment of their citizenry. Hemp, cotton, livestock, to-bacco, barley, and livestock production plummeted or was otherwise turned by military markets and trade policy for the duration. Custom-ary supply and demand, peacetime trading patterns, and the entire re-gional and sectional interrelationships of trade and commerce had been profoundly interrupted or otherwise altered by two years of war. Some people profited while others went hungry. Land went untilled, money depreciated, and hearts hardened into hatred and bitterness, further ac-celerating the cause and effect of resistance, rebellion, and retribution across the land. Travail and sorrow translated into survivor words of bitterness and privation.[30]

The security and happiness of family, church, and state were all rent asunder with little evidence of any immediate reassembly by the end of 1863. Rather, sullen acceptance and perhaps despair symbol-ized a beaten-down populace waiting for the war's surcease. Perhaps the prominent East Tennessee unionist politician T. R. Nelson said it for all the citizenry when he wrote Federal brigadier Samuel P. Carter the day after Christmas 1863. The Union army was more destructive to loyal Tennesseans than the rebels ever were, he complained. Fences were burned, horses stolen, and people were stripped in many instances "of the last vestiges of subsistence, our means to make a crop next year" rapidly destroyed, he suggested. Moreover, "when the best Union men in the country make appeals to the soldiers, they are heartlessly cursed as rebels." John Houston Bills, a West Tennessee landowner, concurred, writing in his diary that both armies took turns stealing his property, "each pretending to fear it may fall into the hands of other and be turned against them." The war had begun a leveling effect on wealth distribution throughout the region, but the process was wrenching. The greatest safety could be found in simply remaining at home. Three or four times Clarksville changed hands, James B. Killebrew noted, but "the Confederates never held the region where we lived except for a few days or weeks at a time after the fall of Fort Donelson."[31]

The end-of-year reports of Secretary of War Stanton and his general-in-chief, Henry Halleck, proclaimed great strides in suppressing rebellion in the Mississippi Valley, in reopening the great river to trade, and in how loyal southerners had been redeemed by force of arms and government

Union men in Alabama greeting Federal gunboats. From *Harper's Pictorial History of the Great Rebellion.*

protection. Yet the dichotomy between reality and hope dogged all levels in Tennessee and Kentucky. Indeed, the Union had militarily rescued Kentucky from the brink of separation as a result of Forts Henry and Donelson and subsequently had conquered much of Tennessee. Some shaky semblance of stable social and commercial intercourse had been restored by the war's third winter. At least major cities, strategic hamlet-towns, and close-in surrounding neighborhoods had adjusted (however grudgingly) to the new conditions of wartime occupation. Louisville, Lexington, Paducah, Nashville, Memphis, Chattanooga, and, lately, Knoxville all lay within national military span of control. Federal land and naval forces patrolled river, rail, and back roads promising "hard war" or harsh retribution to lingering secessionists under General Order 100, as codified by Columbia College legal scholar Francis Lieber. Still, Lincoln himself would extend the olive branch of reconciliation with his "10 percent" formula for restoring rebellious states to the Union at the conclusion of 1863.[32]

Everything rested on submission—to Federal authority and law—with loyalty oaths, slave emancipation, even trade permits and restrictions all equating with unionism. The flow of goods and service generally supported occupation, not restoration of antebellum commerce.

Confederate prisoners at Camp Douglas in Chicago, Illinois. From *Harper's Pictorial History of the Great Rebellion*.

Behind the scenes, of course, Confederate forces remained physically present in northeastern Tennessee as well as wherever Forrest, Morgan, and other raiders might venture. In the shadows lurked rough-hewn flotsam of war, in faded blue and butternut, less given now to lofty ideals and pledges to cause and country and more to plunder, bedlam, and lawlessness. At this point, however, Tennessee and Kentucky only hovered at the fringe of brutalities and atrocities more typically associated with conditions in the trans-Mississippi. In June, Union lieutenant William McCrory of the Seventh Ohio Sharpshooters witnessed the hanging of a felon who had assisted in murdering a civilian who would not divulge where he had hidden his money. The bandits "first cut [the civilian's] ears off and then cut his tongue out and then shot him," recounted McCrory. In this case, both regular armies, not local or irregular authorities, meted out justice. Confederate general Braxton Bragg hanged one perpetrator; Union general George H. Thomas dispatched the other two culprits.[33]

Yet the fiery storm of uncivil war continued to expand. Desperadoes (including deserters from both sides) would soon vie with legitimacy of authorized partisans and raiders. The upper South moved toward a sort of twilight zone of garrisoned towns, no-man's lands, and turmoil marginally controlled or regulated by either military or civilian authority. Erstwhile leaders of partisan contingents often exercised an almost translucent control in the countryside while towns and cities had become, in more cases, the bastions of Federal occupation. Major General William Tecumseh Sherman said it only too well in a letter to his wife in early January 1864: "All that has gone before is mere skirmishing," for the real war "now begins." No amount of poverty or adversity seemed to shake southerners' faith. With their slaves gone, wealth and luxury eclipsed, money valueless, and starvation in full view, as well as "causes enough to make the bravest tremble," he saw no sign of the war's abatement. Such words denoted much of the upper heartland. There remained, however, unresolved pockets like East Tennessee.[34]

CHAPTER 2

Unfinished Business in East Tennessee

Both sides had unfinished business in one crucial section of the Volunteer State. East Tennessee had defied allegiance to either side ever since the state's secession. Division among inhabitants led to violence, destruction of property such as railroad bridges, and a Confederate-imposed "reign of terror" against dissident unionists. In addition, young men rushed to enlist in both armies, just as in Kentucky. Abraham Lincoln sought the liberation of beleaguered East Tennesseans, but his generals balked at the allocation of resources to do so. Major General William Rosecrans and his Army of the Cumberland eventually took the lower end at Chattanooga. Major General Ambrose Burnside's soldiers eventually marched over the mountains to capture Knoxville and dispersed rebel defenders at the upper end. The damage of confiscation, conscription, imprisonment, and restriction on civil liberties had already begun—by Confederate government policies and field representatives. It remained for Burnside and his army to correct such evils—or perpetuate them.

The battles for Missionary Ridge and Lookout Mountain took place late in November just outside Chattanooga. One of Burnside's assistant adjutant generals issued field orders noting President Lincoln's proclamation of "a day of thanksgiving" for November 26. The proclamation cited "the countless blessings vouchsafed the country and the fruitful successes granted to our arms during the past year." "Especially has this army cause for thankfulness for divine protection," intoned Lewis Richmond, "and let us with grateful hearts offer our prayers for its continuance, assured of the purity of our cause and with a firm reliance on the God of Battles."[1]

Four days later, that same God locked Richmond's comrades in combat with James Longstreet's legions at Knoxville. Both seemed in need of divine intervention. In less than twenty minutes bitter fighting for Fort Sanders (named ironically for a Yankee colonel who was related to Confederate president Jefferson Davis), the Army of the Ohio had cause for more rejoicing. In what historian Harold Fink hailed as the climax to the campaign for East Tennessee, Burnside pulled a dramatic "reverse Fredericksburg" on an adversary who, a year before, had selected the superb defensive position behind that Virginia city enabling Lee's Army of Northern Virginia to defeat Burnside and his Army of the Potomac. But four months before Knoxville, Longstreet had himself reluctantly ordered George Pickett's bloody charge at Gettysburg.[2]

Why East Tennessee?

Fink concluded that "the whole East Tennessee campaign is of additional interest because it affords an opportunity to study Longstreet and Burnside," as "corps commanders serving in independent command in the West." Longstreet had come out from Virginia in time to help win the sanguinary contest at Chickamauga in September 1863. His success in exploiting a break in Rosecrans's battle line won him renown among fellow commanders in his new assignment with General Braxton Bragg's Army of Tennessee. But the latter's failure to exploit the victory soon soured Longstreet on Bragg. Longstreet may well have stood at the zenith of his career at this point. Bragg, however, possibly sensed a troublesome rival for command. President Davis's early October visit, to smooth over the rifts in his second army, soon led to the idea of dispatching the Georgian with his two veteran infantry divisions, two artillery battalions, plus Major General Joseph Wheeler's two small cavalry divisions away from the subsequent siege of Rosecrans's army at Chattanooga.

Longstreet's new expedition sought to impose a similar stranglehold on Burnside at Knoxville. Skeptical as to the move, given Bragg's 30 percent battle losses at Chickamauga and an enemy buildup to counter the subsequent siege, yet anxious for independent command, he had acquiesced, and Bragg had been more than willing to let him go. While Longstreet personally wanted to get into Middle Tennessee via Bridgeport, Alabama, and thus work on the Union logistics line, there was merit in dispatching him to restore Confederate control over upper East Tennessee and reestablish the vital rail link with Virginia. One of Bragg's biographers has concluded that the general "probably did not injure his chances at Chattanooga any more by sending [Longstreet] than by keeping him," an astonishing statement given what transpired over the next month's time.[3]

Much of what historian Alexander Mendoza styles a "Confederate Struggle for Command" involving Longstreet and Bragg, as well as internal control of the First Corps of Lee's army, lies beyond the scope of this study. However, reasons and hopes for "Old Pete's" detachment from an army facing imminent Union breakout at Chattanooga suggests much about the role East Tennessee played at the end of 1863. Neither man stood *sans rapproch* for difficulties after Chickamauga. East Tennessee and Knoxville offered opportunities for each of them in his own way. Whether or not Bragg might have selected some other expeditionary leader like Carter Stevenson, who had enjoyed some success by capturing five hundred Yankees and blunting Burnside's thrust toward Chattanooga in a brisk skirmish at Loudon on October 23, remains unanswerable. Stevenson certainly was more familiar with the lower counties of the region. But movement north placed Longstreet and his men closer to their desired return to Virginia, and with Lee importuning Davis, Richmond also liked that idea. True, inadequate transportation and absence of proper maps and intelligence would plague Longstreet. He claimed after the war that Bragg had set him up for failure. Of one thing we may be sure: neither general could or did communicate with the other adequately or helpfully.[4]

Burnside had preceded Longstreet to the west by approximately six months. Exiled after the Fredericksburg debacle in December 1862, he went out to the Department of the Ohio with some latitude of enforcement power for subduing unrest in the southern counties of Kentucky as well as coping with rebel raiders like John Hunt Morgan and John Scott. Ultimately, it fell to his Army of the Ohio, along with a retrieved IX Corps, to move on with Lincoln's pet project of liberating East Tennessee. Marching over the mountains, Burnside succeeded in freeing Cumberland Gap and taking Knoxville in early September, about the same time that Rosecrans originally had chased the Confederates out of Chattanooga. The easterner then wrote Military Governor Andrew Johnson on September 9 that "the place [Gap] surrendered this afternoon *unconditionally* with over two thousand prisoners & small arms & fourteen pieces of artillery." "We have been elegantly received by the whole of East Tenn.," he added, mentioning how "the whole people are crazy to see" the governor.[5]

Fanning out through the region to reestablish national control and succor a strong unionist populace (while suppressing the troubling "secesh" element that had not "refugeed" south or northeast), the Federals still encountered pockets of resistance inspired by the old Fort Donelson hero, Simon Bolivar Buckner, Samuel Jones (moving from southwest Virginia to protect the railroad) and Stevenson closing off access to Chattanooga. Sharp clashes at Rogersville, Sweetwater, London, Lenoir, and Philadelphia punctuated the beautiful October weather and imposed limits upon Burnside's advance. To the north, he tried to clear the route to Virginia, precipitating an engagement with Jones at Blue Springs, nine miles from Bull's Gap on the East Tennessee and Virginia Railroad. Badly dispersed Confederate elements failed to contain Union raids south of Knoxville on the East Tennessee and Georgia Railroad and in skirmishes at Charleston (on the Hiawassee River) and Cleveland. By this time, however, logistical realities had begun to surface as both Burnside's men and Confederates fell to foraging and harassing local civilians.[6]

Bragg sent Longstreet on November 5 to recapture Knoxville just as Grant began seriously preparing to break out of the Chattanooga encirclement. In the view of Longstreet's artillery chief, the redoubtable Edward Porter Alexander, Bragg had dithered for "over forty days of idleness" as "stronger and better men [on the Federal side] had taken hold, and opened up shorter and better lines of communication, and when immense reinforcements had already begun to reach their camp." Writing after the war, the artilleryman thought the Knoxville expedition would have been a cakewalk if undertaken earlier, but now facetiously deemed it "as remarkable a piece of strategy as the war produced." A planned swift strike would degenerate into a foot race with the rain, sleet, snow, and mud of late autumn—all for control of a region different from the rest of the Volunteer State in terms of economics and political sentiment. But historian Robert McKenzie's conclusion that "the blitzkrieg" Bragg envisioned never came off because Longstreet failed to deliver "rapid movements" and "sudden blows," and hence the whole campaign "can only be adjudged an abysmal failure," was hardly apparent at the time.[7]

Historian Jesse Burt viewed East Tennessee, "the earliest settled of Tennessee's grand divisions," as truthfully a romanticized public issue in the North, a geographical entity, a political phenomenon, a strategically important area," and a military problem of the first order for both sides. Southern by geography, genealogy, and temperament, the region arrayed slaveholders and yeomanry tooth by jowl. Fiercely independent yet patriotic in the tradition of forebears like John Sevier, unionist editor-preacher-politician William G. Brownlow had declared in late January 1861, "We are a grain-growing and stock-raising people, and we can conduct a cheap government and live independently inhabiting the Switzerland of America." In fact, East Tennessee, like the rest of southern Appalachia, was a mare's nest of conflicting feelings and emotions, loyalties and politics stretching from family and neighborhood up to region and beyond. "Recollect that East Tennessee is my horror," Major General William T. Sherman would write Ulysses S. Grant on December 1. He added, "That any military man should send a force into East Tennessee puzzles me." Burnside was there and had to be helped, he admitted, but once relieved, "I want to get out, and he should come out too." To Sherman and others, the campaign in that section of Tennessee was always a diversion, a sideshow fraught with political quagmire, bitter partnership, and potential guerrilla ensnarement. Major enemy armies remained the priority of a fighting West Pointer like Sherman.[8]

Essentially loyal to the Union at the onset of the rebellion, over thirty thousand Federal soldiers would come from East Tennessee, or roughly 10 percent of its aggregate population including slaves. In fact, Burnside writing Lincoln from Cumberland Gap on September 10, 1863, declared, "I look upon East Tennessee as one of the most loyal sections of the United States." Its voters had rejected the state secession vote by better than two to one in 1861. It may well have been, as Sam Bollier contends, that while regionalism and nationalism often seemed to conflict, "East Tennessee regionalism was actually conflated with American nationalism during the Civil War. By publicly expressing their Unionist sympathies, "East Tennesseans were able to reconcile their regional identities with their commitment to American nationalism." Yet the same could be advanced for East Tennessee Confederates. Indeed, Tennessee's Appalachia held a significant Confederate population as well. Occupied first by secessionist governor Isham G. Harris's state army in July 1861, it had passed quickly to Confederate control. For the next two years, the Lincoln administration fretted as much about persecuted East Tennessee as it did about border state Kentucky. Confederate authorities meanwhile thought their own policies of conciliation and leniency had been met only by disloyal unionist resistance leading to crackdown and punishment. As Burt would have it, all this "became the subject of poems, melodramatic stories, and extensive newspaper coverage in the North." At the time, Senator Andrew Johnson,

William Brownlow (as editor of the *Knoxville Whig*), exiled U.S. Congressman Horace Maynard, and northern relief societies collecting substantial funds for persecution victims plied Washington with pleas for liberation. Even widely read *London Times* correspondent William Russell caught the East Tennessee fever, preaching that only intervention by force could save this "region of mountaineers and hill people." Federal authorities took two years to alleviate the suffering.[9]

In truth, it had been Sherman's duty as Department of the Ohio commander in 1861 to liberate East Tennessee. The way had not been clear to do so. The task proved no easier for Sherman's successors—Buell and Rosecrans—preoccupied as they were with confronting Bragg's army over the next twenty-four months. So neglect of East Tennessee permitted the Davis government to continue its iron-fisted control over the populace. When unionists turned to sabotage against the railroad and civil disobedience, they were tried and hung or hounded out of their homes and neighborhoods. Russell thought this boded "results of immense important in Kentucky and Tennessee" for the northern cause. Indeed, many unionist martyrs fled over the mountains and, guided by so-called "pilots," made the trek to Kentucky and enlisted in the Union army. Left behind, however, were family and allies. Their stories became legion as the victims caught sight of blue uniforms only infrequently when Union raiders like Brigadier General Samuel P. Carter and Colonel William P. Sanders briefly visited from Kentucky in December 1862 and June 1863, respectively, their mission being to destroy the vital railroad link with Virginia but also to bring succor and hope to suffering loyalists.[10]

There was more to East Tennessee than its persecuted people and their politics. For one thing, the eastern part of the state, although billed as the "Switzerland of America," was anything but wholly mountainous. As Brownlow observed, the region helped feed the deeper plantation South just as Middle Tennessee and Kentucky did, especially when normal commercial ties with the Midwest had been severed by secession and war. Knoxville was the metropolis of the section, profiting from the relationships of agricultural production and commercial shipment via river and rail. Wealthy Monroe County landowner Charles McClung McGhee, for example, moved quickly to take up the economic slack by establishing a pork-processing plant at Knoxville. He apparently prospered through Confederate government contracts, although arrival of Burnside's Federals in September meant the end of that lucrative deal. Moreover, Richmond had established an arsenal of sorts in that city where a fine brick structure housed a storehouse, blacksmiths and carriage-making shops, and fine machine shops doing military work. The Shepard, Maxwell and Hoyt foundry repaired and cleaned unserviceable arms, cast cooking utensils for the troops, and fabricated and repaired gun-carriages and their spare parts as well as machinery and tools for engineer, ordnance, quartermaster, and commissary departments. Coffins, arms chests, packing boxes, and other useful items also came from this complex. Added to such material resources, fully twenty-five thousand men from East Tennessee joined rebel ranks, and they might have been "a well-to-do Knoxville merchant, a learned Decatur lawyer, a backwoods Jefferson County farm boy, or a proud Hawkins County planter's son."[11]

Strategically, in addition to the importance of railroads for lateral movement of troops and communications between eastern and western parts of the Confederacy, East Tennessee offered an inviting gateway for Confederate raids and invasion of Kentucky. Following the near-success of Bragg and Edmund Kirby Smith in the autumn of 1862, other Confederate strategists like Pierre Gustav Toutant Beauregard and various civilian officials dreamt until the final winter of the war of placing the young nation's western frontier squarely upon the banks of the Ohio River. East Tennessee offered a superb launch point for such a quest. However, the Richmond government's primary interest in the region remained the railroad linking Virginia and the Mississippi Valley via Chattanooga. The East Tennessee and Georgia Railroad (Chattanooga to Knoxville, completed in 1855) and East Tennessee and Virginia Railroad (Knoxville to Bristol, finished in 1858) could haul men, materiel, and foodstuffs. Their significance was underscored as early as November 1861, when unionist insurgents burned bridges in Greene County. By 1863, the conjoined railroads remained the only such connection in rebel hands west of the Blue Ridge. So Richmond tried to ensure protection through the forces of Buckner and Stevenson. Once a determined Federal invasion appeared, however, the game was up, and Campbell Wallace, president of the East Tennessee and Georgia Railroad fled with his family, remaining in exile until after the war.[12]

Confederate Resurgence

So the struggle for East Tennessee held great importance as Longstreet tangled with Burnside. As always with military operations, the key would lie with logistics. The care and feeding of the armies, as much as combat valor or operational determination of the generals, marked East Tennessee operations. Longstreet soon experienced the results of inadequate transportation for bringing supplies from north Georgia as well as a dearth of local provisions. He irritated Bragg with constant pleas for help while advancing slowly from Tyner's Station to Sweetwater and beyond. Speed was of the utmost, not just because Bragg told him so but because of Knoxville's stockpile of Yankee supplies and the approaching end of the campaigning season. Burnside's early correspondence also had emphasized the difficulties of long-distance logistics across intervening mountain ranges. The Federal government accordingly had constructed an immense supply dump for five hundred thousand rations at Crab Orchard, Kentucky, over the Cumberlands to the west. Still, both armies lay at the end of long resupply routes. Eventually they would suck dry the East Tennessee economy. "I expect we will see enough soldiering if we stay in E. Tennessee this winter," wrote Pennsylvania infantry corporal Frederick Pettit to his sister from Loudon in October. Everything had to be hauled nearly two hundred miles over the mountains, and "the rebels keep us pretty busy."[13]

Both sides had clearly underestimated logistical difficulties when they advanced against each other in November and December. Burnside's men had hoped to live off the land when they fanned out from Knoxville to tame the region and enlist loyal unionists in their ranks. Pro-Confederates like Dr. J. G. M. Ramsey complained after the war how "they exhausted the smokehouse and cellar of all the necessaries of life, cut down the forests as they pleased, and erected in their fertile fields villas of cabins for their soldiers." The Seventy-Ninth New York "Highlanders" quickly discovered, however, that even local Scottish Americans greeted them with contempt and far from accommodated their needs even by chit or receipt. The New Yorkers experienced further culture shock upon observing a local woman "wipe tobacco juice from her mouth and return her stained hand to the bowl" in which she busily mixed biscuit dough. The Federals expected to be left alone and to enjoy a quiet winter. Requisitioning food and forage during harvest time proved marginally successful, although Burnside estimated that only four days of meat and grain had been the greatest amount he could amass by mid-November. Then Longstreet showed up, not only threatening Knoxville but also disrupting foraging and resupply while at the same time further destroying the civilian food base. One South Carolina colonel reported how the ranks thought the name Sweetwater denoted a land of milk and honey, and artilleryman E. P. Alexander re-

Union supply center in Chattanooga, Tennessee. National Archives and Records Administration.

counted how they expected delicacies like cheese, sardines, and champagne awaiting them in Knoxville. Instead, in worsening fall weather
of chills and rain, they gleaned only what they could beg, buy, or steal
from East Tennesseans or scavenge from the dead in the skirmishes en
route to that city. As pro-Confederate Myra Inman of Cleveland complained, "We will have plenty of corn, potatoes, tallow, pumpkins and
nearly enough to do us another year if we can only keep it from our
soldiers."[14]

The Federals actually had not gotten very far from Knoxville. Local
Confederate resistance and fatigue from the long march from Kentucky
slowed them down. Southwest Virginia offered sanctuary to regional
Confederate forces simply slipping back and forth across the state border with impunity, and there was little that Burnside's men could do,
logistically tied to one hundred miles of available rail line from Loudon
south of Knoxville to Rogersville in the north. At best, probably five
locomotives and twenty-two cars served their needs. Skirmishes and
foraging, as well as recruiting drives among the citizenry, registered
as accomplishments. Whatever had not been abandoned or destroyed

previously by retreating Confederates (such as an invaluable pontoon bridge at Loudon) now fell to Yankee use as Colonel William J. Bolton's Fifty-first Pennsylvania carefully shipped it piecemeal back to Knoxville. Captain Orlando Poe, the army's chief engineer, and Lieutenant Colonel Orville E. Babcock, the IX Corps assistant inspector general, reopened abandoned sawmills and other facilities to fashion timber, forge nails, spin cotton, and make ropes in support of the Federals' efforts to consolidate their defense of the Knoxville region.[15]

Longstreet's advance raised the stakes. Crossing the rain-swollen Holston River west of Loudon on November 13 and 14, the Confederates forced Burnside into action. Tennessee River headwaters confounded the defenders. Burnside first thought about defending the whole region, even crossing the Holstein River and making a stand in Blount County between that stream and the Little Tennessee River until relieved by Grant. Even retreat back to Kentucky offered options. "Old Burn" (as his friend George McClellan liked to call him) really wanted to remain the protector of East Tennessee, and sager counsel came from Assistant Secretary of War Charles A. Dana, Congressman Maynard, Colonel Babcock, and others. Young Assistant Inspector General Lieutenant Colonel James Wilson, in fact, precociously told the Rhode Island general, "Grant did not wish him to include the capture of his entire army among the elements of his plan of operations." So Burnside decided to concentrate at Knoxville, where, according to Dana, he might "continue collecting food and forage and living off the country to the latest moment." Rumor in the ranks had the withdrawal order coming from Washington, but no matter: what this meant, then, was a consolidation of force that had become itself something of a logistical nightmare by early November. With the IX Corps south of the city and the XXIII Corps stretched from Knoxville north, Burnside's original projections for about a week's supply of flour and meat on hand proved totally unrealistic. Quite like the Chattanooga situation, Federal forces in northeast Tennessee found themselves unprepared for a long siege. As it turned out, so was Longstreet.[16]

Orlando Poe described the locale for the Burnside-Longstreet confrontation as "a narrow tableland or ridge, generally elevated about one hundred and fifty feet above the river, but with many points of greater height" extending from a point two miles east of Knoxville, "down the river to Lenoir's, a distance of some twenty-four or five miles." The railroad ran along this valley, he noted. Random encounters with Confederate foraging parties such as at Motley Island ford on the Little

Tennessee River underscored sharply escalating confrontations. Then, Huff's (Hough's) Ferry (November 14), Lenoir's Station (November 15), and Campbell's Station (November 16) became flashpoints in Burnside's fighting retreat back to Knoxville. Suffering from chronic diarrhea dating to the Mexican War, the general had requested relief from command—but not until after the latest emergency. He now intended drawing Longstreet farther away from the Confederate's railhead at Sweetwater and support from Bragg.[17]

After "destroying the pontoon bridge, saw-mills, factories [and] one hundred wagons which had been corralled there laded with provisions" at Lenoir's Station, Colonel William Bolton wrote in his journal for November 15 that troops "cut the spokes of the wheels burnt the harness, tents and officers baggage." The mules were necessary to pull the artillery. Having just drawn five days uncooked rations, the men became human pack animals as barrels of bacon, coffee, and sugar were broken open and distributed to them. What could not be used was destroyed: nothing should be left to the enemy. Even caissons and battery wagons of the artillery would be destroyed eventually. The Federals then began a cheerless night march through mud, darkness, and "more or less musketry firing through the entire night." It became a race with the rebels for the critical chokepoint where the Kingston and Loudon roads converged about a mile southwest of Campbell's Station. It was a close run thing. Burnside's force of barely thirty-five hundred men was stretched to the limit.[18]

The pivotal action came at Campbell's Station and might not have occurred had "Fighting Joe" Wheeler's cavalry been north instead of south of the Holstein on a diversionary mission to Maryville. Or if Lafayette McLaws's infantry had arrived at the pivotal road junction sooner or even had Brigadier General Micah Jenkins (now commanding Major General John B. Hood's division following that general's latest wounding at Chickamauga) outflanked a stubborn defense provided by John Hartranft's Second Division of the Union IX Corps. The Confederates had not anticipated a dogged contest in which veteran Yankee units like the Seventy-ninth New York, stoically "unfurling our colors[,] . . . awaited the advance of the enemy." Darkness ended the combat that cost the Confederates two hundred men, their opponents only half that number (although some figures reversed the ratio). The Federals went their way unopposed for the final fourteen "damp and disagreeable" muddy miles to Knoxville. They had saved their weapons and equipment and what munitions and supplies they could haul with them although Texan John C. West later wrote his wife how "the road is strewn with shells and ammunition from [Lenoir's Station] to Knoxville and there are signs of burning everywhere." Longstreet cast about for blame at this lost opportunity to destroy the opposition, fastening on Brigadier General Evander Law, a rival for Hood's position. He also pilloried his old Georgia comrade McLaws, who equally seemed lacking in ardor. McLaws, in turn, later pointed in the direction of Brigadier General Micah Jenkins. At the time, the hungry and badly shorn and clothed Johnnies merely plodded after the enemy, disappearing in the late November gloom.[19]

As fighting raged at Campbell's Station, Burnside had instructed Poe "to select lines of defense around Knoxville, and have everything prepared to put the troops into position as fast as they should arrive" from the delaying actions below town. Civilians (black and white alike and secessionists as well as unionists) were dragooned into pick and shovel details helping the blue-coated soldiers dig earthworks. Local secessionists like fiery Ellen Renshaw House had never been comfortable with Federal occupation, and she kept track of the confusion and excitement as the investment unfolded. Cavalry and infantry rushing back and forth—"none know what they are after, or where they are going"—was her impression. Every means of conveyance, plus barrels, crates, and cotton bales, were moved into blocking positions astride access roads. Locomotive trucks and driving wheels were fastened with ropes to stakes so that they could be rolled down hill onto any attackers. Ammunition rationing continued at a premium, although "nearly one-half of the troops had two guns each," noted one observer. Skirmishers were issued cotton balls dipped in turpentine so that they could be lit and thrown out to uncover an attacking column, and rockets were placed along the lines for similar purpose. Some prominent unionists, like William G. Brownlow and Thomas A. R. Nelson, simply fled the city, fearing capture should Longstreet take the place.[20]

Burnside had deftly conducted his retirement. Mud had not hindered the rapidity of his march, while logistics and battlefield mistakes apparently cost Longstreet the chance to capture his quarry short of Knoxville's fortifications. Ironically, it would resemble a foretaste to the following year's miscues, ineptitude, and delay accompanying John B. Hood's experience at Spring Hill followed by the Franklin disaster and Nashville coup de grâce in Middle Tennessee. Finger pointing over Lenoir's and Campbell's Stations vied with weary and now-subdued troops seemingly in no particular hurry to finish the march to the city.

There, no fewer than fourteen thousand determined and dug in Federals awaited them. Even Longstreet recognized that he had to methodically reconnoiter and only a siege might give the Confederates any chance at victory. Yet time was not on their side. Longstreet confronted not only Burnside but also the prospect that Bragg could not contain Grant's ever-strengthening army at Chattanooga. The fate of East Tennessee hung upon events at these two cities.[21]

Decision at Knoxville

Situated 150 feet above the Holston River, Knoxville before the war had been a city of over five thousand residents possessed with gas lights, a telegraph company, three banks, and at least eight churches and blessed with rich musical organizations, concerts, and schools, according to E. Katherine Crews. The war added not merely the clatter of soldiers but also their accompanying frivolities, pathos, and disease. Inevitably, as in other occupied upper South cities, by late 1863, churches and schools had been converted to hospitals and open ground had become despoiled by camps, storehouses, and an uncertain ring of fortifications (at first rebel, later Yankee). This then was the atmosphere when skirmishing began on the afternoon of November 17. In the process, Brigadier General William Sanders fell mortally wounded (leading Burnside to honor his sacrifice by changing the name of formerly Confederate Fort Loudon or Buckner). Sanders's seven-hundred-man brigade plus that of Kentucky Brigadier General Frank Wolford stymied the Confederates. Confederate artillerist E. P. Alexander later mourned the death of his West Point friend "Dock" Sanders "but did not know that they were his troops we were fighting until I heard of his death." Meanwhile, Union entrenching continued unabated. Under Captain Poe's critical eye, work parties spent up to eighteen cold and wet hours a day in the festooning hilltops both north and south of the river with forts and redoubts, linked by rifle pits all with clear fields of fire into various creek valleys to their front. Damming of the creeks afforded additional moatlike protection in some quarters, even though "many of the citizens were rebels and worked with a very poor grace," noted Bolton. Elsewhere, the pontoon bridge carefully retrieved from Loudon at the end of October and relaid just west of the mouth of First Creek on November 1 was protected from potential enemy interference by iron cable and log boom. The bridge afforded Burnside the advantage in shifting troops rapidly from either river bank to threatened sectors of the defense line. Federal cavalry screened the south bank of the river and the country beyond. Three Union forts occupied high ground there that Wheeler previously had failed to capture.[22]

Infantryman Pettit of the 100th Pennsylvania not only "found everything in the greatest confusion" at Knoxville when he and his comrades reached there about noon on the sixteenth but also "great determination amongst the troops to hold the place" when they filed into the lines the next day. By night, a chorus of cattle, hogs, horses, and mules intermingled with band music from the campsites of both armies and occasional picket firing. Confiscation and requisition squads ranged over the city looking for food and forage to provision the hungry defenders. It was a "weird reality as upon some horrible phantasm," suggested one defender, as much of the belligerence vanished at nightfall when old veterans fraternized across the lines to "exchange their respective experiences of moving accidents by flood and field." That ceased once more at dawn with everyone "returning to their posts, the exhibition of a head or hand of either side is but an invitation to a hostile bullet." In fact, sharpshooters provided the most deadly activity for much of the siege period. Confederate soldiers might police up Yankee stragglers in their wake, and secessionists such as Dr. J. G. M. Ramsey could filter back to their homes in recaptured areas, yet Longstreet was running out of time.[23]

The fact was that Lee's warhorse had no intention of returning to Bragg's oversight. Nor did he seem unduly concerned about the general situation before Chattanooga or, for that matter, any timetable dictated by the coming East Tennessee winter. Bragg did not press for Longstreet's return until the very eve of the Union breakout on Missionary Ridge/Lookout Mountain. He even moved nearly eleven thousand more men in the direction of Knoxville until Grant's actions forced their recall. He also ordered Sam Jones to send four thousand more to help Longstreet from southwest Virginia. Yet Longstreet seemed content to merely wait for Burnside's starvation, informing Bragg to that effect by telegraph on the twentieth. Staff officers like Colonel Moxley Sorrel complained that his commander moved simply too slowly. True, he had thrown a cordon around his enemy, massing infantry, artillery, and cavalry around the city north of the river while demonstrating with cavalry and infantry against Forts Higley, Dickerson, Stanley, and Hill on the high ground south of the river. In the end, Longstreet would focus upon Fort Sanders and its sector of the defenses that covered the Kingston Pike into Knoxville.[24]

For a time, Burnside continued to receive some food supplies from unionists upriver who merely floated supplies downriver by raft. Then,

Longstreet's encirclement successfully cut one of the Federals' most promising resupply schemes. Burnside's commissary officers previously had devised a plan to herd hogs over the mountains from Kentucky. Some thirty thousand porkers would thus provide a virtually endless supply of meat for the army in East Tennessee. A precedent had been set earlier when IX Corps reinforcements had driven two thousand hogs and six hundred beef cattle behind its main supply train and then professionally slaughtered and salted the meat at Knoxville, possibly using McGhee's old plant. This time, the army contracted drovers to herd a new disjointed and squealing herd over the treacherous mountain paths. They reached the outskirts of the city almost simultaneously with the rebels. Unable to breach the blockade, contractor William Hacker and his crew turned back toward Clinton, Tennessee, and eventually retraced their steps across the mountains with twenty thousand of the original twenty-one thousand hogs. This logistical cause célèbre subsequently survived icy weather, profit-seeking contractors, and Longstreet's arrival only to await resolution of the siege.[25]

Historian Maury Klein termed the events of the next few months starting with Knoxville as "the most bungled, inept, and ill-fated campaign in Confederate Military annals." Confederate artillerist Edward Porter Alexander cited the absence of good maps for cutting off Burnside's retiring forces, but exiled East Tennessee Confederates like Dr. James Ramsey placed blame squarely on the top commander. The physician particularly heaped scorn upon Longstreet in postwar reminiscences, for "he should have made one day's work of it and gone into Knoxville before he paused an hour." The capital error of this general, claimed Ramsey, was his tardiness: "the fault of fat men generally, and especially of the phlegmatic and apathetic." He had more confidence in Carter Stevenson (who by this time had rejoined Bragg's army). In truth, the doctor's feelings may have resulted from Longstreet's snubbing of his advice on map reading. Surely Ramsey could have no real complaint about the Georgian's methodical advance since it afforded him the opportunity to visit his wife and young family at Lenoir's before accompanying the army to Knoxville. Later he returned to exile, attending to official Confederate duties at Atlanta. Ramsey simply reflected East Tennessee secessionists' dashed hopes for redemption via Longstreet's expedition.[26]

A variety of factors, many of them acknowledged in the general's own postwar reflections, explained Longstreet's actions. These included procrastination and inconsistency at the time of the siege, a stubborn reliance on inadequate mapping, and dismissal of advice from local secessionists, all of which were coupled with hope that the town might be starved into submission (punctuated by some short and brilliant assault on Burnside's worn-down defenders). The delays that resulted from waiting for reinforcements were still another factor, and Longstreet's memories of the heavy cost of Gettysburg and Chickamauga further conditioned his response. Finally, late-arriving dispatches (conveyed by the Army of Tennessee's aging chief engineer, Brigadier General Danville Leadbetter, who was familiar with the Knoxville scene from previous duty there) suggested that Bragg was recalling most of the reinforcements destined for Longstreet. Bragg wanted the Georgian to finish his mission and return the main army. Longstreet thought he could still capture Knoxville.[27]

Some Confederates, like Georgian W. R. Stilwell, mused that "it will take a hard fight to get the enemy out of the place." Generally, his comrades were overconfident. They had bested Burnside and his men on too many previous occasions. Chickamauga had restored their faith in themselves after Gettysburg and they had shown their mettle to western Confederates. Others, like Porter Alexander, looked to take Knoxville and the Federals if only "to make Burnside ashamed of himself for something he had done a few months before"—the incarceration of Kentucky *beau sabreur* John Hunt Morgan like a common criminal in the Ohio State Penitentiary. Longstreet, Leadbetter, Alexander, and various division and brigade commanders all reconnoitered Union lines during the early days of the siege. The eastern Confederate officers thought little of westerner Leadbetter's judgment, and from the beginning they had considered an assault on Fort Sanders. Then they shifted to Leadbetter's choice of the Mabry's Hill works at the extreme end of the defenses. However, every approach reminded them of the field over which George Pickett and others had advanced at Gettysburg.[28]

In Alexander's postwar view, "There never was a more complete fiasco than the attempt to find a favorable point for attack," since "everywhere we saw near a mile of open level ground obstructed by a creek & artificial ponds, without cover anywhere, even for skirmishers, & all under fire of formidable breast works on commanding hills." "It required no discussion," Alexander concluded, adding with a hint of distrust of the old regular army engineer, Leadbetter, whose Maine birth rendered him suspect, "even Leadbetter had not a word to say." Eventually everyone returned to the Fort Sanders objective. Alexander, however, claimed that he would go to his grave believing that the Maine Confederate foisted an ill-conceived scheme upon Longstreet, who "af-

The infamous Fort Sanders moat, depicted in a postwar photo with the University of East Tennessee in the background. Library of Congress.

terward preferred to accept the responsibility rather than plead that he had let himself be so taken in." Of course, at the time, they all thought that a quick assault could take the fort.[29]

In truth, Fort Sanders (née Loudon and Buckner) originally had been one of Leadbetter's engineering projects. Atop a nearly two-hundred-foot hill north of the Kingston Road and slightly northwest of College Hill (site of East Tennessee University, later called the University of Tennessee), the two-acre work dominated western Union defenses. Trapezoidal in design with prominent northwest and southwest salients, its twelve-foot parapets had additional cotton-bale strengthening raising the earthworks three additional feet. A dry moat, now rapidly filling with rainwater, some six to eight feet wide and ten feet deep added to its strength. Engineer Poe had additionally strung telegraph wire around tree stumps in front to entrap unwary attackers. Still, those attackers might move quickly under cover to within 80 and 120 yards of the work. After artillery suppression barrages, they could spring a final assault before defenders could recover sufficiently. Or so went the theory. The five-hundred-perimeter-yard fort mounted a dozen field guns but could hold only 450 men. Its open rear gorge permitted rapid reinforcement in time of crisis. Still, its loss might roll up the whole Yankee line.[30]

What Confederate field glasses failed to discern proved the besiegers undoing. The wire entanglements (thought to be blackberry vines, according to one Thirty-sixth Massachusetts major), as well as the true depth of the moat, eluded the final Longstreet-Leadbetter reconnaissance. They simply saw a Union soldier crossing the ditch in front of the northwest bastion and assumed it was no more than five feet deep—no particular obstacle. All the time defenders like the Seventy-ninth New York and 100th Pennsylvania continued to improve Union positions despite inclement weather and incessant rebel sharpshooting. Michigan troops sent out house-burning sorties to remove sniper lairs. One Highlander cook caught a bullet in the neck while smoking his pipe during one such an encounter. Finding himself still alive, he coughed up blood and the offending "minie ball" marched smartly off to the hospital! Then, Confederate plans changed at the eleventh hour.[31]

Weather, lateness in the day, and phlegmatic command postponed any assault on Fort Sanders until the twenty-ninth. Longstreet dropped the idea of artillery preparation altogether. He directed that McLaws's troops drive in Union skirmishers before midnight, form in predawn darkness, and, supported by their own marksmen, simply rush the main northwest salient at daybreak. No need for ladders to scale the ditch, its depth was too shallow anyway. Crazy enough to come out of Bedlam was Alexander's later conclusion, but at the time he had remained merely chagrined that his artillery had been shunted aside. McLaws and Jenkins were skeptical as rumors abounded that Bragg had been beaten at Chattanooga, making further bloodletting needless. Longstreet remained adamant, probably still riled that Burnside had escaped into Knoxville in the first place. The assault "must be made at the time appointed and must be made with a determination that will insure success," he told McLaws irritatedly.[32]

The first part of the scheme succeeded brilliantly. Skirmisher positions fell just after midnight, and shortly after 4:00 a.m., three brigades rushed forward to the fort itself. Their formation was brilliant, thought Major William Franklin Draper later, a line of skirmishers preceding a "a regiment or brigade in column then another skirmish line then a regiment in column." The wire entanglements made short work of the attack's integrity, however, and a disorganized mass of humanity plunged into the deeper-than-anticipated moat, now half-filled with rainwater, its parapet sides rendered slick with overnight ice from buckets of water the "crafty Federals" had dumped on their surface. Lacking scaling ladders, the rebels became sitting ducks for Lieutenant Samuel N. Benjamin's garrison. The young West Pointer coolly employed his lit cigar to personally turn cannon shells into improvised hand grenades which the defenders rained down upon the hapless attackers. In some cases, the doomed rebels threw the missiles back at their assailants. The artilleryman's Parrotts, Napoleons, and ordnance rifles added to the carnage for those still stuck in no-man's land. There was little sense of "giving quarter," as the Yanks coolly shot down one gallant Confederate officer who made it atop the parapet "and stood cheering on his men, encouraging them, alone in the line and unarmed." A witnessing Federal officer thought afterward that never could he "shake hands with the officer [ordering that act] for doing such a cold blooded deed." Altogether, enfilading fire, the telegraph wire, and the moat conditions all brought the Confederate assault to a standstill after about twenty minutes. South Carolina colonel Coward commented that if the attackers ever got into the ditch, "they will be like rats in a cage trap." And so they were.[33]

"Remember James Island," shouted the New Yorkers, alluding to one of their own costly defeats at Secessionville, South Carolina. Indeed, it was a reverse Fredericksburg as the Federals massacred the trapped rebels in Fort Sanders's moat. The unequal fight left approximately one thousand Confederate dead, wounded, and captured to only between twenty-one and forty-two Federals killed and wounded (of the eventual fifteen hundred to two thousand casualty figures for the whole siege). Ninety-eight bodies alone were found in one twenty-foot space of the northwest bastion's moat. Moreover, the defenders had been tenacious in hand-to-hand combat and in their willingness to extend "no quarter." Colonel Bolton termed the affair "a gallant and persistent attack, but it was handsomely repulsed." Infantryman Pettit noted three stand of enemy colors captured in the fort's ditch. Sergeant Francis Judge of Company K of the Seventy-ninth New York received a Medal of Honor five years after the war for seizing the Fifty-first Georgia's flag in the action. Longstreet's aide, Colonel Moxley Sorrel, recorded later that one young Georgia officer actually got through an embrasure "and instantly demanded the surrender of fort and garrison." The defenders, "while making him a prisoner of war," wildly cheered him. Onlookers like Porter Alexander could not believe what they saw—surely the fort had surrendered. Later he would bemoan his own role in not accompanying Jenkins to intercede with Longstreet to secure such implements before the assault. One of McLaws's staffers told Longstreet that it was useless to continue assaults through the entanglements without axes. "Without a second thought, I ordered the recall," Longstreet recounted.[34]

Burnside called a truce at noon to gather dead and wounded. Opponents like Alexander and Sam Benjamin used the occasion to fraternize in no-man's land. Longstreet now dropped any idea of renewing the assault. One captured rebel supposedly told Burnside personally, "General I will tell you our men just swear they are never going into that slaughter pen again, and when they won't go the ball won't roll." Another captive observed wryly, "General Longstreet said we would be in Knoxville for breakfast this morning, and so some of us are." Truth was, as Massachusetts soldier George A. Hitchcock recorded, "Longstreet took the flower of the rebel army and threw them against the fort filled with two or three veteran regiments and Captain [*sic*] Benjamin's battery." Certainly everyone had had his fill of direct assaults on heavily defended positions. A disgruntled Longstreet was left to ponder his next move.[35]

The investment did not end. Soldiers on both sides expected renewed combat, although within half an hour of the failed assault a courier brought word of Bragg's fate at Chattanooga. A telegram from President Davis (relayed through Confederate lines at Rogersville north of Knoxville) stated that the Army of Tennessee had retreated to Ringgold, Georgia. Longstreet was asked to cooperate with his old commander once more. But additional word soon discouraged Longstreet that Grant had cut the roads to Georgia and dispatched Major Generals Gordon Granger and Philip H. Sheridan with the IV Corps, as well as Major General William T. Sherman with the XI and XV Corps, to free Burnside at Knoxville. They had ten days, starting November 28, to do it. News of the relief column soon became known in Knoxville and fighting slackened. Everyone, including contrabands, still worked strengthening fortifications. As historian Robert McKenzie recounts, only hindsight made it become clear "that the twenty minutes of carnage on 29 November marked the defining moment of the Knoxville siege."[36]

Finally, on the afternoon of December 1, large wagon trains of the enemy could be seen moving eastward, observed Union colonel Bolton, "and we think that the siege will be raised soon." This was the fourteenth day of the investment, he said, "and the rations are getting shorter and shorter every day." Burnside's inspirational message, read at dress parade that day, noted "to all the offices and soldiers of the IX Corps, too much praise cannot be awarded, for the heroism, patience and valor displayed by them, on all occasion for the past three weeks." He especially singled out the Fort Sanders garrison. Still, it wasn't until December 5 that Bolton could proclaim that "the siege raised at 4 o'clock A.M. by the enemy retreating in the direction of Strawberry Plains" with his Fifty-first Pennsylvania in hot pursuit. Quite a number of their pickets were captured, he said, "but Longstreet had made good his escape" and the troops returned to camp. "I never felt more relieved in my life than when we found the rebel army gone," observed Fred Pettit, adding, "Thank God for this deliverance was the emotion of my mind." Burnside soon followed with another field order calling upon the Army of the Ohio to "commemorate the series of victories all culminating in the redemption of a loyal district, by inscribing on their Colors and Guidons the comprehensive words, expressive of the grand result 'EAST TENNESSEE.'"[37]

By Sunday December 6, Knoxvillians could emerge from ersatz shelters in cellars and gather together to swap war stories. Naturally, unionists were elated, but to secessionists like Ellen House, "a leaden cloud hangs over our spirits." In distant Washington, Lincoln had rejoiced at first with news of Grant's victory at Chattanooga, but then characteristically reminded his field commander bluntly, "Remember Burnside." All that was now ended, Lincoln's project "nearest and dearest" to him—redemption of East Tennessee for the Union—accomplished. In truth, the word "redemption" may have been slightly premature. At first, Longstreet thought about returning to Bragg's army. When that became impossible because of the army's relocation to north Georgia and Grant's relief column in-between, Longstreet accepted Bragg's November 28 suggestion that he might retire to Virginia and drew off to the northeast. He would not leave the region. Nevertheless, Lincoln recognized the significance of Burnside's victory, calling upon "all loyal" to assemble at their places of worship to "render special homage and gratitude to Almighty God for this great advancement of the National Cause."[38]

The Federals' plight during the siege could be sensed from Colonel Bolton's journal comment on December 6. "We were pretty hard up for rations for both man and beast," he noted. The stark facts were that each man had been allotted one-quart of cornmeal for five days, "four ounces of sugar and two ounces of coffee; bean-bread, hard, one loaf, weighing forty two ounces, for four for each day; two spoonsfull of salt for five days per man"; a little fresh beef "sometimes, at times about ten inches of pork for five days, two spoonsfull of molasses per man; one half plug of tobacco every five days, and at times corn issued to the men on the cob." If a horse or mule dropped a grain of corn from their feed boxes, the soldiers would eagerly pick it up, and even the manure would be searched for corn and pounded into meal. The animals themselves fared no better, feeding on boxes and tailboards of the wagons, eating the ropes and gnawing into the collars for the straw they contained. Knoxville rivaled Chattanooga for privation during the period, as trees were cut down for firewood and half-starved horses and mules were driven to the Holston and slaughtered, their carcasses thrown into the river. Still, there had been lighter moments as when Burnside forced secessionist women of the city to walk directly beneath his headquarters and national flags, as it had been "no uncommon thing for them to spurt their tobacco juice in our faces," Bolton recalled. Chagrined as the secesh were, "all of us from Burnside down to the last private were in good spirits during the entire siege," concluded the Union colonel, as "no man thought of retreat or surrender," being "determined to defend the place."[39]

Longstreet's Campaign to Nowhere

Longstreet opted for continuing pressure on a beleaguered Burnside while at the same time drawing any Yankee relief column farther and farther from Chattanooga. He could help the defeated Army of Tennessee in no better way, he thought. Moreover, by the last day of November, Longstreet also had in hand a dispatch from Grant to Burnside (carefully planted so as to fall into Confederate hands) that had outlined not merely one but purportedly three separate relief columns on their way to Knoxville. Sherman's command moved on the south side of the Tennessee River. A second body, led by cavalry brigadier Washington L. Elliot, marched from Decherd northwest of Chattanooga back through Murfreesboro before heading east across the Cumberland Plateau to Kingston and on into Knoxville. A third force under Brigadier General John G. Foster (the ailing Burnside's designated replacement) would come in from Cumberland Gap. Longstreet intended to meet and destroy Foster. What Longstreet did not realize was a major Confederate command change: Bragg was out as commander of the western army.[40]

On the very day of that change, December 2, Longstreet wrote Bragg outlining how he was "threatened on every side, without communication in any direction." The next day, Army of Northern Virginia commander and Longstreet's nominal chief, Robert E. Lee, weighed in with Richmond authorities, offering his opinion on the "condition of affairs in Georgia and Tennessee." "I think," Lee told President Davis, "that every effort should be made to concentrate as large a force as possible under the best commander to insure the discomfiture of Grant's army." He worried particularly about "our depots of provision and important manufactories" in the Peach State. Indeed, the command situation there, not Longstreet's sideshow, took precedence. With Lee even considered as Bragg's replacement, Longstreet remained tied to forlorn upper East Tennessee.[41]

Meanwhile, Sherman joined Burnside by December 6 after a physically grueling march, according to participants like German Americans John Daeuble and Gottfried Rentschler of the Sixth Kentucky. The relief column "carried on their bodies all their belongings, including flour, half-rations and sixty cartridges per man." They reported quaint towns like Morganton and Maryville "demolished and mostly abandoned" with virtually destitute inhabitants all the way from Chattanooga to Knoxville. "The country people had nothing but meat and corn, and only in small quantities," Rentschler noted. Longstreet's Confederates had cleaned them out. And so "we finally came to Knoxville, almost starved after a 10-day march." Unbelievably, by comparison, the generals eventually enjoyed a sumptuous turkey dinner, seemingly belying the notion that near-starvation attended Union forces at Knoxville. No festivities, however, attended Elliott's relief column battling guerrillas and brutal terrain coming cross country from Murfreesboro.[42]

Longstreet's force had decamped for the upper counties at nightfall on December 4. Jenkins took the lead, McLaws in the rear followed by wagon trains and the whole column screened by Brigadier General William Martin's cavalry. Alexander's men fashioned fake cannon or "quaker guns" to deceive the Federals as to their departure. To their commander, "a couple of [Captain George V.] Moody's 24 pdr Howitzers bellowed our last farewell, and sent two shells that made flashes, like lightening in the dark, where they exploded over the enemy's lines and in five minutes more the last guns were limbered up and the column was in motion." Passage proved slow "between the black dark and the pouring rain and the thick woods," so that the Confederates could do nothing "but let our animals pick their own way." As a result, he missed a hanging party for a Union spy yet endured "a hard night's march" in the cold, over bad roads, faintly illumined and warmed by miles of fences on fire "at the angles where the rails crossed." The shivering column did not stop short of Blaine's Cross Roads, eighteen miles from Knoxville. It was "one of the coldest times I ever saw," confessed Georgian W. R. Stilwell. Longstreet eventually made a stand in the

Rogersville area, where he could both intercept Foster and (he informed Richmond) receive reinforcements and resupply by rail from Virginia. Meanwhile, Burnside regaled Sherman with tours of the Knoxville defenses that had withstood Confederate legions for two weeks.[43]

As Knoxville's residents gaped at the Fort Sanders battle site or marveled at the physical destruction of the siege for dwellings, outbuildings, and landscape, the Federal commanders wondered what to do about the Confederates now in northeast Tennessee. Burnside thought Longstreet was bound for Virginia. He released Sherman back to Grant while retaining Granger's ten-thousand-man IV Corps. His force (or that of Foster when he eventually arrived in Knoxville on the tenth) could hasten rebel departure from the state. Such optimism would now cost the Federals dearly. Neither Burnside's nor Granger's men (who had not replenished their supplies after Chickamauga) could handle winter campaigning. Lacking tents, blankets, or coats, they were in the same predicament as Longstreet's own poorly outfitted veterans. It would befall East Tennessee civilians to succor both bedraggled armies at no small cost to themselves. Sherman, for his part, scarcely protested his return to Grant, for he abhorred East Tennessee as a thankless sinkhole, did not agree with the policy of occupying the region, and thought it should be stripped and abandoned. He allowed his men that opportunity on their march back to Chattanooga. Meanwhile, Burnside entrusted his second-in-command, Major General John G. Parke, with pursuit of Longstreet. On December 12, Grant sent instructions to Foster that retaining Granger, he should "drive Longstreet to the farthest point east you can."[44]

Foster immediately told Grant that "the weather and want of supplies are serious obstacles." Then, as an ailing Burnside made ready to leave Knoxville for his home in Rhode Island on December 12, Longstreet moved to fall upon Parke's destitute force. These eight thousand to nine thousand infantry plus four thousand cavalry had come from the Army of the Ohio, scarcely recovered from the siege and short in all types of supplies. "It is true that we were 'driving' them," contended William Todd of the Seventy-ninth New York, "but they did not run very fast, and our advance troops didn't seem particularly anxious to hurry them." That evening Foster wired General-in-Chief Henry Halleck in Washington, as well as Grant, that "Longstreet is moving leisurely up the valley, foraging as he goes." Union horsemen harassed his rear but could do little given bad roads while poorly shod and physically weakened infantry further handicapped pursuit. Grant fully expected Longstreet to continue on to supply dumps at Bristol, Virginia.[45]

If occasion permitted, Foster hoped to make "a dash at Saltville" in southwest Virginia with his mounted force. Driving snow, cold, and exhaustion of men and animals precluded that result when Parke's people met McLaws's force at Bean's Station, about fourteen miles from Rogersville on December 14. Longstreet had decided to turn back and smite his pursuers. Some five hundred casualties resulted for both sides before the Federals disengaged and retired to the Blaine's Cross Roads–Richland Creek area by nightfall. Eighth Michigan cavalryman Watson B. Smith wrote his father on the twentieth that "the enemy gained no advantage save position at the battle but Longstreet claimed to have come away with sixty-eight captured wagons, about forty of which were loaded with sugar, coffee and other stores. Georgia sharp-shooter William Montgomery remembered the wagon capture because it was "loaded with brown sugar and roasted coffee in the grain." "I was a not long in filling my haversack," he commented. Thus began what one local historian termed a "campaign to nowhere" with Union and Confederates sparring all winter on the axis of the East Tennessee and Virginia Railroad.[46]

Longstreet pointedly informed Richmond that "we shall be obliged to suspend active operations for want of shoes and clothing." Virtually every dispatch laid out the dearth of horseshoes, ammunition, and "so little transportation, that I can barely subsist by using all of my teams to haul flour, corn, & c. and am thus far unable to accumulate supplies." The region seemed to abound with those supplies, yet "the season is so far advanced that I doubt whether any important operations can now be undertaken." He still thought offensively: "If we regain possession of East Tennessee, I think that our position here against the enemy's flank, in case he moves into Georgia, will be a good one, and it will be a good point from which we may threaten the enemy's rear in Kentucky and at Nashville." In the end, however, the southern general disliked "to venture out at so late a period without shoes." He could supply his army for the winter, "and if we can do [no] more we may drive the enemy out for want of provisions, or force him to come out and fight us." The Davis government apparently agreed, telling Longstreet to gather all foodstuffs and animals possible within his lines.[47]

Longstreet's ideas at this point paralleled that of one of the Confederacy's superior military strategists, Pierre Gustav Toutant Beauregard. Chafing in exile while commanding the Department of South Carolina, Georgia, and Florida at Charleston for over two years, this veteran commander had plied Richmond with plans and suggested military alternatives to little avail. In December 1863, he advanced to political friends at the capital, a "sketch of operations" designed to "arrange for a sudden and rapid concentration upon some selected, decisive, strategic point of the theater of war of enough troops to crush the forces of the enemy embodied in that quarter." Knoxville would be that concentration point. Upward of forty thousand men drawn from across the shrinking Confederacy (including Virginia) would join the Army of Tennessee and Longstreet's corps to comprise a formidable strike force of one hundred thousand men. Lapsing into Jominian references to the art of war, Beauregard proposed breaking out of north Georgia and striking from East into Middle Tennessee to overwhelm Grant's forces and either "pursue the routed Enemy with vigor to the Banks of the Ohio and Mississippi" or return "to the several sources the various detachments or quotas for the campaign" as circumstances allowed. Given the immense topographic and logistical obstacles involved, Beauregard still felt "intense anxiety lest golden opportunities shall be lost—lost forever." He regarded "a concentration and immediate mobility that are indispensable to save us." Then, on December 16, General Joseph E. Johnston arrived to take over the Army of Tennessee at Dalton, Georgia, assuming command three days shy of the New Year. He, not Beauregard or Longstreet, would define operations.[48]

Longstreet's idea depended upon finding mules to mount his approximately thirteen thousand infantryman for a thrust across the mountains into Union-occupied Middle Tennessee and on into Kentucky. Received sympathetically by Lee, a more realistic quartermaster eventually quashed the scheme on the grounds there were not enough mules available or even obtainable. Here was apparently another consequence of early Confederate loss of the upper heartland. Lee biographer Douglas Southall Freeman dismissed the fantasy that would only have littered the mountain route "with dead mules and dismounted men." Besides, Longstreet had enough to occupy his time at Rogersville. Troubles with subordinates like McLaws and Law underscored command disharmony. Basically, Longstreet was peeved about not taking Knoxville and unhappy with denial of full independent power. Perplexed by War Department authority accorded Brigadier General John C. Vaughn to mount his brigade for war service, Longstreet fired off a scathing indictment of the mounted arm, particularly the Confederacy's policy of employing partisan rangers.[49]

A confirmed infantry soldier, Longstreet insisted that "our country is completely overrun by cavalry; farms destroyed and forage and subsistence consumed and wasted to such an extent that I am apprehensive that we shall not be able to get along." Partisan cavalry, he commented, often transferred their authority to keep and sell everything that they capture not merely to the enemy's side. "Horses, mules, cattle, and, in some instances, Negroes are taken and sent south and sold," and now the regular cavalry too had taken up the idea, he noted, so that "I fear that this feeling to acquire property is more at heart with much of our cavalry than a disposition to drive the enemy from our soil." He urged disbandment of the partisans or their dispersal so that they might be conscripted into the line infantry. Such terse sentiments met a positive reception in Richmond, although none of this was new. Irregulars ravaged much of the upper South. East Tennessee was only passing through the same trials visited upon other portions of heartland.[50]

With the Confederates in winter quarters by Christmas from Morristown north between the Holston and French Broad Rivers and their opponents occupying the region from Knoxville and Strawberry Plains to Cumberland Gap, both sides turned their attention to basic survival. Impassable streams, bad roads, and scarcity of food and forage hampered both sides, despite a railroad that linked each of them to facilities in their respective rear. Sherman's march to relieve Burnside had been revealing, as "we have eaten and are eating up much meat, meal, four, &c., and though we try to forage on the enemy, I fear we take much of Union people." One Cleveland, Tennessee, resident had complained on November 26 how "the Yankees are taking our corn, potatoes, pork, salt and never pay a cent and besides talk very insulting to us." Chickens, too, and even "Aunt Phoebe's quilt off of her bed" fell prey to the enemy's rapaciousness. She wailed on Sunday, November 29, "We sit in the house with bowed heads while the victorious army passes along with raving manners, and offer up a silent prayer for our country whilst we hear nothing but the exultant shouts of our enemy." They came to town playing Yankee Doodle," she recounted, but she and her family "go to bed with sad hearts but still hoping God has better days for us." It was impossible to do otherwise.[51]

Sherman, at least, had spared the mills "because we hold and may hold the country." After the siege, orders went out from Knoxville that local troops should not attack farm fences for fuel in order "to protect the crops of farmers, who will be entirely destitute during the coming winter unless it is vigorously enforced." That, of course, meant nothing to freezing troops. But, far away in Washington, the Lincoln administration felt that "the holding of East Tennessee, and the prevention of the enemy from getting supplies there, is deemed of the greatest importance."

So while early winter storms slowed most of the operations to that end, Grant sent another senior commander, Major General Philip H. Sheridan, by mid-December to get things in order at Strawberry Plains, Blain's Cross Roads, and vicinity.[52]

The New Year's period was most brutal. German American Gottfried Rentschler noted bitter cold, relentless wind, and little or no issued rations. It was so cold on January 1, he claimed, that "the water in containers next to the fire froze." Reenlistments were due about this time and proved slow to rally for another tour. Complaints were rife about inadequate provisioning of food and clothing by the government and the soldiers conveyed them back home to local newspapers. All that would change but slowly over the next two months as restoration of transportation and expedited resupply occurred all up and down the upper Tennessee Valley. At the end of January, Rentschler correctly predicted (as it would turn out) that "little or nothing will happen before the first of April."[53]

What did occur in part was an upsurge in partisan activity, atrocities against unionists, and re-outfitting of farm fencing in wire by the civilian populace in order to deny the wood to liberating Yankee soldiery. By this time, Grant believed that Foster, Granger, and the others would "be as much force as can be subsisted for the present, and I think abundantly sufficient to keep the enemy from making any inroad, and possibly to drive him entirely out." He had told Halleck optimistically on December 17 that "if Longstreet is not driven from the valley entirely and the road destroyed east of Abingdon [Virginia], I do not think it unlikely that the last great battle of the war will be fought in East Tennessee." Deserter and citizen reports both had suggested Bragg's army was too much demoralized and reduced by desertion to do anything that winter. So planning to visit Nashville and Louisville, Grant would return to Knoxville, "if there is still a chance of doing anything against Longstreet." He badly wanted to move the enemy beyond Saltville that winter, "so as to be able to select my own campaign in the spring instead of having the enemy dictate it for me." He asked his colleague from campaigns on the Mississippi, Rear Admiral David Porter, to send two or three light-draft gunboats over Muscle Shoals to be used on the upper Tennessee, where they would prove of immense service. He even directed Foster to "collect all the stores you can in East Tennessee this winter." They might be needed in the spring.[54]

A Valley Forge Winter

Both armies had orders to provide receipts and requisition only necessities from the inhabitants. Army of the Ohio cavalry corps headquarters near Blain's Cross Roads and the provost marshal of East Tennessee both forbade stealing household effects by "unauthorized persons." Wagoners and wagon masters were singled out as "the worst offenders," with robbery, theft, fraud, and open outrageous violation of all laws characterizing "their conduct in every part of the country." "In behalf of a people who have suffered more than those of any other portion of the United States for their devotion to the Government," Brigadier General Samuel P. Carter, himself an East Tennessean, appealed to Foster to protect the populace from the depredations of an obviously starving and ill-clothed army. And Granger made it abundantly clear the next day in a letter to Army of the Cumberland chief Major General George H. Thomas that his division had been nearly a month without tents and clothing replacement and possessed only limited transportation, thus "being obliged to live upon the country." Pneumonia and diarrhea attended their bivouac, twenty-two miles east of Knoxville with the stock of medicines inadequate to the epidemic. Nearly six hundred of Granger's men lacked shoes; moccasins fashioned from blankets and threadbare summer uniforms, and ponchos but no tents, covered their bodies. Their patriotism was put to the test, they muttered. One cavalry scout brought word that there were numerous gristmills in the vicinity of New Market, eight miles from Strawberry Plans—run by the enemy.[55]

Grant soon grew impatient. A campaign that he proposed to Washington for knifing south to the Gulf of Mexico at Mobile was hung up by Longstreet's tenacious hold in East Tennessee. More active campaigning by the Army of the Potomac in the East promised some relief. Grant promised to rush supplies to Foster and arrived for a personal visit to Knoxville on the last day of the old year. The northern army's quartermaster general, Montgomery C. Meigs, advised Foster from Chattanooga to use pack-mule convoys over the mountains from Kentucky until such time as railroads could be rebuilt from Nashville to Chattanooga and steamboats employed to ferry goods upriver to Knoxville. Foster wrote Secretary of War Edwin M. Stanton on Christmas Day about promptly reimbursing local citizen claims in order to prevent undue suffering among the people. Like Burnside, he too now sought relief from duty due to health. Daily skirmishing and small encounters while on forage expeditions in the Mossy Creek area occupied the troops while their officers complained continuously about "the unauthorized and pernicious manner in which foraging was conducted" near Strawberry Plains.[56]

Prominent East Tennessee unionists like Thomas A. R. Nelson sensed little relief as he recorded how "our fences are burned, our horses are taken, our people are stripped in many instances of the very last vestige of subsistence, [and] our means to make a crop next year are being rapidly destroyed." When the "best Union men in the country make appeals to the soldiers," they were "cursed as rebels," and when certificates were given for property taken, "they are generally far much less than the true amount." "A citizen in attempting to enforce a claim against his Government has to run the gauntlet of 'the circumlocution office,'" Nelson complained. "Discouraged and disheartened, he turns away, feeling that the Government which he loved and honored and trusted, and which never did him any harm before the war, has at last become cruel and unjust, and cares nothing for his sorrows and sufferings."[57]

Union soldiers like Fred Pettit of the 100th Pennsylvania summarized the matter for his family on Christmas Day 1863 from a camp near Blain's Cross Roads. He supposed that all at home "are busy today eating your Christmas cakes, Christmas dinner, and all the other good things which old Christmas is supposed to bring." Then, he suggested, "perhaps you would like to know how we are spending our Christmas in the army." The previous Yule he had dined on pork and beans, but this year "we have been furnished nothing but a small piece of boiled beef" supplemented by "a few crackers, a little cheese and butter" from the sutler. In fact, they had only gotten one-fourth to one-half rations of bread over the past month. So "standing picket all night and making your breakfast and dinner on a small piece of boiled beef without any bread does not go well when you have money in your pocket." Money meant little, since clothing too was at its lowest ebb—toes sticking through both shoes "and everything else in about the same condition." He wasn't complaining, he said, as "this army is now in far better spirits than the Army of the Potomac was at this time last year with plenty of rations and good clothing." "We have beaten the enemy and feel confident of being able to do so still," with reenlistment high due the fact that everyone wanted to "finish what we have begun." The soldiery understood "that it is impossible to get supplies here fast enough for so large an army." Such grim determination was necessary to withstand what would be the coldest winter in some years in the region.[58]

Ironically, Longstreet's men enjoyed a far more sumptuous feast that holiday. Settled into makeshift winter huts around Russellville,

Morristown, and Rogersville, they scavenged the countryside, bringing back turkeys, hams, chicken, molasses cake, gingerbread, cornpone,
and the ubiquitous demon rum. At first, they had lived on parched corn
and "sometimes ¼ lb. of flour," Georgian Will Stilwell observed to his
wife just before Christmas that "our campaign thus far has suffered
from the fact of Bragg's path." By that he meant that when "he fell
back from his position he left our rear exposed and we had to change
our base by a side step to the left," going to Knoxville and "leaving
Burnside's army there and almost starved out." He contended that if
Bragg had held his position at Chattanooga, "I think we would have
captured all of them." Still, "happy and cheerful" was the way one staff
officer characterized the rebels, although several wondered about what
had been accomplished since leaving Chattanooga.[59]

As with Bragg at Chattanooga, the Knoxville result raised generally
unpleasant feelings against Longstreet too. At months end, Longstreet
sought relief from his duties and jokes freely circulated in that city about
"Peter the slow" and being a "slow, old humbug." Certainly winter dol-
drums contrasted with expectant autumn when he and his men had advanced expectantly against Knoxville. Then, Foster's renewed attempt
(at Grant's urging) to push the Confederates beyond Bull's Gap, south-
east of Russellville, pulled the Confederates out of their lethargy. Neither side intended a major battle. So they merely squabbled in the area
of Dandridge, ultimately forcing the Federals to retire toward Knoxville
by midmonth. At least arch secessionists like Eliza Fain inwardly rejoiced that Rogersville and vicinity had passed back under Confederate
protection.[60]

Fighting at Mossy Creek, Fair Garden, Kimbrough's Cross Roads,
Blant's Hill, and Dandridge reflected Union and Confederate desire
to control of the foraging area between the Holston and French Broad
Rivers. While Union cavalry leader Samuel Sturgis consistently claimed
victory over his opponents in the field, his net gain of hard-fought territory seemed to shrink before the Confederates' renewed push that carried all the way to Strawberry Plains, scarcely fifteen miles from Knoxville, at one point. Then both the Richmond government and Johnston
dashed any notion of Longstreet continuing to besiege the city. No additional units were available to reinforce that option, they said. In fact,
by February 20, President Davis specifically ordered Martin's cavalry
back to the main Army of Tennessee. Longstreet petulantly retired to
Bull's Gap with pickets at Russellville and one division plus artillery even
moving as far back as Greeneville, home to Tennessee's Union military
governor Andrew Johnson and termed, by one Virginian, "perhaps the

most intensely disloyal town in E. Tenn." It was virtually deserted at the Confederates' approach. In all, Longstreet considered his new position "unassailable," although that was apparently just what the Federals in Knoxville decided to undertake later in March. By this point, Longstreet and the Confederate high command had given up on retaking Knoxville but clung to the idea of taking the initiative back to Middle Tennessee. Then plans collapsed when Union buildup in Virginia occasioned Longstreet's recall to the Army of Northern Virginia.[61]

Grant, who had originally wanted Longstreet pushed back to Virginia, now decided he could do no further mischief where he was for the winter. Later, a new commander at Knoxville, Major General John Schofield, and a rejuvenated Federal force advanced to challenge Longstreet, arrayed along Bay's Mountain from Rogersville to the Nolichucky River in Greene County. Schofield's goal was Grant's goal: defeat Longstreet, redeem the rest of East Tennessee, and move on to destroy indispensable salt works at Saltville, Virginia. Advancing from Knoxville with the only slightest hint of spring in the air, the Union commander could not believe the destitute scenes of destruction and privation. Beyond Strawberry Plains, he determined the impossibility of attacking the strongly posted Longstreet. Despite minor brushes between the combatants, nothing of consequence resulted from this expedition. East Tennessee unionists like Oliver P. Temple called this mime not really war but one army "doing all it could in a hospitable way to induce the other not to depart, and the other graciously agreed as long as there was anything left to eat."[62]

Temple's contention that would not change until Federal patrols at the end of March and beginning of April discovered that Longstreet was returning to Virginia. In fact, if anything through most of that cold and wet winter, it was more a matter of extending areas for foraging than strategic positioning. With temperatures well below zero almost every night, pickets froze to death at their posts and the dead from the various skirmishes could only be interred with difficulty in countless country graveyards. To Lewellyn A. Shaver of the Sixtieth Alabama camped east of Morristown, "the suffering of Washington's Army at Valley Force, if it equaled, certainly did not exceed that of Longstreet's Army, while located at this place." It was his opinion that "it may be safely asserted that the annals of warfare present few, if any, parallels with this campaign in point of hardship."[63]

Reminiscing in his eighties, sixty-one years after the close of the war, Confederate R. G. Smith of the Cookeville, Tennessee, area said it well concerning the post-Knoxville period: "We were moved from place to place, staying some time at Dandridge [*sic*] than at Morristown where we remained a month, perhaps." It had been "one of the coldest winters I have every experienced," with the mountains covered with snow all the time and "in the valleys the ground was frozen so hard that traveling was difficult. "We had frequent skirmishes with Yankee Cavalry, but these did not amount to much." Eventually Smith and his mates left in the spring, and by May 5 they found themselves in Richmond, Virginia, "a rough miserable looking set of men." While in East Tennessee they were cut off from the outside world, living on what they could pick up from the surrounding country and suffered for both food and clothing. Many were barefoot when they got to the Confederate capital, the merchants there "came with armsful of shoes and gave each needy man a pair." Clothing from the War Department soon appeared so that before long they "were fixed up very well" and ready for the next campaign when Grant moved the Federals overland in eastern Virginia.[64]

In fact, historian Alexander Mendoza paints a more opaque portrait of Longstreet and his First Corps that winter. Suggesting that they may have found a land of milk and honey upon first arrival in the upper counties, all that changed. As Alabama Sergeant W. R. Houghton from Benning's brigade complained, they would have taken bread from a baby "if there had been bread and a baby to be found." Nonetheless, Mendoza credits quartermaster Major Raphael Moses with superhuman efforts to feed, sustain, and clothe Longstreet's men. As with the Army of Tennessee in north Georgia, the legions in East Tennessee settled into a sedentary camp life of letters and packages from home and occasional socials with local belles or they resorted to hard drink and a predictable soldierly disgruntlement about conditions. The incessant alarms and skirmishes probably made for a livelier winter in the upper counties than with Bragg's army, but in all, observes Mendoza, coping with a hostile environment and guerrillas (much less the Yankees) helped improve First Corps cohesiveness as a fighting unit. The winter tested the men's character, but the First Corps "wanted to achieve a victory over the enemy, something that had eluded them for a long time." They probably cared less about any grand strategy of redeeming the heartland and most certainly preserving Confederate banners over a God forsaken, volatile frontier like East Tennessee.[65]

Even a year later, the meaning of the Fort Sanders victory remained etched on Union escutcheons for those still stationed at Knoxville.

Chaplain Henry Cherry of the Tenth Michigan Cavalry was one. From across the river, "Fort Sanders is in full view," he wrote friend Amos Gould at home, "which the Rebels attempted to take by storm, & into the ditch of which were piled 597 men in a few minutes, by being tripped up with a telegraph wire, which was wound from stump to stump near the edge of the ditch, which it is said 1000nds lay in a hollow beyond having their charge impeded by wires fastened near the ground & by this strategy the Rebels under Longstreet were defeated, & Burnside held the city, driving Longstreet's forces beyond Strawberry Plans & afterward to near the Virginia line." It sounded simple in retrospect and, of course, never broached the subsequent suffering and almost purposeless campaigning that signified the rest of the winter's East Tennessee campaign. No matter, Union arms had liberated Knoxville, held it against a veteran foe, and stabilized this last part of the unoccupied Volunteers State, at least in their own minds. What remained was the unresolved process of stabilization and reconstruction for what East Tennesseans called their "upper counties" between Knoxville and the Virginia line (or for that matter most of the region as a whole).[66]

Blending War and Occupation

Mixed signals emerged from the East Tennessee campaign of 1863–64. Longstreet's men "had become a breechesless, shoeless, lousy, starving band, roving all about through the woods, preying on cattle, hogs, sheep and almost every creeping thing they could run across, destroying a ten-acre field of corn with all ease in one night and be squealing for more next morning; sitting around the fire cracking parched corn with as much grace as an old hog ten years old," wrote South Carolina lieutenant Richard Lewis to his mother on the last day of 1863. In fact, their shift beyond Knoxville "was so hasty and through such a poor and exhausted country, we had to resort to the issue of corn, and frequently we got nothing for two or three days, except what the men could steal and forage through the country." The same picture attended their opponents' pursuit. Edward Summers of Company B, Sixth Kentucky Cavalry (U.S.) wrote his cousin back in Bracken County from Mossy Creek on January 11, 1864, "We have bin and are yet pretty hard run for provision [living on half-rations], and have bin for near two months." In truth, he wrote, "we have went as high as three days without a mouth full of anything but parch corn." All that would change, Summers expected, "as soon as we get the Rail Rode Bridge finished a

Cross the Holston river the Cars will be up with Supplies." Summers claimed they had Longstreet's "whole force surrounded and his capture is sure" as "there is no way for him to make his escape." "We would close in on him if we had supplies," he added.[67]

The war's harshness also affected civilians. "I have seen mutch of this world and its buties" but also "witnessed many Dark and Horrible Deeds such as has made my blood run cold," Summers continued. He had viewed so much slaughter and bloodshed "that I have become hardened to it indeed so mutch so tat it don't affect me a bit more to see a man shot down than if he was a hog." Such images spread across the whole upper South stretching from the Mississippi Valley to northeastern Tennessee. The presence of starving, foraging bodies of armed men in uniform (many hardly under control of their officers) introduced turbulence and disruption to expanding circles beyond the battlefield. Mounted raids and guerrilla or partisan activity transcended the accepted rules of warfare. East Tennessee was now added to the oppressive and confiscatory nature of civil-military relations. Surviving accounts and reminiscences like those of J. B. Polley of the Fourth Texas Cavalry, and official reports and correspondence of the armies not unlike the civilian jottings of Myra Inman of Cleveland and Eliza Fain of Rogersville, reflected the shock and disbelief about man's cruelty to man in the seemingly relentless scavenging and foraging that ranked uppermost in affairs that bitter winter. East Tennessee secessionist and sometime treasury agent for the Confederacy J. G. M. Ramsey wrote President Davis on April 13, 1864, about "pro-CSA citizens" in the region suffering at the mercy of unionists and U.S. soldiers with many starving "with no prospects for crops this year." He wanted the government to purchase or impress supplies for distribution by trusted agents. Much could be attributed to a breakdown in military logistics for both armies thereby causing widespread foraging and impressments. Fain more simply commented in her diary two days after Christmas, "I feel God will never bless a people who disregard his commands" since peace could never come "until the fourth commandment is obeyed."[68]

East Tennessee became more than a mere item of interest to politicians and generals. That winter, food, clothing, and shelter became the abiding concern of soldiers and civilians alike, from urban Knoxville to rural farmland stretching from Chattanooga to Bristol and southwestern

Virginia. Knoxville itself felt the health menace of small pox among soldiers, freed people, and even citizenry. Unburied animals and poorly interred dead soldiers provided a public health menace as neither civil nor military authorities did much to alleviate the situation. The White House congratulatory telegram to Grant after Chattanooga had indicated a blunt "Well done. Many thanks to all. Remember Burnside"; yet it had taken over four thousand casualties to redeem East Tennessee. Hardly comparing in ferocity to Shiloh, Perryville, Stones River, or Chickamauga, the statistics of the East Tennessee operation remained a reminder of the cost of finally purging Volunteer State soil of all secessionist spirit. For Lincoln and his generals, it was a matter of regional unionism, as well as strategic importance as the gateway to Georgia. For Davis and his commanders, the issue was not merely retaining a rebellious province, but more the potential of losing a vital rail and communications link between eastern and western portions of a diminishing Confederacy if not an entry point back to Middle Tennessee and Bluegrass Kentucky beyond. It was a matter of survival for the soldiers of drawing "three crackers for two days rations" while their officers' cooks ranged across the country "and buys chickens and all sorts of things good to eat," complained James Whitney of the Forty-fourth Ohio band at Strawberry Plains on January 4. By March, Illinoisan Thomas Berry at Morristown felt "some of the Regiments in the rear ought to be brought to the front so they can learn something about war, the boys of the 83d [Illinois] at Fort Donelson don't know anything about war yet they have learned only the first rudiments as yet." Everyone looked to the return of "veteranized" or reenlisted men to the ranks to relieve the hardships of those in winter encampments like East Tennessee.[69]

At the same time, other issues mattered. Indeed, North Carolina governor Zebulon Vance complained to the rebel War Department how his own borderland mountains were "filled with tories & deserters" and "robbed & eaten out by Longstreet's command." Military advisor Braxton Bragg replied in mid-April that "more harm than good" had resulted from allowing what he termed "reserves" or Home Guard partisans laxity of cooperation with the main army, but little came of it. Wrapped in such considerations were violations of citizens' rights, death on some isolated picket post and battlefield for the soldiery, and the anguish of empty corn cribs, cold hearth stones, and war weariness for the common folk victimized by both sides. Perhaps for this reason, Andrew J. Stephens, orderly sergeant of Company E, Second North Carolina Mounted Infantry (Union) stationed at Cumberland

Gap, wrote in fractured prose to Miss M. J. Brakebill in Knoxville on July 29, 1864, cursing the war's impact and how

> it has deprived many a man of his life and caused thousands of invaledes that their life wil be a misery to them the remainder of their dais whilst the men who Caused the Rebellion to be brought on are not Engaged in it they are lyeing at home resting easy—the war hoop has not rech their dores yet but I don't think that it wil be a grate while til it will re-sound evry where thru out the Confederacy and every Reble in it may feal it.

Union soldiers and loyalist civilians could relate to Stephen's final comment that he wanted to live to see "Every Reble Damnd and delivered and then I want to go Home and see my people."[70]

CHAPTER 3

The Situation at Midwar

Seventy-two-year-old Columbia, Tennessee, farmer Nimrod Porter started his January 1864 diary by noting how the previous year had left many thousands with aching hearts, mourning lost friends and relatives slain or "wounded and carried off the field to die." Countless others had sickened and died in prisons, hospitals, and camps. Said Porter, "History cannot record the great destruction of life that has been occasioned by this most unnatural and wicked war." What dreadful suffering had resulted from the unnecessary conflict, he wrote. No survivor "will be able to give a full picture of its consequences and distresses." He cited widows trying to retrieve property wrenched from them by "the ruthless hands of the soldiery," leaving them and their children "in a state of sufferings." Midnight robberies and lawlessness on the highways "are the order of the day" in every neighborhood, committed "by soldiers belonging to both armies and robbers that don't belong to any army." That such bandits were "trafficking and trading unlawfully having Negroes to steal mules and horses and carry them off to those robbing traders appears to be the order of the day," he observed. Those actions drained the country of all the mules, "leaving us without any chance to live." "Oh, how long will divine providence permit such a state of affairs to continue," wailed Porter.[1]

Those in Confederate ranks could only fume from a distance. Third Tennessee major Flavel C. Barber had noted in his diary from an Army of Tennessee campsite near Dalton, Georgia, on December 3, how "every account from home confirms the tales of desolation and insult and robbery inflicted upon our once happy and prosperous middle Tennessee."

"Truly we have much to bear," he added, asking, "May God give us strength and courage to bear it." Somewhat in contrast, Arkansas colonel Daniel Harris Reynolds penned year-end thoughts at Brandon, Mississippi, "in hopes that 1864 may see the close of the war and our brave and suffering soldiers returned to their homes—and our country beginning to recover from the great burdens that are now weighing her down." He anticipated a "glorious and prosperous" future once Independence was gained since "as a people we have all the elements of greatness." Wondering frankly "how many years will close before our cruel enemies cease a hopeless war" and acknowledge that independence, he observed how his people had suffered many hardships and how "we will be able to bear and will bear many more rather than yield."[2]

Reynolds preferred anything, even death, to submission. May we all have the wisdom and manhood to continue the struggle until we succeed in the great contest, he concluded, "remembering that future generations are alike interested with us in the result." Elsewhere, Private Grant Taylor of the Fortieth Alabama wrote his wife from Dalton about "a heap of dissatisfaction among the troops here," and that "the citizens are generally out of heart off from the army," saying "they will take the oath if the Yankees ever come through here." Tennesseean Barber, captured at Fort Donelson two years before, exchanged and hardened through the successive interval, noted that "all we can do is to fight on and hope and pray for better times next year." Submission had been made impossible "by the conduct of our insolent foe," in his view, and the only tolerable alternative was resistance to the bitter end. "We must fight, we can nothing else, if necessary forever."[3]

By contrast, David F. McGowan of Company I, Forty-seventh Illinois at LaGrange, Tennessee, however, was more upbeat. He told his sister Ellen how the regiment had received a "quite handsome" new flag on December 14, "a present from the children of Peoria." Two days before Christmas he wrote that he had read Confederate president Jefferson Davis's latest speech but not that of his own commander-in-chief. Davis's piece "is quite an able document," he wrote, speaking "quite hopefully of the final independence of the Southern Confederacy." Frankly, he continued, at that moment he wanted simply "to eat Christmas Dinner with you" and suggested that she "eat Double rations and try to imagine that I am there." By January 3, he was freezing, with the thermometer at "eight degrees below zero all day," coming on the heels of balmier weather. "Our tents are very poor protection against cold weather," as he hoped to "never hear any more about the *Sunny*

South." There was plenty of entertainment for them—good singing in camp, theater in town, and "some young ladies in town who play well on the piano"—and he thought he might "try to scrap an acquaintance if they are not too strongly Secesh." He soon gave that up since most of the fair sex had "the everlasting snuff stick in their mouths," though they spit beautifully. The Masons promised to have a big supper soon, but he did not think "they will admit outsiders." He confessed that the theater had gone lame and they anticipated marching orders anyway. Most enlightening of all, McGowan observed, "There is quite an amount of business done here by the citizens." They brought their cotton in and "sell it for greenbacks and then get permission to buy what goods they want for their own use." He did not think it "very good policy to let them trade with us but no doubt many of them would starve if it were not for our men."[4]

Searching for a Strategy

Union commander of the Division of the Mississippi, Major General Ulysses S. Grant, seemed less concerned with Providence and future generations. At the moment, he worried how conditions in Tennessee and Kentucky might affect the war in the West. Confederate general James Longstreet and his East Tennessee army threatened Grant's flank. Union resupply, which ran via fragile rail and river connections from the upper reaches of the Tennessee River at Knoxville back through Chattanooga and north Alabama, then north to a Nashville supply base, and finally on to northern Kentucky and the Ohio River, posed a great hazard for various Union armies in the field. Rebuilding and guarding the railroad from Chattanooga northward with bridges periodically destroyed by rebel raiders, insufficient clothing and provisions for his men, and the fact that "the enemy intend holding a position in this country for the Winter and to make this the great battle field in the Spring" bothered Grant when he wrote his wife, Julia, from a Knoxville visit on the second of the month. Unable to actively campaign at that point, he wanted a cavalry expedition outfitted from loyal Tennesseans in southeastern Kentucky to knife into Longstreet's line of communications at Abingdon and Saltville, Virginia. Then Grant personally took to the wintry roads up through Cumberland Gap to assure loyal Kentucky governor Thomas Bramlette that Kentucky too "is a portion of my command and shall receive hereafter as heretofore all the protection that my forces are capable of giving."[5]

Grant sought manpower for East Tennessee while Bramlette wanted sufficient troops to police his tenuous hold on the Bluegrass. It was the age-old military question—resources for home defense and occupation versus those needed for fighting armies. Civilian governor Bramlette and Tennessee military governor Andrew Johnson both struggled to raise, train, and equip soldiery for winning a war on two fronts—armies versus armies and counter-insurgency and civil support missions. Grant placated Bramlette and by mid-January had 68,000 men facing Confederates in north Georgia and north Alabama with a 9,351-man garrison back at Chattanooga. Thus Grant could write General-in-Chief Henry Halleck in Washington about the supply problem and the ill-advised winter furloughing of a large number of veterans, but also about his vision for the spring.[6]

Grant's trusted colleague of previous campaigns, Major General William Sherman, had gone to Vicksburg, Mississippi, intending an overland campaign into the Magnolia State's interior. Supported by a flying column marching south from Memphis, this move was to be a prelude to securing a line "from Chattanooga to Mobile, Montgomery and Atlanta." "I do not look upon any points except Mobile in the South and the Tennessee in the North as presenting practicable starting points from which to operate against Atlanta and Montgomery," claimed Grant. To do so meant a huge supply buildup and elimination of Longstreet. Halleck had written the previous week alluding to the Trans-Mississippi area "connected with our foreign relations and especially with France and Mexico" (a sensitivity more apparent in the nation's capital than in Tennessee, perhaps). Yet it "must be subordinate and subsequent to those which you have proposed for East and West Tennessee." Headquarters left it to Grant to decide when affairs permitted an advance toward Atlanta or the gulf.[7]

Still, Halleck pressed Grant and Sherman with his own apprehension. "The rebels seem to be making the most desperate efforts for the next campaign," the general-in-chief wrote them. With almost every man of whatever age capable of bearing arms "being pressed into their ranks, by spring their armies will be very considerably increased." By comparison "our people, are acting on the mistaken supposition that the war is nearly ended" and that "we shall hereafter have to contend only with fragments of broken and demoralized rebel armies." Such was the tone in the press and debates in Congress, and without a new conscription law, "our military force in the spring may be relatively much smaller than it now is." With this he cautioned against troop

Nashville and Chattanooga Railroad Depot with the State Capitol Building in the far upper left. National Archives and Records Administration.

dispersal and diversion of effort. He despaired that the East Tennessee situation would prevent accomplishment of the plans for Tennessee, Arkansas, Mississippi, Louisiana, and Texas that winter.[8]

Accordingly, Grant, Sherman, and Major General George H. Thomas, Army of the Cumberland commander at Chattanooga, furloughed only those units who reenlisted en masse while awaiting new contingents arriving for training and amalgamation. Grant blamed Burnside for not annihilating Longstreet when he and Sherman had conferred after raising the Knoxville siege in December. Now, on January 20, he bluntly told Halleck, "I feel no alarm for the safety of East Tennessee, but the presence of Longstreet has been embarrassing in forcing me to keep more troops there than would have been otherwise necessary, and in preventing other movements taking place." Moreover, it had proven taxing to "some of the most loyal people in the United States to support a cause they detest." At least by this time, the two generals could agree with Secretary of the Treasury Samuel Chase about removing trade restrictions in Kentucky and parts of Tennessee. Thomas weighed in, however, that "until the people of Tennessee by their voluntary act return to the Union," he could not concur that it was "prudent to remove the restrictions on trade at any point where trade is not at present permitted."[9]

An overworked Grant sounded tired and irritable in his note to wife Julia from Louisville on February 3. The town was overrun with generals, he said, due to a court of inquiry for Major General Thomas L. Crittenden tainted by the Chickamauga disaster. Grant wanted to get away: "I believe I will move temporarily to some one company post out on the rail-road where no body lives and where but few people are to be seen." He wrote Thomas in late January that Foster, in poor health, seemed incapable of hounding Longstreet "beyond the reach of doing further harm in this state." Frankly, the Georgian was not the only Confederate threat to Grant's plans. A tempestuous rebel frontier stretched from northern Mississippi below Memphis across northern Alabama to north Georgia and up to the foothold held by Longstreet above Knoxville. In the western portion, Generals Stephen D. Lee and Nathan Bedford Forrest (one or the other either "commanding or co-operating"), blocked entry from West Tennessee to Federal expedition-ary commander William Sooy Smith out of Memphis. Their comrade Philip Roddey's sixteen hundred men raided and foraged northward from the Florence, Alabama, area on the Tennessee River west of Chat-tanooga. Conscripting manpower, gathering supplies, and driving unionists and refugee freedmen into Union lines, Forrest claimed in February 1864 that he "succeeded in bringing out of West Tenn 3100 troops at the end of the year" with several hundred more arriving there-after. He had thought back in November that he could raise upward of fifty to one hundred per day to a total of eight thousand if "unmo-lested" by the Yankees, for "the people of West Tennessee generally are loyal to the South." Neither he nor the enemy could control the burgeoning illicit cotton trade, however.[10]

Still, the most serious Confederate challenge lay with the Army of Tennessee, recuperating after its Missionary Ridge collapse. It had new leadership. Braxton Bragg had departed in disgrace, elevated by Presi-dent Jefferson Davis to be his personal military adviser. A diminutive but combative Joseph E. Johnston replaced Bragg soon after Christmas. Neither the president nor the new commander liked one another, and "Little Joe" underestimated the strength of his adversary (around eighty thousand) and his own weakness as perhaps less than fifty thousand of-ficers and men remained in the ranks at Dalton at the New Year. Six thousand prisoners and forty pieces of artillery had been left in Union hands after Missionary Ridge. Other bedraggled, demoralized, and de-feated soldiers had simply left for the duration, Georgians especially. Private Oliver V. Strickland of the Forty-third Georgia wrote home just before Christmas that he would have loved to take the holiday with his family but could not. As Private Grant Taylor of the Fortieth Alabama put it, "in low spirits and generally out of heart," drawing only enough meat and bread for two light meals a day. "I do not see how a government can expect to keep an army together [poorly] fed as we are," he concluded. Indeed, the Army of Tennessee was but a shadow.[11]

The winter of 1863–64 has been portrayed as yet another period of lost opportunities and miscommunication between Richmond and its principal western field commander. Excepting Chickamauga in September, the Army of Tennessee had an unbroken record of two years of failure—great promise always tempered by irresolute chieftains and eleventh-hour defeat. Postdefeat depression attended its officer corps after Missionary Ridge. Bragg had despaired of "politicians for generals and executive officers," while corps commander William G. Hardee admitted his faith in the southern cause was on the wane. Certainly leadership realized the want of supplies posed their greatest difficulty and one well known to their opponents. Brigadier General St. John Richardson Liddell told Hardee how the Federals "did not hesitate to seize or destroy the last hope of supply to the already destitute widow or orphan," which seemed to him to be "a barbarous method of conducting war [that] had been overlooked as obsolete or only a relic of barbarism." Still, a thin shred of irrepressible optimism stirred. A "next-time" mentality mixed with illogic from Richmond to Dalton.[12]

The next round in this cycle started immediately with Bragg's removal. A winter of rebuilding the army flirted with high-sounding plans and schemes incompatible with conditions (army strength and stamina, logistics, weather, and estimation of the enemy). The guiding mantra remained an offensive to redeem Tennessee and Kentucky with the Ohio River as permanent boundary for the Confederacy in the West. Here lay three years of unrequited goals, unresponsive generals, and a spate of strategic schemes from the likes of Davis, Bragg, P. G. T. Beauregard, Robert E. Lee, Longstreet, and others. Here too was the residue of the president's vaunted offensive-defensive grand strategy. Subordinates sometimes saw alternatives more clearly, however.

Liddell, while transferring from the Army of Tennessee back to duty closer to home in Louisiana, wondered why the railroad terminus from Talladega and Selma at Jacksonville, Alabama (a scant sixty miles from Dalton) would not have enabled "us to shift to either one at pleasure, as the movements of an enemy moving between these points indicated the proper course of us? If the enemy attempted to march directly south from Chattanooga, we could strike him nearly at right angles from the east or the west, on whichever side we might happen to be in position," or at least "retard and confuse his offensive plans" possibly even causing a division of the Federals to occupy both roads. The chances and means of procuring supplies, available from Talladega and Selma, were certainly equal to those from Marietta and Atlanta, in Liddell's view. He deliberated about calling the matter to his superiors' attention, but "then it was so plain as to be unmistakable" since "a general's business is to know all the topographical features and railroad communications of the country in which he operates." Not so, apparently, for nobody could move before spring, and renewal of their opponents' offensive juggernaut rendered opportunity moot.[13]

Johnston took command with instructions from Secretary of War James A. Seddon not only to "re-establish hope and inspire confidence" in the ranks through discipline, prestige, and increasing the army's numbers but also to restore and supply deficiencies in ordnance, munitions, and transportation. Don't expect reinforcement, the secretary told Johnston, but "you will be able to assume the offensive" when able. Johnston answered on January 2 that to assume that offensive meant movement into Middle or East Tennessee. Given winter, the mountains, and the enemy positions, that was impractical so that "advancing from Northern Mississippi made more sense. Johnston preferred to beat the enemy in front of him at Chattanooga and then move forward, but everything depended upon finding more manpower. Two weeks later he could see moving via Rome to Huntsville, crossing the Tennessee near Gunters Landing (a scheme later actually embraced by Confederate leaders). Johnston enthused about defeating Sherman and then joining up with Longstreet to cross the Cumberlands, amply supplied from East Tennessee. By mid-March, Davis in consultation with Bragg, Lee, and Longstreet (but independent of consultation with Johnston) produced a scheme whereby the Army of Tennessee, using the railroad from Dalton to Cleveland, Tennessee, could unite with Longstreet at Kingston, west of Knoxville, traverse the mountains and Cumberland plateau, descending to Sparta in Middle Tennessee behind main force Federals, and victual and regroup to claim that region. Davis told Longstreet that "there should be a simultaneous demonstration or actual movement from Miss. into Tenn." Whatever the route, difficulties of terrain, resupply, and an obstinate enemy seemed more evident to Johnston than to anyone else. Moreover, no one seemed aware that the upper heartland might not offer a cornucopia of resources awaiting liberation.[14]

Lee could tell Davis on February 18, "It is very important to repossess ourselves of Tenn, as also to take the initiative before our enemies are prepared to open the campaign." That was as far as he went. Means (supplies) could not produce ends (strategic result) in this case. Whichever route notwithstanding, cutting loose from defending Georgia and the indispensable Atlanta logistical base presumed far too much about winter campaigning in Appalachia. Cavalry raids might achieve limited goals against the enemy but alone could not redeem lost territory. Hostile countryside devoid of provisions to succor the march of an army (however diminished in size) over rough roads through inhospitable terrain would test inadequate logistics. It was all a pipe dream and Johnston knew it. Given potential Federal reaction, Johnston, considered the arguments, weighed the difficulties and effectively blocked all suggestions on plausible grounds of under-strength, ill-provisioned forces and unprepared cavalry and artillery. Spring might be different, with returned soldiery. Stopping the Federals before undertaking a counter-offensive remained Johnston's answer.[15]

Major General George H. Thomas's abortive late February reconnaissance-in-force toward Dalton, as well as Sherman's more audacious move across Mississippi to Meridian (thwarted when Forrest defeated Smith's cavalry column from Memphis), at least spooked Confederate planners. Transfers of men and materiel to counter such threats rather than concentrating offensive power resulted. The president's emissary, Brigadier General William N. Pendleton, communicated Davis's views for "the earliest and most efficient aggressive operations possible" at a conference with Johnston and Wheeler at Dalton on April 15, but overestimates of enemy strength and unpreparedness once again left Johnston willing only to "stand on the defensive till strengthened, watch, prepare, and strike as soon as possible." The die had been cast for a month when Grant went east in March to assume supreme command of all Federal armies. Confederate strategists talked wildly of offensives against Washington itself and otherwise throwing the Federals off balance. But dreams of "going back to Tennessee" dissipated in the winter snows of north Georgia and became moot when spring blossoms presaged renewed Federal movements southward on the rail line to Atlanta as well as in Virginia. The Confederacy could find neither men, materiel, nor risk takers to bring off serendipity. The Confederate moment had passed by May. Johnston gained minimal reinforcement from Mississippi, but Longstreet returned to Virginia, his destiny determined perhaps by Lee's words to Davis on April 15: "If [Longsteet] is able to advance into Tennessee, reoccupy Knoxville, or unite with Genl Johnston, great good may be accomplished, but if he can only hold Bristol—I think he had better be called for a season to Richmond." To Army of Tennessee biographer Stanley Horn, "The opportunity to throw 90,000 Confederate troops—even paper troops—into Tennessee never again presented itself." Thirty years later, Thomas Connelly concluded that the upcoming campaign in Georgia was already over, the "army doomed to defeat." Johnston, he observed, needed good relations with his government, clear understanding of that government's expectations, solid logistical support, and the confidence and loyalty of subordinates. Said Connelly, "He had none of these."[16]

Two Recuperating Armies

The two great contenders in the West went to ground like tired titans after Missionary Ridge. They encamped less than three score miles from one another along the Tennessee-Georgia border. The winter at Dalton produced highs and lows for the Confederate Army of Tennessee. Johnston restored the morale and condition of two army corps, cavalry, and artillery, while to the rear medical director Dr. Samuel H. Stout refurbished Deep South hospitals in anticipation of renewed combat. News reached the army how the Congress in Richmond debated the currency question and repeal of laws allowing exemption from army service. The public press "is violently opposed" to universal conscription, suggested Tennessee private Flavel Barber, because "many editors and printers would be forced into the ranks." He hoped that the politicians would back off as "we ought to bring one hundred thousand fresh men into the field next spring." To that end, Irish American division commander Patrick Cleburne proposed the unprecedented and politically unacceptable plan to arm and enlist slaves with the promise of freedom "within a reasonable time." The proposal itself was couched in obtuse but self-evident language. Many of his fellow officers immediately castigated Cleburne and the government closeted his written proposal. It would not surface until the 1890s, long after he had fallen at Franklin later in 1864 and slavery had ended with the Confederacy's demise. Ironically, the merits of Cleburne's proposal found favor three months after his death, when the Confederate Congress (at Robert E. Lee's urging) authorized arming of slaves. By then, the move would come too late.[17]

While Johnston also dutifully suppressed knowledge of Cleburne's proposal, he saw merit in somehow turning the South's peculiar institution to resources for the army. Retention of blacks as company cooks, pioneers, and laborers promised to yield a 25 percent addition of whites to the ranks in Johnston's view. But in the end, this highly charged issue threatened the very being of the Confederate South and disrupted consensual development among Johnston's subordinates. The proficient Irish American was effectively blackballed within the command hierarchy, although Cleburne's old Fifteenth Arkansas would present their former regimental commander with a one-thousand-dollar sword in mid-April. Tennessee captain Robert D. Smith thought he should have prepared some special speech for the occasion, "but he came out in his old style." Cleburne "is not a fine speaker," commented Smith, but he had very few superiors as a general.[18]

Meanwhile, the hungry, ill-clad, and "disorganized and demoralized mob" of rebels began to recover, and with restored discipline the army overcame thievery in the countryside and defeatism and stagnancy in camp. Religious revivals gladdened hearts. Texas captain Samuel T. Foster recounted how Brigadier General Mark Perrin Lowrey, an ordained Baptist minister, kept "baptizing soldiers all winter, regardless of Cold weather." Playful army-wide snowball fights between units from different states substituted for mortal combat with the Yankees. Johnston's reinstituted dress parades, drills, and target practices, a furlough system, and an amnesty proclamation for all deserters helped rebuild the Army of Tennessee as a unit. The men nestled in snug log huts and laid out company streets and also reconstructed roads south of Dalton by Christmas. This was done "with a view to falling back," carped roving reporter Peter Wellington Alexander. In truth, every possible improvement to the army was essential.[19]

Still, only the single railroad supplied the army from Atlanta and "was taxed to its utmost capacity to even give the men a ration of a pound of meal and a third of a pound of bacon a day," claimed staff officer James Wylie Ratchford. Sumner A. Cunningham of the Forty-first Tennessee (and postwar editor of the *Confederate Veteran*) recalled how after the army had been at Dalton for a few months, forage wagons were sent twenty miles and farther for supplies. "There are a great many things [that] happens in a large army to keep the camp in something to talk about," observed Texan Foster. The army never suffered from raids by Union cavalry. Paperwork, as well as wrangles with state and national officials about logistics and strategy, consumed headquarters more than anything else. Camp rumors that the northern government was executing paroled Vicksburg prisoners recaptured in the battles for Chattanooga stirred soldiers like Grant Taylor since "if they should do it, our government would kill as many of theirs but that would not do our poor fellows any good after they were dead."[20]

If East Tennesseans of the Nineteenth or Middle Tennesseans of the Forty-first Tennessee regiments were any criteria, inebriation, whoring, and unbridled freedom continued until Johnston (as much a strict disciplinarian as Bragg) tightened matters. Harsher punishments (including executions), drills and maneuvers, target practice, and esprit-building dress parades brought the troops back into line as spring campaigning drew closer. Nonetheless, an aborted trip to stop Sherman in eastern Mississippi found Cunningham and the Forty-first devastating "sixty sacks of goobers and four barrels of whiskey" at Atlanta thus producing a warning for Montgomery citizens that "'the meanest men in the Confederacy' were on their way there." The counterploy against Sherman netted little for the rebels in the ranks except, perhaps, correspondence with the fair sex as the soldiers tossed pieces of paper bearing their names and units from troop trains to any women near the tracks. Occasional visits from homefolk (some Tennessee parents successfully negotiated passes through Yankee lines at Chattanooga) or new friends among the north Georgia locals, as well as more clothing and food (thanks to Johnston's efforts), improved the Army of Tennessee's morale.[21]

Desertion loomed large for the army that winter. In truth, "anxiety had replaced anticipation, and personal integrity had replaced sectional pride" as the principal motivational force in the lives of Tennesseans Morgan Leatherman and Resinor Etter at Dalton. Realizing that possible execution and corporal punishment were the plight of deserters, "I have no chance to git out of this civel ware [sic]," Etter jotted in his diary. Leatherman wrote his father that he knew his duty and would not keep the family name "free from all stain of dishonor" such as desertion. An uneven furlough distribution system (one enlisted man out of thirty and one officer among three, which Johnston eventually reduced to only those soldiers who had reenlisted) boosted some spirits although awardees tended to overstay their leave. For those southerners from areas now under Union occupation (the Third Tennessee from the Pulaski area, for instance), furloughs were an illusion. Then, too, Sam Watkins of the First Tennessee Regiment, a native of Maury County, thought the hassle of constantly showing furlough papers at every provost checkpoint while on leave diminished the attraction of this privilege.[22]

Naturally, furloughs could provide their own reward—victuals from home, personal items, and small talk that sustained comrades in the inner circle of mess and tent—if one could get home. Soldiers from

Union-occupied areas and border-states rebels particularly relished seeing kinfolk. Reading materials and newspapers had become scarce in camp (although news seemed to trickle in, even across the lines, as when Flavel Barber noted in his diary how some northern papers were speaking out and declaring the South could never be subjugated, thus urging conciliatory measures to end the war). In fact, toward late winter, every rumor of peace or military advance sent spirits racing across the encampments. Somehow, Captain James I. Hall of the Ninth Tennessee managed to procure "a fine collection of books—some two or three hundred volumes, many of them choice books," which were generally read throughout camp and "afforded our men both amusement and profit." In the spring, they would be boxed and sent to the rear with extra baggage and consequently lost in the course of events.[23]

Most fortunate were several senior officers, like corps commander Hardee and Colonel John C. Brown of the Third Tennessee. They used the winter lull to woo and marry sweethearts. But most of the army remained frozen in time and place, tied down where the army had encamped and consigned to smoky, sooty, and cramped temporary homes for those who remained with the colors. A lucky few secured transfers to the navy. In all, noted Philip Daingerfield of the Thirteenth Arkansas and later Fifth Company, Washington Artillery, "our principal salvation was Joseph E. Johnston!" He turned everything into new life, new hope, new fidelity, new zeal, and "esprit de corps," doing it "for the wreck which Bragg made and then abandoned." Tennessee cavalry captain Thomas B. Wilson observed that "the army was rallied and reorganized at Dalton during the winter." Johnston took a force "pretty badly demoralized and disheartened when it first reached Dalton but by the time the campaign opened in the next spring it had recovered its tone and was a much better organized army than it had ever been under Bragg."[24]

The main Federal camps from around Chattanooga to north of Knoxville and west to the Mississippi mirrored those of their opponents. The primordial needs of food, clothing, and shelter generally offset the ecstasy of victory. Surviving letters, diaries, and memoirs never failed to mention the privations from a "Valley Forge" winter suffered in East Tennessee or a wet and typical holiday season along Tennessee's boundary with Alabama and Mississippi. Federal cavalry, like Jennison's Seventh Kansas "Jayhawkers," spent a discomforting late year expedition trying to disrupt recruiting efforts by Forrest and Stephen Dill Lee in West Tennessee. The cold, frostbite, and a lack of tents and rubber ponchos marked their remembrance of the experience. Invalids in hospital received better food and care, they believed. At Chattanooga, the tasks of improving city defenses, monitoring a small army of prostitutes (many of them destitute southern women with husbands in the Confederate army), waiting for the first relief train on a rebuilt railroad to arrive by mid-January, and even commencement of a national cemetery took place.[25]

The U.S. Christian Commission provided quantities of religious tracts, and Soldier's Libraries sprang up to cater to men's needs. The Fifty-second Illinois organized a Young Men's Christian Association activity at Pulaski with Bible classes vying with noncommissioned-officer schools for the attention of young junior officers like Lieutenant Jerome D. Davis. By spring, baptisms in Chickamauga Creek would follow the pattern set across the lines in the Confederate religious revivals. But until restoration of dependable transport of goods and food could be assured via wagon, rail, and steamboat from major facilities back in the Nashville-Murfreesboro area, the army in blue remained at the mercy of the elements, overworked quartermasters, and questions about perseverance if not survival. By Valentine's Day, at least, "twenty-four freight trains per day run to Chattanooga from Nashville, and army stores are rapidly accumulating here," wrote Major James Austin Connelly of the 123rd Ohio to his wife. Still, he told her, "I actually feel that I have lost a great deal of valuable time *"patrioting"* up and down and over and through the lines of this rebellious Confederacy, and I don't see how I'm going to make it up." He took small consolation in doing his duty for his country.[26]

Other Federals, like Alfred C. Willett of the 113th Ohio, stationed at Stiner's Station, ten miles east of Chattanooga, remained more optimistic. "The Rebels are coming in our lines every Day and giving them Selves up," he wrote a female friend back home, adding that "they think the Southern Confederacy 'bout gone up." We looked to the new recruits for "the Sooner this reblion [*sic*] is put down the bitter [*sic*] it is for all of us[,] then we can return to our Homes in Peace and quietness." Others, like George F. Cram of the 105th Illinois, wrote his mother from Nashville in mid-January: "Military affairs drag slowly and some already think that we shall be obliged to carry on a war of invasion till all the rebellious states are subjugated one by one." He felt it would all be over "before the coming of another year."[27]

Wherever Union contingents garrisoned the occupied South, three-year enlistments were up in the spring, and so the reenlistment process stirred the camps. It was called "veteranizing" or signing up for another tour, observed Constantin Grebner of the Ninth Illinois. The Fourteenth Wisconsin of the Army of the Tennessee was typical, becoming a so-called veteran regiment in December when two-thirds of its members reenlisted and returned to the state with a thirty-day furlough, each reenlistee receiving $302 in bounty money plus the $100 for the first enlistment. However, Howard Hopkins of the Third Michigan Cavalry (stationed where they had been the winter before at La Grange in West Tennessee) vowed not to reenlist until slackers up north came out and did their patriotic duty. In fact, Brigadier General Benjamin Grierson had to reluctantly rally such men with unaccustomed speech making, arousing "all their love of organization—the company, regiment, and the 'old brigade' so that their 'esprit' was kindled all at once." The Army of the Cumberland's small regular army contingents at Chattanooga had no options; their original enlistments had been for up to five years and they watched helplessly as the volunteers partook of furloughs and bounty money. The process varied across the army, although furloughs so appealing for rebuilding morale and restocking the ranks stymied any plans for winter operations.[28]

Even those precious furloughs back north, often involving time-consuming and unpleasant passage to and from camp and home, had value. Stopovers often yielded sights and spectacles, whether a storm-tossed Lake Michigan harbor at Chicago or the imposing State Capitol and Library at Nashville, scarcely imagined by farm boys from the prairies. At Clarksville, Tennessee, the citizenry shrank in horror at the anticipated steamboat passage of their old nemesis, the Fifth Iowa Cavalry, having suffered that unit's heavy-handed occupation visits the previous year. Hawkeye Josiah Conzett noted how "the cry was lock all the doors and look to your chick coops—the Fifth Iowa Jay Hawkers are coming!" Then the men were confined to their boat during a refueling layover. But once these hard bitten, battle-tried veterans reached home, family, good food, church socials, and "the old life" restored manners as well as spirit. Many wanted to stay home and did. Others looked forward to returning for the spring campaign. Eventually even those hapless regulars left on duty with the Chattanooga army received just reward: reduction to three-year terms, bounties, and trade of dull provost duty for Thomas's brief but active midwinter demonstration to Dalton.[29]

Naturally not everyone remained with the colors. James H. Jones of the Fifty-seventh Indiana wrote from Murfreesboro in late January how he would not reenlist "unless they will raise a Company to go threw the north and hang traitors of Secesh or what you will please to call them." German Americans in the Ninth Ohio would simply choose to go home in late May, their term of enlistment over, notwithstanding the needs of Sherman's drive against Atlanta. Earlier, Ohio brigadier John Beatty penned in his diary a month before resigning to return to civil life, "Nothing of interest has transpired today. Bugles, drums, drills, parades—the old story over and over again; the usual number of corncakes eaten, of pipes smoked, of papers respectfully forwarded, of how-do-ye-do's to colonels, captains, lieutenants, and soldiers. You put on your hat and take a short walk. It does you no good. Returning you lie down on the coat and undertake to sleep; but you have already slept too much and you get up and smoke again, look over an old paper, yawn, throw the paper down, and conclude it is confoundedly dull." It was a hard sell between duty, honor, and country and the feeling that duty had been served and someone new had best look after the country. Nevertheless, approximately one in every two western soldiers would reenlist for another tour while only one in fifteen chose to do so in Union armies as a whole.[30]

Winter experiences differed only slightly for Union soldiery posted as railroad guards in "portable towns" of "canvas covers and clapboard sides" like Stiner's Station, Whiteside, or Bridgeport, or in tents on the Memphis and Charleston at LaGrange, Tennessee. Band music and homegrown glee clubs, even theater, kept the ranks entertained while extra drink, food, and merriment attended Christmas celebrations. With the cold new year returned the drudgery of clerking requisition forms, drilling or manning, and improving block houses and fortifications to guard logistical lifelines and features like the great Tennessee bridge crossing at Bridgeport. Relatively untouched north Alabama towns like Huntsville, Scottsboro, Stevenson, and Larkinsville, as well as East Tennessee locations from Wartrace to Blue Springs and Cleveland, witnessed Union soldiery fraternizing with attractive and receptive local belles, exchanging carte-de-visites as well as twirls around the dance floor. Members of the Forty-seventh Illinois at LaGrange received a new flag from the children of Peoria and wondered whether to "veteranize" (reenlist) or just serve out their time unobtrusively in that West Tennessee location. Eastern veterans like Brigadier General Alpheus Williams decided "this railroad guarding is doleful" at Tullahoma, a town with thin, slabby, and shabby houses scattered about, with broken windows and a deserted air about it. Remaining residents "are like the houses, poor white trash," while "the Negro is the only gay dog, keeping up dances every night and having a good time at a cheap rate."[31]

By contrast, Iowan John Campbell marveled at the beauty and technologically advanced "water works" in Huntsville and commented upon "no apparent coldness towards nor contempt for the Yankees manifested" in the congregation of the New School Presbyterian Church he attended on Sundays. Illinoisan David Fisher McGowan at LaGrange echoed his observations, although he was not impressed by the local female habit of "the everlasting snuff stuck in their mouths." Campbell observed a few citizens who refused to take the Yankee oath of allegiance and were unceremoniously sent "beyond the lines" to the Confederacy. And Illinois captain Charles W. Wills told his sister about encountering one refugee Virginia gentry woman who "lives off of the United States Commissary Department, and begs her chewing tobacco of United States Soldiers. She's a Rebel, and talks it with her mouth full of Uncle Sam's bread and bacon." [32]

Railroad bridge at Whiteside, Tennessee. Note the blockhouse on the near side and the fort beyond the bridge. This was typical of Federal bridge and railroad defense in the Western theater of the war. National Archives and Records Administration.

This process of interfacing with the region's inhabitants had been going on for two years, especially where pockets of unionism could be found, like around Shelbyville, Tennessee. Development of reconstruction infrastructure, which included both army largesse and private services of the United States Sanitary Commission, suggested stabilization efforts were well underway behind the advancing Union conquest of people and terrain. Letters from occupation troops stationed across the Alabama line that winter seethed with anger at perceived Copperhead traitorism back home while there were "Alabamians flocking to the old flag," with "whole companies coming in at one drove, from the Rebel army and enlist in ours," saying "they will fight for the old Union 'til the last drop of blood is gone.'" Peorian David McGowan complained to his sister while en route to Tennessee from Louisiana aboard the steamer *Sunshine* on December 3 how "there are so many people [at home] who don't appear to care what becomes of the country while they can make money and take things easy." He admitted that he would "have to drop this subject, it makes me feel bad to think that there are so many men who ought to be in the ranks, that can stay at home when, if they would do their duty, this war might be ended in a few short months." The prospect for more battles, cavalry raids, and guerrilla depredations come spring mingled with the reality of unreconstructed rebels living alongside loyal unionists while drifters, vagabonds, deserters, and outright bandits floated through the war-torn South in numbers equaling men in the ranks on both sides.[33]

The View in the Rear

A two-year occupation of the formerly lush Nashville basin of Middle Tennessee illustrated the situation in the rear. Garrison duty here involved protecting the strategic political and supply center of the upper South. It meant guarding major rail lines that were indispensable to the Union army's survival all the way from north Alabama to Knoxville. The Louisville and Nashville, Nashville and Decatur, and Nashville and Chattanooga Railroads had suffered two years of heavy wear as well as enemy attacks. However, given periods of shoal water in the Tennessee River at Muscle Shoals, Alabama, or Harpeth Shoals near Betystown on the Cumberland, which hampered any dual resupply route via the rivers, and the abysmal roads south and east over the mountains and Cumberland Plateau, there really could be no alternative to rail for sustaining Federal armies from Knoxville to Chattanooga. Finishing the prewar Nashville and Northwestern Railroad from Kingston Springs west of Nashville to the Tennessee River offered the opportunity to circumvent bottlenecks on the Louisville and Nashville north of the latter city. River and rail via a new depot called Johnsonville and thence to the Tennessee capital and on south to the armies held promise. Work lagged through the winter, although by February 1864 a mixture of Missouri and Michigan engineer units, contraband laborers, and uniformed guards from the Twelfth and Thirteenth United States Colored troops laid one-third to three-fourths of a mile of track per day. Grant placed old railroader and now army colonel D. C. McCallum directly in charge, though the project technically belonged to military governor Johnson. The new line would finally open in mid-May, a marvel of fabricating bridges and roadbed over countless stream valleys, warding off partisans and subsisting in a hostile environment of wilderness, unsympathetic populace, accidents, and unpredictable weather.[34]

McCallum may have been the principal Federal official most displeased with conditions on Tennessee railroads in general. He had been sent in December by Secretary of War Edwin M. Stanton to examine "the present condition of affairs connected with the United States military railroad service in the Department of the Cumberland." Reporting back on January 19, he declared that "while the duty is an unpleasant one, the interest of the service and my personal reputation demand a plain statement of the case." Repairs and rebuilding of the Nashville–Chattanooga line had been deferred to similar work on the road to Knoxville. Trains were thus being run at only eight miles per hour over the 151-mile stretch from the state capital to Chattanooga. Accidents occurred virtually every day as the main problem remained the old U-shaped rail on wooden stringers laid imperfectly upon an unballasted mud roadbed that had appreciably decayed over the previous two years of hard use by both Union and Confederacy. Shop deficiencies at Nashville, the desirability of using old Confederate rolling mills at Chattanooga to fabricate new rails rather than robbing them from secondary lines, and the total inadequacy of only seventy locomotives and six hundred freight cars to serve 519 miles of railroad in the department also gained McCallum's ire. He recommended increasing the total to two hundred locomotives and three thousand cars staffed by one thousand men run in the manner of the best northern railroads (with which McCallum had firsthand knowledge). This included superior organization and practical managerial and engineering talent. By early February McCallum found himself elevated to general manager

Return of a Union foraging party. National Archives and Records Administration.

for correcting deficiencies attributed to his predecessor, a less visionary and more lethargic J. B. Anderson.[35]

McCallum first reorganized rail operations into two departments, one for transportation (operation and maintenance of all lines) and a second for construction (reconstruction of railroads "which might fall into our hands as the army advanced"). Of course, the Nashville and North-western remained exempt while under military governor Johnson's charge. When it became operational, it passed to McCallum and the U.S. Military Railroad regime. So all told, McCallum's western rail "empire" would link western river ports and rail connections all the way to the front lines beyond Chattanooga and Knoxville with interim strong points in northern Alabama. McCallum would return an old hand, Adna Anderson (originally president of the Nashville and Chat-tanooga Railroad who had somehow survived from the earliest Confed-erate period), as general superintendent of transportation and mainte-nance of roads in use. He appointed W. W. Wright as chief engineer of construction and carried the organization arrangement all the way down to division and subdivision level (expansible and contractible "to suit the requirements of military movements"). Each division would comprise

five subdivisions numbering engineers, administrative assistants, mechanics, laborers, drayers, and train crews—777 supervisors and work
gangs with each subdivision further broken down into squads under
subforeman. It was a civilian equivalent to a military organization.[36]

McCallum's broader responsibility over railroads in the Departments of the Cumberland, the Tennessee, and the Ohio caused more
difficulty in securing sufficient locomotives and rolling stock. Calls
upon patriotism and well-placed contracts netted 140 additional locomotives and 2,573 cars, but even this proved ultimately inadequate
by spring. Disparity in gauge meant that he could tap only Kentucky
lines having the same five-foot standard as those in Tennessee. An over-
tapped Louisville and Nashville, as well as the Louisville and Lexington
and Kentucky Central lines, had to supply 21 more locomotives and
195 cars for the burgeoning effort. Government purchase eventually
contributed this new equipment. Extensive machine and car shops developed at Nashville and Chattanooga using machinery partly seized or
purchased in the region or obtained from northern manufacturers. At
times, one hundred locomotives and more than one thousand cars were
in Nashville facilities as it formed the main terminal station for five hundred miles of road running throughout the occupied upper heartland.
Similarly, extensive warehouses concentrated the necessary materials to
rebuild or repair track, bridges, buildings, and rail equipment. In fact,
noted McCallum later, "the general intention was to make [Nashville
and Chattanooga] the great centres toward which all operations should
converge; where supplies of all kinds could be obtained in case the roads
were cut in their rear; where repairs of any kind or to any extent could
be made, and in case communication was destroyed between them, operations could be conducted from either with facility in any direction."[37]

The war left abandoned rail lines throughout portions of both Tennessee and Kentucky. McCallum cited other railroads reopened that
winter, including fifty-two miles of the Memphis and Charleston returned to operation from the Mississippi River port to Grand Junction.
Twenty-six miles of the Mobile and Ohio were back in service from
Columbus to Union City. In both cases, however, they merely served
the garrisons of strategic hamlets, pacifying their neighborhoods. They
remained distinct and separate from main army operations and "required and received very little attention as compared with the lines leading to the front," noted McCallum. Indeed, the Nashville and Chattanooga Railroad was "the great main line, over which passed all the
supplies for the armies of the Cumberland, Ohio, and the Tennessee."

Provisions, clothing, camp equipment, animal forage, arms, ammunition and ordnance stores, reinforcements, and the varied miscellanea of campaigning passed to the front assisted by waterborne supplement. In return, sick, wounded, disabled, and discharged soldiers, refugees, and prisoners, as well as materiel, went to the rear via this transport complex. Just how well this logistical lifeline could be maintained and protected once fighting began again in the spring remained to be seen.[38]

The city of Nashville emerged in this period as the centerpiece for the Union rear. William F. King of the 147th Indiana captured the shabby treatment of war imposed on the preconflict "Athens of the South" with narrow, dusty streets and houses "without architectural taste" except for the capitol (itself virtually a bristling fortress of barricades, cannon, and guards), which still commanded "a beautiful view of the surrounding country which is dotted with tents of soldiers as far as you can see." He considered the city cemetery "the most beautiful place I ever saw," even though military now mixed with family plots and it "excites some painful reflections to gaze upon such a city of dead all caused by an unholy war." Down below was the cesspool of "Smokey Row" whereby "there is much demoralization in the army and thousands of young men here are ruined," suggested George Cram. Historian Jeannine Cole has reinforced Cram's assertion with an analysis of legalized prostitution in Nashville and Memphis. Cram, for one, was happier when his unit left the city in late February, passed through unionist-leaning Shelbyville and breathed the cleaner mountain air of the Cumberlands. Obviously, thousand of other transiting men in blue welcomed longer stays in the den of iniquity. But every time soldiers left Nashville, headquarters worried more about the city's protection. Unionist East Tennessee cavalry units now bolstered city defenders, and King's letter to his wife in late March reflected reality: "This city of Nashville is an immense military post with forty thousand troops," besides the numbers of speculators, sutlers, and camp followers. Indeed, Alfred Lacey Hough, Philadelphia commission merchant turned mustering officer for Veteran Volunteers, saw the city and its environs as "an immense storehouse" and "the largest military depot in the world at this moment," with "acres of stuff piled up around the town." He told his wife they must hold Nashville at all cost, and that government employees, as well as a small garrison, were prepared to fight behind fortifications.[39]

Indeed, a city that had seen almost no Confederate protection two years before now became the second most heavily fortified city in North America. Surpassed only by Washington, D.C., it stood unrivaled for

Fort Negley in Nashville. From *Harper's Pictorial History of the Great Rebellion.*

the sophistication of at least one of its works: Fort Negley. Arguably the most magnificently proportioned fort anywhere, it was certainly the greatest inland field fortification constructed of stone. It loomed over the city cemetery so favorably seen by William F. King. Union naval power might control the Cumberland flanks of the city, but Nashville's south-facing forts became the pet projects of professional army engineers. Major James St. Clair Morton, a native Philadelphian and West Point graduate, had commenced the work under orders from Major General Don Carlos Buell. By 1864, the very early battery and street barricade protection effected by Federal troops soon after the city's occupation had been replaced by some twenty heavy forts and redoubts, blockhouses, magazines, as well as guardhouses and stockades defending the railroad bridge across the river. A defending garrison of three thousand soldiers supplemented by two thousand mobile troops and four thousand quartermasters provided a base from which a field army might maneuver and repel attackers. Designed to hold back upward of thirty thousand enemy through heavy cannon, intricately designed and constructed bastions, tunnels, gun platforms, bomb proofs, and small-arms firing slots, Nashville's hilltop fortifications commanded vast cleared fields of fire around the city's south side. These installations also served as beacons of freedom to refugeed blacks who, ironically, became the labor for constructing the very symbols of their salvation.

Also important were the outlying fortifications for Franklin and Murfreesboro. Fort Granger enclosed nearly twelve acres in guarding the Harpeth River rail crossing of the Nashville and Decatur Railroad at Franklin. For a time, equal in importance to Storehouse Nashville was Fortress Rosecrans, thirty miles to the south on the Nashville and Chattanooga at Murfreesboro. This largest enclosed earthen fortification built anywhere during the war sat on high ground about a mile and a half north and west of the Rutherford County courthouse at the center of town. It represented five months of effort in the winter and spring of 1863 to create a sanctuary for the Army of the Cumberland in case of defeat and a supply base for that army and a means of controlling the railroad. Its two-hundred-acre complex included sawmills, commissary depots, storehouses, blockhouses, and redoubts. Its garrison shifted to controlling the countryside, suppressing guerrilla raids on the railroad to the south and servicing the continuous stream of destitute refugees streaming north from Alabama, Georgia, and lower East Tennessee. Fortress Rosecrans's relevance by early 1864 would be apparent should any Confederate army once more come to the upper heartland.[40]

Memories of the Union soldiery that Tennessee winter conveyed in word and picture a point in life's passage that could never be replicated, perhaps. Illinoisan Charles Wills recalled a sometimes tempestuous rivalry between eastern army units and western troops stationed on railroad guard. "The 11th and 12th Corps Potomac men and ours never meet without some very hard talk," he observed, and "to hear our men talk to them when passing them or their camps marching, you'd think the feeling between us and the Rebels could be no more bitter," the westerner concluded. Eloquent Federals like Colonel John Beatty marveled at the wild, "dense wilderness of the Tennessee and Chickamauga [streams] with brooding Lookout with its foothills, spurs, cover, and waterfalls congregating grounds for villains and sneaking thieves; the plumed knights, dashing horse men and stubborn infantry." In the corner where Georgia, Tennessee, and North Carolina came together lay "in former times, a rendezvous for the blacklegs, thieves, murderers, and outlaws," who could simply slip briskly across a state line, one step ahead of the law, he decided. James A. Connolly similarly stood in awe of the former Cherokee land, when encamped at Ringgold, where "save a few scattering houses, nothing but shapeless piles of brick and lone chimneys is left to mark the site of the town," thanks to the war. When pos-

sible, Chickamauga veterans returned to that ill-fated field and
sadly viewed the exposed remains of comrades and the de-
tritus of battle still on view.⁴¹

Others stood in awe on
Lookout Mountain, where pho-
tographers captured the natural
beauty of this locale—a "scene
[that] is truly wonderfully
grand—sublime, beautiful, and
even terrifying," in the mind of
William T. Shepherd of Taylor's
Illinois battery. He told his
father that he and his friends
were "also securing keepsakes,
mementoes &c. in the shape
of canes, pebbles, Flowers &c
&c all of which you shall see
when I come home." Fifteenth

Brigadier General John Beatty, USV.
U.S. Army Military History Institute.

Pennsylvania private Othniel S. Spang, an art teacher from Norristown,
portrayed in his sketchbook the winter starkness of the Sequatchee and
Tennessee Valley region and at least one impression of the primitive
living conditions of the inhabitants. Then, too, official photographs of
George N. Barnard to this day snapshot contemporary views of Nashville, Chattanooga, and Knoxville. Apparently Barnard accompanied
Sherman on inspection of his new Military Division of the Mississippi,
headquartered at Nashville. Barnard provided over one hundred views
of the army of occupation's contribution to the war—forts, structures,
vehicles, people, and, of course, the backdrop scenery that each participant in those photographs would have witnessed through his or her
own eyes.⁴²

The sense of having the soldiers active rather than passively suffering the monotony of winter camps contrasted with all the inertia of
pen and illustrations, of course. Thomas's Dalton foray and the upper
county foraging trials supported that goal. For roving Confederate reporter Peter Wellington Alexander, the Yankee failures, however, "give
us two months more time in which to prepare for the great campaign
of 1864," he assured southern readers hungry for any sign of hope. By
early May, "great activity" betokened "a movement on our side soon,"

wrote Sergeant Ebenezer H. McCall of the Eightieth Ohio from Nashville, citing "a large amount of rations, Hospital stores, Ambulances, and nearly everything needful in battle" having been shipped to Huntsville, "which place I suppose is to be used as a base of supplies." The Fifty-third Indiana was a part of that buildup, moving from Mississippi via boat convoy north to Cairo and Paducah, then up the Tennessee River toward the front. Chaplain William W. Curry, new to the unit, reported an overnight stopover at Clifton, Tennessee, on May 14, showing what "was once a promising village" but with few houses remaining "while many bare chimneys and heaps of rubbish mark the site of those given as a sacrifice to the desolating torch." "If the rebels will not learn to regard the usages of civilized warfare without the stern lesson of retaliation, they must then be taught it thus," he concluded starkly.[43]

Volunteer and Bluegrass in Contrast

Major General Lovell H. Rousseau was a native Kentuckian serving as Nashville district commander in the winter of 1864. His troops were generally well equipped, disciplined, and drilled, he told headquarters at the end of January, except for Colonel William Stokes's Fifth Tennessee Cavalry. Reconstruction of the road to Columbia and progress on building the Nashville and Northwestern Railroad seemed encouraging. Civil-military relations appeared stable except at Gallatin. Elsewhere, "the post commanders were "vigilant in suppressing the rebellion and just in their treatment of the people." Colonel Henry R. Mizner and Major Thomas C. Fitzgibbon and their Fourteenth Michigan at Columbia had captured "more armed rebels" than there were soldiers in their regiment. The disposition of the populace to return to their allegiance "is general and apparent," and throughout the district there "has been no real cause for complaint, the post commanders having been vigilant in suppressing the rebellion and just in their treatment of the people." Based on what he heard on good authority from locals, he thought 80 percent of the people desired restoration of civil authority and the old government and "will say so when the proper occasion is offered." Rousseau did not think, "I am being deceived." The "disorders and confusion incident to the war have caused great suffering, of which they are heartily tired, and are desirous of peace on almost any terms."[44]

The greatest problem seemed to be the slave population, "giving much trouble to the military, as well as to the people." "Slavery is virtually dead in Tennessee," he proclaimed. Still, the blacks leave their homes and "stroll over the country uncontrolled." Hundreds of them neither worked nor were capable of doing so, being supported solely by the government. Many straggling blacks had obtained arms from soldiers. They were insolent and threatening, thus intimidating white families who were not permitted to keep arms or would be afraid to use them if they had them. "The military cannot look after these things through the country, and there are no civil authorities to do it," Rousseau commented. Blacks had begun working for themselves but still lodged with their masters, blithely asserting their right to do so. Moreover, for some time, the soldiery went out into the country, liberated slaves, and brought wagonloads of women and children to Nashville and other army posts. Brigadier General Eleazar Arthur Paine particularly hired slaves back to their owners through printed, blank contracts filled out for the occasion, a practice neither sanctioned nor repudiated by Rousseau. He bridled at forced military enlistment of blacks still in bondage by commanders of colored troops. Basically, Rousseau did not think he could correct the "evils complained of connected with the black population" and remained unwilling to fix any rules in these matters, remedies, he felt, best left to restored civil authority.

Rousseau reported the dire state of rural affairs generally in midstate. Legal and illegal impressments and thefts had left few farm animals available for spring plowing and farmers felt little inclination to purchase replacements in light of future requisitioning. The army needed to stop impressments of the few horses, mules, or oxen still left on Middle Tennessee farms, he contended. "Between the loyal and disloyal no discrimination is made" and "unless an order be made preventing future impressments and protecting the farmers, little or no crops will be produced" in the spring. Moreover, seizing houses in Nashville for commissary and quartermaster storage also seemed bad policy for the government and unjust to the people. Done at enormous expense due to high rents and the cost of removing private property from such places, Rousseau sought construction of cheap, temporary government storehouses. Authorities should not seize a loyal man's storehouse without paying him a fair compensation.

In Rousseau's mind, restoration of civil governance would allow Lincoln's December amnesty idea to take effect if properly administered and implemented, thus leading to assurances of protection. Such would "induce the community almost in a body to voluntarily take that oath," he told Thomas. At present, the proclamation was of little practical utility

98

since nobody had been appointed to administer the oath and no place or time had been fixed for that purpose. Rousseau's observations came from a Union officer from a slave state of moderate persuasion. They were from a soldier-administrator engaged in occupation and early Reconstruction, not a victim or an innocent caught up in a fourth year of war. Loyal, hardworking, even radical when it came to treating secessionists firmly, the Kentuckian was ambivalent in racial attitudes toward wartime-induced social experiments with former slaves yet conservatively inclined to extending the olive branch toward penitent former Confederates. Still, could he have been overly optimistic at conditions and attitudes of Middle Tennesseans around him that winter?

Wartime Tennessee and Kentucky no doubt chafed at Union military presence. The secessionist Volunteer State simmered with volatility under direct military governance. The loyal Bluegrass State festered under increasingly intrusive, nationally imposed dictums and regulations that tested state and local self-rule. Federal presence went only so far in stabilizing conditions in both jurisdictions—the one under a military, the other civil governance. Federal antiguerrilla sweeps, like transitory Confederate cavalry raids and partisan activity, provided no return of law and order or allegiance to one side or the other. In both states, large swaths of territory stood untamed and as a result increasingly passed under the yoke of military control. Military, political, economic, and sociocultural disruption blended as civilian authority sparred with military demands. The emancipation issue morphed into a race question, made worse when Union military recruitment of black and white manpower inflamed the Bluegrass. Trade restrictions and permit systems, breakdown of labor and capital relationships, interruption of the interlocking network of commercial patterns across upper heartland America exacerbated peoples' worries. Just as important were matters of allegiance, sovereignty of the people and their laws. With the army as Washington's instrument to retain Kentucky for the Union, matters of civil liberties (oath of allegiance), amnesty under Lincoln's December proclamation, and procurement of human and material resources (requisition of manpower through conscription quotas, as well as contractual acquisition of materiel from food and forage to other goods and services) became controversial.

Restrictions were nettlesome. Louisville received its first lot of sugar and molasses shipped upriver from New Orleans only on Christmas Eve, despite the fact that the great Mississippi highway for commerce had reopened six months previously with the fall of Vicksburg and Port Hudson. Other affairs remained equally tenuous. True, numerous sales of Bourbon County land, as well as of slaves near Louisville, had continued before the onset of winter. However, Colonel S. D. Bruce ordered the closing of a number of Louisville coffee houses for selling liquor to soldiers in mid-January and distillation of corn in the state soon followed, also by military decree. Revocation would come within a fortnight, while on January 23, the military "permit system" affecting Kentuckians' ability to conduct business was abolished in the Bluegrass. Still, regulations imposed by the military remained an anathema no matter the wartime necessity.[45]

Indeed, Kentucky's schizoid existence could be seen when, on January 7, a communication from "the secretary of the provisional government of the State of Ky." announced that William E. Simmons had been reelected as Confederate senator for six years representing that state in Richmond. At the same time, back in Frankfort, twenty-five separate legislature ballots for United States senator failed to deliver a winner and a special committee began exploring the possibility of moving the state capital to either Louisville or Lexington. Pressure to secure citizen claims for damages by either Federal or Confederate forces or even rebuilding state infrastructure due to military activities seemed to go nowhere while some trade resurfaced, as on March 20, when Dr. L. Herr of Lexington reputedly sold his trotting stallion "Membrino Pilot" to a Chicago buyer for ten thousand dollars. Such transactions hardly affected the common man in most of Kentucky and Tennessee, however. From remote Appalachia to western counties in both states, destitution and famine, persecution and deliverance, as much as survival and sufficiency, dictated people's lives. Barbarism, guerrillaism, and persecution for political beliefs jostled economics for the most attention.[46]

Still, Governor Johnson and Governor Bramlette mainly addressed two issues in the winter of 1864: suppressing dissidence and finding military manpower. Guerrillaism destabilized both of their states, yet for Bramlette, the Negro question, when coupled with Washington's insatiable thirst for cannon fodder, provided constant challenge. Certainly both men remained the bane of rebel sympathizers and insurgency. Bramlette issued a proclamation on January 4 that held secessionist Kentuckians responsible for all guerrilla raids and charged them with aiding and abetting their outrages. For every loyal citizen carried off by guerrillas, he decreed, five "of the most prominent and active rebel sympathizers in the vicinity of such outrage" would be arrested. They would be held hostage to safe return of the captives. Disloyal relatives of guerrillas would be singled out for specific punishment. Bramlette pronounced, "Let them learn that if they refuse to exert themselves actively for the assistance and protection of the loyal, they must expect to reap the *just fruits of their complicity* with the enemies of our State and people."[47]

One contemporary almost immediately editorialized how Bramlette's "proclamation delegates an assumed absolute power over the personal liberty of citizens to irresponsible military officers, and leaves them to select their victims; it provides no form of trial, requires no proof of guilt, indicates no redress nor relief, establishes no safeguards against personal vindictiveness and petty tyranny." Sad was "such unwarrantable assumptions of executive power," especially when it led to an overly zealous military. On January 12, Brigadier General Jeremiah Boyle was temporarily succeeded by Brigadier General Stephen Gano Burbridge as commander of the District of Kentucky. Both men had served in the Union army, and Burbridge by March would embrace Bramlette's interpretation of Kentucky law regarding disloyalty and aiding, harboring, or abetting partisan depredations. As one student of wartime Kentucky alleges, Burbridge "used the [Kentucky legislature's] acts in almost every one of his controversial orders during his military command in Kentucky." Penalties included fines, incarceration, debarment for attorneys, and victim compensation. The devil would lie in interpretation and enforcement. Where relations between civilian and military in Kentucky and between the Frankfort government and Washington quickly grew tense if not intractable, centered on emancipation and recruitment of blacks into the ranks. Here the hearts and minds of Kentuckians seemed intractable.[48]

Bramlette had often bothered generals like Grant and Foster with his prodding about Kentucky security and withholding reinforcements from main army operations. Burbridge had been intended as a temporary palliative but by March 14, Grant decided that "he seems to be doing so well in Kentucky that I think he had better be retained permanently in the command of the district." That would later prove unwise, but at this time Burbridge as the local representative of national government and Bramlette as chief enforcer of the Kentucky constitution and law were simply learning accommodation. Bramlette particularly sought conciliation with Washington regarding enrollment and training of Kentucky blacks in the army (violently opposed by the legislature, if not key conciliators like Lincoln's influential Kentucky friends, John and Joshua Speed, who served as confidantes to the president). With the solidity of the Democracy in the Bluegrass collapsing into two factions and a Lincolnite party of Unconditional Unionism in the ascendancy, Bramlette sent a delegation to explain his state's position to the president. Burbridge, in turn, wired his commander-in-chief, assuring him of "the national ring" to the governor's personal recommendation to Kentuckians to submit quietly to the black enrollment, and "trust the American people to do us the *justice* which the present congress may not do." "Kentucky will do her duty to the Nation," he told the president. The administration need have "no fears about the enrollment in this State." The law would be obeyed. The governor's delegation personally reached a compromise with Lincoln whereby Bramlette assented to the enrollment but in turn received assurances that no enlistments of African Americans would take place as long as Kentucky fulfilled her quota of white recruits. Accommodation on race, recruitment, and antipartisan enforcement would prove as unstable as conditions themselves.[49]

Just how settled were Bluegrass conditions at this time? A tantalizing glimpse of affairs in Lexington, at least, could be seen in mid-April when the local provost marshal, Brigadier General Nathaniel Collins McLean, wrote home to a wife more anxious about their financial conditions in Glendale, Ohio. McLean told her on the eleventh that it was County Court Day and "this starts our fair with people from the country who were to settle accounts today or frolic." It was a great horse day, he noted, with all the fine stock of the neighborhood paraded around. "The sidewalks of the Courthouse Square are filled with furniture and everything else for sale and it looks like an Irish fair more than an American town." But that afternoon he went to a public meeting and listened to prominent locals Dr. Robert J. Breckinridge and Charles Anderson, who "both made stirring and effective appeals but their very speeches brought out in the audience, as a partition or a portion of them, the evidence of a dangerous feeling which must be carefully watched and rigidly put down as Kentucky will blasé [*sic*] up in the rebellion, under a false name."[50]

Writing over succeeding days, McLean noted rumors of a rebel advance from Mount Sterling that, however ridiculous, nevertheless prompted joy or dread among the populace as their loyalties dictated. For McLean, a "feeling of excitement is constantly kept up by the disloyal which prevents the growth of a healthy union sentiment." He thought that "this feeling is largely aided by many officers in our army here who are of the Woolford [Wolford] school." Now and then he heard little remarks of that tenor "which indicate the feeling whilst there is nothing strong enough for me to take hold of," but that he would carefully note so that whenever a good occasion arose, he might "show these gentlemen where they stand." He had in mind a visit to Camp Nelson, eighteen miles distant, he told his wife, but only traveling if he could get an escort, so threatening was the countryside. Even in nominally loyal Kentucky, affairs seemed unstable and loyalties strained. Union officers could not ride about unattended.

Andrew Johnson faced some of the same problems in Tennessee, particularly the question of harsh reprisal for disloyalty and terrorism. As military governor, he had long since become inured to violations of civil liberties. In fact, as Lincoln's viceroy in Tennessee he could always fall back on national policy in that regard. He continued actively vilifying secession and slavery as inhibitors to a new era dawning for the people of his state. By this time, he and others began working actively for that new era. East Tennesseans like Roane County native John A. Campbell urged restoration of civil government and a special convention to dispose of slavery. Major General George H. Thomas also urged restoration of civilian control as "it is my earnest advice that you do so." Johnson accordingly proclaimed the first Saturday in March as Election Day in order to restore republican government via local elections, and he set about laying the groundwork for that event.[51]

Johnson drew upon Lincoln's amnesty proclamation and got the president to clarify its implementation in late January. The military governor, departmental military commander, and all those designated by them could administer its provisions. As Lincoln personally wrote East Tennessean and state attorney general Horace Maynard, "Loyal as well as disloyal should take the oath because it does not hurt them clears all questions as to their right to vote & swells the aggregate number who take it which is an important object." Nonetheless, Johnson still feared that Lincoln's amnesty scheme would reenfranchise former Confederates. Indeed, loyal Memphis editor James B. Bingham wrote Johnson in mid-February how "the rebel [guerrilla] Richardson has instructed his friends in the upper counties to take any oath which may be necessary, but to control the elections by all means." So Johnson imposed more stringent loyalty requirements, layering a new oath into the proclamation. The governor's "ardent desire" or "Damnesty" oath, as it was variously termed, would soon make a mockery and farce of the county elections anyway, much to Johnson's embarrassment. Yet the military governor pressed ahead then with appointment of officials while taking to statewide political stumping. By spring, he would discover Tennessee restorationists bitterly split, particularly in East Tennessee, partially by what Johnson saw to be the problem of Lincoln's amnesty policy and partly by the Negro question. His passage back to self-rule was pockmarked with tactical failures. Little wonder that by May, Johnson would write Lincoln, proposing that "pardons granted to Tennesseans be upon the application of those desiring it directly to the President" thus inducing "a much greater obligation to the Government."[52]

Johnson saw Tennesseans divided three distinct ways that winter. Each demanded separate handling yet integrated accommodation. Unionists were to be assisted and rewarded, secessionists, punished or exiled. Those wavering or downright exploitative (Johnson referred to them as "pig today & pork to-morrow" or unionists when the Federals were about and secessionists when Confederates were close by) posed the dilemma. Indeed, this continuing fact of life confronted both Johnson and Bramlette in their states' responses to the core issue of the "new" reason for war—emancipation and the slavery question. For Johnson the question was wrapped in political overtones as the former slave defender charged ahead, espousing emancipation as a socially liberating force from oligarchic tyranny and economic entrapment. Bramlette faced more delicate sociocultural and economic challenges with the issue of military manpower procurement. The issue became one of public safety to most Kentuckians.[53]

On February 1, Lincoln issued a proclamation ordering a new five-hundred-thousand-man draft slated for March 10 (for three years or the war's duration) in addition to the three hundred thousand men requested the previous October. The Union seemed to be exhausting northern white males, and outcries from industrial towns of the Northeast to farming communities of the Midwest sought alternatives and relief from state quotas. States such as Massachusetts and Michigan looked to recruit African Americans (free or slave) in the South to apply against their quotas. In fact, military liberation of blacks (in effect an ersatz emancipation) first raised Bramlette's ire (and soon thereafter most of Kentucky's slave-owning citizenry) when a Federal agent attempted to recruit able-bodied blacks of the state into the First Michigan Colored Regiment. Bramlette bluntly wrote then-Kentucky district commander Boyle on January 13 that "no such recruiting will be tolerated here. Summary justice will be inflicted upon any who attempt such unlawful purpose." He had told one recruiter the month before that Kentucky would fill its October quota from white men and would not "permit any state which is unwilling to meet the measure of duty by contributing its quota from its own population, to shelter from duty behind the free negro population of Ky." By late March, the governor, in company with a new local military representative, would reverse himself.[54]

The men of the commonwealth had more than fulfilled their duty in the minds of loyal state officials. A total of 54,902 Kentuckians manning fifty-two infantry and fifteen cavalry regiments, as well as six batteries of artillery, wore Union blue, with 39,065 still standing to the colors as of February 1864. Then Lincoln's new March call and his order to resort to the draft soon after April 15 for any deficiency led to the Frankfort-Washington accommodation. But the furies had been let loose in the Bluegrass. African American troops at rebellious Paducah tried to "conscript" black steamboat hands on March 21, leading to a race riot when white troops intervened on behalf of the victims with casualties on both sides. Burbridge had already ordered all impressed blacks be released from their duties and sent home to owners, and on March 10, Kentucky war hero Colonel Frank Wolford of the First Cavalry created a sensation in a political speech, declaring it the citizenry's duty to resist black enrollment as "unconstitutional, unjust, another of a series of startling usurpations" and a violation of their guaranteed rights. Wolford was hence arrested for speaking disrespectfully of the president, then released and remanded to Grant's charge at Nashville before being restored to command by Lincoln himself. However, this fundamental question overhanging the whole South would especially bedevil Kentucky-national relations for the remainder of the war.[55]

Military manpower controversy for Johnson had its own twists. Tennessee had organized and sent loyal volunteer regiments to the regular Union forces. But in so doing, authorities had stripped the state of home protection. So Johnson's utmost concern had always been recruitment of loyal Tennesseans for a "personal" corps of "Union Guards" to act as a pacification, counter-insurgency and stabilization force. Designed for twelve-month service, Johnson's efforts butted against Federal generals like Stephen Hurlbut at Memphis, who wanted Home Guard outfits specifically protecting that city and neighborhood. And, of course, both men competed with the likes of Confederate recruiters and raiders for a draw on available white males. Then there was the question of what to do about freedmen of the Mississippi Valley, also being tapped for Federal "United States Colored Troops" or even northern state quotas against spring conscription. Moreover, on January 7, Johnson's adjutant general, Alvan C. Gillem, reported from Camp Nelson, Kentucky (the large supply depot and troops rendezvous for unionists fleeing East Tennessee), that the pitiful 2,386 cavalry and artillery recruits there "deserve some consideration" and might well be transferred to Nashville for reorganization and preparation for the field rather than languishing where they were. In truth, refugee males in cavalry service at Nashville were so anxious about their persecuted families east of the mountains and restive for furloughs to visit them that they often seemed of dubious value for campaigning. Still others, facing reenlistment demands through attachment to other state regiments, petitioned the governor that they might transfer to Tennessee units. And there were petty problems, like with the Tenth Tennessee Infantry guarding construction of the Nashville and Northwestern Railroad at Sullivan's Branch whose officers complained bitterly in early March about the "tyranny and insolence" of a "pompous, insolent, and abusive Polish-born ex-U.S. regular," now one of their own, who might affect reenlistment among the men. Union Tennessee troops remained shaky at best.[56]

Military necessity caused Secretary of War Stanton to revoke his fall order allowing Johnson to independently draw upon logistical officers at Nashville for his Union Guards. He directed now that all ordnance requisitions, at least, go through the Washington bureau of that arm. Apparently none of this hindered Stokes's much-maligned Fifth Tennessee Cavalry from responding well in late January to Grant's direct request for cleaning out a guerrilla-ridden region between Carthage and Sparta on the western edge of the Cumberland Plateau since the main army's cavalry itself was far distant beyond Chattanooga. But Johnson's March visit to Washington apparently stirred up the War Department concerning arms and equipment for his Guard. At the end of March he contacted the chief of ordnance, Brigadier General George D. Ramsay, about obtaining two thousand additional Merrill, Sharps, or Maynard carbines and horse equipage. The bureaucrat responded only with sabers and subpar Gallagher firearms (at least a newer model using soft metallic as opposed to the old paper cartridges that jammed the weapon). Priorities always went to front-line troops, not those policing the rear. Even some volunteer units labored with obsolete materiel almost to war's end.[57]

Gillem reported on March 11 how the organization of Tennessee regiments at the capital "is progressing well, but there are neither arms nor horses for them here." Those sent directly to the Union armies apparently performed nicely, although others, including Stokes's men, were badly handled by guerrillas on occasion. Colonel John Murphy, another former regular private soldier, seemed to be doing good service with eight hundred or nine hundred men from the Fifth at Clifton on the Tennessee River. Bringing eight Tennessee cavalry regiments of about six thousand together at Nashville, thanks to Major General Thomas's help, Gillem noted how the politically radical Stokes had expressed a desire to aid Johnson in reestablishing civil government and apparently agreed wholeheartedly with greater use of blacks in military service. The notorious Colonel Fielding Hurst and his Sixth Tennessee, on the other hand, continued to terrorize secessionists and loyalists alike in West Tennessee. At least the military governor now enjoyed good relations with the army commander in Tennessee as Johnson recommended to Lincoln on March 21 that the Department of Cumberland ought to be placed under Thomas's command to receive instructions and orders directly from Washington rather than continue under William T. Sherman, the new theater commander. In Johnson's view, Thomas's subordination to Sherman would only induce "disappointment in the public mind & impair the public service." Perhaps Sherman's refusal to liberate East Tennessee from rebel oppression in the fall of 1861 and openly negative attitudes about that section contributed to Johnson's advocacy.[58]

Civilian Perspectives

Two years of Federal occupation in Tennessee and Kentucky had worked hardships on civilians in the upper heartland. Sarah Anne Bailey Kennedy wrote her husband (absent in the Confederate civil service) that their Clarksville, Tennessee, home "would scarcely be recognized by those who left it three years since, business dull, very little social intercourse, and every man for himself seems to be the motto." Amateur concerts and tableaux provided some release, but personal cares about sickly family members, retention of the house against threatened Union confiscation, and the cares of a southern woman left to fend for herself in terms of finances and business decisions all intruded upon her life. True, spring crocuses and violets in her garden promised happier times, but formerly polite townsmen now courting favor with the other side irked her. She no longer received the deference she considered her due.[59]

Kennedy was particularly incensed when one Yankee officer implied that she might intentionally set her chimney on fire so as to burn the whole town down. "This is the first *insult* has been offered me," she wrote her husband, keeping him well informed via a clandestine mail service through the lines. And she told him also about one occasion when a southern woman ("professing to have a husband in the southern army and a loud crying rebel, but of doubtful character"), just to test Kennedy, had queried her about privately selling her household property in anticipation of confiscation. The plucky Clarkesvillian saw through the ploy and later learned the woman was married to a Federal soldier. That same night, however, Kennedy's smoke house was robbed and she mentioned that old-time residents seemed to be moving away—to New York, New Orleans, or Louisville—ostensibly on business but obviously to find a less oppressive habitat. Break-ins and other trials of occupation became almost a way of life for residents of the upper heartland. Moreover, Yankee officers like Colonel William Lowe of the Fifth Iowa Cavalry especially took possession of private houses for headquarters without remorse.

"Gloom reigns in the hearts, and homes, of most of our people," Kennedy wrote her husband on March 19, 1864. Still, widows and widowers were the only ones having a gay time, she said. They are styled something called the rejuvenating club and consumed an oyster dinner at one social event leaving the hostess nothing to share with Kennedy as had been custom. They had cleared the board of all refreshments, leading Kennedy to observe that "juveniles always cleared the table." And Nanny Garland wrote her absent Confederate beau Major John Minor from "Sailor's Rest" downriver from Clarksville how she had not been to town since the previous October but had heard from friends much about Union repression of free speech. She asked Minor to disregard rumors as to the loyalty of the Clarksville girls—their allegiance lay with gray coats and they were not seduced by the occupation boys. She, like many, scorned those males who remained at home and were not in Confederate ranks.[60]

Hard times prevailed elsewhere as well. Over in East Tennessee, Knoxvillians had settled into sullen acquiescence to Union occupation after Fort Sanders, although continuing persecution and confiscation against disloyal residents failed to silence that "very violent rebel" Ellen House's outbursts about the "vile" Yankees. Indeed, short rations for soldiers and civilians alike in that East Tennessee city all winter made for hard feelings. At Gallatin, Tennessee, school girl Alice Williamson similarly spewed venom in her diary against local Union commander Brigadier General Eleazar Paine. Incarceration, even execution of anyone smacking of guerrilla associations (including professed Confederate soldiers), were the order of the day. She noted Johnson's March

"Impressing Negroes to work on the Nashville fortifications." From John Fitch, *Annals of the Army of the Cumberland* (Philadelphia: J. B. Lippincott, 1864).

elections, but since only Union men could vote, "nobody knows how it turned out nor do they care." A new freedmen's school (which she derisively called "Freedmen's University") drew even more of her ire with its northern teachers. And East Tennessee troops now occupied the town. "They are the meanest men I ever saw; but they have one good trait," she thought, as they "make the negroes 'walk the chalk.'" Still, matters improved little by spring for this high-strung unreconstructed rebel: "This is the dullest May-day Gallatin ever seen; no picnics or anything else."[61]

In Kentucky, thirty-seven-year-old Christian County farmer and Methodist circuit rider George Richard Browder also bemoaned the heavy hand of government that assessed "innocent people" to pay loyal Kentuckians for property destroyed by what he simply termed "robbers." He saw one "good & true man" ordered into close confinement as a hostage for another that had burned a third party's house. "Who is to find, or surrender the robber while an innocent man lies in prison," was Browder's question. Young Lexington unionist Frances Peter seemed less concerned about such response to Governor Thomas Bramlette's proclamation ordering the military to immediately arrest at least five rebel sympathizers in the vicinity of any outrage when a loyal citizen was carried off by what were more generally known as southern guerrillas.[62]

Sketch of contrabands coming into camp under the Emancipation Proclamation. Library of Congress.

With a keen eye and ear for gossip and news, Peter recorded in her diary how Grant had appeared in town to unionists' delight in January. Confederate prisoners from Longstreet's corps had been less enthusiastic: "They are wretchedly clad, dirty, miserable, and half starved." Local secessionist ladies busily supplied them food and clothing, she noted. Peter berated Kentucky senator Garret Davis's latest "Copperish" tinge in Congress, where he "delivered some very treasonable resolutions." She quoted Bramlette's vehement opposition to black recruiting in the state and how letters found on captured rebels in Graves County from wives and sweethearts evidenced war weariness while the Yankees had proven kinder than expected. She deplored the absence of a good loyal local newspaper, constant rumors of Confederate invasion, and how the Negro question had occasioned a fistfight between Kentucky and Michigan soldiers stationed in Lexington. "In fact the negroes throughout the country are no longer the humble servants that they used to be," she jotted down on January 27. They "are restless, impertinent and discontented, neglect their work, and run off in great numbers," a comment increasingly made across the Commonwealth as the year unfolded. By March, Peter recorded the appearance of Frank Wolford, who quickly disgraced himself, in her eyes, with "such an address as none but the vilest Copperhead would make, abusing Mr. Lincoln, telling Kentuckians that they ought to arm themselves to resist the enrolling of negroes and setting himself in opposition to the Government." "She will not follow any such lead," Peter suggested, and she predicted that the only thing that Wolford would accomplish "by preaching such a doctrine will be to destroy all hopes of getting compensation for the slaves that are taken by the Government."[63]

Peter wondered why Bramlette sat quietly on the same stage as Wolford lashed out so treasonously. She thought the colonel played into the hands of the secessionists by such behavior: "I suppose they think there will be a counter revolution here against the Government which will greatly aid the rebel army in taking the state out of the Union." Times appeared stormy to Peter, but she expected the old ship of state to once more weather the gale as it had in 1861. She blamed Congress, not Lincoln, for the enrollment law. Kentuckians could not resist carrying that law into effect "without being as much in a state of rebellion as any of the Confederates, and having a Civil War in our midst." That course "would be fraught with evil" in every manner, for emancipation would be necessary and there would be no hopes of compensation and Kentucky troops would be sent out of the state, "the whole State overrun with armies and devastated by war." If Bramlette attempted to resist Congress, he would find Kentucky unionists remembering how they put down previous and secessionist-leaning governor Beriah Magoffin in 1861. Peter decided, "The secesh will make one more attempt to get Ky." It might prove a bloody one, "but come and cost what may, Ky stays in the Union, and will never side with those who resist the government." Alas, Fanny Peter, an epileptic, would not survive to see how her prediction turned out.[64]

The enrollment question, Wolford's apostasy, and heavy-handed military confiscation provided similarly familiar and troubling issues for freshman Kentucky congressman Brutus Clay in Washington that winter. Already having run afoul of Radical Republicans on Capitol Hill as well as conservative Democrats at home, Clay was barraged by family and in-laws for favors as war embroiled the Commonwealth. People wanted trade and passage permits and one relative accosted him concerning the threat to their mutual business interest in Mississippi cotton plantations where confiscation of slave labor by army and navy raiders (under the guise of liberating them from disloyal and inhuman owners) vied with guerrilla harassment to keep planters from raising their crop to sell on the Memphis black market. Rumors of invasion, as well as black enrollment at home, also caught the rookie legislator

Sketch of "reliable" contraband at a cavalry outpost. Library of Congress.

attempting to straddle unconditional unionism yet protect property against unnecessary Federal interference and ersatz emancipation. Like so many Kentucky natives, Brutus Clay did not respond well when eight hundred miles separated him from his duties in governance and his familial and business responsibilities at home.[65]

When winter eventually gave way to spring, two great armies confronted each other in East Tennessee and north Georgia. The Confederacy's forces at most numbered seventy thousand in the Army of Tennessee and Longstreet's command, positioned for both defense and liberation—defense of the Confederate deeper South but also liberation of the Union-occupied upper South. Facing them stood a Union array, one hundred thousand strong, at least, and poised for further conquest more than defense of territory already conquered. The Union grand strategy might hold in upper East Tennessee, but Sherman's plans projected offensive to Atlanta. Neither he nor his chief, Ulysses S. Grant, reckoned the upper heartland had been tamed, but that responsibility now lay with others. Sherman wrote Memphis unionist J. B. Bingham toward the end of January that he did not think Tennesseans were quite ready for "premature State organization" to return to the Union. "What the people want is protection in their homes," he concluded, "and this cannot be promised them till the Armies of [Robert E.] Lee and Joe Johnston are defeated & scattered; and until we can turn our attention to the small bands that now infest the Interior." These lawless bands "intimidate the Courts, Sheriffs, Constables &c.," who alone "can bring protection to life and property." State organizations might determine political questions but would be powerless against Confederate armies who "would pay them little or no respect."[66]

Random events of comity occasionally did occur in the war-torn upper South. The *Chattanooga Gazette* reported a March wedding on Walden Ridge as just "such a rare case of universal *concord* being the result of such universal *discord* whereby citizens, soldiers, deserters, spies and bushwhackers from both sides formed the wedding party. "Scarcely a harsh word was uttered during the whole night," recorded the paper, "all danced together as if nothing was wrong, and parted mutually the next morning, each party marching off separately." This notwithstanding, "considering the great hatred existing between the different parties it is marvelous that bloodshed was not the immediate result."[67]

CHAPTER 4

Hard War Turns Harder

Buoyed by a third star and command of all the armies of the United States, effective March 4, 1864, Ulysses S. Grant left Nashville for Washington. Before departing, however, he had to correct a potentially damaging faux pas by one of his staff. The homes and businesses of known Confederate sympathizers long had been subject to confiscation. Zealously pursuing such action against Dr. W. A. Cheatham, raider John Hunt Morgan's brother-in-law, Brigadier General William F. Smith, had ordered the physician and his wife evicted so Grant and his wife might occupy the property. Feelings ran high against Morgan for his damaging raid north of the Ohio the previous summer. Moreover, the Cheathams had been arrested in May 1863 for corresponding with the raider. The intervention of wife Julia and Grant's own incredulity about Smith's actions soon corrected the situation with a safeguard being put on the Cheatham residence. Grant could ill afford the wrath of a respected Nashvillian, much less his own wife.[1]

Grand Strategic Visions

In early February, Grant as commander of the Military Division of the Mississippi had responded to Indianapolis-based Brigadier General Alvin P. Hovey's observation that "there seems to be a general impression in the North that the rebellion is nearly over and I am afraid it will eventually result in injury to our cause." It was not over, and Grant took pains to assure him that the harsh winter portended an early spring and that he was "very desirous of being ready to take advantage of the first dry roads to commense [*sic*] a campaign." There would be sharp fighting and he needed trained levies "ready for duty from the moment they report for duty." That was where Hovey's professional experience came into play. If the spring fighting proved successful, Grant believed, "the war will be ended within the year; if the enemy gain temporary advantage, the war will be protracted." As top commander, Grant would accompany Major General George Gordon Meade's eastern Army of the Potomac, supervising its moves against Robert E. Lee's Army of Northern Virginia. He would entrust the Western theater to his friend William Tecumseh Sherman, charging him principally with destroying Joseph E. Johnston's Army of Tennessee and capturing the strategic rail and industrial center, Atlanta, Georgia. As for James Longstreet in upper East Tennessee, Grant had fretted all winter with the Confederate's provocative presence. Now, Old Pete would simply return to Lee's fold as the departure of both men caused operations in the West to take a different turn. Grant all along had wanted not only to take down Confederate armies but also to destroy the southern infrastructure supporting those armies. Thus Confederate logistical resources—transportation arteries, factory towns, rail centers, and, of course, the will of the people—would feel Union power. In essence, Union armies would become raiders in themselves, cutting up the lower South and ending on the coast under naval protection. Grant envisioned a strike from Chattanooga to Atlanta and thence through Montgomery, Alabama, to the Gulf Coast. His move east changed the dynamics.[2]

Had Grant remained in the West, Sherman would have commanded the Atlanta column, with Major General James B. McPherson providing the linking force coming north from Mobile, Alabama. Now Sherman would mastermind the whole operation while political general Nathaniel Banks in Louisiana would focus on cleaning up affairs in that state before striking eastward to take the port city of Mobile. The Union navy would continue providing insurance that the western rivers would remain open to logistical support of the Federal grand strategy until such time as it could secure Mobile as a new base for the raiding strategy. Banks soon proved incapable of mounting the Mobile operation, bogging down on the Red River with schemes to procure cotton for a hot market. It devolved upon Sherman to rely upon an insecure line of communications stretching by rail and river back through Tennessee and Kentucky to the Ohio. Occupation of the upper South retained great importance as the principal logistical backdrop to major

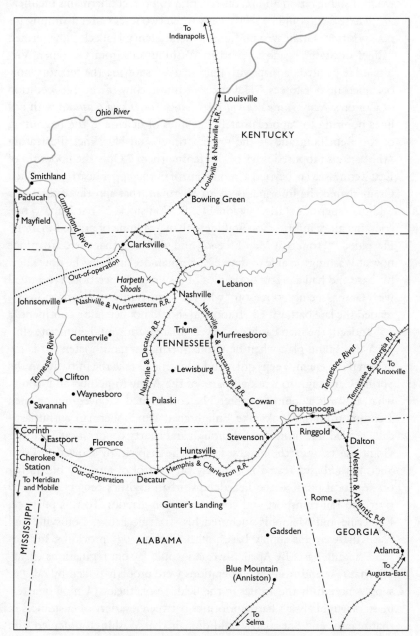

Sherman's lines of communication, 1864. Map by Bill Nelson.

operations. Continuing regional turbulence elevated the equally vital work of stabilization and reconstruction to protect Sherman's lifeline.

These facts could be seen clearly when two weeks after assuming his new position, Grant wrote Major General Henry Halleck (now termed "Chief of Staff" headquartered in Washington), from Culpeper, Virginia. He wanted "a map with lines marked showing the territory now occupied by our forces." Halleck sent him a copy of the 1863 edition of Colton's *New Guide Map of the United States and Canada* with red lines pointing to "approximately our lines of defense at the beginning of the Rebellion, and at the present time" and blue lines illustrating "the various proposed ways of shortening them." Only the upper tip of East Tennessee lay beyond Union control in the upper heartland. When Grant shared the information with Sherman, that apostle of total war told his superior's staffer, Colonel C. B. Comstock, "That map, to me, contains more information and ideas than a volume of printed matter." He added, "From that Map I see *all*, and glad am I that there are minds now at Washington able to devise." Sherman declared that he now knew his base and had a pretty good idea of his lines of operation. He agreed with Grant, seeing no reason "why the same harmony of action [as attended the late battle at Chattanooga] should not pervade a continent."[3]

Indeed, the map easily portrayed what Grant would enunciate simply as his grand plan when he wrote Sherman a month later. "It is my design if the enemy keeps quiet and allow me to take the initiative in the Spring Campaign to work all parts of the Army to-gether, and, somewhat, towards a common center," he commented. Converging on such a common point "looks like Enlightened War," Sherman enthusiastically replied. He promised "thorough and hearty cooperation," sensing Grant was taking "the biggest load." The map clearly showed too that Sherman's "base" rested not merely on control of territory but rather on key focal points—the heartland's urban logistics centers linked by river and rail transport and communication arteries. To this purpose, Knoxville and Memphis anchored his strategic flanks; Louisville and Nashville were his supply bases, with Chattanooga providing his forward staging base. By April, Sherman would lay out regulations ensuring that rear and front-line operations were properly linked by rail "to supply more fully the armies in the field." Nonetheless, Union quartermasters would always battle priorities between a variety of customers in that regard, and Sherman would despair that Washington denied him the services of Louisville quartermaster Brigadier General Robert Allen as his chief logistician for coordinating subfunctionaries in supply requirements of the coming campaign. Sherman became his own chief logistical officer with delegation of power to those who served him.[4]

Logistics depended upon who controlled the rear echelons of supply. Both sides knew this fact dictated affairs for the upcoming campaign. In fact, rail links principally would supply both armies, one northward from Chattanooga and the other from northern Georgia back to Atlanta. Gone now was Sherman's confident statement back in October: "We are much obliged to the Tennessee [River], which has favored us most opportunely, for I am never easy with a railroad which takes a whole army to guard, each foot of rail being essential to the whole." They—meaning the enemy—"can't stop the Tennessee and each boat can make its own game," he had boasted, as he thought "we can clear out anything except occasional shots at passing boats." At that point he had written to Rear Admiral David Porter, his naval comrade in the West, about keeping the western waterways always open to army traffic, as well as regular packet traffic as that "brings private enterprise to the aid of the general purpose." But, declared Sherman, inland water trade regulation belonged to the Treasury Department, not the military, which might interest itself only insofar as that trade might constitute contraband of war. Having a jaded view of "merchants, as a class" as being governed by the law of self-interest, he nonetheless observed that "the real merchant, the man who loves his country as we do, would not ask to send down the river arms or ammunition or anything that would endanger our lives or the lives of our command." By winter and spring, heartland rivers like the Tennessee and Cumberland, even the Mississippi and Ohio, would be far to Sherman's rear on the road to Atlanta. Nonetheless, rivers and rail, as they networked Sherman's logistics in early 1864, remained part of Union and Confederate operational strategy and vital to his success.[5]

Sherman's military division comprised three principal departments —the Cumberland, the Tennessee, and the Ohio. Each had its own army (bearing the same river nomenclature) that would do the fighting, but each department had subordinate administrative frameworks that emerged and changed with the pace and direction of operations. For example, to ensure smoother administrative control, districts and subdistricts such as those at Nashville, Memphis, northern Alabama, and the Etowah came into existence from time to time. Politicians periodically petitioned for reapportionment of counties into a different military district or department (such as was the case in the Jackson Purchase section of western Kentucky) "to insure greater uniformity in orders through the State, so far as they relate to citizens and the elective franchise," as one lawmaker stated it. Grant rejected this overture on the grounds that it "would necessarily begat confusion" for the affected military commander. Operational effectiveness dictated everything as posts at Nashville, Gallatin, Bowling Green, and Clarksville constantly added clerks and paperwork as well as garrisons, underscoring their importance to army operations but often in conflict with the needs of occupation and stabilization. A panoply of troops and logistical and training facilities provided the sinews of war. Loyal unionist and newly recruited African American contingents added diversity to assigned northern volunteer and conscript units. The driver remained, above all, Sherman and his Atlanta campaign.[6]

Federal power still did not conclusively control the heartland. A target of overall Confederate strategic interest and planning, and with infrastructure subject to periodic cavalry raids and ever-present guerrilla activity, many residents of Tennessee and Kentucky still anticipated deliverance. On the other hand, federally garrisoned towns became fortified strategic hamlets and, together with more isolated posts such as Union Fort Donelson, guarded not only rivers and rail but tried to shield the populace from partisans and bandits. More often, they simply served to intimidate that populace with military governance pending reconstitution of civil authority. Southerners had few choices: abandon homes, defy the invader and be exiled south, or accept the hated Yankee oath of allegiance. Such acquiescence meant they might ply trades and vocations and, like unionist neighbors, make room in their homes for refugees as well as northern entrepreneurs exploiting wartime economic opportunities. Chattanooga Presbyterian minister Thomas Hooke McCallie suggested that the "horrid war had desolated everything." His church was used for a hospital, "and no bell rang out on the air, telling us of God, His house, His worship." "The pastors all except myself gone" as "there were no stores open, no markets of any kind, no carriages on the streets, no civil officers and no taxes nor tax collectors, fortunately," he wrote. Strangers filled "our streets, our highways and our houses" as the rattle of spurs and tramp of soldiers "were constantly falling on the earth."[7]

Readiness for Any Threat

Therefore, logistics affected everything in Sherman's domain. Nashville district commander Major General Lovell H. Rousseau's report to Department of the Cumberland commander Major General George H.

Thomas at the end of January underscored that fact when he highlighted construction progress on the Nashville and Northwestern railroad linking Nashville and Johnsonville on the Tennessee River. The line was designed to circumvent a guerrilla-prone bottleneck on the Louisville and Nashville north of the city as well as shoal water in the Cumberland. Thirty-four miles in running order and an additional twenty miles ready for grading and laying rails, as well as fifteen hundred tons of iron in transit from Pittsburgh, Pennsylvania, led First Michigan Engineers and Mechanics commander William P. Innes to think he could "finish the road for business in sixty days." The story of the railroad's construction was told by Mrs. Eben M. Hill, wife of one of the railroad's builders. That saga included life in camps with her four-year-old son and other wives of project officers, riding in the virgin forests of the upper Harpeth Valley, and living in constant fear of hovering partisans. Those connected with the endeavor rejoiced when opening ceremonies at Johnsonville on May 10, gave an excuse for a "rough and primitive dinner" punctuated by flowing champagne, toasts, speeches and everyone feeling happy and brotherly." Military governor Andrew Johnson had done the ceremonial honors and, she observed uncharitably, "had about all he could carry," was practically incoherent, and "mumbled around for a while, and became lachrymose and shed tears, and then turned to a big black Negro standing behind him, threw his arms around his neck and hailed him as a brother." Somehow the line had been completed and would prove indespensible.[8]

Even then the railroad was not turned over to the army until August. The critical issue would be guards for such rail lines, and Rousseau had detailed back in January the problem of protecting railroad bridges against "squads of the enemy going through the country" bent upon interrupting transportation." Rail chief D. C. McCallum too observed how the Nashville and Northwestern "was very much exposed to attacks from guerillas, who at times inflicted considerable damage, and interfered with its operation." Running through an untamed part of Middle Tennessee, the town of Waverly may have been the project's headquarters, but all around lay some of the most infested guerrilla lands in the state. The fate of railroads depended upon road guard garrisons as well as strategic hamlets, as Departmental Assistant Chief of Artillery John Mendenhall's annual report, like Rousseau's, provided Federal perspective on the situation.[9]

Starting with a reconstituted Union Fort Donelson (built between the old rebel works and the town of Dover, Tennessee), the artillerist worked his way south to Bridgeport, Alabama, enumerating the condition of works and facilities, state of garrisons, and number of artillery pieces. He included Donelson, Clarksville, Gallatin, Carthage, Nashville, Murfreesboro, Franklin, Columbia, Tullahoma, Elk River, Decherd, Stevenson, and Bridgeport. Fort Donelson was typical—generally in good condition, magazine large and frequently aired, ammunition well stocked and cared for. The garrison of the Eighty-third Illinois and a battery of the Second Illinois Artillery (four James rifled cannon) were well taken care of, drilled well, and had fine winter huts. Four 24-pounder seacoast and two 12-pounder iron guns and one 8-inch siege howitzer comprised the fort's armament (with "one old 6-pounder iron gun, on a broken carriage" lying near the fort). Why that former Confederate piece had not been policed up by the Federals much earlier remained unclear. Still, Mendenhall's Fort Donelson comments suggested a satisfactory situation.

All told, sixty or more heavy and light cannon and upward of twenty thousand troops defended departmental strong points. By April, estimates along the line of the Nashville and Chattanooga Railroad (by this point like Louisville and Nashville subject to orders from the commanding general and controlled by McCallum, general manager for the U.S. Military Railroad in the region) suggested thinly stretched garrisons protecting bridges and stockades and attractive targets if not for partisans, certainly for heavier enemy forces. Frankly, the isolated garrisons seemed better suited to pacify and intimidate local citizens and deter guerrillas rather than defy any cavalry raids or major Confederate counter-offensive. Sherman's forward deployed army plus natural barriers such as the Tennessee River remained the principal tools for deterrence and defense of the latter threat. Behind the lines, Federal commanders had to assume that a certain level of logistical destruction could be absorbed and repaired quickly, whether from partisans or guerrillas, stretching from north Alabama and Georgia back to the Ohio River.[10]

Forrest Emboldens Confederate Fortunes

Partisans or guerrillas posed as much danger to Federal activities that winter as more organized Confederate cavalry raids or major rebel armies. Still, most of these sunshine patriots preferred hearth and home to cold and snow and were notoriously unreliable when it came to taking orders or effecting coordinated activity. Raiders and partisans had been effective previously when directed against Union lines of communications in Kentucky and Tennessee (although admittedly, the Wheeler/ Forrest winter campaign had ended in disaster at Dover, Tennessee, in February 1863). Little could be done until March, anyway, given the unpredictable weather. It does seem that Richmond and the Confederates allowed Sherman somewhat free rein to build up his offensive against Atlanta. "Fighting Joe" Wheeler's cavalry remained tied to directly supporting Johnston's main army. Bedford Forrest stayed focused on deterring Yankee thrusts out of Memphis. John Hunt Morgan (but lately freed from a Yankee prison after his controversial and largely unsuccessful raid north of the Ohio the previous summer), courted favor in Richmond circles for another spring swing into the Bluegrass. The so-called Kentucky bloc of politicians and generals lobbied the administration for liberation of their home state just as did James Longstreet. But Confederate resources remained allocated to the basic defense of Atlanta or Richmond.

In fact, the Confederacy had too few resources, spread across too many miles of territory with competing priorities from field commanders. A public canvass for volunteers and resources to ride with Morgan, for instance, threatened to undermine the whole effort as some fourteen thousand "volunteers" from army ranks signed up and had to be squelched in order to maintain formal unit strengths. Morgan personally never overcame his image as a freebooter, unwilling as he was to subordinate himself to larger military requirements. His escapade north of the Ohio still carried the taint of robbing private property. Now, at best he could only win reassignment of two brigades in southwestern Virginia plus a mounted battalion from Johnston. There might still be enough for one more Morgan raid into his native Kentucky but nothing approaching a repeat of the Smith/Bragg fall 1862 invasion. Ultimately, such raids would prove transitory and bereft of permanent accomplishment.[11]

One might ask, did not the Confederate high command realize the potential afforded by its premier western cavalryman, Nathan Bedford Forrest? True, this highly independent and self-made great captain was outside any West Point clique. He had defied Jefferson Davis's favorite commander Braxton Bragg, earning exile to a supposed backwash in northern Mississippi. Here he performed well, keeping Sherman's second-rate subordinates, like Stephen Hurlbut, Samuel Sturgis, Cadwallader C. Washburn, and even two better generals bearing the name Smith (Andrew Jackson and William Sooy), at bay. He accomplished wide-ranging sweeps into the swath of territory between the Tennessee and

Mississippi Rivers, however marginal for deterring the main Union efforts elsewhere. Grant and Sherman, for instance, thought that as long as partisans and Forrest's warriors did not interdict river navigation or capture Union strong points from the Ohio to Vicksburg, or more especially enter Middle Tennessee, then upper heartland garrisons could marginalize the threat. Memphis authorities might even go their way, more content to make fortunes from contraband trade in cotton. Yet, Forrest seized opportunities offered him and could have done more with aid from Richmond.

Union Army of the Tennessee commander Major General James B. McPherson, for instance, merely told the Memphis-based Cadwallader Washburn from Huntsville, Alabama, on April 29 that he might not be able to assume the offensive against Forrest "with as much boldness as is desirable" and force him "to fight or be driven out of West Tennessee," but that it was imperative to keep the raider occupied and prevent from "forming plans and combinations" to cross the Tennessee River and break up Sherman's railroad communications. Assume an "offensive-defensive" of watching Forrest closely and strike a blow whenever it could be put to advantage, McPherson urged, thus preventing the raider from being "able to inflict upon us any serious damage." As it would turn out, Forrest's early spring operations produced a level of violence unanticipated by the Federal high command. Eventually, governments in both Richmond and Washington would be drawn to the controversy of harsher war practiced in West Tennessee. But Confederate West Pointers with an abiding grudge against partisans, raiders and free-spirited citizen-soldiers like Morgan and Forrest never acted upon their vast potential for destabilizing and disrupting the upper heartland as preparatory to coordinated permanent redemption or reoccupation of Tennessee and Kentucky.[12]

While East Tennessee stood gripped by bitter winter stalemate and the middle part of the Volunteer State, as well as Bluegrass Kentucky, experienced harsh Union presence, the strip northward from Mississippi between the Mississippi and Tennessee Rivers lay open to any challenger. In fact, West Tennessee and the so-called Jackson Purchase of western Kentucky remained hotbeds of seething rebellion. Only nominally occupied, Union cavalry left this area to support Sherman's Meridian expedition and stir up a hornet's nest in northern Mississippi. Regional rebel authorities therefore scrambled to find men and resources to counter Federal expeditions from Memphis into northern Mississippi while attempting to suppress loyal Tennesseans under a much-despised

Colonel Fielding Hurst in West Tennessee. It was always a nip-and-tuck battle on both counts. In addition, periodic Yankee threats to northern Alabama iron and coal fields, as well as to government works at Talladega, Tuscaloosa, and Selma, prompted that state's congressional delegation to press the Confederate War Department for greater protection. Meanwhile, Lieutenant General Leonidus Polk's Department of East Louisiana, Mississippi, and West Tennessee remained formally short of supplies, horses, and ways to fill the ranks. Except for Forrest, southern fortunes appeared hamstrung in this area.[13]

On January 11, Polk split his cavalry in two, Forrest absorbing the northern half of the department and Major General Stephen D. Lee the southern portion. This, at least, held some promise for overcoming lack of command unity. Forrest took charge on January 26 with a ringing appeal to redeem West Tennessee from the "merciless ravages" of the enemy. He claimed to have ample supply of arms, ammunition, and accouterments as well as "men enough in the department" to drive out the enemy. Richmond already had expressed reservations about the uncontrollable nature of cavalry in Mississippi with respect to civilian property. Johnston had ducked, telling President Davis that "should your Excellency desire to carry back the war into Middle Tennessee, it seems to me that it must be done by assembling as large a force in Northern Mississippi as we can collect there, with a bridge equipage for the passage of the Tennessee," a "larger force, if practicable than Lieutenant General Polk's and mine united," which, of course, was nowhere to be found. Furthermore, Johnston wanted such manpower with his own army. While higher authority dithered, Forrest acted. Asserting that given a month's duration in West Tennessee and Kentucky, he "would have everything in fine condition," including cleansing the area of unionists, Forrest collected three depleted Kentucky infantry regiments of about seven hundred men by mid-March as he and Polk decided upon a bold new raid northward into West Tennessee and Kentucky. His goal would be recruits, remounts, supplies, and reestablishment of Confederate control as well as interference with Andrew Johnson's planned civil elections.[14]

Forrest's dealings with his subordinates remained rancorous that winter. Division commander James Chalmers and brigade leader Robert V. Richardson both incurred their leader's wraith for their tepid response to Forrest's rather strict, frontier-like code of leadership, command, and control. So tension rode northward with the expedition as Forrest moved Kentuckian Abraham Buford's division forward from

Tupelo, Mississippi, by mid-March. "Forrest is on the wing again, no one knows where," young Shelby County native Belle Edmondson noted in her diary on Sunday, March 20. Forrest's ill will only increased as he encountered a West Tennessee overrun by what he called bands and squads of robbers, horse thieves, and deserters "whose depredations and unlawful appropriations of private property are so rapidly and effectually depleting the country." Conditions had changed since his last raid in December. Not only Federal volunteers but also homegrown Tennessee "Tories" and former slaves under arms in blue uniforms now graced Union occupation. This latter phenomenon was especially galling—dishonorable, distasteful, and illegal under southern laws and customs. Retribution glinted in Bedford's eyes as he rode into Jackson, Tennessee, and found a citizenry simply livid at the "outrages committed by the commands of Colonel Fielding Hurst and others of the Federal Army" who Forrest termed "renegade Tennesseans." He would see to justice. To Edmondson, Forrest's coming meant the Yankees "are evidently in a great fright about something."[15]

Forrest communicated his displeasure about Hurst to both the Union commander at Memphis and also to Polk. He ordered his inspector to gather details of crimes against the citizenry. Atrocities had been ostensibly perpetrated against prisoners and the sum of five thousand dollars extorted from Jackson citizens by Hurst and his thugs. The local Yankees had murdered six or seven Confederate soldiers, burned part of the town, and created a general atmosphere of retaliation and intimidation. Hurst, a West Tennessee slaveholding unionist had organized the Sixth Tennessee (Union) Cavalry and used it to terrorize secessionist neighbors. None of the charges now seems the least bit novel. Such travesties took place all across the upper heartland and would only grow worse over time. Particularly bitter neighborly violence on the Cumberland Plateau and west of the Tennessee River suggested the changing nature of civil war. Hurst had bluntly told Military Governor Johnson how persecuted his kind had been since the beginning of the war. He claimed to have nearly one thousand men in his regiment with orders to "proceed to the destruction of all armed enemies to the United States Government," subsisting his command upon the country and taking all serviceable animals for his own and army use ("in every case giving receipts," as was both sides' custom for requisitioning from civilians). He intended to treat peaceable and loyal citizens kindly and protect them against destruction by guerrilla bands infesting the country. Federal authorities doubted the veracity of

West Tennessee unionists and, said Hurst on one occasion to Johnson, "frequently taunt us with being 'Conquered Rebels' and *insinuate* that they had just as lieve [*sic*] have us on the other Side as not." Cavalry division commander Brigadier General Benjamin Grierson (famous for his raid through northern Mississippi the previous year) suggested that Hurst not let his men straggle from camp or go to their own homes and that no foraging parties should be sent out except in charge of officers who would be held accountable for their men. He might attach all loyal Home Guards. Hurst's activities simply reflected local feuding. Still, Forrest declared, "Fielding Hurst, and . . . his command of outlaws, are not entitled to be treated as prisoner's of war."[16]

Federal commanders knew that Forrest was on the move, but they did not know where. For the most part, they thought that he "shows a determination" to cross the Tennessee River and strike the Tennessee and Alabama Railroad. Their counter-efforts may have kept Forrest west of the river mainly gathering resources. He soon moved from Jackson directly north on the rail line to Trenton and brazenly opened a recruiting station virtually under Federal noses. At the same time, he also started picking off small Federal garrisons guarding Mississippi and Ohio river landings and commerce, policing neighborhoods against guerrillas while attempting to underwrite political actions of the Nashville military government. In turn, occupation garrisons provided recruiting stations for implementing key elements of Federal reconstruction.

These various Federal stations administered Lincoln's December 8, 1863, proclamation of amnesty and reconstruction, carefully documenting individuals voluntarily taking the oath while restoring the rights of such citizenry, who were thereby entitled "to protection of government and regarded as loyal." Oath violations would produce trial and punishment by military commission. The garrisons also served to disrupt slavery, although authorities in the District of Nashville, at least, were told to "have as little to do with slaves," leaving it to "masters & slaves to settle their own affairs without military interference." Liberation of aged blacks and children from their homes and relocation as army dependents at army posts had become a drain on supplies, as had slave owners sending their workers to get support from those army posts. Middle Tennessee regulations promulgated by Lovell Rousseau on February 17 also prohibited further impressments of horses and mules surplus to crop raising and "all marauding, so demoralizing to the soldier and so unworthy the brave men had to cease." Conditions varied west of the Tennessee River to some extent. Still, the spirit was similar. Forrest and his command saw Federal activities of this sort inimical to Confederate control.[17]

Johnson personally disdained Lincoln's terms toward traitors and had issued his own proclamation in late January calling for electing county officers on March 5 and requiring voters to take both Lincoln's amnesty oath and his own unique test oath claiming eternal fealty to the United States and its laws. Forrest's presence disrupted the military governor's intentions in West Tennessee. In fact, Forrest's activities rendered the election farcical. Still, Sherman willingly tolerated Forrest's activity, writing the commanding officer at Cairo on March 23, "I am willing he should be up in that neighborhood. If the people don't manifest friendship, don't divert any troops bound up the Tennessee on that account." In addition, local Federal commanders found partisan activities preceded Forrest's arrival and were especially unnerving along the railroad south of Paducah, in areas near Island Number 10 and Columbus, Kentucky, as well as Mayfield, Kentucky. Colonel William H. Lawrence of the Thirty-fourth New Jersey reported from Columbus on March 17 that an aggregate of 846 guerrillas had been counted in the Paris, Tennessee–Mayfield, Kentucky, vicinity heading for Paducah. The small Union garrisons individually could not contest Forrest's coming. Sherman dismissed the threat, but the newly assigned Cairo district commander, Brigadier General Mason Brayman, did not.[18]

Brayman was an old veteran. He had served under Grant at Belmont, Fort Donelson, and Shiloh, later taking charge of the post at Bolivar, Tennessee. He was in Memphis at mid-March then sent to relieve Brigadier General Hugh T. Reid upriver at Cairo, Illinois. Brayman's new assignment stretched 160 miles from the mouth of the Tennessee River just east of Paducah all the way to Island Number 10 and, of course, inland. His garrisons at Paducah, Cairo, Columbus, Hickman, Island Number 10, and Union City totaled 2,329 officers and men. Three-fourths of them were African American and fully 500 personnel had not mustered into service with temporarily assigned officers awaiting formal commissioning. Moreover, half of the white troops were off on detached local duty. Fortifications stood unfinished or neglected with guns dismounted and unfit for service. Ammunition was deficient in number and defective in quality, and most of Brayman's cavalry at Paducah and Union City remained unmounted. Their dispersal for occupation duty made Brayman's units unfit for concentrated combat with Forrest. On paper, of course, Brigadier General Cadwallader C. Washburn's

District of West Tennessee (of the XVI Army Corps) yielded the greatest resources for such work, with nearly 17,600 men (including Brayman's units) listed. Certainly about 8,000 men in Brigadier General C. P. Buckland's District of Memphis and Grierson's nearly 6,000 cavalrymen provided the really organized maneuver force in the region, although many of them had been bested in earlier winter encounters with Forrest. Others had gone home on furlough, and Grierson wrote Sherman on March 23 that "what is left is in poor condition and not very reliable." The cavalryman promised to send Hurst's "800 to 1,000 strong to hang upon, harass, and watch the movements of the enemy." Sherman still told the War Department that "Forrest's cavalry has gone up toward Columbus, where he can do us little harm, and it would be folly for me to push him." There were "troops enough Cairo to reenforce Columbus and Paducah beyond the chance of danger."[19]

Brayman thought his greatest problem lay with protecting the naval and supply facilities at Mound City (eight miles above Cairo and guarded by only fifty invalids). Here stood the major depot for sustaining and repairing the navy's Mississippi Squadron. Captain A. M. Pennock controlled $5 million in public property at the base. Cairo also counted millions in floating "depositories" of arms, munitions, and naval stores as well as shipping and holding army supplies. In fact, this dismal southern Illinois rail terminus had become a wartime boom town with entrepreneurs grown rich on government and private contracts at a junction where steamboat and rail came together to link downriver economic restoration with midwestern prosperity. Observed Brayman, "The operations of the army and navy of the Mississippi and its dependencies on either side depended upon the safety of the public property at the two points named." Although hundreds of miles behind the battlefront, Mound City and Cairo supported the Union raiding strategy, including the ill-fated Red River expedition in Louisiana.[20]

Sounding the alarm, Brayman bluntly reported that the "river towns and those portions of Kentucky and Tennessee not in possession or under the shadow of our arms" were under insurrectionary control. Between those rebels who had taken the oath and stayed within Federal lines "and their brothers who were in arms without, full fraternity and correspondence existed," he contended. Interior portions of the Cairo district were "infested by armed bands of guerrillas, engaged in murder and pillage, and supplied by their friends at our posts with such articles as the spoil of their loyal neighbors failed to yield." The laxity of trade regulations, the activity of the disloyal who had taken the oath but then carried on illicit traffic under Federal protection, "and too often the complicity of our own officers who shared their crimes and their profits" constituted an efficient means "by which disloyalty was fed and the enemy encouraged to remain." Loyal men, he thought, paid the price, as the section was "the scene of constant depredations, spreading alarms, and often exciting expectations of formidable attacks upon our occupied posts."[21]

Ironically, Hurlbut had given dispensation to citizens of Tipton County in the far northwest corner of Tennessee if they enrolled to protect life and property and keep the peace. No Federal troops would enter the county or seize property. Perhaps this move exacerbated conditions alluded to by Brayman. Excepting the Mississippi River traffic, the lack of stabilized economic conditions in the region could be deduced also from Brigadier General Grenville Dodge's comments to Sherman from Athens, Alabama, on March 15 how "there is something wrong about these trading-boats that run up the Tennessee river." The rebels never captured them except for temporary ferry use, and "if half the stories I hear of them are true they are continually violating the trade regulations," hardly expecting to trade with anyone but rebels in the interior anyway.[22]

Forrest exploited such conditions when his expedition entered the area. The raider sent Colonel W. L. Duckworth and five hundred men to capture Union City on the railroad to Columbus. The Confederates appeared before dawn on March 24 and skirmished hotly with Isaac R. Hawkins's command, which they found well entrenched behind ten-foot earthworks enhanced with abatis. Lacking artillery to root out the Federals from their particularly strong redoubt near the town's railway station, Duckworth resorted to customary ruse involving Forrest's usual demand for surrender. Yield or suffer the consequences, went the message to Hawkins, as if his nemesis was once more present. Meanwhile, Duckworth's men thrashed about, cheering and blowing bugles as if twice in numbers while rumors circulated in the Federal command that the rebels had artillery. Easily intimidated (he had been coerced before to surrender to Forrest at Trenton during the Confederate's first foray into the region in 1862), and despite Brayman's telegraphic orders to stand firm awaiting relief, West Tennessean Hawkins buckled once more, even though Forrest personally was nowhere in sight. At 11:00 a.m. he surrendered.[23]

Much was then made of the Seventh Tennessee (Union) Cavalry yielding to the Seventh Tennessee (Confederate) horsemen—West Tennesseans all—and even the rebels' slave cooks supposedly rejoicing at their masters' success. Many in both units were neighbors "with intense ill feeling between them." Still, according to one of Forrest's privates, the captives "bore up manfully and turned out to be jolly good fellows," although one of them contended the officers and men "cried like a whipped child" and cursed Hawkins as a traitor. Hubbard termed Hawkins, a Huntingdon lawyer, Mexican War veteran, and sometime representative to a Washington peace conference in February 1861, "that most gentlemanly Federal officer." By Forrest's estimate capturing "this renegade Hawkins" netted four hundred prisoners, two hundred horses, several hundred stand of arms, and, since Hawkins's men had just received a year's back pay, sixty thousand dollars in cash. Duckworth sent the prisoners south through Trenton and Humboldt, taunting, mistreating, and even robbing them en route. They eventually would end up in Andersonville, Georgia, prison camp. Perhaps a third of them would die within a year of their capture.[24]

Forrest sent a battalion feinting toward Memphis, but Hurlbut and company hardly stirred from that location. Having removed supplies and leveled the fortification at Union City, the Confederates escaped unscathed. Brayman's relief column was barely six miles distant at the time of Hawkins's surrender. Brayman quickly retraced his steps to Columbus. Forrest captured Union City Thursday taking eight hundred prisoners, noted Belle Edmondson in her diary, adding enthusiastically, "God grant he may be successful in all his attempts to garner our lost territory." She said nothing about the roundup of unionist private citizens in Huntington during the succeeding month when Forrest clamped down on disloyalty and collaboration, unionist guerrillaism, and signs of sympathy toward Seventh Tennessee Union prisoners. Alerted to unionist James McCree, who got word to Federal authorities so that they might intercept the POW column, Forrest wanted to hang him but for the intervention of Jackson civilians. As it was, the raider ordered any escaping prisoners shot. His men had other things on their mind, however, as a round of dances and social gatherings greeted Company E of the Seventh (Confederate) moving south through Bolivar. "Many a sweet word spoken upon which, it was hoped, something might be realized 'after the ratification of a treaty of peace,' as the Confederate bills all said," remembered Private Hubbard.[25]

Paducah Defies Forrest

In Forrest's terse words, "I moved now with Buford's division direct from Jackson to Paducah in fifty hours; attacked it on the evening of the 26th [25th]; drove the enemy to their gun-boats and forts; held the town for ten hours, and could have held it longer, but found the small-pox was raging and evacuated the place." He claimed to have captured numerous stores and horses; burned sixty bales of cotton, one steamer, and the dry dock; and captured fifty prisoners. The story was actually a bit more complicated than that. For one thing, it was a tough twenty-six-mile ride to Paducah, where the Federal commander proved to be of sterner stuff than Hawkins at Union City. He also had naval gunfire support in the form of two paddlewheel tinclad steamboats, the *Paw Paw* and *Peosta*. The first boat was only two years old, built in St. Louis and salvaged from hitting a snag in 1863. Equipped with two 30-pounder rifles and six 24-pounder howitzers, it was well known on western waters. The second boat was seven years old, built in Cincinnati, and heavily armed with three 30-pounder rifles, four 32-pounder smoothbores, six 24-pounder howitzers, and two 12-pounder smoothbore field guns.

Yet at first matters went well for the raiders. Arriving about noon on March 25, Forrest's men pushed Federal pickets for about three or four miles back into Paducah while southern-sympathizing residents rejoiced at liberation. For most it was their first sight of Confederate soldiers since their area had come under Yankee domination in mid-1861. The Federal commander, Colonel Stephen S. G. Hicks, hastily withdrew his garrison into a ditch-surrounded, strong earthwork named Fort Anderson (after Kentuckian Robert Anderson, who had ignominiously surrendered Fort Sumter to start the war). Hicks wired Brayman, "I am fully prepared, but am short of ammunition. Send me some more."[26]

Forrest mostly wanted supplies and horses, not a major battle. Some of his men, particularly local Kentuckians, desired otherwise. Without proper reconnaissance, Forrest let the situation slip from his grasp. Hicks's command numbered the 122nd Illinois Infantry (only three companies of which had ever been under fire), Sixteenth Kentucky Cavalry, and First Kentucky Heavy Artillery (Colored), subsequently enrolled as the Eighth Heavy Artillery, U.S. Colored Troops, all garrison troops. The latter unit labored under something of a cloud since Kentucky lay beyond purview of Lincoln's Emancipation Proclamation but not the previous year's confiscation, enrollment, and militia acts.

Recruitment among liberated blacks farther south in the Mississippi Valley by the U.S. Army's adjutant general Lorenzo Thomas and his agents had netted between twenty thousand and twenty-seven thousand such recruits into the ranks. Under confiscation provisions, enlistment in the Union army guaranteed freedom, although runaways to Union labor gangs as well as the military amounted to freedom by default if not legality. Still, open recruitment of slaves found little favor among most Kentucky and Tennessee whites, and loyalist Kentucky governor Thomas Bramlette fought the idea. Adjutant General Thomas, stationed in Louisville, heard arguments from Department of the Ohio commander Ambrose E. Burnside as well as Bramlette, both urging caution about black recruitment in the Bluegrass. Lincoln himself had promised the governor that such recruitment would not take place. It had and the heavy artillerists at Paducah in March were proof. The future would see more.[27]

Forrest intended impacting such endeavors. Possibly, Paducah was the first time Forrest's soldiers confronted blacks in uniform and under arms. At any rate, with such feelings running high, Confederates soon did their best to capture Fort Anderson regardless of the color of the defenders. About midafternoon, after about an hour's sharp skirmishing, Forrest sent his customary demand: "If you surrender, you shall be treated as prisoners of war; but if I have to storm your works, you may expect no quarter." Unabashedly, and perhaps to Forrest's surprise or even consternation, Hicks shot back, "I have been placed here by my Government to defend this post, and in this, as well as all other orders from my superiors, I feel it to be my duty as an honorable officer to obey." It sounded much like Dover, Tennessee, on February 3, 1863, when Colonel Abner Harding of the 83d Illinois defied Wheeler and Forrest.[28]

The Paducah fight now became more general and bloody. Without orders, Confederate Kentuckians under Paducah native Colonel A. P. Thompson rashly attacked the defenders head on. Repulsed three times, Thompson paid for the effort with his life (some said within sight of his home). Hicks expended some twenty-seven thousand rounds of his supply of thirty thousand cartridges and had determined "to receive the enemy on the point of the bayonet, feeling fully determined never to surrender while I had a man alive"—sentiments communicated to the garrison and received "with loud shouts and cheers." Meanwhile, sharpshooters peppered the Union works while Forrest and the main body of Confederates worked the town in search of plunder, supplies and horses. Hicks eventually directed cavalrymen to burn houses within range of the fort and the gunboat captains likewise sprayed the town with heavy fire.

Brayman later wired Hurlbut: "Colonel Hicks had warned the people of the probable necessity of doing this, their rebel instincts rendering it quite certain that the town would have not been thus occupied without their consent." Under such circumstances, "the result is important, and the damage to the town to be scarcely regretted." "I have no regrets for the losses of those who sympathized with the enemy; who invited and welcomed them," he stated in his after-action report, "and am satisfied that the retribution which the necessities of war brought upon the city falls far short of that which justice would warrant." Lieutenant Commander James W. Shirk, commanding the Seventh District, Mississippi Squadron echoed Hicks: "Altogether, I am of the opinion that those inhabitants of Paducah who sympathize with their 'misguided Southern brethren' have received a lesson which thy will not forget in a hurry."[29]

Forrest remained overnight near Paducah and skirmished again with Hicks the next morning before sending a second flag of truce proposing a prisoner exchange (including the Union City prisoners). Thirty-five or forty convalescing Federals in the Paducah general hospital had not made it into Fort Anderson the previous day. Hicks demurred, however, claiming he had no authority to effect an exchange. There the Paducah fight ended. Forrest withdrew to Mayfield and sent another force under Kentucky colonel Adam Buford to pin down the Columbus garrison. Buford proved as incapable of inducing the Federal commander there to surrender as had Forrest at Paducah. Hicks tallied his losses at 14 killed and 46 wounded out of 665 available men, claiming "the most reliable information" suggested that Forrest had lost 300 dead and from 1,200 to 1,500 wounded but was willing to say the total "may be safely set down at 1,500." Breezily, Forrest claimed only twenty-five killed and wounded but more importantly suggested that during his ten-hour visit, he "captured many stores and horses; burned sixty bales of cotton, one steamer, and a dry-dock, bringing out fifty prisoners." Union shelling claimed a hotel, the brewery, and some sixty homes in the process of defending the town. One transiting visitor in May, Private Edgar Eno of the Twelfth Wisconsin, wrote that the town was indeed "badly cut up from the balls and grape that they threw from the gunboats." It was hard to see towns treated that way, he wrote "dear friends at home," "but such is the fruits of rebellion."[30]

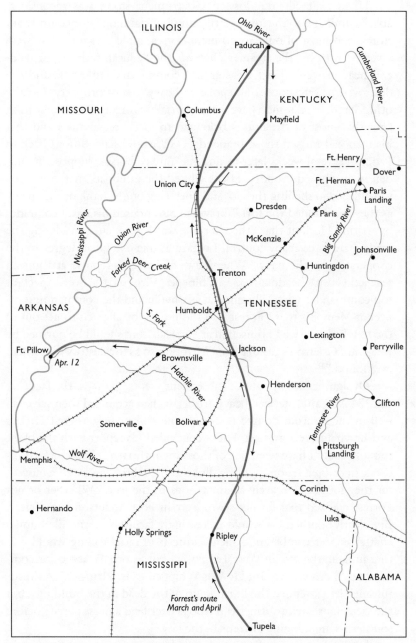

Forrest's raid in West Tennessee and Kentucky, March and April 1864. Map by
Bill Nelson.

Hicks claimed "our loss in Government stores was inconsiderable," admitting to the loss of structures but claiming "our commissary stores, and most of our Government horses, mules, wagons, &c. were saved." Truth be, the steamer *Dacotah,* the Paducah train depot, Federal headquarters, quartermaster and commissary buildings, and the destroyed private houses all spoke to heavy loss of property. On the other hand, Hicks may have been partially correct. Forrest, hearing later that most of the horses belonged to local secessionists and that his men had missed those branded "US," would send Buford back to Paducah several weeks later to find the Yankee horses, supposedly hidden in an unused foundry. Hicks saluted the gunboats that "rendered valuable aid in shelling the city and operating on the flank of the enemy as they surrounded the fort." Brayman also praised his naval comrades by writing Hurlbut that "the river line was kept open, considering the inadequate force at my control, I regard as due in a great degree to the cooperation of the navy." When news of Forrest's repulse at Paducah reached Grant's headquarters in Culpeper, Virginia, the ever-expectant top commander wired Sherman at Nashville and the commanding officer at Memphis that "Forest [sic] should not be allowed to get out of the trap he has placed Himself in at Paducah" but should be pursued by Benjamin Grierson's cavalry from Memphis so as to "destroy him where ever found."[31]

Of significance in light of subsequent events, perhaps, the fact that the 274 African American heavy artillerists had acquitted themselves so well in the fighting despite their greenness likewise garnered Hicks's and Brayman's recognition. Hicks concluded his report with the blunt thought that "I have been one of those men who never had much confidence in colored troops fighting, but those doubts are now all removed, for they fought as bravely as any troops in the fort." Whether or not Forrest realized that former slaves were in Fort Anderson is not clear. But clearly southerners would increasingly face their erstwhile human chattel as peer combatants. Such acid tests of racial feeling would further inflame the war in West Tennessee, but as one *Peosta* sailor commented, "Forrest gives In; He Was Whipped & By Negroes." A dreadful smell had attended the burning up of the dead in the buildings, but the victorious African American troops later held a dress parade before southern-sympathizing citizens in the city.[32]

Forrest furloughed Buford's Kentuckians to remount, refit, recruit, and visit homefolks from Mayfield, Kentucky. He retraced his steps south through Trenton to set up headquarters back at Jackson by early

April. Buford issued a stirring commendation to his men from Mayfield on April 4, proclaiming, "At the very doors of their homes, some
of your comrades laid down their lives to rescue Kentucky from the
iron heels of abolition, despotism, and the rule of the negro." Federal
pursuit proved desultory and fruitless. One of Forrest's subordinates,
Colonel J. J. Neely, badly handled Hurst near Bolivar. A congratulatory
Brigadier General James A. Chalmers exulted, "Colonel Neely drove
Hurst hatless into Memphis, leaving in our hands all his wagons, ambulances, papers, and his mistresses, both black and white," as well as
seventy-five prisoners. Meanwhile, an exiled Tennessean Alvin Hawkins
later complained from Greencastle, Indiana, that Forrest had arrested
and carried off several prominent West Tennessee unionists from Carroll County and suggested to Andrew Johnson that prominent secessionists might be imprisoned or banished south of Union lines until
the captives were released. "Unless a *Rigid System of Retaliation be
adopted and enforced*" it was idle to talk of protecting and encouraging
Union men in Tennessee, observed Hawkins. So it seemed for many
loyal heartlanders that spring.[33]

Point and Counterpoint

Differing perspectives emerged in the wake of Forrest's "Occupation
of West Tennessee and Kentucky" (as southern historian Ralph Selph
Henry termed the February–May time-frame). Secessionists in the region glowed with pride and anticipation. Redemption was at hand.
Belle Edmondson caught the spirit. "Forrest is having glorious victory in Kentucky, Hickman and Paducah both held by our forces," she
crowed, noting how Yankee gunboats were shelling the town. "Father
of justice and mercy crown our enemies with victory, drive the wicked
tyrants from our Sunny land—we humbly crave thy pardon & blessing
—oh! Give us peace," she prayed. Indeed, for all intents and purposes,
Confederates moved freely in the strip of territory between the Mississippi and Tennessee Rivers despite efforts the Union high command
to get subordinates to cooperate in pursuit. By this time Sherman was
fully committed to securing his railroads. He told quartermaster Allen
in Louisville on April 8 that he planned to crack down on civilian traffic
on the railroads even though "I will have down on me all the Christian charities who are perambulating our camps, more to satisfy their
curiosity than to minister to the wants of the poor soldier." Pithily he
added, "My universal answer is that 200 pounds of powder or oats

are more important to us than that weight of bottled piety." Sherman and Grant both felt West Tennessee held sufficient troops to cope with Forrest. They completely misunderstood that subordinates, like Ben Grierson, had only broken-down horses and inadequate manpower to work with.[34]

From Jackson, Tennessee, Forrest clarified his situation in two insightful dispatches, one to his department commander, Leonidus Polk, dated April 4 and a second, back-channel missive to Johnston on April 6. Confident that he could maintain himself against any enemy cavalry sent against him, Forrest told Polk that insufficient clothing, food, quantities of small arms, and lead for ammunition plagued his efforts. He wanted the railroad repaired to Corinth, Mississippi, where a supply base would enable him to "hold West Tennessee against three times my numbers." He could then send back a wealth of conscripts and deserters for infantry service. In the letter to Johnston, Forest used the subterfuge of thanking him for "past favors" and recounted his success with a force of about eighty-five hundred men featuring his brigade of Kentuckians and recalled how another Bluegrass partisan, Colonel Thomas G. Woodward, operating in southern and southwestern Kentucky, was anxious to join Buford. Forrest offered to trade "at least two men for every one of Colonel Woodward's" garnered from the conscripts and deserters in this portion of the state. He boasted that he had possession of everything west of the Tennessee River except the river posts of Memphis, Fort Pillow, Columbus, and Paducah, and noted that his men "are in fine spirits and my command harmonious, and I hope to accomplish much during the spring and summer." Moreover, since the Federals were apparently dispatching their XVI and XX Corps from Memphis to Pulaski and Chattanooga, Forrest's thought that "everything available is being concentrated against General [Robert E.] Lee and yourself." "Am also of opinion that if all the cavalry of this and your own department could be moved against Nashville that the enemy's communication could be utterly broken up," concluded the cavalryman.[35]

Such a move was, of course, what Federal authorities feared most. Sherman personally countered panic in West Tennessee with comments like those to Hurlbut on March 24: "I know that two divisions of white troops with Grierson's cavalry and the blacks can not only hold the river, but act offensively against the enemy." Forrest, he contended "is only after horses and conscripts up in West Tennessee." Hurlbut answered that with Grierson behind him and with infantry support from Memphis, "I think this Forrest movement exaggerated." Yet even

Grierson's orders to Hurst showed hesitancy: hang upon and harass with a view of impeding movements as much as possible, avoid a general engagement and capture foraging parties and stragglers, hold his command in hand, and "do not allow yourself to be drawn into any trap or be surprised." Protect loyal West Tennesseans, instructed Grierson, forage upon the disloyal, and do not permit "your men to straggle or pillage" as any deviation "from this rule may prove fatal to yourself and command." Wild rumors had Forrest even threatening Union Fort Donelson across the Tennessee on the Cumberland River so that Rousseau had ordered five hundred dismounted cavalry and a light artillery battery made ready to reinforce that point. These men were to be mounted by impressing horses in the fort's vicinity, later assigning them to the Sixth Tennessee Cavalry. Sherman tried to orchestrate a cordon around Forrest with gunboats, Grierson's cavalry, and XVI Corps' infantry of Brigadier General James C. Veatch, as well as such outlying garrisons as Fort Donelson. Sherman expected his subordinates to prevent Forrest from crossing the Tennessee and then cut off his retreat. His 4:00 pm. wire to Grant from Chattanooga on March 28 said that if his orders were executed "with rapidity and energy, [they] should result in the dispersion or destruction of his forces."[36]

Partisan activities along the Louisville and Nashville Railroad in southern Kentucky, as well as rumors of Forrest's crossing the Tennessee and Cumberland, spread the contagion of fear that spring. Middle Kentucky commander Stephen. G. Burbridge (as much an anathema to Kentuckians as Hurst was to West Tennesseans and seeking to control the pace of levies on Kentucky blacks despite the need for manpower to counter raiders and guerrillas) told his superiors that he had enough force to protect the railroad despite the incursions. His correspondence parroted Sherman's demands for the pursuit, capture, and destruction of every man in Forrest's command who crossed the Tennessee. Stockade and railroad posts "must be defended if only 50 men have to fight 1,000 men." Rebel raiders would not have sufficient time to linger any place for long.

New intelligence indicated Forrest had temporarily gone to ground in West Tennessee and no river crossings to the east seemed imminent (excepting random small parties that seeped across). Sherman now ordered some troops transferring from lower Mississippi and Red River operations to stop at Memphis. Brigadier Andrew Jackson Smith's division, for instance, would halt for training and re-outfitting, but more specifically for operations against Forrest's northern Mississippi base.

He wanted Smith to raid inland from Vicksburg to Grenada, Mississippi, overcoming any opposition from Forrest, Stephen D. Lee, or Polk while destroying the railroad south of Grenada but preserving that rail town "as at a later period I wish to occupy Grenada and use its railroad to Memphis." Smith was to continue his raid eastward linking up with McPherson at Decatur, Alabama, having eaten out the heart of Forrest's Confederacy. Sherman assumed that Grierson, Veatch, and the gunboats would have broken Forrest.[37]

Departmental returns for federally occupied areas showed plenty of strength on paper as of April Fool's Day. Rousseau's District of Nashville boasted nearly fourteen thousand officers and men and seventy-six guns that could be brought to the chase. Burbridge's Kentucky district's southern and southwestern precincts might throw about five thousand into blocking activities. As in West Tennessee, all of these numbers related to dispersed garrisons rather than a concentrated field force. More immediately, Hurlbut's XVI Corps numbered over thirty-three thousand men and seventy-three cannon tied to garrisons with little stomach for battle, still off on home leave for reenlisting or otherwise unavailable. Grierson's statistics revealed disturbing news about the number and condition of horses: of 4,934 reported mounts scarcely 2,302 proved serviceable. In fact, questions of serviceable mounts, reorganization of units, and upgrading the arms of key veteran contingents with Spencer repeating carbines stood out in dispatches. In West Tennessee, specifically, the Yankees not only were tied down by garrison inertia and fear of a vaunted enemy but also simply lacked adequate means for chasing Forrest's illusive raiders.[38]

Sherman meanwhile learned that Forrest had compromised his telegraphic communications with West Tennessee. Sherman then sent Brigadier General John D. Corse by steamboat to bolster spirits and confidence among stampeded subordinates from Paducah to Memphis. Sherman fairly radiated confidence. He had Grant's "private and confidential" dispatch of April 4 in hand, outlining the general-in-chief's grand strategic design "to work all parts of the army together and somewhat toward a common center." He replied to his chief that "with 10,000 men and two such dashing officers as Corse and [Joseph] Mower, A. J. Smith can whip all the cavalry and infantry (if any) in North Mississippi." Moreover, Sherman beamed, "Old Hicks has done so well that he should have a life estate at Paducah." He had less confidence in Hurlbut and Brayman, deeming them too defensive-minded and easily frightened. Smith's appearance with veterans seasoned in both the Meridian and Red River expeditions "will be a big bombshell in Forrest's camp should he, as I fear he will, elude Hurlbut." Furthermore, local Federal authorities might permit loyal citizens in places like Pulaski, Tennessee, to help stabilize areas by purchasing and keeping arms for suppressing robbers and partisans. They would be of little help against Forrest, and by the end of the first week in April, Forrest had evaded Veatch and Hurlbut altogether. Veatch simply missed contact while waiting at Purdy near the old Shiloh battlefield. Grant expressed misgivings about the Grenada scheme anyway while agreeing that Hurlbut was a weak reed at Memphis.[39]

Sherman finally admitted to Grant on April 9, "Forrest will escape us." When McPherson at Huntsville, Alabama, expressed concern for sufficient force in Memphis, Sherman fired back that with 10,600 troops plus three full regiments of armed citizens and sixty heavy guns, he felt "no apprehension whatever for the safety of that city," but only Hurlbut's timidity and alarmism. He added separately, "The more the enemy's cavalry that keep over toward the Mississippi the better, as our object is to disperse them. They cannot make a lodgment on the river, anyhow, and only wander about consuming the resources of their own people." Hurlbut was all but marginalized in Sherman's mind. Meanwhile, that Memphis political-general plied McPherson with marginalia: district organization of various corps troops, requests for veteran cavalry units like the Third Michigan and Seventh Kansas, consolidation of all African American troops under his command, and the cotton trade from Mississippi plantations. He advanced Forrest's order of battle and ostensible strength (eight thousand effectives: six brigades comprising fifteen regiments) and artillery (four captured 3-inch rifled guns and eight howitzers) and the continuing intelligence that "he proposes to cross at Clifton, at mouth of Big Sandy, and operate in Kentucky and Middle Tennessee." One thing Hurlbut would not do was fight.[40]

A frustrated Sherman wrote McPherson on April 11 suggesting how Hurlbut was "generally willing to order movements, but personally don't direct them." While "lawfully the commander of the Sixteenth Corps, we do not need his personal services." He understood McPherson's embarrassment with the hack subordinate and offered to let Hurlbut down easy before summarily dismissing him from command. Still irritated by Veatch's withdrawal from Purdy (as it "makes Forrest's escape from the trap in which he caught himself easy and certain"), and wishing "we had a bold, dashing officer to put at Memphis," Sherman wondered if there were any units at Cairo that could go up the Tennessee and move inland on Jackson or Paris since that "would disturb Forrest more than anything Hurlbut will do from Memphis." Forrest's force was widely scattered, with many men on furlough stealing horses and recuperating, and thus susceptible to destruction. True, Forrest might cross the Tennessee, "but I don't care if he does." If the raider broke the railroad between Nashville and Louisville "it would not bother us," asserted Sherman, "for we have vast supplies here, and if he comes over to the neighborhood of Pulaski or Columbia we will give him more than he expects." A focused Sherman added, "As we want a surplus of our best troops on the line of the Tennessee." When that was done, "we can give more attention to the Mississippi as against the small bands that threaten it."[41]

Sherman remained optimistic that at some point Forrest "will catch a second edition of Paducah" while responding caustically to reports that had the rebels attacking Columbus and crossing the Tennessee near Hamburg since Forrest could hardly attack on the Mississippi and cross the Tennessee that same day. As spring blossoms signaled seasonal change, Confederate riders from central Kentucky to northern Alabama and Mississippi kept their opponents off pace. Yet the Confederate military was its own worst enemy. Should cavalry support the main armies or conduct these independent raids assisted by partisans and hinterland instability? No doubt Sherman's dispersed rear echelons and line of communication appeared vulnerable. Federal positions of strength themselves forced Confederate dispersion of effort. Concern for strategic interests and resources like central Alabama ironworks vied with political concern about the home front, replenishment of manpower and mounts, and most of all defense of the railroad to Atlanta. McPherson's concentration in the Decatur area of the Tennessee Valley usefully disconcerted both Johnston and Polk. Gadfly Tennessee Confederate governor Isham G. Harris might accompany Forrest much of the time, helping to rally Tennesseans, yet his counterweight came from Alabama senator R.W. Walker and governor T. H. Watts, who badgered their own sector commanders about Federals poised to strike the invaluable iron-producing region of Shelby and Bibb Counties, where destruction of such facilities "would be an irreparable loss to the Government, and would cripple most seriously our military operations."[42]

Furthermore, Johnston complained about losing cavalry to the protection of north Alabama, citing Polk's own February estimate of having fifteen thousand horsemen available for a movement into Middle Tennessee. Polk ordered Stephen Lee to move north from Mississippi to help Forrest, who "will be at Jackson as long as he is permitted to remain there; his object is to raise troops." Then all that changed suddenly as the north Alabama threat forced Polk to order Forrest out of West Tennessee to unite with Lee in opposing an anticipated Federal raid by Grierson and A. J. Smith from Decatur down through Elyton and the Jones Valley. Forrest should bring out as many recruits as possible while leaving a holding force to blunt Hurlbut and other pursuers. Polk also vented about lack of communication with Forrest, although the latter informed headquarters on April 10, "I expect in the course of ten or twelve days to move back into North Mississippi and expect to take out with me at least 2,000 more troops, conscripts and deserters included." Even when writing this letter, Forrest entertained more aggressive moves. By that time, Forrest's command would have reassembled, and the general promised full and thorough reports. Buford in Kentucky, Harris at Paris, and Bell at Bolivar had been the most successful recruiters, he noted, although Forrest doubted the value of extending conscription to sixteen and post-forty-five-year-old white males.[43]

Fort Pillow: "A Great Slaughter Pen"

Forrest informed Polk on April 4, "There is a Federal force of 500 or 600 at Fort Pillow, which I shall attend to in a day or two, as they have horses and supplies which we need." On the tenth, he wrote Lee that he would move against Fort Pillow the following day with two brigades, "the [enemy] force at that point being 300 whites and 600 negroes." Carefully sending a diversion to keep Hurlbut pinned in Memphis, and Buford to threaten Columbus before going on to retrieve the overlooked Paducah horses, Forrest (again accompanied by Governor Harris), took Chalmers with Tyree Bell's and Robert "Black Bob" McCulloch's brigades—some fifteen hundred in number—to reduce Fort Pillow. Bell and McCulloch trudged seventy and fifty miles respectively from separate points through spring drizzle and mud to reach their position about 5:30 a.m. on April 12. "I attacked Fort Pillow on the morning of the 12th" and after a brief fight "drove the enemy, 700 strong, into the fort under the cover of their gun-boats," Forrest reported in his initial after-action dispatch on the fifteenth. He demanded surrender, he continued, which was declined: "I stormed the fort, and after a contest of thirty minutes captured the entire garrison, killing 500 and taking 200 horses and a large amount of quartermaster's stores." Forrest cited his own losses as merely twenty killed and sixty wounded. He noted "over 100 citizens who had fled to the fort to escape conscription ran into the river and were drowned." "The Confederate flag now floats over the fort," he concluded.[44]

In various succeeding reports (including one that he sent to Jefferson Davis), Forrest wrote that the Mississippi had been "dyed with the blood of the slaughtered for 200 yards," as the enemy had "attempted to retreat to the river, either for protection of gun-boats or to escape, and the slaughter was heavy." He betrayed the driving passion behind what actually had transpired by sneering at the large enemy death toll among "Tennessee Tories" and former slaves both in Federal uniform opining: "It is hoped that these facts will demonstrate to the Northern people that Negro soldiers cannot cope with Southerners." Achilles V. Clark of the Twentieth Tennessee Cavalry substantiated the picture of "a great slaughter pen." He suggested that "human blood stood about in pools and brains could hav [sic] been gathered up in any quantity." He had tried to stop the butchery and nearly succeeded, "but Gen. Forrest ordered them shot down like dogs and the carnage continued," he declared, until "our men became sick of blood and the firing ceased." One of Forrest's surgeons, Dr. S. H. Caldwell, painted a more favorable picture of his chief's intervention. Writing to his wife on April 15, Caldwell declared that the garrison refused to surrender, "which [incensed] our men & if General Forrest had not have run between our men & the Yanks with his Pistol and saber drawn not a man would have been spared." Nearly half a century later, one of Forrest's biographers had him avowing in his particular patois at the end of the affair, "We busted the fort, at ninerclock and scattered the niggers," adding that his men "is still a killinam in the woods." Perhaps apocryphal, there was much to explain and little to exonerate about Old Bedford at Fort Pillow.[45]

The name "Fort Pillow" subsequently became known as that era's day of infamy in the North as much as a glorious victory in Forrest lore. The Confederates had constructed river defense works there in 1861 and expanded the complex, ironically naming it for native Tennessean and amateur soldier Gideon Pillow, who at the time served as the district commander and subsequently as part of the brigadier claque that surrendered Fort Donelson to Grant in February 1862. By the time of Forrest's attack two years later, Pillow performed provost marshal work rounding up deserters in the Alabama hill country. Various garrison commanders during Confederate occupancy of the post included Patrick Cleburne, John P. McGowan, and Alexander P. Stewart. Garrison numbers varied from 945 to 3,600 men at different times. Located on the First Chickasaw Bluff forty miles north of Memphis (by direct line, double that by river meanderings), the outer works ran for nearly four miles in a semicircle around the fort. Perhaps three thousand slaves had been employed to build the works.[46]

Federal occupancy began in September 1862. The Fifty-second Indiana garrisoned the place until January 1, 1864, using it as a jump-off point for raiding and suppressing guerrillas in the area. By February, the Hoosiers had been replaced by local homegrown Yankees of Union City loyalist attorney William L. Bradford's battalion. Despite Sherman's order to abandon the post in January 1864, Hurlbut actually strengthened the garrison with Philadelphia abolitionist and army regular Major Lionel F. Booth and his colored Sixth U.S. Heavy Artillery. And more reinforcements had been en route on the actual day of the fight. Hurlbut reasoned that neighborhood stabilization and pacification efforts and protection of river traffic dictated such continued occupation of the positions. A Union gunboat, the *New Era* (a 157-ton former river ferryboat sternwheeler built at Wellsville, Ohio, in 1862 mounting 24-pounder howitzers) under Acting Marshal James Marshall, hovered offshore. Sherman subsequently claimed that he did not know the post had been reoccupied and that "the garrison at Fort Pillow was not part of our army, but a nondescript body, in process of formation and posted there to cover a trading post for the convenience of families supposed to be friendly to us, or, at least not hostile." Nonetheless, a force of about 550 men occupied the inner redoubts, with eight-foot-high ramparts, six-foot ditches, and various buildings serving civilian as well as garrison needs—a strategic hamlet, not a first-rate fortress when Forrest arrived there in April. Although Hurlbut, Booth, and Bradford considered the position defensible, the garrison was no match for the estimated fifteen hundred rebel veterans who surrounded and besieged them. Fort Pillow would be no repeat of Paducah. In fact, Forrest's earlier rebuff, the multiracial and loyalist composition of the garrison, the fort's layout, and the vicious attitudes of Forrest's raiders set the stage for Yankee disaster, later associated with the words atrocity and massacre.[47]

Forrest's reduction of Fort Pillow followed a familiar pattern of besiegement, call for surrender, negotiation and rejection, and final assault. Confederate sharpshooter fire and the press of numbers forced Federal abandonment of the outer works and nearby barracks and supply buildings. Booth was mortally wounded and Bradford assumed command, continuing to negotiate using Booth's name. Final discussions broke down about midafternoon. Forrest sent his usual caveat about not being responsible for the fate of the garrison if it did not surrender, to which Bradford refused. Forrest's men then swept forward and overwhelmed the defenders and the panicked garrison broke for the cover of the riverbank and protective gunfire of the *New Era* as prearranged. At that point, the fighting took an ugly turn, resulting in the controversial slaughter of soldiers and civilians, both black and white. Forrest's initial promise to the defenders that "you will be treated as prisoners of war" had evaporated with further negotiations and disintegrated altogether in the rebel blood lust of victory. Achilles Clark clarified that there had been taunting back and forth during the truce, with Yankees "threatening that if you charge this breast works to show no quarter." When gaining the fort, "our men were so exasperated by the Yankee's threats of no quarter that they gave but little." Fighting eventually blended with surrender and slaughter since no Federal lowered the fort's flag or displayed any white flag. The *New Era* ineffectually supported the garrison as victor and vanquished mingled indiscriminately. Captured cannon added to the Confederates' inventory to play upon the gunboat, which soon withdrew from range, leaving the soldiers to their fate. Forrest lost control of the situation as his men butchered wounded and captives alike. "The poor deluded negros would run up to our men fall upon their knees [*sic*] and with uplifted hands scream for mercy but they were ordered to their feet and then shot down," Clark observed in an oft-quoted comment, with the white men faring "but little better." Federal reinforcements hovered aboard transports as well as the gunboat, incapable of decisive intervention. Some Union prisoners were taken, and the wounded were subsequently exchanged.[48]

Depending upon perspective, one might conclude that atrocities mixed with at least some humanitarian actions at Fort Pillow. Nonetheless, for weeks and months after the fight, this calamity filled newspaper and personal accounts. Even Union POWs like Captain Robert T. Cornwall of the Sixty-seventh Pennsylvania, at Richmond's Libby Prison, recorded in his diary that it was "enough to make one's blood run cold to read the boastful account of the most inhuman murder of five hundred officers and men after they had surrendered, and that, too, by a force ten times as great as that of the garrison." He vowed that "as sure as there is a God in Heaven and brave hearts in the land of the free, there is a great day of retribution coming." Certainly ret-

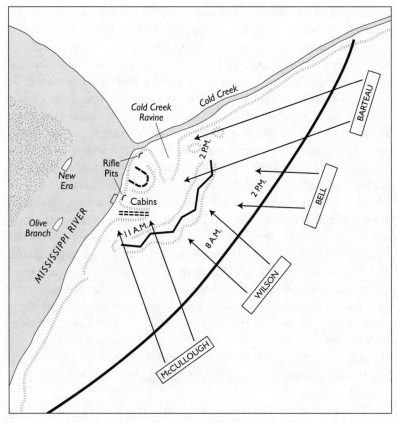

Fort Pillow, April 12, 1864. Map by Bill Nelson.

ribution was on the lips of official Washington, from Capital Hill to the White House. Testimony was taken for congressional investigations and political agendas pointed toward northern national elections in the autumn. President Lincoln rather languidly told his Cabinet on May 3 that it was certain that a large number of "our colored soldiers, with their white offices" were "massacred after they had surrendered." Grant, as senior Union general in the war, demanded retaliation if allegations of Confederate brutality proved verifiable, and he suspended prisoner exchange permanently. Rebel authorities meanwhile ducked responsibility as an attempt was made "to illuminate the heinous act by the prompt tender of thanks to General Forrest from the highly elated rebel Congress," suggested Grierson many years later, thus indicating "the policy of the so-called Confederate government."[49]

The great southern bard and author of "Maryland, My Maryland," James R. Randall, felt compelled to pen "At Fort Pillow," in which he defended against the North's outrage by providing his own rhetorical venom about "the Yankee fiends, that came with fire," and "camped on the consecrated soil" of his home and his mother's grave while defiling his sister's purity. "You shudder as you think upon, the carnage of the grim report, the desolation when we won the inner trenches of the fort" he thundered," but "there are deeds you may not know, that scourge the pulses into strife, dark memories of deathless woe, pointing the bayonet and knife." Still, Sherman (hardly a proponent of black soldiery) apparently decided not to press the issue, having his focus elsewhere. He recorded benignly in his memoirs years later, "No doubt Forrest's men acted like a set of barbarians, shooting down the helpless Negro garrison after the fort was in their possession; but I am told that Forrest personally disclaims any active participation in the assault, and that he stopped the firing as soon as he could." Nearly a century and a half later, Americans continue to wrangle over what happened at Fort Pillow. Fort Pillow became "one of the most studied and highly contentious episodes" in the entire war. George Burkhardt, a student of "black flag warfare," observes wryly that "if 1864 was the prime year for atrocities, April was the worst month," citing not only Fort Pillow but also similar crimes at Poison Spring, Arkansas, and Plymouth, North Carolina.[50]

When the smoke cleared on that April day at Fort Pillow, the Confederates had secured a complete victory, captured a Yankee fort at a cost of an estimated one hundred casualties, and killed, wounded, or captured to nearly five times that number of the enemy (specifically dispatching easily 204 of perhaps 262 black troops engaged). "After the fight," noted participant Dr. S. H. Caldwell, Forrest's men "commenced the plunder of the town," burning the supply facilities and generally pillaging for themselves (although Caldwell complained to his wife that he had nothing he could send home because the weight of all the trophies threatened to break down his mount). Atrocities occurred even subsequent to the fight when as a prisoner Major Bradford was apparently killed by uncontrolled junior rebels once they had left the area. One student of the affair contends that "nearly all historians publishing on the subject today hold that a massacre took place, that some Confederates tried to cover it up, and that some northerners tried to exploit the event to aid the war effort." But whether or not the Mississippi "was dyed with the blood of the slaughtered" or that burnings and burials alive, bayoneting through eyes, and other sundry gory events were true, Paul Ashdown and Edward Caudill contend the stain of Fort Pillow "was also a stain on the Forrest Myth" that began to spread almost instantly after the battle. Historian Albert Castel thought fifty years ago that an "analysis of both the Northern and Southern evidence leads to the conclusion that Forrest's troops, having captured Fort Pillow as a result of superior strength and tactics, out of a combination of race hatred, personal animosity, and battle fury then proceeded to kill a large number of the garrison after they had either ceased resisting or were incapable of resisting." As to Forrest's complicity, Forrest biographer Brian Wills states bluntly, "As commander of the troops on the scene, Forrest was responsible." Or as another student of the affair, John Gauss, notes, as the chief commander at the scene, Forrest "gets full credit for the victory and shoulders the blame for the atrocities."[51]

The battle itself was hardly more than another contribution to the tally sheet of unending violence. It reflected the changing nature of conflict in the heartland by 1864. Fort Pillow epitomized the essence of a people's war, not between "disciplined and civilized armies [that] must be cherished as a force for the common good" (to quote modern British historian John Keegan) but between elements of "savage society." The battle pitted Tennesseans against Tennesseans, loyal unionist southerner against vengeance-seeking rebellious southerner. Above all, Fort Pillow represented a clash over race, between antebellum codes and mores and modernizing human rights. Legally armed white southerners wreaked vengeance against black southerners they felt to be illegally freed, armed, trained, and equipped to wage insurgency against the prevailing sociocultural economic system. Historian of the Tennessee "home-grown Yankees," James Baggett, adds that by slaughtering Bradford's "tories," the Confederates could teach other unionists "the ultimate lesson and end a dire situation for area inhabitants" (adding white Tennesseans' most unpardonable sin of joining with blacks to fight fellow white southerners). Once the battle was joined, "other happenings" encouraged atrocities tracing from rebel hatred and divided loyalties in West Tennessee to leadership failure on both sides "to control its own soldiers," pandemonium, excessive drinking, and victimization. Ultimately, James D. Lockett portrayed Fort Pillow as both a crime against humanity and a military lynching, as the defeated South's first shot in a war to maintain white supremacy.[52]

The aftermath of Fort Pillow proved instructive. Area unionists felt abandoned as other posts contracted and many loyalists simply fled to

Memphis and Paducah. Sherman wrote Halleck and Grant on April 16 how the "force captured and butchered at Fort Pillow was not on my returns at all," being "the first fruits of the system of trading posts designed to assist the loyal people of the interior." All such stations were a weakness and offered tempting chances for plunder. Frankly, he suggested, "our efforts heretofore to cover trading schemes, local interests, and matters of civil reconstruction has almost paralyzed large armies by dividing them up into little squads easy of surprise and capture." They should be "deferred till all large armies of the Confederacy are broken up and destroyed." The navy, however, felt that it had helped thwart Forrest's intent to take Columbus and Paducah simultaneously with Fort Pillow. Local commanders like Fleet Captain A. Pennock and Lieutenant Commanders Le Roy Fitch and James Shirk remained confident that their tinclad flotilla could keep the major rivers open to wartime commerce and military traffic. They had anticipated the raiders capturing ferryboats and other craft so as to attack army and navy shore facilities necessary, if not for Sherman's campaign, at least for continued Federal control of the Mississippi Valley. Yet a fascinating strategic twist on the disaster occurred when a one-legged major general, Dan Sickles (the other leg sacrificed at Gettysburg the summer before), reported back to Lincoln from Memphis at the end of May. "The raid of Forrest upon Paducah and Fort Pillow, it is believed, was undertaken in part to enable him to secure large quantities of goods which had been accumulated by arrangement through disloyal agencies, at points within our lines, along his line of march," he claimed. Sent south by the president to ascertain progress of reconstruction in Union-held cities, the condition of blacks, and the effect of Lincoln's amnesty proclamation (even the effectiveness of Johnson's governorship as well), Sickles felt that Forrest's raid had uncovered scandalous and unproductive "trade with the enemy." Memphis stood as the epicenter, detrimental to not only winning the conflict but also restoring the Union in West Tennessee and northern Mississippi.[53]

Meanwhile, Forrest ordered Chalmers to level Fort Pillow, burn the out buildings, and take captive survivors back to Jackson. Concern about rumored enemy pursuit (possibly even from Middle Tennessee) drove Forrest. Union gunboats scurried to the Fort Pillow site, shelled the empty woods and ravines aimlessly, but retrieved the Union dead and wounded under a flag of truce while in turn communicating the nature of the disaster to the outside world. Forrest had little interest in conveying captured black soldiers back to rightful owners when his army needed their labor. Moreover, he had to respond quickly to Polk's instructions to return to Mississippi, concentrate with S.D. Lee (who on the thirteenth, took command of all Polk's cavalry, including Forrest's band), and blunt the threatened Yankee move on Alabama. On the other hand, he said, "I feel confident of my ability to whip any cavalry they can send against me, and can, if necessary, avoid their infantry." If permitted to remain in West Tennessee at his superior's pleasure, he told Polk, he would welcome having his regular artillery component with him "as I could operate effectively with my rifle battery on the rivers." Still, a sort of triumphal march attended his passage away from Fort Pillow with enthusiastic gatherings hailing the rebels as conquering heroes. Women at Brownsville, Tennessee, honored Forrest with a set of silver spurs made from their sewing thimbles.[54]

Forrest's success kept his opponents practically in a state of siege (Hurlbut's view) and penned up in Memphis (Sherman's observation), although Grierson went out to try to intercept Forrest's retirement. Hurlbut was relieved of command, replaced by Major General Cadwallader C. Washburn, and the dispersal of troops to other points hampered coordinated action. For the most part, the Confederate raiders confined their efforts for the next two weeks mainly to sweeping West Tennessee for conscripts, deserters, and supplies. Federal authorities used the specter of Fort Pillow to inflame and unify African American troops' purpose while clamping down on trade and contact with civilians in the region evacuated by Forrest's raiders. To Belle Edmondson, Forrest's exploits expressed the hand of God, providing salvation for previous sins. "Drive this wicked band from our Sunny Land," she penned in her diary. "Give us Liberty and peace," she wrote, and "make us a Christian nation." She rejoiced how "the Yanks are frightened to death in Memphis" and wished "we could get possession of our city once more." At the same time, she complained that the Yankees "have begun to forage on the Country," making supplies short in Memphis, and that "the negroes have raised the black flag—gone out on a raid after Forrest, and I will bet, but few will ever return." She added, "God grant not one of our dear Soldiers will be sacrificed to those cowardly dogs."[55]

At this point, however, Providence seemed to be ordaining that Federals strike into Alabama, and senior Confederate commanders— Johnston, Polk, and Stephen Lee—debated about either countering the rumored offensive or starting one of their own into Middle Tennessee. Only the necessity of rebuilding the Memphis and Charleston Railroad west to Corinth to ensure proper resupply daunted such undertaking. Except for northern-inspired controversy, Fort Pillow faded from view for the most part as Polk wrote Secretary of War James Seddon about his own elaborate scheme to regain control of the Mississippi from Cairo south with battalions of cavalry and riflemen taking positions "to break up the navigation of the river, to destroy the commerce on the border, and to prevent all efforts at agriculture from being successful." They might even seize river craft and reconstitute a Confederate naval presence. Sherman's anticipated movements in north Alabama and Georgia, local dissidence in Alabama and Mississippi, and the breakdown in civil government, as well as illicit cotton trading with the Federals, kept Confederate commanders off balance as April waned. Forrest, on the other hand, now saw merit in returning south to reorganize and have his command inspected so as to counter War Department suspicion (stoked by Braxton Bragg) that he and his men were simply out of control. Such delay played directly into Sherman's hands.[56]

Forrest's Afterglow

Grant and Sherman acted to clean up the situation in West Tennessee in the wake of Fort Pillow. The general-in-chief told Sherman on April 15, "Forrest must be driven out, but with a proper commander in West Tennessee there is force enough now [to do so]." Sherman should press on with his Atlanta campaign, although if it seemed necessary to detach troops against Forrest, "and make the campaign with fewer men!" Having been told of the Fort Pillow massacre, Grant directed that "if our men have been murdered after capture, retaliation must be resorted to promptly." "Does General Hurlbut think if he moves a part of his force after the only enemy within 200 miles of him that the post will run off with the balance of his force?" Grant queried sarcastically. He told Sherman to relieve the Memphis commander and that he would send Major General Cadwallader C. Washburn, "a sober and energetic officer," to succeed the lethargic inebriant Hurlbut because "there has been marked timidity in the management of affairs since Forrest passed north of Memphis." Sherman ordered Hurlbut upriver to Cairo, as another newcomer, Brigadier General Samuel Sturgis, arrived at Memphis to handle Forrest. Washburn was part of a prominent political family that included Grant's old patron, Illinois congressman Elihu Washburn, and C. C. himself had been a three-term congressman from Wisconsin. Sturgis was a veteran West Pointer, class of 1846, which had numbered among its graduates George B. McClellan and Stonewall Jackson. Something of an inebriate himself when he arrived in Memphis, Sturgis had gained fame with a hard-bitten remark during the Second Manassas campaign in Virginia two years before that he did not care "a pinch of owl dung" about fellow Illinoisan in command, John Pope, veteran of the war in the Mississippi Valley who had been called east by Lincoln to resolve defeats there—and who then failed miserably himself. Washburn and Sturgis arrived in Memphis on April 23 and 24 and began seizing every horse and mule in sight and tapping commands up and down the Mississippi for reinforcements to go after Forrest.[57]

Sensing that the "Forrest Myth" had begun to impact even this pair, Sherman sent word to Washburn not to exaggerate his opponent's strength or his own weakness and not to let Forrest "insult you by passing in sight almost of your command." He told Grant on April 19, "It does seem as though Forrest has our men down there in cow, but I will try new leaders, for I believe our men will fight if led." He counted ten thousand men and seven thousand horses at Memphis (before expropriation) and continued to marvel how the army could continuously destroy so many mounts. Later he would tell Washburn, "Don't hesitate to take horses and everything in the country that will strengthen you. It is only a question of whether you or Forrest shall have them." Grierson, a fan of Hurlbut, had little kind to say about Sturgis and chafed at constraints while the exiled Hurlbut became prickly about "the imputation of 'marked timidity'" and requested a court of inquiry. Grant dismissed that request curtly: "Whether his course was 'timid' or not, it has been unsatisfactory." Even Lincoln refused to intercede when Sherman bluntly told Hurlbut, "The fact that Forrest's and Chalmers' forces, as well as that of [Ben] McCulloch, passed by the flank within 50 miles of Memphis unattacked does show timidity somewhere." Memphis had sufficient force to assure its safety and left at least four thousand infantry and much cavalry with which to have attacked Forrest in the flank going north or returning south. One officer of the Second United States Colored Troops boasted that if Forrest came near the city "he will have a good time," since his regiment was the best drilled in the city, white or black, and given another six months could beat any throughout the army." Simply put, Grant and Sherman were fighters; Hurlbut, a politician and racketeer in uniform, was not. There did seem to be a dearth of cooperation in West Tennessee.[58]

Sherman's orders to Washburn sounded like a repeat of those to Hurlbut and others. In addition to Sturgis's strike force and Grierson's seizure of mules and horses as well as Buckland's infantry preparations, a general buildup would occur as another expedition under Brigadier General Walter Q. Gresham would once more ascend the Tennessee River to cooperate with the Memphis field force. The object as usual, stated Sherman, was to prevent Forrest from getting off with his plunder, and, in fact, "all the force along the Mississippi River must strike at the enemy wherever they can do so to advantage and occupy his attention and keep him busy in that quarter." Paducah, Cairo, Columbus, Memphis, Vicksburg, and Natchez were to be held at all cost. The river navigation would be kept open via such permanent posts, a thorough system of scouting parties and patrols, and the assistance of the gunboats and Marine brigade. "All weak, isolated points which are exposed must be evacuated," said Sherman, returning to his theme that "the plan of establishing small posts on the river is bad, and must not be carried out to any extent." Even Lieutenant Commander Shirk, commanding the Seventh District's Mississippi Squadron of gunboats, repeated the rumor that Forrest was to hold the portion of Tennessee and Kentucky until Polk moved north and secured a Tennessee River crossing so that their combined forces could cross and cut off Sherman's supply line between Nashville and Chattanooga. By April 21, Sherman was apprehensive that Forrest had eluded pursuit. "I fear we are too late," he wrote Washburn, "but I know there are troops enough at Memphis to whale Forrest if you can reach him."[59]

In fact, Washburn already had misgivings, stoked by one of Hurlbut's aides upon his arrival at Cairo. After stating that the reports trickling in about Fort Pillow "make out a much worse case than any of the published accounts" so that the "Sioux Indians after this will be regarded as models of humanity," he expressed reservations about going after Forrest. Reflecting the realities of inadequate resources as conveyed by subordinates Grierson and Buckland, "with the cavalry [at Memphis] there certainly but little can be done toward intercepting raids of the enemy," he wired Sherman on April 21. Upon reaching Memphis, he sounded the same note to higher headquarters as Hurlbut and others: insufficient and poorly mounted cavalry present, the rest home on furlough and altogether but eighteen hundred "very poor" white mounted cavalry, another one thousand dismounted, two thousand white infantry, six hundred white artillery, and thirty-five hundred colored troops. The total, eighty-one hundred, would allow him "to do little but act on the defensive" against Forrest's estimated eight thousand, "all well mounted." Reinforcements from Vicksburg brought only unarmed men and unshod horses. He closed one missive to Grant's headquarters with the all-too-familiar bleat, "While with the force I have here I feel perfectly secure against any mounted force they may bring, I do not feel that I could venture to go in pursuit of Forrest without hazarding the city unless I have more force." To Sherman, on the twenty-fourth, Washburn once more illustrated the quandary of holding Memphis ("on account of the large amount of Government supplies in the city and the prestige which its capture would give the rebs") and simultaneously going after Forrest at Jackson ("Forrest, being able to move more rapidly than our infantry which I send after him, might swoop down upon us here with his whole force"). A more agile Forrest easily enjoyed the upper hand.[60]

An aggrieved Hurlbut at Cairo had it quite on the mark in an April 27 letter to Department and Army of the Tennessee headquarters. Perhaps as a cover for his own deficiencies, he derided Washburn's efforts yet captured the essence of the problem. Grierson's cavalry was of little value, its horses run down and few in number. "All the dash and energy they ever had was taken out by Sooy Smith's misfortune" in conjunction with the Meridian operation earlier. Only the Fourth Missouri, Second New Jersey, Nineteenth Pennsylvania, Sixth Tennessee, and Seventh Indiana could be considered organized, and only the Missourians were "reliable for serious action." Otherwise, detachments of nonveterans lacking sufficient horses and foot-bound infantry provided a maneuver force which by marching off would court "serious disaster." He therefore affirmed "as my deliberate opinion that no movement should be made to bring Forrest to action with less than 5,000 good men, and that it is infinitely better and safer to wait the return of the veteran cavalry, now past due." Intelligence disclosed Confederates repairing railroads and building a base of operations for Forrest at Corinth. Hurlbut's credence was probably long past, yet the need for a counter-offensive seemed palpable.[61]

Other impressions of the raider's impact on affairs trickled in. Grenville M. Dodge, one of McPherson's wing commanders at Athens, Alabama, thought that Forrest had possibly added one thousand or two thousand men to his command since going into West Tennessee. Moreover, "he takes everything without regard to former principles of the owners, and that entire country is feasting him and his officers." Dodge knew "a large number who have professed great 'love' for our flag who have outdone themselves in toadying to Forrest." It would be "a just judgment on West Tennessee if the troops sent there were given orders to burn the entire country, take everything that can walk, and destroy any and everything a rebel can eat or drink or be of any benefit whatever to them." Even Sherman wrote Secretary of War Edwin M. Stanton, "I know well the animus of the Southern soldiery, and the truth is they cannot be restrained." Fort Pillow would make blacks desperate and "when in turn they commit horrid acts of retaliation we will be relieved of the responsibility." Thus far, they had been comparatively well behaved and refrained from "the horrid excesses and barbarities" so dreaded in the southern press. He countered Confederate claims that any position taken by assault was not entitled to quarter by observing that such a rule would have justified slaughter at any places similarly captured by the Federals, such as Arkansas Post and Fort DeRussy. "I doubt the wisdom of any fixed rule by our Government, but let soldiers affected make their rules as we progress," as we "will use their own logic against them, as we have from the beginning of the war." To Sherman, the "Southern army, which is the Southern people, cares no more for our clamor than the idle wind, but they will heed the slaughter that will follow as the natural consequence of their own inhuman acts." Therefore, he instructed McPherson on April 24, "give General Slocum [at Vicksburg] and Washburn [at Memphis] orders to seem most active; to hold there all the enemy possible, even at a small risk to the river, for if we whip Joe Johnston good, everything lying west will feel the blow." The navy would patrol the Tennessee and "the worst we have to apprehend is that Forrest may come across to act against our right flank, but this would be prevented if Washburn [and Slocum] threaten Grenada [Mississippi]."[62]

The Federals in West Tennessee again proved incapable of destroying Forrest. "God bless our little band and crown them with victory," Belle Edmondson wrote. By month's end, McPherson's dispatch to Washburn reflected reality. "You may not be able with the troops at your disposal," he decided, "to assume the offensive with as much boldness as is desirable against an enemy like Forrest, and force him to fight or be driven out of West Tennessee." It was of utmost importance, however, to keep his forces occupied and prevent him from forming plans and combinations to cross the Tennessee River and break up the railroads in Sherman's rear. "By assuming the offensive-defensive—watching him closely and striking a blow whenever it can be put in to advantage—he will be compelled to be on his guard," and not, said McPherson hopefully, be able to inflict upon us any serious damage." Sturgis's promising expedition with three thousand cavalry and thirty-four hundred infantry, as well as twenty cannon out of Memphis, went nowhere. "No news except a rumor that Forrest had beaten the Nigger troops who left Memphis," Belle Edmondson jotted gleefully in her diary. In truth, an advanced party under Colonel Joseph Kargé successfully dislodged some of Forrest's command from entrenchments near Bolivar. Then rain, high water, destroyed bridges, and slow-footed infantry (not to speak of Sturgis's own overnight delay in ordering pursuit) prevented exploitation of Karge's limited success. Forrest's main column escaped. By the end of the first week in May, Sturgis had returned to Memphis, and Forrest settled into camp at Tupelo, Mississippi, his West Tennessee raid ended. "Though we could not catch the scoundrel we are at least rid of him and that is something," Sturgis told superiors. Thoughts of a similar foray into Middle Tennessee still coursed through Forrest's head, however.[63]

In a way, Forrest's retirement fit Sherman's plans, although Sturgis's dispatch a week later probably irritated Uncle Billy when he concluded, "I regret very much that I could not have the pleasure of bringing you his hair, but he is too great a plunderer to fight anything like an equal force, and we have to be satisfied with driving him from the State." Forrest had "not come to West Tennessee for the purpose of fighting, Sturgis maintained, unless it might so happen that he could fall upon some little party or defenseless place, and being well mounted and having, of course, every facility for gaining information of our movements, it is idle to follow him except with an equal force of cavalry, which we have not in that part of the country." The raider might turn on Sherman's communications "and I rather think he will," Sturgis observed, "but see no way to prevent it from this point and with this force." "We will have to be satisfied with driving him from the State." Perhaps Washburn's conclusion was correct on May 8. "The main object of Forrest's visit to West Tennessee, as avowed by himself, was to draw troops from General Sherman, to protect exposed points," said the new Memphis commander. In that "he has signally failed." West Tennessee and Kentucky "are now clear of any organized rebel force, and no place in this district is in danger or in any way threatened," Hurlbut's successor cheerfully advanced.[64]

What did higher command think about all this? Sherman wrote his wife about Hurlbut "ruined by his apathy & fear to go out of Memphis

to fight Forrest." "He seems to have set down on the Defensive," continued the general, "when he had plenty of men who by marching out fifty
miles could have made Forrest quit that Country long before he did.
The mischief done was however to the Negros & People of West Tennessee, rather than to us." Confederate senior leadership saw it rather
differently, rewarding and praising Forrest and his command. Forrest
himself had written President Davis from Jackson on April 15, stating
that at the time "North Mississippi West Tenn and Southern Kentucky,
West of the Tennessee river are free from federal rule and occupation"
with garrisons cowering in Memphis, Paducah, and Columbus. He
proclaimed success in all engagements with "the enemy and the bands
of guerrillas, horse thieves and robbers which infested this region have
been broken up, and dispersed, and many men, heretofore Union in
sentiment, are openly expressing themselves for the south." Recruiting
of volunteers seemed no longer possible, but conscription in the region
"would give us from five to eight thousand men perhaps more." For
such reasons Polk told him on April 24, "Your brilliant campaign in
West Tennessee has given me great satisfaction, and entitles you to the
thanks of your countrymen." The Confederate Congress one month
later bestowed its thanks to the raiders "for their late brilliant and successful campaign in Mississippi, West Tennessee, and Kentucky—a
campaign which has conferred upon its authors fame as enduring as the
records of the struggle which they have so brilliant illustrated." In late
May, in gallant fashion hardly befitting Forrest's rough-hewn image,
the cavalryman sent Confederate first lady Varina Howell Davis the
"beautiful flag of the '62 Illinois,'" captured at Paducah by Tyree H.
Bell's Tennessee brigade. Fort Pillow's infamy entered no one's talk,
other than when Secretary of War Seddon suggested to Davis, "Much
misrepresentation of events . . . has been thrown before the world." In
fact, Forrest at the time stood poised for his finest moment.[65]

CHAPTER 5

The Raiders of Summer and Fall

The summer of 1864 was important for both sides. The war dragged on inconclusively as the Federal presidential election loomed. Delegates to a National Union Convention of mostly Republicans and some War Democrats nominated President Abraham Lincoln as their standard bearer on June 8. In a surprise move, these delegates (possibly with the president's "hidden hand") replaced Vice President Hannibal Hamlin with Tennessee military governor Andrew Johnson in an effort designed to garner voters of diverse political persuasion and to project a uniform war prosecution policy. Just a week before that, dissident radical Republicans had produced a splinter slate of former army generals John Charles Fremont and John Cochrane to reflect their dissatisfaction with emancipation policies and weak conduct of the war. On the final day of August, the regular Democrats selected the popular Major General George B. McClellan and Ohio politician George H. Pendleton for their presidential slate in another anti-administration move. Meanwhile, Union armies could not capture Richmond and Atlanta. Union naval operations tightened the blockade along southern coasts, but several ports still remained active. Nathan Bedford Forrest's lair in northern Mississippi continued intact.[1]

The Confederacy stood defiant. Able only to backpedal before the Union behemoth, its generals still practiced their time-honored summer strategy of raiding Union logistics and disrupting the enemy rear. True, a third raid into Maryland this time actually carried southern arms into Washington's District of Columbia. But then it too flickered out. Summer drought, heat, and timing doomed that attempt to change the course of the war by one of Lee's remaining chieftains, the ever-colorful Jubal Early. He came close, and reverberations of such audacity and near-success after three years of fighting still sent chills through the Lincoln administration. Early hovered all summer as a threat in the lower Shenandoah Valley. Lincoln faced political defeat in the autumn as everywhere the war dragged on.

Union stabilization efforts also remained in flux. Summer witnessed a high level of scouts, expeditions, skirmishes, and raids either emanating from or heading into the upper heartland. In truth, they mostly took place on the eastern and western peripheries. Morgan mounted yet another daring Kentucky foray while Forrest continued his spring-long chess match with Sherman's satrapies in West Tennessee. Rear-echelon forces thwarted Morgan, while northern Mississippi became the killing ground for Forrest. In effect, these sideshows only tangentially brushed the thrust and counterthrust of the main armies. Ironically, they might have been more important strategically but for quirks of fate and timing. In a sense the Confederacy miscued on using a potentially damaging tool like Morgan or Forrest (much less partisans and civilian dissidence) to permanently destabilize the Union rear. The issue hinged on Richmond's internecine skirmishing with field commanders like Joe Johnston and state politicians like Georgia governor Joe Brown as well

Morgan's raiders. From *Harper's Pictorial History of the Great Rebellion.*

as dispersion of effort based on the Confederacy's departmental system of self-defense. For the most part, barring major army counter-offensive, raids themselves were merely transitory.

Johnston claimed later that Bishop-General Leonidus Polk's information about the strength of his cavalry in the spring had led him to hope "that an adequate force commanded by the most competent officer in America for such service," namely Forrest, could be sent for the purpose of breaking up Sherman's railroad in Tennessee and Kentucky. He recalled making that suggestion directly to Davis on June 13 and July 16, as well as through Bragg on four separate occasions in June. "I did so," Johnston claimed, "in confidence that this cavalry would serve the Confederacy far better by insuring the defeat of a great invasion than by repelling a mere raid." Still, nobody up the chain of command from Forrest and Morgan boldly utilized their talents that summer without strings attached and bridles on their actions. In the end, lack of proper command alignments and speed hindered the cooperation necessary to exploit all possibilities.[2]

Still, cavalry raids had various patrons. Alabama governor Thomas H. Watts, for one, wrote Jefferson Davis on July 4 that while confident in Johnston's approach, *"now what is needed, is a force to cut the communications of Sherman & keep them cut."* Forrest and six or eight thousand men offered the means. "Why cannot this be done *now?*" He queried.

Impromptu barricade of bushwhackers. From *Harper's Pictorial History of the Great Rebellion.*

Indeed, rather than direct all possible help to Johnston's army, why not reinforce and utilize Forrest's strike force in the Union rear? Watts might express a willingness "to strip his state of mounted troops if Forrest's force was insufficient," and even Robert E. Lee proffered that much had to be risked to save Alabama, Mobile, and communication with the Trans-Mississippi. "It would be better to concentrate all cavy in Misspi. & Tenn. on Sherman's communications," he said on the twelfth. Even a lowly commissary officer in Meridian, Mississippi, wrote Davis how withdrawal of Federals from west of the Mississippi would enable Confederate forces to similarly shift east of the river "into Ky. And Tenn., destroying depots at Nashville, cutting supply lines at Chattanooga, and uniting with Hood [who eventually replaced Johnston in north Georgia on July 17]" to "capture the whole Yankee army under Sherman." Advice was cheap, resources scarce. Johnston and company somewhat effectively deflected much of this talk of alternatives. This did not mean, however, that Sherman's line of communications and the upper heartland went untouched.[3]

Morgan's Faded Kentucky Glory

While Forrest danced with Federals close to the Mississippi, Morgan's reemergence with a new band of followers opened the summer activities in Kentucky. Morgan's new command, however, was not his select band of old. Richmond authorities faced manpower needs elsewhere, and the simple lack of horses, equipment, and arms yielded mostly Captain J. D. Kirkpatrick's eight-hundred-man battalion of misfits for Morgan's purposes. Months of cajoling, recruiting, and courting public favor (offset by official obfuscation) had mingled with the marital bliss of reunion with his wife, Mattie, after the previous year's capture and imprisonment. But nothing had produced the requisites of a fighting force and Morgan knew it. Criminal depredations accompanied Kirkpatrick's passage from north Georgia to the staging area of East Tennessee and Abingdon, Virginia, according to Morgan's latest biographer, James Ramage. At least, the new command's first actions helped William E. "Grumble" Jones repel counterpart Brigadier General William Averell's Yankee raid on invaluable lead and salt mines in the Wytheville and Saltville area in early May. Still, Morgan itched for the independence enjoyed previously through the favor of fellow Kentuckian Simon Bolivar Buckner as departmental commander. Morgan defied orders to remain on the defensive with Jones. He saw an early June

Confederate raiders twisting railroad track and burning railroad ties. National
Archives and Records Administration.

raid into Kentucky as an opportunity to secure horses and equipment
and alleviate his supply problem in southwest Virginia, rebuild a unified
and fit command through daring action, and humble Yankee authorities, who had become dangerously oppressive to scions of the Bluegrass.
Truthfully, Kentucky public unrest coupled with rumored midwestern
conspiracy of Copperheads seeking a separate peace and end to the war
offered exploitable circumstances. Nonetheless, years later, Davis regretted allowing Morgan his way rather than insisting on even his original
directive, that the raider move through East Tennessee directly against
Sherman's communications. What Morgan really wanted was to regain
personal fame and glory in his home state.[4]

The perceived Yankee reign of terror in Kentucky provided good
cause for a Confederate raid. By spring and summer a schism seemed to
be developing in Bluegrass loyalty. Homegrown colonel Frank Wolford,
as well as Lieutenant Governor Richard T. Jacob, spoke openly against
black recruitment. Governor Thomas Bramlette and Brigadier General
Stephen Burbridge, Kentucky district commander, seemed for the moment in sync on that issue with the politician avowing as early as April 8
that such recruits would be received into U.S. service if offered by their
owners. They would enlist and muster at Camp Nelson in southern

Jessamine County but would then be hustled to training camps at Clarksville, Nashville, and Gallatin in Tennessee. Bramlette appointed a commissioner to visit the camps and to ensure legal owners received proper vouchers and the state would receive credit for Kentucky blacks recruited in Tennessee and other states. For other reasons, both the state legislature and many Union Democrats demanded Burbridge's ouster, and that political party ruptured as a prowar/slave liberation faction formed the Unconditional Union party, embracing the recast Lincoln administration's ticket. By late June, a Union Democratic party, led by Louisville editor George Prentice and Louisville and Nashville Railroad president James Guthrie, as well as the Peace Democrats under Charles Wickliffe and others, had also established their political presence. By this point, too, state issues concerned not just emancipation and black recruitment but also civil liberties to further corrode patriotic Union solidarity. Morgan's threat provided little respite for Washington or Frankfort but potential for Richmond.[5]

Moreover, West Tennessee district leader Brigadier General Cadwallader Washburn interfered with western Kentucky obstreperousness by declaring that the people of the disloyal Purchase region "will not be allowed to sell their cotton and tobacco, or purchase supplies, until they show some friendship for the U.S. government, by driving out the guerrillas and irregular bands of Confederate soldiers who pay them frequent visits." Guerrillaism joined the volatile mix with six-month enrolled militia available for such emergencies. Kentucky inspector general Daniel Lindsey issued a draft postponement dictum on June 6 due to "the scarcity of labor, and the fact that the citizens have so patriotically and nobly responded to the late call for six-months' men." Meanwhile, black volunteering in Lexington was brisk, and a black unit commander at Paducah conducted "impressment" in Union County (with gunboats helping "to persuade the owners to consent to the raid"). Then Morgan and twenty-one hundred well-mounted and -armed soldiers came through Pound Gap, eluded Burbridge's blocking force, and concentrated everyone's focus.[6]

Both national and state authorities watched Morgan apprehensively. All spring and summer unhappy Kentuckians had petitioned their governor about raising home guards and militia to cope with guerrillas. But now there was Morgan again. As early as March, Brigadier General George Crook at Lexington warned the chain of command that the raider "is preparing a raid through Pound Gap on Richmond Ky, Lexington, Frankfort, Bardstown and thence back to Johnston's army cutting railroad from Louisville to Nashville and bridges." There was "a secret organization in Kentucky of from two to three thousand men," with horses and arms, "and will join him there." Morgan "gets positive information from Kentucky twice a week by scouts," was well posted in regard to the number and position of Union forces and would avoid them. Crook claimed the move would be deferred a few weeks while another one-star, Nathaniel C. McLean (a native of southern Ohio and married to a Louisville belle), also wrote from his provost marshal and division command slot in Lexington on April 9 that May would be the time frame, that "there are indications from the disloyal portion of the people, that upon the slightest encouragement I should have my hands full." He told his wife that "I pray they may be disappointed as all future raids will no doubt be attended with more destruction of property and life than any previous ones." He admitted not understanding how Lexington could be defended except by fighting in open fields "with nothing to prevent an enemy from turning your flanks when he pleases." Burbridge moved out to cover Pound Gap, and overall, the Federals outnumbered Morgan by better than five to one throughout the state. Unfortunately, the bluecoats were positioned for peacekeeping and insurgency, not stopping a major raid.[7]

What would be Morgan's final foray took place east of the Kentucky River—a sweep from Hazel Green to Mount Sterling and Lexington thence to Georgetown and Cynthiana on the railroad to Cincinnati before disintegrating into disorderly retirement through Sardis, Morehead, West Liberty, Paintsville, and Pikeville back to Abingdon. Towns were captured, citizenry liberated, and opponents dispersed or captured (including Brigadier General Edward Henry Hobson, Morgan's nemesis, who had taken the cavalier at Buffington's Island during the latter's famous Ohio raid), and railroads and supply lines were disrupted. For a time it seemed like one of Morgan's old strikes. Southern hearts and senses once again thrilled as he accomplished more than any other Confederate in the field that summer. He would soon be invading Maryland and Pennsylvania, they said. Only the final statistic proved more telling. Morgan and his principal subordinates took some twenty-five hundred men into Kentucky and brought back scarcely six hundred. The damage they inflicted on the enemy included government property destroyed, enemy prisoners taken, and Federal stabilization and security operations suspended. In the end Morgan's men, however, damaged their own reputations through lawless, ill-disciplined behavior.[8]

The glorious capture of 380 Federals initially at Mount Sterling and 600 more under Hobson at Cynthiana proved exhilarating, even if involving generally raw levies. Part of Morgan's men unsuccessfully

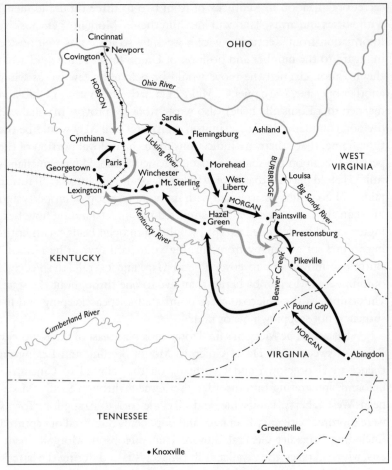

Morgan's Kentucky raid, June 1864. Map by Bill Nelson.

stormed Frankfort, where the governor and enrolled militia joined several hundred blue-coated Kentucky units to beat them off on June 10 and 11. Then Burbridge and his command returned to administer humiliating drubbings to the raiders near both those towns and the Federal Kentuckian received a brevet major generalship for his success. Morgan and the remnants escaped with their reputation for hard fighting and discipline in tatters, sullied even more by bank robberies and the appropriation and wanton destruction of private property. Morgan's disruption of railroad activities sounded good but proved chimerical. His usual authorization for confiscation of U.S. property extended beyond hard goods and animals to government cash (repeating such activities of the previous summer north of the Ohio River) and contrasted with his specific prohibition against plundering private property. His men apparently made no distinction when searching banks and courthouses, homes and businesses in Mount Sterling, Lexington, and Maysville. They netted eighty thousand dollars in assets from the Farmer's Bank of Mount Sterling, for instance. By the time they reached Georgetown, private property generally became open game, with little intervention or prosecution of offenders at the time, due, said Morgan, to the fact that obstinate enemy pursuit would have endangered the whole expedition. Therein lay the rub, as jewelry, clothing, and thousands of dollars in citizen funds left with the rebels with little or no accountability.[9]

Needless to say, Morgan's image of beau chevalier in the minds of his fellow Kentuckians evaporated forever. This disciplinary lapse, however officially explained later on, even soured relations with some of Morgan's subordinates and would lead to charges against the raider pressed all the way to Richmond. Still, many in Morgan's ranks, like Mosgrove of the Fourth Kentucky, decided, "I know that the soldiers who plundered the store at Sardis, thoughtless boys that they were, had shown their gallantry on many a field, and that they were not criminals in the common acceptation of the term." Yet Captain Edward O. Guerrant thought otherwise, muttering in his diary on June 8 how Morgan went to Lexington "to serve that city as Mt. Sterling had been served: bank robbed, stores plundered, universal pillage of private property!" Disgusted with "Morganism," the whole program now seemed to be plundering which old hands termed "bumming." "Evil only can come of such work," Guerrant concluded. Kentucky citizen Pearson Merrell of Pulaski County merely told his uncle and cousins, "I hope [the Union forces] will capture them all an send them all to Cam Duglis [Camp Douglas] where I think they all ought to be." He was most concerned about a bunch of guerrillas terrorizing and killing an old man two or three miles from his place, people saying that "he was kild on his principle an some for his money," certainly both reasons for the mayhem occurring in the Bluegrass.[10]

Biographer James Ramage thinks Morgan simply became lost "in a world of his own," where power, control, and triumph—perhaps overconfidence—intruded upon reality. Morgan would always claim Kentuckians were pro-southern and that the presence of Confederate troops on their soil for just a couple of months would yield twenty-five thousand recruits if not outright secession. But the antics of Morgan's men and Burbridge's firm response prevented either from happening. Morgan and his band dribbled back over the mountains by the end of the month. Investigations into robbery and dispersal of some sixty-two thousand dollars from a Mount Sterling bank, ten thousand dollars more from a Lexington bank, and at least nine thousand dollars from similar facilities at Winchester and Maysville would last virtually to the end of the war. Charges brought against Morgan suggested that he specifically directed Surgeon R. R. Goode of his staff to enter the Farmer's Bank of Kentucky and seize public funds for Confederate use and that Goode took the cash from the Mount Sterling facility, "failing to account for the same, applied said money to his own use." Morgan, ill for most of the summer following the raid, only half-heartedly ordered investigations. He eventually admitted a breakdown in discipline but denied directing any depredations or failing to punish offenders. By autumn, he would be dead, the money only partially restored to Kentuckians and the escutcheons of both he and his command besmirched forever. Neither President Davis's military adviser Braxton Bragg nor Secretary of War James Seddon had ever thought anything positive would come from the operation.[11]

In fact, Bragg remained totally negative toward Morgan's after-action report in early July. Nothing thus far indicated "any satisfactory result" from the raid, he thought, and should Morgan "ever return with his command it will as usual be disorganized and unfit for service until again armed, equipped and disciplined." Such activities always lost a large number of men as prisoners, thus placing the Confederacy at the mercy of the foe, he decided. Had Morgan's men been available to help Jones counter Union invasion of the lower Shenandoah (during which Jones lost his own life at the battle of Piedmont on June 5), "we should probably not have to regret a defeat there and mourn the loss of one of our most gallant leaders, who fell in striving to save that invaluable region from devastation." Private Mosgrove's postwar commentary cited the surprise and capture of two Federal forces offset by "those two serious disasters" at Mt. Sterling and Cynthiana. Morgan may have paroled between twelve and fifteen hundred prisoners by Mosgrove's count, but he had lost about one thousand of his own men, thought the young veteran.[12]

In fact, Colonel William Henry Norris, an army official in Richmond, told Seddon in mid-September that Morgan had taken 800 of his own command and Giltner 1,640 on the Kentucky raid. Giltner returned with 316 men and Morgan with 292, respectively, for a total of 608. They had gleaned but 50 recruits. Little or nothing had been gained for the Confederacy. A chastened Morgan pleaded with Richmond to pardon deserters and others from his command who had been ravaging the upper heartland ever since earlier failures in his home state. But the government had tired of Morgan and his antics. By comparison, Burbridge received the personal thanks of Lincoln, Secretary of War Stanton, and departmental commander John M. Schofield for (as Stanton put it) "the brave and successful operations of the last six days in Kentucky, achievements of valor, energy, and success that will be regarded with admiration by all loyal people of the United States." In the end, Morgan's exploit combined with guerrillaism and profound manifestations of disloyalty to set the stage for increasingly oppressive Union countermeasures in the Bluegrass.[13]

Alarmed by the turmoil, President Abraham Lincoln suspended the writ of habeas corpus and proclaimed martial law in the state on July 5. Burbridge received orders to arrest all citizens giving aid and assistance to armed rebels and inciting insurrection and rebellion. The administration implied that perpetrators included even state government officers and members of the Kentucky delegation to Congress. Burbridge was to use discretion, but rebellion "must be put down with a strong hand" and traitors punished regardless of "rank or sex." Moreover, Western theater commander Major General William T. Sherman told Burbridge that he might instruct all post and district commanders that "guerrillas are not soldiers, but wild beasts, unknown to the usuages of war." So strong were Sherman's feelings that he also noted, "Your military commanders, provost marshals, and other agents, may arrest all males and females who have encouraged or harbored guerrillas and robbers, and you may cause them to be collected in Louisville; and when you have enough—say 300 or 400—I will cause them to be sent down the Mississippi, through their guerrilla gauntlet, and by a sailing ship send them to a land where they may take their negroes and make a colony, with laws and a future of their own." Officials generally were disinclined to condone Bluegrass toleration of dissent.[14]

Forrest's Memphis Raid

Meanwhile, to the south, Confederate forces in Alabama had their hands full countering Federal mounted activity in support of Sherman's advance. Kentucky brigadier Lovell H. Rousseau led a highly successful antirailroad raid south from Decatur, Alabama, in mid-July reminiscent of Brigadier General Benjamin Grierson's expedition the previous year in Mississippi. Federal activity out of Memphis kept Forrest occupied if not exactly suppressed. In this regard, the summer commenced promptly with Brigadier General Samuel Sturgis's expedition from Memphis during the first thirteen days of June. It culminated in a stunning Yankee disaster at Brice's Crossroads, Mississippi, on the tenth. Through superior tactics and grit, Forrest's inferior force soundly whipped Sturgis, inflicting casualties in excess of four thousand, counting prisoners, while taking 250 wagons and ambulances, eighteen artillery pieces, five thousand small arms, three hundred thousand rounds of small-arms ammunition, and a large quantity of artillery projectiles. Grierson noted years later that after Sturgis's return to Memphis, "he was relieved from command, and the heaviest maledictions of the loyal people and press were heaped upon him." Sturgis was an incompetent inebriate to Grierson. Still, Forrest and his men protected vital northern tier agrarian sections of Mississippi and Alabama while, in turn, potentially threatening Sherman's logistics in Middle Tennessee. They certainly disrupted Union stabilization and reconstruction efforts in the upper heartland.[15]

Sherman worried most about Forrest because of "that single line of railroad, four hundred and seventy-three miles long, supplied an army of 100,000 men and 35,000 animals." The Atlanta campaign was "an impossibility without these railroads." Well might Sherman write the War Department that he could not understand how the rebels could defeat Sturgis's eight thousand men, although "Forrest is the very devil, and I think he has got some of our troops under cower." "There never will be peace in Tennessee till Forrest is dead," he decided, and he wanted Forrest followed "to the death, if it cost 10,000 lives and breaks the Treasury." To departmental subordinate James B. McPherson, Sherman commented that a joint army-navy expedition against the port city of Mobile, Alabama, had to be placed on hold. Forrest should be pursued, "devastating the land over which he has passed or may pass, and make him and the people of Tennessee and Mississippi realize that, although a bold, daring, and successful leader, he will bring ruin and misery on any country where he may pause or tarry." If Forrest and the populace were not punished now, "the whole effect of our past conquests will be lost."[16]

With this in mind, a second strong column set out from La Grange, Tennessee, under Major General Andrew Jackson Smith from July 5 to 21, and stymied Forrest in a bloody stand-up fight at Tupelo near

Harrisburg, Mississippi. In a scene reminiscent of Forrest's problems with his superior Joseph Wheeler at the battle of Dover, Tennessee, in February 1863, Forrest now had difficulty with Stephen D. Lee's battle management. Smith's stubborn defense bloodied up to 40 percent of Confederate attackers. The Federals eventually retired back to Memphis, claiming lack of supplies while Forrest suffered a wound during the pursuit. In a sense, both Sturgis and Smith kept the "Old Bedford" (as his men affectionately termed Forrest) occupied as Sherman continued his march on Atlanta. But while striking at the rebel's support base, Smith failed to accomplish Sherman's orders to destroy Forrest. Grierson thought "never was there a better opportunity to destroy Lee and Forrest's army than at that time." Could anyone comply with Sherman's admonition to Cadwallader Washburn, "it is of vital importance that Forrest does not go to Tennessee"?[17]

Smith went after Forrest again at the beginning of August. Starting on July 28, a third expedition, mustering eighteen thousand men and outnumbering Confederates some four to one, headed south from West Tennessee toward Columbus, Mississippi, with the ultimate destination of turning and coming out at Decatur, Alabama. The progress of this month-long march was to be marked with Sherman-like destructive efficiency in the countryside. Like previous Yankee forays, however, logistical overstretch eventually brought the expedition to a standstill. Rainy weather, plus a bold countermove by Forrest eventually caught Smith short. Moreover, Forrest now had a new superior, as Johnston called Stephen D. Lee to corps command following Polk's death on Pine Mountain in Georgia. Forrest's new department chief, Dabney Maury, was a Virginian, willing to defer to his subordinate commander, who seemingly had a better idea of the local situation and could accomplish good results if left on his own. Such promise brought results when Forrest determined upon a bold countermove—capture Memphis, even briefly, and force Smith to abandon his march through northern Mississippi.

Forrest also personally wanted to capture these irritating Memphis generals, Washburn and Stephen Hurlbut (visiting the city en route to a new command downriver). Aided by a rebel element in the city, Forrest might have considered a lengthier stay in the Bluff City, a town he knew only too well as property owner and slave trader there before the war. Federal occupation had changed its tone and especially its antebellum reputation as regional commercial center resting on local cotton production and the transportation afforded by the Mississippi River and east-west Memphis and Charleston Railroad. Wartime Memphis, however, had become a wild and speculative center for contraband trading across the lines with cotton, tobacco, and other tender. Forrest may have been reluctant to impact such benefits for a starving southern civilian populace. Or his purpose may have remained simply military and psychological.[18]

Starting from the college town of Oxford, only lately evacuated by Smith's army, Forrest and perhaps fifteen hundred troopers (about half his available force) departed in pouring rain on August 18. July had already been hot, humid, and extremely wet—typical of a Delta summer—thus hampering military operations for both sides. John Chalmers and the rest remained behind, distracting Smith in the Oxford neighborhood. Crossing swollen creeks and rivers on ersatz pontoon bridges (hastily constructed from cotton gin floors and cabin sides and anchored with "cables" of wild grape and muscadine vines yanked from verdant bottoms) and an occasional surviving ferry, Forrest had to rein in his enthusiastic troopers. "They were making a regular corn shucking out of it," he recalled as he rested his column at Hernando, discerning numbers and disposition of the enemy in and around Memphis from scouts. The rain stopped about twenty-five miles from the city and the men joked about the booty they expected to take there. Their commander, meanwhile, instructed subordinates on their precise roles in the upcoming attack and issued strict orders against plundering, much to the disgust of his grumbling men.[19]

Forrest relied heavily on his two brothers for support. One, Captain William H. Forrest, would take forty scouts, surprise the pickets, and ride quickly and directly to capture Hurlbut at the famous Gayoso House (although actually spending the night elsewhere in the city). Lieutenant Colonel Jesse A. Forrest with the Sixteenth Tennessee Cavalry would move down De Soto Street to the 206 Union Street mansion to take Washburn. Brigadier General Ralph P. Buckland, Memphis district chief (occupying a Court Street residence), was another target. Meanwhile, Colonel J. J. Neely with three regiments would pin down the encamped 137th Illinois (short-term one-hundred-day men) and Lieutenant Colonel T. H. Logwood with the Twelfth and Fifteenth Tennessee Cavalry would follow Billy Forrest to the center of the city, blocking the landing of troops from Yankee transports in the river. Bedford Forrest would stay personally on the outskirts of town with Colonel Tyree H. Bell and two additional cavalry regiments and an artillery section, keeping Federals pinned in their camps while protecting the raiders' line of retreat on the Hernando road. The plan was right and the execution superb as dawn of Sunday, August 21, broke over the city. The only problem proved to be an elusive quarry and a disorganized and disoriented melee downtown.[20]

The three Federal generals (in various state of dishabille) all avoided capture. A dispersed city garrison (never properly disposed to really defend the city) put up a good fight from rallying points like Fort Pickering and provost guard headquarters. Both sides embellished what transpired, although Commander Robert Townsend of the gunboat *Essex*, posted off shore, had it right when he informed his superior Rear Admiral David Porter (commanding the Mississippi Squadron) that "the surprise was the worst and most disgraceful feature of the affair." It became something of a grandstanding operation on the Confederates' part when Billy Forrest rode his horse right into the Gayoso lobby looking for Hurlbut, and pretty much hit or miss with a lot of gunfire, milling around in the dusty streets, and descent into plundering as much as battling the men in blue. "After hurriedly riding about the streets, whooping and yelling and playing pranks when the whim seized them," said cavalryman Benjamin Grierson later, they "vanished like the wind, retreating whence they came." The defenders suffered nearly five hundred casualties (including civilians and blacks) and probably six hundred captives, including many civilians in various stages of night dress. The raiders made off with a large number of horses while sustaining perhaps 35 killed and wounded, although estimates ran as high as 50 killed, 190 wounded, and 25 to 30 captured. Townsend concluded that everyone thought the Memphis militia stood up well to the rebel hellions ("considered very problematical a few days since") while "Forrest's troops displayed dash without stamina; they were audacious, but lacking in determined and persistent effort."[21]

In the account of a Wisconsin soldier identified only as "Mell," the Memphis affair started with dinner the night before at the Gayoso, largely because Hurlbut and staff were there sightseeing aboard the *Mollie Able* ("a beautiful boat, one of the Mississippi 'floating palaces'") and walking to the park to be serenaded by the brigade band while watching "the fair young ladies of Memphis as they promenaded the walks of the park." "We didn't think, when we sat down to dinner at the Gayoso," he told his mother, "that the next morning the Rebel Genl Forrest would take breakfast here." His account of the fighting moved beyond the sensationalism of downtown grandstanding and surprise. His Fortieth Wisconsin formed up, marched against Forrest's covering contingents, and marveled that the enemy's dead and wounded "were mostly dressed in bag-cloth pants & from their *out spread* condition might be said to have laid in *sack* cloth & *ashes.*" Together with its sister Thirty-ninth and Forty-first Wisconsin Regiments, the Fortieth formed a battle line and suffered through an artillery exchange between the second section of the Second Missouri battery and rebel artillery before pursuing Forrest's departing troopers. "They being mounted we were unable again to come up with them," he recounted, suggesting all he secured from the experience was a branch or twig from a nearby bush, knocked down by a rebel shell. He hoped to see the enemy return "as we would be better prepared for them," but there was no danger of that. "They rushed into the city, took fresh horses from the livery stables, all the prisoners, citizens & soldiers they met & dashed out." He supposed that the defying battery "before which we lay was probably to cover their retreat."[22]

Forrest himself appeared atop "King Philip" at one point, brandishing his long cavalry saber and looking "more like a devil incarnate than anything those Yankees ever saw." He and the reserves scattered a desultory pursuit, and pausing to regroup, the raider sent word to Washburn asking for a truce to exchange prisoners. He wanted no such encumbering underclothed, shoeless, and hungry wretches. Washburn demurred but eventually sent food for the captives that also satiated rebel appetites. Meanwhile, Chalmers, although driven south of Oxford, had completely baffled Smith, and the pursuit went nowhere. Washburn later blamed Smith and confused matters when he declared, "I am at a loss to know where [Forrest] means to cross at Panola, or go via Holly Springs." Washburn told Sherman that "to have allowed Forrest to elude [Smith] and march on Memphis is strange; to have failed to intercept him is equally so . . . while refusing responsibility for the Confederates' easy passage in and out of Memphis." He may have been justified in declaring that a ten-mile picket line made "to concentrate at any point sufficient force to present an obstacle to a sudden cavalry dash such as the one just experienced." Buckland more responsibly noted Forrest's well-laid plan, as well as a foggy morning and acoustical shadows so that "the report of small-arms, and even artillery, was heard but a short distance." An unimpressed Sherman wired back that Washburn might send Forrest word that "I admire his dash but not his judgment." "The oftener he runs his head against Memphis the better," growled Uncle Billy, advising "the importance of converting those armories into regular citadels, with loop-holes and flanks." "See to it," he told Washburn.[23]

Rumors that Forrest would return to the city kept Memphis jittery for several days after the raid. Northern and southern newspapers spread word of Forrest's latest exploit to the embarrassment of Union authorities. Washburn used it as a pretext to clamp down on suspect mayor John Park, who was thrown into Irving Block Prison, as were several police thought to have aided and abetted the raiders. Later, in September, a grand jury indicted Forrest in absentia for "maliciously and traitorously" arraying his command with guns, swords, pistols and other warlike weapons" in the streets of the city. Chief Justice of the U.S. Supreme Court, Roger Brooke Taney, eventually told local U.S. marshal W. W. Coleman of West Tennessee "to take the body of Nathan B. Forrest if to be found in your District and him safely keep" for a March 1865 circuit court appearance. All of this was moot at the time, and Forrest and two colleagues would eventually post a ten-thousand-dollar bond in March 1866. But as of the fall of 1864, faux chivalry held sway. In a much publicized incident, Forrest returned Washburn's captured uniform and papers and the Union general, in turn, had Bedford's prewar tailor in the city make up a splendid new uniform from gray cloth for the raider (along with a special sword for the general's assistant, Major John P. Strange). Perhaps the maligned Hurlbut had the last laugh. Jibing superiors and his successor alike, the Illinoisan declared, "They superseded me with General Washburn, because I could not keep Forrest out of West Tennessee, but Washburn cannot keep him out of his bedroom."[24]

Grierson commented sourly after the war that Forrest's column should have been seriously crippled or destroyed but instead was allowed to "go scot-free, returning south the way it came, unmolested and unharmed." Smith's expedition ("gotten up with such trouble and expense") should have gone on with the invasion of the enemy's country but instead retreated. Of course, his frustration that this unfortunate course accomplished nothing "beyond keeping Forrest engaged and away from Sherman's communication," gained "by all the long and fatiguing marches endured by the troops," missed that very point. Dabney Maury's congratulatory dispatch to Forrest—"You have again saved Mississippi. Come and help Mobile"—aptly suggested the importance attached to the Memphis raid. Furthermore (and like Morgan's foray into the Bluegrass), the excursion provided a morale boost for southerners and a fillip for jaded rebel troopers. An instance of brilliant military judgment might again be posterity's conclusion, yet Atlanta was Sherman's and fairly won when Hood evacuated the Georgia city on September 1. Forrest's activities may have kept Mississippi Valley re-inforcements from reaching Sherman that summer, but apparently the Union hero hardly needed them. Furthermore, the contretemps games played between Forrest and the Memphis generals scarcely endangered the lucrative clandestine trade route with northern Mississippi. Prob-ably, Forrest's exploits best signaled belated potential for raiding behind Sherman to shape actions in Georgia as Hood stood poised to fight another day.[25]

Wheeler's Turn

The Confederate command finally responded, sending cavalry directly against Sherman's line of communications. After a singular tactical victory over Federal horsemen in early August, Hood executed a turn about, dispatching Joe Wheeler with the Army of Tennessee's mounted force (some forty-five hundred horsemen) back along the Western and Atlantic to destroy track in an eleventh-hour ploy to save Atlanta. In truth, the troopers were elated to be off on their own looking for pay back "for all the raids they have made on us" and hoping that get-

Major General Joseph Wheeler. Cour-tesy of the Clarksville–Montgomery County Museum, Clarksville, Tenn.

ting in the Yankee rear might cut off supplies "that may be the means of making them fall back from Atlanta." Hood told his cavalry leader to wreck the railroad all the way to Chat-tanooga, cross the Tennessee River, and move upon the rail lines in Middle Tennessee. He was to leave a party of twelve hundred behind for additional destruction and destabilization. A forlorn hope, it might just be worth the chance.[26]

Sherman thought the move played to his own strength. He had guarded against such a contingency with strong rail-road garrisons, stockpiling sup-plies while sending some of his own horsemen to range at will against Hood. Wheeler's Middle Tennessee raid from August 10 to September 2 proved fairly successful at first. Departing Covington, Georgia (east of Atlanta), he cut up the Western and Atlantic Railroad and captured small railroad garrisons and seventeen hundred head of cattle intended for Sherman's men. Yet Union railroad repair crews patched the damage quickly. The appearance of Major General James B. Steedman's pursuers sapped Wheeler's fragile confidence, and while he soon rested his tired troopers at Tunnel Hill just below Chattanooga, the Confederates failed to destroy that rail chokepoint on Sherman's lifeline. Wheeler then left behind two hundred men with orders to wreak havoc every night back down the railroad at some half-dozen specified points. Wheeler claimed that the stay-behinds ran off twenty trains and interrupted communication between Dalton and Atlanta "for no less than two weeks."[27]

Wheeler soon discovered that his timetable depended upon food and forage in a thoroughly picked-over country. Then the rains that plagued Forrest and the Yankees in Mississippi wrought havoc upstream on the Tennessee River. Intending to ford at Cotton Port between Chattanooga and Knoxville, Wheeler had to detour to the French Broad and Holston Rivers north of Knoxville, all of which took time and sapped strength. By this point, rear-echelon Federals were on the alert and mounting pursuit. Wheeler permitted Brigadier General John S. "Cerro Gordo" Williams, a Kentucky attorney before the war, to take two brigades and half the artillery to independently attack Union-held Strawberry Plains and the railroad bridge across the Holston River. A complete failure, Williams never caught up with the fast moving main column crossing the Cumberland Plateau to the Nashville basin. Much of Wheeler's column faded off on tangential moves and little further use to the expedition.[28]

Sherman wired Halleck on August 17 that Wheeler could not disturb Knoxville or Loudon, might hurt some minor points, "but on the whole, East Tennessee is a good place for him to break down his horses and a poor place to steal new ones." He left Wheeler to rear-echelon subordinates who, by contrast, panicked predictably. Responding to a much agitated Stephen Burbridge in Louisville that a combined Wheeler/Morgan column was descending upon him, Sherman wired on August 23, "the enemy cannot spare a large force now to invade Kentucky," "it is a raid designed to make clamor and nothing more." "Of course I cannot turn back for a cavalry raid," he pointed out. General-in-Chief Ulysses S. Grant sounded more concerned, writing from City

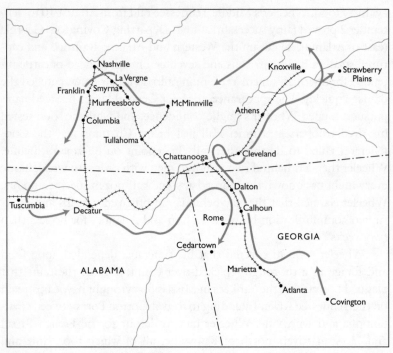

Wheeler's Tennessee raid, August 10–September 2, 1864. Map by Bill Nelson.

Point near Petersburg, Virginia, a week later, "My greatest alarm now is that Wheeler may go into Kentucky." He wondered if sufficient troops could be pulled together throughout the region to stop him. Kentucky was critical that election year summer and, in the minds of Washington, quite wobbly for the Union. Such intervention by the top general only further stirred rear-echelon hand-wringing. Pursuers such as Steedman, Kentuckian Lovell Rousseau, and loyal Tennessean Alvan Gillem eventually succeeded in herding Wheeler's shrinking contingent, although it did create "a clamor." One Chattanoogan accused the raiders of murdering and capturing many Union citizens in Hamilton, Bradley, Polk, and McMinn Counties, robbing all the stores in Athens, stealing everything they could get hold of from Union men and ripping up part of the railroad. But, he wrote on August 25, the raid "is at last a bout plaid out."[29]

Deserters from Wheeler's main column (now easily reduced by a third in strength) claimed that the expedition's goal was going after horses in the Bluegrass. Even military governor Johnson wrote Lincoln that word had Morgan planning to link up with Wheeler's column, "who is now making a raid for the purpose of again entering Kentucky & destroying the Nashville and Louisville RR." Morgan's rebels had been busily threshing and gathering all the straw in upper East Tennessee for that purpose, according to his Tennessee agents. He pointed out how Gillem's pursuers had captured Confederate congressman Joe Heiskell (as well as former congressman Albert G. Watkins) during the interruption of Morgan's plans. "Joe Heiskel [sic] walked to meet us," was the way the news passed along to Lincoln, who replied in typical fashion, asking if that meant "any more than that Joe was scared and wanted to save his skin?" Both Confederate politicians ultimately ended up in jail at Nashville and Knoxville. In any event, Wheeler's officers passed misinformation that John C. Breckinridge and others were moving from the Shenandoah into eastern Kentucky just to throw the Federals off course.[30]

Then Colonel George Dibrell and his command became another casualty, dropping off to capture the Sparta garrison in their home region and recruit while there. They succeeded in receiving such dubious additions as the infamous Champ Ferguson and his irregular band of cutthroats, with whom he apparently had worked the Cumberlands the year before. Dibrell eventually ended up, like Williams, having to double back to East Tennessee with, says Wheeler's latest biographer Edward Longacre, "neither . . . of additional use to Joe Wheeler and his rapidly shrinking force." The Federals held such overwhelming odds that it made an appreciable difference. Strength returns for the Departments of the Cumberland and the Ohio showed each at about sixteen thousand to eighteen thousand officers and men with numerous light and heavy cannon available for defense and interception. It was a really a question of positioning for interception, rapidity of response, and, quite frankly, lack of élan and fighting will among garrison troops and rear-echelon commanders. More often than not, Confederate raiders simply spooked such defenders, who were comfortable in sedentary facilities protection and at most guerrilla policing.[31]

Despite his problems, Wheeler set the pace as various parties struck at telegraph and rail on the Nashville to Chattanooga line as close as eight miles from the state capital. Subordinates claimed that Confederate honor demanded retaking the city, but Wheeler demurred. Perhaps only two thousand defenders manned the fifty-four guns protecting the city, and it was by no means clear that Tennessee district commander

Rousseau had measurably strengthened Brigadier General John F. Miller's city garrison. Still, Wheeler could not risk additional delay or a costly attack with the enemy concentrating against him. He remained risk-averse, declaring, "My troops were not given to me to make a name, but to do what I could for my country." He issued a manifesto calling upon Tennesseans to rally as had their comrades in Georgia and Alabama and let it go at that. Angling now for Franklin and the railroad leading south from Nashville to the Tennessee River and Alabama line, Wheeler ran into a determined railroad garrison just south of the Harpeth River town. Here a third Confederate general went down—the popular and able West Pointer and fellow Alabamian John H. Kelly, lost to a sharpshooter's bullet.

Rousseau and the Federals dogged Wheeler's heels from this point all the way to north Alabama. There was little time to damage rail and telegraph as the raid became rather tattered at this point. Eventually, even the pursuers became convinced that Wheeler's command had disintegrated and broke off the chase. Roddey finally advanced over the Tennessee River from the south, but with little impact. Perhaps five hundred survivors from Wheeler's column went into bivouac near Tuscumbia, Alabama, by mid-September, broken in body and spirit. Dibrell, Williams, and countless smaller bands (estimated at two thousand strong by Union colonel William B. Stokes, Fifth Tennessee Cavalry), plus any irregular partisans temporarily attracted to their ranks, scattered all across Middle and East Tennessee. In truth, the raid appreciably weakened the Confederate mounted arm. Losing over half of his men, depriving Hood of invaluable reconnaissance, and hardly disrupting Federal foraging efforts. Little wonder the diminutive "Fighting Joe" seemed dejected when Forrest met up with him. Bemoaning loss of influence with his troops and "being unable to secure the aid and co-operation of his officers," Forrest believed "it to the interest of the service that he should be relieved of command."[32]

Thoroughly disgusted with what he saw and heard, the ghosts of the Dover raid the previous year seemed to surface when Forrest groused to his latest departmental commander, Richard Taylor, that he had left Wheeler with twenty-three hundred of Forrest's old command when he had been sent to Mississippi after the dispute with Bragg the previous November. "General Wheeler has turned over to me what he has of my old brigade, numbering sixty men," he now offered in September. Taylor replied that he had confidence that Forrest would reorganize the survivors. Dibrell eventually showed up at Greenville, South Carolina, and recounted how he had followed Wheeler into Middle

Tennessee before turning back to East Tennessee with "200 to 300 more recruits, stragglers and absentees," hardly of much use for hitting Sherman's supply lines at this point. Wheeler, like Forrest and Morgan, did not prevent Atlanta's capture or occasion Sherman's recall.

A reinvigorated Wheeler eventually submitted a somewhat self-congratulatory telegram to Hood telling how the longest raid of his military career had been accomplished despite high water, detours, used-up mounts, and persistent pursuit. He claimed six hundred prisoners, one thousand horses and mules, two hundred supply wagons, and the cattle herd as trophies from his escapade—plus, supposedly, two thousand recruits and eight hundred absentees he snagged along the way. "He had been successful thus far in all engagements with the enemy, and had lost no prisoners in action," observed Brigadier General Francis A. Shoup, Hood's chief of staff. Hood, with no time for recriminations, ordered Wheeler, once rested, to get back on Sherman's communication line, which was still vital even though Atlanta had fallen in the interim. Wheeler's absence had cost Hood invaluable intelligence when Sherman sealed off the city. Sherman's rear-echelon log blockhouses together with concentrated pursuit seemingly had thwarted the raiders, a fact quick to be pointed out by historian Joe Baggett. James McDonough and James Jones concluded that more simply, Wheeler had been gone too long and forced to cover too much territory. Still, Sherman's lifeline northward lay open as Hood determined his next move.[33]

Morgan's Demise

By late August and early September, Morgan was back in the news—not with another independent raid but, rather, trying to reclaim East Tennessee in Wheeler's wake. The flamboyant Kentuckian had sought and supposedly been offered some degree of independent action following his Bluegrass fiasco. But as part of Robert E. Lee's Virginia domain, army headquarters viewed him not only as defender of the salt works in the southwest part of the Old Dominion but also as possibly a ranger partner for Jubal Early in lower Shenandoah and north of the Potomac River. On July 11, the very day that "Ole Jube" had been poised to take Washington, Morgan wrote Lee asking, "Where must I strike the enemy?" Kentucky Federals had been drawn toward defending Chattanooga, he thought; Knoxville had only a small garrison. He wondered, "Would it be best to strike at the Baltimore and Ohio Railroad, or move to the rear of Knoxville and operate upon the Nashville road?" But it took seventeen days for Lee to respond, not to Morgan his

subordinate directly but to the
Confederate secretary of war (a
scant thirty miles from Lee's
headquarters), implying that he
had told Morgan to strike the
Baltimore and Ohio Railroad
west of Cumberland, Mary-
land, and then move farther
north into western Pennsylvania. If true, when coupled with
Early still threatening Washington in the Shenandoah, this
move might have offered relief
for Lee's main army besieged at
Richmond and Petersburg. Lee
claimed Morgan's illness had
caused the army commander
to query the raider as to what
other mission he might undertake rather than directing specific action.[34]

Colonel John Hunt Morgan and his
wife, Mattie, shortly after their wedding. Courtesy University of Kentucky
Library.

The impatient Morgan
then applied directly to Rich-
mond for permission to lead five hundred men southward through
North Carolina against Sherman's supply lines. Davis and his secretary of war deferred to Lee again. The latter reiterated his need for
salt works and Shenandoah Valley protection as well as action north
of the Potomac. Time slipped by and Morgan led no independent raid
of his own anywhere. A court of inquiry met in Abingdon to inves-
tigate the Kentucky allegations and the general was suspended from
command. Limited resources, Lee's identification of priorities, mistrust
of Morgan's cooperative abilities, and the general strategic disarray of
the season dictated events. At the time, Morgan reported dutifully
about regrouping his roughly four thousand men, gathering back under military control "strolling bands, calling themselves 'independent
scouts,'" who were prowling about East Tennessee "depredating upon
private property, and under no set of rule or discipline," and beginning the collection of supplies and foodstuffs "as far down toward
Knoxville as practicable." Intrepid East Tennessee unionist William G.
Brownlow sent intelligence to military governor Johnson on August 18

that Morgan at Bull's Gap and Rogersville and John Vaughn at Kings-
port and Jonesboro had their men spread out foraging wheat and oats and
all the cattle and horses too. Brownlow felt "a little uneasy for Gillem"
(who after chasing Wheeler's survivors had remained to reassert Union
control over upper East Tennessee), what with the Confederates going
against him from both front and rear. It would be in East Tennessee
that Morgan would meet his fate.[35]

Morgan defied his suspension putting his faith in spectacular victory over the enemy to redeem his fortunes. He concentrated fifteen
hundred men and two artillery pieces at Johnson City before marching southward hoping to defeat Gillem. The Federals, however, won a
victory at Blue Springs, but both sides knew that some decisive action
would take place in the vicinity of Bull's Gap or Greeneville. An overconfident Morgan led the way through guerrilla-infested countryside and
established headquarters in the large mansion of widowed Catherine
Williams in downtown Greeneville. His troops encamped outside town
with lax security against surprise. And that is precisely what Gillem's
Federals accomplished early on Sunday morning, September 4. Accounts differ as to who betrayed the famed rebel raider, possibly widow
Williams's own daughter, some local unionist's wife, or even an ado-
lescent youth befriended by Union troops in the locale. At any event,
Gillem dispatched two columns to intercept the rebels and one of them
discovered that Morgan was in person at Greeneville. Captain C. C.
Wilcox of the Thirteenth Tennessee (Union) then made a dash in the
gray dawn's drizzle (it had rained heavily overnight, greatly discomforting Gillem's march), surrounded the Williams house, and flushed
Morgan and his staff from their comfortable billets. Private Andrew J.
Campbell of the Thirteenth Tennessee Cavalry and a former rebel conscript, now dressed in a nondescript brown jacket that could have passed
for Confederate garb, spotted a fleeing figure in the garden and shot
him when that the fugitive failed to heed his warning to stop and surrender. At the time, Campbell did not know that fugitive was Morgan.[36]

Captain Henry B. Clay (the great Kentucky statesman's grandson
and member of Morgan's staff) informed Campbell afterward that "you
have just killed the best man in the Confederacy." There were claims
later that Morgan had been shot after surrendering, in direct violation
of the rules of war, a thought eventually refuted by some witnesses from
both sides. Others claimed Morgan was away from his command, some
said even in the arms of the widow Williams. That he "was murdered
there is not the shadow of a doubt," thought Kentucky private Dallas

Mosgrove. Staff captain Edward Guerrant lamented in his diary that after a brilliant career, Morgan fell away from his command, was surprised in bed, and was chased by bloodthirsty ruffians to a vineyard—"and perhaps assassinated!" Whatever the circumstances, the six-foot Kentucky cavalier was dead at age thirty-nine, unceremoniously slung across the pommel of Campbell's mount and carted off as a trophy to Gillem. By now the Federals had all but destroyed Morgan's command itself. The remnants retired to nearby Jonesboro after losing 75 casualties and 106 prisoners. They thought their chieftain had been merely captured.[37]

Gillem too doubted his good fortune at first, until Campbell appeared with Morgan's body. Congratulations were soon passed around, but also denunciation for such unchivalric treatment of the dead foe. Campbell claimed his immediate superiors ordered it. He and Gillem eventually received promotions for their success, but those superiors did not. A Confederate hero was no more, followers lamented. Enemies heralded the end of "a Thief and Coward" (as the *Knoxville Whig* proclaimed). Relief mixed with sorrow in Richmond, for the court of inquiry could now be muted over a fallen hero. Upon learning of the event, Sherman merely grunted, "Good." Earlier, in June, he had suggested when Morgan had been in Kentucky, "I attach little importance to him or his Raid," since his army did not depend on Kentucky resources and "there are plenty of troops there to capture& destroy him. Forrest is a more dangerous man." He had also placed little stock in Gillem's homegrown Yankees, considering them a "refugee hospital for indolent Tennesseans," worthwhile only as a political element. But Gillem and "Andrew Johnson's bodyguards" finished Morgan's threat to Kentucky in East Tennessee.[38]

Morgan's death hardly brought peace to the upper counties, however. Gillem and Morgan's successor, John Vaughn, continued the fight with homegrown units and extreme bitterness on both sides. Gillem was eventually handled roughly in another round of scuffles. Forrest's actions ultimately proved of more interest to commanders like Sherman and Hood. In fact, by the time of Morgan's death, Forrest and his men would be back in the saddle and off on yet another raid, this time in response to long overdue recognition that the Union line of communication back through Tennessee might still be vulnerable. Forrest's forays (first into northern Alabama and Middle Tennessee in September and October then immediately followed by a similar feat into West Tennessee and culminating with his famous Johnsonville exploit in October and November) would prove the Confederacy's high point for this period. Viewed generally by posterity as coming too late to have any meaningful impact on Sherman's activities around Atlanta, they nevertheless stirred the South's spirits at a moment when military reversals and then Lincoln's reelection predicated doom for the experiment in rebellion. Moreover, Forrest accomplished precisely what he personally had said earlier—that he could wreak havoc and force Sherman's attention to his rear. Forrest's latest success may well have forced Sherman's decision to cut loose from an exposed line of communication and strike out to make interior Georgia howl all the way to the sea.[39]

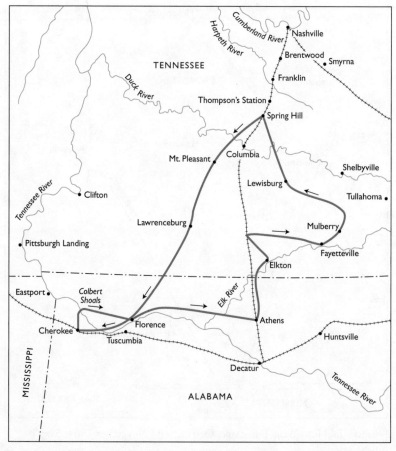

Forrest's raid into central Tennessee, September and October 1864. Map by Bill Nelson.

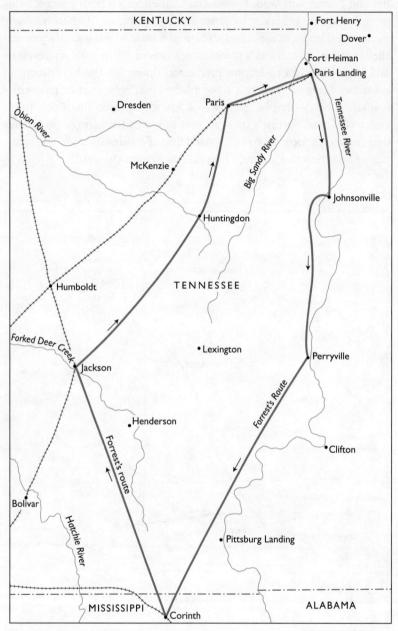

Forrest's raid into West Tennessee, October and November 1864. Map by Bill Nelson.

Forrest Rewrites the Script

Circumstances defined Forrest's actions. Anxious to attend to personal affairs and recover his health yet sensitive to an anguished plea for help from Mobile commander Dabney Maury, Forrest went out of channels to independently write Jefferson Davis on September 5. He asked permission to move on Sherman's supply lines in Middle and West Tennessee. Davis concurred the next day. While Hood and Sherman locked in correspondence about the disposition of Atlanta's citizens after the city's fall and the Georgia governor began making noises about removing his state and its troops out of the war entirely, Forrest might do something to actually affect more positive result. Later in the month, Davis would go to Georgia to try to bolster spirits and develop plans with Hood. For the moment, let Forrest loose, the president wired Taylor, his brother-in-law and now Forrest's new departmental commander.

So Taylor pulled Forrest off a train bound for Mobile at Meridian, Mississippi, and convinced him to take the offensive assignment immediately. At first, Forrest, in Taylor's own words "suggested many difficulties, and asked many questions" and Taylor "began to think he had no stomach for the work." The cavalryman simply wanted to be clear on how he was to cross the Tennessee River and return if pressed by the Federals and how he was to be supplied and deal with prisoners. A sudden fire returned to the raider's eyes when apparently he was satisfied by a railway superintendent that he would be amply supported at least to the Tennessee line. He strode out vowing to march at dawn and "hoped to give an account of himself in Tennessee." Taylor's return wire to Davis was just as melodramatic: "Five minutes after my arrival at Meridian," he claimed, "I issued the orders contemplated . . . [and] the movement is now in process of execution."[40]

Such a promise did not quickly translate to action, however. Forrest needed two weeks to plan and assemble his expedition in northern Mississippi and move it to the jump-off point of Cherokee Station, Alabama, the eastern terminus of a very war-ravaged Memphis and Charleston Railroad. It took most of that time to get the superintendents of that road and an equally battered Mobile and Ohio line working with impressed slave labor and soldiers to make transit possible. Burned out bridges, grass growing on neglected rights-of-way, rails and roadbed in poor shape—the delay at least permitted Forrest to fashion a lean expeditionary force, including dismounted cavalry as infantry in anticipation of capturing mounts from the Yankees. Forrest eventually left bivouac on the morning of September 16, 1864. His 3,542 men carried four days cooked rations and one hundred rounds of ammunition per man. Moving in part via rickety rail as well as nearby roads, the force stopped briefly at Tupelo to hear their commander promise to force the enemy back out of Georgia within sixty days. The Memphis Federals did nothing to hamper them. In fact, Private Milton Hubbard of the Confederate Seventh Tennessee Cavalry observed that "as there was no necessity for rushing, we moved leisurely to Cherokee."[41]

What Forrest learned at Cherokee Station gave him pause. The discussions with Wheeler suggested gathering opposition in Middle Tennessee. Dismay about only sixty survivors from Forrest's original command was offset only partially by addition of the Twentieth Tennessee Cavalry (recruited behind Yankee lines after Chickamauga by officers of the old Forty-eighth Tennessee Infantry) and Colonel James T. Wheeler's First Tennessee Cavalry, which now joined to round up stragglers left behind by that kinsman's recent debacle. P. D. Roddey's nine hundred reinforcements (relieved of summer duty guarding recruit camps) swelled the ranks to nearly five thousand men, give or take. But time seemed of the essence, and stragglers from the ranks who visited local homefolks bothered Forrest as the column resumed its march on September 21. Still, they got across the Tennessee River at Colbert Shoals and to the outskirts of Florence, all within a day of starting. Forrest himself received a hero's welcome wherever he appeared. Mounted on King Philip, he swept into Florence with his escort, delighting streets lined with men, women, and children, "whose shouts were ably supplemented by the yells of the visiting soldiers." Young Milton Hubbard thought such triumph "would mark an event in a life otherwise filled with adventures."[42]

Forrest now struck for Federal targets on the railroad north to the Tennessee line. Indeed, the campaign became one of cherry-picking small Union garrisons guarding bridge crossings, stables, and towns from Athens, Alabama, to Pulaski, Tennessee. The story became the same from September 24 to 27: traditional bluff and awe tactics, easily induced Yankee surrenders at Athens and Sulphur Branch trestle, but no repeat of any Fort Pillow atrocities when the Confederates took U.S. Colored Troops captive. Sherman's supply line may have held up well against local insurgents and random raiders with its stout blockhouses and forts, but not so when attacked by Forrest's formidable band with artillery and an adept commander. Federal property went up in smoke, rails were twisted and rendered useless, and animals and prisoners were swept up in the process. Forrest wired Taylor that he had "entirely destroyed the railroad from Decatur to Pulaski, and five large railroad bridges, which will require sixty days to replace." Angry officers of the surrendered Athens garrison later complained officially to Federal headquarters that Colonel William Campbell's capitulation "was uncalled for by the circumstances, was against our wishes, and ought not to have been made."[43]

Pulaski proved more difficult to capture. Federal reaction had been swift once news of Forrest's advance stirred the chain of command. Sherman and his subordinates directed a concentration of rear-echelon troops in Middle Tennessee and central Kentucky against the threat. Several divisions from Sherman's main army also went back as Generals George H. Thomas, John Schofield, and Lovell Rousseau took over coordinated response. "The policy should be, small but well-commanded bodies in the block-houses, and a movable force to act straight against Forrest, who must scatter for forage," Sherman dictated. Heavy fighting at Pulaski cost Forrest some one hundred casualties and further used up artillery ammunition leading him to wire Taylor on the twenty-seventh that he was transferring attention instead to the line of the Nashville and Chattanooga Railroad at Tullahoma. Reaching Fayetteville the next day, Forrest dispatched two separate parties to wreck the rail and telegraph facilities north and south of Tullahoma. But from this point on, the Federals began to correct the imbalance. By the time the Confederates reached tiny Mulberry, scouts informed Forrest of strong enemy concentration from both Chattanooga and Nashville directions. Perhaps thirty thousand Federals now moved on the raiders.[44]

With Thomas in overall charge of the operation, Rousseau led the endeavor for pressing "Forrest to the death." Thomas doubted that there would ever be a better chance of doing so and Rousseau wired Sherman on September 28 that "Forrest is here to stay unless driven back and routed by a superior cavalry force." This was no mere raid, he contended. "I regard it as a formidable invasion, the object of which is to destroy our lines," which he would surely do "unless met by a large cavalry force and killed, captured, or routed." Frankly, observed the Kentucky Federal, "Forrest's movements are much more cautious than formerly, as he "will not give battle unless he chooses to do so." Apparently, Forrest was choosing to do so, and Sherman typically wired Washington two days later that he took for granted the raid would cut his rail connections but that concentration of force would "prevent his making a serious lodgment." Forrest's cavalry "will travel one hundred miles in less time than ours will ten," Sherman lamented. "I can whip his infantry but his cavalry is to be feared." In a separate telegram to President Lincoln, he observed, "It would have a bad effect if I were to be forced to send back any material part of my army to guard roads so as to weaken me to an extent that I could not act offensively if the occasion calls for it."[45]

Sherman certainly sounded more fatalistic now than when Forrest had rampaged through West Tennessee. Rear echelons in Middle Tennessee seemed unsure of themselves too and at one point had Forrest with eight thousand riders headed for Nashville. The rebel chieftain put out word that he intended "to stay in Middle Tennessee till Sherman comes from Atlanta to drive him away." Brisk recruiting enhanced Forrest's ranks, at least in north Alabama. Yet the farther he stretched, the more he extended his own communication line, the more artillery and small-arms ammunition he expended battering Yankee fortifications, and the more encumbered he became with prisoners and booty (necessarily detailing manpower to escort them south). Sherman and his lieutenants worried about tunnels, bridges, and the track of the Nashville-Chattanooga line; Forrest worried about escape. He soon abandoned any new work and concentrated close to Columbia while preparing to retire back to Alabama and operate against the Memphis and Charleston toward Decatur, where, he said later, "there was a prospect of accomplishing some good." By October 2, Forrest had determined that Columbia and the rest of the railroad to Nashville lay beyond his reach. He turned south, scooping up stray pockets of Federal resistance while deceiving Rousseau as to his intentions.[46]

Regaining the Tennessee River in the vicinity of Florence while Buford and part of the command harassed Huntsville to the east, Forrest confronted high water and even Union gunboats. One naval flotilla convoying another converging column from Johnsonville, Tennessee, under Colonel George B. Hoge ran into Forrest's old preacher-subordinate Colonel D. C. Kelly at Eastport, Mississippi. Well-placed cannon fire disabled the stern-wheel gunboats *Key West* (207-ton paddlewheeler mounting six 24-pounder howitzers, two 24-pounder smoothbores, and a 12-pounder rifle) and *Undine* (179-ton stern-wheeler mounting eight 24-pounder howitzers), blew up artillery caissons aboard the transports *City of Pekin* and *Aurora,* and completely unhinged Hoge's plans. This "battle of Eastport" forced Hoge and his men back downriver to Johnsonville. Forrest escaped and others undertook the tally of another Forrest success. To Sherman, at least, whatever the body count and material statistics, "it will be a physical impossibility to protect the roads now that Hood, Forrest, and Wheeler, and the whole batch of devils are turned loose without home or habitation."[47]

Forrest's official report sounded impressive—some 3,360 of the enemy killed, wounded, or captured at a cost of only 340 losses of his own. Eight hundred horses, eight artillery pieces, two thousand small arms, several hundred saddles, fifty wagons and ambulances, plus large quantities of medical, commissary, and quartermaster's stores constituted the booty. "During the trip my troops supplied themselves with boots, shoes, hats, blankets, overcoats, oil-cloths, and almost everything necessary for their comfort," he observed. The greatest damage to the Federals came from the "complete destruction of the railroad from Decatur to Spring Hill," excepting the great Duck River bridge. Forrest declared, "It will require months to repair the injury done to the road, and may possibly be the means of forcing the evacuation of Pulaski and Columbia, and thus relieve the people from further oppression." Federal reports showed a different perspective.

Admitting to large-scale damage to railroad and rolling stock on the Nashville–north Alabama part of Sherman's logistical lifeline, Brigadier General Daniel C. McCallum, the government's general director of railroads, felt that it would only take a week to fully restore "communication between Chattanooga and Atlanta." A year later, the U.S. Military Railroad chief in the West claimed that between them Wheeler and Forrest really had destroyed only twenty-nine and a half miles of track, and that was rapidly restored. In his view, the effort against Sherman's rear met with only marginal success. The ability of Federal logisticians to stockpile materiel at forward depots plus Sherman's coordination of the rear-echelon containment of Forrest had temporarily staved off disaster. Loss of blockhouses themselves and their garrisons, and the destruction of railroad and government property, was bad enough. An early Forrest biographer John A. Wyeth contended, "Sherman had at least begun to despair of keeping intact his communications from Atlanta to Nashville." Forrest certainly had achieved more than Wheeler, suggests historian Joe Baggett, largely because of boldness, cohesiveness of his command, John B. Morton's superior artillery, and some poor judgment on the part of Union railroad garrisons who chose to surrender rather than fight. Still, Forrest too had been ultimately rebuffed by "troops arriving from multiple locations in Tennessee, Kentucky, and Georgia," whether or not, as Baggett claims, they reflected multiethnic and foreign origins that Forrest's veterans could claim for their misfortune.[48]

The Johnsonville Caper

Frankly, the direction of the war was changing anyway by mid-autumn. Both sides turned to employing their armies, not just the cavalry, as raiding tools. Making Georgia howl was about to be equaled by the Confederate's main army in the West playing hell in Tennessee again. The principal instrument of Confederate success thus far in 1864 had been Forrest and his cavalry. Johnston and then Hood had bitterly contested the road to Atlanta but had failed to secure the city. Forrest, Wheeler, Morgan, and numerous lesser bands of rebel horsemen had taken the war to the enemy's logistics, though with not half the anticipated success. Still, they had tired Sherman and his lieutenants with incessant diversions. Their harassment of the rear had disrupted Yankee concentrations of resources such as Ben Grierson had "recruited, reorganized and brought to a high state of efficiency" at Memphis. The latter "have become a treasure for every major general near to snatch at and appropriate for operations at distant points," he growled later. Countering Sterling Price west of the Mississippi, Hood, and the trio operating on Sherman's rear, Grierson felt his force had been "piecemeal cut and carved up and taken from me, and left subject to the whims of military cormorants who were insatiable and perfectly indifferent to the claims of others."[49]

Forrest pointedly asked for leave on October 8, citing concern for "a large estate in Mississippi" but hinting at the need for rest and recruiting too. He also wished to reconcentrate dispersed riders and reconstitute his artillery. Nevertheless, he acquiesced about a new request from headquarters to "make the trip to West Tennessee." The request stemmed from Davis's impromptu visit to Georgia to buttress civilian spirits and subsequent decision at Hood's headquarters on September 28 that the main army itself should move on Sherman's rear in the Volunteer State. The Confederate high command now envisioned a two-pronged operation by Hood and Forrest to draw Sherman's attention to a threatened Middle and West Tennessee. With Memphis Federals continuing to show only lackadaisical signs of emerging from their lethargy (Grierson noting the dearth of resources to even do so), Washburn sent several regiments on a joint operation to retake Eastport, Mississippi, on the Tennessee River in early October. On the tenth, the gunboats, transports, and Federals were ambushed by Colonel David Kelly's artillerists in one of those rebel turkey shoots that panicked Yankees, embarrassed their commanders, and accomplished nothing. So, the time seemed right for another Forrest dash west of the Tennessee River in the Purchase area. He accordingly received orders on the ninth to do so. securing as many supplies (receipted and paid for in Confederate script) and recruits (in coordination with Brigadier General Gideon Pillow's policing deserters and reserves) as possible from West Tennessee, Forrest was also to "hold the country for a considerable time" (for

View of Paducah, Kentucky, at the confluence of the Ohio and Tennessee rivers and the northern terminus of the Mobile and Ohio Railroad. From *Frank Leslie's Illustrated History of the Civil War.*

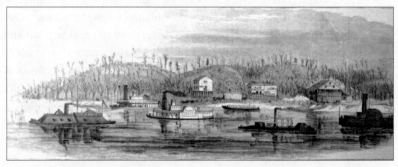

Union gunboats passing supply base at Eastport, Mississippi. From *Harper's Pictorial History of the Great Rebellion.*

which purpose the Mobile and Ohio Railroad might be reconstructed to Jackson with reserves collected to defend it) as well as perhaps cut all railroad communications north of Nashville.[50]

Forrest sent his reply to Taylor three days later, reflecting how out of touch headquarters was with the actual situation in West Tennessee. Absence of slave labor meant Mississippi workers would have to be imported for the railroad support work. Moreover, "the country has been destroyed and "the amount of supplies in that region has been greatly exaggerated," he stressed. His command could be subsisted and more than enough wheat and hogs could be procured beyond civilian needs, but the inhabitants would not accept Confederate paper and would gladly disperse their surplus "to prevent their falling into our hands." The only solution had to be provision of a trading commodity like salt. Then loyal southerners might come forth, interesting themselves "in hunting up and furnishing the Government with every article of supply that they could possibly spare." Apparently patriotism had given way to realism in West Tennessee. To Forrest, his military mission could accomplish more by destroying the large Federal supply base at Johnsonville and the Nashville and Northwestern Railroad link to Nashville on the eastern side of the Tennessee River. Thus "it is my present design to take possession of Fort Heiman, on the west bank of the Tennessee River below Johnsonville, and thus prevent all communication with Johnsonville by transports." Forrest wanted to complete destruction of Sherman's logistics, not merely food gathering, although in planning his operation, he suggested, "I may be able to procure supplies from Kentucky."[51]

Forrest was blunt on several matters. "The great predominating, absorbing desire is to cut Sherman's line of communications," he assured Taylor. He alluded to having just done "something toward accomplishing this result during my recent expedition" and being "anxious to renew the effort at some future day." The desirability of repairing rail and bridging from a sort of a Cherokee-Tuscumbia-Florence "sanctuary" for a return to Middle Tennessee (since his former pursuers had now all "returned to their former positions, and thus afford an opportunity for another expedition") seemed offset by straggling and diversions to help the main army. Citing Roddey's men in particular as dispersed all over the place, with passes or not but wishing no "spirit of unkindness toward that gallant and meritorious officer," Forrest saw such a breakdown in discipline as illustrating a disreputable state of affairs and "humiliating to my feelings," a "burlesque upon military discipline." Between this breakdown in discipline (and there were many freebooters, partisans and wide-ranging foragers generally frequenting this part of the dwindling Confederacy) and the plight of the populace along the Mississippi-Alabama-Tennessee border, regional conditions appeared unstable.[52]

The lack of necessities could be seen everywhere, as in Hood's ranks Stephen D. Lee's corps had to provide "sandals made for the barefooted men of their commands out of green beef-hides" for the offensive. Taylor and Forrest corresponded quite freely about the breakdown in the civilian economy. Citizens resorted to widespread cotton trading with the enemy for survival. "For a distance of twenty miles north and south of the Memphis and Charleston Railroad, from Corinth to Memphis, the people have lost everything they possessed in the way of subsistence, both by the enemy and our own raiding parties," observed Forrest from Corinth on October 18. They were "daily making applications to me for permission to carry cotton above to exchange for meat and the actual necessities of life." Neither Taylor nor Forrest had a satisfactory answer other than to clamp down on issuing passes for such activities, burn or confiscate the cotton and legally try the perpetrators of such "illegal and demoralizing traffic."

Confederate authorities generally could do little for citizenry caught between Union occupation and Confederate raids. Forrest and his expedition confirmed civilian conditions when they reached Jackson, Tennessee. The cavalryman reiterated civilian need for salt, and Taylor confirmed a promise to provide the commodity to the community. But Forrest remained focused on his mission as he told Taylor on October 21 how rehabilitation of rail and telegraph in West Tennessee seemed impossible due to lack of materials. The inhabitants had used the wires for baling cotton and the poles had rotted. Worse than that, Forrest had to release men to go home and procure new horses, thus reducing his overall numbers. At this point, the fast changing strategic picture entered a new phase. Richmond, perhaps equivocal about Hood's performance and abilities, had elevated P. G. T. Beauregard to command of a "Military District of the West." Hood and Taylor would report to him. The Army of Tennessee was moving westward across north Alabama looking for a right hook northward and liberation of the upper heartland. The campaigning season was late, weather was unpredictable and the army would stress an already wobbly logistics system. Moreover, Davis's public morale boosting had alerted Federal authorities to the military move. Forrest was supposed to have completed his mission in West Tennessee by October 26 and reported to Hood for orders—hardly the best arrangement given the distance between raider and main army. Yet Forrest finished his initial mission within the week.[53]

Beauregard wired Confederate adjutant general Samuel Cooper on November 3: "General Forrest reported on 31st ultimo from Paris, Tenn., that he had captured, during two preceding days, on Tennessee River, 2 gunboats and 4 transports, one-half of which are still serviceable." Five days later he added to the news that Forrest had engaged the enemy at Johnsonville, destroying four gunboats of eight guns each, fourteen steamers, and twenty barges in addition to an estimated 75,000 to 120,000 tons of quartermaster and commissary stores at the landing and in warehouses. Even then statistics deceptively explained Forrest's startling success. Forrest's subsequently expanded report of January 12, 1865, sounded considerably more relaxed. By that time, however, his words would have seemed rather pyrrhic to a Confederate cause confronting the overall impact of intervening events in Middle Tennessee between November and the new year. No matter, the Johnsonville raid would echo Forrest's name for the ages.[54]

Much of the Johnsonville success could be attributed to intrepid subordinates like Buford and Chalmers and the adept employment of captured Yankee cannon by acting chief of artillery Captain John Morton, as well as the element of surprise. Then, too, another participant, Colonel Hylan B. Lyon (lately elevated to command of an anachronistically titled "Department of Western Kentucky," headquartered at Paris, Tennessee) attached himself with several hundred reinforcements, just back from a lightning swing through the neighborhood of Clarksville, Tennessee, Eddyville, Princeton, and Elkton, Kentucky. They, like partisans John Chenoweth of Kentucky and Alexander Duval McNairy of Tennessee, disrupted Federal control of the area. Chenoweth battled U.S. Colored Troops recruiters near Fort Donelson while McNairy ripped up portions of the Nashville and Northwestern Railroad near Johnsonville and Lyon recruited Kentuckians while fending off pursuers from various local Union garrisons. Eddyville was Lyon's home, and he captured the local Federal contingent of Kentucky mounted infantry and U.S. Colored heavy artillerists until the gunboat *Brilliant* arrived to take Mrs. Lyon hostage. Lyon then hastily paroled the captives but carried off the black troops. Lyon's joining Forrest added another twist to the story.[55]

Lyon himself was a West Pointer and old army veteran with knowledge not only of his home neighborhood but also of how to site artillery batteries. He supposedly helped Forrest and Chalmers in this regard. But it may have been another local character, known best to the Kentuckian, who also aided the effort. This was the eccentric "Old Jack" or "Captain Jack" Hinson, who supposedly "piloted the way for our guns through Cypress creek swamp to the river bank in front of Johnsonville," noted Forrest's adjutant Major Charles W. Anderson. Known well to Lyon, this somewhat legendary folk hero from the land between the Tennessee and Cumberland Rivers was a Stewart County native and possessed encyclopedic knowledge of all the

Colonel Hylan B. Lyon. Library of Congress.

pathways and terrain in the area. Moreover, at the time of Johnsonville, he was engaged in a personal vendetta against the invaders and occupiers of his native land. A Yankee patrol two years before had executed two of Hinson's sons as "bushwhackers," gruesomely affixing their severed heads to the family's farm gateposts. Hinson swore revenge, secured a special hard-hitting hunting rifle, and began terrorizing army patrols and steamboat passage on the rivers. His gun soon bore thirty-six notches for his prey as Hinson's "clear gray eyes, compressed lips and massive jaws" indicated an avenger not to be trifled with. Forrest and Hinson instantly related to one another—warriors who made their own rules of war in this backwoods guerrilla conflict.[56]

The Johnsonville result disrupted river traffic, captured and destroyed steamboats, and embarrassed the Union navy. Forrest's men operated from positions at old Confederate Fort Heiman (mostly abandoned since the capture of Fort Henry but occasionally used as a Federal campsite for policing the region) and upstream at Paris Landing. All of this preceded the commotion and chaos subsequently caused at an unsuspecting Johnsonville depot across and farther upriver. If the few days on the Tennessee were a turkey shoot for the rebels, the catastrophe visited upon the Federals led by Colonel C. R. Thompson and Lieutenant Colonel Edward M. King told of steamboat captains and gunboat crews deserting their posts under fire, abject ineptness in counterbattery fire from Johnsonville earthworks, and rampant looting of quartermaster supplies by ill-disciplined defenders. A naval board of inquiry later cleared Acting Master John L. Bryan of the *Undine*'s abandonment, capture, and reuse by Forrest's "horse marines." Yet the ill-fated stern wheeler (scarcely a year old and only recently rehabilitated after its near sinking by a snag in the Tennessee), found its 24-pounder howitzers outgunned by the Confederates field artillerists. Unable to protect arriving transports, the Confederates took it, placed it under the command of Frank P. Gracey (one of Forrest's lieutenants, himself a former steamboat captain), and may have considered using it as a ferry boat to transfer the cavalry across the river and even threaten Nashville or to carry supplies back to Hood's army, now thought to be upriver at Tuscumbia, Alabama.

Such goals evaporated with arrival of Union naval reinforcements that, more than anything else, salved damaged egos when the *Undine* like the depot eventually went up in smoke. Still, Forrest's force held the position on the river for several days while flattening the Johnsonville depot across the river with long distance artillery fire and tallying a fine count of destroyed river craft, capture of twenty-six pieces of artillery as well as $6.7 million worth of property. These facts aside, the sensationalism of Forrest's caper possibly exceeded its long-term impact. True, once again, panicky Federals had the devil and an inflated number of Confederates rampaging in disguise, even as far away as Chicago. In actuality, Forrest's greatest accomplishment may well have been as he reported later, "Brigadier General Buford, after supplying his own command, turned over to my chief quartermaster about 9,000 pairs of shoes and 1,000 blankets." That would count more with the ill-clothed and poorly shod Army of Tennessee than all the fireworks at Johnsonville, should the materiel actually reach Hood's ranks.[57]

A disgusted Sherman wrote Grant famously on November 6, "That devil Forrest was down about Johnsonville, making havoc among the gunboats and transports." He ordered Thomas to send Major General John Schofield and the XXIII Corps to counter the raid. J. Andrew Merlin of the Forty-fifth Ohio with that column reported not only the muddiest place he had ever seen upon reaching the destroyed Johnsonville depot but how they had rounded up "about 250 of the employees who had run off and were making for Nashville and had fastened on a lot of blankets, boots, tents, greatcoats, etc.," arrested the sulkers, and thought the colonel commanding the depot "ought to be cashiered and dishonorably dismissed the service." Forrest notwithstanding, and his continued wariness of what Hood and Beauregard intended in north Alabama, Sherman firmly advocated marching through Georgia to the sea. "If I turn back the whole effect of my campaign will be lost," he had wired Grant four days before on November 2d. Schofield's troops and a fleet of gunboats seemed likely "to repair that trouble [at Johnsonville]." He correctly reaffirmed that the line of the Tennessee "was only opened for Summers use, when the Cumberland could not be depended upon." "We now have abundant supplies at Atlanta, Chattanooga and Nashville with the Louisville and Nashville R. Road, and the Cumberland river unmolested," so that Jefferson Davis's threat "to get his Army on my rear or on my communications [is] a miserable failure." After the war, Sherman would begrudgingly admit that Forrest's feat of arms "excited my admiration."[58]

For the moment, in the autumn of 1864, Forrest's self-satisfied command rode south over rain-soaked, almost impassable roads seeking desperately to cross the rising Tennessee waters at Perryville, Tennessee, to knife in among Thomas's hosts gathering in anticipation of Hood's avowed advance. The Union navy's dragnet of all small craft and the flood waters stymied such intentions. So Forrest's men and overworked ox and mule trains plowed slowly through the mud of West Tennessee before finding Hood at Florence, Alabama, by midmonth. Back at Johnsonville, humiliated local Federal commanders put out the fires and reclaimed what they could from the smoldering embers. Events would cause Schofield little pause at the depot and the Federals soon evacuated surviving troops to Nashville for concentration against Hood's gathering storm. Surviving facilities remained for partisans and local inhabitants before the Union Tennessee troops eventually returned to guard the railroad and bridges until the close of the war.[59]

That Forrest's command could so stealthily mount a major expedition and surprise Federal garrisons was a tribute not only to his military acumen but also to the fact that West Tennessee had not been subdued. Given the general lethargy of Memphis commanders, the absence of Federal field intelligence gathering seems unremarkable. Yet, overall, the summer had ended less than auspiciously for a shrinking Confederacy. The bright hopes and promises, even successes and high morale, were gone. The campaign for Atlanta was over, Lee's embattled army losing ground in Virginia with even Early about to be set upon by yet another hero from the West, Philip H. Sheridan. Supplanting Johnston with Hood had ultimately lost Atlanta, and Confederate leaders seemed perplexed as to the next step. Lincoln's reelection now appeared assured as a determined Union effort to push the war to victory seemed immutable. Wizards of the saddle like J. E. B. Stuart in Virginia and Morgan in the West had fallen to enemy bullets along with upper heartland partisan rangers such as Colonel Thomas Woodward killed and comrade Adam R. Johnson blinded and put out of action (some said by friendly fire). So many promising leaders from Albert Sidney Johnston and Thomas Jonathan Jackson to Leonidus Polk had joined the pantheon of Confederate dead, thus affecting surviving operational command and leadership structure. Wheeler stood discredited despite a valiant if disjointed effort and only Hood and his lieutenants together with Forrest remained to carry forward whatever counter-offensive might be mustered in the early fall. Indeed, Forrest's flinty purpose seemed more appropriate now than the often jaunty style of Morgan and Stuart, anyway. Earlier cavalier code had been supplanted by the forays of guerrillas and bushwhackers as well as Forrest's rough-hewn raids.

Little wonder, then, that Federals like trooper Edward Summers of the Sixth Kentucky Cavalry might write his cousin Arthur Johnson in Bracken County on September 22 how Morgan's death, the capture of his staff, and the slaughter of his men, as well as "the total rout and distruction of Wheelers Entire Cavalry force," constituted "the deth blow to the Southern Confederacy throughout the land all that yet remain to be accomplished on our part is to take Richmond Virginia, and the Last Root and Branch of the Southern Confederacy is for ever ded and dambd." But he admitted that Kentucky troops would most certainly vote for George B. McClellan and the Democrats later that fall "if allowed a vote," for they "are getting tired of a protracted war and will support a pease Candidate." At least, he declared, "John Morgan will never bother Kentucky any more."[60]

In all of this, vying for the hearts and minds of southerners seemed to take second place to slaughter on the battlefield and destruction of the southern way of life. Harsh prosecution of civil war and downright disintegration into terrorism and lawlessness emerged from Appalachia to the Mississippi bottoms. Southern leadership concentrated on militarily driving Sherman from Georgia or as Georgia senator Benjamin Hill had told the secretary of war in early July, "when Sherman is driven from Georgia we will recover Tennessee and Kentucky; Grant's army will leave Virginia; Lincoln's power will be broken, his reelection defeated by a straight out peace candidate, and we shall speedily end the war on our own terms." All then, he said, "is lost by Sherman's success and all is gained by Sherman's defeat." Presidential military adviser Braxton Bragg confirmed the prevailing view of focusing on the battlefield. He declared at the end of September that operations in Middle Tennessee "by a force unable to seize and hold the country will not benefit us and will seriously distress our people." Raids were injurious to the troops and unprofitable in results in his eyes. However, using the Selma and Rome rails as a base, "our cavalry could render the use of the Chattanooga railroad very dangerous, if not impracticable," he touted. Sherman had six months' supplies close at hand and "our true field of operations is south of Tennessee." That thought was about to change.[61]

CHAPTER 6

---∞∞∞---

Tennessee's Instabilities

Military governor Andrew Johnson's agenda was generally political and reconstructionist by 1864. His March rebuff in county and district elections hardly deterred him from proclaiming on April 4 that he would appoint suitable persons until regular elections could be held the following January. He then returned to the speech circuit on behalf of holding conventions and other organizing bodies to return unionism to center stage. He pressed emancipation and wrote Lincoln the next day about a Shelbyville meeting where public support exceeded his expectations. Thus he advocated not only a state convention to decide the issue in Tennessee but also congressional action on a constitutional amendment. He further told the president that treason arrests by U.S. marshals seemed to be exerting a powerful influence and hastening restoration more than anything else. On May 19, he exhorted a crowd at the opening of the Nashville and Northwestern Railroad to Johnsonville to "go to the ballot-box and put down this infernal and damnable system of slavery, and restore your State." But, he added ominously, "unless you people show a desire to put down these guerrillas and restore the law no generals can save you from ruin." Do your part and the soldiery would protect and sustain you, he urged.[1]

Shifting Political Tides

The Shelbyville meeting went well, for the area was strongly unionist, or so it was thought. Local commander Major General Lovell Rousseau, a native Kentuckian and a conservative on emancipation, ostensibly made a "fine speech taking high ground on the negro question," which Johnson fancied would set well in Kentucky and Tennessee. The military governor urged Lincoln to take a short leave of absence from presidential duties to speak more widely as "it would do much good in putting down Copperheads and traitors." The governor also wanted an immediate Tennessee convention ending slavery once and for all. But he soon faced opposition in East Tennessee, where the idea of reconvening an 1861 unionist convention at Knoxville produced much rancor and uncertainty as long as James Longstreet's Confederates, guerrillas and rebel vigilantes roamed the area. The point of greatest danger, noted William G. Brownlow, "is the driving of our *Union voters* out of the Country." Thousands were already streaming north of the Ohio and would never get back. The rebels wanted them gone so they might vote unionism down. Another East Tennessean queried in mid-June, "How are the men and regiments that was raised for the express purpose to protect the upper Counties of East Tennessee" being used when they seem to be "guarding the rebels property of Middle Tennessee" while their families "are now exposed to the Rebels, and suffering from their tyrannical [*sic*] rule, being robed [*sic*] & murdered daily by them"? Johnson's sparing a few regiments would stiffen unionist resolve, yet the section continued unready for any state convention.[2]

Resistance continued to be a problem all over the state. Johnson received troubling news of "unprincipled, disloyal and even dishonest" men running Memphis's municipal government, as well as of the impact of Forrest's recent arrest and abduction of prominent unionist citizens in West Tennessee. "I may be mistaken," wrote one exiled Volunteer from Greencastle, Indiana, in mid-May, "that unless a *Rigid System of retaliation be adopted and enforced*," it was idle to talk of protecting or encouraging Union men in his home state as all other means seemed to have failed. Even Johnson drifted when writing Lincoln that the chief executive's December amnesty offer "will be seriously detrimental in organizing the state government" and the army seemed to have gotten as much benefit "that can result from it." Better to let all pardons granted to Tennesseans come from direct application to the president, for as now operated "its main tendency is to keep alive the rebel spirit in fact reconciling none." By June, Johnson had been tapped for the national Lincoln reelection ticket and his speeches breathed unionism and loyalty, death to aristocratic oligarchy and slavery, and gratitude for northern appreciation of what this son of the South might symbolize. He often repeated his much-quoted phrase of yore, "Treason must be made odious and traitors must be punished and impoverished." Further, "their great plantations must be seized and divided into small farms, and sold to honest, industrious men," proclaimed this Union commoner.[3]

Closer to home and the war itself, western commander William Tecumseh Sherman told Johnson to relinquish management of the completed Nashville and Northwestern Railroad to military operation while leaving protection of the line to Rousseau. The goal of circumventing bottlenecks on the Cumberland River and the Louisville and Nashville Railroad had been accomplished, and the new route "will soon be needed to full extent of its capacity" for the continuing Atlanta campaign. Thus the military governor might turn his attention to complaints that units of his own homegrown Governor's Guard, like the Thirteenth Tennessee Cavalry, were replicating Fielding Hurst's West Tennessee thuggery by intimidating and scandalizing citizenry. Wilson countians complained about guerrillas while also deploring the depredations of blue-uniformed Tennesseans raiding homes and stealing horses. Vagrant slaves raised other issues and a certain twilight zone had been reached by mid-1864 for owner and slave, white and black, government officials, humanitarians, soldiery, and partisans proclaiming Confederate allegiance while practicing pure banditry. Economic conditions as much as political sentiments played a hand in this disarray and defied the abilities of men like Johnson to mitigate the consequences.[4]

Truthfully, what to do about slavery plagued everyone, from lowest yeoman farmer to the military governor and army officials. In the words of the editors of *Freedom,* free labor "developed in uneasy coexistence with slavery" in Middle and East Tennessee and northern Alabama. Lincoln's emancipation proclamation applied to neither Tennessee nor Kentucky. Alienation of unionist and presumably redeemable Confederate slave owners always appeared foremost in occupation authority minds. Certainly the general tenor in the Volunteer State could be found in the words of abolitionist and colored troop's recruiter Major George L. Stearns to the American Freedmen's Inquiry Commission at Nashville on November 23, 1863. "Slavery is dead; that is the first thing" and "that is what we all begin with here, who know the state of affairs." Certainly, encouragement of latent unionism conflicted with Tennessee's situation, built upon a slave system. Yet, Stearns was impressed by "the manner in which these people [slaveholders] are cowed" by Federal power even as they entertained a "lingering hope that by some hocus-pocus things will get back to the old state." The greatest problem seemed to be determining equitable wage exchange between owner and slave in the new world of free labor when even the government—demanding and hiring slave labor—had hardly established appropriate commensurate pay. Stearns cited Brigadier General St. Clair Morton's Fort Negley project that had conscripted blacks and worked at least 800 of some 2,768 to their graves without salary over the previous fifteen months. Admittedly, Morton's signature result meant "because, by the building of that fort, at that time, the safety of Nashville was secured, and we were enabled to hold Nashville, instead of making a stand at Fort Donelson."[5]

When asked "about what proportion of Tennessee do we now hold," Stearns admitted that "practically, it is less than half the state," suggesting realistically, "that is, you are safe inside our picket lines, and are not safe anywhere else." The United States government held dominion, but no commissioner could venture forth safely. "The guerrillas are everywhere," so to him, it was best to let slaves work out arrangements for wages with farmers and plantation owners without government involvement. Stearns wanted to recruit black soldiers, not black labor (in direct contrast to Johnson, who thought slaves should provide merely cheap labor, not fighters). But everywhere authorities sought guidance. Brigadier General G. M. Dodge at Pulaski wrote to the army's adjutant general, asking about contract wages and settlement on abandoned land and stating that "negroes will go where they can get paid for their labor—and Government will protect them in doing it." Slave-owning Yankee general Rousseau ranted against fellow brigadier Eleazer Paine's high-handed hiring-out procedures, suggesting a strong sociocultural internal conflict even in Union ranks, particularly among fellow Kentuckians. As Rousseau saw it, "the Negro population is giving as much trouble to the Military as well as to the people." Vagabond blacks, many armed, strolled uncontrolled over the countryside, hundreds supported by the government but neither working nor able to do so, said Rousseau, who concluded that "the military cannot look after these things through the country and there are no civil authorities to do it." Gradually, the private sector made its own course. Abandoned lands in Rutherford County near Murfreesboro witnessed squatters and speculators taking over, arranging wage-scale labor from slaves and exploiting Johnson's authority to seize and use lands. By autumn, slave owners sought some "settled plan" from the government for systemized use of black labor.[6]

Johnson wanted to instill self-reliance, not public dependence, for freed people. He objected to massing them together and thought "they should be scattered as much as possible among the whites" because the influence of the latter upon them would be more beneficial. In his mind, the influences around the blacks "when congregated together [were] not calculated to elevate or improve them." By autumn, the military governor would raise the status of all black Tennesseans to that of pre-war free Negroes. By the first of the year, a state convention would approve a constitutional amendment ending slavery that Tennessee voters would ratify in February 1865. Meanwhile, contraband camps developed, offering fertile labor pools for hiring out or military recruiting. Such camps—at Nashville, Gallatin, Hendersonville, Clarksville, and Pulaski in Tennessee; at Huntsville, Alabama; and at Camp Nelson, Kentucky—were essentially replicated to some extent wherever Union troops were in garrison, including, for instance, Fort Donelson. At war's end, the superintendent of freemen for the Department of the Cumberland would observe to the Freedmen's Bureau Commission that seven formal "Contraband camps" of about 5,500 refugees "carried on without system, without shelter for the people, and apparently, without any definite plan as to their future condition," being "entirely dependent upon the U.S. for support." These camps no doubt stood as a national government reaction to wartime dislocation and need. Such symbols left unresolved what formal Federal responsibilities accompanied wartime transformation from the suppression of rebellion to humanitarian intervention. No easy answers attended that question hovering above both Governor Johnson and the military in 1864.[7]

Fate and national politics largely refocused Johnson's actions that summer and fall. He left cavalry raids and partisans largely to military solution. Despite loyalist citizen urging, he did not interfere with Memphis military commander Cadwallader Washburn's establishment of a civil commission as a military court for civil cases. He received supplications from refugees and families of those serving in Tennessee's Union volunteer units with the armies as well as his own Governor's Guard. Yet he seemed to have no way to soothingly answer those wavering unionists, like Whig politician and Rogersville lawyer John Netherland, who wrote him on July 8, "They say, that the Union men of the South were told, that this war was not waged for the purpose of interfering with the institution of slavery in the south, that *now*, that pledge is violated," and that "we were told when the Union Army came here, that they came as friends, that contrary to that pledge, our fields have been desolated, our horses, and grain all taken from us, our families insulted and impoverished, and that a few rebel guerrillas are allowed to occupy our whole country from Strawberry plains up to the Virginia line" while Johnson sat comfortably behind Nashville's fortifications.[8]

Three hundred and six East Tennesseans signed a petition to Brigadier General Samuel P. Carter, provost martial in East Tennessee, calling attention to their plight. With no help available to gather the impending grain harvest and little corn planted anyway, they asked, "What will the people of that section do, should they receive no aid from the Federal Government, and the rebels are permitted to reap and take what grain is now growing?" What would become of the mothers, wives, sisters, and children of the absent soldiery and refugees? To whom should they look for protection given their loyalty and suffering of persecution for the past three years? Invoking much religious spirit, the petitioners asked for Carter's intercession to secure a force to drive off "the few guerrillas that are now holding" the upper counties of the region. Carter sent the missive to higher headquarters, but Sherman dismissed the loyalists as nothing but a political element and washed his hands of them "except for pay and rations." Johnson had no recourse but to send his own Governor's Guard.[9]

Except, perhaps, for those serving at the front, even loyal Tennesseans training in the Governor's Guard contingent and Johnson's mobilized volunteer units showed signs of stress and strain. R. L. Houston with the Second Tennessee (Union) Infantry at Camp Gillem near Nashville wrote his father in May how he wished he could be home helping with spring chores on the Maryville farm. He could not understand how authorities could furlough men from the Third Regiment and not his own. Earlier in March, he recounted how unionist Tennesseans who had been campaigning in Mississippi had set upon some distant relative living near Aberdeen in that state as "if it was *awlright* for them to take his corn or anything they needed," since the rebels had "*striped* you and I don't care of the Yankees takes everything he has got." It would never do for East Tennesseans to guard East Tennessee, he commented, "for it would please them too well" for retribution; better to have "two Shillings Mishigens" guard the section and "*steel* everything they want for us Tennesseans to guard it." In fact, Houston told his father, he was perfectly willing to let the Michigan Federals "do the fighting after my time is out." Such had become the rather enigmatic attitude that raised doubts about Tennessean resiliency for hard and prolonged fighting."[10]

In the words of *Johnson Papers* editor Leroy P. Graf, "Upper East Tennessee was still under Confederate domination." Guerrilla raids "in which citizens were shot, houses robbed, and everything plundered 'indiscriminately'" affected all directions, from Knoxville, Morristown, Maynardsville, Seviersville, and Athens. Loyalists had departed for the army or some distant refuge, leaving neighborhoods to renegade control. So, the military governor did take steps to liberate that remaining corner of his state from Confederate army control. He sent his own expeditionary force to supplement Union units, and he placed native son Brigadier General Alvan Gillem in charge. Moreover, he responded to increased proposals for organizing Home Guard militia throughout the state for counter-insurgency duty. Enrollment of a city militia had already been going on in Memphis since 1863. Still, here Johnson and Sherman differed as to handling dissident and hostile civilians within Union lines. Create a docile populace and exile recalcitrants north out of the war zone seemed to be Sherman's approach. Johnson advocated the opposite: send them south, pressed back along with the rebel armies. Let rebel authorities "hear their cries of suffering & supply their stomachs & backs with food & raiment," he advanced. At present, "we relieve the Confederate Gov't" and only "add to the rebel or copperhead sentiment & increase opposition to the Government" by shipping them north. Those from East Tennessee should have been sent south, he told Major General George H. Thomas, commanding both the Department and the Army of the Cumberland. "They would rather go anywhere else than south & it would create more terror than sending them north." Sherman changed his tune once Atlanta had fallen. But all summer he opposed sending disloyalists through his lines under a flag of truce.[11]

Farmer Nimrod Porter near Columbia observed that in his neighborhood Union soldiery roamed through, impressing slaves for work details on fortifications in Georgia, and he had contacted army authorities about hiring out his laborers. He caught one Yankee official liberally and illegally cutting timber on his property. Identification of just who was a "guerrilla" and who was a bona fide Union soldier bothered him. Then the various raids by Wheeler, Forrest, and Philip Roddey further confused matters as occupation leaders like Brigadier General Robert H. Milroy mistreated citizens by "taking everything they could get and more than they needed." By September, said Porter, locals expressed displeasure with "Johnson's enrollment and the onset of the draft." Ardent secessionist and novelist Lucy Virginia French in McMinnville at the foot of the Cumberlands, felt the times "so uncertain" that her husband prevailed upon her to move back from Beersheba Springs. They had never psychologically recovered from a winter-time "sacking" of that lovely spa community by rural mountain people egged on by bushwhackers. Bettie Ridley Blackmore lost her rented house near Murfreesboro in the summer because she ostensibly had harbored guerrillas.[12]

"All's Quiet in G. today," Alice Williamson penned in her Gallatin diary on August 15. Union nemesis Eleazar A. Paine had been transferred to wreak havoc in Paducah, Kentucky, with subsequent stationing of both African American and white federal troops in Williamson's area. For the next few months, she diligently noted arrests and executions of ostensible partisans, impressments of citizens' horses and the onset of conscription whereby "the Yankees are drafting everyone between the age of seventeen and fifty" with citizens "running in every direction trying to get to the Southern army." She wondered what the deserters would do now. Then authorities panicked when Wheeler's raiders skirted the area and news that the hated Paine had been dismissed from the army due to malfeasance and misuse of authority followed. Alice wondered why that demon could be sent to Paducah so easily but had been kept so long at Gallatin, where "he did a thousand times worse than there," although in Kentucky, she observed, he stayed "56 days and shot 67 men." She concluded that "the noble hearted patriots who suffered here will never be cared for save by those at home whom their wrongs have made desolate." Speaking of the destitute, newly organized relief societies in Nashville and East Tennessee addressed their plight, although little would be done for black refugees and the animosity toward whites fleeing East Tennessee remained palpable, whether elsewhere in the state or throughout the Ohio Valley.[13]

Disarray Indicators

Everywhere the ugly scars of war bespoke hideous battles, roaming bands of outlaws, efforts of marching armies to live off the land, and the inability of the populace to stop the struggle that most of them had so enthusiastically embraced two years earlier. There was even something of a mixing of clearly defined fighting front, no-man's land between combatant armies and homeland hearth troubled by guerrillas, political irresolution, and economic and sociocultural blight. Clarksville lawyer Joseph B. Killebrew suggested in his autobiography that "the greatest safety in those times was found in remaining at home." Here then lay the upper South in the throes of the fourth year of war, the setting for backyard feuds legitimized by that war, a playground for mobile raiders also living off the land and populated by innocent (or not) civilian victims. Lurking in the shadows were the deserter and criminal flotsam of no particular address, loyalty, or sense of mercy or honor. Fertile croplands stood fallow and fenceless, with little sign of activity. Even centers of habitation rotted in idle abandonment or teemed with squatters devoted to the business of exploiting war in some fashion.[14]

Van R. Willard of the Third Wisconsin recounted arriving in Fayetteville, Tennessee, thirty miles west of Tullahoma in mid-February. He and his mates found what was once "a fine, little city of about two thousand inhabitants," with mostly red brick houses, several stores, a printing office, an academy and other public structures. It was now "deserted by all save rats and mice—not more than half of the people were at home—probably had gone visiting among their friends way down south in Dixie." Centerpiece to "one of the most rabid Rebel counties in the state," the rough and hilly Lincoln County "had been one of the favorite haunts for bushwhackers." A tax of thirty thousand dollars had been levied on the county for the murder of three Union soldiers, and "it was thought best to establish a military post at Fayetteville to facilitate the collecting of the tax and the breaking up of those bushwhacking bands," Willard observed. The collection of the tax was to take place, refugees were to be protected, and the destitute families of men in both armies were to be supplied with food, and for that purpose, contributions were levied on the wealthy secessionists in the neighborhood he recounted. Soon in comfortable quarters with preparations made for building a fort in the public square, Willard further commented that "it was thought advisable to have a few mounted men scout about the country and hunt bushwhackers."[15]

Such scenes could be found all over the Volunteer and Bluegrass states. Incorporating wars within a war, the region overall continued a breakdown of comity and stability. The infamous Champ Ferguson and Tinker Dave Beatty replicated peacetime feuding and provided the tip of a legionary iceberg of desperadoes using the war as a mask for uncivilized behavior. Patrolling the country, protecting wagon trains, or chasing guerrillas became a shadow war beyond official reports and glorious battle remembrance. Fights between army and partisans often claimed innocents, like a Mr. Sexton of Stewart County, Tennessee, cut down while simply fleeing his home when a recruiting party of the Fourth U.S. Heavy Artillery (Colored) had a spat with irregulars in early October. "My men supposing him to be one of the rebels, as he attempted to escape," shot him down claimed Thomas R. Weaver, a Yankee lieutenant colonel. Perhaps a partisan, perhaps not, Sexton met his fate in what historians have styled "war at every door," the "contested borderland," or simply "the uncivil war." Lieber's code or law of war did not govern what Van Willard termed skirmishing "with the bushwhacker gentry."[16]

Federal rear-area security forces (left for logistics protection as well as pacification) confronted such conditions from garrison towns and "strategic hamlets," sporadically penetrating what historian Stephen Ash postulates as a vast no-man's land beyond the pale of both rebel and Yankee authority. Commanders faced difficult choices of not only helping sustain armies but also caring for destitute civilians, often of questionable loyalty, and the ubiquitous refugee. Giles County citizens (of flexible loy-

Sketch of a guerrilla fighter (or deserter). Library of Congress.

alty) received assessments from $100 to $250 each "for the support of Union refugees coming within the lines of" the XV Corps at Pulaski on January 26, 1864. Indeed, over the two-year period since invading the South, Union authorities had developed skills at confronting problems from governance and local economy, law and order absent civilian justice, and provision of basic health and human services never before experienced in such intensity. Nevertheless, they never quite overcame the tyranny of violence and disruption of life chronicled in soldier letters like those of a New Yorker self-styling himself "Blue Jacket." Writing from little-known Jasper, Tennessee, near Chattanooga, the author recounted the basic tragedies visited upon innocents caught up in violence not always of their own choosing. Guerrillas visited one house, killing two white men and a black man, then ravaging and beating two women in the neighborhood. The whites had only recently been discharged from the First Alabama Cavalry (Union), and "their having been in the United States service is probably what prompted these fiends to do the foul deed." The black man, he observed, was murdered "simply for being a negro."[17]

Economic stakes demanded attention from military authorities, possibly more so than the politics that had brought on the war. Subsist the loyal and take from the disloyal became the dictum, although the military might do little about whether a particular farmer thought conditions stable enough to produce for market or even survival. A new local market of military customers offered some hope. More often it became a question of banned or quarantined goods—the illicit trade about which President Abraham Lincoln's special investigator, Major General Dan Sickles, wrote impassionedly to the president in May 1864. He railed against the restored free trade in the war-torn Mississippi Valley because "immense supplies go to the enemy and help to sustain a hostile population." Thus the prevailing dilemma was whether to enforce the laws and regulations or cut a slice of profit from condoning such trade. Regulations were clear, evasion was likewise. Most questionable were cotton shipments into places like Memphis and Nashville, although they in turn permitted commerce in commodities as diverse as whiskey, tobacco, medicines, and cloth. Historian Gerald Capers opined that the significant role of Memphis in the war was its position "as the depot for most of the contraband trade between North and South." But for Sherman's prohibition on the use of the railroads through Kentucky and Tennessee in order to sustain his Atlanta campaign, Nashville and Chattanooga might also have laid similar claims. Yet Memphis stood out as Michigan senator Zachariah Chandler contended that from twenty to thirty million dollars worth of supplies reached the Confederacy through that city alone.[18]

Memphis: Bluff City Uniqueness

If occupied cities and towns from Chattanooga to Clarksville and from Knoxville to Nashville served as military control and logistical centers, surely Memphis provided a most unique function during the war. The antebellum river town, like upstream St. Louis and Louisville, was there because of commercialism—a wedding of river and rail, the juncture of the interior with exterior markets. The war had changed not the fact, only the master of such fate. The military rather than private enterprise dictated wartime activity. Memphis, sometimes styled the

"Charleston of the West" before the war, had been accustomed to free trade up and down the Mississippi. At first both Union and Confederate governments had recognized the attraction of continuing such commerce. Once the nonreconciliation line was crossed in the summer of 1861, however, both sides imposed restrictions. The Confederates banned exportation of cotton, naval stores, sugar, molasses, syrup, tobacco, and rice except through southern ports; the Union stopped trade with the Confederacy except under individual permits issued by the secretary of the treasury. Denial of needed supplies to both sides became an economic strategy of each. Port and trading cities like Memphis suffered accordingly.[19]

Memphians had equivocated about secession at first. As historian Joseph Parks noted, "Loyal Memphians in 1860 believed that the welfare of their city depended on the preservation of the Union, whereas in 1861, they had become convinced that secession and union with the Confederacy were now necessary for the welfare of Memphis." Cotton barons and the cotton boll swayed the citizenry here, unlike in the interior Tennessee River counties of Weakley, Carroll, Henderson, Decatur, and Hardin, which remained pockets of unionism. By the following spring, however, Confederate trade restrictions had strangled business while Union naval interdiction had closed the lower Mississippi to distant European markets (as well as those in the north). When Confederate general Pierre Gustav Toutant Beauregard ordered the burning of stored cotton and splitting open barrels of molasses to deny them to the advancing enemy after Shiloh, Memphians particularly questioned their decision. As lawyer John Hallum petulantly estimated, a postwar value of some $129 million was sacrificed to such military panic. The Union naval victory in the battle of Memphis on June 6, 1862, sealed the city's fate, although some locals anticipated restoration of trade if not prosperity.[20]

Memphians paid the price when the Federals took over the city. The civil administration of Mayor John Park continued under military occupation. Yet Grant, Sherman, and their successors drove rebel sympathizers from houses and occupations, exiling them south to Confederate territory. Those secessionists who remained in the city by the time of Forrest's visit in August 1864 might have welcomed redemption for something more than a short stay. Still, by this time, the whole complexion of society, politics and economics had changed the character of the Bluff City. Import limits were lifted on September 11, subject to a 5 percent tax, and free trade reappeared with the countryside. Memphis, which had served Confederate needs for commerce and production of war materiel, ceased to be that kind of supplier to the conquerors. Instead, it became a forward depot for joint operations in the lower Mississippi Valley. Then, after the fall of Vicksburg and Port Hudson, noted Parks, a "flood of goods immediately began to pour into Memphis," while "just as promptly large quantities poured out of the city into the waiting arms of Confederates and guerrillas." Cotton became the medium of exchange for such transactions.[21]

Viewpoints regarding wartime Memphis lay with the beholder. Virulent rebels such as one Confederate captain's wife living in the city had declared at the end of 1863, "there is a perfect reign of terror" in the city. Principal stores were closed, their contents confiscated, and all trade was conducted through strict occupation controls of a Board of Trade under oath that "the articles mentioned are for family use and not to be taken out of the United States." Swarms of detectives ensured compliance with payoffs for catching the unwary as well as to the provost marshal to get off, "that being the way matters are conducted in Memphis!" Still, "Memphis is a lovely city," proclaimed Sergeant Major Stephen F. Flaherty of the 102nd Illinois as his unit steamed up the Mississippi on April 26 and 27 en route to join Sherman's Atlanta operation. One might pass many pleasant hours viewing beautifully ornamented grounds in which "are embowered the elegant dwellings of her wealthy citizens," he decided. Nowhere else had he seen more tastefully or more richly ornamented grounds, and the city park, known as Court Square, was a lovely "little spot near the levee" reserved from the business district for those "who could not well spare the time necessary to rusticate in the fields and groves beyond the limits of the city."[22]

Flaherty was especially taken with the figure of Andrew Jackson, surrounded by an iron railing in the park and bearing the inscription "The Federal Union: it must be preserved." Tragically, some secessionist had endeavored to obliterate the inscription by defacing it with a bayonet. Still, the Illinoisan refused to think ill of Memphis citizens "who can throw aside the cares of business and devote their energies to beautifying their homes and their city by the introduction of the choicest ornamental trees" and playful, innocent little city pets like squirrels and domesticated wild geese. Memphis "bears few marks of the desolating war that has ravaged the South," declared Flaherty, gazing upon crowded landing, busy levee, and the hurrying, jostling crowd with only the ubiquitous blue uniform, flitting here, there, and everywhere indicating the proximity of war. "Noble business blocks; lovely little cottages; elegant private residences, and the hovels of the poor," blended in a scene that had in it "more beauty than deformity; that is more suggestive of happiness than wretchedness."[23]

Two years of Federal rule reflected changing demographics: eleven thousand original whites and five thousand slaves, but also nineteen thousand newcomers (an influx of vagabond speculators, charlatans, gamblers, and lewd women together with authorized military and Treasury Department officials). The *New York World* styled them a "crowd of sharks, cormorants, sharpers, gamblers, speculators, anxious relatives seeking for sick soldiers," in short, the "most mixed, assorted, and grotesque lot of mortals crowded together imaginable." The newspaper might have added loyalist refugees from the interior to the list. Abandoned rebel houses became abodes for vagrants. The celebrated "Irving Block" prison became housing for every type of civil and political prisoner, regardless of age, race. or sex. Extraction of loyalty oaths (as elsewhere) became mandatory to normal life. Smuggling, spying, and passive resistance by unrepentant original citizens jostled for accommodation with customary business and less savory professions. Change even attended the city newspapers, the traditional *Appeal* having departed with Confederate forces and been replaced by the puppet organs *Bulletin* and *Argus* (the latter becoming "the voice of the occupying army until the end of the war").[24]

As with other occupied Tennessee cities and towns, Memphis also experienced two years of danger to public health. The presence of soldiers, refugees and contraband, vice, and animal waste and offal, claims historian James B. Jones Jr. "made the Bluff City even worse than the conditions of the two capitals: Washington, D.C. and Richmond, Virginia." With a city government unwilling or unable or civilians simply lethargic or unwilling to change habits voluntarily, the Union military had to step in with enjoinders, requirements, and regulation. Responses included street cleaning, vaccination against disease, medical inspections, and appointment of health officers and commissioners. For all their apathy about chasing Nathan Bedford Forrest, commanders such as Brigadier General James C. Veatch and Major General Stephen Hurlburt appeared more proactive concerning urban health. Apparently improvement was somewhat marginal, for Memphis Health Commissioner W. Underwood reported an alarming 463 deaths alone in July 1864 from any variety of causes traceable to poor sanitation and environment. Still, draining cellars, removing offensive flatboats in the river, cleaning and fencing vacant lots, and stopping the disposal of filth at one bridge counted among Underwood's achievements. All of these actions he took absent a modern understanding of germ theory or of how mosquitoes could transmit yellow fever (epidemics of which would devastate the city after the war). Thus, Jones suggests, Underwood's wartime attack on breeding grounds for disease "did all the right things for all the wrong reasons, and his work in Memphis improved sanitation and public health." In this case, Union military occupation was a step in the right direction.[25]

Like other Tennessee cities and towns, Memphis became a tent city for convalescents as Sherman's planning had 24,500 backup hospital beds in Chattanooga, Nashville, and Memphis, just in case. Moreover, the Bluff City's prostitution problem equaled that of Nashville until both came under a system of legal and licensed control. Formerly grand hotels like the Gayoso and Overton (second homes to cotton barons) now served the transient occupation community. Genteel Memphis ladies such as Elizabeth Meriwether, Belle Edmondson, Hannah Henning, Mrs. L.C. Pickett, Felicia Lee Carey Thornton Shover, Ginnie Moon, and Loreta Janeta Velazquez, to name but a few, continued to defy both occupation and the new social climate as the city's Confederate women struggled to keep families and hearth together. They opened their unconfiscated homes to boarders, kept the lamp of education alive while visiting Confederate wounded and prisoners, and continued fundraising efforts for orphans and orphanages.[26]

One phenomenon could be calculated for future problems. The government's concentration of black refugees in camps Fiske and Shiloh near Fort Pickering, Camp Dixie on President's Island west of the fort, and Chelsea in north Memphis inflamed the whites who remained in the city. Part of the Union army's freedmen program, these camps reflected a fundamental population shift. Prior to occupation, city slaves and free blacks "lived in little patches within a perimeter of whites." Black historian Bobby L. Lovett has noted that the camps, seen as a control device by antebellum whites, now "violated this antebellum demographic pattern" and offered "a measure of freedom and cover from watchful white eyes." Inevitably there would be future conflict, he opined, especially when, during the last years of the war, census figures showed a tripling of blacks in the city—by August 1865 reflecting 16,509 African Americans out of 27,703 residents. For the moment in 1864, Union occupation, black regiments garrisoning Fort Pickering, and white counterparts encamped around the city ensured an uneasy lid on the race issue.[27]

Memphis occupation authorities practiced restraint in dealing with the indigenous population, although confiscation of churches (the previous focal point for a system of aid in the Confederate period) and the influx of northern caregivers and reformers of the missionary and freedmen's stripe must have galled the city's first ladies. No longer able to contribute to the Confederate war effort, they carefully avoided friction with the hated occupiers while continuing previous benevolent and charitable aid societies on their own. Occupation of William Richardson Hunt's mansion by the Western Sanitary Commission for a "soldiers' home"—"while he is faithfully serving the Confederacy his commodious dwelling and ornamental grounds are found to be very serviceable as a pleasant home for his enemies," noted one transient Federal—probably irritated them. They offered passive resistance and engaged in clandestine pursuits, all the while suffering the difficulties that one Ohio soldier had discerned very soon after the fall of the city. Writing to his wife, George Cadman noted, "God forbid, my dear, that you should ever live in a country subject to military rule. However kindly the rules are carried out there must of necessity be great hardship." The novel introduction of not only northern volunteers but also locally recruited loyal Tennesseans and eventually freed blacks in blue uniforms to picket the city and garrison protective Fort Pickering provided a stern reminder.[28]

Young David F. McGowan of Company I, Forty-seventh Illinois provided a snapshot of Memphis on Independence Day, 1864. The heat was intense and the day passed with little excitement, he wrote sister Ellen. "There were several salutes fired from the Fort and different Batteries." There were two or three excursion parties and a few private parties "all through exertions of the *soldiers* and *Foreigners*." He thought "the Citizens would much sooner celebrate the day that Fort Sumter was fired on" and noted that the "City of Memphis is a very pretty place, but there is very little of an interesting nature going on" since "most of the Citizens (although they have taken the oath) are very strong secessionists." There "are some fine-looking Ladies in town, though of course I am not acquainted with any of them," he added. Indeed, like sisters and brothers all across the occupied South, old-line Memphians provided a hidden fuse of defiance, sedition, noncooperation, and even espionage awaiting liberation. To be sure, Memphis accommodationists existed too in the name of survival and profit.[29]

Collaboration attends every war and occupation. But during the Federal occupation, Sherman's August 1862 remark to Grant—"What use in carrying on war when our own people are supplying arms and sinews of war?"—undoubtedly prevailed. Sherman referred to the lively contraband trade that only worsened as time went on. Occupation authorities might waver between strict and lenient treatment of the populace and dissatisfaction with Mayor Park's administration as the general state of health and infrastructure of the city declined. A controversial June 1864 mayoral election led a new prefect, Major General Cadwallader Washburn, to suspend parallel governance entirely. But by this point commercial conditions from corrupted trade and profit in a reemerging cotton market enshrouded Memphis and its wartime residents. No wonder political generals like Stephen Hurlbut huddled close to headquarters and profitable enterprise rather than undertake hunting down Forrest and guerrillas.[30]

Detrimental or at least questionable conditions surrounding the contraband and cotton trade periodically assumed center stage. When a convalescing Dan Sickles reported back to Lincoln in May about "goods to the amount of half a million a week went through our lines, sold for currency or exchanged for cotton," he alluded to the Memphis problem. A congressional committee on the conduct of the war estimated $20 to $30 million worth of trade passed through the city en route to Confederacy. Supply boats had almost unrestricted opportunities for such trade on the Mississippi and its navigable tributaries, declared Sickles, "stopping anywhere along the river and dealing with anybody." Both loyal citizenry and occupation officials told him that Memphis "has heretofore been so reliable and constant a source of rebel supplies as to secure for it a comparative exemption from attack by the enemy." Assistant Secretary of War Charles A. Dana called the purveyors of such trade "harpies who follow in the track of the army, and barter the cause for which it is fighting with more the baseness of Judas Iscariot, but without his remorse." When cotton prices rose over one dollar a pound by the end of June, Vermont senator Jacob Collamer wondered why the government did not withdraw its army and simply enlist "a force of Yankee pedlars" who could "go down there and trade them out."[31]

Memphis and wartime, as well as public allegiance, also bothered Confederate authorities. One southern intelligence operative informed his headquarters handlers in mid-March how "immediately upon the withdrawal of the forces of General Forrest from the line of the Tallahatchie a general movement of cotton took place toward Memphis, and not less than 2,000 bales were carried in [to the city]." The excuse for such trafficking with the enemy, he noted, "was the necessity for procuring food and clothing for family use and for relatives in the Confederate army, and in some instances it was true, but in very many cases it was for the purposes of speculation and extortion," and to carry into the city "such information as would be of use to the Yankees in their future raids." He commented that Federals authorities encouraged such activity to obtain cotton, as well as oaths of allegiance from the citizenry, "thus giving foundation to the reports of a returning Union sentiment throughout the country, and by this means encouragement to the Federal administration." Nobody could buy or sell produce or supplies without taking the oath, a "practice [that] is dangerous in its effects and pernicious in its influence," regardless of binding effects, for "it creates them in law, if not in fact, alien enemies, and the operative, H. Winslow by name, had found "that those who associate much with Yankees adopt very many of their opinions." So much so that "some very influential and wealthy citizens" of the river city had returned and taken the oath to secure their property and collect their rents: "Those, too, who were loudest in their professions of attachment to the South, telling of their sacrifices for her welfare and the sons given to sustain her in her hour of trial, but no word has been said of their increased wealth by speculation and extortion." He also vented about how "persons from the South going through the country proclaiming the Southern Confederacy as played out" represented a military despotism and how Confederate soldiers would not fight without being paid in Union greenbacks.[32]

On the other hand, the plight of business in occupied Memphis created conditions ripe for exploitation. Memphis attorney John Hallum (discharged from Confederate service for medical reasons and an oath taker in exchange for five hundred dollars cash) served as something of an intermediary between unethical Union officials and equally immoral speculators and smugglers. There was always some Moses to lead an entrepreneur out of his wilderness of business problems, as Hallum claimed to do "more for the Southern people in an almost incredible short space of time than any thousand soldiers of the rank and file the South ever put in the field." Officials "offered themselves for sale" and he procured them on behalf of the Confederacy, as he spent his time consulting with merchants and blockade runners from an office on the south side of Court Square. Old-line merchants needed help and bridled at oath taking and other restrictions. New businessmen came to town to make money which involved "winking at trade regulations, trading with smugglers, or become smugglers themselves"—in short, forgetting any avowed loyalty to the Union. Bribes to Hurlbut's officials could always secure release from Irving Block prison or evasion of regulations. Hurlbut personally could duck the taint of corruption, although "presumption points with index finger." Jeffrey Lash, his biographer, colorfully observes how Hurlbut, a marginally competent field commander, adeptly hid a "clear pattern of misconduct" at Memphis "under a façade of strict and efficient administration." That Illinois politician-general's fate was sealed when he failed to actively do anything about Forrest. Nonetheless, everyone from Forrest to Hurlbut and below seemed willing to tolerate Yankee-held Memphis as a conduit for the law of supply and demand.[33]

Hurlbut's succession highlighted Memphis as a sinkhole of vice and avarice requiring attention. Washburn concurred that "Memphis has been of more value to the Southern Confederacy since it fell into Federal hands than Nassau." Exchanging cotton at Memphis for money or supplies that could be conveyed to Confederate lines or the hinterland had strengthened the enemy, nullified the naval blockade of southern ports, and weakened and demoralized the Union army. It had become a beacon for spies in the guise of innocent cotton suppliers, he advanced. Washburn, like Sherman before him, wanted total prohibition of commercial intercourse with the rebellious states. And so, on May 10, he decided to close his lines to transit and trade, to take effect in five days. Nobody could enter the city except by special river permit. River trade would be confined to landing at only those points garrisoned by Federal troops between Cairo, Illinois, and White River, Tennessee. Naval patrols by the ram *Monarch* would monitor trade, interdict illegal commerce, and arrest all conscription age males as prisoners of war. "This of course shut out the cotton grower and brought the cotton business to a complete halt," noted historian Joseph Parks.[34]

Sickles thought that while Washburn's tougher policy might alleviate "the evil in his district," he wanted universally "all trade with all persons beyond our lines [to] be interdicted and that commanding officers of squadrons and military districts be held responsible for the enforcement of the prohibition." It might be argued, the New Yorker admitted, that loyal people outside Union lines would suffer, but "those within our lines suffer in the vital injury done to our cause by a concession which benefits a hundred rebels where it relieves one Union man." Not only did the example of "a vast trade carried on with our enemies "sap the energy and enthusiasm of our men in uniform," declared Sickles, but "his intercourse enriches a mercenary horde, who follow in the rear of our forces, corrupting by the worst temptations those in authority, given aid and comfort to the enemy, and relieving that extreme destitution of the insurgent population which would otherwise operate as a powerful inducement toward the restoration of tranquility and order." In line with Sickles views, more universal restrictions soon came from Washington not Memphis.[35]

On July 2, 1864 (a year after Sickles had sacrificed his leg on the second day at Gettysburg), Congress rolled back the executive branch's unlimited power to issue trade permits through the Treasury Department. In a testament to the failure of the permit system, the legislators authorized the president to make such provisions as would supply "the necessities of loyal persons residing in insurrectionary States, within the lines of actual occupation by the military forces of the United States." The commanding general would determine a monthly allotment in advance. In response, Washburn opened a supply store system in Memphis with only those willing to sign yet another loyalty pledge able to conduct business, and then it was limited to imports of only $2 million per month. Clearly not intended to restore Memphis prosperity but to screen out smugglers and the disloyal, accredited merchants would act as "instruments of the Government in carrying out the law, rather than as merchants engaged in prosecution of ordinary lucrative and unrestricted business transactions." Later, Treasury officials were instructed to favor disabled Union soldiers when granting supply store permits. With nearly all the top level military (including Rear Admiral David D. Porter, commanding naval forces on the rivers) clamoring about trade aiding the enemy, Sherman's Military Division of the Mississippi issued a general order at the end of August detailing legal commerce "near armies in the field or moving columns of troops, save that necessary to supply the wants of the troops themselves," and in departments and military districts "embracing country within our military control."[36]

Much seemed familiar about Sherman's directive. Quartermasters and commissaries could forage on the transited landscape "leaving receipts and taking the articles up on their returns." Where cotton was found and transportation to the rear did not interfere with military traffic, a quartermaster could ship that cotton to Nashville or Memphis counterparts, who in turn would invoice it as captured property of the enemy. Military authorities could not claim any private interest in the cotton. As for trade within Union lines, as long as articles were not contraband of war or detrimental to army operations then the military could work with Treasury agents and subagents "to the extent proportionate to the necessities of the peaceful and worthy inhabitants of the localities under conditions of fidelity of the people and maintenance of peace and order." Such trade would cease "when guerrillas are tolerated or encouraged" and "the army or detachments sent to maintain the peace must be maintained by the district or locally that tolerates or encourages such guerrillas."

All military officers would assist Treasury agents in taking possession of abandoned property and estates subject to legal confiscation. Firearms were to be strictly regulated and prohibited in general, for hunting, as an example, but were legal if for self-defense or aiding in the maintenance of peace and safety. Similarly, the sale of medicines and clothing, as well as salt, meats, and provisions, "being quasi-contraband of war," would be regulated by local commanders and Treasury agents. Noncontraband articles like women's and children's clothing, groceries, and imported articles were deemed "too unimportant to be noticed by military men" and left to Treasury agents for action. Finally, trading preference would always be extended to "men who have served the Government as soldiers, and are wounded or incapacitated from further service" while (in a phrase sounding very Shermanesque), "men who manifest loyalty by oaths and nothing more are entitled to live, but not to ask favor of a Government that demands acts and personal sacrifices."

Businessmen could not have been pleased by any of the government actions seeking to close loopholes in the trading across the lines. The local occupation mouthpiece *Memphis Bulletin* tried to console its readers with the notion that they should go ahead and rebuild the cotton market infrastructure in anticipation of better times when Union victory would end wartime restrictions. Cotton exports would increase sevenfold within six months of the rebellion's end, stated the newspaper, and net a $150 million market. Memphis would equal St. Louis and any other midwestern city in population and prosperity so *Bulletin* readers should prepare themselves for this bright eventuality. However, they needed to stop expressing sympathy or support for the guerrillas, take an active role in suppressing bushwhacking and furnish no aid and comfort to the enemy. The only hope for Memphis trade would come as a cooperative effort on the part of all loyal individuals to clear the surrounding countryside of "little pestiferous bands of guerrillas and bandits, whose depredations close it against our commerce." Sullen disloyalty, admitted sympathy with the rebellion, secret aid to the partisans, and denunciation of necessary military rules were not merely criminal but "stupid blunders as well as crimes," proclaimed the newspaper.[37]

Government officials saw their responsibility limited to containing smuggling and contraband trade, satiating the pent-up market demands for cotton while controlling graft, corruption, and profits. Despite continuing efforts to manage the levels of such trade through proscribing excess profits, utilizing the sale of abandoned property to pay for government agents' purchase of products of rebel landowners, and protecting loyal businessmen, the ingenious cotton speculator and smuggler of contraband functioned undaunted in the fall. The future remained to be seen as Confederate fortunes on the battlefield seemed quixotic after the fall of Atlanta. Yet the war was far from over. Washburn rid himself of the troublesome Memphis mayor Park, incarcerating him in Irving Block for "treasonable sentiments, uttered in the most vindictive manner" in addition to personally denouncing the Union general. Unceasing guerrilla incursions led to the use of prominent secessionists as hostages to safe passage of railroad activity. Military enlistment of black and white Memphians kept sentiment high against Union occupation. As historian Parks concluded, "There was little progress in the development of loyal sentiment in Memphis during the last year of the war."[38]

War and Treasury actions could not resolve the fundamental quandary—succoring upper South loyalists through controlled trade while at the same time preventing "aid and comfort" to the enemy via speculators, secessionists, and survivors. In September residents of the Memphis area headed by Chancellor William M. Smith of the Sixth Division petitioned authorities to include all of West Tennessee within the army's occupation zone. Such was the prerequisite for restoring commerce. When outside Union lines, loyalists felt threatened by local rebels who thought they had been turned loose and would not be punished. Moreover, "our people really need supplies," claimed Smith. Similarly, on September 23, other loyalists, like Elijah C. Hurst (the notorious Fielding Hurst's brother), told military governor Johnson how treasury regulations produced great hardship for small West Tennessee cotton growers to traipse their meager yields all the way to Paducah. Why couldn't a supply post be established at Johnsonville that would mutually benefit residents needing supplies and the government wanting cotton? Soon thereafter an assistant special treasury agent at Nashville called attention to the great difficulty in shipping nonregulation goods northward—rags, hides, manufactured yarns, tallow, and other goods—plus a 3 percent trading tax. That John T. Bolinger from Paducah on November 28 and William K. Hall from Columbus, Kentucky, on December 19 continued to complain about the plight of unionists outside occupation jurisdictions suggested no cessation to the problem itself.[39]

Perhaps bureaucratic red tape and jurisdictional boundaries contributed as much to the problem as anything. Lieutenant Isaac R. Hawkins of the Seventh Tennessee Cavalry (Union) told Johnson three days before Christmas that "the orders of the treasury department when they come to receive a military application [for supplies], affect the entire district, and no distinction is made between the *most uncompromising rebel* and an old *Loyal lady, who has given four sons and her husband to her country,* and has been severely punished for doing so." He illustrated his point by showing how one of his subordinates had requisitioned supplies from both the army's western Kentucky district and the Treasury's local customs surveyor to help several widows and solider families beyond Federal lines only to receive the answer, "Under present military regulations family supplies of no kind can be shipped to West Tenn." He complained that "the people of Western Ky, who I think more disloyal than any I have ever seen they can buy salt & almost anything *else at this place* [Paducah]," while a Loyal man who may not live half a mile from him if he reside in Ten', can not get a pound, unless he pay 3 or 400 pr cent and then smuggles it through."

The result to Hawkins was that "the rebels are supplied & the Loyal not," which he did not think right and could not believe that the government would condone. Hawkins was told that "there is twenty five per cent difference in the price of Cotton grown by a Ky rebel and that grown by a loyal man or his widow in Ten, and that per cent is in favour of the rebel," all due to some treasury regulation. That surely required correction, and as "you are the only representative we have," Johnson was supposed to do something about it. There were then serious discrepancies between a Kentucky that had not left the Union but contained more traitorous elements than a Tennessee that had seceded but supposedly harbored pockets of unionism. Political allegiance in the hearts and minds continued to defy officially artificial geographical boundary lines in the upper heartland. The impact by late 1864 could be seen in pockets and dinner pails.[40]

The State of Johnson's State

Here, then, was a war economy that dangerously mixed loyal and disloyal economic activity and average citizenry together with war profiteers. Observes editor Graf of the *Papers of Andrew Johnson,* "insecurity of life and property was undoubtedly the most pervasive concern of the people." He deftly illustrates how, through their views (and with a little imagination), posterity can discern what it was like "to be caught up in the maelstrom of war, in the uncertainties and insecurities of a revolutionary social upheaval." Indeed, Graf's rich introductions offer snapshots of the tribulations of the great and small, rich and poor in the business "of restoring government in the face of guerrilla raids and wide popular resentment." Reconstruction amid undiminished conflict in the upper heartland showed the futility of such efforts until the final fires of rebellion died out. Authorities tried to ensure a modicum of normality in order to eradicate a seedbed for starvation and insurrection. The tentacles of illegal exchange stretched beyond Memphis to other ostensibly pacified communities like Shelbyville and across the tier counties served by the Tennessee River, where it turned eastward. Confederate cavalryman Philip Roddey, for instance, readily distributed wagonloads of boots, shoes, sugar, and salt to both soldiery and civilians as such supplies were brought across lines. "I am told that any man can go to Shelbyville, and get whatever is wanted," Major General John "Blackjack" Logan informed Huntsville, Alabama, headquarters in late February. "In fact," he contended, "captured rebel letters show that the rebel troops across the [Tennessee] River are being supplied bountifully in this way." Yet such trade was more than quasi-military. Breakdown in normal commercial patterns across the occupied South coupled with the realities of succoring noncombatants and combatants (regular and irregular alike).[41]

Neither Johnson nor army authorities in Tennessee (or his elected counterpart Thomas E. Bramlette and uniformed officials in Kentucky) successfully dented the unrelenting disruption and dislocation in the heartland. They certainly tried. During the six months before joining Lincoln on the National Union Party ticket, Johnson's official business primarily involved engaging supplicants (refugees both destitute and persecuted), organizations of loyal Tennessee military units, or his Governor's Guard to repress guerrillas and restore civil law in the state via the political process. Changed wartime conditions introduced by Lincoln's Emancipation Proclamation and suppression of civil liberties, as well as imposition of national conscription, buffeted the East Tennessean's repeated attempts to restore civilian governance. In such instances, Johnson confronted nasty divisions and conflicts in the ranks of his followers, as well as virtually insurmountable public apathy and resentment bolstered by intimidation from hard-line secessionists and their guerrilla allies. In Graf's blunt words, the dedicated and determined war governor acted "in the midst of an unrepentant, nay unregenerate and vengeful, defeated community." The depth of societal division could be found in the pitiful pleas of unionists across the state. Notwithstanding flight to sanctuaries, whether in Kentucky or Union Tennessee enclaves, refugees cried out for help from the confiscation and transfer of absent property. They sought jobs, shelter, and clothing for transient families and professed their fealty and martyrdom to the cause. Such applications tugged at Johnson's patience if not his humanity.[42]

Continued societal instability prohibited any magic formula so long as the war dragged on, guerrillas and bandits intimidated the common citizenry, and Federal actions themselves inflamed hearts and minds. From the earliest, Johnson had thought he needed a state army to suppress the partisans and reestablish law and order. Enlistment of loyal volunteers from Tennessee unionists had only drained men off to the main Federal army—fourteen regiments of cavalry, ten regiments of infantry, five light artillery batteries, and two heavy artillery regiments of African American descent, to be exact. Organized at locales like Nashville and Gallatin, Murfreesboro and Carthage, Knoxville and Strawberry Plains, Jackson, Grand Junction, Bethel, LaGrange, Bolivar, and Trenton, these white and black Volunteer State contingents contributed to the war effort and furnished their share of incompetence, controversial leadership, and logistical headaches, not to speak of credibility—Fielding Hurst's quasi-guerrillas as a case in point. On the other hand, many served ably and honorably and, indeed, helped Lovell Rousseau and others chase raiders Forrest and Wheeler. Still, Tennesseans in blue always remained just beyond military governor Johnson's reach, which was just what the Union high command preferred but could not offset from other resources to satisfy the East Tennessean. In the end, Johnson had to fashion a Governor's Guard and ensure that over time it would become most proficient under West Point brigadier Alvan C. Gillem while best serving the needs of the state, not those of the Yankee high command.[43]

By 1864, relations between Johnson and military authorities like Jacob Ammen at Knoxville, Rousseau and George H. Thomas in Middle Tennessee, and Napoleon J. T. Dana at Memphis had measurably improved since the earlier scuffles with Don Carlos Buell, William Rosecrans, and Nashville's controversial provost marshal, Colonel William Truisdal. Perhaps Johnson learned more patience; perhaps army-civilian chemistry improved. Of course, the governor's old opponents had been sacked and were gone. Still, precedence of war prosecution versus political restoration hardly differed now that Johnson and Sherman fretted about rear-area security, control of the Nashville and

Northwestern Railroad, and guerrilla eradication. When Johnson wrote Secretary of War Edwin Stanton in July about calling a portion of raised volunteers a Governor's Guard under his exclusive control, General-in-Chief Henry Halleck advised against it. This consummate professional predictably complained that such troops left under state and local control were of "little or no use against the enemy" and that inspection reports of the Tennessee cavalry in particular showed them to be "undisciplined, disorganized and worthless for military service." The issue revolved around control and reliability in that case. Still, civil-military relations had improved in-theater.[44]

Johnson sent Gillem and the brigade-sized "Guard" off to rescue East Tennessee from "all bands of lawless persons" (as requested by 306 petitioners on May 28) in early August, and they initially disproved Halleck's thesis. Leaving Gallatin near Nashville on the fourth and traversing the rugged Cumberland Plateau, they advanced all the way to Bull's Gap above Knoxville and Strawberry Plains by the eighteenth—a distance of 218 miles. They dispersed rebels and partisans in hot skirmishes at Rogersville on August 21 and Blue Springs two days later. Gillem claimed his men had gained confidence and experience. By September East Tennessee operations had eliminated John Hunt Morgan and temporarily stabilized conditions, much to the delight of long-suffering East Tennessee loyalists. Then Confederate brigadiers John S. Williams and John C. Vaughn attempted a comeback under pressure to cooperate with the Army of Tennessee's march north to Chattanooga from the smoldering ruins of Atlanta and north Georgia. Gillem routed them and subsequently moved to Greeneville "to insure quiet and give confidence to the people to attend the Presidential election." Fortunes then reversed when a new Confederate commander for southwest Virginia and East Tennessee, the venerable former U.S. vice president, future Confederate secretary of war and general, John C. Breckinridge, rallied Vaughn and others. They staged a counter-offensive, and in a two-day encounter at Bull's Gap, stampeded the Federals back to Strawberry Plains, disgracing Gillem and the Governor's Guard.[45]

Johnson now looked elsewhere for alternatives to the uniformed manpower shortage for shoring up his shaky control of the state. In August he drafted, and the next month maneuvered, a Union state convention to accede to a formal Military Enrollment Proclamation (in effect copying what Hurlbut had commenced the year before with West Tennessee and Kentucky forming Home Guards under militia laws of the two states). Like so many of Johnson's ploys, however, there were various motives and issues rolled into one, although the governor's words were honestly straightforward. "Whereas the rebellion has inaugurated a guerrilla mode of warfare throughout the country, degenerating into the commission of every species of crime known to and punishable by the laws of the land, it is the duty of all good citizens, therefore to unite in one common effort to sustain the civil authority throughout the State, and suppression of these marauding bands, which are preying upon the innocent and defenceless throughout the whole community," stated the dictum of September 13, 1864.[46]

In fact, Johnson's proclamation directed that "all able bodied male persons" (including "white and colored" for the first time in state history) between the ages of eighteen and fifty be enrolled and subject to such duty. Actually it was more a survey of numbers and locations than conscription per se, explained the state adjutant general. Still, the military governor wrote Secretary of War Stanton two days later, "We are organizing the militia of the State for the purpose of restoring the Civil authority & the expulsion of guerrilla bands." He asked that "if there are any arms due the State under the act distributing arms among the several states they could be used to great advantage at this time." Similar requests to army ordnance authorities had yielded only promises, and Johnson wanted something more substantial by early fall as he tried to organize a militia to ensure safe polling stations for the upcoming national presidential election. But as editor Graf observes sagely, "Until the disorders and insecurities created by roving bands of Confederates were quelled, the prospects for successful civil government were dim." Indeed, Johnson's call occasioned mostly bleats of personal safety concerns and complaints about possible persecution exacted upon the loyal populace. Yet another Johnson ploy seemed dead on arrival.[47]

Such facts emerged from the front lines of the guerrilla war. Captain Ben S. Nicklin, Thirteenth Indiana Battery guarding the Louisville and Nashville's South Tunnel near Gallatin, reported attacks on his inadequate garrison of sixty Tennessee mounted infantry (Fortieth Infantry, U.S. Colored Troops) and his battery men. His post had been attacked suddenly at night on October 10, with guerrillas killing four soldiers and two railroad hands at the tunnel. The country to the north was full of the enemy, he noted, as "Governor Johnson's proclamation enrolling the citizens is sending them to the guerrillas and to the rebel army." The country "has not even the germ of loyalty in it, and while the rebels and guerrillas are advised of every movement of our side we can learn nothing of them until too late." "Men that talk loud,

228

both here and at Nashville, of their devotion to the Union, never do an act for its support, but, if their negroes are to be believed, when they are at home stigmatize all as Yankees, and chuckle over the way they get around Federal authorities." Nicklin claimed to have a long list of names together with witnesses and charges showing how the citizens of the locale acted and he promised to try and arrest some of them in the next week. Most of all, he wanted more men, another company, to effectively patrol out twelve to fifteen miles from his post and thus avoid surprises like that of the tenth.[48]

Still, Johnson persevered with what had been uppermost in his mind since arriving in Nashville two years before—restoration of civil governance. Stillborn attempts had attended the intervening time, but by January 1864, Lincoln's amnesty proclamation of the month before provided yet another vehicle. With a baseline figure of 10 percent of the 1860 vote count, Tennessee could then require normal age, sex, race, and guiltlessness of crimes stipulations along with place of residence requirements. Not satisfied with that, Johnson added yet another special franchise oath to the bargain. The wannabe returning citizen would have to "ardently desire" suppression of the insurrection and vow to heartily aid and assist all loyal people in the accomplishment of such suppression. Only one exception existed in Johnson's view: Any East Tennessean in U.S. service would be "prima-facie evidence that he was a Loyal Citizen." Such a "hard oath—a tight oath" apparently bothered Lincoln, yet he acquiesced to the military governor's belief that anything less merely allowed unrepentant secessionists back into normal economic and political life. Both men wanted proof in deeds, not merely words. Johnson's opponents quickly dubbed the move his "Damnesty oath."[49]

Opposition to this hard-line approach had surfaced with the March 1864 local elections. Low voter turnout this time may have resulted less because of guerrilla intimidation and more from moderate unionists and tepid secessionists simply abhorring additional demands of loyalty and Johnson's unionist dictation plus out-of-state soldiery shadowing the polls. Johnson obligingly extended the time for counties and districts to hold their elections, but to little avail. Hard-liners won out wherever elections were held, although the governor resisted extending his proclamation to East Tennessee, being content to listen to advice from local citizens as to appointment of necessary officials. In fact, by summer his effort to return civil government to his state could be seen as abject failure. His unrelenting position on rebellion and repentance, his embrace of emancipation and unrelenting prosecution of the war as part of the Union platform set the tone. As he had told the audience at the opening of the Nashville and Northwestern Railroad at Johnsonville on May 19, unless the people as a whole wanted to suppress guerrillas and restore the law, "no Generals can save you from ruin," he suggested. Following his nomination to the national ticket, he urged loyal men to "control the work of reorganization and reformation absolutely." This left little room in the tent for lukewarm unionists and tepid secessionists.[50]

Momentum independent of Johnson personally began to build by early autumn. "A respectable number of Union men, representing the different sections of Tennessee" met at the State Capital on August 2. They issued a call for a September convention and, while seemingly independent of the governor, were in fact his friends and correspondents. Sam Milligan, Horace Maynard, Joseph S. Fowler, James B. Bingham, and Leonidas C. Houck led the effort that came together in Nashville on September 5–8, and the conclave produced proposals supporting the Baltimore platform of the Union party, state participation in the national election, enrollment and arming of the state militia, and formation at an early date for another convention to revise the state constitution and reorganize the government. The proposals led to further Johnson proclamations, overtaken by the fall's military uncertainties. Moreover, when some twenty-six thousand to forty thousand Tennesseans ostensibly voted in the November presidential election, Congress cast out the ballots. Undeterred, unionists from the eastern part of the state persisted; West Tennesseans avowed support, and only the presence of a major, if final, Confederate counter-offensive at the very gates of the state capital in December held up proceedings. Nevertheless, realistically, as editor Graf observed, "until the disorders and insecurities created by roving bands of Confederates were quelled, the prospects for successful civil government were dim" in the state of Tennessee. Johnson knew it.[51]

CHAPTER 7

---oᴥᴥᴥo---

Kentucky's Lamentations

A late greening spring in Kentucky found similar issues confronting the loyal, civilian government of Thomas Bramlette. What to do about blacks, guerrillas, and national intrusion into state affairs worried officials and the populace. A U.S. district court judge in Louisville had decided on March 1 that anyone taking the oath in response to Lincoln's amnesty proclamation was thereby absolved of "anything standing against him." But perhaps the death of the wife of antebellum conciliator-statesman Henry Clay, on the sixth of April, symbolized a true end to the spirit of compromise and good will among Kentuckians. The question of enrolling blacks against the state's military quotas, the unceasing turmoil of crime, and the actual onset of conscription on May 13 all inflamed the Commonwealth. Union Democrats met in convention in Louisville to prepare for the national Chicago convention and instructed delegates to back former major general George B. McClellan for president and their own governor for his running mate. At the same time, the "Unconditional Union" gathered elsewhere in the river city announced unanimous support for Lincoln's reelection. Prospects of that event coupled with heavy-handed military presence to badly split the state that spring and summer.[1]

Kentuckians' Perspectives

Members of the extended Clay clan reflected the strains and frustrations. Patriarch Brutus, one of the state's congressmen in Washington, was a major slave owner, leery of emancipation much less black military enrollment yet supportive of Lincoln and the Union. His brother Cassius, a strong abolitionist, was off in St. Petersburg as U.S. envoy to the czar of Russia. With sons in both armies, another of Brutus's brood managed a plantation near Paris, Kentucky, and told his father on March 29 that "these are times that but few if any know what is the best to be done" with fewer even knowing how to act "toward the many Lincoln bayonets that now surround our immediate neighborhood." Troops of all kinds and character were there, and he thought "the fair & beautiful fields of old Kentucky must soon be laid waste & annihilation must be the end." He was at least getting on well with the blacks on the place, "but negroes here are generally much demoralized by all doings" with a great deal of stealing in the neighborhood. "It seems as if every fellow is trying to see how much devilment he can do in that way." He, his mother, and the rest of the family tried to figure out the best approach to planting and marketing of crops, anticipating another rebel invasion and how to avoid Brutus's caustic criticism as an absentee landlord. Brutus, of course, had his own frustrations with machinations on Capitol Hill.[2]

Indeed, the Clay portion of Kentucky lay directly in the customary path of Confederate raids out of southwest Virginia and East Tennessee through Pound Gap. If not Longstreet, then some other intruder was anticipated all spring, and the Clay family frantically sought solutions to anticipated rebel confiscation of livestock or premature disposal of the fruits of their labor in fluid markets. Moreover, distant cotton property investments in Mississippi had turned sour with Federal occupation there, blockade of trade and disruption of slave labor. Brutus's brother-in-law Christopher Field had floundered trying to start up such business writing from Memphis on New Year's Day how he wished "the federal lines were closed up so as the people in the Valley could go to work and plant." He thought it very important for us to make cotton during the balance of the war," as "we could then afford to lose our slaves." A great deal of property transaction in Kentucky showed land owners, discouraged and downtrodden, selling out to wealthy neighbors and moving west to find more salubrious living. Then, one of the Clay sons, Ezekiel, who had joined the First Kentucky Mounted Rifles with Humphrey Marshall, would fall badly wounded and captured in fighting in the eastern mountains of the state, thus raising family concern. But mostly, the disintegrating nature of unionism and support for Lincoln bothered the Clay family. Brutus worried that he could not be home helping family, friends, party, and Kentucky cope with its throes of tribulation and change. Christopher Field, hardly a secessionist, concluded, "I do think Mr. Lincoln is pursuing and has been all the time [been on] a very suicidal course to restore the Union." The president was "severing it further & further [with] every act and Proclamation he issues," even though Field too desired reunion.[3]

Uncertainty equally accompanied the lives of Kentucky commoners like Christian County farmer and Methodist circuit rider George Richard Browder as well as young Lexington unionist diarist Frances Peter. Returning home from one trip, Browder noted on April 11 how "robbers have been in again plundering & stealing." Most of his jottings continued that theme, pointing the finger mainly at thieving and cowardly characters shedding Union uniforms for mufti at night while vagrant slaves also preyed upon livestock and corn cribs and more frequently accosted citizens for valuables. He noted how "the papers are full of accounts of pillage & plunder in many parts of Ky." The newspapers in April also recounted Forrest "capturing and killing negro troops," suggesting that "there is a decided lull in negro enlistments." Kentucky blacks, to Browder, suddenly "*seem* more contented" as a result, although "large numbers are dying at Clarksville" Tennessee contraband camps. For Browder, at least, "the unusually backward" weather retarded crop growth and kept him off guard mainly about slave instability. June 8, "a day of strange feelings" said Browder, "found my plantation entirely deserted by negroes—not one left!" Eventually rounded up and returned, this man of God severely reprimanded them while shipping the most uncooperative off to Louisville to be hired out. "I should have been glad if they had gotten safe into Clarksville without my responsibility," he concluded.[4]

Young Fannie Peters, meanwhile, presented another view before her death from epilepsy in early April. The Lexington lass penned final diary entries loaded with political innuendoes and bemoaned the lack of a loyalist newspaper for her family's community, where Union men might "express their sentiments without having to send all the way to Cincinnati to do so." She would not survive to see the startup of the *Lexington National Unionist* that very month and how the new journal would castigate both Bramlette and disgraced homegrown unionist military hero, Colonel Frank Wolford, for their opposition to black recruitment as well as other Lincoln administration policies. She did note the departure of protective Union garrisons southward from Camp Nelson at the end of March and how that promised to open the way for more Confederate invasions. Rebel farmers seemed to be "saving up all the provisions they can," she suggested, as "the secesh seem to expect them." Her doctor father's mill, situated in a rebel-inclined part of the state, was "rather bare of grain just now," but if any raiders did come, said Peters, "they won't find as much to steal from Pa as last time." Indeed, a secessionist uncle near Georgetown had gone to the southern part of the state "ostensibly to buy cattle but I would not be surprised if it was to help the rebels."

Feisty to the last, Peters recounted how the lieutenant governor and Wolford were in town on April 2, appearing for "a rabble rout of secesh to whom they made Copperhead speeches, the subjects of which were mostly abuse of the Govt. & Mr. Lincoln & praise of McClellan." Even those final notes in her life reflected concerns dogging her fellow Kentuckians—fear of more rebel raids, the endless political battles between parties and factions, and loyalism and dissent swirling about "occupied" Kentucky and the nation. Brigadier General Nathaniel C. McLean, late of Burbridge's command, and by April 26 riding with reinforcements to Knoxville and eventually the campaign for Atlanta, wrote his wife from Burnside Point that he did not understand southeastern Kentucky hospitality whereby even the rich of the section took payment for lodging and meals from travelers such as himself. Only starvation would cause him to do so, and it was "this thing of keeping travelers in a way of making money that I do not admire."[5]

Causes of Kentucky's Malaise

In retrospect, various issues embroiled the Commonwealth, including black military enrollment, guerrilla and rebel raids, as well as citizen disloyalty and secret societies. Over the course of the year, Governor Thomas Bramlette and the legislature moved from sometime ally to opponent of the Union military administrators in the state like Brigadier General Stephen Burbridge. Their differences affected civil-military relations but also the future of the people and their state in both war and peace. In one sense, Kentucky mirrored what was happening at the national level concerning war prosecution. Was it to be "harsh" or conciliatory, radical or conservative, the Union as it was or the Constitution as it is? Or was Kentucky witness and participant in a newly emerging relationship between national versus state power? People and events intertwined on issues and solutions, usually absent consensus. Horizontal (within the state) and vertical (national-state) processes played out differently than in Tennessee under Andrew Johnson's military government.

Recruitment of African Americans especially festered with most Kentuckians. Bramlette thought he had worked out an accommodation personally with Lincoln—no black enrollment as long as Kentucky met its conscription quotas with white males. He even permitted the controversial Wolford to recruit a six-month unit while awaiting courts-martial. On June 6, Bramlette had state inspector general Daniel W. Lindsey postpone the June 11 draft on the grounds of "scarcity of labor, and the fact that the citizens have so patriotically and nobly responded to the late call for six-months men." Burbridge and the army immediately proclaimed such short-term cohorts of little value. The general gained Washington's favor for his handling of Morgan's late raid and he told civil administrators that congressional confiscation acts of the past two years plus the outpouring of slave and free blacks for military service enabled him to enroll that part of the population anyway. A predatory expedition by a Paducah colored troops colonel up the Cumberland to impress and enlist slaves further destabilized the situation with Bramlette protesting to Washington and Burbridge ducking responsibility.[6]

War Department inspectors went to Kentucky in July, at least in part to study black enlistment progress. By this time, Burbridge had been breveted major general of volunteers and presided over all recruiting in the state, at least in army eyes. But now competing with Adjutant General Lorenzo Thomas's own efforts to bring in slaves for such purposes throughout the Mississippi Valley, Burbridge claimed he could accomplish more in placating whites in his state as a native Kentuckian than any outsider. By the end of the month, with the judge advocate general pronouncing successful enrollment of ten thousand Kentucky blacks, Burbridge stood so well with Secretary of War Edwin M. Stanton that he was authorized to raise two mounted colored regiments for internal police duty in the state and procure necessary mounts from loyal Kentucky owners with promised reimbursement at war's end. Both actions failed to impress the citizenry.[7]

By this point, other issues intruded on Burbridge's agenda. Morgan's summer raid, the unceasing tide of guerrilla turbulence, rumors of seditious conspiracies, and inflammatory and derogatory anti-administration rhetoric virtually unglued his actions. Aided by Lincoln's habeas corpus suspension, as well as by the perception of the army's own judge advocate general that the state was in a deplorable condition, Burbridge wrote Stanton that he would spare no effort to recruit soldiers, protect loyal citizens, and suppress treasonable and disloyal sentiments and practices. With that he began what became known as a "reign of terror." To make it official, he received special blessings from his direct superior. Starting on June 14, theater commander William T. Sherman told his minion, "Go on, raise the hue and cry, and don't mind the cost of money or horseflesh to hunt down every robber and guerrilla in your State. Make a clean job of it and Morgan and all other such men will let Kentucky alone in all time to come." This would be only the first of Sherman's instructions and comments on the matter.[8]

Parts of the Bluegrass had always been seething beds of secession. That fact had changed but little by 1864, even with Union occupation. West of the twin rivers, the so-called Jackson Purchase, or simply "Purchase," had defied control from Paducah, Memphis, or Frankfort, for that matter. Forrest's successful spring foray lingered in memory, causing Cadwallader Washburn to direct that "the people of that disloyal region, Western Ky., will not be allowed to sell their cotton and tobacco, or purchase supplies, until they show some friendship for the U.S. government, by driving out the guerrillas and irregular bands of Confederate soldiers who pay them frequent visits." Such sentiments fit well with Burbridge's intent as well as those of military governor Andrew Johnson and West Tennessee loyalists. They certainly matched Sherman's views and a strategy that he laid out for Burbridge on June 21.[9]

One wonders if Sherman's words reflected his disappointments with fence-straddling Kentucky neutralism as departmental commander in 1861. Writing from Big Shanty, Georgia, on the road to Atlanta three years later, he reiterated how Kentucky remained in the Union despite coercion to do otherwise. But he suggested the actions of "the so-called partisans or guerrillas are nothing but simple murder, horse-stealing, arson, and other well defined crimes, which do not sound as well under their true names as the more agreeable ones of warlike meaning." He had pressed Governor Bramlette before embarking on a campaign to organize in each county "a small trustworthy band, under the sheriff, if possible, and at one dash arrest every man in the community who was dangerous to it, and also every fellow hanging about the towns, villages, and cross-roads, who had no honest calling, the material out of which guerrillas are made up." The governor had countered "this sweeping exhibition of power" seemed too arbitrary. Thus, thought Sherman, personal liberty had become so secure that "public safety is lost sight of in our laws and constitutions, and the fact is we are thrown back a hundred years in civilization, law, and everything else, and will go right straight to anarchy and the devil if somebody don't arrest our downward progress." "We, the military, must do it, and we have right and law on our side," he announced. "All Governments and communities have a right to guard against real or even supposed danger." Therefore, the "whole people of Kentucky must not be kept in a state of suspense and real danger lest a few innocent men should be wrongfully accused." Such words gave Burbridge license to abuse power.[10]

First, said Sherman, Burbridge should order all his post and district commanders to realize that "guerrillas are not soldiers but wild beasts unknown to the usages of war." To be recognized as soldiers, "they must be enlisted, enrolled, officered, uniformed, armed, and equipped by some recognized belligerent power, and must, if detached from a main army, be of sufficient strength, with written orders from some army commander, to do some military thing." That was precisely what Confederate partisan rangers were supposed to be. Sherman contended that "of course, we have recognized the Confederate Government as a belligerent power, but deny their right to our lands, territories, rivers, coasts, and nationality, admitting the right to rebel and move to some other country where laws and customs are more in accordance with their own ideas and prejudices."

Second, observed Sherman in his inimical fashion, since civil power in Kentucky could not protect life and property or prevent anarchy, "which nature abhors," the military rightfully, constitutionally, and lawfully can intervene and "everybody can be made to stay at home and mind his and her own business." If not, then they "can be sent away where they won't keep their honest neighbors in fear of danger, robbery, and insult." And third, said Sherman to Burbridge, "your military commanders, provost-marshals, and other agents may arrest all males and females who have encouraged or harbored guerrillas and robbers" and "cause them to be collected in Louisville, and when you have enough, say 300 or 400, I will cause them to be sent down the Mississippi through their guerrilla gauntlet, and by a sailing ship send them to a land where they may take their negroes and make a colony with laws and a future of their own." If they would not live in peace "in such a garden as Kentucky," pronounced the general, "why we will kindly send them to another, if not a better land, and surely this would be a kindness and a God's blessing to Kentucky."

Sherman counseled not to allow personalities to mix in the decision; "nor does a full and generous love of country, 'or of the South,' of their State or county form a cause of banishment," he said, but rather "that devilish spirit which will not be satisfied and that makes war the pretext for murder, arson, theft in all its grades, perjury, and all the crimes of human nature." He preferred to allow civil authorities do the task, "but if they will not, or cannot, then we must; for it must be done." There had to be an "end to strife," and the honest, industrious people of Kentucky, and the whole world, "will be benefited and rejoiced at the conclusion, however arrived at." He repeated that he did not object to anyone having "what they call 'Southern feelings,' if confined to love of country, and of peace, honor, and security," and even "a little family pride." But, he preached, these become "crime when enlarged to mean love of murder, of war, desolation, famine, and all the horrid attendants of anarchy." Burbridge soon got the point.

That same day, Sherman ensured that all of his department commanders plus the War Department received a copy of his Burbridge letter. He doubted that Lincoln would sustain him, he told Stanton, "but if he don't interfere is all I ask." "We will never have peace as long as we tolerate in our midst the class of men that we all know to be conspiring against the peace of the State, and yet who if tried by jury could not be convicted." Our civil powers in the South "are ridiculously impotent," he claimed, and "it is as a ship sailing through sea—our armies traverse the land, and the waves of disaffection, sedition, and crime close in behind, and our track disappears." A beginning should be made, "and I am willing to try it, but to be effectual it should be universal." The problem would be "in selecting a place for the malcontents"—Honduras, British or French Guiana, San Domingo, Madagascar, or lower California would do. If the government would not assent and name the land to which Sherman might send a few cargoes, "I will find some island where they will be safe as against the district of my command." He was sure that "one thing is certain, there is a class of people, men, women, and children, who must be killed or banished before you can hope for peace and order, even as far south as Tennessee." Indeed, the Volunteer State, as well as Georgia, soon came under Sherman's draconian plans.[11]

Thus, under directions from Washington as well as Sherman, Burbridge embarked on his crackdown. He wrote Adjutant General Lorenzo Thomas that "until resident rebels in Kentucky are made to suffer in pocket for the depredations committed by guerrillas, it will be impossible to break up the thieving bands with which the State is now infested." So Stanton directed him to "spare no effort to protect loyal citizens, and carry into effect the enlistment of troops, white or black, and suppress treasonable and disloyal practices within your command."

In late June, Halleck, lamenting that Cynthiana citizens had "buried the rebel dead with honors, while our dead were treated with marked insult" during Morgan's late raid, told Burbridge to arrest and send to Washington under proper guard "all persons inciting insurrection or aiding abetting the enemy." He also understood among "these aiders and abettors of rebellion and treason are distinguished officers of the State government and members of the Congress of the United States." They too were to be arrested and shipped to the nation's capital. Any rebellious attempts in Kentucky "must be put down with a strong hand, and traitors must be punished without regard to their rank or sex." A sanguine Sherman told him to "clear out the guerrillas, root and branch, and banish the vagabonds that, under pretense of being Confederates, commit murder and highway robbery, and don't bother too much with the fellows who make money, as they are not a dangerous set." He felt that "their self-interest and fear of danger will keep them quiet enough." The situation only worsened in July when Lieutenant Leroy Fitch of the naval force patrolling western waters pronounced guerrilla control from the Green River to the end of Union County and President James Guthrie of the Louisville and Nashville Railroad requested three hundred repeating rifles from the War Department to protect his trains.[12]

Even more suspicious if not downright dangerous (Halleck's words) was the plot uncovered by military authorities that suggested secret organizations at work in the Midwest and Kentucky to aid the Confederacy. The Knights of the Golden Circle, the Sons of Liberty, and Copperheads had all helped Morgan the year before in his great raid north of the Ohio River and were once again active in the summer of 1864. On July 2, Indiana district commander Brigadier General Henry Carrington noted the cooperative arrangements between these clandestine shadows with some two thousand partisans under colonels George Jessee, Leonidus Sypert, and Adam Rankin Johnson, as well as various guerrilla captains gathered in Kentucky to aid the rumored insurrection. Burbridge sent African American units to Owensboro and Henderson, although Carrington's informant suggested some disarray in the ranks of the plotters (whose Kentucky leader was prominent state judge Joshua Bullitt). They vowed "not to rise up in arms until a Confederate force crossed the Ohio" or "opened up in Kentucky." Carrington marveled "at their knowledge of rebel movements" and at their having either a "wonderful intuition or a perfect system of information."[13]

It should have been no surprise when, on July 16, Burbridge issued General Order 59 in response to "the rapid increase in this district of lawless bands of armed men engaged in interrupting railroad and telegraphic communications, plunder and murdering peaceful Union citizens, destroying the mails, &c." All guerrillas, armed prowlers "by whatever name they be known, and rebel sympathizers" were admonished that future stern retaliatory measures "would be adopted and strictly enforced whenever the lives or property of peaceful citizens are jeopardized by the lawless acts of such men." Rebel sympathizers within five miles of any outrage committed by armed men "not recognized as public enemies by the rules and usages of war" would be arrested and sent beyond United States territory. Moreover, "so much of the property of rebel sympathizers as may be necessary to indemnify the Government or loyal citizens for losses incurred by the acts of such lawless men will be seized and appropriated for this purpose." But most stringent of all, "whenever an unarmed Union citizen is murdered four guerrillas will be selected from the prisoners in the hands of the military authorities and publicly shot to death in the most convenient place near the scene of the outrage." The unionist *Louisville Daily Journal* rhapsodized that General Order 59 "falls like a stream of golden sunshine upon the dark storm clouds of an angry sky."[14]

In practice, however, Burbridge's next moves turned that angry sky even stormier. As his biographer Bryan Bush observes, General Order 59 "caused Confederate prisoners to be mistaken for outlaws and many innocent men paid with their lives." At least sixty-seven prisoners were executed under this order between July 1864 and January 1865. Flimsy evidence, hearsay, or complaints from loyal neighbors or simply rumor that a Confederate Kentuckian had slipped home all gave rise to Burbridge's heavy handed arrests, imprisonment, confiscation of property, and, worst of all, blatant, exemplary execution of prisoners. A week after issuing the general order, Burbridge had John Pierman Powell (aged twenty-three) and Charles William Thompson (aged eighteen) shot for "the atrocious attempt of a gang of guerrilla scoundrels and marauders . . . to murder in cold blood" one James E. Rankin and other outrages in the Henderson neighborhood. Captured ten days before near Owensboro, the pair apparently formed part of a Confederate recruiting detail in the area. Pleas for stays of execution even guerrilla threats notwithstanding, the two went to their deaths and became local martyrs in the eyes of family and friends. Supposedly, retaliatory executions became commonplace, with over fifty victims falling prey to Burbridge's harsh methods. About this time, the equally controversial Brigadier General

Eleazar A. Paine of Gallatin, Tennessee, infamy, took over at Paducah and began his own "fifty-one day's reign of violence, terror, rapine, extortion, oppression, bribery, and military murders," according to Kentucky chronicler Richard M. Collins.[15]

The state of semi-anarchy attending Kentucky by late summer provided the pretext for heavy-handed arrests, persecution of civilians, and, on August 1, even military interference in the polling process for sheriffs and minor county or precinct officers, as well as the Second District Court of Appeals judge. Recruitment of African American mounted units caused impressments of horses from disloyal citizens. As Judge Advocate General Joseph Holt told Stanton from Louisville on July 28, they would be composed of men "almost raised on horseback," of uncompromising loyalty and intimately acquainted with the neighborhood. This move would "prove a powerful instrumentality" in ridding Kentucky of guerrilla bands of robbers and murderers. If nothing more, however, their presence "would exert the happiest influence in favor of the Government policy of employing such colored troops." All such moves predictably drew protests from loyal Kentuckians like the governor and railroad president Guthrie. The arrest of Judge Joshua Bullitt on pretext of treasonous support of copperheadism drew a stern rebuke from Sherman in mid-August concerning who had perpetrated the war in the first place and how Kentuckians now had "a disposition to cry against the tyranny and oppression of our Government" when such could not exist were it not for that war. The rebels seized property, lived off the countryside, and had "introduced terror as part of their system." In unvarnished prose he pronounced "those side issues of niggers, State rights, conciliation, outrages, cruelty, barbarity, bankruptcy, subjugation, &c. are all idle and nonsensical."[16]

It was as simple as a schoolboy's fight, contended Sherman. When one or the other party gives in, "we will be the better friends." He confessed to having more respect for "some of the open enemies" than "for the canting sneaks to my rear" and posited that the question ultimately would be resolved around "shall we have a government that must be obeyed or not." Those answering in the negative or wavering "are enemies or mere denizens of the land, stript of the right of suffrage, debarred from speaking or writing, yea, even from marrying, for I would stop the breed." Peace would have been achieved long since had the populace embraced full occasion instead of "sickly expedients," and "the longer we remained blind to it the longer will be the war, the more of these insidious, mean little side issues that harass you in Kentucky and the fearful load of debt that somebody must pay." Sherman wished all in Kentucky well, he told Guthrie, and intended "to push the main rebel army far from you, and to root out that other class, who, under the plea of being soldiers, are regarded by us as common vagabonds and thieves."

Sherman thought that regular Confederate leaders like Johnston, Lee, or Bragg would not sanction such "dogs as called themselves guerrillas in Kentucky." Therefore he would "sustain General Burbridge if satisfied he is not influenced by mere personal motives," admittedly a concern given his subordinate's nativity. Nothing "has occurred to evince anything of the kind" up to that point, so "Bullitt and the rest must therefore spend some years abroad and take time to study and reflect on the great theory of self-government which began with old Adam and has made precious little progress since." Sherman closed by reiterating how "I should like Governor Bramlette and the real thinking men of Kentucky to know the kindly feelings I entertain toward them, and how earnest is my wish to insure to them tranquility and peace." Whether or not Guthrie and the others would be placated by such words did not matter. The policies and programs sanctioned by Sherman and practiced by his appointees would continue in the commonwealth. The national government seemed convinced of their effectiveness.

Judge Advocate General Holt told Stanton at the end of July how Burbridge's recent orders enforcing indemnity from rebel sympathizers for thefts and robberies of guerrillas, and directing the execution of guerrilla prisoners in retaliation for murders committed by these bands, "cannot fail to produce the happiest effect in mitigating these atrocities." A number of such executions had taken place and the guerrillas had not retaliated. "These outlaws are banded together in the same interest, are animated by the same spirit, and seek the accomplishment of the same guilty ends," he proclaimed. They were "a brotherhood of traitors and felons." Public safety demanded that they should be held accountable "for the crimes of each and all of their members." Burbridge's executions, believed Holt, "have inspired a most wholesome terror, and it is to be hoped that the stern but necessary policy thus inaugurated will be in nothing relaxed." Holt added that both he and Burbridge traced much of the problem to Lincoln's December amnesty proclamation. Burbridge, in fact, calculated "nine-tenths of the guerrillas now infesting Kentucky have taken the oath under that proclamation." But all rebels mocked such oaths "which they take only because they can make them instrumental in advancing their personal interest and treasonable enterprises." So far as Kentucky was concerned, "the rebels have used this proclamation, and the oath under it, only as a means for returning to the state, visiting their friends, making observations upon our military affairs, and then arming, mounting, and equipping themselves either for the Confederate service or for the career of robbers and cut-throats." Both he and Holt urged suspension of amnesty, especially in light of the apparent conspiracy in Kentucky and adjoining states pointing toward armed cooperation with the Confederacy.[17]

Kentucky no doubt had become as rife with the guerrilla pestilence as Tennessee by summer. The *New York Herald* reported on July 27, under the heading "Interesting from Kentucky," how guerrillas ranged the state. Some bona fide partisans like Adam Rankin Johnson and Tom Woodward had been there for several years. The infamous Champ Ferguson similarly had a long track record of mayhem and clan retribution in southeastern Kentucky. Other irregulars appeared in the wake of Morgan's abortive raids or in reaction to Burbridge's clampdown. Names like Henry Clay Magruder, Jerome "Sue Mundy" Clarke, Dick Mitchell, Gabriel Slaughter Alexander, Bill Marion, Samuel Oscar "One-Arm" Berry, James "Jim" Watson, Thomas Carlin Dupoyster, and William Turner now appeared and it wasn't always apparent that targets of their wraith were other combatants. Eventually, even the notorious William Quantrill would wander over from Missouri seeking sanctuary. Hamlets like Bloomfield and Taylorsville south of Louisville became guerrilla nests. Conditions also spawned free-booting counterguerrilla hunters like Major James Bridgewater and Captain Edwin Terrell (a turncoat Confederate) who evoked fear and loathing among the peaceful citizenry as much as the partisans. Kentucky Unionists continued to importune the governor to let them raise self-protection state guards. By midsummer, Kentucky was aflame with this plague—victimizing foes, citizenry, blacks, and whites.[18]

So August found no let-up either in Burbridge's summary punishment or in guerrilla activities, which were aided by drought conditions and low water that permitted the bands to line the banks of the Cumberland and board "nearly every steamboat." Adam Johnson's band seemed particularly precocious, interdicting the Ohio River and even crossing at will into Illinois and Indiana. Burbridge moved to strengthen fortifications at Louisville, Lexington, Mount Sterling, Frankfort, and Louisa in response, as well as to coordinate counterguerrilla operations by subordinates Paine, Hugh Ewing, and Edward Hobson. With Joe Wheeler's move through East Tennessee, Halleck warned Burbridge on the nineteenth, "You must look out for another raid into Kentucky," a possibility also involving Morgan. Then, suddenly, the guerrilla situation changed. A detachment of the Fifty-second Kentucky (U.S.) Mounted Infantry repelled Colonel Thomas Woodward and two hundred men attacking Hopkinsville on August 19, mortally wounding the guerrilla. Adam Johnson's band also was badly handled and dispersed at Grubbs' Crossroads near Canton by the Forty-eighth Kentucky (U.S.) Cavalry two days later, their Confederate chieftain blinded and subsequently captured. He spent the next five months incarcerated in Fort Warren Prison, Boston Harbor, until exchanged in February 1865. Concern about Wheeler and Morgan evaporated, although new fears arose of another move north by Forrest into the Purchase by late month, and the guerrilla bands quickly reformed under new chieftains. Ironically, Richmond would name Johnson commander of the Confederate Military District of Western Kentucky two weeks later with major recruiting and conscription duties, although ultimately Hylan B. Lyon would take his place.[19]

Lieutenant Colonel Thomas G. Woodward, First Kentucky Cavalry, CSA. Courtesy of Courtesy of Clarksville–Montgomery County Museum, Clarksville, Tenn.

A lull in the tempo, however, allowed Burbridge to revisit his earlier quest to devastate southwest Virginia salt works, enticed by Andrew Johnston's military commander Alvan C. Gillem. On September 11, he wrote Halleck from Lexington how the capture and dispersal of what he termed Jessee's force (probably Adam Johnson) left "Kentucky nearly free from guerrillas, and the State quiet." With sufficient guards for the railroads, he proposed moving to Abingdon, Virginia, and Halleck approved the next day, imploring an early move "while Breckinridge's corps is occupied by General Sheridan near Winchester" in the northern Shenandoah Valley. What resulted was an ill-fated month-

long raid, a massacre of Burbridge's black units at the battle
of Saltville, Virginia, and in a
nearby Emory and Henry College hospital (reminiscent of
Fort Pillow) on October 2 and
a severe blow to the general's
reputation. He retreated to a
yet-seething Kentucky, content
merely to issue a warrant for
Champ Ferguson, implicated
in the events surrounding the
massacre.[20]

Brigadier General Adam Rankin
Johnson, CSA (pictured here as a colonel). From Davis, *Partisan Rangers
of the Confederate States Army.*

Meanwhile, Burbridge fur-
thered securitization of the
commonwealth on August 12
by stopping all shipments of
goods or produce without special license, which required a
loyalty oath as well as a dis-
claimer about aiding or abetting the rebellion. Arrest and confiscation
of goods would attend those refusing to comply. By this point, he began treading upon Bramlette's purview with military interference in
local election procedure on August 1, as well as upon the politician's
special project, a Home Guard similar to that of Johnson in Tennessee. Bramlette ordered local officials to report on election meddling,
and twelve days later, Burbridge decided to bring under his supervision
"squads of Federal soldiers and companies of men styling themselves
'State Guards,' 'Home Guards,' 'Independent Companies,'" who were
"roving over the country committing outrages on peaceable citizens,
seizing without authority their horses and other property, insulting and
otherwise maltreating them." Such might be expected of the "traitorous guerrilla robbers and thieves," but not those "armed in the cause of
Union," declared his latest general order somewhat disingenuously. Such
appropriated property would be restored to proper owners and hence-
forth "no property of any kind will be seized or taken from peaceable,
law-abiding citizens of this command without authority in writing from
proper military officials." Aside from whose men were committing the
crimes—Burbridge's or Bramlette's—license to steal no doubt rode with
any Yankee crackdown. All of this had little impact on continuing guer-

rilla activity. But by the end of the month, the "wild riders" of Frank Wolford's old First Kentucky Cavalry (of course without him) had returned from Sherman's army to help restore the peace in their state.[21]

Guerrilla executions renewed, as did guerrilla activity. Captain Jake Bennett led nineteen rangers into Owensboro on August 27, drove off an African American guard and captured and burned a wharf boat containing government stores. They escaped unscathed. Yet push-back against Burbridge, and Paine in particular, began to surface. Bramlette privately warned Burbridge in mid-August "that some of the men who were urging you to make arrests and would have had them made to the greatest extremes are now turned against you and seeking popularity by denouncing your arrests and casting odium upon you." He urged the general to let authorities north of the Ohio move against traitors and conspirators. The *Louisville Democrat* had opined wryly on August 8 that it was strange when citizens rendered so little or no active assistance against guerrillas: "Their inaction is punished by the military as *disloyalty*." It might be patriotic and heroic to take up arms or give information against them; but "who is to protect the man who does this, when the guerrillas assail him the next day?" Protect the helping citizen, otherwise any expectation of his active support was unreasonable, said the newspaper. Then, on the sixteenth, Brigadier General Henry Prince wrote General-in-Chief Ulysses S. Grant from his Columbus, Kentucky, post concerning Paine's reign of terror, including executions and banishments, "with the theory that the sickest patient requires the most violent dosing." Indeed, Paine had been sent to Paducah largely when the Paducah Union League branch complained in early July that "rebels are doing all the business, and they are reaping all the advantages of trade." Like Burbridge, he had been given a free hand and openly ranted in "habitual salutation" about "God-damned" scoundrels and how he would "dig a hole, shoot you, and put you in it." He had hounded the mayor and secessionist-tinged families out of town, often under African American guard, imposed heavy levies on rebel-owned cotton and tobacco in order to compensate unionists for guerrilla depredations, and once paid one thousand dollars to a loyalist woman whose husband had been hung by rebels for his sentiments, declaring, "He would pay her a thousand more." "That's the right kind of doctrine," concluded a headquarters aide A. L. Hunt in mid-August." Apparently, Prince did not think so, however.[22]

Grant responded on September 4, declaring bluntly that Paine had to be removed as "he is not fit to have a command where there is a solitary family within his reach favorable to the Government." His administration will result in huge and just claims for "destruction of private property taken from our friends." Grant thought he would do for "an entirely disloyal district to scourge the people" (alluding perhaps to his tour at Gallatin, Tennessee), "but even then it is doubtful whether it comes within the bounds of civilized warfare to use him." Paine was relieved two days later, though one Paducah unionist protested, claiming that Paine "was ordered here by the President to collect assessments on rebel sympathizers," and if now sent away "the Union men in this end of the State will leave." Under pressure from Bramlette and Burbridge, Kentucky brigadier Speed Smith Fry and Colonel John Mason Brown investigated Paine's conduct. Brown privately told Inspector General Daniel Lindsey bluntly on September 16, "I don't think that Warren Hastings administration in India could present greater enormities of oppression, outrages and wholesale plunder, than Paine's brief reign of terror in this end of Kentucky." Civil officers "who have, for forty years, filled office in all integrity and honor, have been cursed as a humane man would not curse a dog, and ordered with sanguinary threats to resign." But "they braved Paine out" and "refused even to plead innocent in the absence of charges." Businesses were shut up; all rents of property diverted into the hands of the local military; and enormous fines, "in one instance as high as 9000 dollars," were levied and only prevented from being collected by "Gen. Meredith's providential arrival." Men had been shot by Paine "without trial, for offences of which a regular military court had acquitted them." In short, said Brown, "a reign of terror, such as no one can conceive who has not witnessed it, existed." Congressman Lucien Anderson, Provost Marshal R. H. Hall, port surveyor Thomas M. Redd, a major in the Eighth U.S. Colored Heavy Artillery, and other individuals—in addition to Paine—were implicated. Aside from the oppression and executions, Paine's Paducah rivaled Hurlburt's Memphis, perhaps. Paine got a court martial and little else. His milder successor. Brigadier General Solomon Meredith (Indiana commander of the famous eastern army's Iron Brigade) quickly released fifty-some prisoners held at Mayfield and emptied the Paducah guardhouse upon assuming duties on September 8. One relieved Mayfield citizen, Mrs. A. E. Mayes composed a piano forte, fantasie characteristique, "The Contrast," in honor of the change.[23]

As Mayfield historian Lon Carter Barton quoted from the local newspaper years later, one of Paine's uniformed captives, facing execution at the tyrant's hands but invited to drink with him offered the Yankee the following toast: "There is a land of pure delight; where saints immortal reign; a land prepared for black and white; but not for General

Federal fortified court house in Mayfield, Kentucky. Courtesy of Lon Carter Barton.

Paine." And, one of the most sensational complaints about Kentucky military rule surfaced at the Democratic convention in Chicago at the end of August. Former governor Charles A. Wickliffe proclaimed that many of the best and most loyal citizens, including twenty or thirty ladies, lay imprisoned in military prison filth at Louisville. Newspapers were "forbidden to make the slightest allusion to this terrible state of affairs," he announced. The surgeon in charge of the prison debunked the allegations claiming the domicile "a good dwelling house, well ventilated and dry, and as comfortable as could be expected under the circumstances." Yet the allegations and incidents forged ahead. Brigadier Ewing prescribed county courts would levy a sum sufficient to arm, mount; and pay fifty men to be raised and maintained in each county; Bramlette called upon judges and justices to refuse such tyranny; and Lincoln subsequently voided the order. Frank Wolford reentered the fray with renewed inflammatory and disloyal statements and Bramlette denounced radical Rev. Dr. Robert J. Breckinridge's defense of Burbridge's actions with the sentiment, "the reverend politician who has been aptly characterized as 'a weathercock in politics and an Ishmaelite in religion.'" Breckinridge declared that the arrest policy had not gone far enough, invoking the words of Simon de Montfort's indiscriminate slaughter of Frenchmen centuries before: "Kill them *all;* God knows his own." Treat all Kentucky dissidents alike, Breckinridge said, "and if there are any among them who are not rebels at heart, God will take care of them and save them at least." Within two weeks, the minister had been thrown from his horse and rendered hors de combat from the lecture circuit. Many wondered at this manifestation of God's will.[24]

Unceasing guerrilla activity, threat of new Confederate cavalry raids, the run-up to the national election, a newly emerging strain between Bramlette and Burbridge over who could and could not vote, as well as the military interference issue again, arrest of prominent Lexington citizens General John B. Houston, and the well-publicized "Great Hog Swindle of 1864," consumed the Kentucky autumn. *Louisville Daily Journal* editor George Prentice invented the legendary sobriquet "Sue Mundy" for the feminine-like guerrilla Jerome Clarke, and Department of the Ohio commander Major General John Schofield made a brief visit in the state, writing Sherman from Louisville on October 3 about very bad conditions with "criminal looseness, and, in some instances, gross corruption in the administration of military justice." He cited the freeing of public enemies of the worst character upon payment of large fees to lawyers having personal influence with commanding officers while innocents remained in jail for long periods without trial. The provost marshal's department at Louisville and the military police all over the District of Kentucky "appear to have been mainly engaged in trading in negro substitutes and extorting fines for violation of petty regulations." In fact, "the officers of police appear to have performed all the duties of public prosecutors, judge, and receiver of moneys," and while he knew that Burbridge reported directly to Sherman and was sent there by the president and Grant with reference "to the arrest and disposition of disloyal persons under direct orders from your headquarters," Schofield had ordered an investigation since at that moment the commander of the district was notably absent, by this time off on his campaign in southwest Virginia. But it was the "Great Hog Swindle" that grabbed the headlines and incensed Kentuckians the most, it seemed.[25]

At the end of October, just when a new Confederate raid from West Tennessee threatened, Burbridge became involved with a scheme to supply the voracious appetite of the Union army with cheap pork. Conniving with Louisville quartermaster Major H. C. Symonds, Burbridge issued an order effectively shutting down transportation of hogs out-of-state, thus forcing hog farmers to sell to the Union government via a Louisville packing plant at sub-market prices. Price rigging, forced sales via trade permit system, plus the illusion of favoritism toward loyalists all raised Kentuckians' hackles. Bramlette complained all the way to the White House once again about Burbridge's high-handedness, which built upon his September 3 rant about ordinary trade restrictions that "harass the citizen without any compensating public good, and which wear more the phase of subjecting the citizens to odious political tests than looking to the public good." Historian Thomas Clark late called it one of the most "dastardly tricks imposed upon Kentucky during the war." Symonds backed down on unit price and fired the original packing contractors and stopped the monopoly of the agents. He eventually claimed to have saved the government two hundred thousand dollars in the process. But Bramlette told the state legislature that Kentucky farmers had been swindled out of three hundred thousand dollars and the affair would not be forgotten for a generation in the Bluegrass. The swindle certainly added to the feud between governor and general and between the public and the military.[26]

The autumn threat of more Confederate cavalry raids from West Tennessee resulting from Forrest's move toward Sherman's logistics eventually would result in a full-blown incursion by Kentucky's own Colonel Hylan B. Lyon. Burbridge was caught short in manpower, having sent six black and five white regiments in response to Halleck's directive to bolster Thomas's buildup at Nashville "to enable him to meet any forces that Hood may send north." He asked for reinforcements to no avail. He, Meredith, Ewing, and Hobson all had to make do when Lyon eventually appeared, as much on a recruiting drive as intending to attack railroads and other infrastructure. In fact, unpopular Union conscription may have yielded 200 men from Breckinridge, Meade, and Hardin, as well as 278 from other counties, when Lyon passed through Henderson and Morganfield, according to postwar accounts. At least one such recruit, a young Maysville lawyer named S. Thomas Hunt, was captured and with three other Lexington prisoners taken out and shot under Burbridge's direct supervision. Later, when Lyon enforced Confederate conscription laws in the Commonwealth, such draftees deserted in droves. Conscription demands cut both ways as far as Kentuckians were concerned.[27]

All such disruption caused Burbridge to strike back with a vengeance in the weeks leading to the November election. His General Orders 7 and 8 spoke to intolerance of armed citizens' intimidation at the polls and raised the "black flag" of no quarter against armed guerrillas like Sue Mundy, who thought nothing of murdering anyone encountered in a blue uniform and robbing travelers in stagecoaches, as had happened near Shawneetown in early October. No wonder political, military, and economic controversies proved so negative in the national election on the eighth. Even Ewing (Sherman's brother-in-law) wrote Lincoln on November 1 how Burbridge's attitude and action would cost the administration dearly in the state and how the tyrant should be replaced with another more moderate Kentucky Union general, Thomas L. Crittenden. True to prediction, Lincoln lost to McClellan by a margin of 64,546 to 27,797. Turnout reflected a 64 percent drop over 1860, with nine counties showing no returns. Farmer George Browder, who had supported the Democrat, for "he says he will restore the constitution," lamented that the president's reelection "seals the fate of republican government in the U.S." With conscription, the race and slave issue, and travesties committed citizens by the military, Browder wailed, "oh, the horrors & outrages of civil war & abolition power!"[28]

Wither Kentucky?

Bitterness only increased for Kentuckians as fall passed toward winter. Bramlette now pressed both Washington and Grant for Burbridge's relief. He accused military authorities in Kentucky of "indiscriminate arrests of persons purely on account of their favoring the election of McClellan, treating as rebels all who are opposed to Mr. Lincoln's reelection—threatening and bullying the citizens—and menacing the civil authorities and officers of the State, laying unjust political restrictions upon the business and necessary trade of the country, seeking out inventions by which to harass, oppress, and injure those who differ with him in politics." All this produced "a very bad state of feeling, which has required all my skill to keep from manifesting itself in violence." And Burbridge persisted, said the governor, citing the arrest of John Houston and "in many ways sought to provoke collision with civil authorities." The general, he suggested, "has not capacity to comprehend the evils which he is prompted to provoke," instigated by men who "do comprehend and intend them, and who work upon his weakness through his vanity to accomplish them." He is wholly unfit for any command where there is anything at stake which requires "either intellect, prudence, firmness of purpose, justice, or the manliness of the soldier to accomplish." Grant endorsed Bramlette's view, observing, "I have from the start mistrusted General Burbridge's ability and fitness for the place he now occupies," wanting others like Jacob Ammen or Grenville M. Dodge instead. Lincoln weighed in on the Houston issue. Burbridge protested, the president insisted, and Kentucky district division commander Nathaniel C. McLean (returning to Lexington staff duty after less than auspicious field service with Sherman) wrote his wife before Christmas how the general that even he had come to dislike, now seemed very threatened when Bramlette dispatched agents to Washington to have him removed while Burbridge's friends explored his retention or a better command.[29]

Beset with financial difficulties at home, McLean also feared Schofield might supplant Burbridge, although at this point, the Kentuckian still maintained favor. Burbridge ordered investigations of alleged illegal voting and wrote Bramlette soon after the governor's initiation of proceedings against him, "I make no insinuations of dereliction of duty on the part of the civil authorities of the State, but say openly that if the military authorities had received during the past year that hearty and cordial support in their efforts to maintain the Government and preserve the peace in the State which, when I assumed command, I was assured would be afforded by the civil authorities, Kentucky today would not be cursed with the presence of guerrilla bands and her loyal citizens outraged by frequent robberies and murders." Clearly the two men would continue their collision course. But McLean hinted that even the general's "friends are rather lukewarm, and nay consent to his removal without much reluctance provided they can get a man they like in his place." Meanwhile, Burbridge hustled out of the state on yet another attempt to destroy southwest Virginia salt works, and in his absence, noted a postwar Kentucky historian, "the guerrillas seem to have undisputed possession of a large portion of the state." Between the guerrillas and Lyon, Yuletide was not a happy time in the commonwealth. Certainly Union brigadier McLean thought so, absent his wife and children at home in Cincinnati.[30]

Diarist Peter, now in her grave in Lexington, escaped what befell her fellow citizens through this tempestuous period. Other commentators agreed with Congressman Clay's clan, expressing dismay at slaves departing for the army (and their families gaining freedom via congressional mandate of the previous March). Among other things, the ersatz freed people now acquired surnames for the first time. Then, the federal Treasury Department had refused to honor Clay family claims for property losses in Mississippi. But most of all, for this stratum of society, politics burned into their psyche as much as breakdown in law and order nearby. "Strong Union men seemed to be very much outraged at the way things have turned," wrote Louisa A. Keiningham, a friend of Clay's wife, Ann, visiting her at Frankfort, with political affairs "much more excited" at the state capital than home in Paris, Kentucky. She felt uneasy and feared an outbreak before the fall presidential election. Brutus, meanwhile, had campaigned for McClellan, although his kins-man Cassius in St. Petersburg, Russia, felt him wrong both in that re-gard and on the whole slave question.[31]

The general unhappiness concerning "a collision between the civil & military authorities" also could be sensed throughout George Browder's diary entries of the period. Between departing slaves from neighboring farms (thanks to inducements by African American re-cruiters from Clarksville across the Tennessee line), robbers, and Fed-eral soldiers impressing horses and further disturbing normal rural life, Browder had little solace. True, his preaching and husbandry went on. While noting political matters, he remained aloof from partisan com-ment, perhaps fearing authorities' confiscation of his writings or arrest. He was more disturbed with those assessments of neighbors for losses by rebels and guerrillas as "the best, & purest, most honorable, peace-able & quiet men in our country are by that act classed with horse thieves & houseburners & made to pay for what they never did, and as a general rule the damages assessed have been three or four times as much as was sustained." The military, he supposed, "get a large share of the booty."[32]

Browder was also vexed by Lincoln's suspension of the writ of ha-beas corpus and proclamation of martial law. Friends and even Browder's father left for Louisville, New York, and Chicago to look after business interests or prisoner sons or simply "to stay until the great excitement in Ky about the arrests should subside." For "very many prominent citizens of our state have been recently imprisoned by military order, without knowing the charges against them or who accused them, he suggested." Then came the crowning blow: George Richard Browder, family man and man of the cloth, was drafted into the Union army! Conscription took effect in Kentucky on September 5 with "hundreds of young men leaving for the South and married men looking for negro substitutes." He noted guerrillas as threatening the lives of all who put in for Negro substitutes. When his own special plea for exemption failed, he too set out to find someone to take his place in the ranks. He questioned his faith and his loyalty and prayed for personal deliverance "from this great calamity." Eventually financed by friends and relatives, he, like thou-sands of loyalists both North and South, found substitute relief. Never-theless, Browder felt that while he did not like McClellan, he thought him preferable to Lincoln, for he "says he will restore the constitution."[33]

Kentucky should have seceded, claimed those of that persuasion. It did not. Like other border slave states, Delaware, Maryland, and Missouri, it remained in the Union. As such it appeared a pariah in the eyes of many north of the Ohio. Southern by geography, its economics rooted in human bondage, Democratic in politics, and dependent on trade with the warring sections while neutral at the start of the war, Kentucky remained a dark and bloody middle ground for four years. Somewhere between Maryland (only marginally touched by a brother's war), and Missouri (totally engulfed in fratricide), Kentucky became fair game for invading armies and raiders, liberators, emancipators, and business charlatans. Like Tennessee, its citizenry were preyed upon by partisans, guerrillas, and, by 1864, the riff-raff flotsam who were simply robbers and desperadoes. Its people and politicians never quite overcame the stigma that sent an "Orphan Brigade" of Kentuckians to rebel arms and nearly eighty thousand black and white sons to Union banners with another 12,476 serving in Union Home Guard contingents. Others retreated to partisan ranks or plain lawlessness. Legally untouched by Lincoln's Emancipation Proclamation, that very assertion of national power via conscription, suppression of civil liberties, and army recruitment of blacks all rubbed raw. Loyal Kentuckians were split among Radical Republicans (abolitionists), moderates, and conservatives all protesting their fealty to the Union. In a story as fascinatingly complex as that of occupied Tennessee, this swing state of the Clay clan, the Crittenden family, James Guthrie, Henry Prentice, and Frank Wolford, as well as Simon B. Buckner, John C. Breckinridge, John Hunt Morgan, and others, remained sharply divided throughout the conflict. Both presidents, Lincoln and Davis, spent hours fretting about their birth state. Neither administration garnered unfettered allegiance from the Bluegrass.[34]

The trouble lay with the evolving nature of conflict. Kentuckians wanted neutrality or even self-determination of detachment. Neither blue nor gray could permit that stance. As Kentucky historian Lowell Harrison has observed, while the state escaped the war damage of other southern states, "there were few citizens . . . whose lives were not affected in some way by the demands of the great conflict." He decided that while Kentuckians "have long been noted for their unusual political behavior," the intensifying waging of that conflict simply exacerbated the political battles at home. Retaining its prewar civil institutions (unlike secessionist and hence defeated and occupied Tennessee), Kentucky's civil government received severe buffeting from a parallel military administration in its midst as well as the socioeconomic vicissitudes accompanying conflict. In one sense, Kentucky and Tennessee were the same: both exempt from legal but not ersatz emancipation, garrisoning, strained civil-military relations, and race jammed together by the fourth summer of conflict.[35]

In principle, Kentucky retained civilian, representative government, basically embracing a conservative, union democracy. Kentucky's home-front turmoil centered upon civil-military discord. Civil administration best representing Kentuckian attitudes vied with despised military command by Jeremiah Tilford Boyle and Stephen Burbridge (both native Kentuckians), as well as Eleazer A. Paine and Hugh Ewing. An ever-hardening military policy singled out protest and dissidence, account-ability for lawlessness, latent treason, and disruption by raiders and partisans. Hard war views of northern radicals found expression among ultra-unionist, radical native sons of the state, and one may seriously question the handling of Kentucky by Lincoln's administration. Historian E. Merton Coulter astutely suggested much later that the discord lay with clear-cut differences over state versus national governance.[36]

Kentucky's relations with Washington were never close and cordial, Coulter thought, but rather "characterized by mutual distrusts, suspicions, and misunderstandings." He also entitled one of his chapters "commercial restrictions and other military rigors," explaining how "a hundred rules and restrictions were soon hedging the citizen about on every side and making him feel that the Federal forces must have been sent to the state to ruin him and vex him to death rather than to protect him from the Confederates." In fact, this historian spoke frankly of an "army of occupation" in Kentucky, not unlike that sent to Tennessee and other rebellious southern states. Indeed, from the summer of 1862 on, the Federal boundary for restricted commercial area was placed at the Ohio River, not the Cumberland, thus in effect implicating the Bluegrass State as part of the Confederacy. The same demands put upon Tennesseans—loyalty oaths, commercial permits (issued by statewide boards of trade that favored loyal unionists), prohibition in arms and munitions trading, interference with corn distillation production, even the closure of crossroads stores and town markets—befell Kentuckians, thanks particularly to Burbridge and Paine.[37]

Almost all Kentuckians, said Coulter, saw these restrictions emanating from military authorities "from whom it was widely felt nothing good could come" and further reflection of vengeance and personal grudge just as in Tennessee. Ironically, the U.S. Treasury Department on January 8, 1864, had annulled and abrogated all trade restrictions for the Bluegrass thinking the major conflict had pushed far to the south. Hence, Kentucky trade might be reopened safely. Of course, the activities of raiders Forrest, Lyon, and Morgan soon made mockery of such confidence. The ever-present guerrillas further dismantled this theory by summer with Federal military commanders in the state, as well as Washington fact finders like Dan Sickles, convinced that western Kentucky was a sieve through which trading with the enemy was an onerous pursuit. Indeed, the Jackson Purchase strip was a sieve and had been since the beginning of the war. When the Paducah Union League branch complained that "Rebels are doing all the business, and they are reaping all the advantages of trade" in early July, Eleazar A. Paine took charge, prompting the postwar appellation of "fifty-one days' reign" of persecution.[38]

While the Union Democracy, the Peace Democrats (forged from the old States Rights party), and the exceedingly small and unpopular Unconditional Union group of radicals (most closely resembling the national Republican party, perhaps), vied with one another for power during the 1864 presidential election, one might wonder just who was running Kentucky? Bramlette, who originally had strongly supported Washington policies and welcomed formation of unionist Home Guards as armed police the previous year, and who in October of that year had directed arrest of "five of the most prominent and active rebel sympathizers" as hostage for every loyal citizen carried off by guerrillas in any particular neighborhood, became increasingly alarmed as he watched oppressive military implementation of those policies. As Coulter observed, the governor's actions failed to protect the innocent, left proof of guilt, redress, or relief unresolved and eventually "left absolute power over personal liberty in the hands of irresponsible military officers." Kentuckian Maria Knott commented that "people had to vote just as the military saw fit or not at all." Unionist colonel Frank Wolford was hounded out of the army, placed under arrest on occasion, "not for cowardice, not for treason, not for insubordination, but because he spoke in opposition to the policy of Mr. Lincoln & Co," Sidney Clay wrote his uncle Brutus. In fact, that family's letters reflected the festering anxieties generally besetting Kentuckians at this stage: unprotected property and persons, army occupation and oppression, and the threat of enemy raids. But mostly "the treachery of the Gov't. & the audacious villainy of the Republican Reps. in Congress" pointed to one main issue: the emancipation and enrollment of freedmen as soldiers.[39]

Secretary of War Edwin M. Stanton's original directive to

Burbridge, enclosing the president's directive, stated specifically that "you will spare no effort to protect loyal citizens, and carry into effect the enlistment of troops, white or black, and suppress treasonable and disloyal practices within your command." To a man like Burbidge, this was license to rule with blood and iron. His predecessor, Jere Boyle, had established precedent. Lawyer and slaveholder-turned-soldier Boyle had gained fame at Shiloh, but his command of the District of Kentucky from May 1862 to January 1864 showed inept handling of guerrillas and raiders, as well as heavy-handed punishment of persons suspected of disloyalty, use of troops to control elections, and assessment upon nearby citizens for damages caused by guerrillas. In the summer of 1862, Boyle had promised punishment for those harboring or assisting guerrillas and assessment of damages, all subsequently underscored by Bramlette in his proclamation and by the legislature in the 1864 act. Boyle's unpopularity in the Bluegrass resulted in recall to army ranks and subsequent resignation from service back in January. By summer, ironically, he would write Lincoln openly professing the platform of George B. McClellan and the Peace Democrats largely because of the enlistment of black soldiers in Kentucky.[40]

Burbridge, yet another lawyer and farmer in civilian life, and a veteran of Shiloh and of operations on the lower Mississippi, had more success containing John Hunt Morgan's final foray into Kentucky in June and escalated Boyle's hard war policy against his fellow citizens. His actions "earned him the enmity of the duly constituted civil authorities as well as of the populace." And the third member of the hated Kentucky military triumvirate was Eleazer Paine, the sometime Gallatin, Tennessee, tyrant, guardian of the Louisville and Nashville Railroad, and local occupation chief who was sent to tame Paducah and the Jackson Purchase from July to September. Other Federals who rigorously enforced national policies in Kentucky included Thomas Ewing and Edward Hobson. Ewing commanded at Louisville; Hobson operated out of Lexington and had been both Morgan's captor and captive at different points. Together they soured relations with citizens in much the same fashion as Andrew Johnson in Tennessee. Of the lot, Burbridge seemed the most heinous.[41]

By 1864, war had wrought social disruption throughout the Bluegrass. War divided and dispersed families (white and freed people), spawned almost pathologically destructive bitterness and hatred and only very slowly restored trade, commerce, and agriculture (largely rescued by military supply). War often caused the destruction of infrastructure like railroad bridges, canal locks, courthouses, schools, and mills through either military overuse or wanton depredation. Decimation of the equine industry, diversion of agriculture from civilian to military markets, and headline-grabbing corruption in the hog domain dominated the economic picture. More subtly, the war's impact on such sectors as a lucrative hemp industry (used before the war for cotton bailing and bagging as well as maritime cordage) could be sensed only by scarcity of labor, particularly slave workers. If Boyle's well-intended extension of railroads critical to the military effort like the Lebanon-Danville branch of the Louisville and Nashville and the Kentucky Central (from Nicholasville to Danville and Somerset to link Louisville and Knoxville) subsequently faded by June 12, 1864, the stage was set for postwar development from the Ohio southeastward. Nonetheless, to Coulter's generation, "the destructions of war left in their trail blighted hopes and ruined lives, and aroused a feeling of helpfulness among the more fortunate."[42]

Editors of the Maysville *Bulletin* might think something like Burbridge's imposed trade restrictions "will not authorize an interference in the slightest degree with our business" nor would it "apply to the retail trade between a dealer and his customers in a City." Nonetheless, since Union trade restrictions forbade shipments without permits to and from Kentucky and from one point in the state to another, they did hurt trade at river towns like Louisville, Paducah, and Smithland—although Louisville continued as a thriving commercial center, a convenient spot for Union officers to map out grand strategy at the Galt House or, as on May 25, the gathering place for the Union Democrat politicians. Moreover, the city provided a clandestine rendezvous for treasonous Sons of Liberty conspirators who tested incendiary "Greek Fire" on two government warehouses and a private furniture store on July 1, perhaps underscoring authorities' clampdown on treason. Apparently part of the grand "Northwest Conspiracy," such activities further provoked Union authorities into more general paranoia, especially when Morgan's final raid in the Bluegrass seemed tied to both political and terrorist activities. In fact, this threat level prompted Union authorities to plan and construct fortifications at key sites across central and northern Kentucky, particularly guarding the southern and eastern approaches to Louisville under the guidance of army engineer Lieutenant Colonel James H. Simpson and his assistant U.S. engineer, civilian, John R. Gilliss. Still, eleven redoubts and twelve batteries built along a ten-and-a-quarter-mile arc, anchored on the banks of the Ohio River on either side of that city might be termed later "a string of quite unnecessary" works. Certainly, other places could rightly claim more validity given the extent of threat over four years' time.[43]

In fact, Kentucky's defenses provided engineers and bureaucrats a mission in time of peril. The earthen forts, typically named for fallen Union officers (a pattern followed elsewhere), boasted perimeters of 550–700 feet, included a magazine and a well (to provide garrisoning troops the means to endure siege), and could mount up to six guns. Not meant to permanently house assisting troops, these works were mainly rallying points and were apparently unlinked by intervening rifle trenches. Construction once more proved in short supply with resort to impressments of black and white labor. At Louisville, only the guns in Fort McPherson were ever mounted, and newspaper editor Prentice wanted a new line of road-guarding works on high ground well to the forward of the city by time of the system's completion in late fall 1864. In retrospect, the war was waning by this point, even if official Confederate strategies still included some march to the Ohio. That said, guerrilla incursions in the countryside were not finished, and the fort system may be said to have deterred raids into the river town just as at other locales. In the end, the Louisville system guarded a city of storehouses, hospitals, and a wartime population disrupted in its normal pursuits. Simpson's November annual report testified to the threat that caused occupation authorities to divert labor, garrisons, and ordnance from main army needs elsewhere to the south.[44]

As in Memphis, Nashville, and smaller towns in the occupied upper heartland, Kentucky benevolent associations sprang up to succor widows and orphans. Governor Bramlette even suggested slave owners remuneration for military use of their labor be applied to such aid. But Kentucky, like Tennessee, did not cope well with displaced population either psychologically or physically. The two states wartime record with handling black and white refugees bordered on the scandalous. East Tennessee unionist whites fed Kentucky training rendezvous like Camp Dick Robinson with potential soldiery and, eventually their families in many cases, fleeing persecution and guerrilla depredations back home. Similarly, slaves—contraband—from Union-liberated sections to the south, as well as from restless Kentucky, sought refuge at Federal installations like Camp Nelson in Jessamine County. Built on the north side of the Kentucky River palisades at Hickman Bridge on the Lexington-Danville Turnpike, and set up the year before to aid Burnside's expedition to Knoxville and East Tennessee, the camp became redundant to a large extent in the wake of that successful operation. Yet the concentration of facilities and labor (including liberated slaves), and the recruitment of Kentucky's slaves for soldiers, resuscitated the camp in 1864. While Federal authorities dithered that Morgan's last incursion had targeted Camp Nelson, only to discover the installation offered little allure for such raiders, the facilities beckoned black recruits and their families, raising a different set of problems by the summer and fall of 1864.[45]

The social dimension of war illustrated the Federal government's lack of planning for a fundamental stabilization and reconstruction issue: what to do with displaced people. Continual logistical needs of the army and the blatant hostility of white, slave-owning Kentucky to black soldiery led, by November 1864, to expulsions and inhumane living conditions for "freed people" at "contraband" or freedmen's refugee camps like Camp Nelson, as well as at similar facilities at Louisville and Lexington in the Bluegrass, Huntsville in north Alabama, and Nashville, Gallatin, Clarksville, Pulaski, and Memphis in Tennessee. This experiment with humanitarian relief in the wake of combat produced indifference if not criminal neglect of human suffering at some of locations according to an end-of-year assessment by two special War Department commissioners. The private Sanitary Commission and Christian Commission both investigated Camp Nelson, leading to establishment of the camp's Refugee Home along with the logistical requirements for the facility.

Social, economic, and political problems of the commonwealth notwithstanding, the financial position of the state at least remained sound. While expending $3.5 million for military purposes, a 40 percent tax rate enabled debt reduction from 1859 to 1865 in the range of $5.6 to $5.2 million. The Federal government apparently owed the state $1.9 million noted Coulter. Much of this was of small comfort to the average citizen whose investment in property—real and human—suffered great loss by 1864. No wonder Kentuckians feared the heavy impact of emancipation and army occupation. As Bluegrass historians Lowell Harrison and James Klotter so succinctly put it, "Armies cause property losses whether they are friend or foe." Whether fence rails were burned, labor was run off, property was assessed, or crops and livestock were lost, Kentuckians (if not the state itself) underwent staggering revenue losses by 1864. The animosity generated by Federal officials and policies—incalculable in real dollar amounts—turned many citizens against Washington. This fact would reverberate politically long after the fighting ended and onerous legislation "for the duration" passed into memory.[46]

One particular group seemed the most responsible for the unceasing turbulence and dislocation in 1864 Kentucky. That group mixed legally constituted Confederate partisan rangers with a rogue, criminal element that swarmed unchecked across the upper South by midwar. Estimated at about twenty-eight hundred in number, many of these roaming predators remained after Morgan's catastrophic final raid in the state. For example, Morgan had sent Colonel Jack Allen back into the state in late August to round up the flotsam of the raid. "I told them that they were a curse to their friends, to the Confederate government and to everything that they were a curse to society and ought to go," but only 120 recalcitrants showed up at the appointed rendezvous. The rest stayed at their newfound trade, sparing no individual targets, not even the Shaker village of Pleasant Hill, where "booty and plunder may attract their cupidity to our peaceful borders." Periodically visited by both armies during the war, the Pleasant Hill pacifist community remained fairly quiet during the summer of 1864. Then the situation worsened with outrider thievery of horses, particularly galling to the Believer following. On the night of October 7, 1864, former Morgan follower Captain Sam "One-Armed" Berry (himself reared at Pleasant Hill) and accomplices such as Jerome "Sue Mundy" Clarke (a veteran of Fort Donelson and, like Berry, several years in Morgan's cavalry before turning guerrilla) attacked the mail stage over Shawnee Run near the Shaker's mill. Not content to rummage the mail sacks and rob the travelers, the band accosted others in the neighborhood, relieving them of personal belongings and threatening their persons. Bank robberies soon followed and a general tone of lawlessness descended upon the state. Guerrillas, outlaws, and even defending Kentucky Home Guards and Union regiments mixed in inglorious mayhem. Perhaps the only thing of note to emerge from such episodes was creation of a folk hero—Clarke as "Sue Mundy."[47]

Indeed, law-abiding Kentuckians like George Browder suffered through it all. His diary became a litany of robberies and slave treachery, as well as a record of his avoidance of military service. "I will not gird on carnal weapons and go forth to stain my hands in the blood of battle, then return to minister at Gods altar," he wailed in September. His account captured the major issues confronting common Kentuckians little chronicled by later historians. On September 2, Browder went to Russellville to sell his tobacco harvest and pay debts. Many people were in town paying off assessments to indemnify union citizens for

losses by rebels and guerrillas, he noted. One N. H. Waters, "whose negroes house, provisions and happiness are all destroyed in the war, was
assessed $200 more and being unable to pay it has left the country."
Back on April 23, he had bemoaned the escalating horse stealing and
bank heists, citing "bands of soldiers, organized for protection to the
country, steal away from their commands disguised as rebel guerrillas
and rob whatever they can." By autumn, because of military oppression
in Kentucky and imposition of the draft, "great numbers of men are
going to the rebel army; few beside Negroes are going to the other. It
is said that guerrillas threaten the lives of all who put in Negro substitutes [for whites in the draft]." Robber outrages continued, an almost
unbroken litany for the year.[48]

Was the upper heartland ready for Confederate deliverance in late 1864?
Had Union military occupation coupled with guerrilla or partisan disruption created conditions ripe for Confederate liberation? Would persecuted Kentuckians as well as Tennesseans rally should a Confederate
army move north as it had two years before? Perryville lay in memory;
Bragg and Kirby Smith were preoccupied elsewhere. The *Frankfort
Daily Commonwealth* had observed in 1863, "Bayonets, dungeons, and
court martials we fear will not do." Governor Bramlette subsequently
declared that "wanton oppression of citizens, fraud, corruption, and
imbecility, have too frequently characterized the military career of some
[Federal] officers in Kentucky." Yet one Bluegrass Confederate participant in Morgan's final foray, headquarters captain Edward O. Guerrant,
wrote in his diary how "recruiting has about 'played out' in Kentucky."
Few young men could be found and those in "'*delicate health*' (desperately afflicted with '*indisposition*' to *join the army*)." The young men, he
sneered, "are a shameless, spiritless, down headed, subjugated, elegantly
dressed & strarched set of unconscious slaves to Lincoln & his negro
soldiers." But the old men, women, and children, Guerrant thought,
"generally are truly rebel, heart & soul, perhaps more unanimously,
bitterly, & devotedly Southern in sentiment than at any time during the
war." The women and children in particular, "are the only part of the
once gallant, & chivalric people of K'y, who dare speak their sentiments
to their friends even."[49]

   As in Tennessee, some percentage of Kentuckians might have welcomed deliverance, and perhaps more so in 1864 than when Bragg had
appeared in the state. Brigadier General Nathaniel C. McLean cer-

tainly thought so. Writing to his wife from Lexington on December 1 (and virtually every day thereafter for a fortnight), on the one hand he doubted Washington authorities would be "gulled" by Governor Bramlette's profession of loyalty. "If they do, Kentucky may as well be given over to the rebels at once, for Bramlette is surely under their influence." The government, McLean decided "might as well look upon this state as decidedly rebel, and act upon that idea." Two additional years of Yankee oppression (homegrown and imported) had enhanced that possibility. As analyst of Kentucky government, Penny Miller, states perceptively, "Kentucky became an early example of the hostility of an aggrieved, occupied population, depressed and injured by the suppression of a guerrilla war." And as Kentuckian and future Harvard paleontologist and geologist Nathaniel Southgate Shaler later reminisced, "Not only did the Civil War maim the general [class] of Kentuckians to which I belonged, it also broke up the developing motive of intellectual climate of the commonwealth." By 1864, Henry Clay's home place had retreated from comity, civility, and conciliation. It may have been ripe for Confederate takeover.[50]

CHAPTER 8

Playing Hell in Tennessee:
Spring Hill/Franklin

Longstreet did not entirely devote the winter lull of 1863–64 to purging subordinate dissidents and watching Federal activities in East Tennessee. By February, subsisting his army loomed paramount. Yet down time permitted planning to regain the initiative. Longstreet was not alone. He joined a select group that included President Jefferson Davis and his inner circle of advisers, including Braxton Bragg and Robert E. Lee plus senior field commanders Joseph E. Johnston, P. G. T. Beauregard, and Leonidus Polk. Beauregard had ridden this cause since December and may truly have been the only grand strategic thinker in that group. Finding alternatives to static winter encampment and supply problems may have guided deliberations at Longstreet's level. Then, as spring grew closer, loftier aims intruded.

Lofty Goals and Realities

Longstreet especially pushed active and innovative schemes that, in the words of his biographer William Garrett Piston "showed remarkable breadth of vision." A combination of inadequate resources, weaknesses in collaborative action, and competing priorities from other theaters doomed planning to inertia. Still, Confederate leaders had not relinquished their dream of returning to the upper heartland, even permanently establishing their western national frontier on the banks of the Ohio River. Discussion and intent fell prey to events, especially Federal seizure of the initiative by late spring. Six months of subsequent stale-mate in the East and further defeats defending Atlanta simply delayed any Confederate resurgence in the West. Still, the dream remained.[1]

The verbiage expended upon the grand strategic offensive between February and April was impressive. A so-called western bloc of Confed-erate commanders convinced Richmond of the dire threat to the deeper South. Even Lee recognized that both problems and opportunities lay there. On February 18, he wrote Davis in usual quiet understatement, "It is very important to repossess ourselves of Tennessee, as also to take the initiative before our enemies are prepared to open the campaign." He advocated dispatching his old lieutenant Longstreet into Kentucky to do so. Longstreet proposed that a move to Bluegrass be joined by an energized Johnston. Together they might hold the ground until first Grant, later Sherman, had to withdraw to protect logistical lifelines as well as disputed territory. But Lee thought of a large raid rather than permanent reoccupation; Bragg dreamed of redeeming his 1862 failure. Johnston customarily balked because of (1) problems of coop-eration and coordination with Longstreet and (2) his preference for defeating the Yankees coming down the Chattanooga-to-Atlanta rails before undertaking anything so strenuous as a major counter-offensive. Longstreet advocated mounting his infantry on horses and mules drawn from everyone else, including Lee, and by March even pushed for his former boss to join him in a Kentucky endeavor.[2]

Then everyone faced reality—the lack of resources. Intervening mountains also posed an insurmountable barrier as logistical difficul-ties using a Pound Gap avenue to the Bluegrass were compounded by enemy blockage of any direct route via the railroads north through the Tennessee Valley into Middle Tennessee. Longstreet then envisioned coordinated mounted strikes with Wheeler and Forrest. Still, when John Bell Hood reached northern Georgia, he wrote enthusiastically back to Davis how a reinforced move from that locale "should be suf-ficient to defeat and destroy all the Federals on this side of the Ohio River." "I never before felt that we had it so thoroughly in our power," he added. Federal movements ultimately stymied such a move.[3]

Johnston remained recalcitrant, the high command equivocated, and Union supreme commander Ulysses S. Grant's initiative in Virginia spooked Richmond. Longstreet eventually returned to help Lee in the East and the Federals' spring and summer western offensive ground re-lentlessly to conclusion at Atlanta. More deferential in his memoirs than wartime correspondence would suggest, "Old Pete" on at least two occasions underscored a particular grand strategic point. Writing to Confederate quartermaster general A. R. Lawton on March 5 and Brigadier Thomas Jordan (Beauregard's chief of staff for the Department of South Carolina, Georgia, and Florida) three weeks later, Longstreet noted how an early campaign would "have a greater effect upon our people and upon our cause than anything that may happen at a later day." He cited breaking up the "enemy's arrangements early" so that the enemy would recover neither position nor morale "until the Presidential election is over, and we shall then have a new President to treat with." If President Abraham Lincoln had any success, "he will be able to get more men and may be able to secure his own re-election." In that event, the war would go on for four more years. So Longstreet prodded that the South must "exert ourselves to the utmost of our resources to finish the war this year."[4]

Moreover, Longstreet told Jordan, the enemy would be more or less demoralized and disheartened by the great loss of territory sustained by a major Confederate counter-offensive north to the Ohio. The Federals would have great difficulty recruiting fresh manpower before the fall elections "when in all probability Lincoln will be defeated and peace will follow in the spring." Lincoln's political opponents "can furnish no reason at this late day against the war so long as it is successful with him, and thus far it has certainly been as successful as any one could reasonably expect." If, however, noted Longstreet, Lincoln's opponents "were to find at the end of three years that we held Kentucky and were as well to do as at the beginning of the war, it would be a powerful argument against Lincoln and against the war." The Union president's reelection, Longstreet perceptively decided, "seems to depend upon the result of our efforts during the present year; if he is reelected, the war must continue, and I see no way of defeating his re-election except by military success." As his biographer Piston concluded, "The will to victory can be as important as industrial resources, and that it is difficult at best to wage a war without public support." Longstreet might have underestimated the difficulties achieving his goal. He nonetheless recognized that "strategic maneuvers of such dazzling proportions" might collapse northern morale, defeat their sitting president and lead to peace negotiations. What others had dismissed in the spring might still be possible, even after Atlanta's fall before fall rains and winter cold covered the landscape.[5]

The immediate question for both sides after Atlanta was what to do next? Sherman itched to go for the coast—either the gulf or the Atlantic—making Georgia, Alabama, or anywhere else howl. However,

Hood's Army of Tennessee, though beaten, was still intact, and cavalry raids soon intruded. When remaining Federals south of Atlanta began pulling back on September 6, Hood shifted his own forces to Palmetto Station on the West Point Railroad southwest of the city. Here, Hood could maintain a lifeline to resupply of food and munitions from Alabama and Georgia although he was far too weak to directly attack Sherman. Atlanta may have fallen, but the two gladiators remained intact. In turn, Sherman proposed to Washington that he should "remove all the Inhabitants of Atlanta, sending those committed to our cause to the Rear & the Rebel families to the front," allow no trade, manufactories or any citizens there at all" so as to have "the entire use of railroad back as also such corn & forage as may be reached by our troops." Sherman recognized that Atlanta ("which was & is our grand objective point already [being] secure") could not be defended, although his men quickly built a tighter cordon of defensive works than their opponents had erected earlier. He also saw the liability of logistics back to the Ohio River and no other Union operations either for Mobile or in Virginia offered immediate interest. To historian Albert Castel, Sherman was "a victor who cannot exploit his victory, a conqueror who is unable to continue conquering." To American military historian Matthew Forney Steele, Sherman "had not accomplished all, for Hood's army, the chief objective, had escaped." Benson Bobrick, George H. Thomas's biographer, feels he had "not accomplished half."[6]

Logistics continued to dictate options since Sherman had failed "to smash Hood's army or, at the very least, to drive it out of the state," notes Castel. No matter how marginally successful had been Wheeler's attempt to destroy the railroads back in Middle Tennessee, both sides realized that lifeline remained the Yankees' Achilles heel. So while Hood sparred with Sherman's controversial plan to depopulate Atlanta ("that transcends, in studied and ingenious cruelty," stated the Confederate general), both armies rested, happy to be freed even temporarily from endless marches and ever-present prospect of wounding and death. Ultimately, developments unfolded at Palmetto Station that would shape the fate of the upper heartland. The wild card remained Hood and his army; the target of the moment, Sherman's unbroken railroad. In the words of Hood's latest biographer, Brian Craig Miller, Hood simply "needed to orchestrate a military maneuver so bold that it could eradicate the failure at Atlanta not only from the minds of the Confederate citizens, but also alleviate pressure Lee felt as he stood trapped within Petersburg."[7]

If Wheeler earlier had failed to smash Sherman's lifeline, "Cump" Sherman had failed to accomplish General-in-Chief Ulysses S. Grant's original intent that he "break up" the main Confederate army in the West. Still, Sherman proudly told his father-in-law, Thomas Ewing, back in Ohio in mid-September, "The Grand Outlines contemplated these Grand Armies moving on Richmond, Atlanta & Montgomery Alabama, & Mine alone has yet reached its goal." Then he admitted, "I am now at a loss, for the 'next.'" He wrote wife Ellen how he feared the world would conclude "that because I am in Atlanta the work is done." Far from it, he wrote: "We must *kill* these three hundred thousand I have told you of so often, and the further they run the harder for us to get them." Hood's army, like its commander, was crippled and numbered under forty thousand effectives. Hood remained remarkably agile, and Sherman's logistics beckoned, as did redemption of Tennessee and Kentucky. Davis arrived with hope for both.[8]

Davis had visited his second great army previously on such somber occasions: in December 1862, after Bragg's failed Kentucky campaign, and the following October after his pyrrhic Chickamauga victory. As before, the embattled Mississippian now sought to bolster public morale and plot a new strategy of survival. His arrival at Hood's headquarters by 3:00 p.m. on September 25 signified changes were in store. With many in the army clamoring for the return of Johnston to command, and inadequate supply of food, clothing, and ammunition as well as pay causing much grumbling, open controversy had broken out between Hood and senior corps commander William J. Hardee, adding to the grave strategic situation. Suddenly, Davis made decisions that would continue the controversies of how he and the government managed the war. Hood would be retained, Hardee sent to command on the Atlantic Coast and another of the president's old nemeses, P. G. T. Beauregard, brought in to supervise Hood along with Richard Taylor in a new Military Division of the West. Hard drinking but energetic Frank Cheatham would replace Hardee as corps commander. Similar in age to fellow Tennessean Alexander P. Stewart, the army's second corps commander, Cheatham, had served with the army throughout the war. Ten years their junior, was the peripatetic Stephen Dill Lee, sometime artillerist under Robert E. Lee and Nathan Bedford Forest's superior, who had succeeded Hood as a third corps commander back in July. All would figure prominently in the next adventures of the western army.[9]

Since these subordinates had not operated together in this capacity, the next step would require seasoning for this new command structure.

Davis and Hood (before the president and his aides departed for Montgomery at 6:00 p.m. on the twenty-seventh) reviewed the army to both favorable response and dissident jeering of "bring back Johnston." One Texas soldier firmly believed that the president's visit boded ill for the future. They delivered pep talks, witnessed the unshod and disheveled look to the battle-worn force, and developed a preliminary sort of strategy. Hood would expand the raiding operations of Wheeler, Forrest, and Morgan, this time using the whole army. He would head north on the Western and Atlantic, destroying Sherman's railroad, and draw him out of Atlanta to battle north of the Chattahoochee River. For a time, it worked.[10]

Rebel Risk Taking

The Confederates evacuated their Palmetto camps and crossed the Chattahoochee River on September 29–30, easily gobbling up railroad garrisons at Big Shanty, Acworth, and Moon's Station on October 3 and 4. A nonplussed Sherman wired Grant and Washington how he would not be forced to retreat. Why not send an adequate force north to cope with the new threat, destroy Atlanta, "and then march across Georgia to Savannah or Charleston, breaking roads and doing irreparable damage?" We cannot remain on the defensive, he contended. Just four days earlier he had written Lincoln how "it would have a bad effect" to return any material part of his army to guard roads for it would weaken and eliminate his ability to act offensively "if the occasion calls for it." He did dispatch his most dependable subordinate, Thomas, to Nashville to gird Middle Tennessee initially for Forrest's raiders. Sherman then appointed a new face to consolidate cavalry operations—young James Harrison Wilson. Harrison would assist Thomas in preparing the mounted force for Hood's coming.[11]

Yankee defenses stiffened when rebel Major General Samuel G. French's division of Stewart's corps reached Allatoona, thirty miles northwest of Atlanta on October 5. Confederate intent to fill the railroad cut and destroy the railroad bridge over the Etowah River went unrealized, so Hood's main force then moved circuitously to the west through Cave Spring. It met another reverse at Resaca, but recovered momentum at Dalton and Tilton farther north by midmonth. The Dalton garrison included African American troops and a nasty confrontation ensued upon their surrender, although nothing approaching a repeat of the Fort Pillow episode. For a while, Hood appeared to be winning the task of turning Sherman back on himself, thus losing all the previously hard-won ground. Feelings of cheer and despair mixed as the southerners marched northward. Just the opposite attended the boys in blue following them if the thoughts of Private J. J. Werth, less than a month in the ranks of Company F, Forty-third Illinois, were any indication. Writing to a cousin on November 9th from Chattanooga, he gloated how, on the eighteenth of the previous month, Union mounted troops had captured two cannon and the battle flag of the Eighth or Terry's Texas Rangers while killing five, wounding twenty-five or thirty and capturing "quite a number of them." They had pursued the Johnnies as far as Rome, then retired and were on their way back to Nashville, where Thomas was "organizing an Army to operate against Hood [who] from reports he intends going to Ky. But if he does he will never get back as Bragg did. He then told his cousin, "the northern traitors have about played out and the papers this morning speak well for Uncle Abe [since] the States as far as heard from have gone Union." He closed, "I am well and in good spirits hoping the war may soon end."[12]

The same day that Davis appeared at Hood's Palmetto Station headquarters, Richard Taylor, the newly minted commander of the Department of Alabama, Mississippi, and East Louisiana, penned a letter to presidential adviser Braxton Bragg from Selma, Alabama. Taylor spoke tellingly of disarray across the Confederate effort in the West. He cited "frequent changes of commanders and the number of offices acting under orders from the different bureaus at Richmond and independent of the Departmental commander." District and subdistrict commanders functioned semiautonomously, troops were dispersed over the lower South, which prevented concert of action, and "hence the enemy raids the country with impunity in all directions." No sooner had Taylor reached Meridian, Mississippi, then Forrest was ordered to assist Wheeler in attacking Sherman's rear in Tennessee, helped by Phillip D. Roddey, covering his north Alabama district. Unless Sherman "can be forced from his present position," suggested the president's brother-in-law, "there is but little to be accomplished in this Department." He told Bragg that the Confederacy appeared to have "put forth our entire strength on this side of the Mississippi," and if faced with another campaign, "it is difficult to see whence we are to draw reserves to fill up our ranks." The Trans-Mississippi provided the most fertile opportunity "to create a powerful diversion," he thought. Perhaps Beauregard could bring order from such disparities.[13]

Nonetheless, Hood suddenly achieved exactly what Sherman most dreaded. He drew his opponent out of Atlanta, perplexing the Union commander with damage to the railroad at every turn yet never standing to give battle. Much later, Sherman vented that "thirty-five thousand new ties, and six miles of iron," seemed a heavy price to pay for the backpedaling while watching what Hood was doing. And at the time his letters to wife Ellen showed restiveness being on the defensive, dependant upon the moves of a more mobile if inconsistent enemy and anxious to be off on his own hook. Suddenly, after Dalton, Hood slipped southwest to Gadsden, Alabama, by October 19–21 (acquiring "a thorough supply of shoes and other stores" in the process). At this point, Hood noted later, "I determined to cross the Tennessee River at or near Gunter's Landing and strike the enemy's communications again near Bridgeport, force him to cross the river also to obtain supplies, and thus we should at least recover our lost territory." Meanwhile, Beauregard ordered Forrest north into Tennessee. Hood needed his own cavalry to protect trains but "was compelled to delay the crossing and move farther down the river" to meet Forrest. Stiffening Federal opposition and the rain-swollen waters of the Tennessee River also became a factor.[14]

Hood played loose with his own superiors. Beauregard caught up with him at Cave Spring, Georgia, and again at Gadsden, Alabama, and learned that Richmond had acceded to Hood's new scheme for Tennessee. He believed his subordinate when Hood told him that Sherman lacked provisions and forage at Atlanta, his "wheel transportation was in wretched condition," and repair of the railroad between Marietta and Dalton would require five or six weeks. Meanwhile, the Army of Tennessee could destroy the railroad bridges at Bridgeport and across the Elk and Duck Rivers (all before Sherman could finish track repairs below Chattanooga) and force the Union leader "to return to Tennessee to protect his communications and obtain supplies." As Forrest rode into West Tennessee, Taylor moved to secure the railroad communications in Mississippi and Middle Alabama "for the transportation of supplies" to support Hood. President Davis, stump speaking to rally disheartened and almost rebellious Georgians and Alabamians after the fall of Atlanta, publicly leaked Hood's purpose to friend and foe alike. In speeches at Augusta, Georgia, and Columbia, South Carolina, the chief executive noted Hood's "hand upon Sherman's line of communication" and how, within the month, the army would be searching for passage of the Tennessee River headed north. Newspaper accounts alerted Sherman and Grant while the soldiery gleaned as much from captured rebel mail.[15]

Sherman's Response

Sherman wrote Thomas about Hood's moves from Rome, Georgia, on October 29. "No, I want you to be all ready for him if he enters Tennessee," as "he will work as fast as possible, for winter is coming, but he cannot haul supplies and will be dependent on the country," counseled Sherman. He would relieve "Old Pap" of responsibilities for East Tennessee north of Knoxville and wanted his trusted subordinate to concentrate all outlying railroad and occupation garrisons so as to "get about Columbia [Tennessee] as big an army as you can and go at him." He promised to send David Stanley and the IV Corps, as well as John Schofield with the XXIII Corps, back to help Thomas and, in fact, reduced his own Georgia strike force to just fifty thousand men. "Rush things," he ordered subordinates, for intelligence revealed that "the enemy has passed to the west of Decatur, and, therefore, will cross about Florence." Sherman wondered how Beauregard might support this army, but "Jeff. Davis is desperate, and his men will undertake anything possible." With Decatur secure "and a good gun-boat force up at the head of navigation," he thought, "the enemy will be bold to enter Tennessee; but we must expect anything."[16]

During the first week in November, Sherman similarly detailed to Grant all measures designed to cope with Hood, attempting to quell concern that the enemy's field army should be attended to before any great raid to the sea. He reckoned Hood had about thirty thousand men and that Wheeler and Roddey, not Forrest, provided his "eyes and ears" of cavalry. He thought Forrest was "scattered from Eastport to Jackson, Paris and the lower Tennessee," as Thomas had told him about the capture of a gunboat and transports near Johnsonville. He iterated that Stanley with fifteen thousand men, as well as Schofield's ten thousand combatants, had gone back to defend Nashville, Chattanooga, and Decatur ("all strongly fortified and provisioned for a long siege"). He anticipated Hood's cavalry "may do a good deal of damage," but that Wilson's dismounted force could be rebuilt and resupplied from depots in the rear. He anticipated return of two divisions from William Rosecrans in Missouri. He promised his superiors, "I will destroy all the railroads of Georgia and do as much substantial damage as is possible," reaching the seacoast while "trusting that General Thomas, with all present troops and the influx of new troops promised, will be able in a very few days to assume the offensive."[17]

With the telegraph conveying the negotiation between the western armies' commander and Washington, Sherman decided that, "Thomas will have a force strong enough to prevent [Hood's] army reaching any country in which we have an interest and he has orders if Hood turns to follow me, to push for Selma [Alabama]. From his own vantage point, Sherman regarded "a pursuit of Hood as useless," for unless he gave up Atlanta itself, "my force will not be equal to his." Sherman worried on November 6 that he "felt compelled to what is usually a mistake in war—divide my forces," by sending part back into Tennessee while retaining the balance. And he worried that he should have "dogged" Hood "far over into Mississippi, trusting to some happy accident to bring him to bay and to battle." He had dismissed such alternatives as playing into the enemy's hands by "being drawn or decoyed too far away from our original line of advance."[18]

Having "no uneasiness on the score of Hood reaching my main communications," the fact that his army was "in great distress about provisions, as he well must be," that "that devil Forrest" was "making havoc among the Gunboats and Transports" but that Schofield's troops and other arriving gunboats would "repair that trouble," Sherman reminded Grant that "we now have abundant supplies at Atlanta, Chattanooga and Nashville with the Louisville and Nashville R. Road, and the Cumberland River unmolested." The threat to get "on my rear or on my communications was a miserable failure." By November 10, "I also will have the troops all paid, the Presidential election over and out of our way, and I hope the early storms of November, now prevailing, will also give us the chance of a long period of fine healthy weather for campaigning."[19]

Confirming receipt of Grant's go-ahead order of November 2 to march to the sea, Sherman laid the groundwork for baffling the enemy as to his own movements. Alluding to the Confederate president's indiscretion at communicating state secrets in public, an obviously exuberant Sherman wired Assistant Secretary of War Charles A. Dana on November 10, suggesting how since "indiscreet newspaper men" published information too close to the truth, the war department might counteract with other paragraphs "calculated to mislead the enemy." The notion that "Sherman's army has been much reinforced," especially in cavalry, and that he will soon move by several columns in circuit, "so as to catch Hood's army," or that Sherman's destination was not Charleston but rather Selma, where he would meet an army coming north from the Gulf Coast, numbered among Sherman's deceptive suggestions. To the humorless army chief of staff, Henry Halleck, he wired on the eleventh, "All appearances still indicate that Beauregard has got back to his old hole at Corinth, and I hope he will enjoy it," his own army preferring "to enjoy the fresh sweet-potato fields of the Ocmulgee." He had "balanced all the figures well, and am satisfied that General Thomas has in Tennessee a force sufficient for all probabilities." Tomorrow "our wires will be broken, and this is probably my last dispatch." The next day he wrote Ellen, "We start today."[20]

Unforeseen Seasonal Delay

Sherman thought about Confederate trajectory. "I can hardly believe that Beauregard would attempt to work against Nashville from Corinth as a base at this stage of the war, but all information seems to point that way," he wrote Thomas at midnight on November 11 before leaving Atlanta. Apparently lending more credence to the Creole's abilities or control than those of Hood, Thomas "could safely invite Beauregard across the Tennessee River and prevent his ever returning." Sherman still thought public clamor in the South "will force him to turn and follow me," in which case Thomas should cross at Decatur and drive for Selma "as far as you can transport supplies." His notion that Beauregard, not Hood, managed affairs was similarly mistaken. Beauregard later wrote that "a great deal had been left to future determination, and even to luck." "Circumstances will determine when and where" the Army of Tennessee will cross the Tennessee River," he wired Richmond on October 22.[21]

No doubt Beauregard came to believe that both Hood and the president "were not accustomed to command armies in the field, especially armies like ours, for the management of which much had to be foreseen, and much prepared or created." While that could be said of generals and politicians on both sides, Davis, Beauregard, and Hood had little to work with in the case of the upcoming Tennessee campaign. Hood's movement into the Tennessee Valley, presaging the turn northward, soon encountered logistical facts of life—a broken infrastructure for rapid resupply. Federal garrisons and Confederate raiders had eaten out the upper tier counties of Alabama and Mississippi. Hood's westward movement further dictated switching a base of operations from Georgia to Alabama and Mississippi, no mean feat at this stage of the war for the Confederacy. Then, too, without mentioning much in dispatches and reports, Hood encountered Sherman's rear echelons defending river crossings. Inability to cross at Gunter's Landing shunted the Confederates farther west. The march from Gadsden to the vicinity of Decatur, Alabama, consumed the week of October 19–28, important days for fall campaigning, already touched by autumn rains and frost. Then, Brigadier General Robert S. Granger and his Decatur garrison played a pivotal role shaping the fate of Hood's endeavor.[22]

Sherman wired Thomas that Hood would never assault Decatur in force since "Allatoona and Resaca beat him off, and neither was as strong as Decatur." Indeed, heavy skirmishing and intrepid defense by both white and black Federal troops (including Colonel Thomas J. Morgan's Fourteenth U.S. Colored Troops, shifted hurriedly from the Chattanooga garrison), proved Sherman right. Hood again slipped westward, intending first to cross at Lamb's Ferry and then at Bainbridge but finally concentrating at Tuscumbia across from Florence, Alabama. Here he wired Taylor on the last day of October asking for "at once, twenty days' supply of breadstuffs and salt" plus other provisions. The high command had fooled even their own army. Tennessean W. J. McDill (who would not survive the campaign) wrote his sister that "most of us 'eleven dollar' generals expected to cross the line at Guntersville but Gen. Beauregard and Hood out generaled us." The triangle of Bainbridge, Tuscumbia, and Florence now became the final staging area for the rebel army to get across the river. "While en route to Gunter's Landing," said Beauregard, "I learned, casually and to my surprise that the line of march of our forces had been changed to one in the direction of Decatur, at which point I overtook it." He prepared to confront Hood about whether to return to counter Sherman or to press on with the Tennessee operation.[23]

Nearly two months had elapsed since the fall of Atlanta. The protective army for Georgia now stood two hundred miles out of range. The pivotal moment had passed when the Army of Tennessee could have retraced its steps "over roads with all the bridges destroyed, and through a desolated country, affording neither subsistence nor forage" while offering ample opportunity for desertions," observed Beauregard later. At the time, he merely wrote a frustrated note to Davis from Tuscumbia on October 31, asking obtusely, "To prevent confusion, please inform me whether my presence with any army in the field imposes on me the necessity of assuming command, and whether in that case it relieves from duty the immediate commander." Should not "my orders pass merely through that officers, without destroying the existing system of organization?" He and Hood maintained separate headquarters. And Beauregard remained perplexed as to how to direct what continued to be a deteriorating Western theater of operations.[24]

Hood, meanwhile, "unsure of what he wanted to do or where he wanted to go," consistently dodged being pinned down by his new superior. Davis told Beauregard somewhat evasively that he had been placed in command of the armies in a section of the country, stating somewhat obliquely, "When present with either army you must exercise immediate command while there, but to retain the contemplated freedom of motion it was designed that you should not relieve the general of the particular army, but, by retaining the organization, be enabled to leave at any moment without impairing administrative efficiency." That did not help much. Apparently Beauregard made his own choice, informing the president on November 3 that "General Hood having conducted present movement successfully I will not assume immediate command unless circumstances require it; meanwhile I will assist as far as practicable." Later he offered that because of restoration of army morale, by assuming the offensive he would merely remain in the role of helpmate, not director. Hood, having regarded Beauregard more as useful counsel (since his independent correspondence with Richmond underscored his own perceived freedom of action), stood aloof from consultation. On November 3, he ordered the movement into Tennessee to begin the following Saturday, the tenth. "Want of supplies and bad weather have delayed forward movement, which will be resumed soon as practicable," Beauregard wired the War Department the same day he finally got Hood to the conference table. In Richmond, Secretary of War James Seddon, drawing upon War Department reports, told Davis that loss of Atlanta "has freed CSA troops while it has 'chained down our enemies to the tenure of a far inland position . . . in the midst of a hostile population.'" Where Union occupation "has been lightened, in Ky. And Tenn., people are rallying to CSA."[25]

The eventual Beauregard-Hood meeting was supposedly tense but momentous. The gist of the Tennessee campaign as something more than a railroad raid now captured even Beauregard's interest. His superior, said Hood later, "left it optional with me either to divide the army, sending a part after Sherman and to push on with the remainder, or to move at once against Thomas with the entire force." Hood thought his army too small to divide and so informed Beauregard who acquiesced to a general movement either toward Columbia or Pulaski as dictated by enemy action. Forrest would assist by screening of the columns. Faulty intelligence as to Sherman's whereabouts hampered the pair's recognition of the true strategic situation and Richmond's perceptions proved no better. On November 7, Davis wrote Hood (not Beauregard) that no reinforcements had been sent west by Grant, that the president assumed Hood had tried his best against Sherman's communications, and that "if you keep his communications broken he will most probably seek to concentrate for an attack upon you." The prophetic final sentence of Davis's note was what Hood desperately sought: "But if, as reported to you, [Sherman] has sent a large part of his force southward, you may first beat him in detail, and subsequently without serious obstruction or danger to the country in your rear, advance to the Ohio River." Beauregard's dispatches to Richmond sounded repetitive: "Movement into Middle Tennessee is still delayed by want of supplies, bad weather, and impassable roads."[26]

Relations between Hood and Beauregard now became turgid. An attempt by the department commander to review army corps incurred a testy exchange when delay affected tempers. Beauregard officially reported later that, "after consultation with General Hood, I concluded to allow him to prosecute with vigor his campaign into Tennessee and Kentucky." Still, the departmental commander dutifully dabbled in preparation details, helping Hood and Stewart (now encamped north of the river about Florence) to protect the bridgehead and pontoon bridge with torpedoes (mines) and batteries against any Union gunboat intervention. The department's chief engineer, Major General Martin Smith, carefully examined recrossing points stretching from Florence to below Eastport at Savannah, Clifton, and Decatur in case of future need. Roddey's security for Hood's new line of communications from Tuscumbia to Corinth to Meridian, Mississippi, also came under scrutiny as did "the condition of the roads in Middle Tennessee, and also of those districts best able to furnish supplies of provisions and forage for the army." Beauregard had promised Adjutant General Samuel Cooper on November 6 that "the army will cross the river and take up its line of march on the 9th, with fifteen days' rations." A week later it had not moved.[27]

Somewhere during the march west from Decatur, one strategic aim —if it ever was that (and one suspects it may not have been as important in Hood's mind as that of the Richmond administration)—fell moot. Any impact by Hood on northern politics went unmet. On November 8, northerners (many of whom had already gone to the polls in October and soldiers like John T. Croxton's cavalry brigade screening Tennessee crossings between Muscle Shoals and Florence) voted Lincoln in for a second term. The meaning, undeviating prosecution of the war to victory on Union terms, was now patently obvious to everyone, North and South. The people had spoken, and whatever Hood accomplished might no longer affect that result in any significant manner. Perhaps it never could have done so, given the Confederates' inability to move into Tennessee and Kentucky in October. Yet nowhere in the correspondence at the time is there much indication that politics had an impact on Hood plans and movement. In fact, perhaps only Davis and his inner circle had ever really thought a Tennessee invasion might effect that result anyway. Still, Hood might occasion some impasse, some impact leading to negotiated settlement that could temper Old Abe's victory.[28]

By mid-November, Beauregard had disengaged from Hood's operation, shifting to inspecting Confederate affairs in northeast Mississippi while directing other commanders in a widely dispersed theater to practice a Fabian strategy against their opponents in order to shepherd resources. He reached Macon, Georgia, on the twenty-fourth, intending to organize defense against Sherman's juggernaut. For a time, he seemed baffled as to whether Augusta or Macon before deciding the Federals' goal was the coast, not interior towns. Indeed, Beauregard was doing what Hood might have done—defending Georgia. That day, he simply wired Davis, "Have ordered General Hood to take active-offensive in Middle Tennessee to relieve General Lee." Five days later he wired, "No news yet from the Army of Tennessee." The chief executive sent word on the thirtieth (ironically, as the battle of Franklin was being fought) that until Hood reached "the country proper of the enemy" (presumably north of the Ohio, perhaps loyal Kentucky), he could scarcely affect either Sherman's or Grant's operations. Observed Davis, those opponents "would regard the occupation of Tennessee and Kentucky of minor importance."[29]

Just as the operation finally got moving on November 13, Hood wrote Davis explaining his actions. He had intended a Gunter's Landing crossing, but Forrest had not crossed into Middle Tennessee as he had urged on Beauregard, and then high water and the fact that he had had to draw upon supplies "from and through a department not under my command" involved delay and "retarded my operations." He leaned on Forrest's arrival as an excuse. Without his assistance "I cannot secure my wagon trains when across the river." But, he assured the president, "you may rely upon my striking the enemy wherever a suitable opportunity presents, and that I will spare no efforts to make that opportunity." Forrest's arrival on the morning of November 14 "was serenaded by the Tennesseans in the evening, to which he responded in a very encouraging speech." Hood also tendered some remarks. Hidden from view were some stark logistical facts. If Hood worried about protecting his wagon trains, others found additional weaknesses.[30]

Division commander Major General Samuel G. French of Stewart's corps confronted Hood at the November 1 command meeting about the dearth of artillery horses for the intended operation. Writing to the chief of field transportation, Lieutenant Colonel A.H. Cole, in Richmond on November 4, Major E. H. Ewing, the army's inspector of field transportation, regaled that official with "the long and very fatiguing march of over a month" whereby he had "never seen so hard a campaign upon troops and transportation." They covered twenty to twenty-five miles a day with "positive orders not to stop for water until the day's march was finished, which was generally in the night; many animals were even then neglected by the negro teamsters." The result was that the army's horses "are fagged down and many rendered utterly useless," thus causing lost recuperating time around Tuscumbia. Furthermore, Hood demanded that all baggage wagons should be converted to conveyances for ordnance and commissary stores, causing "greater confusion than I have ever seen," continued Ewing. It would "require a first rate Philadelphia lawyer to sift out this conglomeration of trains and tell what transfer have been made," he added. He supposed eventually "we will be able to transport all necessary supplies," but the animal problem was far worse.[31]

Replacement for 360 artillery horses required substitution of mules, and "unless the weather and roads are very favorable," said Ewing, "we will have to leave some of our guns in Tennessee, if our raid is unsuccessful and we be forced to come back humbly." Upward of fifteen hundred animals had been used up on the march from Palmetto, he suggested, "and, the number will be doubled if we make as hurried a trip into Tennessee as it is expected we will." He dismissed the value of the many captured animals ("100 horses and many mules and wagons"), as Hood "steadily refuses to let us have anything to do with them, and nobody else takes any interest about it." Sadly, he noted, many of the horses "are constantly being sold and traded off by parties capturing them." Cole, in turn, wrote his superior, Quartermaster General A. R. Lawton, that such situation "should prepare us for the possible total loss for all useful purposes of the magnificent equipment of field transportation with which the Army of Tennessee started on its recent campaign." By the end of November (after interim events), Secretary of War James A. Seddon caustically commented on the Ewing

and Cole finding: "This is a lamentable exhibition of the losses encountered in a hasty movement, which subsequent difficulties have
probably made in a great measure abortive." Of course, Hood planned
on replenishing horses, rations, and other supplies via Middle Tennessee and enemy depots. "Men would join us, horses could be obtained,
and the men be supplied with shoes and clothing," the general had told
French at the conference. "Out of touch with reality," as historian Ann
Bailey put it.[32]

One Civil War scholar, Frank Vandiver, concluded that Hood's
"attenuated line of communications to his sources of supplies was unequal to a prolonged effort, and certainly to a rapid and efficient effort." Earlier, another student of the Tennessee campaign likewise had
termed Hood's delay at Tuscumbia "militarily puzzling" since it was
"not so much due to lack of supplies, Forrest's absence or the necessity
of repairing the rail gap to Cherokee Station." Rather, claimed Thomas
Hay, "it was anxiety concerning what Sherman would do," otherwise,
he would have advanced sooner, "at least by the 7th of November."
Vandiver seemingly concurred, even suggesting that had Hood been
"thoroughly conscious of his logistical position," there could be scarcely
any doubt that he would have advanced sooner and "might have risked
advancing at some point east of Tuscumbia" to relieve the strain on his
own railroad logistics.

Uncertainty about Sherman notwithstanding, the search for the
ideal crossing hampered by high water and Yankee resistance, as well as
the fateful conclusion to reorient his own logistical line to Mississippi,
occasioned the time-wasting westward trek. Such shift taxed the rickety
Confederate rail system in middle Alabama and Mississippi. Vandiver
gratuitously offered the observation that in so doing, Hood committed the greatest cardinal sin of all. He left exposed the Confederacy's
"Ruhr"—the heart of the Confederate ordnance facilities, like the Macon laboratories and Columbus Arsenal in Georgia, as well as, eventually, the Columbia arsenal in South Carolina and the Fayetteville,
North Carolina, arsenal and armory. All were eventually destroyed by
an unopposed Sherman. That lay in the unanticipated future, however,
as the Army of Tennessee embarked on its Quixote-like quest in November. Only after the fact could historians like Vandiver claim that in
carrying out his Tennessee plan, "it must be concluded that although
determined and reckless in battle, [Hood] was, sadly enough, an irresponsible logistician." Perhaps that alone wrecked the endeavor before
it fairly started.[33]

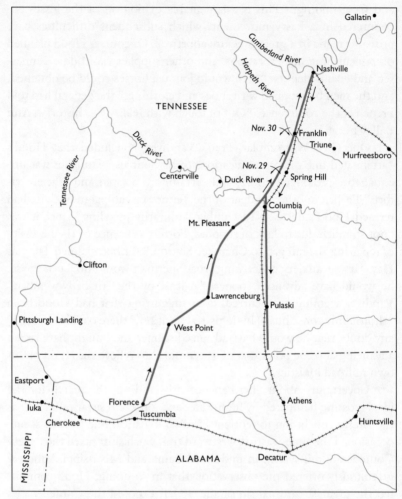

The Tennessee campaign, November and December 1864. Map by Bill Nelson.

Frankly, Hood struck out for Nashville too late in the season and should have known it. Union agents—Croxton's troops and local unionists—as well as fall rains and flood waters damaged the pontoon crossing of the Tennessee in early November. One week's rations on hand were not deemed enough when original estimates sought two weeks supply at least. Hood's strength returned for November 6, 1864, showed "96,481" as present and absent. Yet the only truly meaningful numbers were 44,832 aggregate present, of which 30,500 were termed

1283

"effective." He did not count Forrest, but Beauregard did in a subsequent tally of 34,785 making the trek. Hood's postwar memoirs suggested earlier intentions of taking twenty days of rations in haversacks and wagons, a heavy artillery reserve to cope with gunboats on the Tennessee and to rout his opponents Schofield and Thomas and capture their army before they could reach Nashville. At one point, he spoke of rapidly marching to get in Schofield's rear at Pulaski before the Federals could reach the Duck River crossing. That may have been for Beauregard's benefit, as Hood's superior had harangued him with enjoinders at midmonth to get moving and move fast. Hood knew this while still captivated with grander plans after Nashville, when he would take position in Bluegrass Kentucky near Richmond and threaten Cincinnati while recruiting from Kentucky and Tennessee, especially since "the former State [which] was reported at this juncture, to be more aroused and embittered against the Federals than any other period of the war." He recalled years later the fantasy of moving farther across the mountains to aid Lee in Virginia. First, he needed to beat the Yankees. That proved difficult.[34]

Preparing for the Coming

Federal garrisons all over Tennessee were jittery. Early in the month, soldiers focused on the national election as David M. Wynn of the Forty-fifth Ohio at Pulaski wrote a friend on the eighth how "the soldiers hear in the army of the Cumberlain is all for old Abe Lincoln and we held a Sham Election in our Regt and old Abe got all of the vots." And J. Andrew Morlan of the 107th Illinois, having just reached the ruins of Johnsonville after Forrest's visit, told his parents on the tenth how the regiment had taken a trial vote, with Lincoln garnering 100, "votes for Abe and Andy 143" both, and those for McClellan and Pendleton 43. In his company only one member voted for Little Mac, and Morlan concluded that "any man that voted for Mc voted for the continuation of the war an indefinite length of time." Then, just as suddenly, attention shifted to a greater threat. Treasury special agent William R. Hackley wrote his wife on November 13 that a false alarm with cannon fired, bells rung, and drums beaten two nights before had everyone awake all night in Memphis thinking that Forrest had returned on another raid. "It's Reported that old Hood is adveincing [sic] on this city," Wynn added to his November 8 letter to John Griffith, "and we was ordered to fortify and the Regt. has gone out to work." A Union officer at Benton Barracks in St. Louis told his wife midafternoon on November 22, "Hood is in Tenn and we must watch him, whip him, annihilate him & his army if possible." Sherman was off on his own raid and he could go "where no other general dare look." "God grant he may break the backbone of the rebellion this time and conclude this uncalled for tragedy," he told her. Meanwhile, Thomas scrambled to collect an adequate force south of Nashville to deal with Hood, despite Sherman's confidence that he had provided for such contingency.[35]

Some eight thousand garrison troops at Nashville and various posts in Murfreesboro and Chattanooga, as well as Decatur, Stevenson, Bridgeport, and Huntsville in Alabama, were all at his disposal. Maybe forty-three hundred cavalrymen were available close to the tip of Hood's spear. Brigadier General Edward Hatch counted twenty-five hundred men at Pulaski; Colonel Horace Capron's eight hundred west of that town and Croxton's one thousand at Shoal Creek near Florence provided the forward echelon. They hardly projected a consolidated force-in-being. However, Major General David Stanley's IV Corps (twelve thousand) and Major General John Schofield's XXIII (ten thousand) from Sherman's main army provided the bulk of the upper South defenders. Wilson continued his remounting and rebuilding at Nashville before taking to the field by November 24. Only when the Confederates advanced from Tuscumbia/Florence could Thomas more freely position an army of observation with Stanley and Schofield at Pulaski. Even this situation remained dangerous should the Confederates move quickly and outflank any Union withdrawal back to the state capital. Forrest's Johnsonville raid almost upset the arrangement, anyway. As it was, Schofield had to move quickly to deal with the raider and temporarily leave units at the now-destroyed supply base. Such dispersal threatened Stanley's Pulaski position until Schofield personally arrived and took command there on November 13–14 and Hood's slow movement changed things. Schofield's troops (including the Johnsonville contingent) had positioned at Columbia on the Duck River by the time Hood's columns finally moved north.[36]

As rebel Tom Walker of the Ninth Tennessee recalled, "Although the army was greatly reduced in numbers yet the idea of again entering on Tenn[.] soil made us feel at least we Tennesseans bonant [buoyant] and happy." Forrest's cavalry, having now joined the army, effectively screened Hood's advance against Major General James Harrison Wilson's Federal horsemen. Nevertheless Croxton, Hatch and Capron fell back, disputing Forrest with flashpoints like Campbellsville, Henryville, Fouche Springs, and Mount Pleasant attempting to breach the fog of war. Sleet and snowed began to affect conditions, with the blue-coated troopers outnumbered, dispersed, and often undergunned against their foe. Schofield never quite fathomed Hood's imminent threat. Only by ordering a general withdrawal on November 23–24, could he and his command escape to Columbia. By this point, Wilson had his cavalry deployed behind swollen Duck River.[37]

Despite Forrest's relentless pressure, the Federal army of observation managed to reunite on the Duck River. Meanwhile, Hood's infantry and supply train slogged through enveloping cold, sleet, and snow on wretched roads. Not only Tennessee governor Isham G. Harris but also the controversial Major General Gideon Pillow accompanied the column. (The latter was nursing a broken arm from falling over a fountain in Florence, noted Captain Robert D. Smith of division commander Patrick Cleburne's staff; he had been injured while drunk, according to a slave witness.) These rebels had made it home to what one would term a Middle Tennessee "paradise." Cleburne himself stopped briefly to admire the Polk family's stunning brick St. John's Episcopal Church north of Mount Pleasant and opined, "It would not be hard to die if one could be buried in such a beautiful spot." Within days he would be, dropped with thousands of other men as battles claimed the last flower of the Confederacy's western army. No one knew this at the time as inclement weather settled generally over the landscape by November 27. Three Confederate corps went into position facing Schofield's entrenched Federals south of Columbia on the banks of the Duck River. Having endured a very difficult forty-six mile march from Pulaski to Columbia, Federals like Randolph Rosenberger of the Sixty-fifth Ohio wrote his wife on the eve of his own death the next day at Spring Hill to the north, how he and comrades had gone on picket after digging earthworks and found "the rebels was as thick as a black birds in a corn field." The stage was set for the most climatic moments of the war.[38]

With Wilson's outnumbered cavalry covering Schofield's flanks to the west and east of the town and a stubborn brigade of Kentuckians, Tennesseans, and a smattering of Hoosiers defending the highway crossing on a tongue of land surrounded by the Duck River, Hood seemed unsure if his army would willingly attack fortified positions of the enemy. He called a command conference that evening at the Warfield home east of the Pulaski Pike at Beechlawn. He explained how he intended outflanking his old West Point roommate east of town using Forrest to forge a bridgehead followed by the infantry of Frank

Cheatham and A. P. Stewart as well as Edward Johnson's division from Stephen Lee's corps. The rest of the latter's command plus artillery would pin Schofield in place, lure the Yankees out of their works while the flank column completed the encirclement north of town and river. Schofield, however, was ahead of his old friend. Sensing the danger and concerned that local terrain rendered any defense of Columbia impractical, he wired Thomas, "I shall withdraw to the north bank tonight, and endeavor to prevent him from crossing." By morning of the twenty-eighth, Hood's quarry had eluded him; Schofield again wired his superior that "the withdrawal was completed at daylight this morning without difficulty." As usual, timing was crucial.[39]

Wilson's miscalculation nearly cost Schofield the advantage. Thinking Forrest's aggressive action meant taking the Lewisburg Turnpike directly north to Franklin and thus cut off the army's withdrawal there, Wilson pulled pickets back from the river, giving the Confederates all but uncontested passage of the stream. Undoubtedly Forrest had the advantage and Wilson was too new to the job to thoroughly understand his opponent. Still some of his command, like the Fifth Iowa Cavalry, were seasoned veterans of guerrilla fighting in Middle Tennessee. The Hawkeyes in particular saved the defense during a critical moment when Forrest's troopers pressed Capron's men back across the river at Hardison's Mill. Wilson withdrew, contesting every step to Hurt's Crossroads, easily fifteen miles northeast of Columbia and about five miles from the turnpike crossing at Hardison's Mill. He was completely out of position to screen and scout for Schofield if the Confederates came across the intervening Davis Ford, Huey's Mill, and several other lesser points. Forrest quickly exploited the weakness, driving Wilson's force away from Hood's planned passage of Duck River on the morning of November 29. The armies approached a rendezvous with destiny known as "the Spring Hill affair."[40]

Spring Hill Mysteries

"The enemy must give me fight," Hood told Chaplain Charles T. Quintard, "or I will be at Nashville before to-morrow night." Schofield realized this too, ordering rapid withdrawal as a cold but sunny day broke frost and fog in the Duck River Valley. The so-called mystery or legend, as well as the legacies of Spring Hill, all hinged on roads leading to that sylvan hamlet. They included country lanes and turnpikes, principally the Columbia Pike, paralleling the railroad from town north to Franklin. Yet at play too was the Lewisburg Pike eastward, where Forrest's hip-block had sent Wilson off the playing field. Rally Hill Pike curved westward from the latter highway into Spring Hill. Secondary roads also led there from Hurt's Cross Roads and Mt. Carmel (scene of another of Capron's intrepid rebuffs of Chalmers's horsemen) to the north. And from Carter's Creek Station, midway between Columbia and Spring Hill, a secondary Carter's Creek Turnpike went slightly westward to Franklin, bypassing the Spring Hill bottleneck altogether. Remarkably, by afternoon on November 29, Hood's infantry and cavalry commanded this neighborhood from Duck River northward as they converged on Spring Hill. But they did not close Schofield's principal line of retreat, the Columbia Turnpike. Therein lay the challenge—a race against time, a race ending in resolute Federal defense of Spring Hill mainly against Forrest, and astonishing miscues, miscommunications, and controversy by Hood and his generals.[41]

The bluecoats got to Spring Hill first, but in limited numbers. Alerted by Wilson to the enemy threat that might get behind him and interdict the Columbia-Franklin Pike, Schofield by midafternoon on the twenty-ninth had finally started Major General David Stanley's division and a supply train of eight hundred wagons northward. Stanley placed random infantry, cavalry, and wagon-train guards into defensive positions south and east of Spring Hill during the waning hours of daylight. Hoosier, Illini, Wolverine, and even a unit of loyal Tennessee horsemen performed the task of stopping Forrest's troopers, although Hood directed infantry under Cheatham and others to help put the noose around the Federals. Cheatham and subordinates Cleburne, John C. Brown, and William Bate, even the men of Stewart's corps, received Hood's orders to that effect, although, as it turned out, with completely confusing and uncoordinated result. The upshot was a "total breakdown of communication," which is what the fiasco at Spring Hill "was really about," declared Jerry Keenan in his study of Wilson's cavalry in this campaign. In truth, by midafternoon even Schofield saw the absolute need to get out of Columbia, fretting that perhaps he had tarried too long. Expectant Confederates stood poised to accomplish their task. But as historian Richard McMurry has noted, "The Confederate advance came to a halt with its infantry units scattered over the countryside." Veteran troops "parked in the fields east of the Columbia–Spring Hill Pike, and there they spent the night."[42]

Hood's subordinates sought direction, but their commander thought he had issued such and retired to the Absolam Thompson

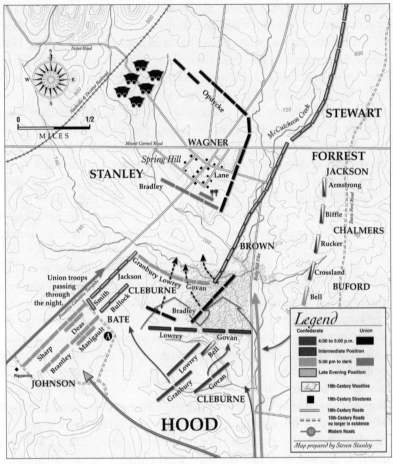

Battle of Spring Hill, November 29, 1864. Map by Steven Stanley and courtesy of the Civil War Preservation Trust.

house, fatigued and perhaps hurting badly from his old war wounds. He left those subordinates and their commands to fumble the opportunity for any number of reasons. These included poor staff work; Federal maneuvers and stalwart defense at key moments of the afternoon and evening that kept principals like Major Generals Benjamin Franklin Cheatham (always accused, it seems, of overreliance on the bottle), William Brimage Bate, and Patrick Ronayne Cleburne at bay; and poor follow-up by Hood and his staff. From the sound of a postwar expostulation of the facts by Tennessee Confederate governor Isham G. Harris, riding with Hood at the time, the heavy skirmishing all afternoon had caused misalignments and Cheatham's stopping short of the turnpike; Cleburne had done no better. Thereafter, Confederate professions of inadequate ammunition and tired troops even by Forrest and Stewart hampered response.

Then too there was a mysterious 3:00 a.m. appearance by a barefoot private, who sought to tell Hood that he had passed undetected through a confused and milling enemy camp and "that they were moving slowly on the road toward Nashville and that he believed a few men could stampede the whole army." Prompted to action, Hood told a staffer, Colonel Penn Mason, to send the soldier and an order to Cheatham to attack at once with "at least a regt. out to fire into them and throw them into confusion." In turn, Cheatham awaited support from Stewart who, ironically, had been told by Hood to rest his men at Rutherford Creek and "not to march his whole corps up to the right." This was Governor Harris's remembrance, at least. And the move failed when Mason admitted later that he had fallen asleep without writing the order! Apparently, everyone did—including Hood—as the Yankees marched past literally under rebel noses. All punctuate a record of mea culpa for the actions of that day and night. As Confederate Major General Samuel G. French wrote sarcastically later, Hood slept, "the heads and the eyes and ears of the army, all dead from sleeping." Bitter was his tone: "Ye gods! Will no geese give them warning as they did in ancient Rome?"

Arguments over blame kept the survivors engaged for years thereafter. And the argument probably will continue in the future. Hood mostly blamed Cheatham, who accepted culpability even though he had never received Mason's unwritten order. Starkly, the facts speak for themselves. Hood had a force of twenty-five thousand men to Stanley's single division of some fifty-five hundred and two hours of daylight remaining to close the trap at Spring Hill. He failed to do so. As Thomas Walker of the Ninth Tennessee put it years later, "Columbia was flanked on the right and we struck the Columbia & Franklin pike at Spring Hill completely in Scoffields [sic] rear about 3 o'clock in evening and from some unknown cause which from that day to this has never been satisfactorially [sic] explained, we lay there until the next morning not over one hundred yards from the pike and witnessed whole of Schoffields [sic] army pass in view without the firing of a gun." Illinoisan Frederick Nathan Boyer captured the event from the other side simply in his diary, noting that as they passed Spring Hill, "we could see the Rebel Campfires, not over a half a mile, I should judge, as we could see the men moving around the fires, and many of our soldiers thought it was part of our Army." The artillery was "wrapped to prevent noise" and nobody was allowed "to speak above a whisper." Being the rear guard, they fortunately got all trains and artillery through without a battle, and after safely running the gauntlet, "we rested but an hour" and resumed the march to Franklin. As Captain Thomas Speed of the Union Twelfth Kentucky wrote his parents later, "At midnight we passed Hoods Army lying *half a mile* from Springhill. We could hardly believe it was the enemy so close were we to them."[43]

Historian Thomas L. Connelly declared solemnly in 1971 that Hood, "sick, tired and distraught" after months of frustration, was "too emotionally unhinged to continue to command." Hood himself admitted later that his Spring Hill plan was fashioned after what he remembered from Virginia—"the well-oiled command relationship of Lee and Jackson." Yet Hood was no Lee and he had no Jackson (at least at corps command). In Connelly's view, at least, the army commander misunderstood "that such maneuvers demanded a well-coordinated and seasoned command staff. According to one of Hood's campaign reports later, "Major General Cheatham has frankly confessed the great error of which he was guilty, and attaches all blame to himself." Or perhaps everyone thought that Schofield and his army would still be there in the morning to stand and fight like valorous combatants were supposed to do. But despite desultory skirmishing (which replicated the whole day's actions and altogether claimed maybe one thousand casualties total for both sides at Spring Hill), the shadowy Yankee column—infantry, cavalry, artillery, and wagon trains—moved on through the muffling darkness and wind.[44]

Another historian of the affair, James McDonough, interprets that shadowy passage somewhat differently from the conventional wisdom. He notes how Major General William R. Bate had deployed skirmishers and actually blocked passage at one point diverting the enemy west of the pike near a Dr. McKessick's place, gaining Spring Hill by a country road. He thinks that Federal contingent may have been Thomas Ruger's division leading Schofield's remaining contingents from Columbia and concludes that this explained why Confederate Major General Edward Johnson subsequently found no Yankees on the pike when he scouted later that night and that perhaps the main force was not on the Columbia–Spring Hill highway anyway. Still, taken all together, the bluecoats knew they were in a very bad situation, "treading upon the thin crust covering a smoldering volcano." By morning of the thirtieth, Schofield and his force reached Franklin. Hood would awaken as "writhy as a rattlesnake" when he learned that his quarry had flown. Taking breakfast at the nearby Nathaniel Cheairs house, he ranted at his subordinates. A much more chastened Hood penned a fortnight later, "Thus was lost the opportunity for striking the enemy for which we had labored so long—the best which this campaign has offered, and one of the best afforded us during the war." Young soldier Tom Walker was perhaps more pensive when years later he referenced Shakespeare "while pondering over the mistery [sic] of that particular part of the campaign": "There is a trade in the affairs of men. When taken at their flood leads on to fortune. Omited [sic] all the rest of their lives are bound in shadows and miseries."[45]

Franklin's Sorry Forever

The mystery, the failed opportunity, and the irony of Spring Hill will always link what came next for Hood. Veterans and historians have seen to that. And they have forever linked the names of two particular Middle Tennessee towns in that saga—Spring Hill and Franklin. Schofield did not intend to fight at Franklin, perhaps ten miles north of Spring Hill and some twenty miles south of fortress Nashville. Arriving in town just before daylight on the thirtieth, he discovered the wagon bridges burnt and fords impassable over a flooded Harpeth River. He set his men to constructing a footbridge for infantry and planking over the railroad bridge for his supply train and artillery. Meanwhile, his little army took out pick and shovel, along with bayonets, to dig a semicircular defense line around the south end of town, anchored on both ends at the river. In front lay a splendid, two-mile, flat, open killing ground. Artillery (including Cockrell's Battery D, First Ohio Light Artillery) in the nearly twelve-acre Fort Granger across the river to the army's backs, as well as indigenous batteries, would provide support fire. The fort, where Schofield eventually established his command post, had an arresting view of the country to the south and had been constructed by U.S. Army Engineer captain W. E. Merrill two years before on Figuer's Bluff to protect the Tennessee and Alabama Railroad crossing. It could support an ample garrison with facilities for seventy thousand rations, a powder magazine for twelve hundred rounds, and a nine-thousand-gallon cistern for water. Now it would just provide fire support and surveillance. Yet only a fool would attack across the open swath of farmland surveyed from Fort Grainger, and Hood had been reluctant to attack fortified lines at Columbia, much less do serious assault at Spring Hill. At least that was the impression that Schofield, Cox, and Stanley held at this point.[46]

Later, Stanley opined that "nothing appeared so improbably as that they would assault," while Cox claimed that "none of us were quick to believe that a *coup de main* would be attempted." The army commander, in fact, took dinner and rest with local unionist Dr. Cliff and his wife in downtown Franklin then moved his headquarters north of the river to Alpheus Truett's house on the east side of the turnpike to Nashville. He obviously anticipated another flank move by Hood to cross downstream as he had at Columbia. About midafternoon, Schofield issued orders for his force to withdraw to the river crossings at nightfall. He would be riding back toward the front line with Stanley when word arrived that the enemy had appeared and deployed for attack. Stanley galloped to the front, Schofield off to his left to Fort Granger where he could watch for that telltale flanking movement, continue orchestrating withdrawal and, overlook the front "nearly to the Columbia pike at the Carter house . . . where communication with the reserves and line of battle could best be had." The calm before the storm came to end.[47]

Hood's men soon appeared on the horizon, embarrassed and angered by their opponents' Spring Hill escape. The seething southern leader determined to destroy the Federals before they could reach Nashville's safety. According to Connelly, he similarly remained committed "to mold the army into his image of the Virginia army as he had known it"—by using frontal assaults and the shedding of blood as "an exercise of discipline" and "a booster of morale." By choice, then, the name "Franklin" would be forever identified with an irate, crippled general and his mad rush to eradicate the scar of Spring Hill and replicate a "New Model Army" patterned on Robert E. Lee's tactical offensive, which, typically, incurred irredeemable losses. He achieved the last part, for Franklin would be a bitterly contested carnage and the sunset of the Confederacy. Recent literature has raised the event to legend and heroic sacrifice, the pivotal event in Hood's campaign. More guarded judgment suggests irrational slaughter defying credulity.[48]

"I will never forget that battle while memory retains its throne or this life shall last," declared Tom Walker. The basic facts of Franklin remain engraved even yet in neo-Confederate theology today. Stewart's corps came through the Winstead hills first, deploying east of the Columbia Pike. Then came Cheatham, who filed to the west of the road. Stephen Lee's trailing corps would serve as a reserve. Altogether the army lacked its artillery support. Without further adieu or even proper

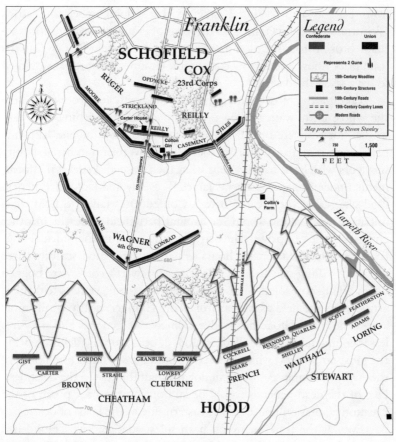

Battle of Franklin, November 30, 1864, initial attack. Map by Steven Stanley and courtesy of the Civil War Preservation Trust.

reconnaissance, Hood launched an eighteen-brigade frontal assault as "all the bands in our army struck up Dixie . . . something we soldiers had never heard before as we were marching into battle," claimed Walker about 4:00 p.m. on November 30. To Major General Samuel French, twenty thousand Confederates moving smartly over the open plain "was a glorious and imposing sight, and one so seldom witnessed, as all were in full view." Even their opponents were impressed as the assault quickly overran two forward-positioned brigades of Brigadier General George D. Wagner's Second Division, IV Corps on a knoll about a mile in front of the main Federal lines, almost upsetting Schofield/ Stanley's initial defense. The routed bluecoats screened the attackers from Federal artillery for a time so that yelping rebels of Patrick Cleburne's and John C. Brown's divisions of Frank Cheatham's corps actually broke through Union defenses around Fountain Branch Carter's solid brick house and nearby cotton gin. Unionist Kentuckians claimed to have saved the day.[49]

Taking "the most withering fire of the war," and wondering how the whole army wasn't killed or wounded before reaching the main works "for we were in full range of shot and shell for one half mile before we arrived at the fortifications," Tom Walker numbered among survivors who lived to tell about what then ensued. Federal reinforcements under Brigadier General James W. Reilly and Colonel Emerson Opdycke sealed the breach, Bates's Confederates failed to hold, thus initiating what many would see as fatal battlefield letdowns in other contests of the campaign. The battle became a toe-to-toe, suicidal slugfest that continued for five hours as participants stood scarcely three feet apart killing one another. Elsewhere, Stewart's corps were bogged down trying to exploit the railroad cut into town, victims to Yankee artillery on the field as well as from Fort Granger, nearly a mile away across the river. Altogether twelve Confederate generals and sixty-five lesser commanders were killed, wounded, or captured (Cleburne being the most prominent) while over six thousand lower ranks (the flower of the Army of Tennessee) were cut down at half the cost to the defenders. Five of the dead generals would be laid out on the back porch of the Carnton plantation house on the eastern side of the fields of death.[50]

Even at the time, many on both sides wondered why Hood had not simply repeated his outflanking of Schofield as he had at Columbia. In fact, Forrest had urged that ploy, but to no avail. A bellicose, unnerved, and perhaps irrational army commander insisted that the Federals were ripe for direct assault. To the west a wide flanking movement by Chalmers's cavalrymen and Bate's infantry "scarcely touched" Federal positions (pulled in close across Carter's Creek and Charlotte Pikes to the riverbank north of town) and so failed to secure position, noted lowly ranker Walker. East of Franklin and north of the river, Forrest's horsemen, divided by Hood to protect his infantry flanks, put only Jackson's division across the river to outflank Schofield from the east. For once, Wilson outnumbered his opponent as he recorded how Hatch and Croxton "made a beautiful fight at the same time, driving the enemy's cavalry across the river with great gallantry." Schofield's earlier opinion that Wilson "was entirely unable to cope" with Forrest vanished dramatically. Hood's stretching his cavalry to bolster a doomed infantry

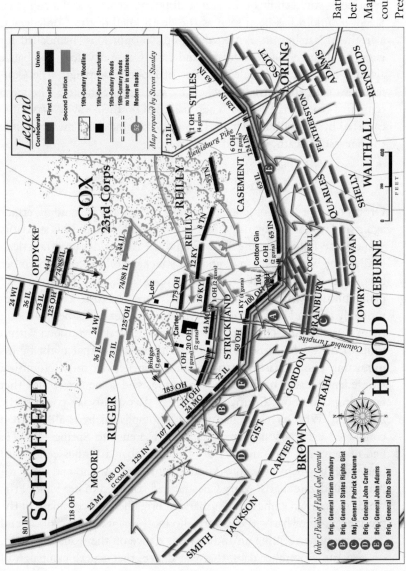

Battle of Franklin, November 30, 1864, final assault. Map by Steven Stanley and courtesy of the Civil War Preservation Trust.

fight could well have changed fate. "But Forrest," notes two students of the battle, "was handcuffed, essentially relegated to the sideline."[51]

Franklin's carnage could be seen all around at Carnton and the Carter place. The McGavock family owners of Carnton would cede land for a final resting place for the multitude of ordinary rebel dead disgorged from neighboring fields and fence rows. The Carter House and outbuildings—centerpiece of the battle and future battlefield preservation—would show bullet and shell holes a century and a half later. Sleepy Franklin has been seen as the death knell of the Confederacy, a frightful last hurrah. A tragedy of epic proportions, bemoaned for generations by neo-Confederates and Lost Cause devotees, the battle actually may not have sealed the fate of Hood's campaign. The Confederates held the battlefield when by midnight, Schofield's battered remnants crossed the Harpeth and hastened on their way to Nashville, escorted by Wilson's horsemen. In Southern minds that meant despite the harvest of death, they had won.

In the Clear Light of Day

Orders held for the Confederates, now with artillery in hand, to attack again at daylight. Only in the morning would Hood and his survivors witness the folly of Spring Hill/Franklin—the rigidly prostrate dead bodies, the writhing injured, and the wreckage of the cold November battlefield. As Tom Walker phrased it years later, the "dead over that plain through which we charged lay in heaps and rows a scene undescribably [sic] sad and horrifying even to a hardened soldier." Among them was Captain Theodoic (Tod) Carter, mortally wounded within sight of his boyhood home and borne there to die that night by his mourning family. Irish American Pat Cleburne, the most promising Confederate leader of the later war period, said some (except for that fatal proposal about freeing and arming slaves) also lay cold on the battlefield. What precisely had Hood accomplished by it all? He had conducted a fairly solid campaign from Florence to Spring Hill. He had maneuvered the Yankees out of their Alabama-Tennessee forward line, flushing them back into Middle Tennessee. At the end of October, Confederate diarist Mary Chesnut had confided to her journal the words of her own embittered husband, a brigadier and confidant of the president (somewhat without portfolio by this stage) how "Hood and Thomas are performing an Indiana war dance on the frontier." Then, on two late November days, that war dance, that superb campaign of

Sam Hood, had disintegrated. "Carnage—loss of generals excessive in proportion to numbers," penned Mary Chesnut. "Can any victory pay for so much death?" was the question asked by prominent Charleston, South Carolina, lawyer Charles Richardson Miles.[52]

What now was to be done with the debris? Hood tersely recorded in two separate after-action reports how he had been ready to renew the battle the next morning, having brought up all his artillery (which he had been reluctant to commit the previous evening "on account of the women and children remaining in the town"). Finding Schofield gone, the wounded cared for, and the dead buried, "we move forward toward Nashville, Forrest with his cavalry pursuing the enemy vigorously." He had but few alternatives, in his own mind, at least. Schofield, on the other hand, felt that "to remain longer at Franklin was to seriously hazard the loss of my army, by giving the enemy another chance to cut me off from reenforcements, which had made three desperate though futile attempts to accomplish." Those reinforcements not forthcoming due to time and distance, it would have been foolhardy to hazard renewed combat on December 1. After all, he had succeeded again in buying time for Thomas to concentrate his "scattered troops at Nashville." He and Thomas had been communicating all day about remaining longer to delay Hood. Thomas wanted three days; Schofield said that he was satisfied that "I have heretofore run too much risk," obviously spooked by the close call at Spring Hill. Between the pair (and notwithstanding the deadly results at Franklin), they decided to continue Schofield's withdrawal back to the Brentwood hills south of Nashville. Wilson's people skirmished briefly with Forrest's advanced units then set up camps around Thompson's Chapel on the Nolensville Pike, two miles from the city. To historians, the significance of Franklin "lay more in the weakening of the Confederate army," which Thomas would soon meet in an even more climatic battle. Of course, the same could be said for Schofield's men. But for Federals in the ranks, like Kentuckian Thomas Speed, they slept as they marched, completely exhausted, having been without sleep for easily thirty-six hours or more and having fought two battles. That, too, memorialized Franklin.[53]

CHAPTER 9

Nashville's Anvil and Hammer

Franklin's tragedy provided the anvil for which the hammer of Nashville administered the crowning blow. Yet nothing was inevitable. Nobody necessarily anticipated that result. Tennessee's capital had long been a beacon—for refugees, freed people, and Confederate generals. Back in May, President Jefferson Davis had approved a proposal "to undertake certain secret service, including the destruction of the enemy's stores collected at Nashville for the ensuing campaign." If it was possible to destroy those stores and impede if not defeat Federal plans for some months to come, "I am of the opinion that the advantage to be gained is worth great hazard in making the attempt," he had written then-departmental commander Leonidus Polk in Alabama. Other plans in that desperate fall of 1864 eventually overtook this particular scheme, originated by unknown Major Jules C. Denis and approved by Major General George B. Hodge. Despite presidential military adviser Braxton Bragg's pessimism that "operations in Middle Tennessee by a force unable to seize and hold the country will not benefit us and will seriously distress our people," the Confederate chief executive's perennial interest in some form of "offensive-defensive" grand strategy had not elapsed after two years of geographical contraction. So John Bell Hood's offensive to take Nashville had gone forward. A major rebel army had not been in the region in over a year. This new attempt would be put to the test in the wake of the Franklin debacle.[1]

In some ways the risk may have been worth it, even after Franklin. That the upper heartland remained unstable could be seen in brushes between occupation garrisons protecting facilities or out on recruiting missions among the vagabond black population and local guerrillas. The gang of Alexander Duvall McNairy constantly harassed workers and guards on the Nashville and Northwestern line that fall. Moreover, rebel partisans always recruited at will among the white populace and thus confrontations were inevitable. For example, on October 11, Colonel T. R. Weaver led such an expedition of his 119th Colored Infantry and men from the Fourth U.S. Colored Heavy Artillery and was attacked near Fort Donelson by a rebel cavalry force under Colonel James Q. Chenoweth. Over in Kentucky's Christian County, farmer C. O'Neal wrote a friend Ben D. Moore, in Drummondville, West Canada (perhaps fleeing to escape Federal conscription), on October 28, calling attention to "a negro raid" out of Clarksville, Tennessee. Occupation authorities traversed the countryside, inducing and finally absconding with all slaves—"three to four wagon loads passing every day"—with slave owners "driving theirs off" to escape the dragnet.

As a result, and helped by an early mid-October frost, the lack of labor destroyed the tobacco crop. Apparently, he said, "the draft is over in this country" what with those Negro raids alleviating the problem of whites to fill the quotas for the county. Guerrillas and vagrant slaves both robbing the citizenry and raiders like Confederate Hylan B. Lyon taking "100 new recruits and 1,000 horses" (resulting in severe retribution by local Yankee colonel Jam Johnson at Hopkinsville who shot two ostensible Confederates) underscored O'Neal's account of a disturbed home land. Moreover, he concluded, "refugees from East Tennessee "are crowding in at Clarksville, so they have to shove the negroes out to make room for them." While O'Neal did not say as much, Federal authorities nowhere had any ironclad grip on the region. Hood and his liberators might well have been welcomed. But they had to capture Nashville and destroy Schofield and Thomas first.[2]

Hood's Stock Taking

At first, a somewhat shell-shocked rebel army meekly followed Schofield toward Nashville's defenses. Only Bedford Forrest pushed the Yankees, while the rest of Hood's army came behind in sequence—Lee, Stewart and Cheatham. They bivouacked in the Brentwood hills by December 1 and pushed on the next day to form a line of battle about two miles in front of Nashville. Lee took the center, resting on the Franklin Pike astride Franklin and Granny White Turnpikes; Cheatham went right across the Nolensville Turnpike, and Stewart moved in on the left, covering the road to Hillsboro. Forrest's horsemen protected both flanks extending to the river. Since the army now lacked sufficient numbers for a continuous front besieging Nashville, a perceptible weakness emerged when the line stopped two miles from the Cumberland on the east and four miles in the west, leaving three major roads open from the south as well as the river, northern railroad, and highway access to the city.

Hood established his headquarters at Colonel John Overton's pleasant plantation "Travelers Rest," just east of the Franklin Pike and about five and a half miles from the city. Built by Overton's father, the influential judge of the same name at the turn of the century, it swirled with gaiety and entertainment, ample food and drink, and even the hint of wedding plans for staff officer Major William Clare and a local Brentwood belle. Sam Hood must have been reminded of his own distant fiancée, Sally "Buck" Preston, as he had promised in January to come back and marry her. By December 5, Hood's engineer, Major Wilbur Fisk Foster, had laid out a line of defense for the army. The shivering yet confident fighting men began constructing "strong detached works" to cover their flanks, intending to enclose them to stop any Federal attempt to attack flank and rear. Hood tried to shield them from Franklin realities and told his chaplain friend Charles Quintard on December 12 that there would be "no more great flanking operations." Rather, the Federals would have to seek out Confederate foes where they might find them with new casualties on the Yankee side.[3]

Some fortunate Confederates like Captain James Litton Cooper of the Twentieth Tennessee had come home. Son of a famous portrait painter in Middle Tennessee, his parents lived at the intersection of the Charlotte Pike and Clifton Road and he remembered his unit taking position west of the Nolensville Pike in full view of not just the famed Fort Negley but also the Capitol and many of the city's best residences. "Very tantalizing indeed it was to be in sight of home and not allowed to be there," he suggested. He and others rested themselves and their horses with the aid of abandoned oats and corn, until "the vile Yankees again disturbed us." Meanwhile, Hood thought that enemy garrisons, cut off at Chattanooga, Knoxville, and Murfreesboro, might soon cause his opponent to undertake an attack to relieve or evacuate those positions. He also felt confident that if Thomas assaulted the Confederate positions, "I could defeat him, and thus gain possession of Nashville with abundant supplies for the army."[4]

Hood sent most of Forrest's cavalry to capture Lovell Rousseau's six thousand men at Murfreesboro, as well as to screen against James

Wilson's cavalry (regrouping at Edgefield across from Nashville) re-crossing the Cumberland to operate on the army's flanks and rear. Hood also noted later in his campaign report how he hoped to capture Murfreesboro "and should then be able to open communication with Georgia and Virginia." Hood was a risk taker but less so after Franklin. In retrospect, few options remained to the crippled general short of admitting failure and retiring behind the sheltering waters of the Duck River or moving entirely to the vicinity of a captured Murfreesboro like Bragg two winters before or even retreating to Alabama.[5]

Interestingly, while Hood used the time after Franklin to write a short report on the campaign thus far, he sent little or no information to his superior P. G. T. Beauregard and only superficially reported both the Spring Hill and Franklin mishaps to Richmond. His communiqués at the time and later concentrated upon logistics: how Middle Tennessee amply supplied his army and how brigade shoe shops had been set up and functioning while captured railroad stock permitted forward supply as far as Pulaski with wagon trains hauling supplies from there. "Having possession of the State," he generously estimated, "we should have gained largely in recruits, and could at an early day have moved forward to the Ohio, which would have frustrated the plans of the enemy, as developed in his campaign toward the Atlantic coast." After the war, Hood would note that his small army could not cross the Cumberland River and move on Kentucky "without first receiving reinforcements from the Trans-Mississippi Department." He felt that few Tennesseans and Kentuckians would rally to his army "since we had failed in the first instance to defeat the Federal Army and capture Nashville." Retreat was out unless for the *"special"* purpose of meeting up with the Texas reinforcements and then return to besiege the Tennessee capital. In truth, Hood would contend, the army's condition rendered "it more judicious the men should face a decisive issue rather than retreat"—in order words, rather than renounce the honor of their cause without having made a last and manful effort to lift up the sinking fortunes of the Confederacy. Such was post hoc thinking. Hood claimed it as his opinion at the time.[6]

Hood used words that betrayed his obsession with "the failure of my cherished plan to crush Schofield's Army before it reached its strongly fortified position around Nashville." Still, that retrospective came later. For all that Beauregard and the War Department knew at the time, he might be succeeding. Even the department commander lived in a fantasy world, writing Richmond on December 4 that Hood "anticipates no difficulty about supplies, and two days later explained why he had not countermanded the campaign into Tennessee in order to use Hood's army to pursue Sherman. Virtually repeating Hood's earlier enunciation of impassable creeks and rivers from Alabama to north Georgia and Sherman's head start on good roads contrasting with the worn-out southern railroads with which Hood's army would have had to navigate, Beauregard added that Thomas (absent Hood's counterforce) could have invaded the richest part of Alabama and captured Montgomery, Selma and Mobile without significant Confederate impact on Sherman's actions. Most of all, Beauregard admitted underestimating Sherman's numbers and overestimating Georgia forces with which he expected to stop the Federal drive to the sea. In fact, Beauregard rested his rationale for Hood on the hope that the Tennessee counterthrust would defeat Thomas and cause Sherman to return to defend Kentucky and perhaps Ohio, thus preventing him from reinforcing Grant in Virginia. Ignorant of conditions in the occupied upper South, Beauregard suggested that "supplies might be sent to Virginia from Middle and East Tennessee, thus relieving Georgia from the present constant drain upon its limited resources." With this, Beauregard continued his passage to defend the southern Atlantic Coast, unaware of events transpiring south of Nashville and helpless to affect their result.[7]

When Hood took position awaiting developments, he essentially duplicated Bragg's static stance two winters before below Murfreesboro. Both generals invited Union response, although unlike Bragg, Hood had a broken army, essentially controlling only a swath of Middle Tennessee back to the Alabama line, if that. Confederate dispatches inferred as much. Isolated Federal railroad garrisons on the route to Chattanooga and other random detachments remained in place by Thomas's orders. With Federal control little affecting the countryside outside their immediate purview during Hood's presence, they blocked complete Confederate reoccupation. Hood might pass the winter there, scantily supplied from a picked-over region just coming out of barren harvest or more especially via the railroad back to Decatur and Cherokee Station, which rebel engineers and logisticians eventually opened past Pulaski to Franklin. But just how well Hood's presence might impact a "redeemed populace" while encamped benignly for the winter, or how dragnets could garner new recruits (or conscripts), was suspect. At one point, even Hood admitted scarcely 164 newcomers to the colors since entering Tennessee, while in one division alone of 296 dismounted cavalry assigned, "all of have deserted except 42 [men]." Nashville newspapers noted an influx of "a troupe of nameless gentry," implying popular response to Hood's "gathering up conscripts with a sweeping hand throughout the counties on his line of march."[8]

Confederate dispatches suggested rejoicing at Hood's coming; Union newspapers in the city implied quite the opposite. Even now, the precise situation remains unclear. That all might not be satisfactory in Hood's wake could be inferred from his instruction to Forrest on December 7 to send Colonel B. J. Hill's command "to Bedford, Giles, and Marshall Counties to break up and destroy the Home Guards in those counties, to collect animals for the army, and to conscribe men liable to military duty." Those unionist Home Guards were "doing great damage to the country and especially to the mills, which are of great use to us. Hill was to put the facilities in running order as soon as possible," implying that Hood planned a long stay in the region. Thus Hood counted on both regional and deeper resupply from Mississippi and Alabama. With the onset of inclement weather by the second week in December, Hood complained to Beauregard that Major L. O. Bridewell was hoarding fifty bales of blankets belonging to the Army of Tennessee back at Augusta, Georgia, and he wanted those ten thousand, plus suits of clothing sent forward. Moreover, his agents scavenged the Deep South for manpower.[9]

Hood might have expected time to rehabilitate his army in the absence of meaningful pushback from Yankee horsemen or Thomas's prompt counterattack. Together with Forrest and ranging partisans (however imperfectly coordinated and controlled), he might conceivably reestablish Confederate control of the immediate heartland in Middle Tennessee. Federal authorities showed little concern for this aspect of the situation. In fact, their focus inside Nashville hinted little at immediate crisis and more at orderly buildup, response to influx of refugees possibly containing subversive elements and normal conduct of trade and transit. However measured and focused Thomas was on military buildup for an attack of his own, the presence of an unchaperoned Hood and his army and the dangers of their settling down for the winter alarmed Washington. Any rebel passage over the Cumberland and continued advance to the Ohio seemed unacceptable given the administration's drive to victoriously end the war.

One civilian, a former Pennsylvania militiaman now working at the Quartermaster's Office of the U.S. Military Railroad in Nashville, wrote his father on December 5 that heavy skirmishing and cannonading occupied the left of the Union line. Hamilton Alricks Jr. had ridden to one high hill while a battery commander he had met in Memphis "shewed me our skirmishers in front about a half a mile and on enquiry I found that was all the troops between us and the rebs." The artilleryman ("for my edification") obligingly "pitched three shells" amid besieging rebels, who "came to the conclusion they had seen enough of the State House which they evidently were looking at as they were opposite a ravine or valley." He and Major General Darius Couch, another Keystoner who happened to be in the city, swapped conversations as Alricks admitted that with "nothing to do at present" he had visited the Tennessee state house and been to the dome with its fine view. While the masonry was pleasing, he said, "I do not admire the shape or proportions of it." His boss read a captured order from S. D. Lee "thanking the Rebs for bravery at Franklin and saying, *We will soon have Nashville and all its stores.*"[10]

Thomas Forges a Thunderbolt

Federal authorities faced two challenges as Hood's army closed on Nashville. The one most closely followed by historians was a predictable military response to a devastated yet still dangerous foe. In fact, from the dispatches at the time, one would never guess that the Confederates not the Federals had been rocked back on their heels by Franklin. Rehabilitation of Schofield's force, especially Wilson's mounted units, as well as mustering of reinforcements from all over the West, protection of lines of communication to a perceivably besieged city, and prevention of Confederate side-slipping across the Cumberland—all this preoccupied the Union command. Furthermore, the chaplain of the Seventy-fourth Illinois said it for all the participants in the road race back from Pulaski: he was "worn out with incessant labors of 2 nights and 3 days," referring in particular to the Spring Hill/Franklin phase of the experience. Kentuckian Thomas Speed noted the same weariness in letters home and reminiscences. Tennessee Union brigadier Joseph A. Cooper's brigade, in fact, reached a devastated Franklin on December 2, discovering that it had missed the battle and was now cut off from Schofield's army. It had to meander through partisan-infested back country before reaching Clarksville on the lower Cumberland, from which it then marched to rejoin comrades-in-arms at Nashville six days later. Meanwhile, A. J. Smith's reinforcing column from Memphis, via side trips west of the Mississippi to St. Louis, wended its slow passage via riverboat, finally reaching Nashville by early December. New arrivals like the Twelfth

Iowa immediately went into position facing Hood's encampments, both sides establishing defensive positions and Hawkeye Henry Grannis expressed surprise, going to fetch water on December 3 "to see the long line of rifle pits that our Brig[ade] threw up last night."[11]

Five days later, Illinoisan Hardin Keplinger of the XVI Corps on the Yankee right wrote his brother how the two armies faced each other across "a valley from a quarter of a mile to two miles in width" with pickets in-between while only occasional artillery exchanges that disrupted none of the soldiers from their cooking, letter writing or card games and simply convinced the defenders that their opponents "have no ammunition to waste." All the wood was about gone on their side of the lines and they "will have to bring it from the north side of the river now," while "those who have to buy wood pay $30 per cord" with "everything high in proportion" within the city. Being confined to camp, Keplinger said they could not get into Nashville proper but that it "is a pretty little city," although "most of the business streets are very narrow which spoils the appearance of the buildings." Nevertheless, the state house was as fine a building as he had ever seen; "the capitol at Springfield won't begin to compare with it." Noting how the rebels had cut off communication with Murfreesboro so that "we can hear nothing of our troops from Murfreesboro to Chattanooga and in Northern Alabama, "We are confident that with our present force [he noted reinforcements would reach them in three or four days] inside our fortifications we can repel all attacks of the enemy."[12]

A second challenge also demanded attention. Union occupation authorities and the citizenry had to address Hood's appearance in terms of saboteurs and rebel sympathizing refugees. These were disruptive political and economic if not military concerns in early December. Lame-duck military governor Andrew Johnson basically left the task of preparation and response to the military, concerning himself more with Brigadier Alvan C. Gillem's reduction of remaining rebel forces in East Tennessee and his anticipated unionist convention in the capital as well as issues of pardon and punishment and other supplication befitting his office. The mantle of dealing with Hood directly fell to Thomas, the methodical and dependable veteran whom Ulysses S. Grant perceived as "no better man to repel an attack" though "too cautious to ever take the initiative."[13]

Certainly the epicenter of Thomas's action was a far cry from Nashville's antebellum appellation as the "Athens of the South." War had obliterated the old rebellious Nashville aristocracy, thanks to two years of coerced loyalty in this Union command and political center, supply depot, refugee terminal, and garrison town. It had all the public health problems of Memphis, with similar rules, regulations, and correctional measures taken by occupation authorities. By the time of Hood's arrival not only were finely attired fast women jostling dour survivors who had not "refugeed south," but "Smokey Row" fleshpots, saloons, and plea- sure palaces were vying with a fortified, hilltop State Capitol Building for the attentions of soldiers, rebel deserters, and fugitives as well as the vanguard of what would later be termed "carpetbag" opportunists from the North. All of them provided ample customers for purveyors hawk- ing all types of goods and services. In some ways, the occupation's legal control system provided the best means of harnessing the raw edged energy of this wartime boomtown. Both general and special orders in the summer of 1864 continued to discourage the guerrilla threat in the countryside through imprisonment in the state penitentiary or hang- ing. Enforcement of the first and second Confiscation acts, as well as the Confederate Sequestration act in seizing forfeited rebel property, coupled with informal seizures and impressments to stifle rebel senti- ments. Harsh measures may have been variously abused or rigorously applied with varying success throughout the upper heartland, but Nash- ville governance established equilibrium, however unpleasant for the remnants of rebellious citizenry.[14]

For one thing, Johnson had seen to it that a loyal city council and set of aldermen had become what historian Gary Shockley calls "lit- tle more than an administrative adjunct of the military government." Newspaper control ensured right thinking, while Johnson's earlier prof- fer of "olive branch in one hand and the Constitution in the other" had given way to sterner measures to control the capital neighborhood in particular. His "Moses of the Colored Men" speech boldly proclaimed "freedom, full, broad, and unconditional, to every man in Tennessee," seconding ersatz military emancipation as legally yet-enslaved African Americans realized that their time as property (of both disloyal and loyal white people) was nearing its end. These so-called contrabands might well contribute to the supplicant challenges of the capital, but they also offered an available labor pool for responding to a rebel army now at the city's gates. Soldiery would do the bulk of the fighting, and black troops as well as white would be part of the Federal response. Both black and white labor would provide support.[15]

Occupation authorities in Nashville, as at Memphis and other urban centers, had long regulated trade and commerce, but Hood's invasion energized new measures. Authorities had legalized and regulated prostitution, the one profession calculated to profit from the huge troop concentration in anticipation of Hood's arrival. In fact, one blue-coated soldier wrote his wife at midmonth how there seemed to be nothing else in town but prostitutes. They monopolized public hacks and theater seats. Dressed to the height of fashion, thanks to their Union officer patrons, they drank and "caroused, singing and hollering like so many drunken men." The physical well-being of garrison and citizens with regard to public health (sanitation, disease, alcohol, crime) increased generally with the crisis-driven influx of soldiers. But the need to clamp down on inflation, due to siege-threatened food and fuel price escalation, led to price controls on December 8. Just seven days before that, General Order 22 decreed that all citizens not legitimately engaged in business or employment or permanently living at Nashville would evacuate to Louisville or other places north of the department. Noncompliance meant removal north of the Ohio River for the duration of the war, and nighttime patrols would sweep up such recalcitrants for exile. Perhaps the ladies of the evening did not prosper after all. Certainly when winter weather suddenly enveloped Nashville at midmonth, city council members feared freezing and starving refugees on the city's streets more than any Trojan horse among the migration from rural to urban scene. Free transportation on the Louisville and Nashville northward and relief donations to aid the poor became part of crisis response. The test to city resources, patience, and abilities seemed acute.[16]

Meanwhile, good reasons lay behind Thomas's military delay. Perhaps more vexed than the "disconsolate man" or "emotionally wrought" individual pictured by historian Wiley Sword, he nonetheless faced great difficulties. Hood had not followed Sherman across Georgia and Sherman had not left the Nashville commander with sufficient or skilled veterans to cope with a major invasion. Sherman assumed that he had done so and too quickly dismissed the recuperative power of Hood's army. Still, like just about everyone in the Union military and political hierarchy, Thomas wanted to finish the business of annihilating rebel arms and the rebellion. Patience wore thin and Thomas was probably no exception. At 8:00 a.m. the day after Schofield's success at Franklin, Thomas wired Grant about rumors concerning the East Tennessee situation (following Breckinridge's rout of Gillem at Morristown in mid-November) and that Lee had evacuated Richmond and was heading in that direction. Major General George Stoneman went to straighten things out in East Tennessee, while Thomas turned to the Middle Tennessee crisis. He had no further news from Schofield's observation army, he said, but "feel sure everything goes well." By 9:30 that night, Thomas sent his operation plan to Henry Halleck in Washington.[17]

Based on the results of the Franklin fight, Thomas determined (1) that "the enemy very far outnumbered" Schofield in infantry and cavalry and (2) to "retire to the fortifications around Nashville, until General Wilson can get his cavalry equipped." Since the navy assured him that ironclads and gunboats would prohibit the enemy from either crossing the Cumberland or blockading it, he could safely await Wilson's refurbishment. If Hood attacks, "he will be more seriously damaged than he was yesterday," while if he remained until Wilson was ready, "I can whip him and will move against him at once." Outlying garrisons from Murfreesboro to Chattanooga and from Bridgeport, Stevenson, and Elk River would similarly deter the Confederates from any diversion. Such would be Thomas's position for all of the two weeks' impasse that followed. Ostensibly understood by Grant and the Washington establishment, Thomas's superiors nevertheless chafed at delay. Their impatience almost cost "Old Pap" his command and seriously endangered Union success.[18]

Secretary of War Edwin Stanton especially reflected administration fears when he wired Grant the next morning at 10:30 about "the disposition of General Thomas to lay in fortifications for an indefinite period" until Wilson got equipped. This appeared to be "the McClellan and Rosecrans strategy of do nothing and let the rebels raid the country." Lincoln wanted Grant "to consider the matter." The general-in-chief did that, concluding that "it looks as if Forrest will flank around Thomas until Thomas is equal to him in cavalry," and in two wires at 11:00 a.m. and 1:30 p.m. on December 2 ever so gently prodded Thomas. "If Hood is permitted to remain quietly about Nashville, you will lose all the road back to Chattanooga, and possibly have to abandon the line of Tennessee," he chided. All well and good if Hood attacks, but if not, Thomas should attack in turn "before he fortifies." It seemed to Grant that after Hood's repulse at Franklin "we should have taken the offensive against the enemy where he was," but Grant admitted to seeing things from great distance. Still, "you will now suffer incalculable injury upon your railroads, if Hood is not speedily disposed of." Put forth every exertion to this end, he directed; arm and put in the trenches the quartermaster employees and citizens and attack. "Should you get him to retreating, give him no peace."[19]

Thomas calmly replied, reiterating Schofield's weakness and stating that he was collecting reinforcements from Chattanooga awaiting arrival of Major General A. J. Smith's troops from the Mississippi Valley but that reinforcements from elsewhere could be gotten only with great difficulty. The fact that he had been given the two weakest corps in Sherman's army plus dismounted cavalry "have enabled Hood to take advantage of my crippled condition." All of this sounded like excuses for inaction to Grant and Washington, even when Thomas iterated that Wilson's men only numbered "about one-fourth that of Forrest's." Therein lay the principal rub—Forrest, not Hood worried the bejesus out of western commanders in the field and Thomas in particular, given the very kinds of damage to railroads, supply depots, and so on that Washington itself warned about.

So the administration and Grant offered suggestions that eventually led to orders about impressing horses in Kentucky and Nashville surroundings (Louisville citizens protested about equine impressments all the way to Secretary of War Edwin Stanton), the dispatch of cavalry from other commands in the West, and signals to everyone that the supreme command expected immediate results. Grant rather weakly suggested that Thomas should be empowered to confiscate mounts with suitable provision of receipts to owners, Halleck pouted about having supplied twenty thousand fresh mounts since September, and Stanton could not fathom why Thomas would not be impressing everything in sight for the emergency since precedents existed. For the better part of a fortnight, everyone sent dispatches, orders, permissions, and threats—desiring to see how Thomas would change the waiting game into action.[20]

Thomas began to better understand Hood's weaknesses by December 5. Captured prisoners claimed that the Confederates relied upon the distant Memphis and Charleston Railroad to Cherokee Station, Alabama, with wagon trains on to the front before Nashville. If an expedition could be started from Memphis against Hood's line of communication, thus cutting his means of supply, "he will run the risk of losing his whole army" if we proved successful "in pushing him back," Thomas told Halleck. Then, Hood directly solicited an exchange of prisoners with the Union commander. Thomas shrewdly shot back that he had captured a large number of such prisoners but that "they have all been sent North, and consequently are now beyond my control." Thus on these two points plus scouting reports as to the exact condition of the rebel defense positions (no earthworks or "only slight affairs" from right to center, strong and entrenched on the left) Thomas sensed vulnerabilities and sought to exploit them.[21]

Logistical Sideshows

In turn, Hood sought to test Thomas's own vulnerabilities with three separate, uncoordinated raids against Union logistics. At least one of them might induce Thomas out of his defense lines to battle in the open. Otherwise, the fortnight spent by Confederate arms before Nashville mostly passed in digging protective positions in the frozen ground while shivering in the dews and damps then ice and snow with only a lucky few like staffer Bromfield Ridley slipping off home for quick visits to secure much-needed clothing and supplies. These detached operations offered some hope of success for the hapless rebels. Hood sent Major General William Bate and Forrest separately to disrupt Yankee communications between Nashville and the isolated Murfreesboro post hoping to prompt Thomas's reaction. Another part of the Confederate cavalry proved once more that it could interdict the river supply route of Union forces in Middle Tennessee despite the United States Navy. A third group of raiders under Hylan B. Lyon ranged farther north from the lower Cumberland into Kentucky. Yet Thomas reported little impact on either logistics or his own situation. At best, perhaps the Confederates kept the Federals off balance. The Murfreesboro diversion actually diminished Hood's capabilities.[22]

In some ways, the most spectacular success replicated the Johnsonville affair as Forrest's trusted chief-of-staff and personal chaplain Lieutenant Colonel David C. "Parson" Kelley ambushed river traffic below Nashville. Late on the afternoon of December 3, cavalry division commander James R. Chalmers dispatched Kelley with three hundred men of Edmund W. Rucker's brigade and H. H. Brigg's section of two 10-pounder Parrott rifles from T. W. Rice's battery to blockade the Cumberland at Bell's Bend downriver from the city. In classic fashion, Kelley emplaced his artillery (soon reinforced by two additional 12-pounder howitzers) upon commanding ground on the south bank behind Samuel Davidson's house close to the Charlotte Pike. Here he could rake the river channel. Kelley also ostensibly deployed "torpedoes" or subsurface mines in the river. The Cumberland was barely seventy-five to eighty yards wide—the perfect blocking spot. Timing cost Kelly an opportunity to bag the largest prize—a sixty-boat troop convoy taking Major General Andrew J. Smith's fourteen-thousand-man

The USS *Fairplay*. U.S. Naval Historical Center.

reinforcement from the Mississippi to their rendezvous with Thomas. Still, the parson would soon underscore local historian Byrd Douglas's comment about "what even a small force in gifted hands" could do against supply lines despite "all the fine gunboats" sent up the river. Within hours of taking position at 5:00 p.m. on December 4, Kelley's guns had forced the surrender of two steamboats, *Prairie State* and *Prima Donna,* which were carrying grain, horses, and mules as well as fifty-six crew members and camp followers.[23]

Kelly's feat underscored Thomas's vulnerability. Indeed, the general had wired Acting Rear Admiral Samuel P. Lee as early as midafternoon of the Franklin battle asking for ironclads to patrol and convoy transports on the Cumberland. He told Halleck at 10:00 p.m. on December 2 how the local naval commander, Lieutenant Commander LeRoy Fitch, commanding Tenth District, Mississippi Squadron, "assures me that he can safely convoy steamers up and down the river" and that the ironclads and gunboats available for riverine defense "are so disposed as to prevent Hood from crossing the river." The navy seemed accommodating, Lee rushing repairs on the ironclad *Cincinnati* to return to support Thomas along with its sister ironclad, the *Carondelet,* and the normal tinclad fleet, the *Fairplay, Moose, Reindeer,* and *Silver Lake.* The Cumberland would be patrolled as high up as Carthage above Nashville to the east. But now Kelley had punctured naval assurances. His action immediately spurred response by both Fitch on the river and Colonel Israel Garrard's Seventh Ohio Cavalry at Hyde's Ferry below Bell's Bend while the rebels unloaded their treasure at Hillsboro Landing, six miles below Bell's Mill.[24]

Within the hour yet another steamer, *Magnet,* also passed Kelly's position, was hit and run into shore four miles below the ambush site. Five hours then passed before word reached Fitch at Nashville. He assembled a task force at Hyde's Ferry and steamed off to do battle despite the darkness and lowering cloud cover. Forty-five minutes after midnight, the Union gunboats opened fire on Kelley's batteries. Exchanges back and forth took place for over an hour and a half. Nobody could see what effect such combat had in the smoke-filled darkness and gloom. Meanwhile,

Lieutenant Commander Le Roy Fitch, USN. Photograph taken after the war, circa 1870. U.S. Naval Historical Center.

the *Fairplay* slipped past to retrieve the captured steamboats at Hillsboro Landing. Both sides claimed some success in the night battle as the captured steamers and their crews were retrieved and the Confederate batteries ostensibly pushed back from the river as Kelley had to dispose of the prized grain before it could be sent off to Hood's army.[25]

Before returning to the fight some twenty-four hours later, Fitch reported heavy Confederate concentrations to both Thomas and Lee, asked the army not to send any more convoys until he had cleaned out these annoyances and made ready an additional ironclad, the *Neosho,* for the task. Sounds of heavy fighting beyond Nashville indicated Forrest at work on the railroad to Murfreesboro and caused delay since the slow speed of the gunboats ensured they would not return from their Harpeth Shoals mission prior to any heavy attack on the city. Meanwhile, Kelley regained his position, accompanied by two more 12-pounder howitzers and Colonel Jacob Biffle's brigade. It was December 6 before Fitch could reengage his nemesis. He did so with both ironclads and tinclads, convoying a bevy of empty steamboats returning to secure more supplies and soldiers at Clarksville. By noon, Fitch battled a wily Kelley, who substituted field artillery mobility for numbers by running his guns along the high ground above Davidson's Landing, thus confusing the Yankees into thinking he had fourteen not six available guns. The *Neosho* stood to the main effort, firing punishing volleys from its Dahlgren smoothbore cannon mounted in a revolving turret but in turn receiving point-blank fire from Kelley's guns, which swept the vessels' decks of everything, including pilot houses. Two crewmen from the ironclad and the *Moose* won the Congressional Medal of Honor for heroism as the cannonade occupied two and a half hours until Fitch withdrew the damaged *Neosho*. In the end, tinclads and steamers returned to Nashville.[26]

Fitch resumed his duel with Kelley in the late afternoon. Employing both ironclads, despite hampered maneuverability in the narrow river bend, the fight seemed less spirited as Kelley's gunners (perhaps running short of ammunition) suffered more casualties than the Union tars despite their repeated hits on the warships. In Chalmers's view, everything now remained unchanged until Biffle's withdrawal on the twelfth, although by then Fitch had shifted his attention upriver from Nashville, tacitly admitting that the navy alone could not lift the river blockade below the city until helped by cavalry to chase Kelley away. The Louisville and Nashville Railroad and roads from the north provided Thomas's sole means of succor. Nobody quite realized that water levels in the river had been dropping anyway so that navigation would be stymied by nature if not from human actions. One thing was sure: Kelley and low water both contributed to Thomas's anxiety and the pressure for offensive action against Hood's army. Help unexpectedly came from simultaneous actions by Forrest and Bate at Murfreesboro.[27]

Forrest and Bate had proceeded with their own diversion. Forrest's actions, in fact, have received more coverage than Kelley's or Lyon's in the history books. Even Bate's forays were subsumed by Forrest's horsemen. At first, Bate's men forced evacuation of Mill Creek blockhouses while dismantling the railroad between Nashville and Murfreesboro. Brisk skirmishing with the Federals on December 4 only faintly foretold stiffening enemy opposition once Forrest appeared with two cavalry divisions and subsequently several infantry brigades. Bate bridled at the new arrangement, then "readily gave cheerful cooperation" for Hood now wanted reduction of the Murfreesboro fortress and garrison. The pair thus settled into the task by December 7, bent upon overawing their opponents and then taking the place. The town's defenders, Lovell Rousseau and Robert H. Milroy, thought otherwise.[28]

Forrest, of course, knew Murfreesboro well. He had raided and captured the resident Union garrison there on July 13, 1862. Now his luck ran out, mainly because the Federals operated from Fortress Rosecrans (previously staffed by convalescents but now hosting perhaps five regiments of four thousand to five thousand men and fifty-seven guns) as well as a fortified courthouse square downtown. They, like everyone else in the Nashville region, had watched Confederates gobbling up hapless railroad garrisons but this time had a counterstroke of their own planned. Pluckier Federal opposition, outnumbering Forrest and well dug in, added to Milroy's determination to redeem a reputation besmirched the previous year during the Gettysburg campaign in the East. Kentuckian Rousseau was never one to cave in willingly so in something styled the "Battle of the Cedars," Milroy's men shattered Bate's infantry (already frayed by Spring Hill/Franklin) who failed to rally to Forrest's personal appearance. The resulting abject rout was "the first time that men had ever broken in Forrest's presence," suggested one biographer.[29]

Legendary tales emerged of Forrest seizing a flag to rally Bates's fugitives while shooting down a cowardly color bearer, King Phillip's snorting and flying hoofs instilling discipline and backbone and Forrest's own typical stormy battle persona. Still, the Federals ultimately retired to their fortress, and a timely rally by the horsemen of Armstrong, Ross, and Buford was eventually rebuffed in the center of town to conclude the fighting. Forrest had been unexpectedly stung while approximately two hundred Confederate prisoners passed into Union hands, more than the relatively few killed and wounded on either side. Bate and his men soon returned under a cloud to the main army while Forrest with his command and two other brigades kept Rousseau and Milroy in place as they destabilized the region as far east as the Stones River confluence with the Cumberland and Andrew Jackson's Hermitage plantation nearby. Foraging and further destruction of the Nashville and Chattanooga Railroad to block reinforcement from the south kept Forrest's cavalrymen busy. Ross's cavalry took a heavily laden supply train of sugar, coffee, bread, and bacon, as well as two hundred thousand rations, about seven miles south of Murfreesboro on December 15. Unfortunately, the supplies were inadvertently burned just when Hood's army needed them, and Old Bedford himself remained unable to assist in ascertaining Thomas's moves at midmonth. By that time, however, as Arkansas private Philip Daingerfield Stephenson declared, "Our independent operations were at an end, and the time had come for Hood to concentrate every available man." A new opportunity for slaughter awaited.[30]

Actually, Hood had intended that a third separate cavalry expedition operate more deeply upon Federal lines of communication north of Nashville, including the Louisville and Nashville and the lower Cumberland River. As early as November 21, with Beauregard's approval, Hood directed Brigadier General Hylan B. Lyon, commanding the Department of Western Kentucky (and personally at that moment in Corinth obtaining arms for his eight-hundred-man/three-artillery-piece contingent based at Paris, Tennessee), to proceed across the Tennessee and Cumberland Rivers between Paducah and Johnsonville to Clarksville, "taking possession of that place, if possible" before placing all the mills in vicinity "grinding at once." He was then to "destroy the railroads between Nashville and Clarksville, and between Bowling Green and Nashville," especially taking care "to keep all the telegraphic communications between these places constantly destroyed." He would conscript and recruit en route but commanding such a poorly organized and undisciplined column required much work. At least a hundred of the men were dismounted, few had blankets or overcoats, and most of them had been in service for only days or at best months. Lyon, of course, had been around since the Fort Donelson surrender in February 1862. He was a West Pointer and commanded Forrest's confidence. His raid proved the final major Confederate offensive burst in the upper heartland.[31]

Departing Paris in West Tennessee about the same time that Kelley ambushed river traffic and Bate and Forrest busily engaged in railroad destruction, Lyon baffled the Federals at first. Kentucky commanders like Stephen Burbridge frantically sought help while Colonel A. J. Smith at Clarksville told superiors, "I fear he may be going to Fort Donelson" en route to Kentucky and suggested shifting the Forty-second Missouri to bolster that river position. While that was done, and some seven hundred Federals prepared to battle the rebels, Lyon had no intention of going to Dover. He at least sent a flag of truce to the fort demanding transfer of one bluecoat charged with killing a combatant after the latter was captured. Winter passage of the rivers mostly slowed the raider's progress. He captured and destroyed four steamers, four barges loaded with forage, and provisions bound for the capital on the ninth at Cumberland City thirty miles downriver from Clarksville—worth $1 million (including the steamboats). He then discovered the Clarksville garrison too strongly posted, while Rear Admiral Lee and the ironclad *Cincinnati* added to Yankee firepower. Lee, in fact, temporarily turned his attention to Lyon instead of Kelly, although the navy's usual bane of low water prevented either interfering with Lyon's crossing or further ascending the Cumberland to help Fitch. Lyon's "already frosted" men kept warm by uncontestedly destroying track and telegraph lines from the Red River bridge at Clarksville northeastward on the Bowling Green–Memphis rail link to its junction with the Louisville and Nashville line to Nashville. At that point, Lyon diverted to Yankee-evacuated Hopkinsville, Kentucky, much-needed shoes and clothing.[32]

Perhaps the lure of his old Eddyville home neighborhood and protect his family from harassing Yankees, the chance to snatch isolated Union garrisons (especially African American) in fortified courthouses of Kentucky or those much-needed supplies drove Lyon at this point. He left one of his two brigades and one piece of artillery under Colonel John Q. Chenoweth to garrison Hopkinsville while he and the other half of the command went after African American garrisons at Cadiz, Princeton, and Eddyville (the Federals fleeing to Smithland and Fort Donelson). The raiders proceeded to burn courthouses at those locales as well as a stockade or corral ("a place of rendezvous for negroes," Lyon called it) at Eddyville. Along the way, he conscripted unwary Kentucky youth (claiming the right to do so as had Forrest and others throughout West Tennessee) with some four hundred such unwilling recruits joining ranks but apparently deserting at the first opportunity. By this point, Lyon's escapade had gained notice in Nashville and Thomas ordered Wilson to send out what amounted to two brigades of the First Cavalry division under Brigadier General Edward M. McCook to "push Lyon to the wall." By December 10, Nashville headquarters learned from Brigadier General Solomon Meredith at Paducah that Lyon was probably headed "to strike the Green River bridge of the L&N in central Kentucky." Within the week, McCook's troopers had bested Chenoweth but, in turn, were harshly used by Lyon returning quickly to rescue his subordinate. Still, based on what they heard from returning colleagues who went out after Lyon "and his band of thieves," some troops like Edward Summers of the Sixth Kentucky Cavalry, left behind at Nashville, thought the whole raid meant mainly a tally of captured rebel men, horses, wagons, and ambulances at little loss in the pursuit through central Kentucky.[33]

Indeed, Lyon's operation was soon rendered moot for directly aiding Hood. The bitter onset of winter weather afflicted the whole region and Lyon claimed that "it was with greatest difficulty" that his men could be made "to move from the fires built along the road." Of course,

Ruins of Christian County Court House in December 1864, a result of Colonel Lyon's court house burning raid. From Meacham, *History of Christian County*, 129.

McCook's pursuit was similarly affected, with the ice and sleet serving as something of a cover for the fact that, at this point, the raider had hardly accomplished anything of his assignment. Perhaps outriders like George Jesse did. Lyon had not captured Clarksville and had not restarted the grist mills, nor had he interdicted Thomas's main lifeline the Louisville and Nashville Railroad. For Hood and his huddled troops far to the south of the raiders, Lyon's actions mattered less than the fact that the weather had likewise delayed Thomas's inevitable assault. Lyon can be faulted for not acting with more alacrity before the storm struck but then no other Confederate in Middle Tennessee particularly did either. As the main army braced for some sort of Federal onslaught at Nashville, Lyon and his raggedly raiders wandered off in central Kentucky and eventually turned back south trying to reach Confederate lines, pushed closely by Federal pursuers. Timing for Hood's coordinated moves seemed as bad as Thomas's counterthrust.

Neither Hood nor Beauregard had indicated a timetable to begin with, suggesting the notion of merely wintering over in the Nashville region. This implied that either Thomas would do nothing or that Hood could beat him (rendered implausible by Spring Hill/Franklin). Even William Rosecrans had eventually responded to Washington's displeasure by venturing out in midwinter to defeat Bragg at Stones River. Remaining static at the end of 1864 would certainly not preclude a repeat for Hood. Still, no sense of urgency went via dispatch riders to Kelley, Lyon or even what would be the Bate-Forrest attempt to destroy the Nashville and Chattanooga Railroad and take Murfreesboro. Thomas received minor tweaking from Hood's detached operations, but little delay in his buildup for the crowning blow to Confederate fortunes. That blow could come none too soon in the view of Grant and the Lincoln administration.

The Decisive Battle of Nashville

Modern interpretation elevating Spring Hill and Franklin to preeminent status in the Tennessee campaign of 1864 notwithstanding, historian Stanley Horn had it correct in suggesting the decisive battle would occur at Nashville. The stakes were still so high after Hood's earlier catastrophe, and he had not been erased from the chessboard of war. Thomas noted in his official report of January 20, 1865, how Hood's position remained unchanged and that nothing of importance took place except occasional picket firing from the third to the fifteenth of December. He further noted that "both armies were ice-bound" for the week preceding the fourteenth when the weather moderated. It was at that point that the Federal commander struck. He consciously avoided reference to the eleventh-hour spate of telegrams concerning his delays, his possible relief of command, and the fact that at varying points Grant raised the prospect of elevating Schofield, John Logan, or even himself to administer the coup de grace to the Army of Tennessee. Grant professed later to be as unsettled by events as at any time in the war and reports from north of the Ohio suggested sabotage against railroads and possible collaboration with Hood or, however implausible in retrospect, that John C. Breckinridge seemed to be moving in that direction. Thus Grant constantly badgered from City Point, "I want General Thomas reminded of the importance of immediate action," to which Halleck replied on the evening of the eighth, "If you wish General Thomas relieved from [command], give the order. No one here will, I think, interfere. The responsibility, however, will be yours, as no one here, so far as I am informed, wishes General Thomas' removal."[34]

The essential fact was that nobody was going to move the "Rock of Chickamauga" until he was good and ready for a sledgehammer blow. He intended such for December 10, although nobody up the chain of command knew it. Grant hemmed and hawed all morning of December 9 and finally ordered Thomas's relief. When he was informed that afternoon, Thomas offered to "submit without a murmur." But the bottom of his reply offered a telling sentence: "A terrible storm of freezing rain has come on since daylight, which will render an attack impossible until it breaks." All that Grant could do was to fret and bluster at Old Pap's slowness (all the while holding the relief order in readiness). In fact, for two previous days Thomas had made noises about attacking, had sent probing reconnaissance by skirmishers supported by artillery and scouted the lines daily himself. He issued preparatory orders for stocking rations, forage while more reinforcements came in from Memphis and St. Louis. Deserter reports noted the rebels trying to take Murfreesboro to winter there rather than Nashville. Only the weather interfered.

Unperturbed at pressure from above or rumors from below, Thomas calmly told attack commanders Schofield, A. J. Smith, J. B. Steedman. and Thomas J. Wood that the severity of the storm precluded the December 10 attack but that "I desire that everything be put in condition to carry out the plan contemplated as soon as the weather will permit it to be done, so that we can act instantly when the storm clears away." Yet conditions were no better for the next three days. Wood reported the ground in his front "is covered with a heavy sleet, which would make the handling of troops very difficult, if not impracticable." Troops could not move with facility so that "an offensive movement would necessarily be feeble, and feebleness of movement would almost certainly result in failure." Grant continued to badger from afar, and Thomas stood his ground, slippery as it was both meteorologically and metaphorically.[35]

The soldiers from both sides used the ice storm to meet and swap tobacco and conversation. With the advent of cold and icy weather, the rebels muddled in makeshift trenches and bivouacs, suffering far more than Hood's staffers back at Traveler's Rest plantation. Conditions were so bleak with Brigadier General Randall Gibson's Louisianans that the cold, poor rations and lack of proper footwear led to burrowing in the frozen earth as well as marginal fashioning of moccasins from uncured hides. Yankees like those in Company C of the Twelfth Iowa likewise made do but with closer proximity to Nashville's supplies and even late morning slumbers in pup tents equipped with fireplaces as they awaited action. They could do little else but wait. Only "midnight requisitioning" from the countryside and an emergency issuance of a beer ration by December 10 kept most Confederates in the ranks. The plundering disturbed Gibson, however, and he ordered the loot given up to "some officer or man who has remained by the Colors and obeyed orders." At least one concerned Nashville family, the Bosticks, sent their daughter through the lines seeking word on sons, Joe and Tom, serving with Hood. Daughter Catherine completed her mission successfully only to be apprehended and sternly reprimanded by occupation authorities for the effort. Apparently, the lull was not universally bad for Illinoisan Frederick Nathan Boyer told how one stormy night he and a captain went to the city to a theater and decided afterward that the four or five mile hike back to camp through rain and mud warranted simply going to a hotel. The next morning he proposed "we go around to Riddle-berger's or Dongana (the two biggest restaurants in town) and get one good square meal, for we may never get another one, as we will have a big battle now soon." His comrade agreed "and we did so, got the best breakfast we could and it cost $11.60 for the two of us and nothing to drink but coffee, and no smokes."[36]

Finally, on December 13, Grant ordered Major General John Logan to proceed to Nashville and relieve Thomas, although some "back-channel" telegrams from Nashville headquarters to Washington should have alerted everyone that a "thaw has begun, and to-morrow we can move without skates." This was good because, while expectations rose that Lyon might soon cut use of the L&N and communication by tele-graph, intelligence also disclosed the rebels shifting their lines a bit, with Hood actually out reconnoitering to construct more earthworks and rumored to be still "confident of taking Nashville." Thomas called his corps commanders together that afternoon, discussed the plan of attack, and issued Special Field Order 342 outlining specific missions. In addition to Smith, Wilson, Wood, Schofield, and Steedman, even Brigadier General John F. Miller, commanding the Nashville post and Brigadier General James F. Donaldson's quartermaster contingents had specific assignments. The great guns of Nashville's forts would provide long-distance suppressant fire. At last, at 8:00 p.m. on December 14, the army commander wired Halleck the words that Washington and City Point anxiously awaited: "The ice having melted away to-day, the enemy will be attacked to-morrow morning." Perhaps sixty-six thou-sand Federals stood ready to smite about twenty-three thousand of their enemy.[37]

When the long-awaited Federal assault came on the warmer yet very foggy morning of Thursday, December 15, there would be no

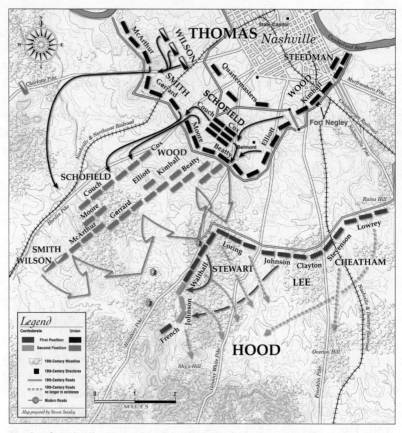

Battle of Nashville, December 15, 1864. Map by Steven Stanley and courtesy of the Civil War Preservation Trust.

sledgehammer blow it seemed. Thomas intended a very simple roll-up of Hood's exposed western flank. Despite Confederate expectations, the opposite flank and direct route to relieve Murfreesboro did not receive Thomas's attention, knowing Rousseau was secure and in no danger of being starved into surrender. He did plan a diversion by Steedman's troops along the Murfreesboro Pike to cover the main buildup west of the Hardin or Harding Pike for the great left sweep. Then, although the troops had been rousted out of bivouac at 4:00 a.m., the dense fog prevented movement for another four hours. Steedman jumped off and almost immediately discovered a well defended anchoring lunette near the Nashville and Chattanooga Railroad rather than an anticipated "log curtain." Confederate arms poured in a deadly fire that decimated particularly attacking U.S. Colored Troops.

Meanwhile, to the west, Twelfth Iowa chaplain Frederick Humphrey recalled poetically how the Union deployment went out "with regimental banners, battle flags and national colors unfurled, and . . . with measured step"—"men, earnest men—men who knew their duty to God and country," clothed in simple blue, soiled by fatigue, symbols of fidelity, and armed with sword, musket, and rifled artillery. They were going into the field to do their duty, in all, "a sublime exhibition of the nation's power." Poetic license of the man of the cloth notwithstanding, the Union flanking advance only inched forward while artillery from Fort Negley and its sister fortifications rained down on the suspected main Confederate lines located on a variety of knolls and heights, like Montgomery Hill to their front. When Wood's IV Corps eventually plunged forward against that 150-foot elevation, the men in blue discovered to their dismay few rebels—merely the remnants of the enemy skirmish line, for the main body had been relocated southward by a mile or so for at least a week. The southerners simply had needed firewood, but this move left their foe with red faces at being outfoxed and poorly served by intelligence. Perhaps Wood had had some indication when the day before he sent Thomas a call for a command briefing to share information with Schofield, Smith, and Wilson on the real state of things to their front. No matter now, with dusk falling, Thomas seemed perplexed that the attack had failed to even reach Hood's principal positions. Unnoticed in the proceedings, Kelley had left the Cumberland, drawn more by the developing battle in his rear than a poorly coordinated attack by Fitch's gunboats and Wilson's Sixth Cavalry division.[38]

For his part, Hood remained preoccupied with headquarters business until signalers flagged news of Steedman's assault about midmorning on the fifteenth. The army commander then hastened to the front. Attaching himself to Stewart's position, he soon realized the masses of blue-coated troops advancing from the north and west suggested that he had bet on the wrong axis of Federal attack. When he tried to shift forces to counter the main enemy movements along the line, he found that any hope of a reverse Franklin was gone. Federal attacks shattered Confederate lines, and by nightfall the day's events suggested that Hood commanded scattering units in much disarray. Stewart's corps lay completely wrecked with only Stephen Lee's corps intact and prepared for further combat. The retiring Confederates rallied on a new line under the shadow of the Brentwood hills. Darkness slowed the Federal momentum. The question was, would Hood order a general retirement or would he stay and face the consequences?

Again, Hood's choices seemed limited; withdrawal would be complete admission of failure and cost him his command, while to remain was gambling that command's fate on a throw of the dice on the morrow. Recognizing Thomas's battle plan, Hood bet on two anchors at opposite ends of a shortened defense line—Peach Orchard hill on Overton's property beyond the Franklin Pike on the east and what would become known as Shy's Hill beyond Granny White Pike on the west. In between, a strong stone wall and ersatz breastworks utilizing ground sloping away toward the attackers would have to provide the main line of defense. Fairly noncommittal about the day's disaster in both his initial dispatches to Richmond and later official report, his dispatches that night indicated that he circulated plans for ultimate withdrawal the following evening and, above all, a call to Forrest "to hold myself in readiness to move at any moment." Hood reestablished headquarters at Judge J. M. Lea's "Lealand" located by Stewart's new position.[39]

The night of December 15–16 was a busy one, in both Washington as at Nashville. Thomas communicated his elation at the day's success to the War Department at 9:00 p.m. "I attacked the enemy's left this morning and drove it from the river below the city, very nearly to the Franklin pike, a distance about eight miles," read his wire to Halleck. Sixteen pieces of artillery, headquarters and other wagons, as well as about one thousand prisoners, had been taken. The troops had behaved splendidly, all taking a share in assaulting and carrying the enemy's breastworks. Then came the words that Lincoln, Stanton, Halleck— and especially Grant—wanted to hear: "I shall attack the enemy again to-morrow, if he stands to fight, and, if he retreats during the night, will pursue him, throwing a heavy cavalry force in his rear, to destroy his trains, if possible." J. C. Van Duzer embellished the news in a later telegram to his telegraph corps superior T. T. Eckert at the capital, and the latter, suppressing Grant's rush to supplant Thomas with a fighter, spread word to the secretary of war and president.

Grant, in the city himself en route to personally relieve Thomas, suffered some embarrassment when Eckert first apprised him of Van Duzer's wire and subsequently with Thomas's own wire in hand. Still, he quickly added congratulations to Stanton's thanks "for the brilliant achievements of the day" and the hope that it would be "the harbinger of a decisive victory that will crown you and your army with honor and do much toward closing the war." The secretary promised a hundred gun salute from Washington's fortress batteries in the morning. Grant, however, could not help himself from continuing to nag Thomas "to

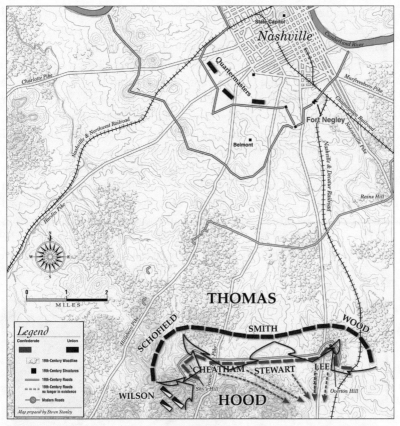

Battle of Nashville, December 16, 1864. Map by Steven Stanley and courtesy of the Civil War Preservation Trust.

push the enemy now, and give him no rest until he is entirely destroyed." Do not stop for trains or supplies, "but take them from the country, as the enemy has done" as "your army will cheerfully suffer many privations to break up Hood's army and render it useless for future operations." "Much is now expected," Grant added, before departing back to City Point. Stanton, for his part, couldn't wait to send a wire to all northern governors announcing the victory. The president's focus was more like Grant's. "You have made a magnificent beginning," he wired Thomas at 11:25 p.m. on December 16. "A grand consummation is within your easy reach. Do not let it slip."[40]

Thomas intended no slippage, though Hood might have taken temporary solace when sunrise the next day again shrouded the ground in mist and the Federals once again dallied in bivouac. The sun burned off the mist and still no attack. Thomas's subordinates ill served their commander's plans. Smith's men hesitated momentarily at Confederates dug in on Shy's hill as well as the breastworks along the main line. Schofield, hardly living up to Grant's expectations (or his own, for he apparently thought later that he could have fought the battle better than Thomas), was spooked by ghosts of Hood's rash attacks at Franklin. He complained about insufficient troops (and perhaps the XXIII Corps was inadequate to the task after that earlier contest) while doing nothing. Worse, he ranked Wilson and held back the brash young cavalry commander to protect the infantry instead of letting him rush on to fulfill Thomas's flank movement. One Federal cavalry brigade had undertaken a reconnaissance, gotten all the way behind Hood's lines to the Granny White Pike, and was poised to cut off the retreat of the entire rebel army. Then the brigade commander pulled back under an

A stereopticon view of the attack by U.S. Colored Troops in the Battle of Nashville. Courtesy of Skip Doscher.

order from Schofield to Wilson and thus lost an early opportunity to affect the course of the day's combat. Vexed once more by his lethargic and skittish juniors, Thomas waited impatiently as light rain began to fall about noon. The soldiery passed their time like their commander in waiting.[41]

Steedman and Wood provided some relief (and tragic entertainment) when the latter impetuously orchestrated a four-brigade assault of Peach Orchard Hill from two directions at midafternoon. Strong abatis and breastworks allowed S. D. Lee's infantrymen (especially Gibson's Louisianans) to gleefully decimate what proved to be largely a U.S. Colored Troops assault. Delivered valorously and stubbornly, it was completely in vain and at variance with Thomas's continued orders to hold in the east and allow Wilson and Schofield to once more envelop Hood's western flank. The destruction of the locally raised Thirteenth Regiment, U.S. Colored Troops with the loss of their prized flag ("presented by the colored ladies of Murfreesboro") was tragic and a feather in rebel caps that afternoon notwithstanding one officer's admiration that "they came only to die." In truth, fully one-third of Union losses in two days of battle at Nashville occurred in the attempt to overrun Peach Orchard hill. Wood may have desired to erase the onus of his misunderstood orders at Chickamauga (costing Rosecrans the battle despite Thomas's heroic rally on Snodgrass Hill, which had earned him the sobriquet "Rock of Chickamauga"). Wood's impetuosity now was not the way to do so.[42]

The tide began to turn when Thomas finally got Wilson moving. His cavalrymen forced Chalmers off a barricaded hill somewhere near the Granny White Pike and thus opened up Hood's left rear. Moreover, the intrepid action of Smith's First Division commander, John McArthur (native Scotsman, later with an ironworks firm in Chicago and a veteran of western battles from Fort Donelson and Shiloh to Vicksburg and one of the army's unsung fighters), cracked the Shy's Hill road block. While Thomas, Schofield, and Wilson discussed the impossibility of doing so, McArthur's men went forward successfully up the north slope of the hill, and Thomas calmly directed Schofield to advance his whole line. At that point, Hood had made another poor decision. Confident that Shy's Hill could defend itself, he pulled back some recently dispatched reinforcements to that position and concerned himself with developments in Stewart's sector. Bate's men once more became the goat of the affair. Amid hand-to-hand fighting, McArthur's men killed Lieutenant Colonel William M. Shy of the Twentieth Tennessee (whose name would forever attach to memory) and Bate's men evaporated in the same fashion as they had several days before at Murfreesboro. Like dominoes, the panic spread to A. P. Stewart's adjacent troops. Within minutes over fifteen hundred infantrymen, eighty-five officers, eight cannon, and at least four flags became trophies of the Federals on Shy's Hill.

McArthur's reinforced attackers then turned and simply rolled up Confederate positions eastward to Peach Orchard Hill. Confederate generals Thomas Benton Smith, Henry Jackson, and Edward Johnson joined the rapidly expanding pool of prisoners. Cheatham dashed by remnants of his command "at full speed saying as he passed take care of yourselves boys the best you can I am going to make that pass through the ridge or die in the attempt and disappeared in our rear," recalled Tom Walker of the Ninth Tennessee. Right then Walker "thought the army was lost beyond all hope." Before long, Wood and Steedman even joined in the progressive attack knocking Lee off John Overton's Peach Orchard hill in the gathering rain and gloom of late afternoon. Many Confederates later expressed surprise at seeing "men & riderless horses rushing in wild confusion" from the woods on their left toward the Franklin Pike. The whole line collapsed en echelon as, even worse, Wilson's cavalry now expedited the rout since they did not have to worry about Forrest's presence. Lee rode fretfully among the fugitives, imploring them to "rally men, rally" as "this is the place for brave men to die." Darkness saved the fugitives as many made "that pass in the ridge" safely. "Thus ended one of the most disastirous [*sic*] battles of the western army," remembered Walker. The Army of Tennessee simply disintegrated before everyone's eyes.[43]

Afterward came the participants' colorful comments about the fiasco. Hood offered in his memoirs that "I beheld for the first and only time a Confederate Army abandon the field in confusion." Confederate corps commander Ben Cheatham observed that it looked "like a flock of wild geese when they have lost their leader." Countless others probably thought as did one disconsolate rebel that he had "never seen an army so confused and demoralized." It was simply "a wide wake nightmare" to another, while a Mississippian discovered that he was the sole survivor of his company, his clothing riddled with bullet holes, his musket splintered. Granny White and Franklin Pikes were awash with abandoned cannon, caissons, wagons, horses, mules, and demoralized defenders chaotically mingled in a rush southward toward safety. Officers tried unsuccessfully to stem the tide and the battle now seemed like a great expelling of wind from a balloon as herded prisoners light-heartedly told their captors that they were finally going in to Nashville. Disdainfully, one Yankee lieutenant held his nose and observed these prisoners were as ragged, dirty, and as smelly as "a flock of sheep on a hot June day." Fully a third lacked shoes, all were cold and hungry, as the two-day battle of Nashville concluded what had begun at Spring Hill and Franklin.

Hood's men had simply had enough. One of Cheatham's brigade commanders, Colonel Andrew J. Kellar, determinedly claimed two days later that "it was not by fighting, nor the force of arms, nor even num-bers, which drove us from the field." He did not elaborate on just what it was, however. Years later, Schofield remembered distinctly a conver-sation he had that afternoon with one captured field officer. Schofield asked him if he recognized the fact that his side was beaten and the prisoner replied simply, "Not till you routed us just now." Schofield doubted the man at the time for they surely recognized their defeat at Franklin or at least the day before at Nashville. Later he concluded, "I doubt if any soldiers in the world ever needed so much cumulative evidence to convince them that they were beaten." That night he told Thomas that he was "satisfied Hood's army is more thoroughly beaten than any troops I have seen."[44]

Such an impression conveyed by telegraph to Washington that eve-ning. Thomas's own recounting of the detailed movements of Decem-ber 17 suggested victory, fatigued troops, that "the greatest enthusiasm prevails," and that pursuit would begin in the morning. Van Duzer's midafternoon wire had been dramatically optimistic given the situation at that moment—Hood fallen back and apparently doing his best to get away, Thomas pressing with great vigor "frequently capturing guns and men," while "everything so far is perfectly successful, and the prospect very fair to crush Hood's army." By midevening, his account detailed each commander's success, the sizable number of captured small arms, where the rebels had stood, and from that information the deduction that "Hood cannot make another such a days fight, while Thomas is in good condition to press him." Van Duzer beamed, "Everybody, white and black, did splendidly." Thomas would report forty-nine pieces of artillery (Hood would admit to fifty), thousands of small arms, and five thousand prisoners from the Nashville affair. He had lost perhaps three thousand casualties with about 10 percent killed in action; eventually a Confederate casualty count calculated perhaps about twenty-three hun-dred killed and wounded.[45]

Annihilation or Escape

Chalmers's small cavalry force, really only Colonel Edmund Rucker's small brigade, provided Hood's immediate rear guard at the end of the fighting. By this time, the full power of Wilson's rejuvenated horsemen had crushed Chalmers's men despite the rebel army commander's order to "hold the granny White Pike at all hazards." Fighting from behind a low barricade, the graycoats proved no match for their opponents as Colonels George Spalding of the Twelfth Tennessee Cavalry (U.S.) confronted his counterpart Rucker as nominal commander of the Twelfth Tennessee Cavalry (C.S.) in one of those quirks of fraternal war. Rucker fell wounded and was captured by others in the Yankee Tennessee outfit, and Wilson later pondered on the "exciting day and night," which he thought vindicated "my policy of concentrating in masses instead of detachments." At the time, Thomas shouted to young Wilson "so that he might have been heard a quarter of a mile: 'Dang it to hell, Wilson, didn't I tell you we could lick 'em, didn't I tell you we could lick 'em?'" In the darkness, he directed his men to "continue the pursuit as far as you can to-night and resume it as early as you can to-morrow morning."[46]

The verdicts of two historians—Stanley Horn's premise that Nashville was the decisive battle of the Civil War and Wiley Sword's comment that it was the war's "most devastating defeat of a major army"—echoed Ohio private Joseph Stewart's sick-bed comment from Murfreesboro to his wife on December 24 that it was "the greatest victory of the war." Still, while Stewart anticipated that Thomas would capture all of Hood's forces before he got out of Tennessee, the combat thus far had not completely destroyed them. Ever churlish toward Old Pap, Grant eyed destruction when he had wired Thomas at 11:00 p.m. on the first night. Nothing more came from Grant until noon on the eighteenth, when he wired that the armies operating around Richmond "have fired 200 guns in honor of your great victory." Even then Grant could not refrain from trumpeting Sherman's accomplishments and further expectations, as well as the perennial concern for Forrest's whereabouts and how "after Hood is driven as far as it is possible to follow him," Thomas should reoccupy Decatur and all other abandoned points. Already one could sense Grant's resignation that annihilation might be impossible. As chapter titles in James Wilson's memoir read forty years later, "Confronting Hood at Nashville" would give way to merely "Driving Hood Out."[47]

At this point, however, from the morning of the seventeenth until the nineteenth of December, a window existed not to merely defeat but to actually destroy the fabled Army of Tennessee. "The whole army was still 'mobized' [*sic*] and devoid of military demeanor," stated one pitiful rebel survivor, apparently kept together by the "cement of common danger." Another, from Bates's division, having thrown away gun and accouterments and run for two days, sat down alone in the woods and took stock. Rolling up his sleeves and examining himself all over, he then vented his "pheelinks": "I am whupped, badly whipped and somewhat demoralized; but no man can say I am scattered." And apparently three distinct encounters punctuated such sentiment over the thirty-mile course from Brentwood back to Spring Hill. Victorious Yankees and defeated rebels fought again at Hollow Tree Gap, four miles north of Franklin, the Harpeth River crossing, and then once farther south, but these skirmishes resulted in no annihilation of a beaten army.

Hood remained undecided about totally quitting the campaign or taking the defensive and regrouping in positions behind the Duck River at Columbia. Unaware of any useful result from Lyon's foray in Kentucky, Hood nevertheless remained seemingly resolute in the face of the Nashville result. His dispatch to Secretary of War James A. Seddon from a command post in the fateful village of Spring Hill on the seventeenth rather unemotionally recounted events. In Wiley Sword's view, Hood neither made mention of a failed campaign, the rout of his army or the threat to his army until it reached the south bank of the Duck at Columbia. He took council from subordinates, watched the army self-dismantle before him, and may have pondered the advice of Nathan Bedford Forrest (now returned to the army and hardly given to equivocation) that if the army commander felt uncertain about holding the state then he should give it up and get the army back behind the shelter of the Tennessee River. At least this was the version told by Dr. Charles Todd Quintard, Episcopal bishop of Tennessee, of Hood's staff.[48]

Such advice, notwithstanding, Hood could personally see the disintegrating situation with every mile. Veteran troops noted how the force had "degenerated to a mob," even the citizenry shunning their approach. Farmer Nimrod Porter near Columbia agreed, jotting in his diary how they were "the worst broke down set I ever saw," taking what little corn was left in the countryside, in fact, "trying to take everything" as they robbed cattle, cows, and calves. "We are badly treated by them," he complained, adding that it was hard work to prevent such thievery. With such scenes around him, Hood made the fateful decision at Columbia on the evening of the eighteenth—retreat to Alabama. Perhaps, said accompanying rebel governor Isham G. Harris, "it is the best we can do." The retreat route provided a rutted, slushy, even frozen highway perhaps reminiscent of Napoleon's retirement from Moscow. Wilson's Yankees substituted for Cossacks on Hood's flanks.[49]

In truth, Thomas himself contributed to the failure to annihilate Hood's mob. Perhaps the elixir of victory on the night of December 16 hampered response; certainly nighttime confusion and mixing of friend and foe, as well as general aversion to night fighting, worked their wiles. Wilson, it seems, was quite ready to begin the work of destruction again the next morning, calling for reveille shortly after 3:00 a.m. Then orders arrived from Thomas during the night that threw off the plan and lost momentum, despite what eventually turned out to be a very productive day of pushing the Confederate rear echelons, gobbling up more prisoners and finding more flotsam of defeat at Franklin and Granny White Pike waysides. If the weather held and the creeks and rivers did not rise, further pursuit might bag Hood's remaining force. But any stiffer Confederate resistance would require the assistance of Thomas Wood's IV Corps. Thomas's error came in directing the army's pontoon train to accompany the pursuit, but using the Murfreesboro, not the Franklin Pike. Major James B. Willett, the train commander wasted precious time and energy going in a divergent direction. Impassability of cross-country roads then confounded this part of the operation, and what with backtracking to Nashville before securing the Franklin road by December 19, the crucial bridging equipment would not catch up with the front of the pursuit until two days later, in essence a week late. Sword suggests Thomas may have been less than forthright in eventually reporting this slip in official dispatches.[50]

Yet Wilson and the pursuers made good headway for several days. The weather essentially held until the nineteenth as the cavalrymen dashed through and around Confederate roadblocks and conducted running battles with the fugitives all the way past Franklin. Then the first serious delay came at the Harpeth River with the retreating Confederates destroying bridges behind them. By this time, both Thomas and infantrymen had joined up and discovered the melancholy, even sickening, reminders left from Schofield's contest in the town. Crowded hospitals, hastily placed wooden grave makers and unsettling destruction marked the fighting's epicenter around the Carter House area. Bodies from the carnage had been simply dumped in the breastwork ditch and improperly covered over with earth. Dr. Belleville Temple of the Thirty-fourth Alabama presided over two thousand sick and wounded at the Episcopal church in town. Ultimately, after several months of such duty, he "was ordered with soldier nurses and convalescent soldiers" to the northern prisoner of war compound at Camp Chase, Ohio. He and the others would eventually be paroled and allowed to go home when the war ended in the spring. But for the moment impressions from Franklin may well have worked upon the psyche of tired pursuers and pursued as they transited the scene in late December 1864.[51]

Retreat to Ignominy

December 19, 1864, arguably proved the breaking point for Hood's survival and Thomas's goal of annihilation. Unappreciated by the distant leaders in Washington and at City Point, and apparently not really anticipated by Thomas's army on the ground, the atrocious weather once again descended upon two armies in motion. Hood's eleven-day retreat to sanctuary below the Tennessee River in north Alabama and eventually encampments at Tupelo, Mississippi, constituted a saga of its own. That anyone survived testified to the fortitude of officers and men. The worst of it commenced south of Columbia starting that day. Rain, sleet, snow, subfreezing temperatures, muddy and rutted roads, and swollen creeks provided the backdrop for the ill-fed, ill-clothed Confederate soldiers who, like their remaining horses and mules, just wanted to escape for another day. They marched not in units but in small clusters of the despairing, many without arms, periodically slaughtering cattle simply to use the hides so that the next day they could "go whistling along with their cowhide slippers as merrily as wedding bells," remembered Walker of the Tennessee Ninth. Desertions and furloughs would lessen their numbers to barely fourteen thousand by trek's end.

Neighborhood residents like Betty Ridley Blackmore wondered at the fate of her son Brom, knowing full well by the rapidly passing soldiers and wagons that Hood had suffered defeat. "Such gloom and sorrow in every heart—nature seems to mourn with us," for "it has been dark and lowering and drizzling for 2 days—not a ray of sunshine, and but little hope in our hearts." She feared the Yankees "will overtake, and destroy a good many" of the army before they could cross the Duck River. That they had not done so already was a testament to divine intervention by nature, perhaps, and fate. The saga was adroitly captured by Wiley Sword when he recounted how an equally despondent Sam Hood had to listen to the mournful chorus of "Yellow Rose of

Texas"—sung from the ranks about marching southward, with hearts full of woe—going back to Georgia to see his "Uncle Joe" (alluding to their late beloved commander, Joe Johnston). You might talk about Beauregard or even Bobby Lee, went the ditty, "but the gallant Hood of Texas, played Hell in Tennessee."[52]

From Franklin on to Nashville and now back south of the Duck River, it had truly been hell in Tennessee for the army of that name. On Christmas Day, Forrest's rear guard unaccountably sent large quantities of abandoned bacon, clothing, and boxes of ammunition up in smoke in the town square at Pulaski. Georgia colonel George H. Olmstead recorded noticing women and children pressed against window panes, watching and weeping at the spectacle. He hoped that none of his kinfolk would ever have to see another day like that. So much for the holiday of peace on earth and good will to men, he sarcastically wrote. Still, the Federal pursuit encountered tougher going once Hood's ragtag crew made it below Columbia. With the weather and road conditions it took them until Christmas Eve to bridge the Duck River and resume pursuit. According to Illinoisan Frederick Boyer, the pontoon bridge was made "out of wagon beds, covered with canvas (great ingenuity of the American Army), and rafts." Even then, logistics problems appeared—shoes wearing out, lack of forage for the animals, combining for Thomas with a resumption of that carping, implied criticism from Washington to make every possible sacrifice and "submit to any hardship and privation to accomplish the great result." Impatiently, Thomas replied, reiterating that "pursuing an enemy through an exhausted country, over mud roads, completely sogged with heavy rains," was "no child's play, and cannot be accomplished as quickly as thought of."[53]

Stiffening resistance at Lynnville on December 20 followed by Richland Creek both between Columbia and Pulaski, then Anthony's Hill on Christmas Day and Sugar Creek the day after (both close to the Alabama line), rebuffed a slowing Federal pursuit. Much of those rebuffs traced to the Forrest's bolstering return. Even Wilson had posed the nagging question at the end of the battle: Just where had Forrest been? He noted that only after the second day's action before the city was Forrest's absence apparent and only two days later did the ranks learn of the Murfreesboro diversion—about a quarter of the investing army, he reckoned. "While it cannot be said with certainty that, had Forrest been present with this force united with that of Chalmers, on the left of Hood's line he would have been able to hold it," suggested Wilson, "it may well be claimed that he could have made a better and more stubborn defense than was made by Chalmers and Ector alone." The specter of Forrest would always hover over any Yankee opponent's response.[54]

The saga ground on toward a bitter conclusion. Another critical milestone came the day after a bleak Christmas. The country and roads south of Pulaski were ice coated, and Hood now moved his pontoon train to the head of the column to ensure its emplacement at Bainbridge, Alabama, on the Tennessee River. A crossing six miles above Florence at the foot of Muscle Shoals would gain sanctuary beyond. Forrest helped with bitter resistance at Sugar Creek on that day, causing Wilson to simply call off further pursuit because of the mounting toll on men and horses. Wood's IV Corps infantry encamped barely out of Pulaski awaiting food and forage coming by wagon train. Federals and Confederates alike now dined on rescued corn cobs from adjacent fields. Wilson later estimated five thousand horses lost in pursuit of Hood, largely due to the debilitating conditions, and it seems that the boys in blue were just as filthy, worn out and about in as wretched condition as their opponents. The best Wilson might do was to detach Spalding with his Twelfth Tennesseans to strike for the river so that Wilson could ascertain "what could be done." If Hood's stragglers stood ripe for one final push to destruction, who might deliver it? As it turned out, neither Wood nor Wilson nor any of the Nashville column. Perhaps that final thrust would come from a joint army-navy expedition sent around by water from Nashville.[55]

Thomas had one final opportunity to destroy his opponent. Halleck had already ordered Major General Napoleon Dana at Memphis to send an expedition to break railroads in Hood's rear. Once again the underutilized and restless Brigadier General Benjamin Grierson showed his best at railroad-busting taking out the Mobile and Ohio in late December and early January. In his personal memoirs many years later, Grierson thought his raid had left Hood and his men "most disagreeably surprised and chagrined to find their railroad communications with the south interrupted, and their much-needed food, clothing, and other supplies destroyed by our audacious raiders." Meanwhile, Thomas requested Admiral Lee on December 17 to let Fitch proceed up the Tennessee with one or two ironclads and gunboats to destroy Hood's pontoon bridge at Florence (as well as falsely reported bridge building at the mouth of the Duck River). The next evening, the general requested the navy to convoy a fleet of transports from Clifton or Johnsonville bound for Florence to block Hood's retreat. Thomas envisioned a double envelopment to cut Hood off from sanctuary by directing Steedman the next day to march to Murfreesboro from the army's concentration at Columbia, thence by rail through Stevenson, Alabama. Gordon Granger's garrison there would take Decatur from P. D. Roddey's Confederates so that Steedman might quickly switch to river transport and further interdict Hood's retreat by destroying any bridges in the Tuscumbia area. In reply to another of Grant's unsubtle proddings, Thomas enthusiastically wired his chief early on Christmas Eve, "I am really very hopeful that either Gen Steedman or Admiral Lee will reach the Tenn. in time to destroy Hoods pontoon bridge, in which event I shall certainly be able to capture or destroy almost the entire army now with Hood."[56]

It was not to be. Neither party accomplished Thomas's goal. Steedman and Granger found that capturing Decatur took longer than antici-pated; indeed so had the rail and steamer trip getting there. Not until evening of the twenty-seventh was that accomplished. More censurable was Admiral Lee's action, for he got into position in time to do damage; then after some desultory exchange between two light-draft gunboats and rebel shore batteries, the sailor decided that foggy weather and a rapidly falling river dictated withdrawal on the twenty-sixth. The next day he remained reluctant to make any lunge toward Hood's bridge at Bainbridge thus earning Wilson's enmity since the locals claimed he could have reached the span without trouble. True, late-arriving orders may have delayed Lee at Eastport on the twenty-sixth awaiting arrival of a Paducah troop convoy and an overland cavalry force (perhaps that of Spaulding). In any event, by late morning of December 28, the last of Hood's rear guard disappeared across the rickety eighty-boat bridge and by midafternoon, and the pontoons had been taken up. The muddy, debris-strewn Tennessee once more defined a "frontier" between Con-federate and Union forces. Thomas received the news of both occur-rences on the afternoon of the twenty-ninth. In the end, an admiral's timidity had allowed Hood again to avoid a fatal blow.[57]

Only one aspect of Hood's invasion remained in play by this time. That was Colonel Hylan B. Lyon's Kentucky foray. While Hood de-stroyed the flower of his army before Nashville, Lyon had continued northeastward from Hopkinsville, knowing that Thomas would send troopers in pursuit. Indeed, diversion of cavalry from the Thomas's own effort against Hood was probably Lyon's singular contribution to the campaign. Certainly scavenging the countryside and towns of west-ern and central Kentucky, plus burning Union-held courthouses and supply facilities, bridges, and facilities of the Louisville and Nashville Railroad, while the stuff of legends, had little effect on the main events. When Lyon's men learned of Hood's disaster at Nashville, shortly before Christmas, they deserted in droves. True, Brigadier General Edward M. McCook and Colonel Oscar H. La Grange never quite caught up with Lyon. The same foul weather that deterred Wilson and the infantry in crossing Duck River in Tennessee similarly impeded La Grange on the Green River. Lyon escaped, did minor damage on the main stem of the Louisville and Nashville Railroad, and then faded southward through Columbia, Burkesville, Livingston, Sparta, McMinnville, and Winchester always just ahead of pursuers at swollen streams yet losing momentum on the way. Like Hood, the raiders eluded Union gunboats on the Tennessee River, crossing at Gunter's Landing, Alabama, having taken one last shot at a Scottsboro, Alabama, Yankee garrison.[58]

Lyon's luck gave out when Colonel William J. Palmer's Fifteenth Pennsylvania Cavalry surprised the troopers encamped on the fifteenth of January at Red Hill. They captured or dispersed the two hundred remaining raiders. Lyon fled to Tuscaloosa, leaving a howitzer, ninety-five prisoners, and 120 "good, but much jaded horses" in Yankee hands. Both McCook and Lyon claimed partial success with their respective sides of the endeavor. The former thought his primary object was accomplished when "the force of general Lyon was dispersed and rendered powerless for further harm." He advised higher headquarters to occupy some parts of western Kentucky "with a small but active force of cavalry, whose duty it shall be to arrest and dispose of everyman who is not known to be a bona fide resident of the neighborhood where he is found." The country could productively subsist a sufficient force, he wrote, and "this is the only way in which these guerrilla bands can be prevented from again concentrating and becoming formidable from their numbers." "Undisciplined and but poorly organized" as they were, Lyon hardly considered himself or his force necessarily guerrillas and boasted of capturing three valuable steamers, burning eight fortified courthouses, several important railroad bridges, depots, stockades, and blockhouses while capturing and paroling 250 prisoners and diverting perhaps 4,500 Union veterans from direct pursuit of Hood. He had enforced the Confederate draft, bringing out 400 Kentuckians, and had secured from a Hopkinsville bank sufficient Federal monies to defray the cost of the expedition, he claimed. He thought he had accomplished everything expected by Hood except "putting the mills in running order near Clarksville, Tenn." When all things were considered pertaining to the expedition, he observed, "it was a success beyond my most sanguine expectations."[59]

Wilson called Lyon an "illusive cuss," and Thomas floridly termed Palmer's final fight at Red Hill "the last blow of the campaign, at a distance of over 200 miles from where we first struck the enemy on the 15th of December, near Nashville." But in western Kentucky, Lyon's passage would be remembered by one later historian's reference to the raider as "the courthouse burnin'est general" in the Confederacy. Whether because some of those symbols of Federal occupation power and governance held indictment papers against Confederate sympathizers or the one in Cumberland County served as Federal commissary and quartermaster facilities or that those in Taylor, Trigg, and Ohio Counties provided the enemy with headquarters and dormitories for transiting troops, even African American soldiers, explanations for Lyon's antics, like those of Morgan, Forrest, Wheeler, and Roddey, proved legion over time. The fortified courthouses provided a pretense for destruction as legitimate military targets. Supposedly court records were spared, but not so citizen treasure, horses, or, according to some accounts, even women's virtue. The main thing, however, was that Hood, Forrest, and now Lyon—all heralds of Confederate resurgence in the West—were no longer a serious threat to the upper heartland.[60]

The day after the battle, trooper Edward Summers of the Yankee Sixth Kentucky Cavalry rode over the Nashville battlefield. Left in charge of camp equipage in the city when his regiment went after Hylan Lyon, he had not participated in the big battle either. But he had his impressions of Thomas's success. "I must say that I never want to witness an other scene like it although I have witnessed worse scenes since I have bin in the Servis," he told his cousin Arthur Johnson. "The ded and wounded wer there all laying on the field weltering in their gore and many of them Literally torne to peases by the Cannon Shots." "Arthur," he concluded, "I honestly believe that the Southern Confederacy is plaid out and that this war will close by the first of June," although "still I may be mistaken." Certainly, Hood's thirty-eight-day attempt to redeem the upper heartland was over. It had been costly. Barely 271 of 673 combatants in Gibson's Louisiana brigade mustered at Tupelo, Mississippi, in early January following the campaign. In fact, Thomas claimed in his final report that 13,189 POWs (including 7 general officers and nearly

1,000 officers of all grades), seventy-two pieces of serviceable artillery, numerous battle flags, and the repatriation of 2,000 enemy deserters had been garnered from the late campaign. All this at a cost not exceeding 10,000 killed, wounded, and missing. Washington, all a-twitter with news that Sherman had taken Savannah and presented to Lincoln as a Christmas present, breathed a sigh of relief. Somewhat facetiously, one of Wilson's staffers suggested that perhaps they might do something similar for New Year's Day with their own latest capture—"the city of Pinhook with all its dependencies and resources"—a caricature of Pinhook Town, Tennessee, a ramshackle three-structure community in direct contrast with the urbane Georgia seaport.[61]

A sense of disgust if not inferiority would always persist over the contrast between attention accorded their own "Old Pap" versus "Cump." The former had not completely destroyed Hood and his army while the latter waltzed to the coast and through the Carolinas. The Nashville army was stuck in what Wilson termed a land with neither holiday dinners, steaming hot punch, nor revelry, a mercy that found "hog and hominy" to keep body and soul together in a land of poor whites with neither turkeys nor chickens "and not enough girls within twenty miles for a country dance." Solace might be found in the words that Admiral Lee sent Secretary of the Navy Gideon Welles from Clarksville on the Cumberland at 1:00 p.m. on the eighteenth. "The country people along this river confidently expected Hood to drive the Union forces out of Tennessee and Kentucky," he told his superior. "The great disappointment at General Thomas' victories will probably cause the Kentuckians, Tennesseans, and North Alabamians to desert and disperse Hood's command." Both Lee and Thomas pointed out that "no Tennessee troops had come to the river since Hood's defeat." To them, Hood's defeat had all but ended the rebellion in the region. Thomas felt his opponent's army was a disheartened, disorganized, half-armed, and barefooted mob that sought every opportunity to fall out and desert their cause. After the war, Hood told a New Orleans interviewer that it had all been simply a forlorn hope with his duty to see it through. In any event, the campaign ended officially on New Year's Eve.[62]

CHAPTER 10

From War to Reconstruction

Three days into the New Year, a *National Intelligencer* reporter noted that Nashville, "one of the most ardent rebel cities in the South" now presented a "forlorn condition" after the battle. Its citizenry was critical of Hood's conduct of the late campaign. Andrew Johnson, vice president–elect and Tennessee's military governor, pronounced of the battle of Nashville, "Its withering influence upon rebels is more decreed than anything which has transpired since the beginning of the rebellion." Gloom did settle over the Southern public. Yet the rebel *Augusta (Ga.) Constitutionalist* in mid-January claimed the spirit of the people as evidenced both in the advance and withdrawal of Hood's army was "in the highest degree, patriotic" and ready to suffer a still greater accumulation of insult and oppression." Such sentiment echoed from the *Charleston (S.C.) Mercury.*[1]

On New Year's Day 1865, Sixth Kentucky (U.S.) trooper Edward Summers wrote his cousin Arthur Johnson: "What fiew [*sic*] of Hoods army that is Left is Now at the Mussle Sholes on the Tennessee River and are Completely Surrounded by Our forces it is thouh [*sic*] that he will Loose his whole army soon he only has about 18,000 men left him out of 40,000." But the battered Confederate Army of Tennessee escaped to Tupelo, Mississippi. Recriminations about the failed campaign began almost immediately. John B. Hood blamed others; others blamed Hood. His campaign report, written in mid-February, recorded correctly that "from Palmetto to Spring Hill the campaign was all that I could have desired." He then lapsed into fantasy, stating that Nashville could still have been a complete victory and that "it is my firm conviction that, notwithstanding that disaster, I left the army in better spirits and with more confidence in itself than it had at the opening of the campaign." Hood penned the report in Richmond, Virginia. On Friday the thirteenth of the previous month, he had requested relief. The government had obliged quickly. Crippled in spirit and body, Hood departed the army he had destroyed. That army was itself soon broken up. Remnants went on one final mission: stopping Sherman's march north through the Carolinas. Franklin and Nashville had sounded the death knell for the Army of Tennessee and war in the upper heartland.[2]

Making Assessments

Army of Tennessee headquarters reported a strength figure for the period ending January 20 at 27,764, with only 19,973 effectively present. At least West Tennesseans and many of Nathan Bedford Forrest's worn-down lot got a thirty-day furlough to visit their homes before enduring a rickety travel system to catch up with the now-dwindling army once more under Joe Johnston's command. Some survivors, like General Stephen D. Lee, eventually got leave to recuperate and court Regina Harrison, the premier belle of Columbus, Mississippi. The rest of the survivors, Major James Wylie Ratchford, for example, remembered making themselves comfortable for several weeks at Tupelo before the transfer east. Forrest's Third Texas Cavalry, still intact and undaunted, occupied forward positions at Eastport, Mississippi, on the Tennessee River before being withdrawn to hinterland Mississippi and eventually sent home to the Lone Star State. The trail home already had begun for many dejected rebels, weary of war and defeat, conscious that their side had lost, and anxious to look after the families and prepare for spring planting. Desertion, the unspeakable "D" word in military circles in any era, commanded Confederate arms after Franklin-Nashville. To Mark Weitz, historian of the Confederate desertion story, "the massive desertion of Tennessee troops" in the aftermath of Hood's campaign "had apparently struck." Perhaps so, but larger numbers of the latter would simply fade off home or join the ranks of bandits, felons, and irregulars.[3]

Statistics can be imprecise, but as Weitz notes, Hood discovered that what the Union had not killed or wounded, "desertion threatened to take away as large numbers of soldiers crossed the Union lines in Tennessee." Apparently, Confederates left in droves and as late as mid-February some of Forrest's commanders tried to induce infantry absentees back to the colors. Brigadier General W. H. Jackson publicly proclaimed, "I appeal to your pride as Tennesseans—troops that have never faltered." He promised reprieve, for "let not your action by remaining at home in this hour of our country's trial cast a stigma upon the fair name of West Tennessee—a name won by the gallant deeds of yourselves and our fallen heroes." Come join him, he suggested, "let us act together and strike a manly blow for independence." Some answered in person, others joined the partisans or faded from view.[4]

Meanwhile, P. G. T. Beauregard, Hood's superior, claimed that his subordinate had never kept him properly appraised of his actions and categorically commented sourly in mid-April (after the war was actually over) that "the offensive in Middle Tennessee could only [have been] successful if undertaken and at once and executed with energy, without any division or material diminution of our forces." Had the original plan as conjured by Hood been implemented, "without undue delay and modifications and with vigor and skill," then not only would the specific campaign have ended differently but Sherman most likely would have been compelled to return to Middle Tennessee, the strategic intent in the first place. None of the fault for the actual result, Beauregard hastened to imply, attached to the gallant and heroic survivors or the dead. The implication was, as Hood himself told Texans at the end, "all my fault." Indeed, most of those in the ranks thought so too. Told at one point by Hood how the cards had been fairly dealt but Thomas beat the game, one irate private rejoined, "Yes, general, but the cards were damned badly shuffled." Clearly, Hood had been the dealer.[5]

Mississippi senator James Phelan sent President Jefferson Davis an impassioned letter from Meridian on January 17 stating bluntly that the "present unhappy condition" of Hood's army could scarcely be magnified. While its physical wants seemed to have been well supplied after the retreat, "its spirit and morale are gone." Having conversed with many intelligent officers, as well as soldiers passing through the town on furlough or special duty, "all—all agree" that the army was merely a mob without spirit but much mutinous anger and without any hope or concern for the future. In fact, Colonel William R. Miles had recently returned from Corinth, Mississippi, where soldiers' opposition to further prosecution of the war and a burning desire to get home coupled with a resolve to escape from the ranks. "An utter contempt of all military discipline," especially among subordinate officers, was "palpable and universal." Hundreds passing through Meridian also declared openly their determination never to return to Hood's army except at the point of a bayonet, and stragglers and deserters were "go-ing off in squads at every opportunity" and, if caught, only tried again. Hood might not think the morale was bad, and Phelan attributed such obstinacy to a brave heart and being shielded from the truth. Only one thing could restore efficiency, arrest desertion, and recall the absent to the colors, said the politician, and that was restoration of Joe Johnston its command.[6]

Phelan argued that he had not seen a single officer or man who did not declare that such a move "furnished the only hope for the salva-tion of the army." It would "send a thrill of gladness thro the ranks unequalled during the war." Disaffection would cease and the thou-sands of absentees "who are plundering the land and spreading despair over the country" would flock to Johnston's standard. But be quick, he urged, for the army of the West was "melting away daily," and if moved to Georgia as anticipated, "a miserable remnant will only reach the state" for desertions would be rife. If Johnston returned to com-mand and the army remained stationary in northern Mississippi, desert-ers would return, the spirit of army and people both would be revived, a complete reorganization effected and the Army of Tennessee would once more be "as effective a force, for the spring campaigns as any other, of equal numbers, now in the field."

Phelan's prescription may have been right. Johnston returned to army command, but not in the dwindling Confederate West. Only Richard Taylor, Nathan Bedford Forrest, and a few other western chief-tains were left to galvanize Confederate fortunes around Home Guards and tattered remnants of once-proud fighting forces. Could they do so? Neither Richmond nor the senior generals wanted to entrust defense to roving bands of partisans and ubiquitous outlaws, bandits, and thugs. Certainly that was not what Phelan or anybody else with seniority and rectitude had in mind. That possibility existed, however, when veterans like Nashvillian James Litton Cooper underscored Phelan's contentions as "thoroughly demoralized, and [with] only the semblance of disci-pline maintained." He "found the whole county filled with soldiers." Personally "unpleasantly situated" and "completely disgusted with Our Brigade head quarters," having "few friends remaining with the [Twen-tieth Tennessee] and caring "very little whether I stayed with it or not," Cooper and his kind were ripe for going home or joining guerrillas. He furloughed for three or four weeks before eventually returning to the army by March. "In the first of April came the beginning of the end," he noted in memoirs penned the following year. "We had anticipated for some time the dissolutions of our hopes in regard to a future confederacy, but we scarcely expected such a complete falling to pieces as did happen."[7]

Hood's defeat had repercussions even at a distance. Washington artillerist Edward Apps, referring to the succession of defeats—Nashville, Savannah, and Fort Fisher—wrote from Lee's lines at Petersburg, Virginia, that while "the cause does not look as bright as I had hoped it would be at the close of the campaign," thanks to God, "the Yankees have gained nothing from this army, its reputation is still untarnished." And David Pierson told his father from Alexandria, Louisiana, on January 11 that he presumed "all the bad news that was on hand about a week ago" concerning Sherman's capture of Savannah and Hood's defeat in Tennessee had reached home. "Men of sense and position" now talked freely about "our being whipped and such" had not been the case before, and "it clearly shows the ominous state of affairs." The cause was "in a bad fix," and everybody knew and felt it. If something was not speedily done, all would be lost. He thought Congress in Richmond would now make a desperate effort to obtain European assistance by abolishing slavery. In anticipation, some parties there in Louisiana "are hurrying off their negroes to Westen. Tex. to sell for gold." Pierson was surely correct about the Confederacy's fate, perhaps less so that anything could be done unless by fighting generals like Johnston or Stephen Lee. Worse even than allowing slaves into the ranks as soldiers, Grant Taylor wrote his wife from Spanish Fort, Alabama, would be any transfer to the Army of Tennessee, "and be under old Hood and I do not like that."[8]

Ironically, recriminations also sullied the victorious Union side. Despite what Russell F. Weigley suggested was "probably the most complete battlefield victory of the war"—or even British scholar Peter Parish's thought that Thomas "came nearer than any other general in the Civil War to the complete destruction of an opposing army"—the Union high command had expected annihilation of Hood's army. They failed to understand at a distance how bad weather, abysmal ground conditions, and weary Union forces could not accomplish the impossible, even when Thomas explained that fact repeatedly. By the time Surgeon George E. Cooper's after-action report underscored Thomas in April, the question was moot. Cooper's recitation of "disagreeable weather" leading to "severe affections of the pulmonary viscera, fevers, rheumatism, and diarrheas" during the pursuit, the burden of rebel wounded and cold weather followed by "rain, rain, rain, and as a sequence mud"—no matter a superbly organized hospital arrangement supporting Thomas—was fact. Weather had been a determining factor in Thomas's actions. Yet Grant, Halleck, Stanton, and Lincoln at the time remained dyspeptic about George H. Thomas's faults. His perceived lethargy to do battle, then to provide the coup de grâce to the defeated, were bad enough, but senior leaders bridled when Thomas simply wanted to go into winter quarters on the Alabama line to recuperate for another campaign. Grant said absolutely not, and Thomas's general fecklessness, as well as chief of staff Henry Halleck's caustic comments about Thomas's inability to live off the land on a winter campaign into the heart of Alabama and even Schofield's peevishness toward his former field commander, further dishonored "Old Pap's'" achievement. John Watkins of the Nineteenth Ohio detected the tone when he wrote his fiancée Sarah Probert from Clifton on the Tennessee River on January 15, "It seems that the authorities think that Thomas has force enough with him to take care of any rebel force that may show itself in the west." Watkins's unit and others could do better work elsewhere, said army leadership.[9]

True, Grant had finally told Secretary of War Edwin M. Stanton on December 23 that he thought "it would now be appropriate to confer on General Thomas the vacant major generalcy in the Regular Army" because at that time "he seems to be pushing Hood with energy, and I doubt not but he will completely destroy that army." Of course, that had not occurred. Still, New York legislators more lavishly plied honors upon Thomas and his men "for the skillful manner in which his army was conducted to the line of the Cumberland, and then hurled with resistless valor upon the rebel host, stripping them of artillery and scattering them as fugitives over a country they had proudly boasted of conquering." Schofield unofficially hinted via back channels to Grant on the twenty-seventh that since Thomas "contemplates a 'spring campaign' using his own command," Schofield believed "such a campaign would not be an economical or advantageous use of so many troops." He wanted to take his men to aid Grant directly in Virginia. And who among western generals did not? Memphis cavalry general Ben Grierson repeatedly sought such a change simply to be out from under a precocious James Wilson. But sowing such seeds of dissension did little credit to either subordinate. Schofield thought Thomas had left him unsupported in the latter stages of the campaign from Pulaski to Nashville. He knew where his professional future lay, and it was not in the West and certainly not under Thomas's command. The two men had different personalities: Schofield itched for fame and attention, and Thomas did not.[10]

Snide comments passed among Grant, Halleck, and Sherman for the next several weeks as the high command perpetuated their common belief in Old Pap's sluggishness and abject failure on pursuit. Thomas was cast aside, and his army, after a few weeks on garrison duty along the line of the Tennessee River in north Alabama, like its opponent was broken up and dispersed to other commanders for more aggressive use. Even Wilson would garner more glory in the final western operations than his chief when his independent strike force of 13,500 Spencer-wielding raiders destroyed the Selma, Alabama, and Columbus, Georgia, munitions centers in late March and April, creating perhaps the war's "most strategically effective expedition, according to historian Edward Longacre. Wilson's troopers also erased their old nemesis Nathan Bedford Forrest in the process, for neither this wizard nor his command formed the potent weapon of the past. In the end, Thomas was left in Nashville commanding two departments and few men and played no further combat role in the diminishing contest. Historian Wiley Sword, indeed, has had the final word on his contribution for saving the upper heartland. Pointing to Thomas's unprecedented victory during the Civil War—nay, all of American history to that point—Sword suggested the destruction of nearly two-thirds of Hood's army warranted better from his government. "There perhaps never beat a heart more worthy and true than that of the outcast Virginian," claims Sword, "who had triumphed over mind and matter at Nashville."[11]

Reshaping the West

Forrest took over in the wake of Hood's departure. On January 24, he became commander of the District of Mississippi, East Louisiana, and West Tennessee, issuing a manifesto against disorder and brigandage. He threatened to exterminate roving bands of deserters, absentees, stragglers, robbers, and horse thieves. By February 3, he had set up the District of North Mississippi and West Tennessee under Brigadier General Marcus J. Wright, although such reorganization hardly mattered by that point. Yankee actions in Alabama drained Forrest's attention and resources. Sherman's army no longer depended upon a line of logistics back to the Ohio River. So Thomas's new role became one of merely assisting others. He took charge of the Department of the Cumberland, which included Tennessee and portions of northern Georgia, Alabama, and Mississippi. Wilson's cavalry started winter camps for sixty days "to Rest and Recroot" (thought Kentucky trooper Edward Summers, having marched seventeen days "through a perfect wilderness and over the Damdest Roads that mortal man ever see"—a trek that saw their wagon trains and mules constantly miring in quicksand and mud from Nashville to Waterloo, Alabama, and then Eastport, Mississippi). The higher command, however, had other plans. A new department and commander were set up for Kentucky, also under Thomas absent Sherman. Confusingly, however, the arrangement left "posts on the east bank of the Mississippi subject to Department of the Gulf commander, Major General Edwin Canby's "orders for protecting the navigation of that river." All else was Thomas's responsibility. Grant wanted a winter campaign, and in addition to Wilson's thrust using contingents from north Alabama and the Memphis region, Thomas was to help Canby against Mobile and relinquish more men and materiel (mainly David Stanley's IV Corps) to Major General George Stoneman's operations in East Tennessee. Here the rebuilding of railroads and another long line of communications from Knoxville and Chattanooga supported Grant's vision of a possible spring campaign blocking fleeing Confederate forces from Virginia. Even then, thinning resources—particularly horses—affected plans and orders. As elsewhere in occupied Tennessee, Stoneman's men were told they were now in a country regarded by the government as conquered, despite continuing counterguerrilla sweeps. That meant that a loyal state organization existed and the inhabitants were under the protection of Union forces. In East Tennessee, troops were prohibited from stealing fences and the horses and mules that would be needed for spring plowing in the nominally loyal area.[12]

Thomas sent a note to Military Governor Andrew Johnson on the night of December 30 from Pulaski stating that since the enemy had been pushed entirely out of Tennessee, he thought that "immediate measure be taken for the reorganization of the civil government of the State," as it was desirable to move the army as close to the enemy as possible and civilians take over. "All should certainly now feel that the establishment of rebel authority in the State of Tennessee is hopeless," he pressed, "and their own interests should induce them to return to their allegiance to the United States, and restore peace to their state without any further quibbling." Johnson seemed ready as he and the general had already exchanged notes concerning the freeing of unmustered Confederate conscripts dragooned during Hood's advance into the state who had subsequently deserted or were captured in that debacle. It would have a good effect to set such persons at liberty, thought the governor, and Thomas agreed. Johnson wrote Thomas on New Year's Day about steps taken "for the reorganization of the State."[13]

As occupation troops like Sixth Kentucky cavalryman Summers at Eastport, Mississippi, fretted only about inadequate food ("we drop out of camp and kill a fine deer every few days" and are "hard run for bread, sugar and coffee," even getting "quite bare for clothing," with many of the boys barefooted) and "Guirriller Bands" locally and back home in Kentucky, even the Union navy began to rethink its role on western waters. Unable to interdict either Hood's retreat or Lyon's passage, the service returned to traditional, if reduced, patrol and convoy duty. It explored adding ten new vessels to the Mississippi squadron in the New Year in order to counter guerrillas and clandestine contraband trade in the upper heartland. Proximity to the Mound City, Illinois, naval station, as well as to Cairo facilities, worried Rear Admiral Samuel P. Lee and his subordinates regarding disloyal elements threatening and seizing arms and equipment there. They sought more robust administration and law and order ashore, while Lee worked out specific joint service cooperation with generals Thomas and Canby for the greater Mississippi Valley. His main concern was that "Forrest and his gang be entirely cleaned out of western Kentucky and Tennessee," and he wished that a naval magazine and earthworks be reintroduced at Johnsonville should that base be reactivated. Thomas asked that he resume convoy support for Wilson's northern Alabama recuperation and buildup, but large shifts of troops to other theaters soon allowed Lee to move his focus back from Eastport, Mississippi, to Mound City. Guerrillas might periodically interrupt Mississippi River traffic at Tiptonville in northwest Tennessee and elsewhere, but as Lee told Secretary of the Navy Gideon Welles on January 22, "The intercourse between the military and naval branches of the service during the recent campaign has been of a most pleasing and cordial character."[14]

Still, Lee avoided sending any additional vessels to help the hardworking Lieutenant Commander Le Roy Fitch police the Cumberland. He told his subordinate on February 1 that "the military authorities should take action regarding the occupation of towns by guerrillas." Where practical, Jack Tars might join soldiers in counter-insurgency sweeps, but gunboats and steamers should only convoy mobile mounted units for such missions. Acting Volunteer Lieutenant H. A. Glassford (one of Fitch's subordinates) did carry Thomas's personal message to the upper Cumberland when on reconnaissance by the USS *Victory* in

March. He stopped at local farmhouses hoping to spark cooperation against the partisans. In East Tennessee a strange twist surfaced that same month when a Richmond-dispatched incendiary group (possibly preceding Lee's intended retreat from Virginia) appeared on the upper Tennessee River with a large yawl, hoping to burn steamers and then go ashore and destroy logistical facilities and stores at Chattanooga. The plot failed when loyalists apprehended the mission. And in April, an army-navy expedition under Brigadier General Embury D. Osband returned from a sweep to Brownsville, West Tennessee, having captured a colonel, a major, four captains, two lieutenants, and twelve men, including the infamous guerrilla Joseph Luxton. Luxton confessed to burning the steamer *St. Paul* on the Hatchee River, so "General Osband hung him from a cottonwood tree [at Randolph] and his body is still hanging from the tree."[15]

To help the army counter guerrillas, vagabonds, and thieves (with the trading area at the mouth of the Obion and the lower Cumberland Valley being areas of heavy activity), the navy also reorganized for its mission. Lee's command now stretched over eleven districts from New Orleans northward. Commander Andrew Bryson's Eighth District, extending from Memphis to Mound City, counted six gunboats. Lieutenant Commander R. Boyd Jr. had the largest number of boats (ten) in the Ninth District, stretching from Mound City to Mussel Shoals on the Tennessee River. Lieutenant Moreau Forrest led the Eleventh District upriver from Mussel Shoals with four boats. Finally, Fitch commanded only three boats (although some of the most heavily armed) in the Tenth District, which included the Cumberland and upper Ohio Rivers. Minor changes in numbers continued until war's end.[16]

By the end of February, Lee actually anticipated "the vigorous progress of the campaign in the East will probably either soon close the rebellion or transfer its leaders and their arms to within the reach of this squadron in their next necessary movement to cross the Mississippi in support of the last part of their policy, to establish firmly a military monarchy in the neighboring quarter." Still, he did not "desire to avoid the discharge of the patriotic duty connected with its defeat." Word came from Washington later in April that Confederate president Jefferson Davis and his Cabinet, escorted by five hundred cavalry, might flee west to join the Confederate Trans-Mississippi command of Kirby Smith before making either for Mexico or Cuba. Lee indicated his squadron's readiness to intercept, and Thomas, in an uncharacteristic spate of sardonic humor declared, "If Davis escapes through my lines,

Canby's and [Lee's], he will prove himself a better general than any of his subordinates." Lee thought that if Smith accepted overtures based on terms accorded his own distant cousin, "the rebellion is at an end even if Jeff. Davis succeeds in reaching the Trans-Mississippi Department." By May 5, the Navy Department planned to shrink the admiral's squadron to twenty-five vessels and Lee concentrated strength on the lower Mississippi by withdrawing boats from the upper heartland. The rebel leadership never exited Georgia, the Franco-Mexican question loomed larger, and by June 5, Assistant Secretary of the Navy Gustavus V. Fox directed that the inland river squadron be shrunk to just fifteen vessels. Three weeks later, that number dropped to five. Demobilization of the brown water navy was in full swing.[17]

Commoners' Musings

Occupation troops resumed their boredom after Hood's scare. A thirty-three-year-old Federal prison registrar at Clarksville sought to memorialize the broader meaning of the episode in verse. Composing his doggerel on December 18, James Hearst panned the new technology of telegraphy to illustrate how one corner of the war focusing on localized guerrilla interruptions to river and rail traffic remained nonetheless connected with events and people elsewhere. He started his ditty with "running to the depot" to watch timetables and people crowd around the office regardless of weather—"scrambling for the papers though they are full of fables," for "oh, but this is jolly waiting for the mail!" His jottings passed to gangs of guerrillas who "cut our rail roads daily" while "hordes of rebble [*sic*] Soldiers, roving found so gaily" swarm the river bottoms, driving "our transports back." He then moved to wider vistas: Hood vowing to take Nashville, but "guess old 'Pappy Thomas' wants to see him try it!" Meanwhile, "Lyons in Kentucky—thinks it a pity, he can't get into Clarksville as he's passing by it." Lyons "don't like Co. [A. J.] Smith" or his six-hundred-strong Eighty-Third Illinois because "thinks him hard on traitors," and the Illini garrisoning the town and Fort Donelson "because it never surrenders." Hearst suggested that former garrison commanders like S. D. Bruce were "abolition haters."[18]

Hearst captured other news: Sherman down in Georgia, Grant "encircling Richmond in his patient manner," Sheridan in the Shenandoah, and Rosecrans in Missouri, as well as "what's [Stephen] Burbridge doing" in southeastern Kentucky and does Breckinridge menace him?" What really peaked his interest was Washington and "what is Congress doing? Making rowdy speeches, Strong on the 'spread eagle' weak in legislation?" "Robed [*sic*] by Speculators—bled by heartless leaches," Hearst wondered, "virtue in the Mopes alone can save the Nation?" And what of Europe, he posed, "growles [*sic*] the British Lyon (beast or politician) but glad he's lost his teeth." "Is neighbor Maxamilian [*sic*] diplomacy still trying" to own Mexico, "hiding Austrian claws French velvet underneath?" Then the sardonic Hearst ended with, "How goes everything—is the world still jogging" [on]? Since telegraphs and railroads, boats and rivers fail with even "the grape vine's down" with "everything is clogging," he thought, "oh, but this is jolly waiting for the Mail." Less cavalier, perhaps, would be the comment of one secessionist Clarksville civilian upon witnessing some returning local deserters from Hood's unsuccessful foray: "If we judge the Confederacy by this section, the army must be greatly depleted."[19]

One Yankee lieutenant, Frank A. Handy, went out to the Nashville battlefield a month after the fight to find complete destruction on local farms, buildings gone, and not a vestige of a fence left. "The country that had been "highly picturesque and very beautiful indeed" was no longer, as "the Demon of War has spread ruin and desolation over it." Three months later, William H. Green of Company F, Forty-fifth New York Veteran Volunteers made a similar pilgrimage to the sight of Union victory, noting "the field is [still] covered with dead horses and bones of all kinds," although he saw no skulls and presumed the men were all buried. He was mostly impressed with a devastated civilian cemetery with wooden headboards replacing marble ones and so picked flowers there that he then sent his sister, asking her to press and lay them away for his return home. This scene, replicated across the Nashville region, hardly differed from that just below Franklin, with convalescents still occupying space in Franklin's buildings.[20]

Yet heartlanders themselves took Hood's intrusion in stride, depending upon where and who they were. Middle Tennesseans had obviously been more closely affected by the passage. Maury County, Tennessee, farmer Nimrod Porter anticipated peace and serenity after several years of war. Spring planting would beckon, as would a return home for most white and black refugees from the invasion. Southern Kentucky farmer-preacher George H. Browder noted nothing specific in his diary about the Franklin disaster and only the rumors of how "Genl Hood's rebel army besieges and threatens Nashville and a change in power is expected here." He cited government impressments of horses as well as truculent blacks in his neighborhood, while finding his congregations "really more interested in the exciting rumors that flood the country and the heavy cannonading near Nashville than in the sermon." By December 5, Browder had sensed the "great excitement" with rebels reportedly shelling Nashville and crossing the Cumberland." Union troops seemed to be "moving in haste and horses are being gathered up in all directions" as he personally hid his one poor blind nag and another elderly mare from the press gang. The Federals, he said, "tell us the rebels are coming" and all "is apprehension and suspense." Lyon's occupation of Hopkinsville had citizenry and soldiers fleeing while merchants at little Elkton "had packed their goods on wagons to send off." "All is excitement and suspense," he continued on December 12, while the next day he penned how McCook's passage through Russellville en route to deal with Lyon had "robbed the people on the route of horses, bacon, fowl etc. in the most reckless manner," with strangers crowded into the town, "flying the rebel conscript."[21]

By the twenty-second, Browder was noting the cold, rainy, and generally disagreeable weather while pillorying bandits rampaging through his neighborhood robbing and plundering houses. His final comment on the war for the year noted, "Hood is badly defeated and traveling southward. There is a general sadness & misgivings among Southern people." He then returned to common living: marrying a young couple as "matrimony revives," enjoying his children's anticipation "of what Santaclaus had brought" (candies, nuts, and toys), and a return to normalcy. A week later he suggested that "everybody seems quiet and calm, although the war rages and we look for increasing troubles." His entry for New Year's Day 1865 may well have reflected most heartlanders' feelings, blue and gray. "Hail another year," he wrote, "may peace return this year to our native land!" "I pray God, the horrors and miseries of last year may not be enacted in this," George Browder preached to a flock at Hadensville that cold and bright Sabbath morning. He spotted some federal soldiers patrolling and pretending to be looking for a squad of rebels, but mostly "they inquired of me where they could get a New Year's dinner!" Browder would turn thirty-eight that month. The war had not yet ended for either he or other heartlanders quite yet.[22]

Indeed, affairs wandered in different directions as Military Governor Andrew Johnson pointed out to the army's adjutant general in Washington on January 16 that "the contrabands in East and Middle Tennessee require some better supervision than they now have." Hood's invasion had brought an influx from the Pulaski contraband camp overburdening the Nashville facility. Reuben D. Mussey was sent to straighten matters out, although freed people continued to suffer bad conditions there and at Camp Nelson, Kentucky, where a refugee home for blacks would be established early in the new year. Citizens like conservative unionist and Nashville lawyer Balie Peyton anticipated an early end to the war. Civilian petitions to Johnson increased concerning a restoration of commerce and trade from Memphis, and former first lady Sarah Polk in Nashville repeated her December request in early March to be allowed to sell a meager one hundred bales of cotton "to provide the means to live on." Remaining Federal garrison and logistical troops returned to mundane chores and concerns after Hood's visit. Thad Roberts of the 148th Illinois worried about an epidemic of smallpox in the city, although the January diary entries of Colonel Robert Galbraith of the Fifth Tennessee (Union) Cavalry mostly noted "nothing of consequence" except perhaps winter high water in the Cumberland River. Lieutenant Owen J. Hopkins of the 182nd Ohio wrote his fiancée in mid-January how his life as regimental quartermaster "is so monotonous when there is no variation from the same routine of business, among his abstracts, vouchers, invoices, receipts, and returns." Six months later, David Jones of the Nineteenth Pennsylvania Cavalry would still report to his wife that his unit remained encamped on properties of rebel general Ben Cheatham and his sons, where Union soldiers had cut down a prize orchard, leaving a splendidly built brick spring house still standing.[23]

In the distant Union prisoner-of-war camp, Johnson's Island, Ohio, on Lake Erie, Captain Thomas Jones Taylor of the Forty-ninth Alabama had concluded on Christmas Day 1864 that prisoners were coming in faster than the previous year, when Missionary Ridge had yielded its crop of captured rebels. Now it was Nashville's turn. Hood was falling back "somewhat demoralized by a series of bloody but unprofitable battles." Still, thought Taylor, the Confederacy had demonstrated that it could stand a hard pounding and survive so it "now seems to be the question whether the north can afford to pound so long as we can stand up under the operation." James Hearst at Clarksville and Tom Taylor at Johnson's Island could each take detached views, the one an occupation soldier, the other a combat POW. But the people of the heartland remained in the thick of unresolved conflict.[24]

Return to Tennessee Guerrillaism

Hood's rebuff had settled the invasion question but not general disquietude. Federal authorities no longer had to fear either main force or large bodies of raiders. But troops not transferred to other, more active theaters of operation returned to pacification and mopping up guerrillas. Political persecution, as well as brigandage and devastation, tested the ability of authorities in both Tennessee and Kentucky to take the next step in the stabilization and reconstruction process pointing toward eventual reconciliation. A recital of such activities went something like this. McMinnville unionists William Bosson and John B. Armstrong warned Governor Johnson in late January that "numerous bands of desperate men sloughed off from [Hood's] retreating army were terrorizing loyalist men and women" in the area now that Federal units "had been withdrawn to counter the invasion." McMinnville had but recently experienced the wrath of two hundred to three hundred such armed men who visited the town, burned "a block of valuable buildings & murdered a federal soldier." The pair warned that any restoration of public elections could not take place under those conditions. They urged the return of garrisons for McMinnville, Sparta, Cookeville, and Livingston with a body of one hundred men at each place, supported from the country and "by this harmonious action drive the Guerellas from the County & give a feeling of Security to the people till such time as a civil organization of the Counties would render the presence of a military force unnecessary." Their missive obviously had not reached its reader, when the next day Johnson ordered those elections.[25]

Stepped-up counterguerrilla military sweeps now took place. Lieutenant Colonel J. H. Blackburn led an expedition through the McMinnville neighborhood prior to the Bosson/Armstrong letter to Johnson but they left no garrisons and the partisans merely returned in their wake. Blackburn told the governor about a welcoming reception by locals and suggested that many perpetrators of violence claimed to be Federal soldiers who honestly thought harsh treatment of the populace would induce loyalty. He believed otherwise that only "a complete revolution in public sentiment, in favor of the Union," would be to assure the obedient that they would be protected while severely punishing those "who willfully violate the laws or usages of the Government." Perhaps that was really what Bosson and Armstrong had in mind too. Captain Robert H. Clinton of the Tenth Tennessee took a similar expedition of mounted Indiana and Tennessee troops out of the Tennessee Barracks near Nashville and roamed Charlotte, Dickson, and Humphreys Counties finding Home Guards guarding Nashville and Northwestern Railroad bridges and ensnaring random bands of guerrillas. Six weeks later, with Johnson's blessing, Clinton importuned Secretary of

War Edwin M. Stanton directly to recruit a special contingent armed with Spencer repeating rifles and he "could in a short time clear the large scope of Country lying between the Cumberland and Tennessee Rivers of all Bushwachacking and Guerella parties who are doing an immense damage by murdering and Robbing the Citizens and gobbling up small parties of Federal soldiers who are garding points on the various Rail Roads and other places that have too be garded."[26]

Similarly, Colonel Robert Mix's Eighth Michigan Cavalry went on patrol from Edgefield south through Murfreesboro before fanning out from Lebanon then south to Shelbyville and Pulaski in order to "pick up the many stragglers from the rebel army who are understood to be lurking in the country, especially Tennessee cavalry under Lieutenant Colonel Withers, understood to be scattered through Davidson, Williamson, Wilson and Rutherford counties." The Twelfth Regiment, U.S. Colored Troops, took over guarding construction parties returning the Nashville and Northwestern Railroad to operation, while scouts attempted to clear bushwhackers like the Bob Riggs gang from around Franklin. February was an especially busy antiguerrilla month, although crafty, experienced partisans such as Duval McNairy continued to elude capture. Also, from East Tennessee, future elected governor William G. Brownlow warned in early February that Bradley and Hamilton Counties were overrun with partisans "and unless there is better management in that District, there will be no voting" in the elections Johnson intended for later that month.[27]

The infestation continued unabated once winter turned to spring and conditions improved for tracking down the lawless. Patrols into guerrilla nests west of Pulaski, between the Tennessee and Duck Rivers, in Lincoln County, and along the Alabama line, as well as from Cumberland Gap and staging points like Memphis and Nashville, took time and resources. Prominent citizens in Davidson, Rutherford, and Williamson Counties continued to have "to show cause" why they should escape exile beyond Union lines for questionable loyalty or activities. With horses always in short supply, the patrols and sweeps commenced on mules or on foot with other mounts seized en route (receipts given and indiscriminate pillage strictly forbidden). In East Tennessee, the Tenth Michigan Cavalry, Seventh Tennessee Mounted Infantry, and Company I, Second Ohio Heavy Artillery saw some action in the vicinity of Athens when guerrillas "obstructed the track between every train near Cleveland, but did not show themselves." Yet Middle Tennessee authorities reduced railroad garrisons on the

Nashville and Chattanooga Railroad between the capital and the Duck River in February. Bushwhackers picked off railroad guards and apparently even had enough audacity to attend civilian dances and other social activities within thirty miles of Nashville in February. Gillem and Stoneman undertook to reconstruct the East Tennessee and Virginia Railroad north of Bulls Gap in East Tennessee and clean out Confederate forces toward Bristol, Virginia, under William "Mudsill" Jackson, John Echols, and John C. Vaughn, even after Robert E. Lee's surrender in early April. Counterguerrilla operations from Memphis continuously probed for Colonel Ben Chenoweth's rebels in that corner of Tennessee. Elsewhere infamous irregulars like Cushman, Perdham, Gatewood, Joel Cunningham, Texas Ranger Root, and East Tennessee felons Dr. J. P. Legg and P. H. Starnes eventually began to surrender or were exterminated. In the no-holds-barred war, Federal superiors consistently praised subordinates for taking no prisoners.[28]

Furthermore, Union Home Guards in counties such as Coffee, Lincoln, Bedford, Franklin, Marshall, Grundy, Warren, and Cannon in Tennessee joined the Federal policing effort. "The home guards," noted one provost marshal, "have through their company courts settled fairly, justly, and amicably many claims" which had been brought for adjudication against guerrillas and bandits. He was convinced, in fact, that the workings of such a device "generally restores to a great extent that good feeling and amity so essential to the welfare of a united people." Perhaps, he also asserted, "the people or home guards have rallied to the assistance of some of our troops, and aided and assisted in driving and killing the guerrillas, by whom our troops were at times repulsed." Official reports and other public documents attest to the focus, intensity, and varying levels of success in helping corral horse thieves and deserters turned criminals from both sides during the remaining months of actual war and transition to peace. Certainly a return of some local county courts in Sumner and Lincoln Counties suggested recovery from Wheeler, Forrest, and Hood, as well as some suppression of guerrillas.[29]

The hot blush of rebellion began to fade by March, especially after the surrender of Lee and Johnston in April. Grant ordered all surplus transport transferred to Arkansas and New Orleans en route to counter the French threat in Mexico. But in the upper heartland, law enforcement, a lessening of ill feeling engendered from the conflict, and meting out compensation for suffering and property losses had to await restoration of civil authority. Continuing cavalry sweeps (many dismounted) would continue for weeks and even months. But so would violence with derailment of a Louisville and Nashville train on April 7 (killing two of the crew) and another three weeks later near Clarksville. The Eighty-third Illinois garrison at Fort Donelson trapped guerrillas on White Oak Creek, burning them out of a barn hideout. Another contingent battled Carney's pack south of the Cumberland, and purported depredations surfaced in early May near Tullahoma. News of the Confederate capitulation only slowly reached partisans in the bush. Delicate surrender negotiations with Federal authorities often consumed great time and trouble.[30]

Memphis authorities noted on April 17 that the fall of Richmond and the capture of the principal Confederate army and all fortified places in the so-called Confederacy east of the Mississippi River signified "the utter and hopeless prostration of the rebel power." All further fighting by rebels within West Tennessee "must be from a spirit of pure malice and revenge for purposes of robbery and plunder, and not in any hope of accomplishing any public good to any State or government." The pace of surrendering Confederates quickened thereafter as detachments of Forrest's command came into Federal lines seeking parole. Those continuing to fight the liberal amnesty terms offered by the United States government could only be regarded as guerrillas and murderers. Some of those roving about West Tennessee inciting the citizenry claimed to be prisoners of war when taken. At one point they had a deadline of until April 25 to lay down their arms, after which they would be held for trial as felons and "common enemies of mankind." Applications began to appear (through citizens) from guerrillas asking for terms of surrender so that they could again become peaceful citizens. Thomas joined the solicitation for guerrilla surrender by May 1, and Lieutenant General Ulysses S. Grant advised subdistrict authorities at Clarksville on May 5 that "as a cheap way to get clear of guerrillas that a certain time be given for them to come in, say the 20th of this month, up to which time their paroles will be received, but after which they will be proceeded against as outlaws."[31]

Federal policies only slowly emerged after Appomattox with regard to surrender of outlying Confederates, possession of firearms, and appearing publicly in gray uniforms. Large-scale guerrilla surrenders now took place in Tennessee, including those of Duvall McNairy and partisans Cross and Miller at Franklin on May 15 and Captain Jacob C. Bennett's seventeen followers at Carthage on the twenty-first. Captain Bruce Phillips and Jerry Stone, infamous partisans in the Fort Donelson area, surrendered there on the twelfth, although publishers of the Eighty-third Illinois newspaper at Clarksville could not resist the comment, "It is a pity that [Philipps] has not graced the end of a rope long since." Perhaps the most infamous of all, Champ Ferguson, acquired "outlaw" status from Major General Lovell Rousseau on May 19 and was not subject to quarter. Nevertheless, Colonel Joseph Blackburn and the Fifth Tennessee Mounted Infantry undertook a sweep through White, Overton, Fentress, and Montgomery Counties "for the purpose of restoring quiet to that region" and captured Ferguson. They sent him to Nashville, arrested for murder and various atrocities. His celebrated trial dragged on until his ultimate execution as a war criminal in late October. Bedford County native Thomas Carrick, a sometime guerrilla or bushwhacker, reluctantly gave up at the end of May with sour sentiments about the "dirty whelps that invaded our country." Eventually, even "regulators" like Captain George King of Rutherford, Tennessee, gave up, turning to diary tales of local vigilantism against presumed wrongs on neighbors and relatives. Even as late as July, sweeps from Memphis aimed at destroying guerrilla remnants roaming Perry and Wayne counties and a portion of Hardin County from their lair in south Hickman County and near Williamsport in Maury County. The flames of guerrillaism eventually transferred to postwar vigilantism, whether of the regulator or white supremacist ilk, acting as local societal management tools just as they had during the war.[32]

Kentucky's Descent into Chaos

About the time that Hood had besieged Nashville, mounting uproar in Kentucky captured Washington's attention. Letters from both Governor Bramlette and a Kentucky delegation called upon the secretary of war and the president for "a change of policy in the military administration" of their state. In short, they wanted Brigadier General Stephen Burbridge replaced. One of the secretary's own minions in Louisville, Major E. H. Luddington, reported on December 7 on six distinct issues in the Bluegrass: condition of the state, temper of the people, character of the troops in the state, civil administration, military administration, and suggestions as to policy. His views had formed, he said, "after consultation with many influential citizens of different localities and of conflicting opinions." Luddington frankly stated that "there is scarcely any security for person or property" in Kentucky. In every county, guerrillas were destroying property and taking lives "of all who have been or now are, in the U.S. Armies." The citizenry was so bitterly arrayed against each other as "to afford immunity, if not assistance to those desperadoes," each party "glad to see men of the other murdered."[33]

Luddington thought that Kentuckians had remained in the Union simply "to preserve slavery and avoid becoming the theater of war, although strongly in sympathy with the rebellious States." Velvet glove or rose-water humoring of the state during the first two years of conflict had kept the peoples' allegiance. When the government attempted to draft men or enlist slaves, however, "the true feeling of the people" came out. Resistance and denunciation of the administration became more pronounced than the original rebels, he thought, unknowingly underscoring why Hood had wanted to move there in the first place. As for the character of troops raised to monitor the situation, they were all one-year troops, raised in the state, penny-packeted about so as to be ineffective, poorly officered, drilled, and, in fact, "merely a uniformed mob." Serving at home with their local prejudices, they regarded only their own interests, not those of the country. They punished local enemies, not guerrillas, capturing few men under arms but rather unarmed people and plundering at their own discretion. As a result, such actions exasperated the citizenry against the government so that "the very troops it employs to serve it prove its worst enemies."

Luddington had few kind words for Governor Bramlette, who "prefers union to rebellion, but loves slavery also." With the politician's eye set on a U.S. Senate seat, "he has slender capacity, great vanity, and greater ambition" as his policy "is simply self first, State second, Union last." Also, since "he has not backbone enough to make a direct issue with the Administration . . . its policy need not be affected in any way by his views." As for district commander Burbridge's military administration, Luddington thought he might have relied too much on others' advice, thus displaying great vacillation on occasion. His management style had produced inefficiency and an evident want of capacity or energy among subordinates. Still, hated as he was by a popular majority ("that signifies nothing if he pursues a policy stringent and impartial"), there seemed no reason for his removal, although the inspector did think "the substitution of a man stronger in capacity and character would be an advantage."

Luddington's prescription for Kentucky lay with an absolute necessity to crush the guerrilla problem by allocating one hundred non-Kentucky mounted and well-led troops per county. He recommended reassignment of all Kentucky units out of the state and no more mustering of such Home Guards, but rather volunteer contingents credited to Federal service. Third, he noted how "noisy and active sympathizers with rebels and rebellion should be dealt with most rigorously" (presumably just what Burbridge was doing) while favoring active and dependable Union men in the state. The policy of the Lincoln administration should be rigidly enforced and the state managed under one established policy. If Bramlette arrayed himself against the administration, the major told Stanton, there should be no hesitancy in superseding him.

Here then was the typical circular problem facing both authorities and the public. Guerrillaism (pseudo-Confederatism) caused mayhem in the community, and in turn, military authorities applied indiscriminate force, thereby evoking civilian displeasure, protest from Frankfort, resistance at home, more incursions, and more retribution. If anything, Kentucky's approach mirrored that in Tennessee, except one state was under national rule and the other ostensibly was not. Military governor Johnson and the regular Union military authorities in Tennessee were as one with antiguerrilla policy. But Kentucky civil government bridled at the Union's military implementation of just about any authority in the Bluegrass State, even though the basic issue was laid out so well by Thomas Speed, an early Kentucky unionist and historian. Speed later claimed that "from 1862 until the end of the war, Kentucky was overrun and infested with these irregular bands, who always claimed to be 'Confederate soldiers' when captured, and, in fact, were operating in Kentucky after their own peculiar manner by the express authority of the Confederate government." Speed noted that in 1864 and early 1865, Kentucky "was full of bands of Confederates, operating as they saw fit." He admitted that Confederate authorities commissioned men to recruit in Kentucky, although once there, they might not have entertained such noble service.[34]

Speed then recited the litany publicized also in Collins's *Annals of Kentucky:* Confederate partisans and Lyon's raiders had wantonly burned thirteen courthouses and nine other structures, there had been no fewer than "twenty instances of wanton plundering of towns by the same," and fifteen unionists had been killed. By contrast, Speed quoted Collins as citing no killings and burnings and only one plundering by Union Home Guards in the state and only one accidental courthouse burning by Federal soldiers. On the other hand, Basil Duke, one of Morgan's finest officers and, more personally, his brother-in-law, also weighed in after the war on the whole Kentucky guerrilla problem, contending that naturally troops on short rations, wearing inadequate clothing, paid in waste paper, and "hardened to the licentious practices of cruel warfare" would be "frequently tempted to violate the moral code." Deserting, they would be feted as guerrillas by a "mistaken and foolish admiration" from the people, and Kentucky just before the close of the war had teemed with such characters. "It was of no use to threaten them with punishment," as "they had no idea of being caught," Duke said. Then, betraying an animus that would sour much of postwar Kentucky, Duke reflected how Burbridge had "shot all he could lay his hands on, and for their sins, many prisoners (guilty of no offence), selected at random or by lot from the pens where he kept them for that purpose, were butchered by this insensate bloodhound."[35]

Burbridge no doubt had terrorized Kentucky citizens in late 1864. So the new year found Governor Bramlette requesting and receiving permission from Washington to raise five thousand of his own troops for state protection. Such a levee would not interfere with Federal enlistment in Kentucky, he claimed. He promised cooperation with Burbridge and other national military forces in case of invasion and suppression of guerrillas. A Radical Union state convention applauded Burbridge's promise to arrest fugitive dissident Judge Joshua F. Bullitt should he return to the state, and Bramlette's annual message to the legislature on January 6 publicly enumerated state grievances against Burbridge. Black recruitment, issuance of illegal trade permits, and arbitrary arrests and incarceration may have sounded familiar to Kentuckians, but the Great Hog Swindle surfaced for the first time, raising a storm of indignation across the commonwealth. Burbridge and Bramlette now engaged in renewed charges and countercharges, obstructionism, and noncooperation over such issues as disbandment of state troops, general interpretation of state-federal prerogatives, and the development of the parallel state military force.[36]

Amid the swirl of growing controversy, Burbridge continued his scourge of anything remotely Confederate. He and the most respected Kentuckian in gray, now Major General John C. Breckinridge, corresponded over whether or not to hang prisoners of war in each other's hands. All the while Burbridge felt the pressure of Louisville unionists to have the city's elite southern-leaning merchant class pay assessments for destitute refugee families, as well as the never-ending threat from guerrillas (such as the notorious Jerome Clarke, or "Sue Mundy," a nom de guerre invented by Louisville editor George Prentice to denigrate the feminine-appearing insurgent), who murdered and robbed at will. On February 6, Burbridge issued orders citing Lincoln's anticipated establishment of martial law in the state and demanding disbandment of any state troops and the return of their arms. Bramlette immediately wrote Stanton about the "unwarranted assumption of power by an imbecile commander." The secretary of war then informed Burbridge that his order was premature regarding the president's proclamation and that he should revoke it and abstain from further actions. By this point, even Lincoln had had enough of Stephen Burbridge. On February 7, Stanton informed Major General John Palmer that he would supersede the Kentucky commander. Fifteen days later, Palmer took over and Burbridge went on leave pending return to the field. Major General Thomas eventually told the Kentuckian to remain in Lexington awaiting orders—orders that never came.[37]

"Thank God and President Lincoln," trumpeted the press. To be sure, Burbridge's relief pleased moderates and dissidents and incensed the radicals. Stanton's orders to Palmer pointed at improving state-federal relations and a more judicious use of arrests and trials, although felons and guerrillas were still to be pursued to the death. The discipline and organization in all Union units in the state needed attention, and the continued recruitment of blacks for military duty, relief of destitute unionists, and reimposition of martial law meant that conditions hardly seemed any different than they had been under Burbridge. Palmer's vow to stabilize law and order, as well as political conditions, would prove hollow. Perhaps his appearance only promised more comity. In the end, notes Burbridge's biographer, Palmer's predecessor, with a good combat record, carte-blanche authority from "Cump" Sherman to stop guerrilla warfare and treason, generally supported but often opposed by civil government from Frankfort to Washington, "was left alone, with no command and hated in his home state." Except for Hylan Lyon's disruptive raid, the Bluegrass in the new year seemed riven mostly by a brand of strife enveloped in myths and perceptions of motives and actions, disregard of civil liberties, thuggery cloaked in blue and gray, and leaders ranging from scoundrels to migrant criminals to well-meaning but agenda-prone politicians and generals.[38]

By this point, Kentucky guerrillas, like those in Tennessee, were simply defying authority. In fact, when a Sullivan County, Tennessee, doctor warned Andrew Johnson about traveling the Louisville and Nashville Railroad to his inaugural, he specifically cited "some of the *worst* men in Kentucky that are to be found upon earth, and they *hate* you, and would make any *Sacrifice* to get you." The fight with guerrillas thus passed to combat between uniformed, legal officials and bandits and felons posing as partisans and freedom fighters. It was more a policing action than war issue. With guerrilla names as legion here as in Tennessee—"Sue Mundy," Henry Metcalfe, Samuel Oscar "One-Armed" Berry, Henry Clay Magruder, Bill Marion, Ben Wigginton, and William Henry Turner, all successors to the famed and more creditable Adam Rankin and Tom Woodward—the historical record indicates only marginal control of the state by proper authority. In Appalachia, Champ Ferguson and Dave "Tinker" Beattie waged their own vendettas, certainly beyond control. Union Home Guard captain Edwin Terrill, termed by one author "a braggart, a thug and a villain" and as disreputable as the men he chased; Major James H. Bridgewater; Colonel Harvey M. Buckley and his Fifty-fourth Kentucky Mounted Infantry; and Lexington operations coordinator Brigadier General Edward Hobson—all earned reputations for firm if sometimes punitive reaction to the never-ending challenge. Out-of-state outfits like the Thirtieth Wisconsin joined with home-grown Kentucky contingents in hunting the lawless, and on January 13, a Major Walker Taylor tendered his services "and those of his Confederate soldiers" to protect the citizens of Hardinsburg in Breckinridge County from the outrages of guerrillas.[39]

Distinguishing who might be legitimate and who was simply a desperado confounded everyone this late in the war. Apparently, Confederate colonel Robert J. Breckinridge bore orders from the Confederate secretary of war dated January 6 to round up all supposed rebel recruiters in the Bluegrasss when captured near Versailles later in February. And if they failed to obey his orders, they might be reported to Federal authorities as unrecognized by Richmond and thus not eligible for POW status. Yet "rigorous retaliatory warfare against all guerrillas, raiders, and predatory bands of assassins and robbers" was what extremist elements like the Radical Union party's state convention wanted. At least one innocent from Breckinridge's mission went to the gallows thanks to Burbridge. Still, efforts eventually tricked Clarke into surrender (claimed sympathizers) and hung him (essentially as a war criminal) at Louisville on March 15. Events on the national stage brought but marginal peace for pardons and paroles, and it did not prevent a skirmish near Uniontown in early May and a chase across the Green River that eventually lead to one band's dispersal, though not before casualties occurred on both sides, including a much-lamented Sergeant Grant Abbey of Company A, Eighty-third Illinois, one of the famed antiguerrilla units in the western army.[40]

Palmer might well issue an order at the end of April easing the "power of arrest" enforcement since "there is no dignity or justice in pursuing foolish people for foolish words." But he well understood that "the bands now prowling through the country are simply guerrillas and robbers" and were to be treated as such, that is, "allowed to surrender for trial." In fact, some of the bands terrorizing Kentucky in the first part of 1865 were no longer even Kentuckian. Sometime in mid-January, the infamous Colonel William Quantrill and remnants of his bloodthirsty crew from Kansas and Missouri had slipped across the Mississippi at Shawnee Village on Devil's Bend, twenty-five miles north of Memphis. Eluding Federal patrols and aided by anyone styled a southern sympathizer, they crossed into Kentucky near Canton, claiming to be the Fourth Missouri (Union) Cavalry. Suggesting their ultimate destination might be Virginia, their more immediate goal seemed to be stealing horses and survival. They even may have secretly entertained notions of assassinating Lincoln. Riding with the crew were Frank James (brother Jesse had ostensibly remained west of the Mississippi to join regular Confederate arms), and at one point they accosted a prominent horse breeder, English-born Robert Attcheson Alexander, at Woodburn Farm near Lawrenceburg in the Bluegrass section on a rainy Thursday evening, February 2, 1865. Alexander had already been visited by Sue Mundy's group and had organized his own protective force at his stud farm. He even had been able to avoid Federal horse sweeps. The Quantrill-Mundy party, however, made off with sixteen of Alexander's prize stock. Ten of the horses were later recovered from skirmishes between Union Home Guards and the robbers, but thousands of dollars in investment were lost and at least two other horses were killed in this raid. A thoroughly nonplussed and grieving Alexander moved the rest of his horses to safety north of the Ohio. Quantrill and Mundy had exacted an even heavier toll. Broken in spirit, Alexander died two years after the war, his death attributable in part to Quantrill's visit.[41]

Quantrill's criminals continued their outlaw ways well past the Woodburn Farm incident. They terrorized a swath of Spencer, Nelson, and Mercer Counties. Quantrill celebrated Lincoln's assassination until Union guerrilla hunter Edwin Terrill (under Palmer's orders and as unsavory as Quantrill himself) caught up with him at the farm of James H. Wakefield near Bloomfield, Kentucky, on May 10. Mortally wounded in a melee, Quantrill was captured and taken to a military prison hospital in Louisville, where he died on June 6 and was buried in an unmarked grave. Frank James and fifteen others from the Missouri gang remained at large until their surrender to a Union outpost at Bardstown,

Kentucky, on July 26. Few unionists either west of the Mississippi or in Kentucky would have concurred with the assessment of John McCorkle, one of Quantrill's riders, that "the spirit of one of the truest, bravest men that ever lived passed from earth to appear before his maker and render an account for the deeds done here." Terrill continued his crusade in search of more partisans. Kentuckians, at least rejoiced at being freed of Quantrill.[42]

In the words of one historian, "The longer the war continued, the more it descended into gangsterism." Magruder, Berry, and other guerrillas might be eventually captured, pardoned, imprisoned, or hung. Yet incidents continued, like one on May 5, involving guerrillas tearing up the track on the Ohio and Mississippi Railroad on the Ohio side of the river fourteen miles below Cincinnati, robbing passengers and a safe of money and valuables and thirty thousand dollars in U.S. bonds, and escaping across the river into Boone County, Kentucky. Likewise, derailment and pilferage of a train on the Memphis branch of the Louisville and Nashville similarly raised law and order questions. Was this banditry or residual guerrillaism? The point of usefulness much less legality had passed with Confederate surrender. When Colonel George M. Jesse and Captain Moses D. Webster sought to negotiate for terms in mid-April, Palmer simply told Burbridge (still in some official capacity at Lexington) that he expected "the absolute submission" of such officers and men to the government as "I do not desire any neutrals here." Each individual would surrender arms and horses: "I am not willing that these men should go abroad in the department with their belts full of pistols to overawe the unarmed and defenseless people of the State." Those guilty "of crime against the rules of civilized warfare" would answer to charges before a commission. "The general idea," proclaimed Palmer bluntly, "is that the people of Kentucky must hereafter be unreservedly for the Government. All others must leave the state."[43]

Even in the sunset days of the Confederacy such an experienced hand as Nathan Bedford Forrest admitted to Richmond how the formal "experiment" to raise and organize troops for the army in a distinct military district in southern Kentucky and West Tennessee by Adam Johnson and subsequently Hylan Lyon had been "a complete failure." Such recruiting efforts by "would-be colonels" delegated to "would-be captains and lieutenants" only created squads of men "who are dodging from pillar to post, preying upon the people, robbing them of their horses and other property, to the manifest injury of the country and our cause," observed Forrest. Deserters from his Kentucky brigade (scarcely three hundred men at that point) had "attached themselves to the roving bands of guerrillas, jayhawkers, and plunderers who are the natural offspring of authorities given to parties to raise troops within the enemy's lines." Forrest wanted revocation of authority to raise troops within enemy lines, mustering officers ordered out and troops sent in to bring out deserters and break up the bands of lawless men "who not only rob the citizens themselves, but whose presence in the country gives a pretext to Federal authority for oppressing the people."[44]

In the end, martyrdom attached to those executed by Burbridge and Palmer under the guise of war and the restoration of law and order. Their names and places of "execution" included Charles W. Thompson and John Perman Powell (Henderson); B. Grisley Wooten and William Woods (Georgetown); Harvey Thomas (Russellville); Richmond Berry and John May Hamilton (Bloomfield); George W. Wainscott and John and William Lingenfelter (Williamstown); J. Bloom and W. B. McGlassin (Franklin); Julias Radas, John Brooks, Francis M. Holmes, and Andrew Jackson Slaton (Guston–Brandenburg); John Lancaster (Louisa); Lindsey Duke Buckner, Wilson P. Lilly, Sherwood Hadley, and William C. Blincoe (near Jeffersontown); James Fielding Brewer and Thomas Bassett (Hopkinsville); Elijah Horton, S. Thomas Hunt, William Jones, and Thornton Rafferty (Frankfort); William Long, William Tighe, William D. Darbrow, and R. W. Yates (Pleasureville); M. and J. Jackson, G. Rissinger, and N. Adams (Midway); [?] Tindle, [?] Pakhurst, and [?] Warford (near Bloomfield); Joseph Hopkins, John W. Sipple, and Sam Stagdael (near Bloomfield); J. Peters and Richard Cheny (near Syms Camp Creek, Metcalf County); Brothers Horton, Tom Forrest, and John Fry Moore (near Henderson); Walter Garth Ferguson and William P. McGee (Lexington); Lycurgus Morgan, John Henn, A. B. Tudor, W. T. Thorton, W. B. Dunn, and Jacob Baker (Greensburg); J. E. Hall (LaGrange); [?] Allen (Christian County); Nathaniel Marks (Louisville); James Jameson and David N. Reese (unknown); and Daniel Hanes (Hanson). Three martyrs were officers, one was a seventy-year-old minister, and the others variously had associations with both regular and irregular Confederate cavalry. Many of the executions took place summarily in the field, some in conspicuous public space, possibly some in prison dark. All reflected the controversial nature of a fratricidal war beyond the glories of regular battle.[45]

Adjusting to Defeat and Victory

Americans were ready for something to happen by March. The war dragged on yet seemed about to end. In Nashville, news of freshets washing out the Nashville and Northwestern Railroad trestles and the discounted value of quartermaster vouchers on street corners caused consternation, pleasing only brokers and speculators. The city quartermaster, Captain John H. James, complained all the way to now–vice president Johnson in Washington that no funds had been provided for liquidation of claims for animals and forage purchased by the former military governor's Tennessee troops for use in East Tennessee. This now hampered his settlement with loyal citizenry. John Overton of Traveler's Rest outside town came through Yankee lines at Memphis and applied to take the amnesty oath. He was denied yet again. The plethora of Union newspapers at the state capital seemed to saturate the public patronage market. Then news of Richmond's capture prompted Johnson's public confidence on April 3 that "we are now winding up a rebellion—a great effort that has been made by bad men to overthrow the Government of the United States." Army correspondents in the city noted passage of the IV Corps en route to Texas to counter French intrusion in Mexico. One Nashville hospital steward was torn between helping process invalids and what he anticipated as a pleasant trip to Texas.[46]

Private Marcus Parmele of the Seventy-fourth Illinois, detailed to the medical director's office in Nashville, noted wistfully that only three of his chums "since our group of boys came out in 1862" were still living, and were now all together in the city. They had made a life for themselves there, socializing off-duty with locals at weekly Sabbath attendance at a Presbyterian church. But they were ready for mustering out and coming home, he told an aunt. Private Henry D. Palmer, due to be mustered out of Company C, 176th Ohio in June wrote friends on February 24 about getting into new barracks on the southern edge of the city where their two days on and two days off patrol duty centered on "our business is to go up and down the streets and stop all disturbances if we find any body drunk we march them to headquarters [as] we like to find a man with shoulder straps tight." Nimrod Porter of Maury County noted some bridge rebuilding in March, and Beech Grove residents in Lincoln County that same month saw "our little village is brushing up wonderfully, plenty of stores & goods" and pasture land, possibly refenced, suggesting enterprise similar to that which restored Pulaski from confusion and idleness immediately after Hood's passing. But Porter was less sanguine, suggesting that "we are gitting [sic] along in the crop line but slow" as "very few of the citizens are trying to raise a crop in this country." The handwriting was on the wall regarding the rebellion, however. On April 3, Rear Admiral Lee ordered a salute of thirty-six guns fired at noon in honor of Grant's taking Richmond. Four days later he ordered his flagship *Black Hawk* to fire off one hundred rounds to mark Lee's surrender at Appomattox. The Tennessee legislature reconvened on April 6, "amid the thunders of Artillery—fired in honor of the deathblow that had Just been given to a gigantic Conspiracy—and the acclamations of a people emerging from the thralldom of Slavery that enshrouded them for ages, and entering on an epoch of freedom, the light of which is destined to illuminate the world." Knoxville cannon also thundered their "demonstrations of joy," although one chaplain there lamented that "Grant should have offered any other than unconditional surrender, & then let the Government show such mercy & leniency as might be wise & proper." East Tennessee legislators petitioned the U.S. postmaster general to reopen post offices on the railroad east of Knoxville and at points off the rail lines.[47]

Then, suddenly, the upper heartland plunged into grief as bunting and fireworks gave way to mourning guns, crepe on uniforms, flags at half-staff, and funeral dirges. Parmele had written an aunt from Nashville on April 11 how "This City, in unison I presume with the whole Country, has been unspeakably Jubilant for several days past, over the recent signal victories and well they may, for the end is now very near." The next day he told other relatives, "I notice by the paper that you are all rejoicing at home as well as we are here over the capture of Lee and surrender of his whole army." This might not "release us before our service expires but I think we shall see no more field services." Then news of Abraham Lincoln's assassination cast its pall. On the nineteenth, Parmele wrote how locally the balmy spring was overshadowed "in expressing the public sorrow of our City—in a more organized and imposing manner—for the lamented death of President Lincoln." He told how he and his mates had taken a window spot on the third floor of one of their quarters overlooking the square to watch the memorial procession in honor of the fallen leader. "The procession was immense and I think the most imposing pageant I ever witnessed," he said. It was an hour and a half in passing, "commencing at 10.20 o'clock." First came the soldiery, "marching with reversed arms" to the solemn dirge, then "muffled drums." Then Generals Rosecrans and Thomas and their staffs, "members of the State Legislature, various civic orders and societies, five companies, etc.— minute guns, and tolling bells and universal drapery of woe, added to the solemnity of the occasion." At the same time, Parmele told relatives back in Rockford, Illinois, "I thought of so many similar scenes all over the Country, and of you all at home." Then the twenty-two-year-old and his colleagues returned to their impatient waiting for mustering out. That would not come until June.[48]

President Lincoln's assassination profoundly affected the nation, the South, and Kentucky and Tennessee. All public business was suspended in Memphis, as it was in Nashville on April 20, when a similar mourning procession wound its way through downtown. Nashville unionists attacked and even killed several people who dared to defame the martyred president (something not noted by Parmele). The climate throughout the region remained tense after the surrenders and Lincoln's murder. Retribution hung in the air when Eli Thayer wrote Johnson in April 15, quoting the East Tennessean's earlier bold statement about punishment of treason. "Their great plantations must be seized and divided into small farms, and sold to honest, industrious men," Thayer raged, for "the day of redemption and deliverance, the day of hope and aspiration to the poor oppressed people of the Southern States has now come." The result of the war had to be the establishment of justice and democratic equality for all. Readjustment and reconciliation would emerge differently from that singular foul deed at Ford's theater in Washington. Johnson would ultimately turn away from vindictive policies and alienate many seeking such retribution. In the aftermath of a forced succession, he welcomed "assurances of my profound esteem and hearty support" from an old colleague in Nashville, George H. Thomas, and loyalist meetings like that in Clarksville, organized by chancery clerk and master of Dickson County Richard M. Baldwin and local lawyer James O. Shackelford.[49]

One incident on Easter Sunday at Trinity Episcopal Church in Clarksville illustrated this highly charged, even irrational, atmosphere. Red and white geraniums, spiria, and lilies of the valley decorated the baptismal font (along with other colored blossoms), as was church tradition for that holy day. But Union soldiers in the congregation felt that such bouquets were "designedly placed there as representing the Rebel colors." Dr. Mary E. Walker, famed female medic succoring hospital patients in the city, took special umbrage and the issue spiraled out of control, making the Louisville newspapers with claims of innocence by both sides. The soldiers' demand to bring forward the national colors along with the collection plate and all the flowers for the priest's blessing only further inflamed the congregation's hearts and senses. Local post commander Colonel Andrew Jackson Smith of the Eighty-third Illinois entered the picture, and the anger about the president's assassination boiled over in this establishment church's sanctuary of southern rectitude. Irreconciliation, as much as grief and disgust, for the moment, seemed to pervade the upper heartland as overt hostilities wound down.[50]

Lincoln's death was not the only tragedy that had an impact on America's heartland and, most especially, Tennessee's Queen City on the Mississippi that April. The steamboat *Sultana,* heavily laden with paroled Union prisoners from Vicksburg, blew apart early on the morning of April 27, having just left Memphis. The night was overcast, the spring flood waters dark and cold. The boat's operators and acquiescent army administrators had allowed too many people aboard—1,866 war-weary veterans, 85 crew members, 75 civilians, and 160 animals—in space registered for only 300 passengers. Forced draft, boat overload, and faulty boilers did what no rebel bullet had accomplished: more than 1,500 men were lost, leaving yet more midwestern households with a vacant chair as war legacy. Washburn wrote Brigadier General William Hoffman, commissary general of prisoners in Washington, on May 14 that 12 commissioned officers and 757 enlisted men constituted the number of paroled prisoners saved from the *Sultana*—"the worst maritime disaster in the history of this nation."[51]

Before long, the western waterways witnessed further effects of postwar demobilization. Admiral Lee wrote Thomas on May 19 that if there was no military necessity for continuing naval expense of four gunboats above Mussel Shoals, the Navy Department wanted them "dismounted" and turned over to the Quartermaster Department. Grant thought it unnecessary to have any warships on any river but the Mississippi at this point, and by the twenty-second, a convoy of rebel prisoner steamers to Memphis occupied captains of the gunboats *Fairplay* and *Abeona.* The naval station at Memphis was deactivated, and late in June the navy raised the ordnance from the wrecks resulting from Forrest's Johnsonville raid the previous fall. The navy began relinquishing western waters back to peacetime, commercial intercourse.[52]

On April 17, Grant wired Thomas that "the freedom of Va. from occupation by an armed enemy renders the occupation of East Tennessee in large force longer unnecessary." He should concentrate the IV Corps back to Nashville, even though "it is desirable to hold all the territory we now have in sufficient force to protect it against roving bands that may yet infest the country." By the end of the month, he told Thomas to "induce all armed bands of men in Tenn. Alabama and everywhere in reach of your command to come in and surrender their

Arms on the terms made by Lee & Johnston." On May 9, perhaps because troops of his command were denied the grand reviews accorded Meade's and Sherman's armies at Washington, Thomas held his own at Tennessee's capital. The next day he issued a stirring, congratulatory general order.[53]

To the IV Corps, Old Pap expressed his pride and admiration, "excited by their brilliant and martial display." Sounding hardly like the dour, perceptively sluggish field commander, Thomas waxed eloquently:

> As the Battalions of your magnificent Corps swept successively before the eye, the coldest heart must have warmed with interest in contemplation of those men, who had passed through the varied and shifting scenes of this great, modern tragedy, who had stemmed with unyielding breasts the rebel tide threatening to engulph the land-marks of Freedom; and who, bearing on their bronzed and furrowed brows the ennobling marks of the years of hardship, suffering and privation, undergone in defence of freedom and the integrity of the Union, could still preserve the light step and wear the cheerful expression of youth.
>
> Though your gay and broidered banners, wrought by dear hands far away, were all shred and war-worn, were they not blazoned on every stripe with words of glory, —Shiloh, Spring Hill, Stone River, Chickamauga, Atlanta, Franklin, Nashville, and many other glorious names too numerous to be mentioned in an order like this.
>
> By your prowess and fortitude you have ably done your part in restoring the golden boon of peace and order to your once distracted but now grateful country, and your Commander is at length enabled o give you a season of well-earned rest.
>
> But, soldiers, while we exult at our victories, let us not be forgetful of those brave, devoted hearts which, pressing in advance, throbbed their last amid the smoke and din of battles; nor withhold our sympathy for the afflicted wife, child, and mother, consigned, far off at home, to lasting, cruel grief.

Now came the moment for inventorying infrastructure and taking stock. By June, the mustering office of IV Corps had issued detailed instructions to its regiments for how, when, and in what priority to send the troops home. Meticulous administration was the army's forte. Office clerks tallied such things as formal fortification construction and railroad conditions under military management and control. Some heartland cities numbered among the heaviest fortified sites in North America. An earlier recital of protection for northern and central Kentucky cities like Covington, Lexington, the Newport approaches to Cincinnati, Ohio, Camps Nelson and Burnside, the Louisville and Nashville and Kentucky Central Railroads, Bowling Green, Munfordville, and even Glasgow could now be updated and accounts squared. This report suggested thirty-eight field forts and batteries mounting 155 field and fortress cannon and mortars spread across Kentucky. A similar idea of the extent of Federal fortifications in Tennessee might be gained from the various reports of Brigadier General Z. B. Tower, inspector general of fortifications for the Military Division of the Mississippi, rendered in May and June 1865. Tower pointed out the strengths and weaknesses of the Tennessee-wide fortifications, noting in one case that "for so important a place, held so long by our troops, the Nashville defenses certainly were not pushed forward as much as they should have been" and that "little aid is given by commanding officers of posts when those posts are not in the front or constantly exposed." He overlooked the fact that the dozen or so forts and batteries had helped stop Hood the previous December. He surely overestimated the resiliency of railroad defenses, doubting "if in any other department such lines have been so thoroughly guarded against surprise or raiding parties." Forrest had proven otherwise.[54]

Tower's reports heralded the positioning of fortifications for both protecting military depots and lines of communication as well as monitoring civilian neighborhoods. The most complete fortification in Tennessee, he boasted, was Fortress Rosecrans at Murfreesboro. The Johnsonville and Clarksville works had been rendered obsolete by events; Fort Donelson retained overcapacity, as the garrison "controlled to some extent the country about and especially the narrow strip toward the Tennessee and had a favorable influence upon the navigation of the Cumberland." Railroad blockhouses had been rebuilt after Hood's destructive path with forty-seven, mostly double-storied structures from Nashville to Chattanooga. Fortifications at Pulaski, Franklin, and Gallatin numbered among posts available for postconflict retention (apparently stabilizing communities). Others, like Decherd, Elk River, Tullahoma, Duck River, and Lavergne, seemed not to merit attention.

East Tennessee included sixteen works guarding Knoxville, "the keep" of the region. Most important was the city of Memphis, Tower advanced, observing (much as he did about Nashville) the sense of importance confounded by relative defenselessness for the whole period of the war. One fort, Fort Pickering, had provided depot protection, as well as control of the city, should the enemy appear there. "As Memphis will be one of the principal places in Tennessee to be occupied for the next year, perhaps for a series of years by a large garrison, and as it will doubtless be the headquarters of the District of West Tennessee, and perhaps of Northern Mississippi, as well as a depot," said Tower, "Fort Pickering will be retained and garrisoned," thus warranting Federal government attention. Elsewhere, however, customary postwar governmental pecuniary would dictate result.

Much of what Tower and others (like George N. Barnard, with his photographs of cities, bridges, and other sites in Tennessee) reported or captured in word or picture held importance for postwar Federal military presence as well as redevelopments in the upper heartland. More useful to restoration of private sector normalcy, however, would be similar reports by other government officials, such as L. H. Eicholtz, acting chief engineer for government railroads. Eicholtz enumerated damages and repairs to U.S. Military Railroad lines after Hood's visit. Six thousand feet of bridges destroyed by the Confederates had been rebuilt only to fall prey to winter/spring floods, while the loss of the Red River bridge at Clarksville to Lyon's raiders caused that line to be abandoned west of Springfield. Destruction in East Tennessee had produced large scale rebuilding with all sorts of improvements such as more sidings, an engine house and a large reservoir at Chattanooga adding to railroad infrastructure with postwar potential. He summarized work in that region in March and April to ninety-four miles of track opened and repaired, twelve miles of track rebuilt, forty-four hundred linear feet of bridging constructed, twenty thousand cross-ties cut and delivered, fifty-seven thousand cubic feet of timber cut for bridging, nineteen switches put in, and five water tanks erected. He mentioned erecting a permanent turnpike bridge across the Duck River at Columbia. Using a Howe truss of three spans (each 112 feet in length) with the bolts and castings of bridges destroyed on the Nashville-Decatur rail line, the new highway bridge was a "strong and permanent structure of 350 feet" costing about $50 per linear feet. Eicholtz "respectfully suggest[ed] charging the turnpike company or corporation of Columbia with [that cost]."[55]

In a sense, then, the Union army and navy had fulfilled a historic role in nation building. Locales differed as to when civil authority would be restored. It was early March in Montgomery, Robertson, Sumner, Smith, Mason, Jackson, and Williamson Counties, where civil courts had been organized, although Stewart County, site of the Fort Donelson battle, still did not have civil government at the end of May. In West Tennessee, toughening martial law by the end of March focused on protecting civilian traders "from the hungry swarm of sharpers who infest the lines." Absent any organized hostile force within the district, "citizens will be allowed to come freely to Memphis and dispose of their products and take back a limited amount of family supplies." Repair of the Memphis and Charleston Railroad from the city to La Grange and reopening of the Memphis and Ohio, Memphis and Louisville, and Mobile and Ohio lines; encouragement of restoration of county courts and administration of civil laws; and farm cultivation absent further "arbitrary seizures of private property of any kind, particularly horses, mules, and oxen" all numbered among the directions sent from Thomas to local West Tennessee district commander Cadwallader C. Washburn. Restrictions on trading in gold were lifted in mid-April in West Tennessee, the Memphis enrolled militia was disbanded in early May, and on the twelfth the military lifted the requirement for passes to enter and leave the Queen City.[56]

Still, restoration of civil government remained spotty in Tennessee. Stephen A. Ash, preeminent student of the subject, concludes that chaotic conditions, thanks to guerrillas and criminals, kept county governmental impact confined to county seats. "For the same reason," he contends, "the revived state government, although it went into operation in early April, had little active support and little impact outside of that city and the garrison towns." Lee Anderson of the 153rd Illinois at Tullahoma wrote a cousin on March 22, 1865, "Most of the people in this part of the world have fled, either North or South, and if they every return they will find a sorry looking place, fences gone, plantations destroyed, buildings burned & their *niggers free,* & in short everything is entirely 'gone up,' & what 'twas white trash' is left, as ignorant as the heathen themselves." In walking the streets, "¼ the persons you meet are soldiers ⅖ negroes and the rest are mostly 'American citizens of African decent.'" Federal military support of civil authority reached a point where no more refugees would be sent north at public expense since "the country is now quiet, and such as are here are advised to return home and do something for themselves." Directed at the swollen, wartime itinerant population that had flocked to Memphis, authorities felt that "there is employment for all in the country who are willing to work; it is not too late in the season to make crops; millions of acres are lying waste for lack of labor; those that can work must or starve, black or white." As part of the government's postwar effort to get people back home, there would be no encouraging "thriftlessness or idleness by supporting those that are able to support themselves." Rather, transport to the country would be furnished those who wanted to go as far as the railhead and two day's rations would be issued to all who left.[57]

Peace slowly returned the heartland to normalcy. Illinois soldier M. J. Vance wrote his father on May 19 from Camp Harker, Nashville, that restive comrades awaited back pay and discharge and if authorities planned to convey the captured President Jefferson Davis through that city as rumored, "they had better keep him pretty well guarded if they want to have the satisfaction of hanging him." Meanwhile, local farmers "have planted their corn and it is up and looks well" and "they are going in to farming a little more extensive this spring than they have since the war." He especially cited "a great many contractors from the north down here raising cotton," with his unit's old camp at "Murfreesboro is all in cotton by this time," as he supposed their old regimental commander Lyle T. Dickey "has a farm rented down by Huntsville and is planting it in cotton." Yet in Memphis, one lady dismayingly wrote her niece in Columbia, Tennessee, about the expense and difficulties of travel, the city filling up with returning Confederate soldiers and "old citizens returning to their homes," and "towns below here are garrisoned by federal troops of *color*." Former Confederate lieutenant colonel W. T. Avery of the Forty-second Tennessee returned to the city, took the amnesty oath on June 3, and immediately applied to Brigadier General W. W. Orme supervising, special agent of the Treasury Department (and a prewar young lawyer favorite of Abraham Lincoln back in Illinois), for recovering his confiscated property: "a four story brick store house situated on the West side of Main Street between Court & Jefferson Streets" as well as a lot just outside the city.[58]

Revival of individual lives and fortunes would vary. Two daughters and wives of the Nashville elite, Rachael Craighead and Elizabeth Harding, both soon returned to opera attendance and other activities that survived occupation. They, like other women, would be swept up in postwar Confederate remembrance, perhaps a post hoc reaction to wartime events in the upper heartland. Unionist daughter Maggie Lindsley married a Yankee officer and would ultimately depart her home city.

A broken and discouraged Lucy Virginia French "was weary, hope-less, and desperate" in McMinnville. Like others, she resented fortunes made by compromising Tennesseans such as Adelicia Acklen of Belmont (just outside Nashville), who parleyed her plantation's cotton through both Confederate and Union hands to become one of the wealthiest women in the South. French's Memphis sister and her husband had ventured in cotton speculation (no matter how illegal) to emerge from the war in similar comfort. But French and her husband wondered, "For what? Did God permit this war? Shall we ever find out why it was allowed?" Other survivors, however, looked less to mourning "years of hardship, privation and sorrow" than to a brighter future. As some Volunteer State correspondents emphasized to Vice President–elect Johnson, restoration of normal trade without wartime restrictions would not only improve their own lot but also win back a wavering and dissident citizenry.[59]

James Wortham and John W. Bowen wrote to this effect from Shelbyville on January 9, 1865. Two days later, Robert R. Pittman, an exiled Memphis cotton factor and commission merchant in St. Louis, spoke confidently of how permitting the people to carry their products to market "& sel [sic] or ship to whom they please as they do in the other borders states of Ky. & Mo" would be good. He saw that this course would bring large revenue to the government besides "*mixing* those people up by commercial intercourse with those of the Northern states & thereby producing a better feeling and understanding amongst them." John A. Jackson, a Pulaski manufacturer of Onasburgs Sheet-ings and Threads ("a coarse durable cotton fabric in plain weave" used for "bagging and industrial purposes") wanted to ship his product through Federal lines, for "there is no Speculation in this matter, only . . . employment to a class of good, but poor Citizens." On March 10, unionist John O. Noble wrote to the new vice president from Hunts-ville, Alabama, asking for dispensation to avoid a loss of 25 percent plus internal revenue and permit fees in shipping eight hundred bales of Tennessee River cotton from Decatur to the Nashville exchange. With Lincoln's intercession, he might sell to the government and gain the whole purchase price less the fees and costs for transportation. "I think I have done Enough for our Government to Entitle me to this favor from the Hands of the Govt[.]," he suggested.[60]

So long as Tennessee (much less Kentucky) had been a war zone (and in active insurrection), Lincoln had ducked the issue of lifting trade restrictions. In some ways, however, it was more a matter of jurisdiction.

The president, secretary of war, or Congress thrashed out the issue while corrupted Treasury field agents thoroughly embarrassed the administration. No matter the reason—the loyalty or the state of occupation or jurisdiction or even ethics of federal bureaucrats—it seemed that amelioration could be effected only after Appomattox and Johnson's ascendancy to the White House. On April 24, now-president Johnson ordered military and civil officials to expedite passage of twenty-five thousand bales of Alabama and Georgia cotton belonging to Kentuckian William L. Vance, brother-in-law to Memphian Robertson Topp, into Union lines to sell it to government agents. He further responded to the state chairman of the Ways and Means Committee, who had asked for relief from the 3 percent tariff on goods coming into Tennessee, by scribbling on the incoming telegram that such would be removed since "Tennessee will be taken out of the States now in inserectn [sic]." On April 29, Johnson issued the blanket executive order removing certain restrictions on trade, leaving exempted items as contraband of war, "arms, ammunition, and all articles from which ammunition is manufactured, gray uniforms and cloth, locomotives, cars, railroad iron and machinery for operating railroads, telegraph wires, insulators and instruments for operating telegraph lines." Johnson realized that key tools of modern conflict had to be controlled by central authority even unto the return of peace. Everywhere, however, amnesty oath-taking remained a prerequisite to restoration of rights and privileges, and only Johnson's more blanketed May 29 proclamation guaranteed complete removal of trade restrictions. Nevertheless, in analyzing the army and presidential amnesty offers in this regard, historian Patrick O. Daniel concludes, "the record is nonetheless interesting in that it illustrates the eagerness of southerners to secure their livelihoods and return to normal trade relations with the rest of the country."[61]

The return of peace caused further structural adjustments in civil-military relations, so crucial to any passage from insurrection to restoration. For the time being, five principal individuals would largely provide the direction and pace of reconstruction in the heartland. Military Governor Andrew Johnson (until he moved to Washington), followed by his duly elected successor William G. Brownlow and General Thomas, would dictate for the Department of the Cumberland and state of Tennessee, while Governor Bramlette and General Palmer (along with Thomas) would guide Kentucky's transition. Johnson and Thomas were as one in sentiment and voice from the beginning. Both were southerners and pragmatic individuals. The governor had followed

Thomas's end-of-year enjoinder to restore civil rule quickly by pressing Major General J. T. Dana at Memphis to join in exempting civil officers, judges, and clerks in that district from the military draft. Dana hoped to help "with you in your work of re-organizing the Loyal Element." Johnson pressed Lincoln to have the army expand Thomas's authority to include the Memphis area. Since Hood's appearance had put off holding Johnson's Union convention to prepare the way for state government restoration, the somewhat fractious delegates finally met in Nashville on January 9.[62]

Coming concurrently with the city's African American celebration of the Emancipation Proclamation's anniversary, the Union convention adopted two state constitutional amendments abolishing and prohibiting slavery and involuntary servitude, as well as prohibiting the legislature from passing future laws that recognized the "right of property in man." This "Liberty and Union" convention further nullified secession and alignment with the Confederacy. It repudiated Confederate debt, affirmed Johnson's appointments as "acting governor" until successors could be elected or appointed but held back from according freedmen any franchise. The outgoing military governor was determined to push his agenda of restoration when on January 26 he ordered regular elections so that loyal Tennesseans, at least, might have an opportunity to return the state to civil law. Unionists would have a chance to vote in a state constitutional referendum on February 22, and selection of civilian governor and legislature was set for March 4. Proof of loyalty remained the prerequisite for franchise so that a Washington's Birthday vote ratified the convention's dictates. Future state historian Walter Durham sardonically noted, "a loyalty oath had again done its work." Still, approval of the constitutional amendments by a wide margin vindicated Johnson's efforts and repaid him for the "defamation and obloquy of which he has been the especial target in his State," announced *Nashville Times and True Union* editor on February 27.[63]

Johnson left for Washington two days later. In January he had informed the president of his efforts to bring back civil administration, although Lincoln had anticipated having to appoint a military governor successor (something Johnson stubbornly ducked). The Union Free State Convention that month had appointed three commissions to visit the capital and present specific requests: (1) that the president declare Tennessee no longer in insurrection, (2) that the president influence completion of a railroad from Knoxville to Nicholasville, Kentucky, as a military measure (to obviously succor loyal populations in East

Tennessee and Western North Carolina), and (3) that payment of claims for property taken by the army from loyal citizens of the state be secured. The wheels of restoration ground slowly in the latter instance, but late in January, Johnson moved ahead, reestablishing civil courts of law in the state with various appointments. Moreover, he reestablished a state militia of some 18,625 white and black enrollees after receiving his state adjutant general's favorable report about Union volunteers in the absence of any duly constituted peacetime contingent

Tennessee held its own reunion inaugural with the convention's candidate, East Tennessee unionist preacher and editor William G. "Parson" Brownlow, sweeping into office unopposed as Johnson's successor. Vilified in the South for brash statements calling for "grape for the rebel masses and hemp for their leaders," Brownlow was best known nationally for his 1862 "celebrated tour," which had helped catalyze northern will for the war as well as publicize the plight of persecuted East Tennessee unionists. Ever controversial and often the bitter political rival of many in high office (including Johnson, although eventually he was supported by the same), Brownlow now enjoyed wild celebrations by his supporters in Nashville even though there had been little interest across the state in his election, given the absence of opposition candidates. In fact, back in February, one of Johnson's confidants, James Bingham from Memphis, warned that "the onerous conscripting for the militia, the draft, and the present condition of the State, all tend to make a small vote probable." Nonetheless, perhaps both Johnson and Brownlow saw this election as a revolutionary overthrow of oligarchic Middle and West Tennessee planter power. In any event, during the weeks that followed, freedmen continued to celebrate deliverance, the first general assembly since 1861 convened, victory parades filled Nashville streets, and Brownlow was inaugurated governor on April 5. "Political power was returned from Washington to Tennessee," held by the unionist minority. That power also ratified the Thirteenth Amendment banning slavery in the United States forever that same gubernatorial inauguration day, and eventually sent two new senators to the nation's capital.[64]

To some degree occupied and separatist Tennessee contrasted with unoccupied and loyal Kentucky. Tennessee transitioned quickly from military to civil governance but in the hands of radical Republicans not conservative Democrats. Kentucky proved the opposite, embedding over the course of 1865 a seemingly neo-Confederate regime with power but in reality showing an antifederal, independent streak of uniquely Kentucky loyalist independent conservatism. Civil governance and military rule had always been at variance if not open confrontation in the Bluegrass. War's end changed little despite commonality of purpose (Union victory) and Burbridge's replacement. Part of the problem may have been the radicalization and politicization of Kentucky unionist citizen-soldiers like Jeremiah Boyle, Frank Wolford and Stephen Burbridge (and a similar segment of the population) versus the petulant loyalism of Governor Bramlette (and his camp of conservative citizenry). The virulent fever of the Radical Union political faction further destabilized any transformation from war to peace.

Virtually every late war issue, from guerrilla suppression and capricious military action against dissident citizenry to the recruiting of Kentucky blacks short of formal emancipation, as well as the Great Hog Swindle perpetrated by a small clique of army quartermasters and other corruption, festered civil-military relations in the transition from war to peace. Efforts to ratify the Thirteenth Amendment foundered in legislative truculence. At least an effort to establish an agricultural college at Lexington as part of Kentucky University suggested more progressive attitudes toward a postwar future. A major fire that destroyed Louisville's famed hostelry, the Galt House, on January 11 may have been symbolic of the continuing storm that transitioned war to peace in the Commonwealth. Cries of military interference with commerce and even politics continued to surface as late as the summer, one chronicler declaring starkly that General Palmer "seems to act as if he a were the *autocrat* of Kentucky, instead of military commandant."[65]

Military authorities seemed particularly fearful of the free election of the legislature on August 7. As in Tennessee, proof of loyalty seemed to attend franchise, with Bramlette's late July proclamation disqualifying any Kentuckian who had served the Confederacy either in military or civil capacity. Union soldiery (especially African American), as well as "thought police" freely working the polls and intimidating would-be voters, led to "a strong feeling of dissatisfaction at and disapprobation of the governor's course" manifesting itself on the street and in the press, even in the ensuing legislature, where conservatives held slim margins over radicals in both houses. Ironically, by autumn "some of the very men who were among the foremost to welcome and cajole the petty tyrant [Palmer]" when he succeeded Burbridge "are now willing to see the latter re-instated in preference." As one modern author declares, "During the last years of the war, [loyal] Kentucky was under military occupation," and apparently postwar Kentucky continued to be "an early example of the hostility of an aggrieved, occupied population, depressed and injured by the suppression of a guerrilla war." Hostilities did not end with the war, observes analyst Penny Miller. Indeed, when habeas corpus restrictions were lifted for all northern and border states on December 1, 1865, only Kentucky and the District of Columbia were not among them.[66]

On the State of Two States

Official statements provide a sense of the situation in Tennessee and Kentucky at the end of the rebellion. Andrew Johnson, former U.S. senator and wartime military governor of the Volunteer State, now the vice president of the United States, declared at his swearing in on March 4, "It is the doctrine of the Federal Constitution that no State can go out of this Union; and moreover Congress cannot eject a State from this Union. Thank God, Tennessee has never been out of the Union!" Johnson admitted, "It is true the operations of her government were for a time interrupted; there was an interregnum; but she is still in the Union, and I am her representative." Back home, he gained much favor among unionists when he pronounced that "Tennessee was in the Union and had *never been out*." To Colonel R. M. Edwards of the Fourth Tennessee Cavalry, that one sentence to loyal men of the South was "all the law and prophets" (paraphrasing Mathew 22:40). Johnson's focus remained obviously constitutional and political, and his elevation to the national scene did not capture the true picture back home with regard to sociocultural and economic conditions. Those problems were left to his civil successor, William G. Brownlow. Problems confronting both Brownlow in Tennessee and Thomas Bramlette in Kentucky included rebuilding war-struck communities, suppressing residual turmoil, and treating the demands and needs of constituents, white and black, Union and Confederate.[67]

When the celebrations subsided, Brownlow sent a lengthy and suggestive message on many issues. For one thing, "secession is an abomination that I cannot too strongly condemn, and one that you cannot legislate against with too much severity," he told the legislators. He cited the blood and carnage, the paralyzed commerce, the destroyed agricultural pursuits and "many of the pursuits of life," the suspended "whole trade and business of our country," and the lessened value of property as a result. Secession and war, said the new governor "has involved the South in irretrievable bankruptcy and ruin." In characteristic

Brownlow rhetoric, he noted secessionist and Confederate persecution of Tennesseans for unionist sentiments, the exile of loyalists, the sacrifices (still continuing) by those forced into uniform, and the thousands of Union refugees populating the capital—men, women, and children, brokenhearted, naked, and starving, having fled before the fire and sword of guerrillas and partisan criminals. He particularly excoriated those "citizen rebels" and "home traitors" who remained under Federal largesse, living in ease and comfort, wielding an overruling social influence while clandestinely trading with and informing the enemy. That said, however, he advised that those responsible for the war's tragedy be excluded entirely from state governance and that former rebels should comport themselves as appreciative of whatever retribution for their treason might be foregone through sympathy and pity.[68]

Brownlow prioritized the need of the legislature to ratify the Thirteenth Amendment in order to protect the newly freed from those who had fought to enslave them and "show the emancipated slave no quarter." He wanted strong actions taken against "the roving bands of guerrillas, and squads of robbers and murderers who frequent those counties and portions of counties remote from our military forces." Their depredations had created a diaspora of loyal citizens seeking new homes among strangers of the northwestern states. The inadequacy of prewar criminal laws to the new situation demanded capital punishment for horse stealing, house breaking, and highway robbery. Furthermore, reorganization of the state militia and military contingency fund also stood high on the new governor's agenda. Resuscitation of state finances and a state debt of nearly $7 million generally required attention and, of course, emancipation under recent state law would dislocate computation of taxables for both former owners and the newly liberated as wage earners. Brownlow suggested holding Confederate officers and directors personally responsible for bank and railroad losses as he underscored the need to quickly rehabilitate those pillars of economic stability and opportunity. He was harsh in restricting franchise and disenfranchising the disloyal in order to ensure against reemergence of a prewar oligarchy that had led the state astray. Finally, Brownlow wanted to send U.S. senators and representatives back to Washington to explore institutions serving the criminal and disabled segments and, especially, to revive a virtually destroyed East Tennessee University at Knoxville. He closed by invoking divine will, the earnest and cordial cooperation required of state and federal authorities, and the legislators' responsibilities for confronting "the condition of the State, the evils that environ

us, and the measures of legislation needed for averting and ridding ourselves of them." To William Brownlow, "the interests of the State, and
the just rights of the people, should be sacredly and vigilantly guarded,
no matter who suffers ruin and disgrace."

In Kentucky, unionist governor Bramlette had perhaps already
given his own "state of the state" message in January. It would have
changed little in three months. Yet after April, Bramlette's message
might have moved close to sister state Tennessee's issues: the destruction and need for rebuilding economically, integrating the returning
veterans (of both sides), and, even more omnipresent, the freedmen's
problem. In both states, testimonials could be seen from fenceless fields
lying fallow in neglect, abandoned if not ruined properties of all classes,
countless grave markers, and vagabond whites and blacks (many of
them maimed) seeking to restructure lives, fortunes, and even families.
Wreckage of all sorts, human and physical, marked both postwar states.
A certain shock mixed with relief everywhere that the combat ended.
"It is all over now. It seems like a dream. What shadows we pursue!"
was how returning journalist Albert Roberts captured a facet of the
postwar aura. How long, however, would it take to recover?[69]

The *Memphis Appeal,* the peripatetic newspaper that exiled south
during the war, returned to print on November 5, 1865. Prominent
Tennesseans and Confederate officers like Gideon J. Pillow of Maury
County, Robert V. Richardson of Memphis, and Captain Thomas J.
Brown of Giles County had founded the American Cotton Planters'
Association that September in New York for the express purpose of
securing financial backing to resume the production and marketing of
cotton. Indeed, the Bluff City parleyed the lucrative wartime contraband trade in that commodity into a solid startup for the postwar period. William Beverley Randolph Hackley, who had gone to Memphis
as Treasury agent in 1863 specifically "to make money" in excess of his
small government salary, collaborated in the legendary fraud and graft
of the city before striking out on his own after the war. The flow of
cotton became a flood as the war drew to a close and trade reopened in
March. Apparently the winter had been tough on merchant paybacks to
government officials like Hackley. By May, however, he could write his
wife that all restrictions on commerce east of the Mississippi (save for
guns and ammunition) had been lifted and Confederates arrived daily
in Memphis seeking parole. He noted Forrest was paroled and back on
his farm in Cohoma, Mississippi. But, said Hackley, "I fear when the
troops are all sent home whenever that may be that there will be many

murders." The Confederates "have the same *feeling* they ever had and have only given up their arms because they cannot longer fight but they hate the men who have staid at home and will fight them upon small provocation. They hate them even more than they do the Yanks." Nonetheless, he anticipated "the difference between cotton grown by compensated labor[,] and the old will be abolished and with it the last of the Treasury regulations will be repealed" by midsummer.[70]

Elsewhere, in southeastern Tennessee, Thomas Crutchfield discovered in the wartime destruction of his Amnicola farm near Chattanooga a surviving Merino lamb, which had escaped soldiers' dinner pots. It became the nucleus of new breeding stock for wool and recovery for his family and livelihood. Putnam County, Tennessee, defied the trend of poor corn crops that year with high yield by late summer and did even better the following season, with tobacco joining the fungibles. Piece goods became available again in general stores, although "most freedmen were illiterate, penniless, and unaccustomed to the total responsibility of caring for themselves and their families." The federally mandated Freedmen's Bureau, created in March 1865 for emergency relief for both races via negotiated work contracts, medical aid, and black education, seemed promising. Congress extended the life of this relief agency for a second year. One Sumner County, Tennessee, Confederate advised another on July 16, 1865, about selling land and properties since "the destruction of our system of labor and the prostration resulting from the general destruction of property must throw large bodies in the market at greatly depreciated prices." Now was the time to "lay hold of it," for it "is a country in which people will live while they live anywhere." Indeed, in addition to returning battered native sons, outsiders—carpetbaggers—would sense opportunities afforded by a heartland revolution that overturned the old and opened new vistas for venturesome entrepreneurs.[71]

Stephen Burbridge's brother wrote him about relocating to Memphis to profit from the renewed cotton trade. He did not do so. But a prewar Maine transplant to Minnesota who had passed briefly through Nashville in 1862 with the Union army returned to the city at war's end to become a resident, working in the "claims business," a lucrative reconstruction endeavor seeking redress for damages suffered in the conflict. For a time, English-born Illinois soldier William H. Bradbury also lingered in the city, eyeing similar opportunities before finally departing home to family and eventually relocating to Kansas. Nonetheless, Nashville remained attractive and reconnected with Edgefield by a rebuilt bridge across the Cumberland, thus allowing resumption of the prewar development boom in that community. Yankees and carpetbaggers acquired large tracts of land in the new suburb (thanks to the prewar owners losing their land and wealth) and, in turn, resold the land at public auctions, often held on the grounds of the downtown Nashville courthouse. Young industry sprang up on both Nashville and Edgefield waterfronts.[72]

Everywhere in the upper South, people like forty-eight-year-old Hanna W. Swan of Knox County in East Tennessee took the loyalty oath. She received President Andrew Johnson's pardon when she renounced owning or using slaves, all costs from previous legal proceedings, and any attempt to recover any property seized by the government during the war. Michigan cavalry chaplain Henry Cherry wrote home in early May from East Tennessee how "the Universities, Colleges, & Academies, & schools have all collapsed, & will have to be reorganized." He wanted to assist but was deterred by simple economics. Others were less benevolent. Quartermaster James H. Wisewell wrote his father in early May, "Why is it? Rebels are pouring in here by hundreds every day and the authorities instead of hanging them are turning them loose to murder & plunder loyal citizens as they have done heretofore." Since the new civilian governor was trying to form a twenty-thousand-man militia, he thought he and associates would have good connections. "So what if this cruel war is over it does not through [sic] me out of a fat office." In September, Knoxvillian Joseph King wrote a Hartford, Connecticut, business connection that "the temper of this community has improved materially recently" with even the *Knoxville Whig* tempering its tone. A local judge had sentenced a person from a neighboring county to the penitentiary for six years for stealing two sides of bacon from a neighbor, declaring "that a rebel stood before the law the same as a Union man, and that there was no law that allowed one citizen to rob another because of his political opinions." King thought this had always been the case before the law, "but the other has been the practice recently with this charge regarded as very favorable to order against the mob." With radical unionists and blacks now in control, no wonder that Governor Brownlow found himself deluged with requests for positions in his new administration.[73]

Northern visitors also began to travel below the Potomac and Ohio Rivers. Seeking perhaps the fate of a loved one who had not returned from the war, these pilgrims keyed upon battle sites and associated graveyards, especially since the government had begun national cemeteries. Black labor combed the areas of carnage for nonbleached bones from shallow graves, often disturbed by rooting wild hogs as well as by rain and wind. One of the travelers to "the desolate south" was writer John T. Trowbridge, who made it to the Western theater only in the late fall and winter of 1865. Traversing Tennessee from east to west through the middle, Trowbridge best captured in anecdotes the indispensability of mules, the homespun "domestic" cloth that served all classes, the absence of free schools but abundance of primitive churches, and, above all, the centrality of the Negro problem, mostly for the lower element rather than those now dispossessed of that labor force. True, Knoxville, Chattanooga, Murfreesboro, Nashville, and Memphis all had the look of towns that for too long had been occupied by soldiery and war's infrastructure. Railroad travel was rickety and ramshackle, and the New Englander's account read like a travelogue with activity, optimism, and the future writ large. His words projected wide-eyed naïveté, as might be expected, and aside from visits to battlefields like Chickamauga, Stones River, and Shiloh, Trowbridge talked much less about the politics than the economics of reconstruction. [74]

Returning cropland prosperity, built upon a new system of contract labor and ownership, and the absolute conviction of Tennessee whites that slavery had been better for the Africans jumped from Trowbridge's portrayal. Of course, he could only anticipate how Memphis would soon regain its "dominant position in the economy of the Mid-South," how the prewar plantation economy would give way "to large farms" feeding the largest spot cotton market in the world. Memphis over the next century would become the scene of hectic activity in the autumn market season; it would become the world's largest producer of cottonseed products as well as a great cotton warehousing center. All that lay in the future, with fame and fortune continuing to rest on the backs of African American labor. In 1865, opportunity lay with Horatio Algers, not backward-focused historians. Chaplain Henry Cherry of the Tenth Michigan Cavalry was one such case.[75]

Stationed at Knoxville, Cherry noted on May 2, 1865, that "the matter of 'reconstruction' will involve a great many very nice points in law & morals and in practicability also for what will work pretty well in one neighborhood will not reach the peculiarities of another." He sensed that it would involve "an innumerable set of questions both in state & church" and, he might have added, society. His regiment moved westward in Tennessee during the summer, and the fall found him anticipating final muster-out at Memphis. The Michiganders had been at nearby Jackson for five weeks, "a wealthy & very beautiful place said to be the handsomest town in Tennessee." But Cherry found the people very different from those in East Tennessee: "aristocratic, and are to day as rebellious in spirit as they were four years ago." Bitterness of feeling existed to a surprising extent as these Tennesseans seemed to wonder why Davis and the Confederacy had failed. He attributed that to lack of newspapers, and thus the people were yet as ignorant of the true state of affairs as though they lived in Greenland.[76]

Cherry concluded to friend Amos Gould back home that West Tennesseans knew the Confederacy had somehow ended, but "they do not know on whom to spit their venom." So they vented their spleens and astonished the minister with epithets "not less than 500 times, most scornfully & bitterly repeated" against the freedmen, abolitionists, and Yankees. "Memphis too is a very determined rebel town, & I think there will yet be serious trouble," Cherry declared, for they were inventing all sorts of ways to prove that the former slave "wont work unless he is made to work" and seemed determined to prove it. "Great disaster will follow," he added. Indeed, he might have been talking as much about anywhere else in both Volunteer and Bluegrass States. Infamous race riots at Franklin and Memphis, the founding of white supremacist organizations like the Ku Klux Klan, the reduction of freed people to peonage and poverty, and the eclipse of the Freedmen's Bureau in the upper heartland, as well as the profoundly bitter polarization over ratification and implementation of Fourteenth and Fifteenth Amendments, which ensured citizenship and suffrage for blacks, ultimately produced a destabilizing and disturbing postconflict Reconstruction era in the upper heartland.[77]

Maury County farmer Nimrod Porter sagely observed in his journal on April 29, 1865, "It is now pretty well understood [that] the Southern Confederacy has gone up & peace of some sort either for well or for woe, will take place . . . shortly." Confederate Tennessee governor-in-exile Isham G. Harris addressed Forrest's shrunken command in Alabama four days later. "He spoke despondently," recorded cavalryman John Johnston. "Our prospects are growing darker and darker each day." It seemed that "our cause is hopeless, but we will stand at our post until we shall see the last curtain fall over the last act of this tremendous but unfortunate drama." They had entered the Confederate army "under a firm conviction of the justice of its cause," and four years of toil, blood, and disaster had not changed his opinion. "We feel that the cause of liberty sinks with the Confederate Government; a few more days will end the disastrous revolution." Indeed, it did for the last holdouts of the Lost Cause.[78]

The serious war for the upper heartland that had begun in February 1862 at Forts Henry and Donelson passed quickly to occupation and then more slowly through stabilization and the even greater ignominy of Franklin and Nashville. At some point in between, reconstruction but not recovery commenced in Tennessee and Kentucky. Even the return of peace was fractious. So formal Reconstruction pointing toward eventual reconciliation took more than double the time of the war itself. Perhaps the road to reconciliation required even a full century. With good reason, the overall legacy of the Civil War nationally might actually be tallied only with an inauguration of an African American president two hundred years after the birth of the emancipationist–war president Abraham Lincoln. Milestones, legacies, legends, and myths only attenuate America's—and by association, the upper heartland's—maturation in that regard.

Ironically, Nathan Bedford Forrest, the greatest survivor of battles in the heartland from Fort Donelson to Franklin, had the final say. He surrendered his men in May and the last correspondence entry in the federal government's *Official Records* volume of that theater contains the thoughts and words of this penultimate son and soldier of the upper heartland. Addressing his "soldiers," he did not think it necessary to refer to the causes that reduced them to this extremity, "nor is it now a matter of material consequence to us how such results were brought about." "That we are beaten is a self-evident fact," he observed. "The government which we sought to establish and perpetuate is at an end." It was now "your duty and mine to lay down our arms, submit to the 'powers that be,' and to aid in restoring peace and establishing law and order throughout the land." Not to do so guaranteed imprisonment, so Forrest sincerely hoped that every officer and soldier "will cheerfully obey the orders given and carry out in good faith all the terms of the cartel "with Federal authorities."[79]

Forrest then imparted his own view of the future. "Civil war, such as you have just passed through, naturally engenders feelings of animosity, hatred, and revenge," he advanced. It was "our duty to divest ourselves of all such feelings, and so far as in our power to do so to cultivate friendly feelings toward those with whom we have so long contested and heretofore so widely but honestly differed." Neighborhood feuds, personal animosities, and private differences should be blotted out, and "when you return home a manly, straightforward course of conduct will secure the respect even of your enemies." Whatever responsibilities may be owed to the government of the United States, to society or to individuals, "meet them like men," he urged. That the attempt to establish a separate and independent confederation had failed should not detract from having "done your duty faithfully and to the end will in some measure repay for the hardships you have undergone" In parting, the "wizard of the saddle" acknowledged his men's zeal, fidelity, and unflinching bravery as "the great source of my past success in arms." His soldiers' courage and determination as exhibited on many hard-fought fields "has elicited the respect and admiration of friend and foe." "You have been good soldiers, you can be good citizens," admonished Forrest. "Obey the laws, preserve your honor, and the Government to which you have surrendered can afford to be and will be magnanimous."

There would be many like Forrest and Cherry who would be drawn to Memphis. In fact, one such migrant and member of Forrest's own command was Denmark, Tennessee, native John Johnston. When he reached home from the defeated cause in mid-May, "I had no plans, no property, and nothing to do." But he had a letter from his brother-in-law, B. M. Estes in the Bluff City, inviting him to come get business training or preparation for the law. So about a week later Johnston went with buddy Billy Henry and several other Denmark folks "with their wagons loaded with cotton bales" to Memphis, no railroads being yet in operation. He was twenty-three years of age, with a "small trunk, containing all my worldly belongings." And so he arrived on the first day of June, ripe from rebel defeat, and joined the denizens of a New South, their eyes uplifted toward the future, if admittedly still wedded to profits from cotton bolls.[80]

Postscript: A Brave New World

The great Prussian war theorist Karl Marie von Clausewitz declared that war was simply an extension of politics or that war was politics by other means. If so, then the Tennessee and Kentucky experience might suggest that reconstruction is an extension of war by other means. Unification had defeated secession by 1865. And Union nationalization or nation building had overcome sectionalism and Confederate separatism. But it had not defeated rebellion. Sullen acquiescence and insurgency replaced direct military combat. Government policies during the war may have suppressed open belligerence. National governmental intrusion in loyal border states, as well as wartime occupation in states that departed the Union (some might even argue Kentucky, which did not), left a residue of hate, resistance, and a festering dissatisfaction with emancipation, confiscation, and the loss of civil liberties. The Civil War ensured survival of one United States; it did not necessarily produce one people. Confederate battlefield defeat gave way to transmogrified resistance in the wake of Appomattox. Racism, economic privation, and political redemption provided a different kind of postwar world. They supplanted the great constitutional issues that had caused secession and war.

Today, government officials, as well as students of the Reconstruction era, identify a litany of actions accompanying Reconstruction. According to Dr. Marie Richards, a foreign service officer and trained historian, actions could include:

1. reconstituting civilian political authority and sovereignty, including a new constitution if necessary;
2. democratic election of national and local government (where they preexisted);

3. reconstituting courts;
4. reconstituting civilian law enforcement (police);
5. rebuilding destroyed infrastructure;
6. reestablishing local and distant trade and commerce;
7. stabilizing currency and financial system;
8. identifying displaced persons, returning refugees, social reintegration, and settling land disputes;
9. disarming militias;
10. reintegrating former military personnel into civilian economy and society;
11. restoring pensions for the disabled and their families;
12. lifting restrictions on freedom of speech and publication and reopening newspapers;
13. reestablishing local revenue sources to support government (i.e., customs, sales, income taxes);
14. reopening schools, universities, and places of worship; and
15. refocusing hospitals and public health system to civilian needs.

Fundamental differences among military operations, occupation, stabilization, and reconstruction, as defined above, attend today's view. In fact, there seems a tandem-like effect, and the Federal government of the 1860s obviously did not have responsibility for or any interest in modern-day perception of actions. Most actions, if taken at all, were for the most part left to the states, local authorities, or the private sector. Budgetary retrenchment, demobilization of a war machine, and a return to traditional American antistatism could be (and was) expected in 1865.[1]

The problem the South faced at the end of hostilities might be found in the words of two southerners at the time. Writing to newly minted president Andrew Johnson on April 20, 1865, retired Lowell, Kentucky, merchant James H. Spillman spelled it out from the commoners' perspective. There were three antagonistic southern entities—rebels, union men, and blacks. "If ever they harmonise," he suggested, "it will be what I do not expect," for one might as well try to mix water and oil. The rebel element has had the ascendancy always and if they cannot retain it, they will leave, he suggested. Yet if they do have it then another war might be expected at a future day. Union men, to Spillman, must be *"the Party."* He advised Johnson, "If you br[in]g the leaders to a just punishment or anough [*sic*] of them to cause the balance to leave or submit you may manage them" since "we all know in the South a tyrant can not be trusted[.]" If the North forgave and trusted them, "then we are as a people gone up," for there had to be "some severity," although "of course it might be carried too fair." Four days later, Johnson informed a visiting delegation of "loyal Southerners" (repeating his earlier and unchanging position) that "it is time our people were taught to know that treason is a crime—not a mere political difference, not a mere contest between two parties, in which one succeeded, and the other has simply failed." "They must know it is treason, for if they had succeeded, the life of the nation would have been reft [*sic*] from it, the Union would have been destroyed." Back in February, he had assured his Tennessee Governor's Guard that the days of the slave oligarchy were past, that there would be no compromise, no settlement that would preserve even a remnant of that aristocracy which had ruled the South for so long. Here was the restoration challenge—fair but measured punishment leading to recognition that reunification brought responsibilities and acquiescence to the finality of battlefield results.[2]

A young Hopkinsville, Kentucky, lass named Augusta wrote her cousin Heddie Thompson on November 17, 1865, apologizing for "a very uninteresting letter," as "there is nothing to tell about since the war has stopped." She really did not know what the newspapers "can get to put in them." At some point, the rest of the United States simply said enough to the high cost of solving "the Southern problem" and turned its back on freed people, loyal unionists, and unrepentant rebels alike. The saga of the upper heartland from antebellum secession to war and ultimately reunion would prove intricate and stretch well into the twentieth century. Many in the heartland carried on with the words of one Tennessean Annie E. Law, who during the war had penned "Kentucky," a poignant poem capturing perhaps an opposite approach to Johnson and Spillman. "Kentucky! Old Kentucky! Once our loved sister state," went her opening lines, "the northern foe now holds thee; with hands and bands of hate." "They have spent the base endeavor to make thy children slaves, and through thy lovely valleys, lay thy Heroes in their graves," went the opening stanza. Successive stanzas recounted the conventional chorus of chains of oppression and tyranny, bondage, vengeance, and martyrdom.

Law then advanced a stirring third stanza:

> Then Kentucky, lov'd Kentucky
> The South now calls to thee
> To join thy destinies with ours,
> And swear thou wilt be free:
> We'll welcome thee, we'll welcome thee
> To thy honored place of yore,
> At the Eden of the sunny South
> Our sister—free once more.[3]

Prominent Kentucky historian E. Merton Coulter later observed that "Kentucky waited until after the war was over to secede from the Union," or so it seemed to his generation. More recently Michael A. Flannery explained a "post-bellum secessionist *mentalté*" pervading the state as if in some sort of penance for its wartime wavering and suffering under Union control. He pointed to a subsequent integration with the rest of the South over "the perfunctory legal acknowledgement of federal supremacy by agreeing to the thirteenth through the fifteenth amendments" (however dilatory even in that regard) so that the South "was permitted to maintain its old sociopolitical structure largely intact." Even Kentucky's returning Union veterans acquiesced to the rise of old Confederate prominence in state and local politics as well as socioeconomic control.[4]

Both Tennessee and Kentucky reached some form of immediate postwar readjustment within the year after Appomattox. David G. Burnet, former president of the Republic of Texas, wrote the now-imprisoned former Confederate president Jefferson Davis from Washington on October 16, 1865, noting that, like Alabama and Georgia, West Tennessee had "both prosperous and destitute regions; Kentucky has but little to complain of." Seating of a delegation in Congress in July 1866 constituted recognition that the Volunteer State in fact "was thereafter considered competent to manage its own affairs" and thus escape reimposition of military government like elsewhere in the South. Federal presence remained, in either the War Department's increasingly controversial Freedmen's Bureau or in the residual presence of U.S. troops. Formation of the Tennessee State Guard under Governor William Brownlow did not preclude Federal military presence in the Volunteer State until at least the election fall of 1876, although its numbers were small and shrank steadily. From a postwar high of

16,065 troops in a ratio of fifteen black to two white units in September 1865, the national government still maintained five posts of 370 men in October 1868 and even one remaining post for only 47 personnel as late as October 1876. Military presence, whether national or state, suggested the armed underwriting of political, social, and economic power restoration.[5]

Kentucky's experience substituted gubernatorial-legislative conflict for the wartime state-federal imbroglios. Coulter, Flannery, and others traced such direction to events beginning with President Abraham Lincoln's agreement with Governor Thomas Bramlette and Conservative demands for Stephen Burbridge's removal. President Johnson's subsequent lifting of martial law and restoration of the writ of habeas corpus in the fall of 1865 in turn set in motion the return of former Confederates' citizenship via a circuit court declaration that the governor-imposed expatriation restriction was unconstitutional (it was unconditionally repealed in December). The state legislature then passed an act allowing ex-Confederate soldiers to bring suit against unionists who had violated their rights through illegal arrest and seizure of property. The state now seemed solidly in the hands of former Confederates, it having been presented to them by the legislature. What they had not won in four years of war was now handed to them almost as recompense for their loss, or so run some explanations for postwar Kentucky affairs.[6]

Within two years, Democrats formerly denied their congressional seats had been returned to those positions and Kentucky began "casting herself in the role of Southern protector and defender," dispatching aid to prostrated sisters like Georgia via a revitalized Louisville and Nashville Railroad (offered free on board in the process). Hardly remarkable in hindsight, continued military presence and rule—even martial law—after Appomattox perpetuated wartime bitterness among a citizenry acutely conscious of their independent tradition of self-government. Nashville native and historian Thomas L. Connelly called this a peculiarly "Kentucky Mind," not neo-Confederatism. Connelly interpreted this carryover resentment of wartime interference from Washington as administered through Union generals such as E. A. Paine, James Brisbin, Jeremiah Boyle, Stephen G. Burbridge, and John Marshall Palmer. These figures, some even Kentucky natives, all had advanced national government actions as legitimate moves to win the war, suppress rebellion and lawlessness, and revolutionize a socioeconomic system via de facto emancipation. Conservative Kentuckians resented what they saw manifested by enforced martial law, suspension of the writ of habeas corpus, military interference with elections, widespread high-handed arrests of suspected disloyals even from among prominent citizenry, unwanted extension of Freedmen's Bureau activities from neighboring Tennessee, and civil rights amendments to both state and national constitutions.[7]

Palmer particularly viewed emancipation as his personal mission, further exacerbating the incipient racism predictable from a revolution of such magnitude. He granted free railroad passes to freedmen in search of work elsewhere. Blacks thus deserted Kentucky in droves, seeking wages and jobs north of the Ohio and in the East since fugitive slave laws no longer obtained. They saw such passes as "freedom papers," thereby making the pass system "an effective instrument to complete the destruction of slavery in the state," according to Victor Howard. Home state economic needs for cheap labor of any kind at war's end aside, the social climate of prejudice and racial oppression ensured white man's governance, "incapable of embracing either racial equality or a commitment to balance individual liberties with social justice." The fight over the Thirteenth Amendment and disgust over unremunerated emancipation flowed together with an ever-burgeoning lawlessness from wartime guerrillaism and domestic turbulence. Vigilantism led to the Ku Klux Klan and the open persecution of blacks as well as radical whites, just as in Tennessee. Perhaps both Radicals and Conservatives simply wished to impose some social order—but under each one's own rule set.[8]

Anecdotal Impressions

Restoration to the Union continued a recital of wartime episodes. By June 6, Sixth Kentucky cavalryman Edward Summers, now company orderly sergeant, was preparing rolls for mustering out both veterans and recruits. He was already thinking about his earlier communiqués to cousin Arthur Johnson about moving west from Kentucky to find new farmland away from border-state turmoil. Wartime grudges carried over in Monroe County, Tennessee, too, with the murder of the Union deputy provost marshal of the county, Joseph Divine. Wartime leader of home defense against bushwhackers and guerrillas, Divine received corporal punishment ostensibly for helping arrest the family of the region's Confederate brigadier, John C. Vaughn, and deporting them from their home. So the bitter four year struggle in East Tennessee, which had witnessed bridge-burner hangings, suppression of civil liberties by Confederate authorities, and retaliation and flight by unionists, transformed into words of affidavits from Divine's widow (herself slipping eventually into pension fraud), suggesting the bitterness, destitution, and destruction awaiting the section's soldiery when they returned. Indeed, the home-grown Yankee Tennessee units were disbanded in major cities like Nashville, Chattanooga, and Knoxville to return (in the words of historian James Alex Baggett) to issues of "pride, politics and pensions"—of the eastern portion of the Volunteer State in particular. While Baggett may correctly assert that "not all Union cavalry veterans were by any stretch of credulity bitter or vindictive," certain evidence suggests that their home-front counterparts— much like those they opposed—may well have harbored spite.[9]

The epilogue of Kentucky's punishment of its former guerrillas was equally fascinating. Jerome Clarke's close sidekick, Henry Magruder, was "one of the last people to die as a result of the Civil War," executed after a few puffs on a cigar on October 29, 1865, thus joining the infamous Champ Ferguson in eternity. Solon Thompson, Henry Metcalf, Henry Turner, Nathaniel Marks, J. H. Vincell, Henry Spaulding, Jake Bennett, Robert Britton, Joseph R. Jonigan, Eliab Garret, "Black" Dave Martin, Thomas L. Henry, and even "One-Armed" Sam Berry escaped the noose, although they were tried, threatened with execution, or even finally incarcerated for lengthy terms for wartime crimes. Lost in family or local lore, their stories have but recently been rescued from obscurity while hardly history's exoneration.[10]

Restoration of the Union rode on anecdotes as had the war itself. Johnson, as president, would resolve the question of restoring Nashville's McKendree Methodist Church property to the national affiliation upon demonstration of loyalty. Confederate general's wife Lezinka Brown Ewell had to await similar dispensation until 1866 for the former military governor's use of her city mansion. Moreover, observes one historian, the state capital's Fort Negley and its sister forts "were not monuments that a defeated South wanted to preserve." Renamed Fort Harker in 1865, this post lingered actively for two years and then was abandoned, becoming ironically a secret meeting spot for local Ku Kluxers for another two years. Happily, the site later became a favorite Sunday picnicking area for Nashville families, much as it had been before the war. The Nashville and Northwestern Railroad eventually converted back to civilian use, expanded as it had been by the military from Kingston Springs to Johnsonville. By June 1865, rail service to the northeast via the Virginia and Tennessee Railroad would reopen, thereby shortening travel to the nation's capital by seven hundred miles. Less anecdotal, in fact, was the larger undertaking all over the South caught by John T. Trowbridge in his *A Picture of the Desolated States and the Work of Restoration* (1866): policing of bodies from the battle-fields and properly honoring their sacrifice for whichever cause they had embraced.[11]

Identifiable and unidentifiable bones, shreds of clothing, and human remains would be gathered into national cemeteries at Nashville, Stones River, Knoxville, and Chattanooga, at least for the Union dead. The Nashville National Cemetery alone came to hold more than sixteen thousand Union burials, nearly thirty-six hundred of them unknown. For erstwhile rebels, their fate was more ignominious: family and church graveyards and forgotten corners of forgotten fields, except perhaps for that shrine of self-destruction at Franklin. At a time when most of the houses and other structures downtown seemed almost beyond repair and the doors of battered St. Paul's Episcopal Church would remain closed for several more years, there, in 1866, local Franklin citizens led by John and Carrie McGavock gave land on their Carnton plantation (where the generals had been laid out on the back porch after the battle) for a Confederate cemetery. Mrs. McGavock began almost a sacred crusade to organize and keep careful records of the reburials. Almost fifteen hundred remains became the centerpiece of a poignant tribute to the tragedy of that battle, even though many families came and exhumed loved ones for transport home. Thirty miles away in Nashville, initial burial of both Union and Confederate dead in the city cemetery eventually resulted in transfer to the national cemetery and a "Confederate Circle" in Mt. Olivet Cemetery, surrounding a forty-five-foot-tall granite monument topped by a Johnny Reb statue. Of course, Clarksville too saw hallowed ground for Confederate dead in the city's burial ground.[12]

The flood of reburials would eventually spawn the great memorialization movement for blue and gray, with separate special days set aside for decoration and remembrance. As with most things after the war, a requisite amount of predictable, if unfortunate, feuding and prejudice attended the honoring of black as well as white war dead. Ubiquitous Confederate memorial statuary sprang up in every town square, but not so much for the South's loyal unionists in blue. Commemoration and preservation of the actual fields of strife themselves lay in the distant future, as passage of years and aging of the participants caused a veterans' movement to consecrate their sacrifice with national and state military parks and battle sites. The passage toward reconciliation would ultimately be served by decoration days, memorializations, and battle-field preservation. Tennessee and Kentucky would not be excluded. As told by National Park Service historian Timothy B. Smith and others, the succession of preserving heartland battlegrounds in the 1890s, starting with Chickamauga and Chattanooga, Shiloh, and Vicksburg, would eventually embrace Stones River and Fort Donelson in the next century.[13]

What began at Fort Donelson in 1862 led to the establishment of a national cemetery in 1867, gracing the very ground that had previously been a Federal fort (not the more famous Confederate bastion perhaps a mile away). Just as important, that Yankee Fort Donelson (and its role in stabilizing and beginning reconstruction for the between-the-rivers section of Tennessee and Kentucky) had subsequently fostered a freedmen's community, not unlike at Fort Negley in Nashville and in places from Camp Nelson, Kentucky, to shanty satellites to Federal logistical centers. Lost except to family lore through the years, it was sizable and spawned the later black community in the expanding town of Dover. Only fitting, the Union Fort Donelson site provided postwar ground for reburial of 670 Union soldiers (512 unknowns) gleaned from the 1862 and 1863 battlefields, local cemeteries, hospital cemeteries, adjacent freed persons' settlement, and other places, including a school. Five known and nine unknown U.S. Colored Troops number among burials, for the second Fort Donelson had been the muster ground for USCT recruits during its tenure.[14]

No battle monuments would appear at Fort Donelson for seven decades after the war. Like Franklin and Nashville, postwar generations of southerners chose to ignore, not memorialize, such disasters. Northerners, who even today lack specific monuments to their efforts at the three battle sites, looked to bloodier, larger, and more famous fields of strife for commemoration. The original Confederate earthworks returned to nature—neglected sentinels to folly, defeat, and surrender. Only by the late 1920s and early 1930s would the bitter gall of defeat evaporate when local citizenry plumbed for a national park. In 1933, members of the Tennessee Division of the United Daughters of the Confederacy would erect "an altar of remembrance" to southern soldiers who fought and died at Fort Donelson. In fact, the story of nationalization of the Middle Tennessee battlefields provides a fascinating study in contrasts. Stones River had been proposed from the 1890s, while a Nashville Battlefield Association had plumbed for its national designation as early as 1909. Ironically, Fort Donelson and Nashville, the preeminent "bookend" events for the Civil War in the upper heart-land, worked against each other when it came to preservation. Timing was decisive when separate legislation for the pair reached the House of Representatives' Committee on Military Affairs for determination in early 1928. The proactive and very vocal pleas of the vice president general of the Daughters of the American Revolution, southerner Mrs. F. Gillentine, to portray a Nashville National Military Park as an effort in national unity with Fort Negley at its core ran into congressional reluctance to preserve too many battle monuments. Alabama representative Lister Hill particularly brushed aside this "gesture towards solidarity" (Gillentine's phrase) by asking if she realized that the committee had reported out the Fort Donelson bill scant weeks before. Committee chair John M. Morin of Pennsylvania then offered to give the Nashville idea "very careful consideration" and the matter died.[15]

Fort Donelson went on to become the national battlefield we know today. Nashville remained to be paved over, cut up for suburbia, and only lately—like Franklin—given some rebirth of concerted action by local preservation activists like Save the Franklin Battlefield, Inc. and the Battle of Nashville Preservation Society, as well as local Civil War roundtables working with city and private citizenry. Fort Negley garnered greater attention and partial restoration through the Works Progress Administration in the 1930s, then lapsed into neglect by the City of Nashville during the years of Jim Crow and segregation until a recent renaissance with brilliant interpretation and a modicum of restoration. As local writer Terry Baker has declared, it provides "a fair idea of what it was like in 1864," when shivering Confederates like Sam Watkins "had to sleep in the open, without the luxury of a fire," and stood looking at it and felt the impact of its heavy guns. If, as Timothy B. Smith so quaintly turned the phrase, "it seems one reason Nashville died was because Fort Donelson lived" (to which might be added Franklin), the approach of the Civil War's sesquicentennial suggests great possibilities through private, local, state, and federal partnering for according these sites their rightful place. Here one might reflect upon the commencement and the conclusion of the tempest that signified the nation's rite of passage. Each of the three events provided signposts or mile markers on that passage.[16]

Perhaps even those signposts fail to convey a continuous reinterpretation of what was and is important to know about war, stabilization, and reconstruction. African American heartland slaves built the original Confederate fort, and the capture of that fort opened a Pandora's box about what to do with human bondage. Former slaves shed their blood in Union blue, storming rebel lines at Nashville two years later, as had at least one enlightened white southerner, Patrick Cleburne, two weeks earlier at Franklin—dying for a cause mandated by slavery. After the fall of Fort Donelson, the upper South disintegrated into lawless guerrillaism, reflected in the conflict of the shadowy Jack Hinson or counter-insurgent Fifth Iowa Cavalry and Eighty-third Illinois Infantry and the Kentucky turbulence of Mundy, Quantrill, and Ferguson. And so, yet another theme of war emerged, that of stabilization, of winning hearts and minds of the civil populace, as well as eliminating what some styled partisan action and others called banditry and terrorism. Hinson himself survived the war, went home after his vendetta, was never prosecuted, and died of a heart attack at his house on White Oak Creek on April 28, 1874, a monument in a way to hundreds, maybe thousands, of his citizen comrades as freedom fighters. Their only memorials would come with gravestones in family or public cemeteries such as those of Confederate martyrs Charles W. Thompson and Pierman Powell, victims of Stephen Burbridge's reign of terror, buried in a Roman Catholic cemetery in Curdsville, Kentucky.[17]

Home Guardsman, partisan, patriot, freedom fighter, or just plain vindictive murderers would attend the memory of individuals like Hinson or Ferguson and become lost in legend. Hinson's haunts around sleepy Dover would exchange the rattle of musketry for a return of steamboat whistles around the bend, signifying the restored lifeblood of economy and society (white and black) for the postwar heartland. It was here that Ulysses S. Grant had earned his sobriquet "Unconditional Surrender" and launched his path to higher command, successive victories, and, by 1868, the road to the White House. He had departed that road that led eventually to Franklin and Nashville, yet the veterans who had given him his initial successes on the Tennessee and Cumberland Rivers never left his memory. Office seekers saw to it. But Grant was like that—befriending almost to a fault and ever willing to help those who had helped him. Perhaps he never knew or visited that national cemetery on the banks of the sylvan Cumberland, but he remained with the fallen in spirit and memory.[18]

Still, war's end for Tennessee and Kentucky had not come at Fort Donelson (as it might have) in 1862. Plentiful symbols across the upper South attest to the fact that nearly a sesquicentennial distance from time and events has not dulled sensibilities to remembering, "lest we forget." John Overton's Traveler's Rest, Adelicia Acklen's Belmont, Sunnyside, and the famous Belle Meade plantation (just like Carnton at Franklin) all survived the war, especially the last major battles in the Western theater. Today we may view their past splendor—monuments to a slave society that was blown away with the winds of war, a war that shaped civilian society as well as the postbellum rise of a New South. Southern civil as well as military cemeteries and town square monuments portray northward-facing Gray Heroes at the "parade-rest" position to memorialize valor and sacrifice. Bethel cemetery in Knoxville does—a statue existent long after Fort Sanders became part of the city's urban and university landscape. The fort may have vanished, but Civil War Trails markers, Longstreet's Bleak House headquarters on Kingston Pike, and Fort Dickerson in South Knoxville keep the flame of memory alive as the nation, Tennessee, and Kentucky enter the Civil War sesquicentennial period.[19]

"Lest We Forget"

Unlike countless silent sentinels, nay, perhaps even more the heroic equestrian renditions of Nathan Bedford Forrest in Memphis or John Hunt Morgan in Lexington, the most poignant reminders of Claude Bower's aptly titled (if textually scarred) classic *The Tragic Era* stand conceivably at Dover and Nashville. At the former, behold the pointed shaft at Fort Donelson bearing the epitaph for the failed Confederacy: "There's no holier spot of ground than where defeated valor lies." In a suburban neighborhood at the latter stands an even more poignant tribute to the war's culminating years. Buffeted by generations of controversy over why one would even memorialize the South's most disastrous defeat, as well as a modern storm of nature and a forced relocation from interstate highway construction, stands the Battle of Nashville Peace Monument. Located at Granny White Pike between Clifton Lane and Battlefield Drive, this simple monument concludes any tour of the events of 1864–65.

Five years before the Fort Donelson UDC tribute, the Nashville Ladies Battlefield Association in 1926 had attempted to establish "the only monument of its type" dedicated not just to the soldiers of Union and Confederacy who fought in the battle of Nashville but also to the American soldiers who fought in World War I. It epitomized the idea of reconciliation, as the bronze sculpture by Italian Guiseppi Moretti portrayed a youth holding the reins of two horses—North and South—and featured the word "Unity," with the stone obelisk topped by an angel. In the end, that was what was achieved by four years of carnage,

Modern-day photograph of the Battle of Nashville Peace Monument. Photograph by Steve
Rogers.

of battles, skirmishes, feuds, atrocities, destruction, and bitterness,
costing a generation of lives, livelihood, and contention between races
and brothers. A war of rebellion, insurrection, independence, liberation, and national unification ended with Unity (or so they hoped in
1926 and so we believe today). Is this the unrequited legacy of war in
the upper heartland? The expenditure of national treasure and time
to accomplish nation building, democratization, and freedom abroad
remains arguably as unfinished as the task at home. Yet as former Confederate president Jefferson Davis told a Chattanooga, Tennessee, audience on July 26, 1870, "It is not the part of brave men to brood over
the sorrows of the past, but rather to look forward with bright hopes
for the future."[20]

Notes

—⌘—

Preface

1. Jeffrey D. Marshall, ed., *A War of the People: Vermont Civil War Letters* (Hanover, N.H., 1999), 40.
2. S. J. Sievers, *Benjamin Harrison: Hoosier Warrior, 1833–1865* (Chicago, 1952), 268–70. For a cartographic portrayal of war zones and frontiers in the upper heartland, see Kenneth C. Martis, *The Historical Atlas of the Congress of the Confederate States of America: 1861–1865* (New York, 1994), maps 19, 21, 23 on pp. 48, 50, 52.
3. Recent touchstones for studying these campaigns include Alexander Mendoza, *Confederate Struggle for Command: General James Longstreet and the First Corps in the West* (College Station, Tex., 2008); Richard McMurry, *Atlanta 1864: Last Chance for The Confederacy* (Lincoln, Neb., 2000); and Anne J. Bailey, *The Chessboard of War: Sherman and Hood in the Autumn Campaigns of 1864* (Lincoln, Neb., 2000).
4. Anne Norton, *Alternative Americas: A Reading of Antebellum Political Culture* (Chicago, 1986), chap. 9; Francis Lieber's thoughts in U.S. War Department, *The War of the Rebellion: A Compilation of the Official Records of the Union and Confederate Armies* (Washington, D.C., 1880–1901), ser. 3, vol. 2:301 (hereafter referred to as *ORA*, followed by series number, volume number, part number, page number); David Bosco, "Moral Principle vs. Military Necessity," *American Scholar* 77 (Winter 2008): 25–34; Theodore Ayrault Dodge, *A Bird's-Eye View of Our Civil War* (Boston, 1883), 334.
5. Joseph B. Killebrew autobiography, 191, Southern Historical Collection, University of North Carolina, Chapel Hill (hereafter referred to as SHC/UNC).
6. See for example, Burrus M. Carnahan, *Lincoln on Trial: Southern Civilians and the Law of War* (Lexington, KY, 2010); Frank G. Hoffman, "Hybrid vs. Compound War—The Janus Choice: Defining Today's Multifaceted Conflicts," *Armed Forces Journal*, Oct. 2009, 14–18, 44;

Robert Wilkie, "Hybrid Warfare: Something Old, Not Something New,"
Air and Space Power Journal 23 (Winter 2009): 14–17; Keith Poulter
et al., "Irregular Warfare, 1861–1865," *North & South* 11 (June 2009):
17–29; Daniel Sutherland, "The Savage War," *North & South* 11 (Aug.
2009): 68–76; Editors, "An Alternative Strategy," *North & South* 11
(Aug. 2009): 14–21, 42; Clay Mountcastle, *Punitive War: Confederate
Guerrillas and Union Reprisals* (Lawrence, Kans., 2009); Cynthia A.
Watson, *Nation-Building: A Reference Handbook* (Santa Barbara, Calif.,
2004); Nina M. Serafino, *Peacekeeping and Related Stability Operations:
Issues of U.S. Military Involvement*, CRS issue brief for Congress (Wash-
ington, D.C., Jan. 30, 2006); Ralph Wipfli and Steven Metz, "Coin of
the Realm: U.S. Counterinsurgency Strategy," colloquium brief (Carlisle
Barracks, Pa., 2007); Greg Kaufman, ed., *Stability Operations and State-
Building: Continuities and Contingencies* (Carlisle Barracks, Pa., 2008);
Patrick M. Cronin, *Irregular Warfare: New Challenges for Civil-Military
Relations*, Strategic Forum, Institute for National Strategic Studies, No.
234 (Washington, D.C., 2008); Mark Moyar, *A Question of Command:
Counterinsurgency from the Civil War to Iraq* (New Haven, Conn.,
2009); and Shannon A. Brown, ed., *Resourcing Stability Operations and
Reconstruction: Past, Present and Future* (Washington, D.C., 2007).
7. "A Rebel Girl on Union," *83rd Illinoisan*, Apr. 21, 1865.

1. The Henry-Donelson Legacy

1. Jean V. Berlin, *A Confederate Nurse: The Diary of Ada W. Bacot, 1860–
1863* (Columbia, S.C., 1994), 84–85; John David Smith and William
Cooper, eds., *A Union Woman in Civil War Kentucky: The Diary of
Frances Peter* (Lexington, Ky., 2000), 8; Walter T. Durham, "Looking
Every Minute for Them to Come," *Tennessee Historical Quarterly* (Summer 2000): 109.
2. The story of the Forts Henry and Donelson campaign may be found in
the author's *Forts Henry and Donelson: The Key to the Confederate Heartland* (Knoxville, Tenn., 1987). Albert Castel presents an intriguing
vignette, "The Mule Goes to War," in *Winning and Losing in the Civil
War: Essays and Stories* (Columbia, S.C., 1996), chap.10, which suggests
a largely overlooked result from the early loss of the upper heartland as
denial of mules to Confederate military use.
3. George Eagleton, Day Book, Feb. 16, 17, 1862, quoted in Alden Pearson
Jr., "A Middle-Class, Border-State Family During the Civil War," *Civil
War History* (Dec. 1976): 322; James A. Hoobler, "The Civil War Diary
of Louisa Brown Pearl," *Tennessee Historical Quarterly* 38 (Fall 1979):
314.
4. Robert Partin, "The 'Momentous Events' of the Civil War as Reported
by a Confederate Private-Sergeant," *Tennessee Historical Quarterly* 18

(Mar. 1959): 79; Thomas Black Wilson, "Reminiscences," 22, 25, SHC/
UNC; Glenn Linden and Virginia Linden, eds., *Disunion, War, Defeat,
and Recovery in Alabama: The Journal of Augustus Benners, 1850–1885*
(Macon, Ga., 2007), 76–77.

5. B. F. Welker to sister, Feb. 27, 1862, William Swanzey to wife, Mar. 2,
1862, and J. N. and E. J. Carothers to James McCallum, Mar. 19, 1862,
all in author's files.

6. For traditional paeans to Johnston, see William Preston Johnston, *The
Life of Gen. Albert Sidney Johnston* (New York, 1878), chaps. 19–37;
Charles P. Roland, *Albert Sidney Johnston: Soldier of Three Republics*
(Austin, Tex., 1964), chaps. 15–17; and Larry J. Daniel, "'The Assaults
of the Demagogues in Congress': General Albert Sidney Johnston and
the Politics of Command," *Civil War History* 37 (Dec. 1991): 328–35.
Compare these to the more critical portrayals in Thomas L. Connelly,
Army of the Heartland: The Army of Tennessee, 1861–1862 (Baton Rouge,
La., 1971); Steven E. Woodworth, *Jefferson Davis and His Generals: The
Failure of Confederate Command in the West* (Lawrence, Kans., 1990),
chaps. 4–7; Woodworth, "When Merit Was Not Enough: Albert Sidney
Johnston and Confederate Defeat in the West," chap. 1 in *Civil War
Generals in Defeat*, ed. Woodworth (Lawrence, Kans., 1999); Albert Cas-
tel, *Articles of War: Winners, Losers and Some Who Were Both During the
Civil War* (Mechanicsburg, Pa., 2001), chap. 9; and Stephen D. Engle,
"'Thank God, He Has Rescued His Character': Albert Sidney Johnston,
Southern Hamlet of the Confederacy," in *Leaders of the Lost Cause: New
Perspectives on the Confederate High Command*, ed. Gary W. Gallagher
and Joseph T. Glatthaar (Mechanicsburg, Pa., 2004), 133–63.

7. N. F. Cheairs to "My Dear Daughter," Apr. 22, 1862, and "Personal Experiences in the War Between the States," in *I'll Sting If I Can: The Life
and Prison Letters of Major N. F. Cheairs, C.S.A.*, ed. Nathan Cheairs
Hughes Jr. (Signal Mountain, Tenn., 1998), 35, 63.

8. Wilson, "Reminiscences," 22, SHC/UNC; George W. Johnson to wife,
Feb. 15, 1862, Filson Club, Louisville, Ky. (hereafter referred to as FC);
Thomas Hopkins Deavenport diary, 11, Tennessee State Library and
Archives, Nashville (hereafter referred to as TSLA); Nathan Cheairs
Hughes Jr., *I'll Sting If I Can: The Life and Prison Letters of Major N. F.
Cheairs, C.S.A.* (Signal Mountain, Tenn., 1998), 25, 78, 96, 145; John
Henry Guy prison journal, and Guy to Father, Mar. 21, 1862, both
Virginia Historical Society, Richmond; Daniel E. Sutherland, *A Savage
Conflict: The Decisive Role of Guerrillas in the American Civil War* (Cha-
pel Hill, N.C., 2009), 77, 88.

9. Ulysses S. Grant, *Personal Memoirs* (New York, 1885), 1:316–18. Events
of the period can be followed in Stephen D. Engle, *Struggle for the
Heartland: The Campaigns from Fort Henry to Corinth* (Lincoln, Neb.,
2001).

10. "Regular" to editor, Apr. 8, 1862, and "H" to editor, Apr. 10, 1862, *New York Sunday Mercury,* in *Writing and Fighting the Civil War: Soldier Correspondence to the New York Sunday Mercury,* ed. William B. Styple (Kearny, N.J., 2000), 83–85; Partin, "Momentous Events," 74, 77.

11. Events of the counteroffensive period can be followed in Earl J. Hess, *Banners to the Breeze: The Kentucky Campaign, Corinth and Stones River* (Lincoln, Neb., 2000); James Lee McDonough, *War in Kentucky: From Shiloh to Perryville* (Knoxville, Tenn., 1994); McDonough, *Stones River: Bloody Winter in Tennessee* (Knoxville, Tenn., 1980); Peter Cozzens, *The Darkest Days of the War: The Battles of Iuka and Corinth* (Chapel Hill, N.C., 1997); Peter Cozzens, *No Better Place to Die: The Battle of Stones River* (Urbana, Ill., 1990); Roger Pickenpaugh, *Rescue by Rail: Troop Transfer and the Civil War in the West, 1863* (Lincoln, Neb., 1998); and Partin, "Momentous Events," 79.

12. Sutherland, *Savage Conflict,* 93–95; Robert R. Mackey, *The Uncivil War: Irregular Warfare in the Upper South, 1861–1865* (Norman, Okla., 2004), introduction, esp. p. 5; James D. Brewer, *The Raiders of 1862* (Westport, Conn., 1997), introduction. See also Benjamin Franklin Cooling, *Fort Donelson's Legacy: War and Society in Kentucky and Tennessee, 1862–1863* (Knoxville, Tenn., 1997), 64–77.

13. Terry Baker, "Fort Negley: Sole Survivor of Nashville's Civil War Defenses," *Nashville Retrospect* 1 (Dec. 2009): 7.

14. Armstead L. Robinson, *Bitter Fruits of Bondage: The Demise of Slavery and the Collapse of the Confederacy, 1861–1865* (Charlottesville, Va., 2005), 109, 127–28, 303n9; U.S. Senate, *Preliminary Report on the Eighth Census 1860,* by Joseph G. Kennedy (Washington, D.C., 1862), 131, 134–35.

15. William F. Smith to H. M. Cist, Nov. 1, 1888, Catalog 33, Fall 2001, Brian and Maria Green, Inc., Kernersville, N.C., copy in author's files.

16. *ORA,* ser. 4, vol. 2:1003; Robinson, *Bitter Fruits of Bondage,* 123–34, and chap. 10; U.S. Senate, *Preliminary Report,* tables 9–41, inter alia. The story of the middle period of the Civil War in the upper heartland may be followed in Cooling, *Fort Donelson's Legacy.*

17. James Welch Patton, *Unionism and Reconstruction in Tennessee* (Chapel Hill, N.C., 1934), 29–31; Thomas B. Alexander, *Political Reconstruction in Tennessee* (Nashville, 1950), 15.

18. Patton, *Unionism and Reconstruction in Tennessee,* 31–33; James E. Sefton, *Andrew Johnson and the Uses of Constitutional Power* (Boston, 1980), 88–89.

19. Patton, *Unionism and Reconstruction in Tennessee,* 32; Stephen V. Ash, *Middle Tennessee Society Transformed, 1860–1870* (Baton Rouge, La., 1988), 97–98.

20. Patton, *Unionism and Reconstruction in Tennessee*, 35–36; Sefton, *Andrew Johnson*, 90–93; Alexander, *Political Reconstruction in Tennessee*, 15.

21. Patton, *Unionism and Reconstruction in Tennessee*, 37–42; Sefton, *Andrew Johnson*, 94–96; Ash, *Middle Tennessee Society Transformed*, chap. 5.

22. Patton, *Unionism and Reconstruction in Tennessee*, 42–43; Sefton, *Andrew Johnson*, 96–97. On the East Tennessee story, see Digby Gordon Seymour, *Divided Loyalties: Fort Sanders and the Civil War in East Tennessee* (Knoxville, Tenn., 2003).

23. E. Merton Coulter, *The Civil War and Readjustment in Kentucky* (Gloucester, Mass., 1966), 154; Penny W. Miller, *Kentucky Politics and Government: Do We Stand United?* (Lincoln, Neb., 1994), 25; Lowell H. Harrison, *The Civil War in Kentucky* (Lexington, Ky., 1975), ix.

24. Coulter, *Civil War and Readjustment*, 146–48, chap. 8.

25. Ibid., 171; *Frankfort Tri-Weekly Commonwealth*, Feb. 13, 1863.

26. Coulter, *Civil War and Readjustment*, 170–78; William Marvel, *Burnside* (Chapel Hill, N.C., 1991), 246–66.

27. Coulter, *Civil War and Readjustment*, 179 (quoting Bramlette in *Frankfort Daily Commonwealth*, Dec. 8, 1863); Lowell H. Harrison and James C. Klotter, *A New History of Kentucky* (Lexington, Ky., 1997), 206.

28. Coulter, *Civil War and Readjustment*, 224; Ash, *Middle Tennessee Society Transformed*, chaps. 5, 6, 7.

29. Bob Womack, *Call Forth the Mighty Men* (Bessemer, Ala., 1987), 323–24; John S. Otto, *Southern Agriculture During the Civil War Era, 1860–1880* (Westport, Conn., 1994), chap. 2; Coulter, *Civil War and Readjustment*, chap. 12.

30. Thomas W. Knox, *Camp-Fire and Cotton-Field: Southern Adventure in Time of War* (New York, 1865), 193; Coulter, *Civil War and Readjustment*, 239.

31. *ORA*, ser. 1, vol. 31, pt. 3:508; Joseph B. Killebrew autobiography, 191; John Houston Bills diary, Oct. 19, 1863, SHC/UNC.

32. *ORA*, ser. 3, vol. 1:1038–40, 1128. On implications of Lieber, General Order 100, and the heartland, see Cooling, *Fort Donelson's Legacy*, 218–22, 257.

33. Synopsis, William McCrory letter, June 6, 1863, Item 107, Catalog 33, Summer 2001, Brian and Marian Green, Inc., Kernersville, N.C., copy in author's files.

34. Sherman to wife, Jan. 12, 1864, in M. A. DeWolfe Howe, ed., *Home Letters of General Sherman* (New York, 1909), 287–88; James B. Martin, "Black Flag Over the Bluegrass: Guerrilla Warfare in Kentucky, 1863–1865," *Register of the Kentucky Historical Society* 81 (1988): 353.

2. Unfinished Business in East Tennessee

1. *ORA*, ser. 1, vol. 31, pt. 3:248. The East Tennessee campaign may be
followed in detail in both parts of *ORA*, vol. 31, as well as in Seymour,
Divided Loyalties. Operations around Chattanooga and the siege of that
city are covered in James Lee McDonough, *Chattanooga: A Death Grip
on the Confederacy* (Knoxville, Tenn., 1984); Peter Cozzens, *The Ship-
wreck of Their Hopes: The Battles for Chattanooga* (Urbana, Ill., 1994);
and John Wilson, *Chattanooga's Story* (Chattanooga, Tenn., 1980).
2. Harold S. Fink, "The East Tennessee Campaign and the Battle of Knoxville in 1863," *East Tennessee Historical Society Publications* 29 (1957): 83.
3. Judith Lee Hallock, *Braxton Bragg and Confederate Defeat* (Tuscaloosa,
Ala., 1991), 2:126. See also James Longstreet, *From Manassas to Appomattox* (Philadelphia, 1895), chaps. 32 and 33; William Garrett Piston,
*Lee's Tarnished Lieutenant: James Longstreet and His Place in Southern
History* (Athens, Ga., 1987), 73–76; Jeffrey D. Wert, *General James
Longstreet: The Confederacy's Most Controversial Soldier: A Biography*
(New York, 1993), 323–28, 338–39; and James Wylie Ratchford, *Memoirs of a Confederate Staff Officer: From Bethel to Bentonville*, ed. Evelyn
Ratchford Sieburg (Shippensburg, Pa., 1998), 44–46.
4. Mendoza, *Confederate Struggle for Command*, 106–14.
5. Leroy P. Graf and Ralph W. Haskins, et al., eds., *The Papers of Andrew
Johnson*, 16 vols. (Knoxville, Tenn., 1967–2000), 6:359; Marvel, *Burnside*, chap. 5; *ORA*, ser. 1, vol. 31, pt. 1:339–40, and pt. 2:3.
6. Wert, *General James Longstreet*, 329–39; Robert Tracy McKenzie, *Lincolnites and Rebels: A Divided Town in the American Civil War* (New
York, 2006), 153–57.
7. McKenzie, *Lincolnites and Rebels*, 157; Gary W. Gallagher, ed., *Fighting
for the Confederacy: The Personal Recollections of General Edward Porter
Alexander* (Chapel Hill, N.C., 1989), 307, 312.
8. Charles F. Bryan Jr., "East Tennessee in the Civil War: A Social, Political and Economic Study" (Ph.D. diss., Univ. of Tennessee, 1978), 19;
ORA, ser. 1, vol. 31, pt. 3:297; E. Merton Coulter, *William G. Brownlow: Fighting Parson of the Southern Highlands* (Chapel Hill, N.C., 1937;
Knoxville, 1999), chaps. 7–9. Rediscovery of war in this region may be
found in W. Todd Groce, *Mountain Rebels: East Tennessee Confederates
and the Civil War, 1860–1870* (Knoxville, Tenn., 1999); Noel C. Fisher,
*War at Every Door: Partisan Politics and Guerrilla Violence in East Ten-
nessee, 1860–1869* (Chapel Hill, N.C., 1997); and Sean Michael O'Brien,
*Mountain Partisans: Guerrilla Warfare in the Southern Appalachians,
1861–1865* (Westport, Conn., 1999).
9. *ORA*, ser. 1, vol. 30, pt. 3:513; Verton M. Queener, "East Tennessee Sentiment and the Secession Movement," *East Tennessee Historical Society's
Publication* 20 (1948): 59–63; James L. Baumgardner, "Abraham Lincoln,

Andrew Johnson and the Federal Patronage," *East Tennessee Historical Society's Publication* 53 (1973): 51–60; Jesse Burt, "East Tennessee, Lincoln and Sherman, Part I," *East Tennessee Historical Society's Publication* 38 (1962): 3–7, 22 (quoting Russell, *London Times,* Nov. 9, 1861). See also James G. Randall, *Lincoln the President* (New York, 1945), 2:266–67; Carl Sandburg, *Abraham Lincoln: The War Years* (New York, 1939), 1:211; Daniel W. Crofts, *Reluctant Confederates: Upper South Unionists in the Secession Crisis* (Chapel Hill, N.C., 1989), 21–25, 62–63, 131, 133, 148–49, 152, 342–45, 347–50; John D. Fowler, *Mountaineers in Gray: The Nineteenth Tennessee Volunteer Infantry Regiment C.S.A.* (Knoxville, Tenn., 2004), chap. 1, and 39–44; Charles F. Bryan Jr., "'Tories' Amidst Rebels: Confederate Occupation of East Tennessee, 1861–1863," *East Tennessee Historical Society's Publications* 60 (1988): 2–22; Noel Fisher, "'The Leniency Shown Them Has Been Unavailing': The Confederate Occupation of East Tennessee," *Civil War History* (Dec. 1994): 275–91; McKenzie, *Lincolnites and Rebels,* 144–45; and Sam Bollier, "'Our Own Paradise Invaded': Imagining Civil War Era East Tennessee," *Tennessee Historical Quarterly* 68 (Winter 2009): 408.

10. William Garrett Piston, *Carter's Raid: An Episode of the Civil War in East Tennessee* (Johnson City, Tenn., 1989); *ORA,* ser. 1, vol. 23, pt. 1:386, 388; David C. Smith, *Campaign to Nowhere: The Results of General Longstreet's Move into Upper East Tennessee* (Strawberry Plains, Tenn., 1999), chap. 1; Larry N. Crouch, "The Merchant and the Senator: An Attempt to Save East Tennessee For the Union," *East Tennessee Historical Society's Publications* 54 (1974): 53–76; McKenzie, *Lincolnites and Rebels,* chaps. 4 and 5.

11. Richard A. Sauers, ed., *The Civil War Journal of Colonel William J. Bolton, Fifty-First Pennsylvania, April 20, 1861–August 2, 1865* (Conshohocken, Pa., 2000), 153–54; William MacArthur Jr., "The Early Career of Charles McClung McGhee," *East Tennessee Historical Society's Publications* 53 (1973): 10–13; Palmer H. Boeger, "General Burnside's Knoxville Packing Project," *East Tennessee Historical Society's Publications* 43 (1963): 76, 77; W. Todd Groce, "Confederate Faces in East Tennessee: A Photographic Essay," *Journal of East Tennessee History* 65 (1993): 3–5; McKenzie, *Lincolnites and Rebels,* chap. 1.

12. William L. Katchersid, "Major Campbell Wallace: Southern Railroad Leader," *Tennessee Historical Quarterly* 67 (Summer 2008): 91–95. Fisher, *War at Every Door,* and O'Brien, *Mountain Partisans,* also provide insights.

13. Smith, *Campaign to Nowhere,* 2; William G. Gavin, ed., *Infantryman Pettit: The Civil War Letters of Corporal Frederick Pettit, Late of Company C, 100th Pennsylvania Veteran Volunteer Infantry Regiment, "The Roundheads," 1862–1864* (Shippensburg, Pa., 1990), 125; Mendoza, *Confederate Struggle for Command,* 114–16.

14. Myra Inman, *Myra Inman: A Diary of the Civil War in East Tennessee,* ed. William R. Snell (Macon, Ga., 2000), 222–23, 225; Asbury Coward, *The South Carolinians: Colonel Asbury Coward's Memoirs,* ed. Natalie Jenkins Bond and Osmun Latrobe Coward (New York, 1968), 93; Gallagher, *Fighting for the Confederacy,* 320, also 312–13; William B. Hesseltine, ed., *Dr. J. G. M. Ramsey: Autobiography and Letters* (Nashville, 1954), 146, 158; *ORA,* ser. 1, vol. 31, pt. 1:259; William Bilby, "Blue Bonnets Over the Border," *Military Images* (July/Aug. 1984): 11; Gavin, *Infantryman Pettit,* 125; Sauers, *Civil War Journal,* 140.

15. Sauers, *Civil War Journal,* 145–46, 148; Fisher, *War at Every Door,* 126–27; Watson B. Smith to Father, Nov. 5, 1863, University of Tennessee Library, Special Collections, Knoxville (hereafter referred to as UTLK).

16. Sauers, *Civil War Journal,* 143–49; *ORA,* ser. 1, vol. 30:718, and vol. 31, pt. 1:258–61, 265–66, 273, pt. 2:30, and pt. 3:128, 138; James R. Montgomery, "The Nomenclature of the Tennessee River," *East Tennessee Historical Society's Publications* 51 (1979): 151–52; Watson B. Smith to Father, Nov. 5, 1863, UTLK.

17. Mendoza, *Confederate Struggle for Command,* 117–21; McKenzie, *Lincolnites and Rebels,* 158–59.

18. Gerald L. Augustus, *The Loudon County Area of East Tennessee in the War, 1861–1865* (Paducah, Ky., 2000), chap. 8; Sauers, *Civil War Journal,* 149–50; Gavin, *Infantryman Pettit,* 126; Orlando M. Poe, "Personal Recollections of the Occupation of East Tennessee and the Defense of Knoxville," in *War Papers: Michigan Military Order of the Loyal Legion of the United States,* vol. 1, paper 8, by Michigan Commandery (Detroit, 1889), 3, 6, 11, 17–19; James I. Baldwin III, *The Struck Eagle: A Biography of Brigadier General Micah Jenkins and a History of the Fifth South Carolina Volunteers and the Palmetto Sharpshooters* (Shippensburg, Pa., 1996), 244–46.

19. Mendoza, *Confederate Struggle for Command,* 119–21; Fink, "East Tennessee Campaign," 93–94; John C. Oeffinger, ed., *A Soldier's General: The Civil War Letters of Major General Lafayette McLaws* (Chapel Hill, N.C., 2002), 220–21; Baldwin, *Struck Eagle,* 247; Gavin, *Infantryman Pettit,* 126–27; W. Mark McKnight, *Blue Bonnets O'er the Border: The Seventy-Ninth New York Cameron Highlanders* (Shippensburg, Pa.: White Mane Publishing, 1998), 109–10; Sauers, *Civil War Journal,* 150–51; John C. West, *A Texan in Search of a Fight: Being the Diary and Letters of a Private Soldier in Hood's Texas Brigade* (Waco, Tex., 1906), 132; J. Gray Lane and Morris M. Penny, *Law's Alabama Brigade in the War Between the Union and the Confederacy* (Shippensburg, Pa., 1996), chap. 11; *ORA,* ser. 1, vol. 31, pt. 1:273–75, 483, 527.

20. Daniel E. Sutherland, ed., *A Very Violent Rebel: The Civil War Diary of Ellen Renshaw House* (Knoxville, Tenn., 1996), 38–47; Sauers, *Civil War Journal,* 152–53; McKenzie, *Lincolnites and Rebels,* 160–61.

21. Mendoza, *Confederate Struggle for Command*, 123–24.
22. *ORA*, ser. 1, vol. 31, pt. 1:492; Poe, *Recollections*, 17–19; Gallagher, *Fighting for the Confederacy*, 317–18; Sutherland, *Very Violent Rebel*, 40–41; E. Katherine Crews, "Musical Activities in Knoxville, Tennessee, 1861–1891," *East Tennessee Historical Society's Publications* 34 (1962): 58; Mendoza, *Confederate Struggle for Command*, 126–27.
23. "The Siege of Knoxville, Tenn.," Document 19, in Frank Moore, ed., *The Rebellion Record: A Diary of American Events* (New York, 1865), 8:251–55; Ronald G. Watson, ed., *From Ashby to Andersonville: The Civil War Diary and Reminiscence of George A. Hitchcock* (Campbell, Calif., 1997), 149–56; McKenzie, *Lincolnites and Rebels*, 162–65.
24. Seymour, *Divided Loyalties*, 127–29; Augustus, *Loudon County*, 83–84; G. Moxley Sorrel, *At the Right Hand of Longstreet: Recollections of a Staff Officer* (New York, 1905), 212–13; Charles A. Earp, "A Confederate Aide-de-Camp's Letters from the Chattanooga Area, 1863," *Journal of East Tennessee History* 67 (1995): 116–19.
25. Boeger, "General Burnside's Knoxville Packing Project," 76–81.
26. Hesseltine, *Dr. J. G. M. Ramsey*, 149–51; Fink, "East Tennessee Campaign," 97–102; Seymour, *Divided Loyalties*, 131, 133, 137–38.
27. Gallagher, *Fighting for the Confederacy*, 323–24; McKenzie, *Lincolnites and Rebels*, 165–66.
28. McKenzie, *Lincolnites and Rebels*, 166–67; Ronald H. Moseley, ed., *The Stilwell Letters: A Georgian in Longstreet's Corps, Army of Northern Virginia* (Macon, Ga., 2002), 233; Mendoza, *Confederate Struggle for Command*, 127–28.
29. Gallagher, *Fighting for the Confederacy*, 324–27.
30. Mendoza, *Confederate Struggle for Command*, 127–28.
31. McKnight, *Blue Bonnets*, 114–15; Sauers, *Civil War Journal*, 153; Seymour, *Divided Loyalties*, 142; John Chapman to father and brother, Dec. 9, 1863, Federal Collection, TSLA; postwar comments by Brevet Brigadier General William Franklin Draper, n.d., author's files; Duane E. Shaffer, "Storming Fort Sanders," *Military History* 22 (Nov. 2005): 47–52; Sorrel, *Right Hand of Longstreet*, 212–13; Funk, "East Tennessee Campaign, 106–8.
32. Longstreet to McLaws, Nov. 28, 1863, Lafayette McLaws Papers, SHC, with a version in *ORA,* ser. 1, vol. 31, pt. 1:494, all cited in Mendoza, *Confederate Struggle for Command*, 132–33; McKenzie, *Lincolnites and Rebels*, 167–70.
33. Coward, *South Carolinians*, 101, quoted in Mendoza, *Confederate Struggle for Command*, 134; McKenzie, *Lincolnites and Rebels*, 167–69; Draper comments, author's files.
34. McKnight, *Blue Bonnets*, 115–21; Gavin, *Infantryman Pettit*, 129–30; Sauers, *Civil War Journal*, 155; Gallagher, *Fighting for the Confederacy*, 329; Sorrel, *Right Hand of Longstreet*, 214–15; Mendoza, *Confederate Struggle for Command*, 134–35.

35. Watson, *From Ashby to Andersonville,* 156–59; Baldwin, *Struck Eagle,* 249–51; McKnight, *Blue Bonnets,* 115–16 Sauers, *Civil War Journal,* 155; Sorrel, *Right Hand of Longstreet,* 114.

36. Fink, "East Tennessee Campaign," 105–10; Seymour, *Divided Loyalties,* 173; Mendoza, *Confederate Struggle for Command,* 135–37; William Smith to H. M. Cist, Nov. 1, 1888; "A Marylander in Tennessee," in *Maryland in the Civil War: A House Divided,* ed. Robert I. Cottom Jr. and Mary Ellen Hayward (Baltimore, 1994), 97–98; Joseph R. Reinhart, ed. and trans., *Two Germans in the Civil War: The Diary of John Daeuble and the Letters of Gottfried Rentschler, Sixth Kentucky Volunteer Infantry* (Knoxville, Tenn., 2004), 27; McKenzie, *Lincolnites and Rebels,* 171.

37. Seymour, *Divided Loyalties,* 173–75; Sauers, *Civil War Journal,* 155–59; Gavin, *Infantryman Pettit,* 131.

38. McKenzie, *Lincolnites and Rebels,* 172.

39. Sauers, *Civil War Journal,* 158–59; Seymour, *Divided Loyalties,* 174.

40. *ORA,* ser. 1, vol. 31, pt. 3:758–61, 767–68; Mendoza, *Confederate Struggle for Command,* 137–38.

41. *ORA,* ser. 1, vol. 31, pt. 3:769–70.

42. John W. Rowell, *Yankee Artilleryman: Through the Civil War with Eli Lilly's Indiana Battery* (Knoxville, Tenn., 1975), 147–52; John W. Rowell, *Yankee Cavalrymen: Through the Civil War with the Ninth Pennsylvania Cavalry* (Knoxville, Tenn., 1971), 157–59; Reinhart, *Two Germans in the Civil War,* 19–25, 29–30; Fink, "East Tennessee Campaign," 103–13.

43. Gallagher, *Fighting for the Confederacy,* 330–31; Moseley, *Stilwell Letters,* 235.

44. *ORA,* ser. 1, vol. 31, pt. 3:387; Fink, "East Tennessee Campaign," 112–14; McKenzie, *Lincolnites and Rebels,* 173–75.

45. *ORA,* ser. 1, vol. 31, pt. 3:391–93, 401, 819–20, 837; Mendoza, *Confederate Struggle for Command,* 141–42.

46. Smith, *Campaign to Nowhere,* chap. 3; Watson B. Smith to Father, Dec. 20, 1863, UTLK; Mendoza, *Confederate Struggle for Command,* 138–47; George F. Montgomery Jr., ed., *Georgia Sharpshooter: The Civil War Diary and Letters of William Rhadamanthus Montgomery, 1839–1901* (Macon, Ga., 1997), 11.

47. *ORA,* ser. 1, vol. 31, pt. 3:817–18.

48. *ORA,* ser. 1, 31, pt. 3:812–16, 835–38, 842–44, 873; Mendoza, *Confederate Struggle for Command,* 178–82.

49. Fink, "East Tennessee Campaign," 116; Castel, *Winning and Losing in the Civil War,* 145–46; Piston, *Lee's Tarnished Lieutenant,* 76–84; Mendoza, *Confederate Struggle for Command,* 150–70.

50. *ORA,* ser. 1, vol. 31, pt. 3:871–72.

51. Inman, *Myra Inman,* 231; *ORA,* ser. 1, vol. 39, pt. 3:382.

52. *ORA*, ser. 1, vol. 31, pt. 3:379–80, 381–83, 394, 396, 402, 408–9, 410, 425–27, 533–36.

53. Reinhart, *Two Germans in the Civil War,* 31–61, inter alia.

54. *ORA*, ser. 1, vol. 31, pt. 3:429–30, 433.

55. *ORA*, ser. 1, vol. 31, pt. 3:441–42, 447–49; Lorle Porter, *A People Set Apart: Scotch-Irish in Eastern Ohio: From the Forks of the Yough to the Killing Fields of Georgia* (Zanesville, Ohio, 1998), 559–60.

56. *ORA*, ser. 1, vol. 31, pt. 3:457–58, 460–61, 463–64, 472, 473, 476, 480–83, 488, 502–3, 506–8, 519, 537–39, and pt. 1:625–41, 646–61; Smith, *Campaign to Nowhere,* 35–36.

57. *ORA*, ser. 1, vol. 31, pt. 3:507–8.

58. Gavin, *Infantryman Pettit,* 132–33, 179–84.

59. Moseley, *Stilwell Letters,* 237.

60. John N. Fain, ed., *Sanctified Trial: The Diary of Eliza Rhea Anderson Fain, a Confederate Woman in East Tennessee* (Knoxville, Tenn., 2004), 136–45; Wert, *General James Longstreet,* 367–368; West, *Texan in Search of a Fight,* 135, 136–37; Mendoza, *Confederate Struggle for Command,* 174–78.

61. Smith, *Campaign to Nowhere,* 176–77; Rowell, *Yankee Artillerymen,* chaps. 9 and 10; Rowell, *Yankee Cavalrymen,* chap. 17; Lynda Lasswell Crist et al., eds., *The Papers of Jefferson Davis* (Baton Rouge, La., 1999), 10:290–94; *ORA*, ser. 1, vol. 32, pt. 2:541–42, 566–67, 653, 760–61, 789–90, 791–92, 809–10, and pt. 3:582–83, 586–87, 590–91, 613–15, 618, 627–28, 636–42, 649, 653–54, 680, 738, 756, and vol. 33:1285, 1286–87.

62. Smith, *Campaign to Nowhere,* 95–96, 187–92; Baldwin, *Struck Eagle,* 260–61; Mendoza, *Confederate Struggle for Command,* 197–98.

63. Lewellyn A. Shaver, *A History of the Sixtieth Alabama Regiment* (Montgomery, Ala., 1867), 3, 43; Mendoza, *Confederate Struggle for Command,* 184–90.

64. R. G. Smith, "Civil War Record," Aug. 1936, Records of Middle Tennessee Civil War Veterans, vol. 3, typescript copy, Historical Records Survey, Nashville, 1939, UTLK.

65. Mendoza, *Confederate Struggle for Command,* 184–96; M. B. Houghton and W. R. Houghton, *Two Boys in the Civil War and After* (Montgomery, Ala., 1912), 68, 69.

66. Henry Cherry to Amos Gould, Mar. 27, 1865, UTLK.

67. Edward Summer to Arthur Johnson, Jan. 11, 1864, author's files; Richard Lewis, *Camp Life of a Confederate Boy, of Bratton's Brigade, Longstreet's Corps, C.S.A.* (Charleston, S.C., 1883), 75–80, 85–86.

68. Fain, *Sanctified Trial,* 135–36; J. B. Polley, *A Soldier's Letters to Charming Nellie* (New York, 1908), 182; Inman, *Myra Inman,* 239–56; Crist et al., *Papers of Jefferson Davis,* 10:338; James B. Jones, "The Struggle

for Public Health in Civil War Tennessee Cities," *West Tennessee Historical Society Papers* (2008): 64–65.

69. James Whitney to sister, Jan. 4, 1864, and Thomas Berry to wife, Mar. 17, Apr. 2, 1864, all in author's files.

70. *ORA,* ser. 1, vol. 31, pt. 3:25; Smith, *Campaign to Nowhere,* 193; James F. Davidson, "Michigan and the Defense of Knoxville, 1863," *East Tennessee Historical Society's Publications* 35 (1963): 47–48; Crist et al., *Papers of Jefferson Davis,* 10:356.

3. The Situation at Midwar

1. Nimrod Porter diary, Jan. 1864 entry, SHC/UNC.

2. Flavel C. Barber, *Holding The Line: The Third Tennessee Infantry, 1861–1864,* ed. Robert H. Ferrell (Kent, 1994), 148, 150, 151, 168; Daniel Harris Reynolds Journal, Dec. 31, 1864, Reynolds Papers, University of Arkansas Library Archives, Fayetteville, quoted in James Willis, *Arkansas Confederates in the Western Theater* (Dayton, Ohio, 1998), 461–62.

3. Ann K. Blomquist and Robert A. Taylor, eds., *This Cruel War: The Civil War Letters of Grant and Malinda Taylor, 1862–1865* (Macon, Ga., 2000), 214.

4. David F. McGowan to Sister Ellen, Dec. 15, 23, 1863, Jan. 3, 1864; McGowan to sister, Jan. 15, 1864, McGowan to Sister Fannie, Jan. 19, 1864, all author's files.

5. *ORA,* ser. 1, vol. 32, pt. 2:85–86, and pt. 3:27–28, 30, 32, 43, 88–89, 96, 101; John Y. Simon, ed., *The Papers of Ulysses S. Grant,* 31 vols. (Carbondale, Ill., 1967–1982), 10:3–17, 510–11.

6. *ORA,* ser. 1, vol. 32, pt. 2:282–83.

7. Simon, *Papers of Ulysses S. Grant,* 10:17–19; *ORA,* ser. 1, vol. 32, pt. 2:122–23, 126–27, 138, 142–43, 149–50, and ser. 3, vol. 4:41, 42.

8. Simon, *Papers of Ulysses S. Grant,* 10:26–29, 30–33, 54–55.

9. Ibid., 10:24–35, 512–13.

10. Ibid., 10:36–77, 514–15, 518–23; *ORA,* ser. 1, vol. 31, pt. 1:620–21, and pt. 3:620–21, 646, 694, 789–90; *ORA,* vol. 32, pt. 1:347, pt. 2:142, 193–94, 201–2, 512–13, 529, 546–47, 609, 614, 617, 648, 650, 673, 796, 738, 753.

11. Blomquist and Taylor, *This Cruel War,* 207–8; Gary Ray Goodson, *The Georgia Confederate 7000,* pt. 2, *Letters and Diaries* (Shawnee, Okla., 1997), 61, 62; Mark A. Weitz, *A Higher Duty: Desertion among Georgia Troops during the Civil War* (Lincoln, Neb., 2000), 65–79, 81, 91. On strength figures, see *ORA,* ser. 1, vol. 31, pt. 3:850, 870–71, 883, and vol. 32, pt. 2:282–83; and Crist et al., *Papers of Jefferson Davis,* 10:144–47.

12. Nathaniel C. Hughes, ed., *Liddell's Record: St. John Richardson Liddell, Brigadier General, CSA, Staff Officer and Brigade Commander Army*

of Tennessee (Dayton, Ohio, 1985), 164; Stanley F. Horn, *The Army of Tennessee* (Indianapolis, 1941), 305–11; Thomas L. Connelly, *Autumn of Glory: The Army of Tennessee, 1862–1865* (Baton Rouge, La., 1971), 277–89; Judith Hallock, *Braxton Bragg and Confederate Defeat* (Tuscaloosa, Ala., 1991), vol. 3, chap. 8.

13. The tangled story of Confederate assessments of the situation, discussion of plans and lost time can be followed in *ORA*, ser. 1, vol. 30, pt. 4:762; 31, pt. 3, 764, 795, 803, 809, 839, 842, 850, 860, 890; vol. 32, pt. 2:514, 541, 637–42, pt. 3:502, 627, 648, 654–57, 667, 679, 683–707, 736, 744, 753, 755, 772–74, 788, 800, 817, 818; and vol. 52, pt. 2:573–74, 575, 581, 644, 664; and Hughes, *Liddell's Record*, 164–69.

14. For additional perspective, see Albert Castel, *Decision in the West: The Atlanta Campaign of 1864* (Lawrence, Kans., 1992), chaps. 1–4; McMurry, *Atlanta 1864*, chap. 2; James Lee McDonough and James Pickett Jones, *War So Terrible: Sherman and Atlanta* (New York, 1997), 68–72; and Stephen Davis, *Atlanta Will Fall: Sherman, Johnston and the Yankee Heavy Battalions* (Wilmington, Del.: Scholarly Resources, 2001), 26–34. See also Crist et al., *Papers of Jefferson Davis*, 10:145, 149–50, 174–75, 215–16; and *ORA*, ser. 1, vol. 32, pt. 2:667, and vol. 52, pt. 2:634–35, 637–41.

15. Connelly, *Autumn of Glory*, 301–11; Craig L. Symonds, *Joseph E. Johnston: A Civil War Biography* (New York, 1992), chap. 17; Crist et al., *Papers of Jefferson Davis*, 10:241, 244.

16. Connelly, *Autumn of Glory*, 281; Horn, *Army of Tennessee*, 321; Crist et al., *Papers of Jefferson Davis*, 10:349.

17. Barber, *Holding the Line*, 153. On Cleburne and emancipation, see Bruce Levine, *Confederate Emancipation: Southern Plans to Free and Arm Slaves during the Civil War* (New York, 2006), esp. chap. 1; Muriel Phillips Joslyn, ed., *A Meteor Shining Brightly: Essays on Maj. Gen. Patrick R. Cleburne* (Milledgeville, Ga., 1998), appendix; and Barbara C. Ruby, "General Patrick Cleburne's Proposal to Arm Southern Slaves," *Arkansas Historical Quarterly* 20 (Fall 1971): 193–212.

18. Jill K. Garrett, transcriber, *Confederate Diary of Robert D. Smith* (Columbia, Tenn., 1997), 118–19; Levine, *Confederate Emancipation*, chaps. 1–4.

19. William B. Styple, ed., *Writing and Fighting the Confederate War: The Letters of Peter Wellington Alexander, Confederate War Correspondent* (Kearny, N.J., 2002), 206; Norman D. Brown, ed., *One of Cleburne's Command: The Civil War Reminiscences and Diary of Capt. Samuel T. Foster, Granbury's Texas Brigade, CSA* (Austin, Tex., 1980), 69; Blomquist and Taylor, *This Cruel Civil War*, 210; Barber, *Holding the Line*, 154–58; Andrew Haughton, *Training, Tactics and Leadership in the Confederate Army of Tennessee: Seeds of Failure* (London, 2000), chap. 10; Glenna R. Schroeder-Lein, *Confederate Hospitals on the Move:*

Samuel H. Stout and the Army of Tennessee (Columbia, S.C., 1994), 130–35; Nathan Cheairs Hughes Jr., *The Pride of the Confederate Artillery in the Army of Tennessee* (Baton Rouge, La., 1997), chap. 11; Kenneth Radley, *Rebel Watchdog: The Confederate States Army Provost Guard* (Baton Rouge, La., 1989), 137.

20. Goodson, *Georgia Confederate 7,000*, 65–66; Russell K. Brown, "*Our Connection with Savannah*": History of the First Battalion Georgia Sharp-shooters, 1862–1865 (Macon, Ga., 2004), chap. 4; Bromfield L. Ridley, *Battles and Sketches of the Army of Tennessee* (Mexico, Mo., 1906), 289–94; Ratchford, *Memoirs of a Confederate Staff Officer*, 50; Connelly, *Autumn of Glory*, 318–21; *ORA*, ser. 1, vol. 52, pt. 3:586–92; Symonds, *Joseph E. Johnston*, 254–55; Jeffrey N. Lash, *Destroyer of the Iron Horse: General Joseph E. Johnston and Confederate Rail Transport, 1861–1865* (Kent, 1991), chap. 4; Sumner A. Cunningham, *Reminiscences of the Forty-First Tennessee: The Civil War in the West*, ed. John A. Simpson (Shippensburg, Pa., 2001), 66–72; James M. McCaffrey, *This Band of Heroes: Granbury's Texas Brigade, C.S.A.* (College Station, Tex., 1996), 99.

21. Fowler, *Mountaineers in Gray*, 129–32; John A. Simpson, *S. A. Cunningham and the Confederate Heritage* (Athens, Ga., 1994), 34–35.

22. Sam Watkins, *Co. "Aytch": Maury Grays, First Tennessee Regiment; or, A Side Show of the Big Show*, ed. M. Thomas Inge (New York, 1999), 113–16; Ridley, *Battles and Sketches*, 282–88; Larry J. Daniel, *Soldiering in the Army of Tennessee: A Portrait of Life in a Confederate Army* (Chapel Hill, N.C., 1991), 112–13, 119–23; Garrett, *Confederate Diary of Robert D. Smith*, 104–14, 116, 119, 123; Barber, *Holding the Line*, 155–71, inter alia; James Van Eldik, *From the Flame of Battle to the Fiery Cross: The Third Tennessee Infantry with Complete Roster* (Los Cruces, N.M., 2001), chap. 16; Womack, *Call Forth the Mighty Men*, 363–64; William C. Davis, *The Orphan Brigade: The Kentucky Confederates Who Couldn't Go Home* (Garden City, N.Y., 1980), 213–16; Radley, *Rebel Watchdog*, 227, 228, 238; Nathaniel Cheairs Hughes Jr., ed., *The Civil War Memoir of Philip Daingerfield Stephenson, D.D.* (Conway, Ark., 1995), 153–62.

23. James R. Fleming, *Band of Brothers: Company C, Ninth Tennessee Infantry* (Shippensburg, Pa., 1996), 60–61; Barber, *Holding the Line*, 159, 163, 164–65, 166–67, 170–71, 172, 177; Mark K. Christ, ed., *Getting Used to Being Shot At: The Spence Family Civil War Letters* (Fayetteville, Ark., 2002), 75–77, 91–93.

24. Thomas B. Wilson, "Reminiscences," 75, SHC/UNC; Hughes, *Philip Daingerfield Stephenson*, chaps. 12 and 13, esp. p. 152.

25. Stephen Z. Starr, *Jennison's Jayhawkers: A Civil War Cavalry Regiment and Its Commander* (Baton Rouge, La., 1973), 279–82; Wilson, *Chattanooga's Story*, 119; James A. Hoobler, *Cities Under the Gun: Images of Occupied Nashville and Chattanooga* (Nashville, 1986), 129; Kirk C.

Jenkins, *The Battle Rages Higher: The Union's Fifteenth Kentucky Infantry* (Lexington, Ky., 2003), 204, 205.

26. Paul A. Angle, ed., *Three Years in the Army of the Cumberland: The Letters and Diary of Major James A. Connolly* (Bloomington, Ind., 1959), 163, 168; Julie A. Doyle, John Davis Smith, and Richard M. McMurry, eds., *This Wilderness of War: The Civil War Letters of George W. Squier, Hoosier Volunteer* (Knoxville, Tenn., 1998), 75–76; Donald Odell Virdin, ed. and comp., *The Civil War Correspondence of Judge Thomas Goldsborough Odell* (Bowie, Md., 1992), 104–23; Jack K. Overmyer, *A Stupendous Effort: The Eighty-Seventh Indiana in the War of the Rebellion* (Bloomington, Ind., 1997), 132–39; J. Merle Davis, *Davis: Soldier, Missionary: A Biography of Rev. Jerome D. Davis, D. D., Lieutenant-Colonel of Volunteers and for Thirty-Nine Years a Missionary of the American Board of Commissioners for Foreign Missions in Japan* (Boston, 1916), 64, 65.

27. Jennifer Cain Bohrnstedt, ed., *Soldiering with Sherman: Civil War Letters of George F. Cram* (DeKalb, 2000), 65; Charles E. Willett, ed., *A Union Soldier Returns South: The Civil War Letters and Diary of Alfred C. Willett, One Hundred and Thirteenth Ohio Volunteer Infantry* (Johnson City, Tenn., 1994), 39; Porter, *People Set Apart*, 558–74.

28. Mark W. Johnson, *That Body of Brave Men: The U.S. Regular Infantry and the Civil War in the West* (New York, 2003), chap. 9; Castel, *Decision in the West*, 10–12; Constantin Grebner, *"We Were the Ninth": A History of the Ninth Regiment Ohio Volunteer Infantry, April 17, 1861 to June 7, 1864* (Kent, Ohio, 1987), 169–79; Howard Hopkins to Abbue Watson Clyde, Jan. 17, 1864, UTLK; Bruce J. Dinges and Shirley A. Leckie, eds., *A Just and Righteous Cause: Benjamin H. Grierson's Civil War Memoir* (Carbondale, Ill., 2008), 225–27.

29. Josiah Conzette memoirs, typescript, 68, 71, State Historical Society of Iowa, Iowa City; Mark Grimsley and Todd D. Miller, eds., *The Union Must Stand: The Civil War Diary of John Quincy Adams Campbell, Fifth Iowa Volunteer Infantry* (Knoxville, Tenn., 2000), 152–59.

30. John Beatty, *Memoirs of a Volunteer, 1861–1863,* ed. Harvey S. Ford (New York, 1946), 264–72; James M. McPherson, *Battle Cry of Freedom: The Civil War Era* (New York, 1988), 730–39; James Jones to Father and Mother, Jan. 25, Feb. 28, Mar. 24, and Apr. 10, 1864, Indiana Historical Society, Indianapolis.

31. Milo M. Quaife, ed., *From the Cannon's Mouth: The Civil War Letters of General Alpheus Williams* (Lincoln, Neb., 2005), 284–95, esp. p. 288; David F. McGown to sister, Dec. 15, 23, 1863, Jan. 15, 19, 1864, all in author's collection; Porter, *People Set Apart*, 560–63, 568–69; Byron R. Abernathy, ed., *Private Elisha Stockwell, Jr. Sees the Civil War* (Norman, Okla., 1958), 67n8, 69–73; Glenn W. Sunderland, *Five Days to Glory* (South Brunswick, N.J., 1970), 115–34; Garland A. Haas, *To the Mountain*

of Fire and Beyond: The Fifty-Third Indiana Regiment from Corinth to Glory (Carmel, Ind., 1997), 114, 120–21; Leland W. Thornton, *When Gallantry was Commonplace: The History of the Michigan Eleventh Volunteer Infantry, 1861–1864* (New York, 1991), chap. 18.

32. McGowan to sister, Jan. 19, 1864, author's files; Mary E. Kellogg, comp., *Army Life of an Illinois Soldier, Including a Day-by-Day Record of Sherman's March to the Sea: Letters and Diary of Charles W. Wills* (Carbondale, Ill., 1996), 203–6, esp. p. 225; Grimsley and Miller, *Union Must Stand*, 142–56.

33. McGowan to sister, Dec. 3, 1863, author's files; William Walton, ed., *The Letters of Edwin Weller from Antietam to Atlanta* (Garden City, N.Y., 1980), 64–80; Philip J. Reyburn and Terry L. Wilson, eds., *"Jottings from Dixie": The Civil War Dispatches of Sergeant Major Stephen F. Fleharty, U.S.A.* (Baton Rouge, La., 1999), 155–57.

34. Joe R. Bailey, "Union Lifeline in Tennessee: A Military History of the Nashville and Northwestern Railroad," *Tennessee Historical Quarterly* 67 (Summer 2008): 106–23; Mark M. Krug, ed., *Mrs. Hill's Journal: Civil War Reminiscences* (Chicago, 1980), 206–301.

35. War Department, *Reports of Bvt. Brig. Gen. D. C. McCallum, Director and General Manager of the Military Railroads of the United States and the Provost Marshal General in Two Parts*, pt. 1 (Washington, D.C., 1866), 8–9.

36. Ibid., 10–13.

37. Ibid., 19.

38. Ibid., 20–21.

39. Robert G. Athearn, ed., *Soldier in the West: The Civil War Letters of Alfred Lacey Hough* (Philadelphia, 1957), 186; Bohrnstedt, *Soldiering with Sherman*, chap. 6, esp. pp. 65–66, 73, 79; William and John Chapman to father, Mar. 20, Apr. 1, May 10, 1864, Account 918, F-22-6, Federal Collection, TSLA; William F. King to wife, Mar. 28, 1864, Indiana Historical Society, Indianapolis; Walter T. Durham, *Reluctant Partners: Nashville and the Union, July 1, 1863 to June 30, 1865* (Knoxville, Tenn., 2008), 8–10, 24–28, 80–85; Mark Zimmerman, *Guide to Civil War Nashville* (Nashville, 2004), 10–11, 14, 15, 29, 49; Hoobler, *Cities Under the Gun*, 15–19, 126–29; Jeannine Cole, "'Upon the Stage of Disorder': Legalized Prostitution in Memphis and Nashville, 1863–1865," *Tennessee Historical Quarterly* 68 (Spring 2009): 40–65.

40. Zimmerman, *Guide to Civil War Nashville*, 34–37, 71, 72; Hoobler, *Cities Under the Gun*, 25, 34, 35, 42–43, 53, 56–57, 111, 112; Baker, "Fort Negley," 7; Lenard E. Brown, "Fortress Rosecrans: A History, 1865–1990," *Tennessee Historical Quarterly* 50 (Fall 1991): 135–41; Frank L. Byrne, ed., *The View from Headquarters: Civil War Letters of Harvey Reid* (Madison, Wis., 1965),112–20.

41. Connolly, *Three Years in the Army of the Cumberland*, 178; Beatty, *Memoirs of a Volunteer*, 266–67.

42. Albert Castel, *Tom Taylor's Civil War* (Lawrence, Kans., 2000), 110; James C. Kelly, "A Union Soldier's Sketchbook of the Chattanooga Region," *Tennessee Historical Quarterly* 51 (Fall 1997): 157–60; Hoobler, *Cities Under the Gun,* 12–13.

43. Haas, *To the Mountain of Fire and Beyond,* 118; Ebenezer H. McCall to Father, May 4, 1864, Fall 1998 catalog, George C. Esker Antiques, La Place, La.; letters from the Sixth Missouri Infantry, Correspondence of Private Thomas Coleman, and Cyrus Gowdy to cousin, Apr. 18, 1864, all Catalog 49, Spring 1997, Theme Prints, Ltd., Bayview, N.Y.; Styple, *Writing and Fighting the Confederate War,* 207–8; Willett, *Union Soldier Returns South,* 32–51; Jedediah Mannis and Gallen R. Wilson, eds., *Bound to Be a Soldier: The Letters of Private James T. Miller, One Hundred and Eleventh Pennsylvania Infantry, 1861–1864* (Knoxville, Tenn., 2001), 129–37; William Alan Blair, ed., *A Politician Goes to War: The Civil War Letters of John White Geary* (University Park, Pa., 1995), 151–71; Kellogg, *Army Life of an Illinois Soldier,* 217, 223, 225; Porter, *People Set Apart,* 540.

44. *ORA,* ser. 1, vol. 32, pt. 2:267–70.

45. Lewis Collins and Richard H. Collins, *Collins' Historical Sketches of Kentucky,* 2 vols. (Covington, Ky., 1874), revised as *The History of Kentucky by the Late Lewis Collins, Revised . . . and brought down to 1874 by his son Richard H. Collins* [*History and Annals of Kentucky*], 2 vols. (Covington, Ky., 1882), 1:129–30.

46. Ibid., 1:129–32.

47. Ibid., 1:130.

48. Bryan S. Bush, *Lincoln and the Speeds: The Untold Story of a Devoted and Enduring Friendship* (Morley, Mo., 2008), 116–21; *ORA,* ser. 1, vol. 32, pt. 2:10, 37, 62, 85–86, 160, 195, 361, 394, 401, 410, 486, 497, and pt. 3:41–43.

49. *ORA,* ser. 5, vol. 3:188–89; Collins and Collins, *History and Annals of Kentucky,* 1:132.

50. N. C. McLean to wife, Apr. 11, 12, 15, 1864, author's files.

51. Graf and Haskins, *Papers of Andrew Johnson,* 6:548–51, 564–65, 574–90, 594–96.

52. Ibid.. 6:568–72, 593, 596, 600–602, 612–14, 618, 625, 628, 638–39; McKenzie, *Lincolnites and Rebels,* 189–93.

53. Graf and Haskins, *Papers of Andrew Johnson,* 6:xxxix–xli, l–li, 548–51, 553, 594–95, 638–39, 658–59.

54. Collins and Collins, *History and Annals of Kentucky,* 1:130.

55. Ibid., 1:132.

56. Graf and Haskins, *Papers of Andrew Johnson,* 6:533–43, 545–46, 553; James Alex Baggett, *Homegrown Yankees: Tennessee's Union Cavalry in the Civil War* (Baton Rouge, La., 2009), 2, 10–12, 41–56, and conclusion.

57. Graf and Haskins, *Papers of Andrew Johnson,* 6:573, 591, 598–600, 626, 633.

58. Ibid., 6:643–47, 648–50, 651–52.
59. Sarah Kennedy to husband, Jan. 18, Feb. 11, Mar. 7, 18, 19, 29, May 1, 8, 13, June 8, 9, 1864, all in Kennedy Papers, Confederate Collection IV—B-2, Box 10, Folder 8; Nick Barker diary, entries for Feb. 5, Mar. 2, June 26, 1864, both in Manuscript Collections, TSLA.
60. Nanny Garland to Major John Minor, May 19, 1864, Sailor's Rest Papers; Sarah Bailey Kennedy to husband, May 19, 1864, Kennedy Papers, both in Manuscript Collections, TSLA.
61. Alice Williamson diary (transcription), 1–19, Special Collections, Duke University Library, Durham, N.C. (hereafter referred to as DUL); Nimrod Porter diary, Jan. 1864 entry, SHC/UNC; McKenzie, *Lincolnites and Rebels,* chap. 7.
62. Smith and Cooper, *Union Woman in Civil War Kentucky,* 181–82; Richard Troutman, ed., *The Heavens Are Weeping: The Diaries of George R. Browder, 1852–1886* (Grand Rapids, Mich., 1987), 173.
63. Smith and Cooper, *Union Woman in Civil War Kentucky,* 186–87, 194–95.
64. Ibid., 197–98.
65. Mary Clay Berry, *Voices from the Century Before: The Odyssey of a Nineteenth Century Kentucky Family* (New York, 1997), 345–79.
66. Brooks D. Simpson and Jean V. Berlin, eds., *Sherman's Civil War: Selected Correspondence of William T. Sherman, 1860–1865* (Chapel Hill, N.C., 1999), 591.
67. *Chattanooga Gazette,* Mar. 17, 1864.

4. Hard War Turns Harder

1. Julia Dent Grant, *The Personal Memoirs of Julia Dent Grant (Mrs. Ulysses S. Grant),* ed. John Y. Simon (New York, 1975), 127; Durham, *Reluctant Partners,* 41–42; McMurry, *Atlanta 1864,* chap. 2.
2. Simon, *Papers of Ulysses S. Grant,* 10:96–97, 218–19; McDonough and Jones, *War So Terrible,* 14–20.
3. U.S. War Department, *Atlas to Accompany the Official Records of the Union and Confederate Armies* (Washington, D.C., 1891–95), Plate CXXXV-A; *ORA,* ser. 1, vol. 32, pt. 3:161–62, 279–80, 435–36, and notes, as well as vol. 33:721.
4. George C. Thorpe, *Pure Logistics: The Science of War Preparation* (Washington, D.C., 1986), 21–26.
5. *ORA,* ser. 1, vol. 25:474.
6. Frank J. Welcher, *The Union Army, 1861–1865: Organization and Operations,* vol. 2, *The Western Theater* (Bloomington, Ind., 1993), 3, 20–28, 128, 206–21; *ORA,* ser. 1, vol. 32, pt. 3:708.
7. Hoobler, *Cities Under the Gun;* McCallie, quoted in Wilson, *Chattanooga's Story,* 114.

423

8. *ORA,* ser. 1, vol. 32, pt. 2:267–69; Krug, *Mrs. Hill's Journal,* 279–80; McCallum, *Reports of . . . and the Provost Marshal General,* pt. 1, 23; Martis, *Historical Atlas,* maps 19 and 20 and Appendix II.

9. *ORA,* ser. 1, vol. 32, pt. 2:90–95, 502–3, 645, and pt. 3:190–91, 473; Graf and Haskins, *Papers of Andrew Johnson,* 6:630–31.

10. *ORA,* ser. 1, vol. 32, pt. 2:90–95, 502–3, 645, and pt. 3:190–91, 473; Graf and Haskins, *Papers of Andrew Johnson,* 6:630–31.

11. James A. Ramage, *Rebel Raider: The Life of General John Hunt Morgan* (Lexington, Ky., 1986), chap. 17; John P. Dyer, *From Shiloh to San Juan: The Life of "Fightin' Joe" Wheeler* (Baton Rouge, La., 1941), chap. 7; *ORA,* ser. 1, vol. 32, pt. 3:582, 587, 781.

12. *ORA,* ser. 1, vol. 32, pt. 3:536; Robert Dunnavant Jr., *The Railroad War: N. B. Forrest's 1864 Raid Through Northern Alabama and Middle Tennessee* (Athens, Ala., 1994), 6–7.

13. *ORA,* ser. 1, vol. 32, pt. 2:512–13, 515–16, 524–25, 540, 556, 561, 563, 572, 604, 615, 616.

14. *ORA,* ser. 1, vol. 32, pt. 2:626, and pt. 3:210, 561; Andrew Nelson Lytle, *Bedford Forrest and His Critter Company* (New York, 1931), 270; Baggett, *Homegrown Yankees,* 196.

15. *ORA,* ser. 1, vol. 32, pt. 3:117–19, 609, 616, 617, 622, 663, 664; Loretta and William Galbraith, eds., *A Lost Heroine of the Confederacy: The Diaries and Letters of Belle Edmonson* (Jackson, Miss., 1990), 98–99, 100. This period is retold in Lytle, *Bedford Forrest,* chap. 17; Robert Selph Henry, ed., *As They Saw Forrest: Some Recollections and Comments of Contemporaries* (Jackson, Tenn., 1956), 43–46, 153–55; John A. Wyeth, *That Devil Forrest: Life of General Nathan Bedford Forrest* (New York, 1959), chap. 14; Brian Steel Wills, *A Battle from the Start: The Life of Nathan Bedford Forrest* (New York, 1992), chap. 9; Jack Hurst, *Nathan Bedford Forrest: A Biography* (New York, 1993), sec. 19; Lonnie E. Maness, *An Untutored Genius: The Military Career of General Nathan Bedford Forrest* (Oxford, Miss., 1990), chap. 13; Paul Ashdown and Edward Gaudill, *The Myth of Nathan Bedford Forrest* (Lanham, Md., 2005), chap. 2; and Robert M. Browning Jr., *Forrest: The Confederacy's Relentless Warrior* (Washington, D.C., 2004), chap. 4.

16. *ORA,* ser. 1, vol. 32, pt. 1:67–69; Graf and Haskins, *Papers of Andrew Johnson,* 6:685–86; Baggett, *Homegrown Yankees,* 196–198, also 34–37, 167–68, 173, 178–79.

17. General Order Number 3, Feb. 17, 1864, District of Nashville, in *Clarksville Gazette,* Feb. 27, 1864.

18. *ORA,* ser. 1, vol. 32, pt. 1:485, 491–92, 493–94, 495–96, and pt. 3:85, 86, 91, 92, 94, 95, 99, 103–5, 110–17, 122–28; Patton, *Unionism and Reconstruction in Tennessee,* 43–44.

19. *ORA,* ser. 1, vol. 32, pt. 1:508, and pt. 3:132, 136, 195–97, 561, 565–66.

20. In addition, see T. K. Kionka, *Key Command: Ulysses S. Grant's District of Cairo* (Columbia, Mo., 2006), 207–8.

21. *ORA*, ser. 1, vol. 32, pt. 1:508–9.

22. *ORA*, ser. 1, vol. 32, pt. 3:87, 150.

23. *ORA*, ser. 1, vol. 32, pt. 1:503, 509–10, 540–46, 574–78, 607, 611–12, and pt. 3:131, 163; Wyeth, *That Devil Forrest,* 301–4; Maness, *Untutored Genius,* 217–23; and Lonnie E. Maness, "A Ruse that Worked: The Capture of Union City in 1864," *West Tennessee Historical Society Papers* 30 (1976): 91–103.

24. Maness, "Ruse that Worked," 91–103; Peggy Scott Holley, "The Seventh Tennessee Volunteer Cavalry: West Tennessee Unionists in Andersonville Prison," *West Tennessee Historical Society Papers* 52 (1988): 39–58; John Milton Hubbard, "Private Hubbard's Notes," and William Witherspoon, "Reminiscences of a Scout, Spy and Soldier of Forrest's Cavalry," both in Henry, *As They Saw Forrest,* 154 and 101–8, respectively; Charles L. Lufkin, "West Tennessee Unionists in the Civil War: A Hawkins Family Letter," *Tennessee Historical Quarterly* 46 (Spring 1987): 33, 38–39; Crist et al., *Papers of Jefferson Davis,* 10:346n8; Baggett, *Homegrown Yankees,* 199–208.

25. Hubbard, "Private Hubbard's Notes," 154–55; also Witherspoon, "Reminiscences of a Scout, Spy and Soldier," 108; Galbraith, *Lost Heroine of the Confederacy,* 102.

26. *ORA*, ser. 1, vol. 32, pt. 1:547, 607, and pt. 3:151, 158–69; John E. L. Robertson, *Paducah, 1830–1980: A Sesquicentennial History* (Paducah, Ky., 1980), 59–60; Paul H. Silverstone, *Warships of the Civil War Navies* (Annapolis, Md., 1989), 168, 180.

27. Michael T. Meier, "Lorenzo Thomas and the Recruitment of Blacks in the Mississippi Valley, 1863–1865," in *Black Soldiers in Blue: African American Troops in the Civil War Era,* ed. John David Smith (Chapel Hill, N.C., 2002), chap. 9, esp. p. 263–64; Frederick H. Dyer, comp., *Compendium of the War of the Rebellion* (New York, 1959), 3:1722.

28. *ORA*, ser. 1, vol. 32, pt. 1:547, also 505–7, 510, and pt. 3:153–54, 156, 157; Robertson, *Paducah,* 57–59; Wyeth, *That Devil Forrest,* 304–5; Robert Selph Henry, ed., *"First with the Most" Forrest* (Indianapolis, 1944), 240–41; Lytle, *Bedford Forrest,* 273–74; Thomas Jordan and J. P. Pryor, *The Campaigns of Lieut.-Gen. N. B. Forrest and of Forrest's Cavalry* (New Orleans, 1868), 413–14; Maness, *Untutored Genius,* 224–27; Wills, *Battle from the Start,* 176–77.

29. *ORA*, ser. 1, vol. 32, pt. 1:505, 511, 548; U.S. Navy Department, *Official Records of the Union and Confederate Navies in the War of the Rebellion* (Washington, D.C., 1894–1927), ser. 1, vol. 25:195–202, esp. p. 299 (hereafter referred to as *ORN,* volume number, page number).

30. Edgar Eno, *Civil War Letters* (Hillsboro, Wis., 1998), 104; *ORA*, ser. 1, vol. 32, pt. 1:607; Lytle, *Bedford Forrest*, 274; Crist et al., *Papers of Jefferson Davis*, 10:346n11.

31. *ORA*, ser. 1, vol. 32, pt. 1:549, and pt. 3:155

32. *Peosta* sailor's letter, Mar. 31, 1864, Item 185, Catalog 5, 1997, Brian and Maria Green, Inc., Kernersville, N.C., copy in author's files.

33. *ORA*, ser. 1, vol. 32, pt. 3:733, and vol. 52, pt. 2:649–50; Graf and Haskins, *Papers of Andrew Johnson*, 6:698–99; William W. Chester, "The Civil War Skirmish Near Bolivar, Tennessee: March, 1864," *Journal of the Jackson Purchase Historical Society* 21 (June 1993): 10–15; Chalmers quoted in Lytle, *Bedford Forrest*, 274; Baggett, *Homegrown Yankees*, 198.

34. *ORA*, ser. 1, vol. 32, pt. 3:165, 171, 178, 199–200, 213, 220, 230, 301; Galbraith, *Lost Heroine of the Confederacy*, 103, also 104, 105, 111; Dinges and Leckie, *Just and Righteous Cause*, chap. 10.

35. *ORA*, ser. 1, vol. 52, pt. 2:653, and vol. 32, pt. 1:608–9.

36. *ORA*, ser. 1, vol. 32, pt. 3:138, 140, 144–46, 154–55, 165, 167, 168–71, 174.

37. *ORA*, ser. 1, vol. 32, pt. 3:173, 181, 185–87, 188–95, 196, 202–3, 204–5, 206, 242–43, 244–45.

38. *ORA*, ser. 1, vol. 32, pt. 3:204–10, 244–45, 255–58.

39. *ORA*, ser. 1, vol. 32, pt. 3:244–46, 247–52, 254, 274, 275–90.

40. *ORA*, ser. 1, vol. 32, pt. 3:290–326.

41. *ORA*, ser. 1, vol. 32, pt. 3:325, also 334–35, 340, 345, 346–49.

42. *ORA*, ser. 1, vol. 32, pt. 3:349, 350–51, 355–60, 732, 733–35, 739, 751, 752, 763–66.

43. *ORA*, ser. 1, vol. 32, pt. 3:757–58, 770, 782.

44. *ORA*, ser. 1, vol. 32, pt. 3:770.

45. Forrest quoted in J. Harvey Mathes, *General Forrest* (New York: D. Appleton, 1902), 382; Achilles V. Clark to sister, Apr. 14, 1864, Manuscripts Collections, TSLA; *ORA*, ser. 1, vol. 32, pt. 1:609–12; S. H. Caldwell to wife, Apr. 15, 1864, copy, Works Progress Administration, Civil War Records of West Tennessee, vol. 4, Historical Records Survey, Nashville, 1939, UTLK.

46. John Cimprich, "Fort Pillow During the Civil War," *North & South* 9 (Dec. 2006): 60–69; Edward F. Williams III, *Confederate Victories at Fort Pillow* (Memphis, 1973), 1–18, 20; also Baggett, *Homegrown Yankees*, 196, 211–15.

47. Contemporary documentation on the fight may be followed in *ORA*, ser. 1, vol. 32, pt. 1:554–74, 586–608, 609–23, and pt. 3:336–37, 346–48, 361–62, 364, 366–67, 375–76, 439, 546, 547; *ORN*, ser. 1, vol. 26:214–37; and such reminiscences as Charles W. Anderson, "The True Story of Fort Pillow," *Confederate Veteran* 3 (Sept. 1886): 322–26; also Silverstone, *Warships of the Civil War Navies*, 175.

48. Modern analysis of the battle should be followed in the various biographies of Forrest, plus Richard L. Fuchs, *An Unerring Fire: The Massacre at Fort Pillow* (Rutherford, N.J., 1994); John Gauss, *Black Flag! Black Flag! The Battle at Fort Pillow* (Lanham, Md., 2003); Andrew Ward, *River Run Red: The Fort Pillow Massacre in the American Civil War* (New York, 2005); John Cimprich, *Fort Pillow: A Civil War Massacre and Public Memory* (Baton Rouge, La., 2005); "The Fort Pillow Massacre: Assessing the Evidence," in Smith, *Black Soldiers in Blue: African American Troops in the Civil War Era* (Chapel Hill, N.C., 2002), chap. 5; William R. Brooksher, "Betwixt Wind and Water: A Short Account of Confederate Major General Nathan Bedford Forrest's Attack on Fort Pillow," in *The Price of Freedom: Slavery and the Civil War,* vol. 1, *The Demise of Slavery,* ed. Martin H. Greenberg and Charles G. Waugh (Nashville, 2000), 287–97; Roy Morris Jr., "Fort Pillow: Massacre or Madness?" *America's Civil War,* Nov. 2000, 26–32; Albert Castel, "The Fort Pillow Massacre: A Fresh Examination of the Evidence," *Civil War History* 4 (Mar. 1958): 37–50; Lonnie E. Maness, "The Fort Pillow Massacre: Fact or Fiction," *Tennessee Historical Quarterly* 45 (Winter 1986): 287–316; John Cimprich and Robert C. Mainfort, "Dr. Fitch's Report on the Fort Pillow Massacre," *Tennessee Historical Quarterly* 44 (Spring 1985): 27–39; John Cimprich and Robert C. Mainfort, eds., "Fort Pillow Revisited: New Evidence About an Old Controversy," *Civil War History* 28 (Dec. 1982): 293–306; Charles L. Lufkin, "'Not Heard from Since April 12, 1864': The Thirteenth Tennessee Cavalry, U.S.A.," *Tennessee Historical Quarterly* 45 (Summer 1986): 133–51; Noah Andrew Trudeau, "'Kill the Last Damn One of Them': The Fort Pillow Massacre," in *With My Face to the Enemy: Perspectives on the Civil War,* ed. Robert Crowley (New York, 2001), 382–94; Kenneth Bancroft Moore, "Fort Pillow, Forrest, and the United States Colored Troops in 1864," *Tennessee Historical Quarterly* 54 (Summer 1995): 112–23; also Clark to sister, Apr. 14, 1864, Manuscript Collections, TSLA; and Baggett, *Homegrown Yankees,* chap. 13.

49. Dinges and Leckie, *Just and Righteous Cause,* 232; Thomas M. Boaz, *Libby Prison and Beyond: A Union Staff Officer in the East, 1862–1865* (Shippensburg, Pa., 1997), 134; "Statement as to Major Bradford," n.d., Nutt Papers, SHC/UNC.

50. George S. Burkhardt, "No Quarter! Black Flag Warfare 1863–1865," *North & South,* 10 (May 2007): 15; Paul Ashdown and Edward Caudill, *The Myth of Nathan Bedford Forrest* (Lansdowne, Md., 2005), 33; Randall's poem in Faith Barrett and Cristanne Miller, eds., *"Words for the Hour": A New Anthology of American Civil War Poetry* (Amherst, Mass., 2005), 140–42.

51. Castel, "Fort Pillow Massacre," 50; Brian S. Wills, "Fort Pillow Massacre," in *The Confederacy* (New York, 1993), 223–24; Cimprich, *Fort*

Pillow Massacre, 104–5; Ashdown and Caudill, *Myth of Nathan Bedford Forrest,* 34; Caldwell to wife, Apr. 15, 1864, typescript copy, Historical Records Survey, Nashville, 1939, UTLK.

52. James D. Lockett, "The Lynching Massacre of Black and White Soldiers at Fort Pillow, Tennessee, April 12, 1864," *Western Journal of Black Studies* 22 (Summer 1998): 84–93; Baggett, *Homegrown Yankees,* 327; John Keegan, "Rules of Engagement," letter to the editor, *Economist,* Oct. 23, 1993.

53. *ORA,* ser. 1, vol. 39, pt. 2:60–61, and vol. 32, pt. 3:382, 443, 448, 449, 451, 452; Graf and Haskins, *Papers of Andrew Johnson,* 6:687n4.

54. Lytle, *Bedford Forrest,* 280; ORA, ser. 1, vol. 32, pt. 1:608, 778–79, 780, 786–87.

55. Galbraith, *Lost Heroine of the Confederacy,* 113, 114, 115, 118, 123, 124; Dinges and Leckie, *Just and Righteous Cause,* 232–33.

56. *ORA,* ser. 1, vol. 32, pt. 3:798–801, 809, 811, 817–23, 824–26, 833–34, 836–37, 855–56; Henry, *As They Saw Forrest,* chap. 28.

57. Simon, *Papers of Ulysses S. Grant,* 10:290–91; *ORA,* ser. 1, vol. 32, pt. 3:366, 367, 381–83, 402, 403; Jeffrey N. Lash, *A Politician Turned General: The Civil War Career of Stephen Augustus Hurlbut* (Kent, Ohio, 2003), chap. 4, esp. pp. 142–43; Dinges and Leckie, *Just and Righteous Cause,* 232–35.

58. *ORA,* ser. 1, vol. 32:405–6, 410–11, 415–16, 425–26, 427–28, 430, 453; Calvin A. Campbell to William W. Martindale, Apr. 16, 1864, courtesy Maj. Arthur Edinger, USMC (Ret.), copy in author's files.

59. *ORA,* ser. 1, vol. 32, pt. 3:428, 431, 433, 441.

60. *ORA,* ser. 1, vol. 32, pt. 3:462–63, also 440, 441, 484, 516.

61. *ORA,* ser. 1, vol. 32, pt. 3:517–18; Dinges and Leckie, *Just and Righteous Cause,* 232–36.

62. *ORA,* ser. 1, vol. 32, pt. 3:479, also 428, 442, 464, 479, 481, 482, 483, 519, 529, 536, 537, 541.

63. *ORA,* ser. 1, vol. 32, pt. 1:693–703, esp. p. 697, also pt. 3:481, 482, 483; Galbraith, *Lost Heroine of the Confederacy,* 122, 124; Francis C. Kajencki, "The Man Who Beat the Devil," *Civil War Times* 37 (Oct. 1998): 40–43.

64. *ORA,* ser. 1, vol. 32, pt. 1:695, 697; Dinges and Leckie, *Just and Righteous Cause,* 235–41.

65. *ORA,* ser. 1, vol. 32, pt. 1:629; Simpson and Berlin, *Sherman's Civil War,* 626; Galbraith, *Lost Heroine of the Confederacy,* 126; Crist et al, *Papers of Jefferson Davis,* 10:342, 436–37, 569.

5. The Raiders of Summer and Fall

1. E. B. Long, *The Civil War Day by Day: An Almanac, 1861–1865* (Garden City, N.Y.: Doubleday, 1971), 511–12, 516–18; 563–64; Matt Speizer,

"The Ticket's Other Half: How and Why Andrew Johnson Received the 1864 Vice Presidential Nomination," *Tennessee Historical Quarterly* 65 (Spring 2006): 42–69.

2. Joseph E. Johnston, "Opposing Sherman's Advance to Atlanta," in *Battles and Leaders of the Civil War,* ed. Robert Underwood Johnson and Clarence Clough Buel (New York, 1884), 4:276; *ORA,* ser. 1, vol. 38, pt. 4:753, 755, 770, 772, 777, and vol. 52, pt. 2:678, 679.

3. Crist et al., *Papers of Jefferson Davis,* 10:498–500, 513, 515, 517, 554.

4. Ibid., 10:513, 535–36; Ramage, *Rebel Raider,* 200–212; Robert O. Neff and Edith Elizabeth Pollitz, *The Bride and the Bandit: The Story of Mattie Ready of Murfreesboro, Tennessee, Wartime Bridge of General John Hunt Morgan* (Evansville, Ind., 1998), 260–77.

5. Bush, *Lincoln and the Speeds,* 121–23; Collins and Collins, *History and Annals of Kentucky,* 1:133–35.

6. Collins and Collins, *History and Annals of Kentucky,* 1:134.

7. Ramage, *Rebel Raider,* 215–17; *ORA,* ser. 1, vol. 39, pt. 2:34, 36, 39, 40, 41, 43, 44, 46, 48, 76–77, 174, 203, and pt. 3:14–15, 75, 288, 569–73 (for the official reports of Morgan's campaign, see pt. 1:19–84); N. C. McLean to wife, Apr. 9, 1864, author's files; George Crook to Stephen Burbridge, letter and telegram, both dated May 18, 1864, T. L. Woodward to Governor Bramlette, n.d., W. W. Tice to D. W. Lindsey, Feb. 19, 1864, J. H. Holloway to D. W. Lindsey, Mar. 10, 1864, Stephen E. Jones to Governor Bramlette, Apr. 28, 1864, T. S. Bells to Stephen Burbridge, May 16, 1864, R. V. Grinder to Governor Bramlette, May 20, 1864, Truitt Thomas to Governor Bramlette, June 13, 1864, J. Stuarts to D. W. Lindsey, July 6, 1864, Mason Hedrick to Governor Bramlette, July 13, 1864, James V. McKasson to Governor Bramlette, July 18, 1864, all in Civil War Guerrillas, Correspondence File, Kentucky Adjutant General Records, Kentucky Military Museum, Frankfort.

8. Ramage, *Rebel Raider,* 218–24; Neff and Pollitz, *Bride and the Bandit,* 271–84; William C. Davis and Meredith L. Swentor, eds., *Bluegrass Confederate: The Headquarters Diary of Edward O. Guerrant* (Baton Rouge, La., 1999), chap. 22; and Edward O. Guerrant, ed., "Diary of Edward O. Guerrant Covering the June 1864 Kentucky Raid of General John Hunt Morgan," *Register of the Kentucky Historical Society* 85 (Autumn 1987): 322–58; and George Dallas Mosgrove, *Kentucky Cavaliers in Dixie: Reminiscences of a Confederate Cavalryman* (Louisville, Ky., 1895), chaps. 14–30, esp. pp. 134–38. Some Federal observations appear in Frank F. Mathias, ed., *Incidents and Experiences in the Life of Thomas W. Parsons from 1826 to 1900* (Lexington, Ky., 1975), chap. 11.

9. Ramage, *Rebel Raider,* 218–34; *ORA,* ser. 1, vol. 39, pt. 1:73–84; Collins and Collins, *History and Annals of Kentucky,* 1:134–35.

10. P. Merrell to "Dear unkle an Cousins," June 23, 1864, author's files; Davis and Swentor, *Bluegrass Confederate*, 464; Mosgrove, *Kentucky Cavaliers*, 174.

11. *ORA*, ser. 1, vol. 39, pt. 1:84.

12. Mosgrove, *Kentucky Cavaliers*, 166; *ORA*, ser. 1, vol. 39, pt. 1:84.

13. *ORA*, ser. 1, vol. 39, pt. 3:27, also pt. 1:84; Crist et al., *Papers of Jefferson Davis*, 10:608.

14. Collins and Collins, *History and Annals of Kentucky*, 1:135.

15. Wyeth, *That Devil Forrest*, 352–74; Wills, *Battle from the Start*, 202–17; Browning, *Forrest*, 61–67; Dinges and Leckie, *Just and Righteous Cause*, chap. 11, esp. p. 255.

16. *ORA*, ser. 1, vol. 38, pt. 4:474, and vol. 39, pt. 2:121, 123; William T. Sherman, *Memoirs of General William T. Sherman* (New York, 1875), 2:399; Eric William Sheppard, *Bedford Forrest: The Confederacy's Greatest Cavalryman* (New York, 1930), 195.

17. Forrest's summer operations can be followed in *ORA*, ser. 1, vol. 39, pt. 1:84–231, 247–351, and 370–401, plus the standard Forrest biographies, Jordan and Pryor, *Campaigns of Lieut.-Gen. N. B. Forrest*, chaps. 15–18; Lytle, *Bedford Forrest*, chaps. 17–20; Henry, *"First with the Most" Forrest*, chaps. 17–21; Henry, *As They Saw Forrest*, 112–36, 158–59; Maness, *Untutored Genius*, chap. 9; Wills, *Battle from the Start*, chaps. 10, 11; Hurst, *Nathan Bedford Forrest*, 183–217; Browning, *Forrest*, chap. 5; Dinges and Leckie, *Just and Righteous Cause*, chap. 12.

18. Succinct accounts of the Memphis raid include Jack D. L. Holmes, "Forrest's 1864 Raid on Memphis," *Tennessee Historical Quarterly* 18 (Dec. 1959), 295–321; see also Juan Rayner, "An Eye-Witness Account of Forrest's Raid on Memphis," *West Tennessee Historical Society Papers* 12 (1958): 134–37; Crist et al., *Papers of Jefferson Davis*, 10:625; Dinges and Leckie, *Just and Righteous Cause*, 279–81.

19. Holmes, "Forrest's 1864 Raid," 300–304; Dinges and Leckie, *Just and Righteous Cause*, 277–81.

20. Dinges and Leckie, *Just and Righteous Cause*, 298, 304–8.

21. *ORN*, ser. 1, vol. 26:517–19; also *ORA*, ser. 1, vol. 39, pt. 1:468–84; Dinges and Leckie, *Just and Righteous Cause*, 280.

22. "Mell" to "Mother," Aug. 22, 1864, author's files.

23. *ORA*, ser. 1, vol. 39, pt. 2:296, also 282, 310; Dinges and Leckie, *Just and Righteous Cause*, 280–81.

24. Holmes, "Forrest's 1864 Raid," 310, 318–20, citing William Forse Scott, *The Story of a Cavalry Regiment: The Career of the Fourth Iowa Veteran Volunteers from Kansas to Georgia, 1861–1865* (New York, 1893), 299, for camp humor at Washburn's expense, also 318–20; Hurst, *Nathan Bedford Forrest*, 215; Wills, *Battle from the Start*, 247–49; *ORA*, ser. 1, vol. 39, pt. 2:296.

25. *ORA,* ser. 1, vol. 39, pt. 2:796–796; Dinges and Leckie, *Just and Righteous Cause,* 280–81.

26. See Edward G. Longacre, *A Soldier to the Last: Maj. Gen. Joseph Wheeler in Blue and Gray* (Washington, D.C., 2007), 165–69, quoting John W. Cotton, *"Yours Till Death": Civil War Letters of John W. Cotton",* ed. Lucille Griffith (University, Ala., 1951), 117; on southern politicians and better use of the cavalry, see *ORA,* ser. 1, vol. 52, pt. 2:685–86, 704–7, 736–40; Baggett, *Homegrown Yankees,* chaps. 14 and 15.

27. *ORA,* ser. 1, vol. 38, pt. 3:958; Longacre, *Soldier to the Last,* 71.

28. Dyer, *From Shiloh to San Juan,* 146–54; Young, *Confederate Wizards,* chap. 11.

29. Graf, *Papers of Andrew Johnson,* 7:118–19; *ORA,* ser. 1, vol. 39, pt. 2:262, 268, 269, 272–74, 278–82, 283–86, 290–92, 294, 299–313; Longacre, *Soldier to the Last,* 172–73; Baggett, *Homegrown Yankees,* 260–70.

30. Graf, *Papers of Andrew Johnson,* 7:120, 125; *ORA,* ser. 1, vol. 39, pt. 2:303.

31. *ORA,* ser. 1, vol. 39, pt. 2:406–8, 561.

32. *ORA,* ser. 1, vol. 38, pt. 5:741–45, and vol. 39, pt. 1:485, 488, 496, 501–2, 804, and pt. 2:325–34, 335–36, 338, 341, 346, 348, 355, 359, 360, 365, 371, 378, 380–82, 384, 385, 390, 393, 401, 422, 423, 434, 439, 440, 456, 458, 460, 464, 466–70, 485, 490–92, 494–97, 506, 518, 522, 533, 859; Graf, *Papers of Andrew Johnson,* 7:153–54.

33. *ORA,* ser. 1, vol. 39, pt. 2:829–30, 845–46, 859, 873, and vol. 38, pt. 3:960–61; Longacre, *Soldier to the Last,* 172–75; Baggett, *Homegrown Yankees,* 271; McDonough and Jones, *War So Terrible,* 288.

34. *ORA,* ser. 1, vol. 39, pt. 2:701–33; Ramage, *Rebel Raider,* 226–27.

35. *ORA,* ser. 1, vol. 39, pt. 2:722–23, 727–28, 729–30, 735, 740–42, 746–47; Ramage, *Rebel Raider,* 728; Graf, *Papers of Andrew Johnson,* 7:101, 113–14.

36. Ramage, *Rebel Raider,* 231–38; Neff and Politz, *Bride and the Bandit,* 286–96; ORA, ser. 1, vol. 39, pt. 1:488–92; Davis and Swentor, *Bluegrass Confederate,* chaps. 23 and 24; Mosgrove, *Kentucky Cavaliers,* chaps. 33–35; Gary Robert Matthews, *Basil Wilson Duke, CSA: The Right Man in the Right Place* (Lexington, Ky., 2005), 173–74; *ORA,* ser. 1, vol. 39, pt. 1:484–86, 488–90; Baggett, *Homegrown Yankees,* 327.

37. Davis and Swentor, *Bluegrass Confederate,* 520–21; Mosgrove, *Kentucky Cavaliers,* 178–79.

38. Ramage, *Rebel Raider,* 242–44; Simpson and Berlin, *Sherman's Civil War,* 647; *ORA,* ser. 1, vol. 32, pt. 3:536, and vol. 38, pt. 4:462.

39. Wyeth, *That Devil Forrest,* 451.

40. *ORA,* ser. 1, vol. 39, pt. 2:818–19, 873; Wyeth, *That Devil Forrest,* chap. 18; Wills, *Battle from the Start,* 249–50; Dunnavant, *Railroad War,* 28–32.

41. John Milton Hubbard, "Private Hubbard's Notes," in Henry, *As They Saw Forrest*, 196–97.

42. Dunnavant, *Railroad War*, 32–33.

43. *ORA*, ser. 1, vol. 39, pt. 1:510–30, esp. pp. 523–25; Wills, *Battle from the Start*, 251–51; Henry, *"First with the Most" Forrest*, 354–56; Baggett, *Homegrown Yankees*, chaps. 8 and 17.

44. Operations may be followed in *ORA*, ser. 1, vol. 39, pt. 1:504–49, 585, and pt. 2:428–544 inter alia, and 859, 862, 867, 870, 871, 873–74, 876, 879, and pt. 2:428–550 inter alia, 429, 442, and esp. p. 480; Wills, *Battle from the Start*, 253–57; John Watson Morton, *The Artillery of Nathan Bedford Forrest's Cavalry* (Nashville, 1909), chap. 17; and Dunnavant, *Railroad War*, chaps. 6 and 7.

45. Simpson and Berlin, *Sherman's Civil War*, 726; *ORA*, ser. 1, vol. 39, pt. 1:506–7, and pt. 2:517; Jennifer Cain Bohrnstedt, ed., and Kassandra R. Chaney, comp., *While Father Is Away: The Civil War Letters of William H. Bradbury* (Lexington, Ky., 2003), 191, 193, 194, 195, 197.

46. *ORA*, ser. 1, vol. 39, pt. 2:546–47; Wyeth, *That Devil Forrest*, 360–62; Dunnavant, *Railroad War*, chap. 9.

47. *ORA*, ser. 1, vol. 39, pt. 3:162, also pt. 2:539–40; *ORN*, ser. 1, vol. 26:582–87; Wills, *Battle from the Start*, 257–61; Silverstone, *Warships of the Civil War Navies*, 173, 179.

48. Baggett, *Homegrown Yankees*, 284–85; Bohrnstedt and Chaney, *While Father Is Away*, 196; Maness, *Untutored Genius*, 305; *ORA*, ser. 1, vol. 39, pt. 1:548; Wyeth, *That Devil Forrest*, 451.

49. Dinges and Leckie, *Just and Righteous Cause*, 283.

50. *ORA*, ser. 1, vol. 39, pt. 1: 539–41, and pt. 2:807, 810; ORN, ser. 1, vol. 26: 582–84; Wills, *Battle from the Start*, 261–63; Wyeth, *That Devil Forrest*, 452–53; Henry, *"First with the Most" Forrest*, 366–67; Lytle, *Bedford Forrest*, 342–45; Hurst, *Nathan Bedford Forrest*, 223–24; Nathaniel Cheairs Hughes Jr., with Connie Walton Moretti and James Michael Browne, *Brigadier General Tyree H. Bell, C.S.A.: Forrest's Fighting Lieutenant* (Knoxville, Tenn., 2004), 179–80; David W. Higgs, *Nathan Bedford Forrest and the Battle of Johnsonville* (Nashville, 1976), 2, 52, 261; Dinges and Leckie, *Just and Righteous Cause*, 283–93; Ben Earl Kitchens, *Gunboats and Cavalry: A History of Eastport, Mississippi* (Florence, Ala., 1985), 121–25.

51. *ORA*, ser. 1, vol. 39, pt. 3:815; Silverstone, *Warships of the Civil War Navies*, 179.

52. *ORA*, ser. 1, vol. 39, pt. 3:658–59, 816–17, 824–26, 829–30, and pt. 2:827–28, 860–62.

53. *ORA*, ser. 1, vol. 39, pt. 3:837–38, also 828–29, 834, 841–47, 850, 852–53, 855–57, 858, 853–64, 866–67.

54. *ORA*, ser. 1, vol. 39, pt. 3:879, and pt. 1:868–69.

55. *ORA*, ser. 1, vol. 39, pt. 1:856–58, 876–78, and pt. 3:156, 279, 284, 343, 384, 392, 426, 435; Edward M. Coffman, ed., "Memoirs of Hylan B. Lyon, Brigadier General, C.S.A.," *Tennessee Historical Quarterly* 18 (Mar. 1959): 35–46.

56. Ridley, *Battles and Sketches*, 596–98; Tom C. McKenney, *Jack Hinson's One-Man War: A Civil War Sniper* (Gretna, La., 2009), chap. 9.

57. *ORA*, ser. 1, vol. 39, pt. 1: 870–75; *ORN*, ser. 1, vol. 26:582–690; for analyses of the Johnsonville event, see Donald H. Steenburn, *Silent Echoes of Johnsonville: Rebel Cavalry and Yankee Gunboats* (N.p.: by the author, 1994), as well as coverage in Maness, *Untutored Genius*, 305–16; Jordan and Pryor, *Campaigns of Lieut.-Gen. N. B. Forrest*, chap. 22; Lytle, *Bedford Forrest*, chap. 22; Wyeth, *That Devil Forrest*, chap. 19; Wills, *Battle from the Start*, 263–73; Browning, *Forrest*, 81–84; Ashdown and Caudill, *Myth of Nathan Bedford Forrest*, 45–46, 89–90; and Joan Wenner, "The gunboat *Undine* traded sides during an 1864 raid by Nathan B. Forrest along the Tennessee River," *America's Civil War*, Sept. 2004, 14, 16, 72.

58. Sherman, *Memoirs* 2:164; *ORA*, ser. 1, vol. 39, pt. 3:595, 658–61; J. A. Morlan to Parents, Nov. 10, 1864, author's files.

59. Steenburn, *Silent Echoes of Johnsonville*, 100–103.

60. Edward Summers to Arthur Johnson, Sept. 22, 1864, author's files.

61. *ORA*, ser. 1, vol. 52, pt. 2:706, 748.

6. Tennessee's Instabilities

1. Graf and Haskins, *Papers of Andrew Johnson*, 6:658–59, 701.

2. Ibid., 6:663–66, 669–79, 707, 711, 734, 735, 736, 741, 74, 745–47, 751–55. On Shelbyville loyalties, see A. Jane Townes, "Was Shelbyville Really a Union Town in a Confederacy County? New View on a Middle Tennessee Community in 1862," *Tennessee Historical Quarterly* 69 (Summer 2009): 130–51.

3. Graf and Haskins, *Papers of Andrew Johnson*, 6:695, 698–99, 723–29, 756–59.

4. Ibid., 6:737, 742–43, 755–56.

5. Ira Berlin, et al., *Freedom: A Documentary History of Emancipation, 1861–1867*, ser. 1, vol. 2, *The Wartime Genesis of Free Labor: The Upper South* (Cambridge, U.K., 1993), 367–86, 411–31, esp. p. 418.

6. Ibid., 415–24, 424–25, 429–31.

7. Ibid., 372, 394–96, 408, 412–15, 630, 649n, 650, 651n, 652, 655–56; Susan Hawkins, "The African American Experience at Forts Henry, Heiman, and Donelson, 1862–1867," *Tennessee Historical Quarterly* 61 (Winter 2002): 222–41.

8. Graf, *Papers of Andrew Johnson*, 7:26–27; also 4–7, 13–15, 25, 28–30, 30–32, 33, 34, 35, 39–41, 41–43, 44–45, 53–54, 60–61, 61–67.

9. *ORA,* ser. 1, vol. 39, pt. 2:75–76, 80.

10. R. L. Houston to father, Mar. 23, May 3, 1864, Civil War Records Survey, East Tennessee, vol. 1, Historical Records Survey, Nashville, 1939, UTLK.

11. Graf, *Papers of Andrew Johnson,* 7:56–57, 70, 78–79, 80–81, 92, 97, 117–18.

12. Sarah Ridley Trimble, ed., "Behind the Lines in Middle Tennessee, 1863–1865: The Journal of Bettie Ridley Blackmore," *Tennessee Historical Quarterly* 12 (Mar. 1953): 48–80; Herschel Gower, ed., "The Beersheba Diary of L. Virginia French, Part II, Winter, Spring, and Summer 1864," *East Tennessee Historical Society's Publication* 54/55 (1982–85): 3–25; Nimrod Porter diaries, May 26, June 2, July 4/5, 27, Aug. 18, 21, 23, 25, 30, Sept. 2, 4/5, 7, 9, 17, 19, 23, 25, 26, 28, 29, 1864, SHC/UNC; Nick Barker diary, June 26, 1864, Manuscript Collections, TSLA; Graf, *Papers of Andrew Johnson,* 7:66n3; A. S. Harrell to wife, Nov. 23, Dec. 22, 1863, Mar. 20, 1864, and Sarah Catherine Delozier Millican, July 31, 1864, all in Civil War Record Survey, East Tennessee, vol. 1, Historical Records Survey, Nashville, 1939, UTLK.

13. William A. Strasser, "'A Terrible Calamity Has Befallen Us': Unionist Women in Civil War East Tennessee," *Journal of East Tennessee History* 71 (1999): 82–83; Alice Williamson diary, Aug. 15, 23, 30; Sept. 1, 5, 12, 16, 17, 20, 22, 27, 1864, DUL.

14. Joseph B. Killebrew autobiography, 191, SHC/UNC; Sievers, *Benjamin Harrison,* 269–70; Martis, *Historical Atlas,* maps 19, 21, and 23 on pp. 48, 50, 52; Stephen V. Ash, *When the Yankees Came: Conflict and Chaos in the Occupied South, 1861–1865* (Chapel Hill, N.C., 1995), 78.

15. Steven S. Raab, ed., *With the Third Wisconsin Badgers: The Living Experience of the Civil War Through the Journals of Van R. Willard* (Mechanicsburg, Pa., 1994), 238–39; Martis, *Historical Atlas,* maps 13, 15, and 17 on pp. 42, 44, 46.

16. Raab, *Third Wisconsin Badgers,* 239; *ORA,* ser. 1, vol. 39, pt. 1:857–58 (on the Sexton incident). On irregular warfare in general, see Mackey, *Uncivil War;* Daniel E. Sutherland, ed., *Guerrillas, Unionists, and Violence on the Confederate Home Front* (Fayetteville, Ark., 1999); Kenneth W. Noe and Shannon H. Wilson, eds., *The Civil War in Appalachia: Collected Essays* (Knoxville, Tenn., 1997); O'Brien, *Mountain Partisans;* Brian D. McKnight, *Contested Borderland: The Civil War in Appalachian Kentucky and Virginia* (Lexington, Ky., 2006); Fisher, *War at Every Door;* Groce, *Mountain Rebels;* Philip Shaw Paludan, *Victims: A True Story of the Civil War* (Knoxville, Tenn., 1981); Peter F. Stevens, *Rebels in Blue: The Story of Keith and Malinda Blalock* (Dallas, 2000); Thurman Sensing, *Champ Ferguson: Confederate Guerrilla* (Nashville, 1942); and Altina L. Waller, *Feud: Hatfields, McCoys, and Social Change in Appalachia, 1800–1900* (Chapel Hill, N.C., 1988).

17. William Styple, ed., *Correspondence to the New York Sunday Mercury* (Kearny, N.J.: Belle Grove, 2000), 280–81; and, more generally, Ash, *When the Yankees Came,* esp. chap. 3, and Ash, *Middle Tennessee Society Transformed,* chaps. 5–7. See also Durham, *Reluctant Partners,* chaps. 6–10; and *ORA,* ser. 1, vol. 32, pt. 2:228–29.

18. Gerald M. Capers Jr., *The Biography of a River Town: Memphis: Its Heroic Age* (Chapel Hill, N.C., 1939), 152, 155, 258n108; Graf and Haskins, *Papers of Andrew Johnson,* 6:687n4.

19. Joseph H. Parks, "A Confederate Trade Center under Federal Occupation: Memphis, 1862–1865," *Journal of Southern History* 7 (Aug. 1941): 290, citing *ORA,* ser. 4, pt. 1:341–42, 529; W. Raymond Cooper, "Four Fateful Years—Memphis, 1858–1861," 36–75, esp. pp. 74–75, and James S. Matthews, "Sequent Occupance in Memphis, Tennessee 1819–1860": 112–34, both in *West Tennessee Historical Society Papers* (1957); Ronald W. Waschka, "River Transportation at Memphis Before the Civil War," *West Tennessee Historical Society Papers* 45 (1991): 1–18; Bette B. Tiley, "The Spirit of Improvement: Reformism and Slavery in West Tennessee," *West Tennessee Historical Society Papers* (1974): 41; Frederick Lee Coulter, *Years of Crisis, 1860–1870,* vol. 2, *Memphis, 1800–1900,* ed. Joan Hassel (New York, 1982), chap. 4; Nancy D. Baird, "A Kentucky Physician Examines Memphis," *Tennessee Historical Quarterly* 37 (Summer 1978): 190–202.

20. Parks, "Confederate Trade Center," 290–91, quoting John Hallum, *The Diary of an Old Lawyer* (Nashville, 1895), 186.

21. Parks, "Confederate Trade Center," 292–300, 306–7.

22. Reyburn and Wilson, *"Jottings from Dixie,"* 199; Ada Sterling, ed., *A Belle of the Fifties: Memoirs of Mrs. Clay of Alabama, Covering Social and Political Life in Washington and the South, 1853–66* (New York, 1904), 222–23.

23. Reyburn and Wilson, *"Jottings from Dixie,"* 200.

24. Joseph Parks, "Memphis Under Military Rule, 1862–1865," *East Tennessee Historical Society's Publications* 14 (1942): 33–34, 54–55; Robert Bailey, "The 'Bogus' Memphis *Union Appeal:* A Union Newspaper in Occupied Confederate Territory," *West Tennessee Historical Society Papers* (1978): 32–47; George Sisler, "The Arrest of a Memphis *Daily Appeal* War Correspondent on Charges of Treason," *West Tennessee Historical Society Papers* 11 (1957): 76–92; Thomas Harrison Baker, *The Memphis Commercial Appeal: The History of a Southern Newspaper* (Baton Rouge, La., 1971), chap. 6; B. G. Ellis, *The Moving Appeal: Mr. McClanahan, Mrs. Dill, and the Civil War's Great Newspaper Run* (Macon, Ga., 2003); James A. Wax, "The Jews of Memphis: 1860–1865," *West Tennessee Historical Society Papers* 3 (1949): 39–89; Sterling Tracy, "The Immigrant Population of Memphis," *West Tennessee Historical Society Papers*

4 (1950): 72–82; *New York World,* quoted in *Memphis Bulletin,* Feb. 12, 1863.

25. Jones, "The Struggle for Public Health in Civil War Tennessee Cities," 64–84.

26. James Boyd Jones Jr., "A Tale of Two Cities: The Hidden Battle Against Venereal Disease in Civil War Nashville and Memphis," *Civil War History* 31 (Sept. 1985): 270–76; Patricia M. LaPointe, "Military Hospitals in Memphis," *Tennessee Historical Quarterly* 42 (Winter 1983): 325–42; Lee Meriwether, "Recollections of Memphis," *West Tennessee Historical Society Papers* (1949): 90–109; Darla Brock, "'Our Hands Are at Your Service': The Story of Confederate Women in Memphis," *West Tennessee Historical Society Papers* 45 (1991): 19–34.

27. Bobby L. Lovett, "Memphis Riots: White Reaction to Blacks in Memphis, May 1865–July 1866," *Tennessee Historical Quarterly* 38 (Spring 1979): 9–10; George Graham Perry III, "A Bend in the River: An Investigation of Black Agency, Autonomy, and Resistance in Memphis, Tennessee (1846–1866)," *West Tennessee Historical Society Papers* 62 (2009): 56–57.

28. George Cadman to wife, June 30, 1872, George Cadman Papers, SHC/ UNC; Brock, "Our Hands Are at Your Service," 28–34; Reyburn and Wilson, *"Jottings from Dixie,"* 200–201.

29. David F. McGowan to Sister Ellen, July 6, 1864, author's files.

30. *ORA,* ser. 1, vol. 37, pt. 2:178–79.

31. *ORA,* ser. 1, vol. 39, pt. 2:60–61; Graf and Haskins, *Papers of Andrew Johnson,* 6:687n4; *Congressional Globe,* 38th Cong., 1st sess., 3224, July 28, 1864.

32. *ORA,* ser. 1, vol. 32, pt. 3:633–36.

33. Lash, *Politician Turned General,* 177; Hallum, *Diary of an Old Lawyer,* 281–85.

34. Parks, "Confederate Trade Center," 309–10; *ORA,* ser. 1, vol. 39, pt. 2:27–28.

35. *ORA,* ser. 1, vol. 39, pt. 2:22–23, 27–28; *Memphis Bulletin,* July 27, 1864.

36. *ORA,* ser. 1, vol. 39, pt. 2:314–15; U.S. House, Ex. Doc. 3, 38th Cong., 2nd sess., 3422–25; *Congressional Record,* 38th Cong., 1st sess., Appendix, 256–57, July 28, 1864; *Memphis Bulletin,* Aug. 19, 30, Sept. 1, 25, 26, Oct. 15, 1864.

37. *Memphis Bulletin,* June 16, 19, 22, Sept. 26, 27, 1864, quoted in Parks, "Confederate Trade Center," 309–10.

38. Parks, "Memphis Under Military Rule," 56–58, esp. p. 57; Parks, "Confederate Trade Center," 31–32; Bobby L. Lovett, "The West Tennessee Colored Troops in Civil War Combat," *West Tennessee Historical Society Papers* 34 (1980): 67–70.

39. Graf, *Papers of Andrew Johnson,* 7:184–85, 318–19, 342–43, 348–49.

40. Ibid., 7:348–49.

41. *OR A,* ser. 1, vol. 32, pt. 2:477–78; Simon, *Papers of Ulysses S. Grant,* 10:106–7. The state of economic and commercial restoration generally can also be discerned from Graf and Haskins, *Papers of Andrew Johnson,* 6:555–56, 610, 611, 630–31, 631–32, 638, 651–52, 702–3, and Graf, *Papers of Andrew Johnson,* 7:xl, lxx, 15–17, 22–23, 29–30, 39, 44, 60–61, 79–80, 91, 92, 161–62, 182–83, 185, 205, 259–60, 264, 277, often to include comments on the refugee problem.

42. Graf, *Papers of Andrew Johnson,* 7:lxx. Supplicant issues emerge in Graf and Haskins, *Papers of Andrew Johnson,* 6:533–36, 538, 545–46, 559, 601–2, 603–4, 606–9, 623–24, 635–37, 653, 655, 657, 664–65, 667–68, 679–80, 684, 685, 707–10, 711–12, 729, 736, and Graf, *Papers of Andrew Johnson,* 7:5–6, 13n2, 15–17, 30, 31–32, 44–45, 48–49, 57, 60, 71, 107, 157–58, 166, 180, 182–83, 184, 185, 186, 188, 319–20, 342–43, 348–49.

43. The ever-present backdrop of partisan warfare appears graphically in Graf and Haskins, *Papers of Andrew Johnson,* 6:566–67, 645, 648–50, 652, 654, 711, 729, 737, 742–43, and Graf, *Papers of Andrew Johnson,* 7:47–48, 56–57, 79, 80–81, 86–87, 104–6, 133–37, 139–40, 166–67, 172–73, 174–75, 180, 184, 200, 201, 238, 239–40, 256–60, 267, 277, 316–18, 326–27. Development of Tennessee union volunteers can be followed in Graf and Haskins, *Papers of Andrew Johnson,* 6:537, 538–39, 540–45, 554, 625–26, 632–34, 643–45, 656, 710–11, 742–743, 746–47, 750, and Graf, *Papers of Andrew Johnson,* 7:17–18, 34, 46, 47, 70, 86–87, 97, 100–101, 113, 123, 133, 134–37, 161–62, 179–80, 189, 197, 198–99, 200, 236, 238, 240–41, 245, 264, 277, 285–86, 290–91, 299–300, 301, 305–6, 308, 316–19. See also Dyer, *Compendium of the War of the Rebellion,* vol. 3, 1636–1647.

44. Graf, *Papers of Andrew Johnson,* 7:34–35 (esp. note 4) and xxxviii–xxxix, 46–47, 48–49, 61, 70, 189–90, 200, 312.

45. *OR A,* ser. 1, vol. 39, pt. 1:485–87, 844–57, 885–97.

46. Graf, *Papers of Andrew Johnson,* 7:159–61.

47. Ibid., 7:xxix, 159–60, and, with other militia-related correspondence, 17–18, 28–30, 77–78, 118–19, 159–61, 162, 167–68, 184, 189–201, 231, 258, 299–300, 353.

48. *OR A,* ser. 1, vol. 39, pt. 1:842–43.

49. Graf and Haskins, *Papers of Andrew Johnson,* 6:xlii–xliii, 574–90, 593, 594–96, 656, 699.

50. Ibid., 6:701–723, 728.

51. Graf, *Papers of Andrew Johnson,* 7:xxix.

7. Kentucky's Lamentations

1. Collins and Collins, *History and Annals of Kentucky,* 1:133–34.

2. Berry, *Voices from the Century Before,* 378–405.

3. Ibid., 351–52.

4. Troutman, *Diaries of George R. Browder,* 175–80.

5. N. C. McLean to wife, Apr. 26, 1864, author's files; Smith and Cooper, *Union Woman in Civil War Kentucky,* 201–3.

6. Collins and Collins, *History and Annals of Kentucky,* 1:134; Bryan S. Bush, *Butcher Burbridge: Union General Stephen Burbridge and His Reign of Terror Over Kentucky* (Morley, Mo., 2008), 112–13.

7. *ORA,* ser. 1, vol. 39, pt. 2:153–54.

8. *ORA,* ser. 1, vol. 39, pt. 2:116.

9. Collins and Collins, *History and Annals of Kentucky,* 1:134–35; Graf and Haskins, *Papers of Andrew Johnson,* 6:737n2.

10. *ORA,* ser. 1, vol. 39, pt. 2:135–36.

11. *ORA,* ser. 1, vol. 39, pt. 2:131–32.

12. *ORA,* ser. 1, vol. 39, pt. 2:140–41, 144–45, 163, 178, 198; Bush, *Butcher Burbridge,* 123 (quoting *Louisville Daily Journal,* July 20, 1864).

13. *ORA,* ser. 1, vol. 39, pt. 2:236–38.

14. Ibid., 174.

15. Collins and Collins, *History and Annals of Kentucky,* 1:136; Bush, *Butcher Burbridge,* 102, 123–26; Execution List, Civil War Guerrillas, Correspondence File, Kentucky Adjutant General Records, Kentucky Military Museum, Frankfort.

16. *ORA,* ser. 1, vol. 39, pt. 2:247–49; Collins and Collins, *History and Annals of Kentucky,* 1:137–38; Bush, *Butcher Burbridge,* 102.

17. *ORA,* ser. 1, vol. 39, pt. 2:212–14.

18. Thomas Shelby Watson with Perry A. Brantley, *Confederate Guerrilla Sue Mundy: A Biography of Kentucky Soldier Jerome Clarke* (Jefferson, N.C., 2008), 23–43; New York *Herald,* July 28, 1864.

19. ORA, ser. 1, vol. 39, pt. 2:817; William J. Davis, ed., *The Partisan Rangers of the Confederate States Army: Memoirs of General Adam R. Johnson* (Louisville, Ky., 1904), 178–79; 196–98; Collins and Collins, *History and Annals of Kentucky,* 1:139.

20. *ORA,* ser. 1, vol. 39, pt. 1:552–64, and pt. 2:243–44, 250, 254–55, 257–59, 263, 268, 272–74, 280–84, 286, 301, 308–9, 316, 320, 322–23, 330–31, 338–39, 345, 350, 360–62, 367, 375; Bush, *Butcher Burbridge,* 124–241, and chap. 8; Thomas D. Mays, *Cumberland Blood: Champ Ferguson's Civil War* (Carbondale, 2008), chap. 8; James L. Head, *The Atonement of John Brooks: The Story of the True Johnny "Reb" Who Did Not Come Marching Home* (Geneva, Fla., 2001), 199–201; Collins and Collins, *History and Annals of Kentucky,* 1:138–39.

21. Collins and Collins, *History and Annals of Kentucky,* 1:138–39; Bush, *Butcher Burbridge,* 131, 140; *ORA,* ser. 1, vol. 39, pt. 2:375.

22. A. L. Hunt to mother, Aug. 14, 1864, A. L. Hunt Papers, SHC/UNC; Thomas Bramlette to Stephen Burbridge, Aug. 15, 1864, Stephen Burbridge Papers, Filson Club, Louisville.

23. Mrs. A. E. Mayes, "The Contrast," bound music of Lottie Hays, Kentucky Library, Western Kentuck University, Bowling Green; H. Robinson to Governor, Aug. 8, 1864, James N. Wilson to Governor, Oct. 8, 1864, R. J. Breckinridge to Stephen Burbridge, Nov. 6, 1864, J. J. Borrell to D. M. Lindsey, Nov. 17, 1864, Richard D. Brown to Governor, Nov. 29, 1864, W. Randolph to Stephen Burbridge, Dec. 1, 1864, all in Civil War Guerrillas, Correspondence File, Kentucky Adjutant General Records, Kentucky Military Museum, Frankfort; Collins and Collins, *History and Annals of Kentucky,* 1:136, 140–41; Robertson, *Paducah,* 63–65; *ORA,* ser. 1, vol. 39, pt. 2:171, 260–61, 342, 349; Lon Carter Barton, "The Reign of Terror in Graves County," The Register of the Kentucky Historical Society 46 (Apr. 1948): 484–95.

24. Collins and Colins, *History and Annals of Kentucky,* 1:139–42.

25. *ORA,* ser. 1, vol. 39 pt. 3:47; Collins and Collins, *History and Annals of Kentucky,* 1:140–44; Watson with Brantley, *Confederate Guerrilla Sue Mundy,* 56–57.

26. Coulter, *Civil War and Readjustment,* 319; *ORA,* ser. 3, pt. 4:688–90; Collins and Collins, *History and Annals of Kentucky,* 1:144–45; Thomas Clark, *A History of Kentucky* (Lexington, Ky., 1954), 346.

27. Collins and Collins, *History and Annals of Kentucky,* 1:144–45; Bush, *Butcher Burbridge,* 157; *ORA,* ser. 1, vol. 39, pt. 3:253, 343–44, 355–57, 383–84, 472–77.

28. Collins and Collins, *History and Annals of Kentucky,* 1:146; Troutman, *Heavens Are Weeping,* 182, 184–90.

29. N. C. McLean to wife, Dec. 1, 8, 9, and 14, 1864, author's files, and Dec. 12, 1864, Historical Shop, Metairie, La., Spring 2009, 89–90, copy in author's files; *ORA,* ser. 1, vol., 39, pt. 3:724–25, 739, 749.

30. Collins and Collins, *History and Annals of Kentucky,* 1:159; McLean to wife, Dec. 7, 10, 14, and 20, 1864, author's files; *ORA,* ser. 1, vol. 39, pt. 3:760–61.

31. Berry, *Voices from the Century Before,* 406–15, 416–18; Troutman, *Heavens Are Weeping,* 184.

32. Troutman, *Heavens Are Weeping,* 180–84.

33. Ibid., 182, 184–90.

34. Coulter, *Civil War and Readjustment,* chaps. 1–12; Harrison, *Civil War in Kentucky;* Harrison and Klotter, *New History of Kentucky,* chap. 13; William F. Fox, *Regimental Losses in the American Civil War, 1861–1865* (Albany, N.Y., 1898), 498.

439

NOTES TO PAGES 255–66

35. Harrison, *Civil War in Kentucky,* 80.
36. Coulter, *Civil War and Readjustment,* chap. 9, esp. p. 183; Harrison, *Civil War in Kentucky,* chap. 5; *ORA,* ser. 1, vol. 32, pt. 3:7–8, 384.
37. Coulter, *Civil War and Readjustment,* chaps. 10 and 11, esp. p. 215–24; *ORA,* ser. 3, vol. 4:688–90.
38. Collins and Collins, *History and Annals of Kentucky,* 1:136.
39. Berry, *Voices from the Century Before,* 349–418, esp. p. 371, 381, 383, 389–92, 409; *ORA,* ser. 1, vol. 32, pt. 3:41–42, 46–147, and vol. 39, pt. 2:181; Harrison, *Civil War in Kentucky,* 85, quoting Maria Knott to Samuel, Aug. 5, 1863, Knott Collection, Kentucky Library, Western Kentucky University, Bowling Green; Coulter, *Civil War and Readjustment,* 230–32.
40. Ezra J. Warner, *Generals in Blue: Lives of the Union Commanders* (Baton Rouge, La., 1964), 40; *ORA,* ser. 1, vol. 39, pt. 2:159–60, 163.
41. Warner, *Generals in Blue,* 54–55, 355–56; Coulter, *Civil War and Readjustment,* 228.
42. Coulter, *Civil War and Readjustment,* chap. 12, esp. p. 251–52; James F. Hopkins, *A History of the Hemp Industry in Kentucky* (Lexington, Ky., 1951), chaps. 5 and 6, esp. pp. 195–96.
43. Robert Emmett McDowell, *City of Conflict: Louisville in the Civil War, 1861–1865* (Louisville, Ky., 1962), chap. 12; Maysville (Ky.) *Bulletin,* Oct. 13, 1864.
44. McDowell, *City of Conflict,* 171–75; *ORA,* ser. 1, vol. 39, pt. 3:769–77.
45. Richard D. Sears, *Camp Nelson, Kentucky: A Civil War History* (Lexington, Ky., 2002), Historical Introduction, 37–168.
46. Harrison and Klotter, *New History of Kentucky,* 207; Collins and Collins, *History and Annals of Kentucky,* 1:130, 135.
47. John Sickles, *The Legends of Sue Mundy and One Armed Berry: Confederate Guerrillas* (Merrillville, Ind., 1999), chaps. 1–3; Thomas D. Clark, *Pleasant Hill in the Civil War* (Pleasant Hill, Ky., 1972), 60–62.
48. Troutman, *Heavens Are Weeping,* 190, also 176, 183–84, 185.
49. Coulter, *Civil War and Readjustment,* 238, quoting Bramlette's message to the legislature, Jan. 6, 1865, as carried in the Lexington *Observer and Reporter,* Jan. 28, 1865, and Frankfort *Daily Commonwealth,* June 8, 1863; Davis and Swentor, *Bluegrass Confederate,* 473.
50. Miller, *Kentucky Politics and Government,* 25; Nathaniel Southgate Shaler, *The Autobiography of Nathaniel Southgate Shaler with a Supplementary Memoirs by His Wife* (Boston, 1909), 76–77.

8. Playing Hell in Tennessee

1. Piston, *Lee's Tarnished Lieutenant,* 82–86; Herman Hattaway and Archer Jones, *How the North Won: A Military History of the Civil War* (Urbana, Ill., 1983), 482–85.

2. *ORA,* ser. 1, vol. 32, pt. 3:607.

3. The whole correspondence trail may be followed in *ORA,* ser. 1, vol. 32, pt. 2:789–92, 800, 802, 808–9, 813–16, and pt. 3:582, 584, 586–87, 588–89, 594–95, 598–99, 606–8, 613–14, 618, 627–28, 636–42, 653–54, 655, 656, 674–76, 679–80, 736–37, 748; and Clifford Dowdey and Louis H. Manarin, eds., *The Wartime Papers of R. E. Lee* (Boston, 1961), 667, 675, 691.

4. *ORA,* ser. 1, vol. 32, pt. 3:588, 679–80; Longstreet, *From Manassas to Appomattox,* 542–47.

5. Piston, *Lee's Tarnished Lieutenant,* 86.

6. Benson Bobrick, *Master of War: The Life of General George H. Thomas* (New York, 2009), 257; Matthew Forney Steele, *American Campaigns* (Washington, D.C., 1931), 1:255; Castel, *Decision in the West,* chap. 10, esp. pp. 548–50; Simpson and Berlin, *Sherman's Civil War,* 696–703; McDonough and Jones, *War So Terrible,* 310–16.

7. Simpson and Berlin, *Sherman's Civil War,* 704–11; Charles Edmund Vetter, *Sherman: Merchant of Terror, Advocate of Peace* (Gretna, La., 1992), 228–33; Brian Craig Miller, *John Bell Hood and the Fight for Civil War Memory* (Knoxville, Tenn., 2010), 140, 141–46.

8. Simpson and Berlin, *Sherman's Civil War,* 711, 717; *ORA,* ser. 1, vol. 39, pt. 1:807, and pt. 2:879–80, also 842–44, 847, 850–51, 860, 862, 867.

9. Bailey, *Chessboard of War,* 17–20. In addition to the Bailey study, other prominent campaign analysis may be found in Thomas Robson Hay, *Hood's Tennessee Campaign* (New York, 1929); Connelly, *Autumn of Glory,* pt. 4; William R. Scaife, *Hood's Campaign for Tennessee* (Atlanta, 1986); Wiley Sword, *Embrace an Angry Wind: The Confederacy's Last Hurrah: Spring Hill, Franklin, and Nashville* (New York, 1992); and Winston Groom, *Shrouds of Glory: From Atlanta to Nashville: The Last Great Campaign of the Civil War* (New York, 1995); Thomas Speed, "Hood's Error," *Louisville Courier-Journal Supplement,* Apr. 2, [?] clipping; and "The Battle of Franklin," *New York Times,* Nov. 13, 1882.

10. Eric A. Jacobson and Richard A. Rupp, *For Cause and for Country: A Study of the Affair at Spring Hill and the Battle of Franklin* (Franklin, Tenn., 2006), 31–39; Miller, *John Bell Hood,* 146–48.

11. See Baggett, *Homegrown Yankees,* 289–90.

12. J. J. Weith to cousin, Nov. 9, 1864, author's files; Johnson and Rupp, *For Cause and for Country,* 39–42; Simpson and Berlin, *Sherman's Civil War,* 726–27, 729–30; operations in northern Georgia and northern Alabama can be followed in official reports, *ORA,* ser. 1, vol. 39, pt. 1:576–827; Miller, *John Bell Hood,* 148–50.

13. Richard Taylor to Braxton Bragg, Sept. 25, 1864, Taylor Letterbook, Manuscripts, Rare Book and University Archives Branch, Tulane University Library, New Orleans.

14. *ORA,* ser. 1, vol. 39, pt. 1:802–3; Simpson and Berlin, *Sherman's Civil War,* 729–47; Miller, *John Bell Hood,* 150–51.
15. Thomas Speed to parents, Nov. 1, 1864, FC; James R. Bentley, ed., "The Civil War Memoirs of Captain Thomas Speed," *Filson Club Quarterly* 44 (July 1970): 255; *ORA,* ser. 1, vol. 45, pt. 1:647; Bailey, *Chessboard of War,* 21–22.
16. *ORA,* ser. 1, vol. 39, pt. 3:477, 498–99, 594–95; Simpson and Berlin, *Sherman's Civil War,* 747–48n.
17. *ORA,* ser. 1, vol. 39, pt. 3:576–77, 594–95, 658–61.
18. *ORA,* ser. 1, vol. 39, pt. 3:658–61.
19. *ORA,* ser. 1, vol. 39, pt. 3:658–61.
20. Simpson and Berlin, *Sherman's Civil War,* 758; *ORA,* ser. 1, vol. 39, pt. 3:727, 740.
21. *ORA,* ser. 1, vol. 39, pt. 3:841, also 746–47; Alfred Roman, *The Military Operations of General Beauregard* (New York, 1884), 2:281, 287–91.
22. *ORA,* ser. 1, vol. 45, pt. 1:648.
23. Bailey, *Chessboard of War,* 42–43; ; Miller, *John Bell Hood,* 150–51; *ORA,* ser. 1, vol. 39, pt. 3:858, 865–66, 868, 870–71, 879; W. J. McDill to sister, Oct. 3, 1864, Civil War Records of West Tennessee, vol. 4, typescript copy, Historical Records Survey, Nashville, 1939, UTLK.
24. *ORA,* ser. 1, vol. 39, pt. 3:870, 874, 879, 880, and vol. 45 pt. 1:649–50.
25. *ORA,* ser. 1, vol. 45, pt. 1:650; 39, pt. 1:803, and ser. 4, vol. 3:756–71; Connelly, *Autumn of Glory,* 484–87.
26. *ORA,* ser. 1, vol. 39, pt. 1:803, and pt. 3:903, also vol. 45, pt. 1:649–50; Sword, *Embrace an Angry Wind,* 66.
27. *ORA,* ser. 1, vol. 39, pt. 1:799, and vol. 44:931–33.
28. On the election, see David E. Long, *The Jewel of Liberty: Abraham Lincoln's Re-election and the End of Slavery* (Mechanicsburg, Pa.: Stackpole Books, 1994), 248, 256–59; John C. Waugh, *Reelecting Lincoln: The Battle for the 1864 Presidency* (New York: Crown, 1997), 346–61; Roman, *Military Operations of General Beauregard,* vol. 2, chap. 41.
29. *ORA,* ser. 1, vol. 44:890, 905, 920, 921, 931–33, 959.
30. *ORA,* ser. 1, vol. 39, pt. 1:808, pt. 3:898, 904, 905–6, 908, 913–14, and vol. 45, pt. 1:648.
31. *ORA,* ser. 1, vol. 39, pt. 3:888–89; Samuel G. French, *Two Wars: An Autobiography of Gen. Samuel G. French* (Nashville, 1901), 290.
32. John B. Hood, *Advance and Retreat: Personal Experiences in the United States and Confederate States Armies* (New Orleans, 1880), 270, 281; *ORA,* ser. 1, vol. 39, pt. 3:889–90; French, *Two Wars,* 290; Bailey, *Chessboard of War,* 45.
33. Frank Vandiver, "General Hood as Logistician," *Military Affairs* 16 (Spring 1952): 10–11; Hay, *Hood's Tennessee Campaign,* 61, 65.

34. *ORA*, ser. 1, vol. 39, pt. 3:893, also 896–987 for Stewart's corps in particular.

35. David M. Wynn to John Griffith, Nov. 8, 1864, J. A. Morlan to Parents, Nov. 13, 1864, "Henry" to "Well, My Precious Mollie," Nov. 22, 1864, all in author's files.

36. Jacobson and Rupp, *For Cause and for Country,* 50–54; Scaife, *Hood's Campaign for Tennessee,* 19; Walter J. Fraser Jr. and Pat C. Clark, eds., "The Letters of William Beverley Randolph Hackley: Treasury Agent in West Tennessee, 1863–1866," *West Tennessee Historical Society Papers* 25 (1971): 101; Baggett, *Homegrown Yankees,* 291–92.

37. The early action in the campaign can be followed well in Jerry Keenan, *Wilson's Cavalry Corps: Union Campaigns in the Western Theatre, October 1864 through Spring 1865* (Jefferson, N.C., 1998), chaps. 2–4; Baggett, *Homegrown Yankees,* 291–94; T. J. Walker, "Reminiscences," typescript, n.d., 24, UTLK.

38. Jacobson and Rupp, *For Cause and for Country,* 59–75; Randolph Rosenberger to wife, Nov. 28, 1864, files, Carter House Museum, Franklin, Tenn.; Garrett, *Confederate Diary of Robert D. Smith,* 164–66.

39. Jacobson and Rupp, *For Cause and for Country,* 75–77; Bentley, "Civil War Memoirs," 256–57.

40. Jacobson and Rupp, *For Cause and for Country,* 77–80, 85; Keenan, *Wilson's Cavalry Corps,* 44–54; Baggett, *Homegrown Yankees,* 293–94.

41. The Spring Hill affair has received much attention. See W. J. McMurray, "Causes of Failure at Spring Hill," *Confederate Veteran* 12 (Aug. 1904): 395–96; J. P. Young, "Hood's Failure at Spring Hill," *Confederate Veteran* 16 (Jan. 1908): 25–41; Thomas Robson Hay, "The Battle of Spring Hill," *Tennessee Historical Magazine* 7 (July1921): 74–91; David E. Roth, "The General's Tour—The Mysteries of Spring Hill, Tennessee," *Blue & Gray Magazine* 2 (Oct.–Nov. 1984): 12–39; and Jamie Gillum, *The Battle of Spring Hill: Twenty-Five Hours to Tragedy* (Franklin, Tenn., 2004); also Jacobson and Rupp, *For Cause and for Country,* chaps. 3–5; Keenan, *Wilson's Cavalry Corps,* chap. 5; Bailey, *Chessboard of War,* 81–88; Connelly, *Autumn of Glory,* 494–502.

42. Richard M. McMurry, "Spring Hill, Tennessee (TN035), Maury County and Spring Hill, November 29, 1864," in *The Civil War Battlefield Guide,* ed. Frances H. Kennedy (Boston, 1998), 394; Baggett, *Homegrown Yankees,* 294–95.

43. Thomas Speed to parents, Dec. 2, 1864, Speed Papers, FC; Frederick Nathan Boyer diary, Nov. 30, 1864, copy, author's files; Walker, "Reminiscences," 24–25; French, *Two Wars,* 291–92; Miller, *John Bell Hood,* 152–53; James L. McDonough, "West Point Classmates—Eleven Years Later: Some Observations on the Spring Hill-Franklin Campaign," *Tennessee Historical Quarterly* 28 (Summer 1969): 190–92; McMurray,

"Spring Hill," 393–95; Terry L. Jones, ed., *Campbell Brown's Civil War: With Ewell and the Army of Northern Virginia* (Baton Rouge, La., 2001), 163–72; *ORA*, ser. 1, vol. 45, pt. 1:712–13, 742–43; Campbell Brown, "Spring Hill—Reminiscence of May 5, July 25, 1888," Military Reminiscences, 1-A-5, Folder 4, Box 2, Campbell Brown Papers, Manuscript Collections, TSLA.

44. Connelly, *Autumn of Glory*, chap. 17, esp. p. 502.

45. McDonough, "West Point Classmates," 191–92; Walker, "Reminiscences," 24–25.

46. Information on Fort Granger derived from on-site park historical markers.

47. McDonough, "West Point Classmates," 192–93, 194–95.

48. Connelly, *Autumn of Glory*, 503–5, esp. p. 504; Miller, *John Bell Hood*, 153–57. Franklin may be explored in more detail for example in Jacobson and Rupp, *For Cause and for Country*, chaps. 7–11; James Lee McDonough and Thomas L. Connelly, *Five Tragic Hours: The Battle of Franklin* (Knoxville, Tenn., 1983); Jacob D. Cox, *The Battle of Franklin, Tennessee, November 30, 1864: A Monograph* (New York, 1897); Sims Crownover, "The Battle of Franklin," *Tennessee Historical Quarterly* 14 (Dec. 1955), reprinted by Carter House Foundation, 1955; David R. Logsdon, ed. and comp., *Eyewitnesses at the Battle of Franklin* (Nashville, 1996); and James B. Knight, *The Battle of Franklin: When the Devil Had Full Possession of the Earth* (Charleston, S.C., 2009).

49. Walker "Reminiscences," 25, UTLK; French, *Two Wars*, 293–301, esp. p. 295; Thomas Speed to parents, Dec. 1864, FC; Bentley, "Civil War Memoirs," 259–60; Miller, *John Bell Hood*, 155.

50. Walker, "Reminiscences," 26.

51. Jacobson and Rupp, *For Cause and for Country*, 381–82; Keenan, *Wilson's Cavalry Corps*, 59–66; Baggett, *Homegrown Yankees*, 295–96.

52. C. Vann Woodward, ed., *Mary Chesnut's Civil War* (New Haven, Conn., 1981), 660, 691, 692; Walker, "Reminiscences," 26.

53. Bentley, "Civil War Memoirs," 261; *ORA*, ser. 1, vol. 45, pt. 1:343–44, 654, 658; Baggett, *Homegrown Yankees*, 296, 301–2.

9. Nashville's Anvil and Hammer

1. *ORA*, ser. 1, vol. 52, pt. 3:748, 664–65. In addition to modern studies of the 1864 campaign noted in the previous chapter, significant work specific to the battle for Nashville includes Stanley F. Horn, *The Decisive Battle of Nashville* (Baton Rouge, La., 1956), Paul H. Stockdale, *The Death of an Army: The Battle of Nashville and Hood's Retreat* (Murfreesboro, Tenn., 1992), James Lee McDonough, *Nashville: The Western Confederacy's Final Gamble* (Knoxville, Tenn., 2004); and Zimmerman, *Guide to Civil War Nashville*. With respect to Davis, see Joseph G. Dawson III,

"Jefferson Davis and the Confederacy's 'Offensive-Defensive' Strategy in the U.S. Civil War," *Journal of Military History* 73 (Apr. 2009): 591–607. On Hood, see Miller, *John Bell Hood,* 158–62.

2. C. O'Neal to Ben D. Moore, Oct. 28, 1864, in Charles Mayfield Meacham, *A History of Christian County, Kentucky, from Oxcart to Airplane* (Nashville, 1930), 141–42; Tennessee Civil War Centennial Commission, *Tennesseans in the Civil War* (Nashville, 1964), pt. 1, 370–71; Davis, *Partisan Rangers,* 184–87.

3. Wilbur F. Creighton Jr., "Wilbur Fisk Foster: Soldier and Engineer," *Tennessee Historical Quarterly* 31 (Fall 1972): 267.

4. William T. Alderson, ed., "The Civil War Diary of Captain James Litton Cooper, September 30, 1861 to January 1865," *Tennessee Historical Quarterly* 15 (June 1956): 168.

5. *ORA,* ser. 1, vol. 45, pt. 1:654, 658.

6. Hood, *Advance and Retreat,* 299–300.

7. *ORA,* ser. 1, vol. 44:932–33, and vol. 45 pt. 2:647, 656–57; T. Harry Williams, *P. G. T. Beauregard: Napoleon in Gray* (Baton Rouge, La., 1955), 244–47.

8. *ORA,* ser. 1, vol. 45, pt. 2:685, also 665, 671, 673; *Nashville Daily Times and True Union,* Dec. 2, 3, 6, 19, 20, 1864, cited in Gary C. Shockley, "The Union Legal Response to Hood's Invasion of Tennessee," *Tennessee Historical Quarterly* 66 (Spring 2007): 32.

9. *ORA,* ser. 1, vol. 45, pt. 2:660, 685.

10. Hamilton Alricks Jr. to Father, Dec. 5, 1864, author's files.

11. Unidentified letter, Chaplain, Seventy-Fourth Illinois, Dec. 1, 1864, excerpt, author's files; Ben H. Severance, "Tennessee's 'Fighting Joe': The Civil War Experience of General Joseph A. Cooper," *Tennessee Historical Quarterly* 54 (Fall 2005): 192; Thomas Speed to Horace Speed, Dec. 7, 1864, FC; Bentley, "Civil War Memoirs," 261; Charles B. Clark and Roger B. Bowen, *University Recruits, Company C, Twelfth Iowa Infantry Regiment, U.S.A., 1861–1866* (Elverson, Pa., 1991), 292.

12. Hardin Keplinger to Brother, Dec. 8, 1864, copy, author's files.

13. *ORA,* ser. 1, vol. 45, pt. 2:96; Graf, *Papers of Andrew Johnson,* 7:325–39, inter alia; Peter Maslowski, *Treason Must Be Made Odious: Military Occupation and Wartime Reconstruction in Nashville, Tennessee, 1862–1865* (Millwood, N.Y., 1978), 121, 141–42.

14. A superb portrait of Civil War Nashville can be gleaned from two volumes by the Tennessee state historian Walter T. Durham: *Nashville: The Occupied City, 1862–1863* (Knoxville, Tenn., 2008), and *Reluctant Partners.* See also Jones, "The Struggle for Public Health in Civil War Tennessee Cities," 85–101.

15. Shockley, "Union Legal Response," 22–28.

16. Ibid., 28–36; Cole, "Upon the Stage of Disorder," 52.

17. *ORA*, ser. 1, vol. 45, pt. 1:36–37, 344; Wiley Sword, "The Battle of Nashville: The Desperation of the Hour," *Blue & Gray Magazine* 11 (Dec. 1993): 12–20, 38–50, esp. p. 19.

18. *ORA*, ser. 1, vol. 45, pt. 2:3.

19. *ORA*, ser. 1, vol. 45, pt. 2:16–17.

20. *ORA*, ser. 1, vol. 45, pt. 2:17–18, 139; modern historical interpretations can be followed in Stephen E. Ambrose, *Halleck: Lincoln's Chief of Staff* (Baton Rouge, La., 1962), 189–95; Curt Anders, *Henry Halleck's War: A Fresh Look at Lincoln's Controversial General-in-Chief* (Carmel, Ind., 1999), 624–35; John F. Marszalek, *Commander of All Lincoln's Armies: A Life of General Henry W. Halleck* (Cambridge, Mass., 2004), 215–17, 238–39.

21. *ORA*, ser. 1, vol. 45, pt. 2:55–57.

22. *ORA*, ser. 1, vol. 45, pt. 1:654, 764; Jordan and Pryor, *Campaigns of Lieut.-Gen. N. B. Forrest*, 636.

23. Byrd Douglas, *Steamboatin' on the Cumberland* (Nashville, 1961), 164–66, esp. p. 165; Myron J. Smith, "Le Roy Fitch Meets the Devil's Parson: The Battle of Bell's Mills, December 4–6, 1864," *North & South* 10 (Jan. 2008): 43–53; *ORA*, ser. 1, vol. 45, pt. 1:764; Wyeth, *That Devil Forrest*, 482, 484–85.

24. *ORN*, ser. 1, vol. 26:636–40; *ORA*, ser. 1, vol. 45, pt. 2: 18, 30, 31, 37, 41, 43, 128, 129.

25. *ORN*, ser. 1, vol. 26:641–48.

26. *ORN*, ser. 1, vol. 26:649–50.

27. *ORA*, ser. 1, vol. 45, 2:764; *ORN*, ser. 1, vol. 26: 649–50, 651–63; Smith, "Le Roy Fitch," 50; Jordan and Pryor, *Campaigns of Lieut.-Gen. N. B. Forrest*, 636.

28. *ORA*, ser. 1, vol. 45, pt. 1:35–36, 744–45, 755; Hughes, *Philip Daingerfield Stephenson*, 292–94; Van Eldik, *From the Flame of Battle*, 198; Brown, "Fortress Rosecrans," 138; Kenneth A. Hafendorfer, *Nathan Bedford Forrest: The Distant Storm: The Murfreesboro Raid of July 13, 1862* (Louisville, Ky., 1997), 32–38, 55–57.

29. Herbert S. Norris and James R. Long, "The Road to Redemption," *Civil War Times* 26 (Aug. 1997): 32–38, 55–57; Van Eldik, *From the Flame of Battle*, 262.

30. Hughes, *Philip Daingerfield Stephenson*, 311; Lytle, *Bedford Forrest*, 360–61; Wyeth, *That Devil Forrest*, 483–89; Van Eldik, *From the Flame of Battle*, 265; Martha L. Crabb, *All Afire to Fight: The Untold Tale of the Civil War's Ninth Texas Cavalry* (New York, 2000), 273–75.

31. *ORA*, ser. 1, vol. 45, pt. 1:803, 952, 1214, 122.

32. *ORA*, ser. 1, vol. 45, pt. 1: 803–6, and pt. 2:73, 98–101, 138, 140, 143, 145, 177; Coffman, "Memoirs of Hylan B; Lyon," 35–53; B. L. Roberson, "The Courthouse Burnin'est General," *Tennessee Historical Quarterly* 23 (Dec. 1964): 372–378.

33. Edward Summers to Arthur Johnson, Jan. 1, 1865, author's files; *ORA,* ser. 1, vol. 45, pt. 1:747, 771, 792, 804, and pt. 2:126, 140–41, 165, 176–77; unidentified news clipping, Lt. Col. George H. Purdy file, and diary, Oliver P. Haskell, Dec. 1–16, 1864, both Indiana Historical Society, Indianapolis; S. Haycroft journal, typescript pp. 36–37, Filson Club, Louisville; James M. Walker to D. W. Lindsy, Jan. 3, 1865, Civil War Guerrillas, Correspondence File, Kentucky Adjutant General Records, Kentucky Military Museum, Frankfort.

34. *ORA,* ser. 1, vol. 45, pt. 2:96–97, also 83, 113; Bob Holladay, "The Question of Stanley Horn," *Tennessee Historical Quarterly* 69 (Summer 2009): 198–209.

35. *ORA,* ser. 1, vol. 45, pt. 2:132–33, also 84, 87, 96–97,104, 114–16, 117, 118, 119, 121, 124, 131–32, 143, 155, 180.

36. Frederick Nathan Boyer diary, Dec. 14, 1864, copy, author's files; Ridley Wills II, *Old Enough to Die* (Franklin, Tenn., 1996), 144; M. Jane Johansson, "Gibson's Louisiana Brigade During the 1864 Tennessee Campaign," *Tennessee Historical Quarterly* 64 (Fall 2005): 190; Clark and Bowen, *University Recruits,* 293–95.

37. Figures cited by Battle of Nashville Preservation Society and Civil War Roundtable, Inc. and the Metropolitan Historical Commission, *Driving Tour and Map of the Battle of Nashville, Dec. 2–16, 1864,* pamphlet (Nashville, 2002), map. See also *ORA,* ser. 1, vol. 45, pt. 1:36, 359, and pt. 2:180, also 103, 133, 147, 171, 173; Wills, *Old Enough to Die,* 144.

38. Smith, "Le Roy Fitch," 50; Sword, "Battle of Nashville," 38–39; *ORA,* ser. 1, vol. 45, pt. 1:38–39, 59–90 inter alia, 128–30, 155–56, 180–81, 184–85, 344–45, 359, 360, 405–6, 550–51, 561–62, and pt. 2:184, 196–208; Humphrey quoted in Clark and Bowen, *University Recruits,* 296.

39. *ORA,* ser. 1, vol. 45, pt. 1:660, 675, 688, 691, 694–95, 697–98, 701, 702, 709–10, 722–23, 747, 756.

40. *ORA,* ser. 1, vol. 45, pt. 2:194–96, 210–13, 227, 228.

41. Sword, "Battle of Nashville," 45–46;

42. Ibid., 46–47;

43. Ibid., 47–48; Johansson, "Gibson's Louisiana Brigade," 192–93.

44. *ORA,* ser. 1, vol. 45, pt. 2:215, 707; John M. Schofield, *Forty-Six Years in the Army* (Norman, Okla., 1998), 248; Sword, "Battle of Nashville," 48, 50.

45. *ORA,* ser. 1, vol. pt. 2:210, 227, 699.

46. James Harrison Wilson, *Under the Old Flag: Recollections of Military Operations in the War for the Union, the Spanish War, the Boxer Rebellion, etc.* (New York, 1912), 2:122–23, 125–26.

47. *ORA,* ser. 1, vol. 45, pt. 2:248, as well as 210, 227–47 inter alia.; Joseph Stewart to Wife and Family, Dec. 24, 1864, UTLK. For analysis of later historians' conclusions about the decisiveness of the battle, see John D.

Fowler, "'The finishing stroke to the independence of the Southern Confederacy': Perceptions of Hood's Tennessee Campaign," *Tennessee Historical Quarterly* 64 (Fall 2005): 216–35.

48. Sam Davis Elliott, ed., *Doctor Quintard, Chaplain C.S.A. and Second Bishop of Tennessee: The Memoir and Civil War Diary of Charles Todd Quintard* (Baton Rouge, La., 2003), 201; Sword, *Embrace an Angry Wind*, 405–8; *ORA*, ser. 1, vol. 45, pt. 2:699; Bate's division veteran recounted from the *Augusta Sentinel* in Paducah, *Federal Union*, Apr. 1, 1865.

49. Nimrod Porter diary, Dec. 18–20, 1864, SHC/UNC; Sam R. Watkins, *"Co. Aytch": Maury Grays, First Tennessee Regiment; or, A Side Show of the Big Show*, ed. Ruth Hill Fulton McAllister (Franklin, Tenn., 2007), 270.

50. *ORA*, ser. 1, vol. 45, pt. 2:214; Sword, *Embrace an Angry Wind*, 400.

51. Sword, *Embrace an Angry Wind*, 402–30; War Record of Dr. Belleville Temple, War Records of Tennesseans, Tennessee Woman's Historical Association, Sept. 30, 1914, author's files.

52. Trimble, "Behind the Lines in Middle Tennessee," 78; Sword, "Battle of Nashville," 50; Sword, *Embrace an Angry Wind*, 422; Walker, "Reminiscences," 27.

53. *ORA*, ser. 1, vol. 45, pt. 2:295–96; Charles H. Olmstead, *The Memoirs of Charles H. Olmstead*, ed. Lilla M. Hawes (Savannah, Ga., 1964), 171; Frederick Nathan Boyer diary, Jan. 2, 1865, copy, author's files.

54. Wilson, *Under the Old Flag*, 119–20; Sword, *Embrace an Angry Wind*, chap. 35; Scott Walker, *Hell's Broke Loose in Georgia: Survival in a Civil War Regiment* (Athens, 2005), 213–17.

55. Sword, *Embrace an Angry Wind*, 419–20; Wilson, *Under the Old Flag*, 141–43; Porter, *People Set Apart*, 726–28; Abernathy, *Private Elisha Stockwell Jr.*, 136–46.

56. *ORA*, ser. 1, vol. 45, pt. 2:307, 339.

57. *ORA*, ser. 1, vol. 45, pt. 1:506, and pt. 2:260–64, 306, 341, 356–57, 370–71, 373, 419, 507–8; *ORN*, ser. 1, vol. 26:671–82.

58. Roberson, "Courthouse Burnin'est General," 376–78; Coffman, "Memoirs of Hylan B. Lyon," 48–51; *ORA*, ser. 1, vol. 45, pt. 1:791–806.

59. *ORA*, ser. 1, vol. 45, pt. 1:805–6.

60. Hall Allen, *Center of Conflict: A Factual Story of the War Between the States in Western Kentucky and Tennessee* (Paducah, Ky., 1961), 146; Keenan, *Wilson's Cavalry Corps*, chap. 11; *ORA*, ser. 1, vol. 45, pt. 1:46; Betty J. Gorin, *"Morgan Is Coming!" Confederate Raiders in the Heartland of Kentucky* (Louisville, Ky., 2006), pt. 9.

61. Edward Summers to Arthur Johnson, Jan. 1, 1865, author's files.

62. *ORA*, ser. 1, vol. 45, pt. 1:46, and pt. 2:263, 371, 403; Johansson, "Gibson's Louisiana Brigade," 193–94; Hood's obituary, *New Orleans Daily Picayune*, Aug. 31, 1879, morning edition, cited in Miller, *John Bell Hood*, 162–63.

10. From War to Reconstruction

1. Crist et al., *Papers of Jefferson Davis*, 11:250, fn. 5; *ORA*, ser. 1, vol. 45, pt. 2:471; Miller, *John Bell Hood*, 163–67.
2. *ORA*, ser. 1, vol. 45, pt. 1:664; Edward Summers to Arthur Johnson, Jan. 1, 1865, author's files.
3. Mark A. Weitz, *More Damning than Slaughter: Desertion in the Confederate Army* (Lincoln, Neb., 2005), 278–79.
4. Ibid., 258–59; McCaffrey, *This Band of Heroes*, 148–49; Douglas Hale, *The Third Texas Cavalry in the Civil War* (Norman, 1993), 267–68; Crabb, *All Afire to Fight*, 284–91; Ratchford, *Memoirs of a Confederate Staff Officer*, 69–70; Herman Hattaway, *General Stephen D. Lee* (Jackson, 1976), 149–53; T. J. Walker, "Reminiscences"; Brown, *"Our Connection with Savannah,"* 146–49; *ORA*, ser. 1, vol. 45, pt. 1:664.
5. W. J. Worsham, *The Old Nineteenth Tennessee Regiment, C.S.A.* (Knoxville, Tenn., 1902), 158; *ORA*, ser. 1, pt. 2:649, 655, 656; Hood quoted in John R. Lundberg, *The Finishing Stroke: Texans in the 1864 Tennessee Campaign* (Abilene, Tex., 2002), 119.
6. James Phelan to Jefferson Davis, Jan. 17, 1865, Manuscript Collections, FC.
7. Alderson, "Civil War Diary of Captain James Litton Cooper," 171–73.
8. Blomquist and Taylor, *This Cruel War*, 299, 323–25; Thomas W. Cutrer and T. Michael Parrish, eds., *Brothers in Gray: The Civil War Letters of the Pierson Family* (Baton Rouge, La., 1997), 221–22; Levi T. Schofield, "Selections from Documents in the Museum of the Confederacy Collections: In the Field and on the Town with the Washington Artillery," *Civil War Regiments: A Journal of the American Civil War* 5 (1996):148–49.
9. Bobrick, *Master of War*, chap. 11; John Watkins to Sarah Probert, Jan. 15, 1865, UTLK; Sword, "Battle of Nashville," 50; Russell F. Weigley, *A Great Civil War: A Military and Political History, 1861–1865* (Bloomington, Ind., 2000), 416; Peter J. Parish, *The American Civil War* (New York, 1983), 483; *ORA*, ser. 1, vol. 45, pt. 1:108–11, and pt. 2:377–78, 402–3, 419–20, 441–42.
10. Donald B. Connelly, *John M. Schofield and the Politics of Generalship* (Chapel Hill, N.C., 2006), 148; Schofield, *Forty-Six Years in the Army*, 272–75.
11. Sword, *Embrace an Angry Wind*, 425; *ORA*, ser. 1, vol. 45, pt. 2:318, 378–79; Edward G. Longacre, *Mounted Raids of the Civil* War (South Brunswick, N.J., 1975), chap. 12; Abernathy, *Private Elisha Stockwell Jr.*, 148–53.
12. *ORA*, ser. 1, vol. 34, pt. 1:48; vol. 36, pt. 1:51–52; vol. 38, pt. 1:40, 49, pt. 1:773, 777, 778, 783, 810, 848, 854, 875, pt. 2, 3–6, 9–21, 28, 29–30, 35–36, 37–40, 46–47, 52, 55, 59, 62, 66, 83, 94, 106, 109, 120–21, 134, 138–39, 153–54, 171, 237–38, 805, 824, 869, 881, 907, 916; and

vol. 57, pt. 2:859–60; Clark and Bowen, *University Recruits,* 307–9; Edward Summers to Arthur Johnson, Jan. 27, Feb. 4, 1865, author's files.

13. *ORA* ser. 1, vol. 45, pt. 2:421, 308, 319.

14. *ORN,* ser. 1, vol. 27:28, as well as 1–20, 57, 58–59, 65, 144–45; Edward Summers to Arthur Johnson, Mar. 1, 6, 1865, author's files.

15. *ORN,* ser. 1, vol. 27:87–89, 104, 185–87, 200; *ORA,* ser. 1, vol. 45, pt. 2:10.

16. *ORN,* ser. 1, vol. 27:36, 51, 56, 78, 113–15, 128–29, 174.

17. *ORN,* ser. 1, vol. 27:65, 92, 104–5, 160–64, 165, 166–67, 176–77, 185, 193, 198–99, 201, 202–3, 205–7, 210–11, 257, 259–60, 278.

18. Wentworth S. Morris, "The Davie Home and the Register of the Federal Military Prison at Clarksville," *Tennessee Historical Quarterly* 8 (Sept. 1949): 248–51, esp. p. 251.

19. Unidentified to John Minor, Jan. 25, 1865, Sailor's Rest Plantation Papers, Manuscript Collections, TSLA.

20. William H. Green to Sister, Mar. 14, 1865, author's files; Frank A. Handy diary, Dec. 24, Jan. 12, 1865, DUL.

21. Troutman, *Heavens Are Weeping,* 190; Nimrod Porter diary, Dec. 16, 22, 1864, and Mar. 7, 21, 1865, SHC/UNC.

22. Troutman, *Heavens Are Weeping,* 191, 194.

23. Otto F. Bond, *Under the Flag of the Nation: Diaries and Letters of Owen Johnston Hopkins, a Yankee Volunteer in the Civil War* (Columbus, Ohio, 1998), 240; Walter T. Durham, *Balie Peyton of Tennessee: Nineteenth Century Politics and Thoroughbreds* (Franklin, Tenn., 2004), 215; Robert Galbraith diary, Jan. 1865, Thad Roberts to Cousin, Jan. 24, 1865, and David L. Jones to wife, June 3, 1865, all in UTLK; Graf, *Papers of Andrew Johnson,* 7:406–7, 417, 497–98; Sears, *Camp Nelson, Kentucky,* li–liii and chap. 4.

24. Lillian T. Wall and Robert M. McBride, eds., "'An Extraordinary Perseverance': The Journal of Capt. Thomas J. Taylor, C.S.A.," *Tennessee Historical Quarterly* 31 (Winter 1972): 357.

25. Graf, *Papers of Andrew Johnson,* 7:431–32, 436–38, 470, 471–72.

26. Ibid., 7:441–42, 446–47, 448–51, 448–51, 460.

27. Ibid., 7:461; *ORA,* ser. 1, vol. 45, pt. 2:526–27, 528–29, 557, 601, and vol. 49, pt. 1:5–10, 13–19, 54–56, and pt. 2:528–29, 601.

28. *ORA,* ser. 1, vol. 45, pt. 2:626, and vol. 49, pt. 1:9, 10, 13–15, 15–17, 19–31, 33, 34, 37–38, 44–46, 47, 54, 73, 74, 75, 326–30, 337, 338, 392, 507, 587–88, 609, 611, 629, 632–33, 656, 665–66, 705–6, 715, 726, 766, 784, 809–10, 842–43, 856, 961–62, 1006–8, 1264.

29. Stephen V. Ash, "The Aftermath: Middle Tennessee, December 1864 to May 1865," *Papers of the Battle of Nashville 140th Anniversary Symposium* (Nashville: Tennessee Historical Society, 2004); *ORA,* ser. 1, vol. 31, pt. 3:292–93.

30. *ORA,* ser. 1, vol. 48, pt. 2:107; vol. 49, pt. 1:74, pt. 2:103–4, 409–10, 413, 465, 692–93, 723, 737, 807, and pt. 2:382–83; *Cincinnati Gazette,* Mar. 8, 1865; "A Fiendish Outrage," "Guerrilla Outrage," and "Guerrilla Chase," all in *83d Illinoisan,* Apr. 7 and May 5, 1865.

31. *ORA,* ser. 1, vol. 49, pt. 2:389, 418–19, 671, 875–76; *ORN,* ser. 1, vol. 27:176, 177–84, 185, 208–9.

32. Thomas Carrick file, Civil War Questionnaires, Confederate, TSLA; *ORA,* ser. 1, vol. 49, pt. 2:10, 31, 99, 104, 366, 381, 406, 418–19, 427–28, 441–42, 512–13, 528–29, 557, 723, 739, 830–31, 832, 843, 904–5, 931; *ORN,* ser. 1, vol. 27:85, 87–89, 102, 134–35, 136, 148, 149, 151–52; *Chattanooga Daily Gazette,* June 1, 1865; Gaylon Neil Beasley, *True Tales of Tipton: Historical Accounts of Tipton County, Tennessee* (Covington Tenn., 1881), 51–53; "Capt. King's Diary," Dec. 1826, typescript, Tennessee Gibson County, Historical Records Survey, Memphis, UTLK; Sensing, *Champ Ferguson,* chaps. 2, 18, 19; Mays, *Cumberland Blood,* chap. 9.

33. *ORA,* ser. 1, vol. 45, pt. 2:93–94.

34. Thomas Speed, *The Union Cause in Kentucky, 1860–1865* (New York, 1907), 260–63; Collins and Collins, *History and Annals of Kentucky,* 1:150–54.

35. Basil W. Duke, *A History of Morgan's Cavalry* (Cincinnati, 1867), 530.

36. Bush, *Butcher Burbridge,* chap. 10; Collins and Collins, *History and Annals of Kentucky,* 1:150–58.

37. *ORA,* ser. 1, vol. 49, pt. 1:667, 688, 732, 741, 742, 753, 756, 761, 780; Bush, *Butcher Burbridge,* 189–90.

38. *ORA,* ser. 1, vol. 49, pt. 1:670–72; Bush, *Butcher Burbridge,* 190; *Louisville Daily Press,* July 25, 1864.

39. Collins and Collins, *History and Annals of Kentucky,* 1:150–58; Graf, *Papers of Andrew Johnson,* 7:484; Watson with Brantley, *Confederate Guerrilla Sue Mundy,* chaps. 20–36 inter alia.

40. "Another Skirmish" and "Death of Grant Abbey," both in *83d Illinoisan,* May 12 and 19, 1865, respectively; Watson with Brantley, *Confederate Guerrilla Sue Mundy,* chap. 32; John Sickles, *The Legends of Sue Mundy and One Armed Berry: Confederate Guerrillas* (Merrillville, Ind., 1999), 1–35.

41. William Preston Mangum II, "Disaster at Woodburn Farm: R. A. Alexander and The Confederate Guerrilla Raids of 1864–1865," *Filson Club History Quarterly* 70 (Apr. 1996): 143–85; O. S. Barton, *Three Years with Quantrill: A True Story Told by His Scout John McCorkle* (Norman, 1992), chap. 13; Watson with Brantley, *Confederate Guerrilla Sue Mundy,* 144–49; Sickles, *Legends of Sue Mundy,* 36–57.

42. Stuart W. Sanders, "Quantrill's Last Ride," *America's Civil War* (Mar. 1999), 48; Barton, *Three Years with Quantrill,* 206–13; Watson with

Brantley, *Confederate Guerrilla Sue Mundy,* 152–58, 162, 166, 178–79, 181–87, 188, 199–203, Sickles, *Legends of Sue Mundy,* 57–59, 65–69.

43. *ORA,* ser. 1, vol. 49, pt. 2:346, 356–57.

44. Scott J. Lucas, "'Indignities, Wrongs, and Outrages': Military and Guerrilla Incursions on Kentucky's Civil War Home Front," *Filson Club History Quarterly* 73 (Oct. 1999): 376.

45. See Stewart Cruickshank and James L. Head's appendix in Head, *Atonement of John Brooks,* 195–211.

46. "Ed" to "Dearest Neely," Apr. 21, 1865, compliments of Maj. Arthur Edinger, USMC (Ret.), copy, Marcus Parmele to "Dear Aunt," Apr. 11, 1865, both in author's files; Graf, *Papers of Andrew Johnson,* 7:543.

47. *ORN,* ser. 1, vol. 27:149, 151, 152; *ORA,* ser. 1, vol. 49, pt. 2:366; Henry Cherry to Amos Gould, Apr. 11, 1865, UTLK; "Surrendered," *83d Illinoisan,* May 12, 1865; Graf, *Papers of Andrew Johnson,* 7:524–25, 526–28, 532, 537, 543–44, 548–49, 617–18, 630–34; Nimrod Porter diaries, Nov. 27, Dec. 2, 7, 16–26, 1864, Jan. 1, Feb. 19, Mar. 11, 20, 31, 1865, SHC/UNC; Frank A. Handy diary, Mar. 20, 1865, DUL; Henry D. Palmer to "Dear Friends," Feb. 24, 1865, author's files.

48. Parmele to "Dear Aunt," Apr. 11, 1865, Parmele to Charlie and Maria, Apr. 19, May 10, June 7, 1865, and Parmele to Parents, May 28, 1865, all in author's files.

49. Graf, *Papers of Andrew Johnson,* 7:561–62, 575.

50. "Communicated" and "Letter from Dr. Mary Walker," *83d Illinoisan,* Apr. 21 and 28, 1865, respectively.

51. *ORA,* ser. 1, vol. 48, pt. 1:441, also 220–21, 223–24; three recent studies of the *Sultana* explosion should be compared for statistics and tales of survivors of the disaster. Chester D. Berry, ed., *Loss of the Sultana and Reminiscences of Survivors* (Knoxville, Tenn., 2005); Jerry O. Potter, *The* Sultana *Tragedy: America's Greatest Maritime Disaster* (Gretna, La., 1997); and Gene Eric Salecker, *Disaster on the Mississippi: The Sultana Explosion, April 27, 1865* (Annapolis, Md., 1996).

52. *ORN,* ser. 1, vol. 27:208–9, 213, 217, 218, 252–53, 260–61, 273–74, 283–84, 285–86, 310–11.

53. *ORA,* ser. 1, vol. 49, pt. 2:522, 523; Headquarters Department of the Cumberland, General Orders 30, May 10, 1865, copy, Parmele Papers, author's files.

54. *ORA,* ser. 1, vol. 39, pt. 3:769–77, and vol. 49, pt. 2:213–16, 375, 499–503, 775–81, 898–901, 977–81; J. W. Chickering, IV Corps Muster Office, Instructions, June 22, 1865, author's files.

55. *ORA,* ser. 3, vol. 5:44–48, and ser. 1, vol. 49, pt. 2:890–92.

56. *ORA,* ser. 1, vol. 49, pt. 1:813, 828, 895–96, and pt. 2:168–69.

57. *ORA,* ser. 1, vol. 49, pt. 1:890–91; Ash, "Aftermath"; Lee Anderson to Cousin Nelson, Mar. 22, 1865, author's files.

58. Petition, W. T. Avery to W. W. Orme, June 3, 1865, M. J. Vance to Father, May 19, 1865, and "Aunt Maggie" to "My Own Dear Mamie," May 21, 1865, all in author's files.
59. Connie L. Lester, "Lucy Virginia French: 'Out of the Bitterness of My Heart,'" in *The Human Tradition in the Civil War and Reconstruction,* ed. Steven E. Woodworth (Wilmington, Del., 2000), 148–50; Carole Bucy, "Rachel Carter Craighead and Maggie Lindsley: The Female Experience in Occupied Nashville," *Papers of the Battle of Nashville 140th Anniversary Symposium* (Nashville, 2004).
60. Graf, *Papers of Andrew Johnson,* 7:380–81, 406–7, 477, 515–16.
61. Patrick W. O'Daniel, "Loyalty a Requisite: Trade and the Oath of Allegiance in the Mid-South in 1865," *West Tennessee Historical Society Papers* 60 (2007): 35–46, esp. p. 46; Graf, *Papers of Andrew Johnson,* 7:629–30, 661, 669–70.
62. Welcher, *Union Army, 1861–1865* 2:20–28, 76–77, 128–37, 145–52; James E. Sefton, *The United States Army and Reconstruction, 1865–1877* (Westport, Conn., 1967), 11, 155–56.
63. Durham, *Reluctant Partners,* 268–70; Graf, *Papers of Andrew Johnson,* 7:372, 404–5, 406, 407–10, 436–38, 464, 487–91.
64. Durham, *Reluctant Partners,* 270–71, 281–82, 284–85; Forrest Conklin, "'Grape for the Rebel Masses and Hemp for their Leaders'; Parson Brownlow's Celebrated Tour of Northern Cities, 1862," *Journal of East Tennessee History* 77 (2005): 44–93; Wilson D. Miscamble, "Andrew Johnson and the Election of William G. ('Parson') Brownlow as Governor of Tennessee," *Tennessee Historical Quarterly* 17 (Fall 1978): 308–20; Graf, *Papers of Andrew Johnson,* 7:385–91, 404, 406, 453–56 , 475–76.
65. Collins and Collins, *History and Annals of Kentucky,* 1:151–63, esp. p. 162; Miller, *Kentucky Politics and Government,* 24–28.
66. Readers should consult chap. 9, "Ending a Rebellion," in Stephen C. Neff's fascinating *Justice in Blue and Gray: A Legal History of the Civil War* (Cambridge, Mass., 2010), as well as Miller, *Kentucky Politics and Government,* 25, and Collins and Collins, *History and Annals of Kentucky,* 1:162–63.
67. *Congressional Globe,* 38th Cong., 2nd sess., 1394–95; Graf, *Papers of Andrew Johnson,* 7:521.
68. State of Tennessee, *Acts of the State of Tennessee Passed at the First Session of the Thirty-Fourth General Assembly for the Year 1856* (Nashville, 1865), 1–15, esp. pp. 1–3; Alexander, *Political Reconstruction in Tennessee,* 71.
69. R. A. Halley, "A Rebel Newspaper's War Story: Being a Narrative of the War History of the Memphis Appeal," *American Historical Magazine* 2 (Apr. 1903), reprinted in Tennessee Historical Commission and Tennessee Historical Society, *Tennessee Old and New: Sesquicentennial Edition, 1796–1946* (Nashville, 1946), 2:247–72, esp. p. 271.

70. Fraser and Clark, "Letters of William A. Beverley Randolph Hackley," 90–107; Mary Wilkin, "Some Papers of the American Cotton Planters' Association, 1865–1866," *Tennessee Historical Quarterly* 7 (Dec. 1948): 335–61.

71. George Winchester to Alfred Royal Wynne, July 16, 1865, George W. Wynne Papers, TSLA; Mary Jane DeLozier, "The Civil War and Its Aftermath in Putnam County," *Tennessee Historical Quarterly* 38 (Winter 1979): 454; Sarah M. Howell, "Daughter of Amnicola: Sallie Crutchfield Gaut, *Tennessee Historical Quarterly* 64 (Summer 2005): 126.

72. Mark B. Riley, "Edgefield:" A Study of an Early Nashville Suburb," *Tennessee Historical Quarterly* 37 (Summer 1978): 137; George Winchester to Alfred Royal Wynne, July 16, 1865, George W. Wynne Papers, TSLA; Robert M. McBride, "'Northern, Military, Corrupt, and Transitory': Augustus E. Alden, Nashville's Carpetbagger Mayor," *Tennessee Historical Quarterly* 37 (Spring 1978): 65; Bohrnstedt and Chaney, *While Father Is Away,* chaps. 12–15 inter alia.

73. H. H. Thomas to William Brownlow, Jan. 28, 1865, Henry C. Cherry to Amos Gould, May 2, 1865, Joseph L. King to John Bracklesly, Sept. 30, 1865, and Hannah W. Swann grant of pardon and amnesty, Oct. 27, 1865, all in UTLK; James H. Wisewell to father, May 2, 1865, DUL.

74. John T. Trowbridge, *The Desolate South, 1865–1866,* ed. Gordon Carroll (New York, 1956), chaps. 16, 17, 19, 20, 22, and 23.

75. Mrs. Harry Woodbury, "A Note on Shelby County," *Tennessee Historical Quarterly* 38 (Spring 1979): 80.

76. Henry Cherry to Amos Gould, May 2, Nov. 1, 1865, Henry Cherry Papers, UTLK; also William E. Hardy, "The Toils and Opportunities of War: A Michigan Chaplain in Civil War East Tennessee," *Journal of East Tennessee History* 77 (2005): 49–93.

77. James B. Jones Jr., "The 'Battle' of Franklin: A Reconstruction Narrative," *Tennessee Historical Quarterly* 64 (Summer 2005): 110–19; Lovett, "Memphis Riots," *THQ* 38 (Spring 1979), 9–33.

78. Nimrod Porter diary, Apr. 29, 1865, SHC/UNC; Alderson, "Civil War Reminiscences of John Johnston," *Tennessee Historical Quarterly* 14 (June 1955): 173.

79. *ORA,* ser. 1, vol. 49, pt. 2:1289–90.

80. Alderson, "Civil War Reminiscences of John Johnston," 174–75.

Postscript: A Brave New World

1. The author is indebted to Dr. Marie Richards, foreign service officer of the Department of State, for this clarification. Marie Richards to author, e-mail, Oct. 13, 2009, author's files.

2. Graf, *Papers of Andrew Johnson,* 7:492, 596, 631.

3. Poem, Annie E. Law, "Kentucky," n.d., Richard M. Saffell Papers, UTLK; Augusta to Haddie, Nov. 17, 1865, author's files.

4. Coulter, *Civil War and Readjustment,* 329; Michael A. Flannery, "Kentucky History Revisited: The Role of the Civil War in Shaping Kentucky's Collective Consciousness," *Filson Club Historical Quarterly* 71 (Jan. 1997): 27–51, esp. p. 37–40.

5. Sefton, *United States Army and Reconstruction,* appendix B; Coulter, *Civil War and Readjustment,* 296; Alexander, *Political Reconstruction in Tennessee,* 121; Crist et al., *Papers of Jefferson Davis,* 12:136.

6. Coulter, *Civil War and Readjustment,* chaps. 13 and 14; Harrison, *Civil War in Kentucky,* 106.

7. Thomas L. Connelly, "Neo-Confederatism or Power Vacuum: Post-War Kentucky Politics Reappraised," *Register of the Kentucky Historical Society* 64 (Oct. 1966): 257–60.

8. Hambleton Tapp and James C. Klotter, *Kentucky: Decades of Discord, 1865–1900* (Frankfort, Ky., 1977), chap. 1; Ross A. Webb, *Kentucky in the Reconstruction Era* (Lexington: Univ. Press of Kentucky, 1979), chaps. 1 and 2; Victor B. Howard, "The Civil War in Kentucky: The Slave Claims His Freedom," in *The Price of Freedom: Slavery and the Civil War,* vol. 2, *The Preservation of Liberty,* ed. Marlin H. Greenberg and Charles G. Waugh (Nashville: Cumberland House, 2000), esp. pp. 24–27; Stuart Seely Sprague, "Slavery's Death Knell: Mourners and Revelers," *Filson Club History Quarterly* 65 (Oct. 1991): 441–73.

9. Baggett, *Homegrown Yankees,* epilogue, esp. p. 395; Robert A. Wasmer, "Partisan Warfare in Monroe County, Tennessee, During the Civil War: The Murder of Joseph M. Divine," *Tennessee Historical Quarterly* 68 (Spring 2009): 67–97; Robert Scott Davis, "Joe Ritchey of Tennessee: An American Desperado in Legends, the Newspapers, And a Federal Pension File," *Tennessee Historical Quarterly* 69 (Summer 2009): 152–73; Edward Summers to Arthur Johnson, June 6, 1865, author's files.

10. Watson with Brantley, *Confederate Guerrilla Sue Mundy,* epilogue.

11. Bobby L. Lovett, "Nashville's Fort Negley: A Symbol of Blacks' Involvement with the Union Army," *Tennessee Historical Quarterly* 41 (Spring 1982): 20–21; Graf, *Papers of Andrew Johnson,* 7:426–29, 675; Dickson Humphreys and Cheatham County Chambers of Commerce, *Tennessee Civil War Railroad: In Service to a Cause; Experience the Conflict,* brochure (Ashland City, Tenn., n.d.).

12. Battle of Nashville Preservation Society, *Driving Tour and Map of the Battle of Nashville;* Williamson County Convention and Visitors Bureau, *The Battle of Franklin, November 30, 1864: A Self-Guided Driving Tour* (Franklin, Tenn., n.d.).

13. Timothy B. Smith, "Civil War Battlefield Preservation in Tennessee: A Nashville National Military Park Case Study," *Tennessee Historical Quarterly* 64 (Fall 2005): 236–47. See also Ronald F. Lee, *The Origin and Evolution of the National Military Park Idea* (Washington, D.C.:

National Park Service, 1972); and Dean W. Holt, *American Military Cemeteries: A Comprehensive Illustrated Guide to the Hallowed Grounds of the United States, Including Cemeteries Overseas,* 2nd ed. (Jefferson, N.C., 2010).

14. Susan B. Hawkins, "The African American Experience art Forts Henry, Heiman, and Donelson, 1862–1867," *Tennessee Historical Quarterly* 61 (Winter 2002): 222–41.

15. U.S. House, *Hearing Before the Committee on Military Affairs on H. R. 10291,* 70th Cong., 1st sess. (Washington, D.C., 1928), 1–7.

16. Smith, "Civil War Battlefield Preservation," 245, 247; Baker, "Fort Negley," 7.

17. Bush, *Butcher Burbridge,* 102, 126; McKenney, *Jack Hinson's One-Man War,* 326–48.

18. Hinson obituary, *Clarksville Weekly Chronicle,* May 16, 1874; for invocation of service with Grant at Fort Donelson, see, for example, letters in Simon, *Papers of Ulysses S. Grant,* 21:7n, 82n, 103n, 104n, 324n, and 22:65n, 156n, 312n, 445, 467.

19. Calvin Chappelle, "Preserving History: Knoxville Foundation Saves Mabry-Hazen House," *Civil War Courier,* June 2008, 1, 29–30; Matt Lakin, "Civil War Trails Markers to Be Unveiled Today," *Knoxville News Sentinel,* July 11, 2010.

20. Quoted in *Chattanooga Times,* July 27, 1870; Crist et al., *Papers of Jefferson Davis,* 12:484; Battle of Nashville Preservation Society, *Driving Tour and Map of the Battle of Nashville;* "The General's Tour—The Battle of Nashville," *Blue & Gray Magazine* 11 (Dec. 1993): 57.

Bibliography

Manuscript Collections

Author's files. Originals and copies.

Hamilton Alricks Jr.; "Angie" to "Addie"; Lee Anderson; Augusta (Hopkinsville, Ky.); "Aunt Maggie" to "My Own Dear Mamie"; W. T. Avery; Lon Carter Barton; Benjamin Batchelor; Belleville Temple; Thomas Berry; Frederick Nathan Boyer (copy); J. N. and E. J. Carothers; J. W. Chickering; Thomas Coleman; Stewart Cruickshank; Levi Darrah; William H. Dorris; William Franklin Draper; Arthur Edinger; Frank Flint; D. P. Goodsell; Brian and Maria Green, Inc., Kernersville, N.C., catalogs; William H. Green; "Henry" to "Well, My Precious Mollie"; Historical Shop, Metairie, La., catalogs; B. R. Hieronymous; Sam Hood; D. Huff; Hardin G. Kiplinger; Lewis and Jacob Low; W. D. McCord; David F. McGowan; Nathanial Collis McLean; "Mell" to "Mother"; Pearson Merrell; J. A. Morlan; M. A. Myers; A. Newell; New York, Eleventh Cavalry; Olde Soldier Books, Gaithersburg, Md., catalogs; Henry D. Palmer; Parmele Family; Eilene Patch; Y. Pyles; John B. Rice; H. Roberts; James Ross; Joseph Rubenfine, West Palm Beach, Fla., catalogs; M. H. Sanborn; Edward Summers; Theme Print, Ltd., Bayside N.Y., catalogs; M. J. Vance; J. J. Weith; James Whitney; D. M. Wynn; Samuel C. Zinser

Carter House Museum. Franklin, Tenn.

Randolph Rosenberger

Duke University Library. Durham, N.C. (abbreviated in notes as DUL).

Stephen Gano Burbridge; Frank A. Handy; Walter M. Howland; John C. Pedrick; Hubert Saunders; W. W. Scott; Alice Williamson; James H. Wisewell

The Filson Club. Louisville, Ky. (abbreviated in notes as FC).

Stephen Gano Burbridge; William C. Elliott; Filson Club Scrapbook; S. Haycroft; Louisville Letters—Phillips Thurston Gates; James Phelan; Thomas Speed; James O. Walton

Indiana Historical Society. Indianapolis.
   Hugh Bay; Cornelius Corwin; Hugh Gallagher; Alva C. Griest; James
   Henry Harris; Oliver P. Haskell; Sanders Hornbook; Martin Luther
   Hursh; Andrew Jackson Johnson; James H. Jones; William F. King;
   Robert Houston Milroy; Peter L. Moore; New Albany and Portland
   Ferry Company; George H. Purdy; Alanson R. Rynum; Benjamin
   Shaffer; Aurelius Lyman Vorhis; Sylvester Wills; Walter P. Wilson;
   David M. Wynn
Kentucky Historical Society. Frankfort.
   Kentucky Military Museum, Kentucky AGO Files
Knox College. Galesburg, Ill.
   Philip Sidney Post
State Historical Society of Iowa. Iowa City.
   Josiah Conzette; Oscar A. Langworthy
Tennessee State Library and Archives. Nashville (abbreviated in notes as TSLA).
   MANUSCRIPT COLLECTIONS: Nick Barker; A. C. Brown; Campbell Brown;
   James B. Brownlow; Benjamin Franklin Cheatham; Samuel Alonzo
   Cooke; Jesse Cox; Rachel Carter Craighead; Eastman Family; Peter
   Ferguson; Figuers Family; Lillian Davis Galbraith; Jill McKnight
   Garrett; Sallie Ivie; Sarah Ann (Bailey) Kennedy; Washington Matthews;
   McEwen; Morey; Mary T. Orr; Leonidus Polk; Sailor's Rest Plantation;
   Sketches—Biography; Ernest Wiggers
   CONFEDERATE COLLECTION: *Clarksville Gazette,* Feb. 27, 1864; John E.
   Duling; Alfred Fielder; J. C. Frasier; W. D. Gale; Glenn H. Reams;
   William A. Smith; J. H. Stibbs; Thomas Black Wilson
   FEDERAL COLLECTION: William H. Chapman; J. C. Harwood
Tulane University Library. New Orleans.
   Louisiana Historical Association; Richard Taylor
United States Military Academy Library. West Point, N.Y.
   Nathan Bedford Forrest Cavalry Corps Order Book
University of North Carolina, Chapel Hill. Southern Historical Collection
   (abbreviated in notes as SHC/UNC).
   Beatty; Ellison Capers; J. H. Colett; Aristide Hopkins; Joseph B.
   Killebrew; William Henry King; Murphey; Leroy Moncure Nutt;
   James W. Patton; Nimrod Porter; Isaac N. Rainey; Semmes; Watson;
   Wilson
University of Tennessee Library. Special Collections, Knoxville (abbreviated
   in notes as UTLK).
   Advocate and *Family Guardian* newspapers, Jan.–Mar. 1864; J. D.
   Banks; Job Barnard; John Bell Brownlow; Henry Cherry, B. W. Chidlaw;
   Civil War Records (East, Middle, West Tennessee), Works Progress Ad-
   ministration, Historical Records Survey, Nashville; Allen J. Clifton;
   William Cosgrove; Elizabeth Baker Crozier; Harry C. Cushing; East
   Tennessee Claims Books, 1865–1879; Thomas J. Eastes; Henry Elliott;

John W. Fox; Robert Galbraith; J. C. Gates; William H. Green; Amos
Guthrie; Jonathan D. Hale; Jethro T. Hill; Howard Hopkins; Michael
Houck; David L. Jones; John Jones; Joseph Linn King; John McNickle
Laird; John P. Lathrop; George Laubach; Kate Livingston; Loudon
Bridge/Civil War Collection; Andrew J. Mackay; Alfred B. McCreary;
David A. Moulton; Charles H. Pierce; James Pritchard; Robert A. Ragan;
E. H. Rennolds; R. B. Rosenburg; Jacob Rowland; Hugh Ryan; Robert
Saffell; Pembroke S. Scott, John Shrady; Mary Francis (Fannie) Smith;
Watson B. Smith; E. Waldo Stacy; Andrew J. Stephens; Joseph and
Martha Stewart; Oliver P. Temple; H. H. Thomas; Julius E. Thomas;
Union Soldier's Letter from Knoxville, Oct. 29, 1863; Alfred E. Waldo;
John Waliken; T. J. Walker; Wartburg (Tenn.); John Watkins; George
Henry Weekes; Henry B. Wetzell; Eleanora Williams; W. W. Woodruff
Western Kentucky University Library. Bowling Green.
Lottie Hays

Government Documents

Barnes, Joseph K., preparer. *The Medical and Surgical History of the War of
the Rebellion (1861–1865): Surgical Volume, Parts I–III.* Washington,
D.C.: Government Printing Office, 1870.
Belknap, William W. *Legends of the Operations of the Army of the Cumberland.*
Washington, D.C.: Government Printing Office, 1869.
Cronin, Patrick M. *Irregular Warfare: New Challenges for Civil-Military
Relations.* Strategic Forum, Institute for National Strategic Studies, No.
234. Washington, D.C.: National Defense Univ. Press, Oct. 2008.
Serafino, Nina M. *Peacekeeping and Related Stability Operations: Issues of
U.S. Military Involvement.* CRS issue brief for Congress. Washington,
D.C.: Congressional Research Service, Jan. 30, 2006. Update.
State of Tennessee. *Acts and Resolutions of the State of Tennessee Passed at the
Extra Session of the Thirty-Fourth General Assembly, July 1866.* Nashville:
S. C. Mercer, 1866.
———. *Acts of the State of Tennessee Passed at the First Session of the Thirty-
Fourth General Assembly for the Year 1865.* Nashville: S. C. Mercer, 1865.
U.S. Congress. House of Representatives. *Hearing Before the Committee on
Military Affairs on H. R. 10291.* 70th Cong., 1st sess. Washington, D.C.:
Government Printing Office, 1928.
U.S. Congress. Senate. Ex. Doc. 28. *Letter of the Secretary of War, . . . Copy
of Report of Special Committee upon the Condition and Treatment of Col-
ored Refugees in Kentucky, Tennessee and Alabama, February 27, 1865.*
38th Cong., 2nd sess., 1865.
———. *Preliminary Report on the Eighth Census, 1860,* by Joseph C. G.
Kennedy. 37th Cong., 2nd sess. Washington, D.C.: Government Print-
ing Office, 1862.

U.S. Navy Department. *Official Records of the Union and Confederate Navies in the War of the Rebellion*. 31 vols. Washington, D.C.: Government Printing Office, 1908–22.

U.S. War Department. *The War of the Rebellion: A Compilation of the Official Records of the Union and Confederate Armies*. 129 vols. Washington, D.C.: Government Printing Office, 1880–1901.

U.S. War Department. Secretary of War. Appendix to the Report of . . . Accompanying Message of the President to the 29th Cong., 1st sess. *Reports of Bvt. Brig. Gen. D. C. McCallum, Director and General Manager of the Military Railroads of the United States and the Provost Marshal General in Two Parts. Part I*. Washington, D.C.: Government Printing Office, 1866.

Books

Abbott, Richard H. *The Republican Party and the South, 1855–1877: The First Southern Strategy*. Chapel Hill: Univ. of North Carolina Press, 1986.

Abernathy, Byron R., editor. *Private Elisha Stockwell, Jr. Sees the Civil War*. Norman: Univ. of Oklahoma Press, 1958.

Agassiz, George R., editor. *Meade's Headquarters 1863–1865: Letters of Colonel Theodore Lyman from the Wilderness to Appomattox*. Boston: Atlantic Monthly Press, 1922.

Aldrich, C. Knight, editor. *Quest for a Star: The Civil War Letters and Diaries of Colonel Francis T. Sherman of the Eighty-Eighth Illinois*. Knoxville: Univ. of Tennessee Press, 1999.

Alexander, Thomas B. *Political Reconstruction in Tennessee*. Nashville: Vanderbilt Univ. Press, 1950.

———. *Thomas A. R. Nelson of East Tennessee*. Nashville: Tennessee Historical Commission, 1956.

Allen, David C. *Winds of Change: Robertson County, Tennessee in the Civil War*. Nashville: Land Yacht Press, 2000.

Allen, Hall. *Center of Conflict: A Factual Story of the War Between the States in Western Kentucky and Tennessee*. Paducah, Ky.: Paducah Sun-Democrat, 1961.

Ambrose, Stephen E., editor. *Halleck: Lincoln's Chief of Staff*. Baton Rouge: Louisiana State Univ. Press, 1962.

———. *A Wisconsin Boy in Dixie: Civil War Letters of James K. Newton*. Madison: Univ. of Wisconsin Press, 1961.

Anderson, Ephraim McD. *Memoirs: Historical and Personal; including the Campaigns of the First Missouri Confederate Brigade*. St. Louis Times, 1868. Reprint, Dayton, Ohio: Morningside Bookshop 1972.

Andrews, Matthew Page, compiler. *The Women of the South in War Times*. Baltimore: Norman, Remington, 1920.

461

Bibliography

Angle, Paul M., editor. *Three Years in the Army of the Cumberland: The Letters and Diary of Major James A. Connolly.* Bloomington: Indiana Univ. Press, 1959.

Ash, Stephen V. *Middle Tennessee Society Transformed, 1860–1870: War and Peace in the Upper South.* Baton Rouge: Louisiana State Univ. Press, 1988.

———. *When the Yankees Came: Conflict and Chaos in the Occupied South, 1861–1865.* Chapel Hill: Univ. of North Carolina Press, 1995.

———. *A Year in the South: Four Lives in 1865.* New York: Palgrave Macmillan, 2002.

Ashdown, Paul, and Edward Caudill. *The Myth of Nathan Bedford Forrest.* Lanham, Md.: Rowan & Littlefield, 2005.

Ashley, Joe, and Lavon Ashley, editors and compilers. *Oh for Dixie! The Civil War Record and Diary of Capt. William V. Davis, Thirtieth Mississippi Infantry, C.S.A.* Colorado Springs, Colo.: Standing Pine Press, 2001.

Asprey, Robert B. *War in the Shadows: The Guerrilla in History.* Garden City, N.J.: Doubleday, 1975.

Athearn, Robert G., editor. *Soldier in the West: The Civil War Letters of Alfred Lacey Hough.* Philadelphia: Univ. of Pennsylvania Press, 1957.

Augustus, Gerald L. *The Loudon County Area of East Tennessee in the War, 1861–1865.* Paducah, Ky.: Turner Publishing, 2000.

Avary, Myrta Lockett, editor. *Recollections of Alexander H. Stephens.* Baton Rouge: Louisiana State Univ. Press, 1998.

Ayers, Edward L. *What Caused the Civil War? Reflections on the South and Southern History.* New York: W. W. Norton, 2005.

Bacon, Benjamin W. *Sinews of War: How Technology, Industry, and Transportation Won the Civil War.* Novato, Calif.: Presidio, 1997.

Baggett, James Alex. *Homegrown Yankees: Tennessee's Union Cavalry in the Civil War.* Baton Rouge: Louisiana State Univ. Press, 2009.

Bailey, Anne J. *The Chessboard of War: Sherman and Hood in the Autumn Campaigns of 1864.* Lincoln: Univ. of Nebraska Press, 2000.

Baker, Thomas Harrison. *The Memphis Commercial Appeal: The History of a Southern Newspaper.* Baton Rouge: Louisiana State Univ. Press, 1971.

Baldwin, James J., III. *The Struck Eagle: A Biography of Brigadier General Micah Jenkins, and a History of the Fifth South Carolina Volunteers and the Palmetto Sharpshooters.* Shippensburg, Pa.: Burd Street Press, 1996.

Banasik, Michael E. *Cavaliers of the Brush: Quantrill and His Men.* Vol. 5 of *The Civil War West of the River,* edited by Michael E. Banasik. Unwritten chapters. Iowa City: Camp Pope Bookshop, 2003.

Barber, Flavel. *Holding the Line: The Third Tennessee Infantry, 1861–1864.* Edited by Robert H. Ferrell. Kent: Kent State Univ. Press, 1994.

Barton, O. S. *Three Years with Quantrill: A True Story Told by His Scout John McCorkle.* Norman: Univ. of Oklahoma Press, 1992. Armstrong, Mo.: Armstrong Herald Print, 1914.

Battle of Nashville Preservation Society and Civil War Roundtable, Inc., and the Metropolitan Historical Commission. *Driving Tour and Map of the Battle of Nashville, Dec. 2–16, 1864.* Pamphlet. Nashville, 2002.

Bauer, K. Jack. *Soldiering: The Civil War Journal of Rice C. Bull.* Novato, Calif.: Presidio, 1977.

Beach, Ursula Smith. *Along the Warioto, or a History of Montgomery County, Tennessee.* Clarksville: Clarksville Kiwanis Club and Tennessee Historical Commission, 1964.

Beasley, Gaylor. *True Tales of Tipton: Historical Accounts of Tipton County, Tennessee.* Covington, Tenn.: Tipton County Historical Society, 1981. Reprint, Charleston, S.C.: History Press, 2007.

Beasley, Paul H., compiler. *Marks, Landmarks, and Markers: A Guide to the Civil War in Nashville and Davidson County.* Nashville: n.p., n.d.

Belz, Herman. *Reconstructing the Union: Theory and Policy during the Civil War.* Ithaca: Cornell Univ. Press for American Historical Association, 1969.

Berlin, Ira, and Barbara J. Fields, editors. *Free at Last: A Documentary History of Slavery, Freedom, and the Civil War.* New York: New Press, 1992.

Berlin, Ira, Barbara J. Fields, Thavolia Glymph, Joseph P. Reidy, and Leslie S. Rowland, editors. *The Destruction of Slavery.* [Freedom: A Documentary History of Emancipation, 1861–1867, Series 1, vol. 1.] New York: Cambridge Univ. Press, 1985.

Berlin, Ira, Steven F. Miller, Joseph P. Reidy, and Leslie S. Rowland, editors. *The Wartime Genesis of Free Labor: The Upper South.* [Freedom: A Documentary History of Emancipation, 1861-1867, Series 1, vol. 2.] New York: Cambridge Univ. Press, 1993.

Berlin, Ira, Joseph P. Reidy, and Leslie S. Rowland, editors. *The Black Military Experience.* [Freedom: A Documentary History of Emancipation, 1861–1867, Series 2.] New York: Cambridge Univ. Press, 1982.

Berry, Chester D., editor. *Loss of the Sultana and Reminiscences of Survivors.* Knoxville: Univ. of Tennessee Press, 2005.

Berry, Mary Clay. *Voices from the Century Before: The Odyssey of a Nineteenth-Century Kentucky Family.* New York: Arcade Publishing, 1997.

Berry, Sue, and Martha Fuqua, editors and compilers. *Homespun Tales: The Battle of Franklin.* Franklin, Tenn.: Pioneers' Corner Association, 1989.

Bigham, Darrell E. *On Jordan's Banks: Emancipation and Its Aftermath in the Ohio River Valley.* Lexington: Univ. Press of Kentucky, 2006.

Birtle, Andrew J. *U.S. Army Counterinsurgency and Contingency Operations Doctrine, 1860–1941.* Washington, D.C.: Center of Military History, United States Army, 1998.

Blackburn, J. K. P. *Terry's Texas Rangers: Reminiscences of . . .* Reprint, Austin, Tex.: Ranger Press, 1979.

Blackwell, Samuel M., Jr. *In the First Line of Battle: The Twelfth Illinois Cavalry in the Civil War.* DeKalb: Northern Illinois Univ. Pres, 2002.

Blair, William Alan, editor. *A Politician Goes to War: The Civil War Letters of John White Geary.* Univ. Park: Pennsylvania State Univ. Press, 1995.

Blomquist, Ann K., and Robert A. Taylor. *This Cruel War: The Civil War Letters of Grant and Malinda Taylor, 1862–1865.* Macon: Mercer Univ. Press, 2000.

Boaz, Thomas M. *Libby Prison and Beyond: A Union Staff Officer in the East, 1862–1865.* Shippensburg, Pa.: Burd Street Press, 1997.

Bobrick, Benson. *Master of War: The Life of General George H. Thomas.* New York: Simon and Schuster, 2009.

———. *Testament: A Soldier's Story of the Civil War.* New York: Simon and Schuster, 2003.

Bohrnstedt, Jennifer Cain, editor. *Soldiering with Sherman: Civil War Letters of George F. Cram.* DeKalb: Northern Illinois Univ. Press, 2000.

Bohrnstedt, Jennifer Cain, editor, and Kassandra R. Chaney, compiler. *While Father Is Away: The Civil War Letters of William H. Bradbury.* Lexington: Univ. Press of Kentucky, 2003.

Bond, Otto F., editor. *Under the Flag of the Nation: Diaries and Letters of Owen Johnston Hopkins, a Yankee Volunteer in the Civil War.* Columbus: Ohio State Univ. Press, 1998.

Bowers, Byron. "Battle of Franklin, Tenn." *Franklin Review-Appeal,* Feb. 24, 1972, 2.

Boynton, H. V. *Sherman's Historical Raid: The Memoirs in the Light of the Record.* Cincinnati: Wilstach, Baldwin, 1875.

Bradley, Michael R. *With Blood and Fire: Life behind Union Lines in Middle Tennessee, 1863–65.* Shippensburg, Pa.: Burd Street Press, 2003.

Brandt, Nat. *Mr. Tubbs' Civil War.* Syracuse: Syracuse Univ. Press, 1996.

Bresnahan, James C., editor. *Revisioning the Civil War: Historians on Counter-Factual Scenarios.* Jefferson, N.C.: McFarland, 2006.

Brewer, James D. *The Raiders of 1862.* Westport, Conn.: Praeger, 1997.

Brown, Norman D., editor. *One of Cleburne's Command: The Civil War Reminiscences and Diary of Capt. Samuel T. Foster, Granbury's Texas Brigade, CSA.* Austin: Univ. of Texas Press, 1980.

Brown, Russell K. *"Our Connection with Savannah": History of the First Battalion Georgia Sharpshooters, 1862–1865.* Macon: Mercer Univ. Press, 2004.

Brown, Shannon A., editor. *Resourcing Stability Operations and Reconstruction: Past, Present, and Future.* Washington, D.C.: Department of the Army, 2006.

Browning, Robert M., Jr. *Forrest: The Confederacy's Relentless Warrior.* Washington, D.C.: Brassey's, 2004.

Buck, Irving A. *Cleburne and His Command.* New York: Walter Neale, 1908.

Buell, Thomas B. *The Warrior Generals: Combat Leadership in the Civil War.* New York: Random House, 1997.

Burt, Jesse C. *Nashville: Its Life and Times.* Nashville: Tennessee Book, 1959.

Bush, Bryan S. *Butcher Burbridge: Union General Stephen Burbridge and His Reign of Terror Over Kentucky.* Morley, Mo.: Acclaim Press, 2008.

———. *Lincoln and the Speeds: The Untold Story of a Devoted and Enduring Friendship.* Morley, Mo: Acclaim Press, 2008.

Byrne, Frank L., editor. *The View from Headquarters: Civil War Letters of Harvey Reid.* Madison: State Historical Society of Wisconsin, 1965.

Caldwell, James E. *Recollections of a Life Time.* Nashville: Baird-Ward Press, 1923.

Caney, Donald L. *The Old Steam Navy.* Vol. 2, *The Ironclads 1842–1885.* Annapolis, Md.: Naval Institute Press, 1993.

Capers, Gerald M., Jr. *The Biography of a River Town: Memphis: Its Heroic Age.* Chapel Hill: Univ. of North Carolina Press, 1939.

Carley, Kenneth. *Minnesota in the Civil War.* Minneapolis: Ross & Haines, 1961.

Carnahan, Burrus. *Lincoln on Trial: Southern Civilians and the Law of War.* Lexington: Univ. Press of Kentucky, 2010.

Carpenter, John A. *Sword and Olive Branch: Oliver Otis Howard.* Pittsburgh: Univ. of Pittsburgh Press, 1964. Reprint, New York: Fordham Univ. Press, 1999.

Carpenter, Noel. *A Slight Demonstration: Decatur, October 1864, Clumsy Beginning of Gen. John B. Hood's Tennessee Campaign.* Austin, Tex.: Legacy Books and Letters, 2007.

Carroon, Robert G., editor. *From Freeman's Ford to Bentonville: The Sixty-First Ohio Volunteer Infantry.* Shippensburg, Pa.: Burd Street Press, 1998.

Castel, Albert. *Articles of War: Winners, Losers, and Some Who Were Both During the Civil War.* Mechanicsburg, Pa.: Stackpole Books, 2000.

———. *Tom Taylor's Civil War.* Lawrence: Univ. Press of Kansas, 2000.

Cater, Douglas John. *As It Was: Reminiscences of a Soldier of the Third Texas Cavalry and the Nineteenth Louisiana Infantry.* Austin, Tex.: State House Press, 1990.

Christ, Mark K., editor. *Getting Used to Being Shot At: The Spence Family Civil War Letters.* Fayetteville: Univ. of Arkansas Press, 2002.

Cimprich, John. *Fort Pillow, a Civil War Massacre, and Public Memory.* Baton Rouge: Louisiana State Univ. Press, 2005.

———. *Slavery's End in Tennessee, 1861–1865.* Tuscaloosa: Univ. of Alabama Press, 1985.

Cisco, Walter Brian. *States Rights Gist: A South Carolina General of the Civil War.* Shippensburg, Pa.: White Mane Publishing, 1991.

Clark, Charles B., and Roger B. Bowen. *University Recruits, Company C, Twelfth Iowa Infantry Regiment, U.S.A., 1861–1866.* Elverson, Pa.: Mennonite Family History, 1991.

Clausewitz, Karl Marie von. *On War.* Edited and translated by Michael Howard and Peter Paret. Princeton: Princeton Univ. Press, 1984.

Coakley, Robert W. *The Role of Federal Military Forces in Domestic Disturbances, 1789–1878*. Washington, D.C.: U.S. Army Center of Military
History, 1988.

Coffman, Richard M., and Kurt D. Graham. *To Honor These Men: A History
of the Phillips Georgia Legion Infantry Battalion*. Macon: Mercer Univ.
Press, 2007.

Cogswell, Leander W. *A History of the Eleventh New Hampshire Regiment
Volunteer Infantry in the Rebellion War, 1861–1865*. Concord, N.H.: Republican Press Association, 1891.

Collins, Lewis, and Richard H. Collins. *Collins' Historical Sketches of Kentucky*. 2 vols. Covington, Ky.: Collins, 1874. Revised as *The History of
Kentucky by the Late Lewis Collins, Revised . . . and brought down to 1874
by his son Richard H. Collins [History and Annals of Kentucky]*. 2 vols.
Covington, Ky.: Collins, 1882.

Connelly, Donald B. *John M. Schofield and the Politics of Generalship*. Chapel
Hill: Univ. of North Carolina Press, 2006.

Connelly, Thomas Lawrence. *Autumn of Glory: The Army of Tennessee, 1862–
1865*. Baton Rouge: Louisiana State Univ. Press, 1971.

Cooling, Benjamin Franklin. *Fort Donelson's Legacy: War and Society in Kentucky and Tennessee, 1862–1863*. Knoxville: Univ. of Tennessee Press, 1997.

———. *Forts Henry and Donelson: The Key to the Confederate Heartland*.
Knoxville: Univ. of Tennessee Press, 1987.

Cottom, Robert I., and Mary Ellen Hayward, editors, *Maryland in the Civil
War: A House Divided*. Baltimore: Maryland Historical Society, 1994.

Coulter, E. Merton. *The Civil War and Readjustment in Kentucky*. Chapel
Hill: Univ. of North Carolina, 1926. Reprint, Gloucester, Mass.: Peter
Smith, 1966.

———. *William G. Brownlow: Fighting Parson of the Southern Highlands*.
Chapel Hill: Univ. of North Carolina Press, 1937. Reprint, Knoxville:
Univ. of Tennessee Press, 1999.

Coward, Asbury. *The South Carolinians: Colonel Asbury Coward's Memoirs*.
Edited by Natalie Jenkins Bond and Osmun Latrobe Coward. New York:
Vantage, 1968.

Cox, Jacob D. *The Battle of Franklin Tennessee, November 30, 1864: A Monograph*. New York: Charles Scribner's Sons, 1897. Reprint, Dayton, Ohio:
Morningside Bookshop, 1983.

Cozzens, Peter, and Robert I. Girardi, editors. *The New Annals of the Civil
War*. Mechanicsburg, Pa.: Stackpole Books, 2004.

Crabb, Martha L. *All Afire to Fight: The Untold Tale of the Civil War's Ninth
Texas Cavalry*. New York: Post Road Press, 2000.

Creekmore, Betsey Beeler. *Knoxville*. Knoxville: Univ. of Tennessee Press,
1958.

Crist, Lynda Lasswell, et al., editors. *The Papers of Jefferson Davis*. 12 vols. to
date. Baton Rouge: Louisiana State Univ. Press, 1971–2008.

Crocker, Helen Bartter. *The Green River of Kentucky.* Lexington: Univ. Press of Kentucky, 1976.

Crofts, Daniel W. *Reluctant Confederates: Upper South Unionists in the Secession Crisis.* Chapel Hill: Univ. of North Carolina Press, 1989.

Cross, C. Wallace. *Cry Havoc: A History of the Forty-Ninth Tennessee Volunteer Infantry Regiment, 1861–1865.* Franklin, Tenn.: Hillsboro Press, 2004.

Crouse, Ethelbert. *Reminiscences, 1861–1865: An Adventure with Guerrillas.* Antwerp, Ohio: A. N. Smith, Argus Office, 1899.

Crowson, Noel, and John V. Brogden, editors and compilers. *Bloody Banners and Barefoot Boys: "A History of the Twenty-Seventh Regiment Alabama Infantry CSA," The Civil War Memoirs and Diary Entries of J. P. Cannon, M.D.* Shippensburg, Pa.: Burd Street Press, 1997.

Crumb, Herb S., and Katherine Dhalle, editors. *No Middle Ground: Thomas Ward Osborn's Letters from the Field (1862–1864).* Hamilton, N.Y.: Edmonston Publishing, 1993.

Cumming, Kate. *Kate: The Journal of a Confederate Nurse.* Edited by Richard Barksdale Harwell. Baton Rouge: Louisiana State Univ., 1959.

Cunningham, Sumner A. *Reminiscences of the Forty-First Tennessee: The Civil War in the West.* Edited by John A. Simpson. Shippensburg, Pa.: White Mane Publishing, 2001.

Current, Richard Nelson. *Lincoln's Loyalists: Union Soldiers from the Confederacy.* Boston: Northeastern Univ. Press, 1992.

Curry, Leonard P., *Rail Routes South: Louisville's Fight for the Southern Market, 1865–1872.* Lexington: Univ. of Kentucky Press, 1969.

Curry, Richard O., editor. *Radicalism, Racism, and Party Realignment: The Border States During Reconstruction.* Baltimore: Johns Hopkins Univ. Press, 1969.

Cutrer, Thomas W., editor. *Longstreet's Aide: The Civil War Letters of Major Thomas J. Goree.* Charlottesville: Univ. Press of Virginia, 1995.

Cutrer, Thomas W., and T. Michael Parrish, editors. *Brothers in Gray: The Letters of the Pierson Family.* Baton Rouge: Louisiana State Univ. Press, 1997.

Cuttino, George Peddy, editor. *Saddle Bag and Spinning Wheel: Being the Civil War Letters of George W. Peddy, M.D., Surgeon, 56th Georgia Volunteer Regiment, C.S.A. and His Wife Kate Featherston Peddy.* Macon: Mercer Univ. Press, 2008.

Daniel, Larry J. *Cannoneers in Gray: The Field Artillery of the Army of Tennessee, 1861–1865.* Tuscaloosa: Univ. of Alabama Press, 1984.

———. *Days of Glory: The Army of the Cumberland, 1861–1865.* Baton Rouge: Louisiana State Univ. Press, 2004.

———. *Soldiering in the Army of Tennessee: A Portrait of Life in a Confederate Army.* Chapel Hill: Univ. of North Carolina Press, 1991.

Davenport, F. Garvan. *Cultural Life in Nashville on the Eve of the Civil War.* Chapel Hill: Univ. of North Carolina Press, 1941.

BIBLIOGRAPHY

Davis, J. Merle. *Davis: Soldier, Missionary: A Biography of Rev. Jerome D. Davis, D. D., Lieutenant-Colonel of Volunteers and for Thirty-Nine Years a Missionary of the American Board of Commissioners for Foreign Missions in Japan.* Boston: Pilgrim Press, 1916.

Davis, Kathleen, editor. *Such Are the Trials: The Civil War Diaries of Jacob Gantz.* Ames: Iowa State Univ. Press, 1991.

Davis, William C., editor. *Diary of a Confederate Soldier: John S. Jackman of the Orphan Brigade.* Columbia: Univ. of South Carolina Press, 1990.

Davis, William C., and Meredith L. Swentor, editors. *Bluegrass Confederate: The Headquarters Diary of Edward O. Guerrant.* Baton Rouge: Louisiana State Univ. Press, 1999.

Davis, William J., editor. *The Partisan Rangers of the Confederate States Army: Memoirs of General Adam R. Johnson.* Louisville, Ky.: G. G. Fetter, 1904. Reprint, Austin, Tex.: State House Press, 1995.

Davis, Worthington. *Camp-Fire Chats of the Civil War.* Hartford, Conn.: Park, 1887.

Dawson, Francis W. *Reminiscences of Confederate Service, 1861–1865.* Edited by Bell I. Wiley. Baton Rouge: Louisiana State Univ. Press, 1980.

DeWees, Joseph, editor. *Joshua DeWees: His Civil War Diary.* Nashville, Ind.: Brown County Printing, 1991.

Dinges, Bruce J., and Shirley A. Leckie, editors. *A Just and Righteous Cause: Benjamin H. Grierson's Civil War Memoir.* Carbondale: Southern Illinois Univ. Press, 2008.

Dinkins, James, and Stephen D. Lee. *The Balaclava of America: Reminiscences of the Battle of Franklin, November 30, 1864.* New Orleans: Picayune, 1903.

Dodge, Theodore Ayrault. *A Bird's-Eye View of Our Civil War.* Boston: Houghton, Mifflin, 1883.

Dollar, Kent T., Larry H. Whiteaker, and W. Calvin Dickinson, editors. *Sister States, Enemy States: The Civil War in Kentucky and Tennessee.* Lexington: Univ. Press of Kentucky, 2009.

Douglas, Byrd. *Steamboatin' on the Cumberland.* Nashville: Tennessee Book, 1961.

Doyle, Julie A., John David Smith, and Richard M. McMurry, editors. *This Wilderness of War: The Civil War Letters of George W. Squier, Hoosier Volunteer.* Knoxville: Univ. of Tennessee Press, 1998.

Dunnavant, Robert, Jr. *The Railroad War: N. B. Forest's 1864 Raid Through Northern Alabama and Middle Tennessee.* Athens, Ala.: Pea Ridge Press, 1994.

Durham, Rogers S., editor. *The Blue in Gray: The Civil War Journal of William Daniel Dixon and the Republican Blues Daybook.* Knoxville: Univ. of Tennessee Press, 2000.

Durham, Walter T. *Balie Peyton of Tennessee: Nineteenth Century Politics and Thoroughbreds.* Franklin, Tenn.: Hillsboro Press, 2004.

————. *Nashville: The Occupied City, 1862–1863.* Nashville: Tennessee Historical Society, 1985. Reprint, Knoxville: Univ. of Tennessee Press, 2008.

————. *Rebellion Revisited: A History of Sumner County, Tennessee from 1861 to 1870.* Franklin, Tenn.: Hillsboro Press, 1982.

————. *Reluctant Partners: Nashville and the Union, July 1, 1863 to June 30, 1865.* Nashville: Tennessee Historical Society, 1987. Reprint, Knoxville: Univ. of Tennessee Press, 2008.

Dyer, John P. *The Gallant Hood.* Indianapolis: Bobbs-Merrill, 1950.

————. *Shiloh to San Juan: The Life of "Fightin' Joe" Wheeler.* Baton Rouge: Louisiana State Univ. Press, 1941.

Elliott, Sam Davis, editor. *Doctor Quintard, Chaplain C.S.A. and Second Bishop of Tennessee: The Memoir and Civil War Diary of Charles Todd Quintard.* Baton Rouge: Louisiana State Univ. Press, 2003.

————. *Soldier of Tennessee: General Alexander P. Stewart and the Civil War in the West.* Baton Rouge: Louisiana State Univ. Press, 1999.

Ellis, B. G. *The Moving Appeal: Mr. Mclanahan, Mrs. Dill, and the Civil War's Great Newspaper Run.* Macon: Mercer Univ. Press, 2003.

Einhoff, Christopher J. *George Thomas: Virginian for the Union.* Norman: Univ. of Oklahoma Press, 2007.

Eno, Edgar. *Civil War Letters.* Hillsboro, Wisc.: Hillsboro Historical Society, 1998.

Fain, John N., editor. *Sanctified Trial: The Diary of Eliza Rhea Anderson Fain, a Confederate Woman in East Tennessee.* Knoxville: Univ. of Tennessee Press, 2004.

Faust, Drew Gilpin. *Mothers of Invention: Women of the Slaveholding South in the American Civil War.* Chapel Hill: Univ. of North Carolina Press, 1996.

Field, Henry M. *Bright Skies and Dark Shadows.* New York: Scribner's, 1890.

Fisher, John E. *They Rode with Forrest and Wheeler: A Chronicle of Five Brothers' Service in the Confederate Western Cavalry.* Jefferson, N.C.: McFarland, 1995.

Fisher, Noel C. *War at Every Door: Partisan Politics and Guerrilla Violence in East Tennessee, 1860–1869.* Chapel Hill: Univ. of North Carolina Press, 1997.

Fitzgerald, Michael W. *Splendid Failure: Postwar Reconstruction in the American South.* Chicago: Ivan R. Dee, 2007.

Fleming, James R. *Band of Brothers: Company C, Ninth Tennessee Infantry.* Shippensburg, Pa.: White Mane Publishing, 1996.

Fleming, Samuel M., Jr. *The Reminiscences of Sergeant Newton Cannon.* Edited by Campbell H. Brown. Franklin, Tenn.: Carter House Association, 1963.

Fletcher, William A. *Rebel Private: Front and Rear: Memoirs of a Confederate Soldier.* Beaumont, Tex.: By the author, 1908. Reprint, New York: Penguin Books, 1977.

469

BIBLIOGRAPHY

Forrest, Nathan Bedford. *Gunboats and Cavalry: The Story of Forrest's 1864 Johnsonville Campaign as told to J. P. Pryor and Thomas Jordan.* Edited and reprinted by E. F. Williams and H. K. Humphreys. Memphis: Nathan Bedford Forrest Trail Committee, 1965.

Fowler, John D. *Mountaineers in Gray: The Nineteenth Tennessee Volunteer Infantry Regiment, C.S.A.* Knoxville: Univ. of Tennessee Press, 2004.

Fox, William F. *Regimental Losses in the American Civil War, 1861–1865.* Albany, N.Y., 1898.

Franklin, John Hope, editor. *The Diary of James T. Ayers, Civil War Recruiter.* Springfield: Illinois State Historical Society, 1947.

Freehling, William W. *The South vs. the South: How Anti-Confederate Southerners Shaped the Course of the Civil War.* New York: Oxford Univ. Press, 2001.

Freeman, Douglas Southall, editor. *Lee's Dispatches: Unpublished Letters of General Robert E. Lee, C.S.A. to Jefferson Davis and the War Department of the Confederate States of America, 1862–1865.* New York: G. P. Putnam's Sons, 1957.

French, Samuel G. *Two Wars: An Autobiography of Gen. Samuel G. French.* Nashville: Confederate Veteran, 1901.

Frey, Jerry. *In the Woods Before Dawn: The Samuel Richey Collection of the Southern Confederacy.* Gettysburg, Pa.: Thomas Publications, 1994.

Fuchs, Richard L. *An Unerring Fire: The Massacre at Fort Pillow.* Cranbury, N.J.: Associated Univ. Presses, 1994.

Furman, Jan, editor. *Slavery in the Clover Bottoms: John McCline's Narrative of His Life During Slavery and the Civil War.* Knoxville: Univ. of Tennessee, 1998.

Galbraith, William, and Loretta, editors. *A Lost Heroine of the Confederacy: The Diaries and Letters of Belle Edmondson.* Jackson: Univ. Press of Mississippi, 1990.

Gallagher, Gary W., editor. *Fighting for the Confederacy: The Personal Recollections of General Edward Porter Alexander.* Chapel Hill: Univ. of North Carolina Press, 1989.

Garrett, Jill K., transcriber. *Confederate Diary of Robert D. Smith.* Columbia, Tenn.: Captain James Madison Sparkman Chapter, UDC, 1997.

Gauss, John. *Black Flag! Black Flag! The Battle at Fort Pillow.* Lanham, Md.: Univ. Press of America, 2003.

Gavin, William Gilfillan, editor. *Infantryman Pettit: The Civil War Letters of Corporal Frederick Pettit, Late of Company C, 100th Pennsylvania Veteran Volunteer Infantry Regiment, "The Roundheads," 1862–1864.* Shippensburg, Pa.: White Mane Publishing, 1990.

Gay, Mary A. H. *Life in Dixie During the War.* Atlanta: Foote and Davies, 1894.

George Henry. *History of the Third, Seventh, Eighth and Twelfth Kentucky C.S.A.* Louisville, Ky.: C. T. Dearing Printing, 1911.

Gillum, Jamie. *The Battle of Spring Hill: Twenty-Five Hours to Tragedy*. Franklin, Tenn.: By the author, 2004.

Girardi, Robert I., and Nathaniel Cheairs Hughes Jr., editors. *The Memoirs of Brigadier General William Passmore Carlin, U.S.A.* Lincoln: Univ. of Nebraska Press, 1999.

Glatthaar, Joseph T. *Forged in Battle: The Civil War Alliance of Black Soldiers and White Officers*. New York: Free Press, 1990.

———. *Partners in Command: The Relationships Between Leaders in the Civil War*. New York: Free Press, 1994.

Gleeson, Ed. *Rebel Sons of Erin: A Civil War Unit History of the Tenth Tennessee Infantry Regiment (Irish) Confederate States Volunteers*. Indianapolis: Guild Press of Indiana, 1993.

Goodloe, Albert Theodore. *Confederate Echoes: A Soldier's Personal Story of Life in the Confederate Army from the Mississippi to the Carolinas*. Washington, D.C.: Zenger Publishing, 1893.

Goodson, Gary Ray, Sr., editor and compiler. *The Georgia Confederate 7000*. Pt. 2, *Letters and Diaries*. Shawnee, Okla.: By the author, 1997.

Gorin, Betty J., *"Morgan Is Coming!" Confederate Raiders in the Heartland of Kentucky*. Louisville, Ky.: Harmony House, 2006.

Graf, Leroy P., Ralph W. Haskins, et al., editors. *The Papers of Andrew Johnson*. 16 vols. Knoxville: Univ. of Tennessee Press, 1967–2000.

Grant, Julia Dent. *The Personal Memoirs of Julia Dent Grant (Mrs. Ulysses S. Grant)*. Edited by John Y. Simon. New York: G. P. Putnam's Sons, 1975.

Grebner, Constantin. *"We Were the Ninth": A History of the Ninth Regiment, Ohio Volunteer Infantry, April 17, 1861, to June 7, 1864*. Edited and translated by Frederic Trautmann. Kent: Kent State Univ. Press, 1987.

Green, Arthur E. *Southerners at War: The Thirty-Eighth Alabama Volunteers*. Shippensburg, Pa.: Burd Street Press, 1999.

Greenburg, Martin H., and Charles G. Waugh, editors. *The Price of Freedom: Slavery and the Civil War*. Vol. 1, *The Demise of Slavery*. Nashville: Cumberland House, 2000.

Greene, John T., editor. *The Ewing Family Civil War Letters*. East Lansing: Michigan State Univ. Press, 1994.

Greenwell, Dale. *The Third Mississippi Regiment—C.S.A.* Pascagoula, Miss.: Lewis Printing Services, 1972.

Grimsley, Mark. *The Hard Hand of War: Union Military Policy Toward Southern Civilians, 1861–1865*. New York: Cambridge Univ. Pres, 1995.

Grimsley, Mark, and Todd D. Miller, editors. *The Union Must Stand: The Civil War Diary of John Quincy Adams Campbell, Fifth Iowa Volunteer Infantry*. Knoxville: Univ. of Tennessee Press, 2000.

Groce, W. Todd. *Mountain Rebels: East Tennessee Confederates and the Civil War*. Knoxville: Univ. of Tennessee Press, 1999.

Groom, Winston. *Shrouds of Glory: From Atlanta to Nashville: The Last Great Campaign of the Civil War*. New York: Atlantic Monthly Press, 1995.

Haas, Garland A. *To the Mountain of Fire and Beyond: The Fifty-Third Indiana Regiment from Corinth to Glory.* Carmel: Guild Press of Indiana, 1997.

Hackemeyer, Kurt H., editor. *To Rescue My Native Land: The Civil War Letters of William T. Shepherd, First Illinois Light Artillery.* Knoxville: Univ. of Tennessee Press, 2005.

Hafendorfer, Kenneth A. *Nathan Bedford Forrest: The Distant Storm: The Murfreesboro Raid of July 13, 1862.* Louisville: K. H. Press, 1997.

Hale, Douglas. *The Third Texas Cavalry in the Civil War.* Norman: Univ. of Oklahoma Press, 1993.

Harrison, Lowell H. *The Civil War in Kentucky.* Lexington: Univ. Press of Kentucky, 1975.

———. *Lincoln of Kentucky.* Lexington: Univ. Press of Kentucky, 2000.

Harrison, Lowell H., and James C. Klotter. *A New History of Kentucky.* Lexington: Univ. Press of Kentucky, 1997.

Hattaway, Herman. *General Stephen D. Lee.* Jackson: Univ. Press of Mississippi, 1976.

Haughton, Andrew. *Training, Tactics and Leadership in the Confederate Army of Tennessee: Seeds of Failure.* London: Frank Cass, 2000.

Hay, Thomas Robson. *Hood's Tennessee Campaign.* New York: Walter Neale, 1929. Reprint, Dayton, Ohio: Morningside Bookshop, 1976.

———, editor. *Pat Cleburne: Stonewall Jackson of the West.* Jackson, Tenn.: McCowat-Mercer Press, 1958.

Head, James Louis. *The Atonement of John Brooks: The Story of the True Johnny "Reb" Who Did Not Come Marching Home.* Geneva, Fla.: Heritage Press, 2001.

Heleniak, Roman J., and Lawrence L. Hewitt, editors. *Leadership During the Civil War.* Themes in Honor of T. Harry Williams. Shippensburg, Pa.: White Mane Publishing, 1992.

Heller, Charles E. *Portrait of An Abolitionist: A Biography of George Luther Stearns, 1809–1867.* Westport, Conn.: Greenwood, 1996.

Henderson, Mary Bess McCain, Evelyn Janet McCain Young, and Anna Irene McCain Nahelhoferu. *Dear Eliza . . . : The Letters of Mitchel Andrew Thompson, May 1862–August 1864.* Ames, Iowa: Carter Press, 1976.

Henry, J. Milton. *Land Between the Rivers.* Paducah, Ky.: Taylor Publishing, 1977.

Henry, Robert Selph, editor. *As They Saw Forrest: Some Recollections and Comments of Contemporaries.* Jackson, Tenn.: McCowat-Mercer Press, 1987.

———. *"First with the Most" Forrest.* Indianapolis: Bobbs-Merrill, 1944.

Herr, Kincaid. *The Louisville and Nashville Railroad, 1850–1963.* Louisville, Ky.: L&N Publications Relations Department, 1964.

Hesseltine, William B., editor. *Dr. J. G. M. Ramsey: Autobiography and Letters.* Nashville: Tennessee Historical Commission, 1954.

Higgs, David N. *Nathan Bedford Forrest and the Battle of Johnsonville.* Nashville: Tennessee Historical Commission, 1976.

Holberton, William B. *Homeward Bound: The Demobilization of the Union and Confederate Armies, 1865–1866.* Mechanicsburg, Pa.: Stackpole Books, 2001.

Holmes, Henry McCall. *Diary of . . . Army of Tennessee Assistant Surgeon, Florida Troops, with Related Letters, Documents, etc.* State College, Miss.: n.p., 1968.

Holt, Dean. *American Military Cemeteries: A Comprehensive Illustrated Guide to the Hallowed Grounds of the United States, Including Cemeteries Overseas.* Jefferson, N.C.: McFarland & Co., 1992, 2009

Hoobler, James A. *Cities Under the Gun: Images of Occupied Nashville and Chattanooga.* Nashville: Rutledge Hill Press, 1986.

Hood, John Bell. *Advance and Retreat: Personal Experiences in the United States and Confederate States Armies.* New Orleans, Hood Orphans Memorial Fund, 1880. Reprint, Lincoln: Univ. of Nebraska Press, 1996.

Hood, Sam. *A Brief Defense of John Bell Hood and the 1864 Tennessee Campaign.* Ashland, Ky.: John Bell Hood Historical Society, n.d.

Hopkins, James F. *A History of the Hemp Industry in Kentucky.* Lexington: Univ. Press of Kentucky, 1951.

Horn, Stanley F. *The Army of Tennessee.* Indianapolis: Bobbs-Merrill, 1941.

———. *The Decisive Battle of Nashville.* Baton Rouge: Louisiana State Univ. Press, 1956.

Houghton, M. B., and W. R. Houghton. *Two Boys in the Civil War and After.* Montgomery, Ala.: Paragon, 1912.

Howard, Victor B. *Black Liberation in Kentucky: Emancipation and Freedom, 1862–1864.* Lexington: Univ. Press of Kentucky, 1983.

Howe, M. A. De Wolfe, editor. *Home Letters of General Sherman.* New York: Scribner's, 1909.

Howell, Alice Hunt Lynn. *Adventures of a Nineteenth-Century Medic: The Life and Times of Dr. William Hunt, 1810–1882.* Franklin, Tenn.: Hillsboro Pres, 1998.

Hughes, Nathaniel C. *Liddell's Record: St. John Richardson Liddell, Brigadier General, CSA, Staff Officer and Brigade Commander Army of Tennessee.* Dayton, Ohio: Morningside, 1985.

———, editor. *The Civil War Memoir of Philip Daingerfield Stephenson, D.D.* Conway, Ark.: UCA Press, 1995.

Hughes, Nathaniel C., with Connie Walton Moretti and James Michael Browne. *Brigadier General Tyree H. Bell, C.S.A.: Forrest's Fighting Lieutenant.* Knoxville: Univ. of Tennessee Pres, 2004.

Humphreys, Dickson, and Cheatham County Chamber of Commerce. *Tennessee Civil War Railroad: In Service to a Cause; Experience the Conflict.* Brochure. Ashland City, Tenn.: Waveryly, Dickson, n.d.

Hurst, Jack. *Nathan Bedford Forrest: A Biography*. New York: Alfred A. Knopf, 1993.

Inman, Myra. *A Diary of the Civil War in East Tennessee*. Edited by William R. Snell. Macon: Mercer Univ. Press, 2000.

Inscoe, John C., and Robert C. Kenzer, editors. *Enemies of the Country: New Perspectives on Unionists in the Civil War South*. Athens: Univ. of Georgia Press, 2001.

Jacobson, Eric A., and Richard A. Rupp. *For Cause and for Country: A Study of the Affair at Spring Hill and the Battle of Franklin*. Franklin, Tenn.: O'More Publishing 2006.

James, James R. *To See the Elephant: The Civil War Letters of John A. McKee (1861–1865)*. Leawood, Kans.: Leathers Publishing, 1998.

Jenkins, Kirk C. *The Battle Rages Higher: The Union's Fifteenth Kentucky Infantry*. Lexington: Univ. Press of Kentucky, 2003.

Joes, Anthony James. *Guerrilla Conflict Before the Cold War*. Westport, Conn.: Praeger, 1996.

Johnson, Leland K. *The Headwaters District: A History of the Pittsburgh District, U.S. Army Corps of Engineers*. Pittsburgh: U.S. Army Corps of Engineers, 1979.

Johnson, Mark W. *That Body of Brave Men: The U.S. Regular Infantry and the Civil War in the West*. New York: Da Capo Press, 2003.

Jones, Jenkin Lloyd. *An Artilleryman's Diary*. Madison: Wisconsin History Commission, Feb. 1914.

Jones, Mary Miles, and Leslie Jones Martin, editors. *The Gentle Rebel: The Civil War Letters of First Lt. William Harvey Berryhill, Co. D, Forty-Third, Mississippi Volunteers*. Yazoo City, Miss.: Sassafras Press, n.d.

Jones, Terry L., editor. *Campbell Brown's Civil War: With Ewell and the Army of Northern Virginia*. Baton Rouge: Louisiana State Univ. Press, 2001.

Jones, Wilmer L. *After the Thunder: Fourteen Men Who Shaped Post-Civil War America*. Dallas, Tex.: Taylor, 2000.

Jordan, Thomas, and J. P. Pryor. *The Campaigns of Lieut.-Gen. N. B. Forest and of Forrest's Cavalry*. New Orleans and New York, 1868. Reprint, Dayton, Ohio: Morningside Bookshop, 1977.

Joshi, S. T., and David E. Schultz, editors. *A Sole Survivor: Bits of Autobiography by Ambrose Bierce*. Knoxville: Univ. of Tennessee Press, 1998.

Joslyn, Muriel Phillips. *Charlotte's Boys: Civil War Letters of the Branch Family of Savannah*. Berryville, Va.: Rockbridge Publishing, 1996.

———, editor. *A Meteor Shining Brightly: Essays on Maj. Gen. Patrick R. Cleburne*. Milledgeville, Ga.: Terrill House, 1998.

Kaufmann, Greg, editor. *Stability Operations and State Building: Continuities and Contingencies*. Carlisle Barracks, Pa.: U.S. Army War College Strategic Studies Institute, 2008.

Keenan, Jerry. *Wilson's Cavalry Corps: Union Campaigns in the Western Theatre, October 1863 through Spring 1865*. Jefferson, N.C.: McFarland, 1998.

Kellogg, Mary E., compiler. *Army Life of an Illinois Soldier Including a Day-by-Day Record of Sherman's March to the Sea: Letters and Diary of Charles W. Wills*. Carbondale: Southern Illinois Univ. Press, 1996.

Kennedy, Francis H., editor. *The Civil War Battlefield Guide*. Boston: Houghton Mifflin, 1998.

Kionka, T. K. *Key Command: Ulysses S. Grant's District of Cairo*. Columbia: Univ. of Missouri Press, 2006.

Kirke, Edmund. *Down in Tennessee and Back by Way of Richmond*. New York: Carleton, 1864.

Kirkead, Elizabeth Shelby. *A History of Kentucky*. New York: American Book, 1896.

Kitchens, Ben Earl. *Gunboats and Cavalry: A History of Eastport, Mississippi*. Florence, Ala.: Thornwood Book Publishers, 1985.

Knight, James B. *The Battle of Franklin: When the Devil Had Full Possession of the Earth*. Charleston, S.C.: History Press, 2009.

Krug, Mark M., editor. *Mrs. Hill's Journal: Civil War Reminiscences*. Chicago: R. R. Donnelley & Sons, 1980.

Kwasny, Mark V. *Washington's Partisan War, 1775–1783*. Kent: Kent State Univ. Press, 1996.

Laine, J. Gary, and Morris M. Penny. *Law's Alabama Brigade in the War Between the Union and the Confederacy*. Shippensburg, Pa.: White Mane Publishing, 1996.

Laquer, Walter. *Guerrilla: A Historical and Critical Study*. Boston: Little, Brown, 1976.

Larimer, Charles F., editor. *Love and Valor: The Intimate Civil War Letters Between Captain Jacob and Emeline Ritner*. Western Spring, Ill.: Sigourney Press, 2000.

Lash, Jeffrey N. *Destroyer of the Iron Horse: General Joseph E. Johnston and Confederate Rail Transport, 1861–1865*. Kent: Kent State Univ. Press, 1991.

———. *A Politician Turned General: The Civil War Career of Stephen Augustus Hurlbut*. Kent: Kent State Univ. Press, 2003.

Lawson, Lewis A. *Wheeler's Last Raid*. Greenwood, Fla.: Penkeville Publishing, 1986.

Le Duc, William G. *Recollections of a Civil War Quartermaster*. St. Paul, Minn.: North Central Publishing, 1963.

Leeper, Wesley Thurman. *Rebels Valiant: Second Arkansas Mounted Rifles (Dismounted)*. Little Rock, Ark.: Pioneer Press, 1964.

Lepa, Jack H. *Breaking the Confederacy: The Georgia and Tennessee Campaigns of 1864*. Jefferson, N.C.: McFarland, 2005.

Leslie, Edward E. *The Devil Knows How to Ride: The True Story of William Clarke Quantrill and His Confederate Raiders.* New York: Random House, 1996.

Lewis, Lloyd. *Sherman: Fighting Prophet.* New York: Harcourt, Brace, 1932.

Lewis, Richard. *Camp Life of a Confederate Boy, of Bratton's Brigade, Longstreet's Corps, C.S.A.* Charleston, S.C.: News and Courier Book Presses, 1883.

Linden, Glenn, and Virginia Linden, editors. *Disunion, War, Defeat and Recovery in Alabama: The Journal of Augustus Benners, 1850–1885.* Macon: Mercer Univ. Press, 2007.

Lindsley, Margaret. *"Maggie!": Maggie Lindsley's Journal, Nashville, Tennessee, 1864, Washington, D.C., 1865.* Southport, Conn.: Muriel Davies Mackenzie, 1977.

Logsdon, David R., editor and compiler. *Eyewitnesses at the Battle of Franklin.* Nashville: Kettle Mills Press, 1996.

Longacre, Edward G. *From Union Stars to Top Hat: A Biography of the Extraordinary General James Harrison Wilson.* Harrisburg, Pa.: Stackpole Books, 1972.

———. *Mounted Raids of the Civil War.* South Brunswick, N.J.: A. S. Barnes, 1975.

———. *A Soldier to the Last: Maj. Gen. Joseph Wheeler in Blue and Gray.* Washington, D.C.: Potomac Books, 2007.

Longstreet, James. *From Manassas to Appomattox: Memoirs of the Civil War in America.* Philadelphia: J. B. Lippincott, 1895.

Losson, Christopher. *Tennessee's Forgotten Warriors: Frank Cheatham and His Confederate Division.* Knoxville: Univ. of Tennessee Press, 1989.

Lovett, Bobby L. *The African-American History of Nashville, Tennessee, 1780–1930: Elites and Dilemmas.* Fayetteville: Univ. of Arkansas Press, 1999.

Loving, Jerome M., editor. *Civil War Letters of George Washington Whitman.* Durham, N.C.: Duke Univ. Press, 1975.

Lowery, Thomas P. *The Story the Soldiers Wouldn't Tell: Sex in the Civil War.* Harrisburg, Pa.: Stackpole Books, 1994.

Lundberg, John R. *The Finishing Stroke: Texas in the 1864 Tennessee Campaign.* Abilene, Tex.: McWhiney Foundation Press, 2002.

Lytle, Andrew Nelson. *Bedford Forrest and His Critter Company.* New York: Minton, Balch, 1931.

Mack, Charles R., and Henry H. Lesesne. *Francis Lieber and the Culture of the Mind.* Columbia: Univ. of South Carolina Press, 2005.

Mackey, Robert R. *The Uncivil War: Irregular Warfare in the Upper South, 1861–1865.* Norman: Univ. of Oklahoma Press, 2004.

Magee, Benjamin F. *History of the Seventy-Second Indiana: Wilder's Lightning Brigade.* LaFayette, Ind.: S. Vater, 1882. Reprint, Huntington, W.Va.: Blue Acorn Press, 1992.

Major, Duncan J., and Robert S. Fitch. *Supply of Sherman's Army during the Atlanta Campaign*. Fort Leavenworth, Kans: Army Service School Press, 1911, and United States Army Command and General Staff College, 1978.

Maness, Lonnie E. *Untutored Genius: The Military Career of General Nathan Bedford Forrest*. Oxford, Miss.: Guild Bindery Press, 1990.

Mannis, Jedediah, and Galen R. Wilson, editors. *Bound to Be a Soldier: The Letters of Private James T. Miller, One Hundred and Eleventh Pennsylvania Infantry, 1861–1864*. Knoxville: Univ. of Tennessee Press, 2001.

Marshall, Anne E. *Creating a Confederate Kentucky: The Lost Cause and Civil War Memory in a Border Stare*. Chapel Hill: Univ. of North Carolina Press, 2010.

Marshall, Jeffrey D., editor. *A War of the People: Vermont Civil War Letters*. Hanover, N.H.: Univ. Press of New England, 1999.

Marszalek, John F. *Commander of All Lincoln's Armies: A Life of General Henry W. Halleck*. Cambridge: Belknap Press of Harvard Univ. Press, 2004.

———. *Sherman: A Soldier's Passion for Order*. New York: Free Press, 1993.

Maslowski, Peter. *Treason Must Be Made Odious: Military Occupation and Wartime Reconstruction in Nashville, Tennessee, 1862–65*. Millwood, N.Y.: KTO Press, 1978.

Mason, T. David. *Sustaining the Peace After Civil War*. Carlisle Barracks, Pa.: U.S. Army War College Strategic Studies Institute, 2007.

Massey, Mary Elizabeth. *Refugee Life in the Confederacy*. Baton Rouge: Louisiana State Univ. Press, 1964.

Massey, Ross. *Nashville Battlefield Guide*. Nashville: Tenth Amendment Publishing, 2007.

Mathias, Frank E., editor. *Incidents and Experiences in the Life of Thomas W. Parsons from 1826 to 1900*. Lexington: Univ. Press of Kentucky, 1975.

Matthews, Gary Robert. *Basil Wilson Duke, CSA: The Right Man in the Right Place*. Lexington: Univ. Press of Kentucky, 2005.

Mattis, Kenneth C. *The Historical Atlas of the Congresses of the Confederate States of America, 1861–1865*. New York: Simon and Schuster, 1994.

Mays, Thomas D. *Cumberland Blood: Champ Ferguson's Civil War*. Carbondale: Southern Illinois Univ. Press, 2008.

McCaffrey, James M. *This Band of Heroes: Granbury's Texas Brigade, C.S.A.* College Station: Texas A&M Univ. Press, 1996.

McDonough, James Lee. *Nashville: The Western Confederacy's Final Gamble*. Knoxville: Univ. of Tennessee Press, 2004.

McDonough, James Lee, and Thomas L. Connelly. *Five Tragic Hours: The Battle of Franklin*. Knoxville: Univ. of Tennessee Press, 1983.

McDowell, Robert Emmett. *City of Conflict: Louisville in the Civil War, 1861–1865*. Louisville, Ky.: Louisville Civil War Round Table, 1962.

McKenney, Tom C. *Jack Hinson's One-Man War: A Civil War Sniper*. Gretna, La.: Pelican, 2009.

McKenzie, Robert Tracy. *Lincolnites and Rebels: A Divided Town in the American Civil War*. New York: Oxford Univ. Press, 2006.

———. *One South or Many? Plantation Belt and Upcountry in Civil War-Era Tennessee*. New York: Cambridge Univ. Press, 1994.

McKitrich, Eric L. *Andrew Johnson and Reconstruction*. Chicago: Univ. of Chicago Press, 1960.

McKnight, Brian D. *Contested Borderland: The Civil War in Appalachian Kentucky and Virginia*. Lexington: Univ. Press of Kentucky, 2006.

McKnight, W. Mark. *Blue Bonnets O'er the Border: The Seventy-Ninth New York Cameron Highlanders*. Shippensburg, Pa.: White Mane Publishing, 1998.

McMillan, Malcolm C., editor. *The Alabama Confederate Reader*. Tuscaloosa: Univ. of Alabama Press, 1963.

McMurry, Richard M. *Atlanta 1864: Last Chance for the Confederacy*. Lincoln: Univ. of Nebraska Press, 2000.

———. *John Bell Hood and the War for Southern Independence*. Lexington: Univ. Press of Kentucky, 1982.

Meacham, Charles Mayfield. *A History of Christian County, Kentucky, from Oxcart to Airplane*. Nashville: Marshall & Bruce, 1930.

Mendoza, Alexander. *Confederate Struggle for Command: General James Longstreet and the First Corps in the West*. College Station: Texas A&M Univ. Press, 2008.

Meriwether, Elizabeth Avery. *Recollections of 92 Years: 1824–1916*. McLean, Va.: EPM, 1994.

Metropolitan Historical Commission and Tennessee Historical Society. *The Civil War Battle of Nashville: A Self-guiding Driving Tour*. Nashville, 1983.

Miller, Brian Craig. *John Bell Hood and the Fight for Civil War Memory*. Knoxville: Univ. of Tennessee Press, 2010.

Miller, Penny M. *Kentucky Politics and Government: Do We Stand United?* Lincoln: Univ. of Nebraska Press, 1994.

Montcastle, Clay. *Punitive War: Confederate Guerrillas and Union Reprisals*. Lawrence: Univ. Press of Kansas, 2009.

Montgomery, George F., Jr., editor. *Georgia Sharpshooter: The Civil War Diary and Letters of William Rhadamanthus Montgomery, 1839–1906*. Macon: Mercer Univ. Press, 1997.

Morrison, Marion. *A History of the Ninth Regiment Illinois Volunteer Infantry, with the Regimental Roster*. Carbondale: Southern Illinois Univ. Press, 1997.

Morton, John Watson. *The Artillery of Nathan Bedford Forrest's Cavalry*. Nashville: Publishing House of the M.E. Church, South, 1909. Reprint, Oxford, Miss.: Guild Bindery Press, 1992.

Moseley, Ronald H., editor. *The Stilwell Letters: A Georgian in Longstreet's Corps, Army of Northern Virginia*. Macon: Mercer Univ. Press, 2002.

Mosgrove, George Dallas. *Kentucky Cavaliers in Dixie: Reminiscences of a Confederate Cavalryman*. Louisville, Ky.: Courier-Journal Job Printing, 1895. Reprint, Lincoln: Univ. of Nebraska Press, 1999.

Moyar, Mark. *A Question of Command: Counterinsurgency from the Civil War to Iraq*. New Haven: Yale Univ. Press, 2009.

Nashville, Tennessee, Chamber of Commerce. Special Committee. *Report of . . . on the Advantages of Nashville as a Suitable Place for a Permanent Army Post and Encampment*. Nashville: Marshall & Bruce, 1898.

Neff, Robert O. *Tennessee's Battered Brigadier (The Life of General Joseph B. Palmer)*. Edited by Martha O. Hewes. Nashville: Historic Travelers' Rest, 1988.

Neff, Robert O., and Edith Elizabeth Pollitz. *The Bride and the Bandit: The Story of Mattie Ready of Murfreesboro, Tennessee, Wartime Bride of General John Hunt Morgan*. Evansville, Ind.: Evansville Bindery, 1998.

Neff, Stephen C. *Justice in Blue and Gray: A Legal History of the Civil War*. Cambridge, Mass.: Harvard Univ. Press, 2010.

Newton, Steven H. *Lost for the Cause: The Confederate Army in 1864*. Mason City, Iowa: Savas Publishing, 2000.

Noe, Kenneth W., editor. *A Southern Boy in Blue: The Memoir of Marcus Woodcock, Ninth Kentucky Infantry (U.S.A.)*. Knoxville: Univ. of Tennessee Press, 1996.

Noe, Kenneth W., and Shannon H. Wilson, editors. *The Civil War in Appalachia: Collected Essays*. Knoxville: Univ. of Tennessee Press, 1997.

Norton, Anne. *Alternative Americas: A Reading of Antebellum Political Culture*. Chicago: Univ. of Chicago Press, 1986.

O'Brien, Sean Michael. *Mountain Partisans: Guerrilla Warfare in the Southern Appalachians, 1861–1865*. Westport, Conn.: Praeger, 1999.

Oeffinger, John C., editor. *A Soldier's General: The Civil War Letters of Major General Lafayette McLaws*. Chapel Hill: Univ. of North Carolina Press, 2002.

Oliver, Robert T., editor. *A Faithful Heart: The Journals of Emmala Reed, 1865 and 1866*. Columbia: Univ. of South Carolina Press, 2004.

Olmstead, Charles H. *The Memoirs of Charles H. Olmstead*. Edited by Lilla M. Hawes. Collection of Georgia Historical Society, vol. 14. Savannah: Georgia Historical Society, 1964.

Otto, John Solomon. *Southern Agriculture During the Civil War Era, 1860–1880*. Westport, Conn.: Greenwood Press, 1994.

Overmyer, Jack K. *A Stupendous Effort: The Eighty-Seventh Indiana in the War of the Rebellion*. Bloomington: Indiana Univ. Press, 1997.

Paludan, Phillip Shaw. *Victims: A True Story of the Civil War*. Knoxville: Univ. of Tennessee Press, 1981.

Parrish, Peter. *The American Civil War.* New York: Holmes and Meier, 1983.

Patton, James Welch. *Unionism and Reconstruction in Tennessee.* Chapel Hill: Univ. of North Carolina Press, 1934.

Phillips, Jason. *Diehard Rebels: The Confederate Culture of Invincibility.* Athens: Univ. of Georgia Press, 2007.

Pickenpaugh, Roger. *Rescue by Rail: Troop Transfer and the Civil War in the West, 1863.* Lincoln: Univ. of Nebraska Press, 1998.

Piston, William Garrett. *Carter's Raid: An Episode of the Civil War in East Tennessee.* Johnson City, Tenn.: Overmountain Press, 1989.

———. *Lee's Tarnished Lieutenant: James Longstreet and His Place in Southern History.* Athens: Univ. of Georgia Press, 1987.

Polley, J. B. *A Soldier's Letters to Charming Nellie.* New York: Neale, 1908.

Porter, David D. *The Naval History of the Civil War.* New York: Sherman Publishing, 1886.

Porter, Horace. *Campaigning with Grant.* New York: Century, 1897.

Porter, Lorle. *A People Set Apart: Scotch-Irish in Eastern Ohio: From the Folks of the Yough to the Killing Fields of Georgia.* Zanesville, Ohio: New Concord Press, 1998.

Potter, Jerry O. *The* Sultana *Tragedy: America's Greatest Maritime Disaster.* Gretna, La.: Pelican, 1997.

Priest, John Michael, editor. *Stephen Elliott Welch of the Hampton Legion.* Shippensburg, Pa.: Burd Street Press, 1994.

Puck, Susan T., editor. *Sacrifice at Vicksburg: Letters from the Front.* Shippensburg, Pa.: Burd Street Press, 1997.

Pula, James S. *For Liberty and Justice: The Life and Times of Wladimir Krzyzanowski.* Chicago: Polish American Congress Charitable Foundation, 1978.

Quaife, Milo M., editor. *From the Cannon's Mouth: The Civil War Letters of General Alpheus S. Williams.* Lincoln: Univ. of Nebraska Press, 2005.

Quint, Alonzo H. *The Potomac and the Rapidan: Army Notes, 1861–3.* Boston: Crosby and Nichols, 1864.

Raab, Steven S., editor. *With the Third Wisconsin Badgers: The Living Experience of the Civil War Through the Journals of Van R. Willard.* Mechanicsburg, Pa.: Stackpole Books, 1994.

Radley, Kenneth. *Rebel Watchdog: The Confederate States Army Provost Guard.* Baton Rouge: Louisiana State Univ. Press, 1989.

Rafuse, Ethan S., editor. *The American Civil War.* Burlington, Vt.: Ashgate, 2005.

Ramage, James A. *Rebel Raider: The Life of General John Hunt Morgan.* Lexington: Univ. Press of Kentucky, 1986.

Ratchford, James Wylie. *Memoirs of a Confederate Staff Officer: From Bethel to Bentonville.* Edited by Evelyn Ratchford Sieburg. Shippensburg, Pa.: White Mane Publishing, 1998.

Reinhart, Joseph R., editor and translator. *Two Germans in the Civil War: The Diary of John Daeuble and the Letters of Gottfried Rentschler, Sixth Kentucky Volunteer Infantry.* Knoxville: Univ. of Tennessee Press, 2004.

Reyburn, Philip J., and Terry L. Wilson, editors. *"Jottings from Dixie": The Civil War Dispatches of Sergeant Major Stephen F. Fleharty, U.S.A.* Baton Rouge: Louisiana State Univ. Press, 1999.

Rice, Ralsa C. *Yankee Tigers: Through the Civil War with the One Hundred and Twenty-Fifth Ohio.* Edited by Richard A. Baumgartner and Larry M. Strayer. Huntington, W.Va.: Blue Acorn Press, 1992.

Richardson, Frank. *From Sunrise to Sunset: Reminiscence.* Bristol, Tenn.: King Printing, 1910.

Robertson, James I., Jr., and Richard M. McMurray, editors. *Rank and File: Civil War Essays in Honor of Bell I. Wiley.* San Rafael, Calif.: Presidio, 1996.

Robertson, John E. L. *Paducah, 1830–1890: A Sesquicentennial History.* Paducah, Ky.: By the author, 1980.

Robinson, Armstead L. *Bitter Fruits of Bondage: The Demise of Slavery and the Collapse of the Confederacy, 1861–1865.* Charlottesville: Univ. of Virginia Press, 2005.

Rollins, Richard, editor. *Black Southerners in Gray: Essays on Afro-Americans in Confederate Armies.* Redondo Beach, Calif.: Rank and File Publications, 1994.

Rosenburg, R. B., editor. *"For the Sake of My Country": The Diary of Col. W. W. Ward, 9th Tennessee Cavalry, Morgan's Brigade, C.S.A.* Murfreesboro, Tenn.: Southern Heritage Press, 1992.

Rowell, John W. *Yankee Artilleryman: Through the Civil War with Eli Lilly's Indiana Battery.* Knoxville: Univ. of Tennessee Press, 1975.

———. *Yankee Cavalrymen: Through the Civil War with the Ninth Pennsylvania Cavalry.* Knoxville: Univ. of Tennessee Press, 1971.

Royster, Charles. *The Destructive War: William Tecumseh Sherman, Stonewall Jackson, and the Americans.* New York: Alfred A. Knopf, 1991.

Salecker, Gene Eric. *Disaster on the Mississippi: The Sultana Explosion, April 27, 1865.* Annapolis, Md.: Naval Institute Press, 1996.

Sauers, Richard A., editor. *The Civil War Journal of Colonel William J. Bolton, Fifty-First Pennsylvania, April 20, 1861–August 2, 1865.* Conshohocken, Pa.: Combined Publishing, 2000.

Scaife, William R. *Hood's Campaign for Tennessee.* Atlanta: By the author, 1986.

Schofield, John M. *Forty-Six Years in the Army.* New York: Century, 1897. Reprint, Norman: Univ. of Oklahoma Press, 1998.

Schultz, Duane. *Quantrill's War: The Life and Times of William Clarke Quantrill, 1837–1865.* New York: St. Martin's, 1996.

Scott, Samuel W., and Samuel P. Angel. *History of the Thirteenth Regiment Tennessee Volunteer Cavalry.* Blountville, Tenn.: Tony Marion, 1973. Reprint, Philadelphia: P. W. Ziegler, 1903.

Scott, William Forse. *The Story of a Cavalry Regiment: The Career of the Fourth Iowa Veteran Volunteers from Kansas to Georgia, 1861–1865.* New York: G. P. Putnam's Sons, 1893.

Sears, Richard D. *Camp Nelson, Kentucky: A Civil War History.* Lexington: Univ. Press of Kentucky, 2002.

Sears, Stephen W., editor. *For Country, Cause and Leader: The Civil War Journal of Charles B. Haydon.* New York: Ticknor & Fields, 1993.

Sefton, James E. *Andrew Johnson and the Uses of Constitutional Power.* Boston: Little, Brown, 1980.

———. *The United States Army and Reconstruction, 1865–1877.* Westport, Conn.: Greenwood, 1967.

Sensing, Thurman. *Champ Ferguson: Confederate Guerrilla.* Nashville: Vanderbilt Univ. Press, 1942.

Sessarego, Alan. *Letters Home III, Camp Life and Battles: Original Letters and Photographs from America's Civil War.* Gettysburg, Pa.: By the author, 2000.

Severance, Ben H. *Tennessee's Radical Army: The State Guard and Its Role in Reconstruction, 1867–1869.* Knoxville: Univ. of Tennessee Press, 2005.

Seymour, Digby Gordon. *Divided Loyalties: Fort Sanders and the Civil War in East Tennessee.* Knoxville: Univ. of Tennessee Press, 1963. Reprint, Knoxville: East Tennessee Historical Society, 2002.

Shaler, Nathaniel Southgate. *The Autobiography of Nathaniel Southgate Shaler with a Supplementary Memoir by His Wife.* Boston: Houghton Mifflin, 1909.

Sickles, John. *The Legends of Sue Mundy and One Armed Berry: Confederate Guerrillas.* Merrillville, Ind.: Heritage Press, 1999.

Siddali, Silvana R. *From Property to Person: Slavery and the Confiscation Acts, 1861–1862.* Baton Rouge: Louisiana State Univ. Press, 2005.

Sievers, Harry J., S.J. *Benjamin Harrison: Hoosier Warrior, Through the Civil War Years, 1833–1865.* Vol. 1. 1952. Reprint, New York: Univ. Publishers, 1960.

Silverstone, Paul H. *Warships of the Civil War Navies.* Annapolis, Md.: Naval Institute Press, 1989.

Simon, John Y., editor. *The Papers of Ulysses S. Grant.* 31 vols. Carbondale: Southern Illinois Univ. Press, 1967–2009.

Simpson, Brooks D., and Jean V. Berlin. *Sherman's Civil War: Selected Correspondence of William T. Sherman, 1860–1865.* Chapel Hill: Univ. of North Carolina Press, 1999.

Simpson, Brooks D., LeRoy P. Graf, and John Muldowny, editors. *Advice After Appomattox: Letters to Andrew Johnson, 1865–1866.* Special vol. 1 of the *Papers of Andrew Johnson.* Knoxville: Univ. of Tennessee Press, 1987.

Skoch, George, and Mark W. Perkins, editors. *Lone Star Confederate: A Gallant and Good Soldier of the Fifth Texas Infantry.* College Station: Texas A&M Univ. Press, 2003.

Smith, David C. *Campaign to Nowhere: The Results of General Longstreet's Move into Upper East Tennessee*. Strawberry Plains, Tenn.: Strawberry Plains Press, 1999.

———. *Lilly in the Valley: Civil War at Mossy Creek*. Rogersville, Tenn.: East Tennessee Printing, 1986.

Smith, John David, editor. *Black Soldiers in Blue: African American Troops in the Civil War Era*. Chapel Hill: Univ. of North Carolina Press, 2002.

Smith, John David, and William Cooper Jr., editors. *A Union Woman in Civil War Kentucky: The Diary of Frances Peter*. Lexington: Univ. Press of Kentucky, 2000.

Smith, Margaret Lyons. *Miss Nan: Beloved Rebel*. Johnson City, Tenn.: Overmountain Press, 1986.

Smith, Samuel D., "Excavation Data for Civil War Era Military Sites In Middle Tennessee." In *Look to the Earth: Historical Archaeology and the American Civil War,* edited by Clarence R. Geier Jr. and Susan E. Winter, 60–75. Knoxville: Univ. of Tennessee Press, 1994.

Smith, Timothy B. *A Chickamauga Memorial: The Establishment of America's First Civil War National Military Park*. Knoxville: Univ. of Tennessee Press, 2009.

Snepp, Daniel W. *Evansville's Channels of Trade and the Secession Movement, 1850–1865*. Indianapolis: Indiana Historical Society, 1928.

Sorrell, Moxley G. *At the Right Hand of Longstreet: A Confederate Staff Officer*. Edited by Peter S. Carmichael. Lincoln: Univ. of Nebraska Press, 1999.

Speed, Thomas. *The Union Cause in Kentucky, 1860–1865*. New York: G. P. Putnam's Sons, 1907.

Starr, Stephen Z. *Jennison's Jayhawkers: A Civil War Cavalry Regiment and Its Commander*. Baton Rouge: Louisiana State Univ. Press, 1973.

———. *The Union Cavalry in the Civil War*. Vol. 3, *The War in the West, 1861–1865*. Baton Rouge: Louisiana State Univ. Press, 1985.

Steele, Matthew Forney. *American Campaigns*. Washington, D.C.: Infantry Journal, 1931.

Steenburn, Donald. *The Man Called Gurley: N. B. Forest's Notorious Captain*. Meridianville, Ala.: Elk River Press, 1999.

———. *Silent Echoes of Johnsonville: Nathan B. Forrest, Rebel Cavalry and Yankee Gunboats*. N.P.: By the author, 1994.

Sterling, Ada, editor. *A Belle of the Fifties: Memoirs of Mrs. Clay, of Alabama, Covering Social and Political Lie in Washington and the South, 1853–66*. New York: Doubleday, Page, 1904.

Stevens, Peter F. *Rebels in Blue: The Story of Keith and Malinda Blalock*. Dallas: Taylor, 2000.

Stockdale, Paul H. *The Death of an Army: The Battle of Nashville & Hood's Retreat*. Murfreesboro, Tenn.: Southern Heritage Press, 1992.

Stocker, Jeffrey D., editor. *From Huntsville to Appomattox: R. T. Coles's History of the Fourth Regiment, Alabama Volunteer Infantry, C.S.A., Army of Northern Virginia.* Knoxville: Univ. of Tennessee Press, 1996.

Stone, Richard G., Jr. *A Brittle Sword: The Kentucky Militia, 1776–1912.* Lexington: Univ. Press of Kentucky, 1977.

Storey, Margaret M. *Loyalty and Loss: Alabama's Unionists in the Civil War and Reconstruction.* Baton Rouge: Louisiana State Univ. Press, 2004.

Styple, William B., editor. *Writing and Fighting the Civil War: Soldier Correspondence to the New York Sunday Mercury.* Kearny, N.J.: Belle Grove, 2000.

Sullivan, David M. *The United States Marine Corps in the Civil War: The Third Year.* Shippensburg, Pa.: White Mane Publishing, 1998.

Sunderland, Glenn W. *Five Days to Glory.* South Brunswick, N.J.: A. S. Barnes, 1970.

Sutherland, Daniel E. *A Savage Conflict: The Decisive Role of Guerrillas in the American Civil War.* Chapel Hill: Univ. of North Carolina Press, 2009.

———, editor. *Guerrillas, Unionists, and Violence on the Confederate Home Front.* Fayetteville: Univ. of Arkansas Press, 1999.

———. *A Very Violent Rebel: The Civil War Diary of Ellen Renshaw House.* Knoxville: Univ. of Tennessee Press, 1996.

Sword, Wiley. *Embrace an Angry Wind: The Confederacy's Last Hurrah: Spring Hill, Franklin, and Nashville.* New York: Harper Collins, 1992.

Symonds, Craig L. *Joseph E. Johnston: A Civil War Biography.* New York: W. W. Norton, 1992.

———. *Stonewall of the West: Patrick Cleburne and the Civil War.* Lawrence: Univ. Press of Kansas 1997.

Tanner, Robert G. *Retreat to Victory? Confederate Strategy Reconsidered.* Wilmington, Del.: Scholarly Resources, 2001.

Tapp, Hambleton, and James C. Klotter. *Kentucky: Decades of Discord, 1865–1900.* Frankfort: Kentucky Historical Society, 1977.

Tarrant, E. *The Wild Riders of the First Kentucky Cavalry.* Louisville: Carothers Press, 1894.

Taylor, Benjamin F. *Mission Ridge and Lookout Mountain with Pictures of Life in Camp and Field.* New York: D. Appleton, 1872.

———. *Pictures of Life in Camp and Field.* Chicago: S. C. Griggs, 1888.

Taylor, Paul. *Orlando M. Poe: Civil War General and Great Lakes Engineer.* Kent, Ohio: Kent State Univ. Press, 2009.

Taylor, Richard. *Destruction and Reconstruction: Personal Experiences of the Late War.* New York: D. Appleton, 1879.

Temple, Oliver P. *East Tennessee and the Civil War.* 1899. Reprint, Johnson City, Tenn.: Overmountain Press, 1995.

Tennessee Civil War Centennial Commission. *Tennesseans in the Civil War: A Military History of Confederate and Union Units with Available Rosters of Personnel, Part I.* Nashville: Tennessee Civil War Centennial Commission, 1964.

Tennessee Historical Commission and Tennessee Historical Society. *Tennessee Old and New: Sesquicentennial Edition, 1796–1946.* Nashville: Tennessee Historical Commission and Tennessee Historical Society, 1946.

Tenney, W. J. *The Military and Naval History of the Rebellion in the United States.* New York: D. Appleton, 1866.

Thatcher, Marshall P. *A Hundred Battles in the West: St. Louis to Atlanta, 1861–65: The Second Michigan Cavalry.* Detroit: By the author, 1884.

Thomsen, Brian M., editor. *Shadows of Blue and Gray: The Civil War Writings of Ambrose Bierce.* New York: Tom Doherty Associates, 2002.

Thornton, Leland W. *When Gallantry Was Commonplace: The History of the Michigan Eleventh Volunteer Infantry, 1861–1864.* New York: Peter Lang, 1991.

Thorpe, George C. *Pure Logistics: The Science of War Preparation.* Washington, D.C.: National Defense Univ. Press, 1986.

Tierney, John J., Jr. *Chasing Ghosts: Unconventional Warfare in American History.* Washington, D.C.: Potomac Books, 2006.

Tower, R. Lockwood, editor. *A Carolinian Goes to War: The Civil War Narrative of Arthur Middleton Manigault, Brigadier General, C.S.A.* Columbia: Univ. of South Carolina Press, 1983.

Trelease, Allen W. *White Terror: The Ku Klux Klan Conspiracy and Southern Reconstruction.* Baton Rouge: Louisiana State Univ. Press, 1971.

Troutman, Richard, editor. *The Heavens Are Weeping: The Diaries of George R. Browder, 1852–1886.* Grand Rapids, Mich.: Zondervan, 1987.

Trowbridge, John Townsend. *The Desolate South, 1865–1866: A Picture of the Battlefields of the Devastated Confederacy.* Edited by Gordon Carroll. New York: Duell, Sloan and Pearce; Boston: Little, Brown, 1956.

———. *The South: A Tour of Its Battlefields and Ruined Cities, a Journey through the Desolated States, and Talks with the People.* Edited by J. J. Segars. 1867. Reprint, Macon: Mercer Univ. Press, 2006.

Trudeau, Noah Andre. *Like Men of War: Black Troops in the Civil War, 1862–1865.* New York: Little Brown, 1998.

———. *Out of the Storm: The End of the Civil War, April–June 1865.* Boston: Little Brown, 1994.

———. *Southern Storm: Sherman's March to the Sea.* New York: Harper Collins, 2008.

Tunnell, Ted., editor. *Carpetbagger from Vermont: The Autobiography of Marshall Harvey Twitchell.* Baton Rouge: Louisiana State Univ. Press, 1989.

Turner, Nat S., III., editor. *A Southern Soldier's Letters Home: The Civil War Letters of Samuel A. Burney, Cobb's Georgia Legion, Army of Northern Virginia.* Macon: Mercer Univ. Press, 2002.

Urwin, Gregory J. W., editor. *Black Flag Over Dixie: Racial Atrocities and Reprisals in the Civil War.* Carbondale: Southern Illinois Univ. Press, 2004.

485

Vale, Joseph. *Minty and the Cavalry: A History of Cavalry Campaigns in the Western Armies*. Harrisburg, Pa.: Edwin K. Meyers, 1886.

Van Eldik, James. *From the Flame of Battle to the Fiery Cross: The Third Tennessee Infantry with Complete Roster*. Los Cruces, N.M.: Yucca Tree Press, 2001.

Van West, Carroll, editor. *Tennessee History: The Land, the People and the Culture*. Knoxville: Univ. of Tennessee Press, 1998.

Virdin, Donald Odell, editor and compiler. *The Civil War Correspondence of Judge Thomas Goldsborough Odell*. Bowie, Md.: Heritage Books, 1992.

Wakelyn, Jon L., editor. *Southern Unionist Pamphlets and the Civil War*. Columbia: Univ. of Missouri Press, 1999.

Walker, Scott. *Hell's Broke Loose in Georgia: Survival in a Civil War Regiment*. Athens: Univ. of Georgia Press, 2005.

Walton, William, editor. *A Civil War Courtship: The Letters of Edwin Weller from Antietam to Atlanta*. Garden City, N.Y.: Doubleday, 1980.

Ward, Andrew. *River Run Red: The Fort Pillow Massacre in the American Civil War*. New York: Viking Penguin, 2005.

Waring, George E., Jr. *Whip and Spur*. New York: Doubleday and McClure, 1897.

Warwick, Rick., compiler. *Freedom and Work in the Reconstruction Era: The Freedmen's Bureau Labor Contracts of Williamson County, Tennessee*. Murfreesboro: Heritage Foundation of Franklin and Williamson County, Tennessee, 2006.

———. *Williamson County: The Civil War Years Revealed Through Letters, Diaries and Memoirs*. Murfreesboro, Tenn.: Heritage Foundation of Franklin and Williamson County, 2006.

Washburn, Wiley A. *Memoirs of the Civil War*. Lufkin, Tex.: Lufkin, 2000.

Waters, Charles M., author and editor. *Historic Clarksville: The Bicentennial Story, 1784–1984*. Clarksville, Tenn.: Historic Clarksville Publishing, 1983.

Watkins, Sam. *Co. "Aytch": Maury Grays, First Tennessee Regiment; or, A Side Show of the Big Show and Other Sketches*. Edited by Ruth Hill Fulton McAllister. Nashville: Methodist Publishing House, 1882. Reprints, New York: Plume, 1999; Franklin, Tenn.: Providence House, 2007.

Watson, Cynthia A. *Nation-Building: A Reference Handbook*. Santa Barbara, Calif.: ABC Clio, 2004.

Watson, Ronald G., editor. *From Ashby to Andersonville: The Civil War Diary and Reminiscences of George A. Hitchcock, Private, Company A, Twenty-First Massachusetts Regiment, August 1862–January 1865*. Campbell, Calif.: Savas, 1997.

Watson, Thomas Shelby, with Perry A. Brantley. *Confederate Guerrilla Sue Mundy: A Biography of Kentucky Soldier Jerome Clarke*. Jefferson, N.C.: McFarland, 2008.

Weigley, Russell F. *A Great Civil War: A Military and Political History, 1861–1865*. Bloomington: Indiana Univ. Press, 2000.

Weitz, Mark. *A Higher Duty: Desertion Among Georgia Troops During the Civil War.* Lincoln: Univ. of Nebraska Press, 2000.

———. *More Damning than Slaughter: Desertion in the Confederate Army.* Lincoln: Univ. of Nebraska Press, 2005.

Wekcher, David A., editor. *A Keystone Rebel: The Civil War Diary of Joseph Garey, Hudson's Battery, Mississippi Volunteers.* Gettysburg, Pa.: Thomas Publications, 1996.

Welcher, Frank J. *The Union Army, 1861–1865: Organization and Operations.* Vol. 2, *The Western Theater.* Bloomington: Indiana Univ. Press, 1993.

Wert, Jeffrey. *General James Longstreet: The Confederacy's Most Controversial Soldier: A Biography.* New York: Simon and Schuster, 1993.

West, John C. *A Texan in Search of a Fight: Being the Diary and Letters of a Private Soldier in Hood's Texas Brigade.* Waco, Tex.: J. S. Hill, 1901.

Westervelt, William B. *Lights and Shadows of Army Life: From Bull Run to Bentonville.* Edited by George S. Maharay. Shippensburg, Pa.: Burd Street Press, 1998.

Whiting, William. *Military Government of Hostile Territory in Time of War.* Boston: John L. Shorey, 1864.

Wilkinson, Warren, and Seven E. Woodworth. *A Scythe of Fire: A Civil War Story of the Eighth Georgia Infantry Regiment.* New York: William Morrow, 2002.

Willett, Charles E., editor. *A Union Soldier Returns South: The Civil War Letters and Diary of Alfred C. Willett, One Hundred and Thirteenth Ohio Volunteer Infantry.* Johnson City, Tenn.: Overmountain Press, 1994.

Williams, Edward F., III, editor. *Confederate Victories at Fort Pillow.* Memphis, Tenn.: Historical Hiking Trails, 1973.

Williams, T. Harry. *P. G. T. Beauregard: Napoleon in Gray.* Baton Rouge: Louisiana State Univ. Press, 1955.

Williamson County Convention and Visitors Bureau. *The Battle of Franklin, November 30, 1864: A Self-Guided Driving Tour.* Franklin, Tenn., n.d.

Willis, James. *Arkansas Confederates in the Western Theater.* Dayton, Ohio: Morningside, 1998.

Wills, Brian Steel. *A Battle from the Start: The Life of Nathan Bedford Forrest.* New York: Harper Collins, 1992.

Wills, Ridley, II. *Old Enough to Die.* Franklin, Tenn.: Hillsboro Press, 1996.

Wilson, James Harrison. *Under the Old Flag: Recollections of Military Operations in the War for the Union, the Spanish War, the Boxer Rebellion, etc.* Vol. 2. New York: D. Appleton, 1912.

Wilson, John. *Chattanooga's Story.* Chattanooga, Tenn.: Chattanooga News-Free Press, 1980.

Wilson, Suzanne Colton, compiler, and J. Ferrell Colton and Antoinette G. Smith, editors. *Column South with the Fifteenth Pennsylvania Cavalry: From Antietam to the Capture of Jefferson Davis.* Flagstaff, Ariz.: J. F. Colton, 1960.

Wingfield, Marshall. *General A. P. Stewart, His Life and Letters*. Memphis: West Tennessee Historical Society, 1954.

Wood, W. J. *Civil War Generalship: The Art of Command*. Westport, Conn.: Greenwood, 1997.

Woodward, C. Vann, editor. *Mary Chesnut's Civil War*. New Haven: Yale Univ. Press, 1981.

Woodworth, Steven E., editor. *The Human Tradition in the Civil War and Reconstruction*. Wilmington, Del.: SR Books, 2000.

Womack, Bob. *Call Forth the Mighty Men*. Bessemer, Ala.: Colonial Press, 1987.

Worsham, W. J. *The Old Nineteenth Tennessee Regiment, C.S.A.* Knoxville: Paragon Printing, 1902.

Wyeth, John Allan. *That Devil Forrest: Life of General Nathan Bedford Forrest*. 1899. Reprint, New York: Harper and Brothers, 1959.

Wynne, Lewis N., and Robert A. Taylor, editors. *This War So Horrible: The Civil War Diary of Hiram Smith Williams*. Tuscaloosa: Univ. of Alabama Press, 1993.

Yater, George H. *Two Hundred Years at the Falls of the Ohio: A History of Louisville and Jefferson County*. Louisville, Ky.: Filson Club, 1997.

Young, Bennett H. *Confederate Wizards of the Saddle: Being Reminiscences and Observations of One Who Rode with Morgan*. Boston: Chapple Publishing, 1914. Reprint, Dayton, Ohio: Morningside, 1988.

Young, J. P. *The Seventh Tennessee Cavalry (Confederate): A History*. Nashville: Publishing House of the M.E. Church, South, 1890. Reprint, Dayton, Ohio: Morningside Bookshop, 1976.

Zimmerman, Mark. *Guide to Civil War Nashville*. Nashville: Battle of Nashville Preservation Society, 2004.

Articles and Essays

Abbott, Martin, editor. "The South as Seen by a Tennessee Unionist in 1865: Letters of H. M. Watterson." *Tennessee Historical Quarterly* 18 (June 1959): 148–61.

Alderson, William T. "The Civil War Diary of Captain James Litton Cooper, September 30, 1861 to January, 1865." *Tennessee Historical Quarterly* 15 (June 1956): 141–46.

———. "The Civil War Reminiscences of John Johnston, 1861–1865." *Tennessee Historical Quarterly* 14 (Sept. 1954): 244–76.

Alexander, Thomas B. "Kukluxism in Tennessee, 1865–1869." *Tennessee Historical Quarterly* 8 (Sept. 1949): 195–219.

———. "Neither Peace Nor War: Conditions in Tennessee in 1865." *East Tennessee Historical Society's Publications* 21 (1949): 33–51.

———. "Strange Bedfellows: The Interlocking Careers of T. A. R. Nelson, Andrew Johnson, and W. G. (Parson) Brownlow." *East Tennessee Historical Society's Publications* 51 (1979): 54–77.

Andrews, Peter. "The Rock of Chickamauga." *American Heritage* 41 (Mar. 1990): 81–91.

Ash, Steven V. "A Community at War: Montgomery County, 1861–1865." *Tennessee Historical Quarterly* 36 (Spring 1977): 30–43.

———. "Postwar Recovery: Montgomery County, 1865–70." *Tennessee Historical Quarterly* 36 (Summer 1977): 208.

Bagby, Milton. "A Setting for Disaster." *Civil War Times Illustrated* 36 (Feb. 1998): 26, 28, 30, 60–62.

Bailey, Anne J. "The Mississippi Marine Brigade: Fighting Rebel Guerrillas on Western Waters." *Military History of the Southwest* 22 (Spring 1992): 31–42.

Bailey, Joe R. "A Military History of the Nashville and Northwestern Railroad." *Tennessee Historical Quarterly* 67 (Summer 2008): 106–23.

Bailey, Thomas E. "Engine and Iron: A Story of Branchline Railroading in Middle Tennessee." *Tennessee Historical Quarterly* 28 (Fall 1969): 252–68.

Baker, Terry. "Fort Negley: Sole Survivor of Nashville's Civil War Defenses." *Nashville Retrospect* 1 (Dec. 2009): 7.

Barton, Lon Carter. "The Reign of Terror in Graves County." *Register of the Kentucky Historical Society* 46 (Apr. 1948): 484–95.

Bates, Walter Lynn. "Southern Unionists: A Socio-Economic Examination of the Third East Tennessee Volunteer Infantry Regiment, U.S.A., 1862–1865." *Tennessee Historical Quarterly* 50 (Winter 1991): 226–39.

Bearss, Edwin C. "Bedford Forrest and His 'Critter' Cavalry at Brice's Cross Roads." In *Leadership During the Civil War,* edited by Roman T. Heleniak and Lawrence T. Hewitt, 73–84. Shippensburg, Pa.: White Mane Publishing, 1992.

Bejach, Lois D. "Civil War Letters of a Mother and Son." *West Tennessee Historical Society Papers* 4 (1950): 50–71.

———. "The Journal of a Civil War 'Commando' DeWitt Clinton Fort." *West Tennessee Historical Society Papers* 2 (1948): 6–32.

Bentley, James R., editor. "The Civil War Memoirs of Captain Thomas Speed." *Filson Club Quarterly* 44 (July 1970): 235–72.

Berkeley, Kathleen Christine. "Elizabeth Avery Meriwether, 'An Advocate for Her Sex': Feminism and Conservatism in the Post-Civil War South." *Tennessee Historical Quarterly* 43 (Winter 1984): 390–40.

Betts, Vicki, editor. "The Civil War Letters of Elbridge Littlejohn, Part 2." *Chronicles of Smith County, Texas* 28 (Summer 1979): 11–50.

Bigelow, Martha Mitchell. "Freedmen of the Mississippi Valley, 1862–1865." *Civil War History* 8 (Mar. 1962): 38–47.

Blankenship, Gary. "Colonel Fielding Hurst and the Hurst Nation." *West Tennessee Historical Society Papers* 34 (1980): 71–87.

Boeger, Palmer H. "General Burnside's Knoxville Packing Project." *East Tennessee Historical Society's Publications* 35 (1963): 76–84.

Bollier, Sam. "'Our Own Paradise Invaded': Imagining Civil War Era East Tennessee." *Tennessee Historical Quarterly* 68 (Winter 2009): 391–40.

Bolte, Philip L. "Dismount and Prepare to Fight Gunboats." *Civil War* 65 (Dec. 1997): 23–65.

Boone, Jennifer J. "'Mingling Freely': Tennessee Society on the Eve of the Civil War." *Tennessee Historical Quarterly* 51 (Fall 1992): 137–46.

Bosco, David. "Moral Principle vs. Military Necessity." *American Scholar* 77 (Winter 2008): 25–34.

Bradley, Michael, and Milan Hill, "Shoot If You Can By Accident." *North & South* 3 (Nov. 1999): 33–48.

Bratcher, James T. "An 1866 Letter on the War and Reconstruction." *Tennessee Historical Quarterly* 32 (Mar. 1963): 83–86.

Brooksher, William R., and David K. Snider. "Devil on the River." *Civil War Times Illustrated* 15 (Aug. 1976): 12–19.

Brown, Lenard. "Fortress Rosecrans: A History, 1865–1990." *Tennessee Historical Quarterly* 50 (Fall 1990): 135–41.

Bryan, Charles F., Jr. "'Tories' Amidst Rebels: Confederate Occupation of East Tennessee, 1861–63." *East Tennessee Historical Society's Publications* 60 (1988): 3–22.

Burgess, John W. "A Civil War Boyhood: Soldier of the Union." *Atlantic Monthly* 151 (Mar. 1933): 367–68.

Burgess, Tim, editor. "Reminiscences of the Battle of Nashville." *Journal of Confederate History* 1 (Summer 1988): 152–68.

Burkhardt, George S. "No Quarter! Black Flag Warfare 1863–1865." *North & South* 10 (May 2007): 12–29.

Burt, Jesse C. "East Tennessee, Lincoln, and Sherman, Part II." *East Tennessee Historical Society's Publications* 35 (1963): 54–75.

———. "Sherman, Railroad General." *Civil War History* 2 (Mar. 1956): 45–54.

Campbell, James B. "East Tennessee During the Radical Regime, 1865–1869." *East Tennessee Historical Society's Publications* 20 (1948): 84–102.

Cartwright, Thomas Y. "Franklin: The Valley of Death." *Hallowed Ground* 5 (Spring 2004): 28–31.

Castel, Albert. "The Fort Pillow Massacre: A Fresh Examination of the Evidence." *Civil War History* 4 (Mar. 1958): 37–50.

Chester, William W., editor. "The Civil War Skirmish Near Bolivar, Tennessee: March, 1864." *Journal of the Jackson Purchase Historical Society* 21 (June 1993): 10–15.

———. "H. R. A. McCorkle: The Civil War Diary of a C.S.A. Private." *Journal of the Jackson Purchase Historical Society* 19 (June 1991): 21–28.

Cimprich, John. "Fort Pillow During the Civil War." *North & South* 9 (Dec. 2006): 60–70.

———. "Military Governor Johnson and Tennessee Blacks, 1862–1865." *Tennessee Historical Quarterly* 39 (Winter 1980): 459–70.

Cimprich, John, and Robert C. Mainfort. "Dr. Fitch's Report on the Fort

Pillow Massacre." *Tennessee Historical Quarterly* 44 (Spring 1985): 27–39.

Cimprich, John, and Robert C. Mainfort, editors. "Fort Pillow Revisited: New Evidence About an Old Controversy." *Civil War History* 28 (Dec. 1982): 293–306.

Clark, Sam L., and H. D. Riley Jr. "Outline of the Organization of the Medical Department of the Confederate Army and Department of Tennessee." *Tennessee Historical Quarterly* 16 (Mar. 1957): 55–82.

Coffman, Edward M., editor. Memoirs of Hylan B. Lyon Brigadier General, C.S.A." *Tennessee Historical Quarterly* 18 (Mar. 1959): 35–53.

Conklin, Forrest. "Footnotes on the Death of John Hunt Morgan." *Tennessee Historical Quarterly* 35 (Winter 1976): 376–88.

———. "'Grape for the Rebel Masses and Hemp for Their Leaders': Parson Brownlow's Celebrated Tour of Northern Cities, 1862." *Journal of East Tennessee History* 77 (2005): 44–93.

Connelly, Thomas L. "Neo-Confederatism Or Power Vacuum: Post-War Kentucky Politics Reappraised." *Register of the Kentucky Historical Society* 64 (Oct. 1966): 257–69.

Connor, Sam. "Cleburne and the Unthinkable." *Civil War Times Illustrated* 36 (Feb. 1998): 45–48.

Cooling, B. Franklin. "The 'Decisive' Battle of Nashville." *Hallowed Ground* 5 (Spring 2004): 21–27.

Cooper, Constance J. "Tennessee Returns to Congress." *Tennessee Historical Quarterly* 37 (Spring 1978): 49–62.

Copeland, James E. "Where Were the Kentucky Unionists and Secessionists?" *Kentucky Historical Society Register* 71 (Oct. 1973): 344–63.

Copley, John M. "Battle of Franklin, with Reminiscences of Camp Douglas." *Journal of Confederate History* 2 (1989): 27–53.

Coppock, Paul R. "The Kilgore Killing." *West Tennessee Historical Society Papers* 15 (1961): 40–54.

Crabb, Alfred Leland. "The Twilight of the Nashville Gods." *Tennessee Historical Quarterly* 15 (Dec. 1956): 291–305.

Craig, Berry F. "The Jackson Purchase Considers Secession: The 1861 Mayfield Convention." *Register of the Kentucky Historical Society* 99 (Autumn 2001): 339–61.

Creighton, Wilbur. "Wilbur Fisk Foster: Soldier and Engineer." *Tennessee Historical Quarterly* 31 (Fall 1972): 261–75.

Crownover, Sims. "The Battle of Franklin." *Tennessee Historical Quarterly* 14 (December 1955): 291–322.

Cubbison, Douglas R. "John Bell Hood and the Campaign in North Alabama and Middle Tennessee, October–November 1864." *Military History of the West* 34 (2004): 51–74.

Culp, Frederick M. "Captain George King's Home Guard Company." *West*

Tennessee Historical Society Papers 25 (1961): 55–78.

Cummings, Charles M. "Otho French Strahl: 'Choicest Spirit to Embrace the South.'" *Tennessee Historical Quarterly* 24 (Winter 1965): 341–55.

Dalton, Robert E. "A Note on Fayette County." *Tennessee Historical Quarterly* 32 (Winter 1973): 389–90.

Davidson, James. "Michigan and the Defense of Knoxville, Tennessee, 1863." *East Tennessee Historical Society's Publications* 35 (1963): 21–53.

Davis, Louise. "The Battle of Nashville . . . 110 Years Later." *Nashville Tennessean,* Dec. 15, 1974, 10–18.

Davis, Robert Scott. "Joe Ritchey of Tennessee: An American Desperado in Legends, the Newspapers, and a Federal Pension File." *Tennessee Historical Quarterly* 69 (Summer 2009): 152–73.

Dawson, Joseph G., III. "Jefferson Davis and the Confederacy's 'Offensive-Defensive' Strategy in the U.S. Civil War." *Journal of Military History* 73 (Apr. 2009): 591–607.

DeLozier, Mary Jean. "The Civil War and Its Aftermath in Putnam County." *Tennessee Historical Quarterly* 38 (Winter 1979): 436–61.

Dinkins, James. "Destroying Yankee Gunboats." *Confederate Veteran* 37 (Sept. 1930): 341–44.

Donnelly, Ralph W. "Local Defence in the Confederate Munitions Area." In *Military Analysis of the Civil War: An Anthology,* by the editors of *Military Affairs.* 239–51. Millwood, N.Y.: KTO Press, 1977.

Doolittle, Charles C. "The Defense of Decatur, Alabama." In *Sketches of War History, 1861–1865: Papers Prepared for the State of Ohio Commandery of the Military Order of the Loyal Legion of the United States, 1888–1890,* vol. 3, by Loyal Legion of the United States, Ohio Commandery, edited by Robert Hunter, 264–77. Cincinnati: Robert Clarke, 1890.

Doster, James F. "The Chattanooga Rolling Mill: An Industrial B-Product of the Civil War." *East Tennessee Historical Society's Publications* 36 (1964): 45–55.

Dunlap, Sam B. "Missouri Battery in the Tennessee Campaign." *Confederate Veteran* 12 (Aug. 1904): 389.

Durham, Walter T. "The Battle of Nashville." *Journal of Confederate History* 1 (Summer 1988): 119–51.

———. "Civil War Letters to Wynnewood." *Tennessee Historical Quarterly* 34 (Spring 1975): 32–47.

Editor, *North & South.* "An Alternative Strategy?" *North & South* 11 (Aug. 2009): 14–21, 42.

———. "Irregular Warfare, 1861–1865." *North & South* 11 (June 2009): 3, 17–28.

Eisterhold, John A. "Fort Heiman: Forgotten Fortress." *West Tennessee Historical Society Papers* 28 (1974): 43–54.

Evans, David. "Wool, Women, and War." *Civil War Times Illustrated* 26

(Sept. 1987): 38–42.

Fain, John N. "The Diary of Hiram Fain of Rogersville: An East Tennessee Secessionist." *Journal of East Tennessee History* 69 (1997): 97–114.

Feistman, Eugene G. "Radical Disfranchisement and the Restoration of Tennessee, 1865–1866." *Tennessee Historical Quarterly* 12 (June 1953): 135–51.

Fink, Harold S. "The East Tennessee Campaign and the Battle of Knoxville." *East Tennessee Historical Society's Publications* 29 (1957): 79–117.

Fisher, Noel. "Definitions of Loyalty: Unionist Histories of the Civil War in East Tennessee." *Journal of East Tennessee History* 67 (1995): 58–88.

Flannery, Michael A. "Kentucky History Revisited: The Role of the Civil War in Shaping Kentucky's Collective Consciousness." *Filson Club History Quarterly* 71 (Jan. 1997): 27–51.

Fowler, John D. "'The finishing stroke to the independence of the Southern Confederacy': Perceptions of Hood's Tennessee Campaign." *Tennessee Historical Quarterly* 64 (Fall 2005): 3, 216–35.

Fraley, Miranda L. "The Legacies of Freedom and Victory Besieged: Stones River National Cemetery, 1865–1920." *Tennessee Historical Quarterly* 64 (Summer 2005): 134–64.

Frank, Fedora Small. "Nashville Jewry During the Civil War." *Tennessee Historical Quarterly* 39 (Fall 1980): 310–22.

Fraser, Walter J., Jr. "Barbour Lewis: A Carpetbagger Reconsidered." *Tennessee Historical Quarterly* 32 (Summer 1973): 148–68.

Fraser, Walter J., Jr., and Mrs. Pat C. Clark, editors. "The Letters of William Beverley Randolph Hackley: Treasury Agent in West Tennessee, 1863–1866." *West Tennessee Historical Society Papers* 25 (1971): 89–107.

Frink, C. S. "Organization of the Surgical Department in the Field, and the Experience of Its Offices in the Battle of Franklin." In *Sketches of War History, 1861–1865: Papers Prepared for the State of Ohio Commandery of the Military Order of the Loyal Legion of the United States, 1888–1890,* vol. 4, by Loyal Legion of the United States, Ohio Commandery, edited by W. H. Chamberlin, 418–28. Cincinnati: Robert Clarke, 1896.

Futrell, Robert J. "Federal Military Government in the South, 1861–1865." *Military Affairs* 15 (Winter 1951): 181–90.

Gallagher, Gary W. "Disaffection, Persistence, and Nation: Some Directions in Recent Scholarship on the Confederacy." *Civil War History* 55 (Sept. 2009): 329–53.

Garrett, Jill K. "St. John's Church, Ashwood." *Tennessee Historical Quarterly* 29 (Spring 1970): 3–23.

Gaston, Kay Baker. "A World Overturned: The Civil War Experience of Dr. William A. Cheatham and His Family." *Tennessee Historical Quarterly* 50 (Winter 1991): 3–16.

Gates, John M. "Indians and Insurrectos: The U.S. Army's Experience with

Insurgency." *Parameters of War: The Journal of the Army War College* 13 (1983): 59–68.

Gildrie, Richard P. "Guerrilla Warfare in the Lower Cumberland River Valley, 1862–1865." *Tennessee Historical Quarterly* 59 (Fall 1990): 161–76.

Gordon, Ralph C. "Hospital Trains of the Army of the Cumberland." *Tennessee Historical Quarterly* 51 (Fall 1992): 147–56.

———. "Nashville and the U.S. Christian Commission in the Civil War." *Tennessee Historical Quarterly* 55 (Summer 1996): 98–111.

Gower, Herschel. "Belle Meade: Queen of Tennessee Plantations." *Tennessee Historical Quarterly* 22 (Sept. 1963): 203–22.

———, editor. "The Beersheba Diary of L. Virginia French, Part II, Winter, Spring, and Summer, 1864." *East Tennessee Historical Society's Publication* 54/55 (1982–85): 3–25.

Gracey, Julien F. "Capture of the Mazeppa." *Confederate Veteran* 13 (Dec. 1905): 566–70.

Grimsley, Mark. "'Rebels' and 'Redskins,' U.S. Military Conduct toward White Southerners and Native Americans in Comparative Perspective." In *Civilians in the Path of War*, edited by Mark Grimsley and Clifford J. Rogers, 137–61. Lincoln: Univ. of Nebraska Press, 2002.

Groce, W. Todd. "Confederate Faces in East Tennessee: A Photographic Essay." *Journal of East Tennessee History* 65 (1993): 2–33.

Guerrant, Edward O., editor. "Diary of Edward O. Guerrant Covering the June 1864 Kentucky Raid of General John Hunt Morgan." *Register of the Kentucky Historical Society* 85 (Autumn 1987): 322–58.

Hagerman, Edward. "Field Transportation and Strategic Mobility in the Union Armies." *Civil War History* 34 (June 1988): 143–71.

Halley, R. A. "A Rebel Newspaper's War Story: Being a Narrative of the War History of the Memphis Appeal." In *Tennessee Old and New: Sesquicentennial Edition, 1796–1946*, vol. 2, by Tennessee Historical Commission and Tennessee Historical Society, 247–72. Nashville: Tennessee Historical Commission and Tennessee Historical Society, 1946. Originally published in *American Historical Magazine* 2 (Apr. 1903).

Hardy, William E. "The Toils and Opportunities of War: A Michigan Chaplain in Civil War East Tennessee." *Journal of East Tennessee History* 77 (2005): 49–93.

Harper, Herbert L. "The Antebellum Courthouses of Tennessee." *Tennessee Historical Quarterly* 30 (Summer 1971): 3–25.

Harris, William C. "East Tennessee's Civil War Refugees and the Impact of the War on Civilians." *Journal of East Tennessee History* 64 (1992): 3–19.

Harrison, Lowell H. "The Diary of an 'Average' Confederate Soldier." *Tennessee Historical Quarterly* 29 (Fall 1970): 256–71.

Hattaway, Herman. "Dress Rehearsal for Hell." *Civil War Times* 37 (Oct.

1998): 34–39, 74–75.

Hawkins, Susan. "The African American Experience at Forts Henry, Heiman, and Donelson, 1861–1867." *Tennessee Historical Quarterly* 61 (Winter 2002): 222–41.

Hay, Thomas Robson. "The Battle of Spring Hill." *Tennessee Historical Magazine* 7 (July 1921): 74–91.

Hermsdorfer, Sally Sartain. "For 'The Cultured Mothers of the Land': Racist Imagery in the Old South Fiction of Tennessee Suffragist Elizabeth Avery Meriwether." *Tennessee Historical Quarterly* 57 (Fall 1997): 183–95.

Hesseltine, W. B. "Tennessee's Invitation to Carpet-Baggers." *East Tennessee Historical Society's Publications* 51 (1979): 78–91.

Hightower, T. H. "Lynch's Battery at Bull's Gap." *Confederate Veteran* 25 (Aug. 1917): 345, 385.

Hoffman, Frank G. "Hybrid vs. Compound War—The Janus Choice: Defining Today's Multifaceted Conflicts." *Armed Forces Journal,* Oct. 2009, 14–18, 44.

Holladay, Bob. "The Question of Stanley Horn." *Tennessee Historical Quarterly* 69 (Summer 2009): 198–209.

Holley, Peggy Scott. "The Seventh Tennessee Volunteer Cavalry: West Tennessee Unionists in Andersonville Prison." *West Tennessee Historical Society Papers* 42 (1988): 39–58.

Holmes, Jack D. L. "Forrest's 1864 Raid on Memphis." *Tennessee Historical Quarterly* 18 (Dec. 1959): 295–321.

———. "The Underlying Causes of the Memphis Race Riot of 1866." *Tennessee Historical Quarterly* 17 (Sept. 1958): 195–221.

Hoobler, James A. "The Civil War Diary of Louisa Brown Pearl." *Tennessee Historical Quarterly* 38 (Fall 1979): 308–21.

Horn, Stanley F. "Nashville During the Civil War." *Tennessee Historical Quarterly* 4 (Mar. 1945): 3–22.

———. "The Papers of Major Alonzo Wainright." *Tennessee Historical Quarterly* 12 (June 1953): 182–84.

Howell, Elmo. "William Faulkner's General Forrest and the Uses of History." *Tennessee Historical Quarterly* 29 (Fall 1970): 287–94.

Howell, Sarah M. "Daughter of Amnicola: Sallie Crutchfield Gaut." *Tennessee Historical Quarterly* 64 (Summer 2005): 121–33.

———. "John C. Gaut: Wielding Justice in Tennessee, 1861–1869." *Tennessee Historical Quarterly* 67 (Spring 2008): 3–21.

Howes, Edward H., and Benjamin F. Gilbert, editors. "Land and Labor in Kentucky, 1865: Letters to George Lewis Greathouse." *Register of the Kentucky Historical Society* 48 (Jan. 1950): 25–31.

Hughes, Susan Lyons. "My Old Kentucky Home—At War." *North & South* 4 (Jan. 2001): 59–67.

Huston, James A. "Logistical Support of Federal Armies in the Field." *Civil*

War History 7 (Mar. 1961): 36–47.

Jacobson, Timothy C. "Joseph Buckner Killebrew: Agrarianism in the New South." *Tennessee Historical Quarterly* 33 (Summer 1974): 157–74.

Jaronski, Stefan T. "Mail from Hood's Tennessee Campaign." *Confederate Philatelist* 41 (Nov.–Dec. 1996): 211–16.

Jenkins, Kirk C. "Commands: The Union soldiers of the Fifteenth Kentucky often fought gray-clad men from the same county as themselves." *America's Civil War,* Sept. 2004, 18–20, 68.

Johansson, M. Jane. "Gibson's Louisiana Brigade During the 1864 Tennessee Campaign." *Tennessee Historical Quarterly* 64 (Fall 2005): 187–95.

Johnson, Leland R. "Civil War Railroad Defenses in Tennessee." *Tennessee Valley Historical Review* 2 (Summer 1972): 20–26.

Jones, James Boyd, Jr. "The 'Battle' of Franklin: A Reconstruction Narrative." *Tennessee Historical Quarterly* 64 (Summer 2005): 110–19.

———. "Municipal Vice: The Management of Prostitution in Tennessee's Urban Experience, Part I: The Experience of Nashville and Memphis, 1854–1917." *Tennessee Historical Quarterly* 50 (Spring 1991): 33–41.

———. "A Tale of Two Cities: The Hidden Battle Against Venereal Disease in Civil War Nashville and Memphis." *Civil War History* 31 (Sept. 1985): 270–76.

———. "The Third Battle of Franklin, September 27, 1923." *Tennessee Historical Quarterly* 57 (Fall 1997): 172–81.

———. "The Struggle for Public Health in Civil War Tennessee Cities." *West Tennessee Historical Society Papers* 60 (2007): 62–108.

Jones, Robert. "The Press in the Election: Ending Tennessee's Reconstruction." *Tennessee Historical Quarterly* 65 (Winter 2006/2007): 320–41.

Jones, Robert, and Mark E. Byrnes. "'Rebels Never Forgive': Former President Andrew Johnson and the Senate Election of 1869." *Tennessee Historical Quarterly* 66 (Fall 2007): 251–69.

Jones, William S. "The Civil War in Van Buren County, 1861–1865," *Tennessee Historical Quarterly* 67 (Spring 2008), 57–64.

Kajencki, Francis C. "The Man Who Beat the Devil." *Civil War Times* 37 (Oct. 1998): 40–43.

Kelly, James C. "A Union Soldier's Sketchbook of the Chattanooga Region." *Tennessee Historical Quarterly* 51 (Fall 1992): 157–60.

———. "William Gannaway Brownlow, Part II." *Tennessee Historical Quarterly* 43 (Summer 1984): 155–72.

Kelly, R. M. "A Brush with Pillow." In *Sketches of War History, 1861–1865: Papers Prepared for the State of Ohio Commandery of the Military Order of the Loyal Legion of the United States, 1888–1890,* vol. 3, by Loyal Legion of the United States, Ohio Commandery, edited by Robert Hunter, 319–32. Cincinnati: Robert Clarke, 1890.

Ketchersid, William L. "Major Campbell Wallace: Southern Railroad Leaders." *Tennessee Historical Quarterly* 67 (Summer 2008): 91–105.

Kime, Marlin G. "Sherman's Gordian Knot: Logistical Problems in the Atlanta Campaign." *Georgia Historical Quarterly* 70 (Spring 1986): 102–10.

Kiser, John W. "Scion of Belmont." *Tennessee Historical Quarterly* 38 (Spring 1979): 34–61.

Kornell, Gary L. "Reconstruction in Nashville, 1867–1869." *Tennessee Historical Quarterly* 30 (Fall 1971): 277–87.

Lafferty, W. T. "Civil War Reminiscences of John Aker Lafferty." *Register of the Kentucky Historical Society* 59 (Jan. 1961): 1–28.

Lakin, Matt. "Civil War Trails Markers to Be Unveiled Today." *Knoxville News Sentinel,* July 11, 2010. Available online at http://www.knoxnews.com/news/2010/jul/11/civil-war-trails-markers-set-to-be-unveiled/.

LaPointe, Patricia M. "Military Hospitals in Memphis, 1861–1865." *Tennessee Historical Quarterly* 42 (Winter 1983): 325–42.

Lash, Jeffrey N. "'The Federal Tyrant at Memphis': General Stephen A. Hurlbut and the Union Occupation of West Tennessee, 1862–64." *Tennessee Historical Quarterly* 48 (Spring 1989): 15–18.

LeForge, Judy Bussell. "State Colored Conventions of Tennessee, 1865–1866." *Tennessee Historical Quarterly* 65 (Fall 2006): 231–53.

Leftwich, William Groom, Jr. "The Battle of Brice's Cross Roads." *West Tennessee Historical Society Papers* 20 (1966): 5–19.

Livingood, James W. "Chattanooga, Tennessee: Its Economic History in the Years Immediately Following Appomattox." *East Tennessee Historical Society's Publications* 15 (1943): 35–48.

Lovett, Bobby L. "Memphis Riots: White Reaction to Blacks in Memphis, May 1865-July 1866." *Tennessee Historical Quarterly* 38 (Spring 1979): 9–33.

———. "The West Tennessee Colored Troops in Civil War Combat." *West Tennessee Historical Society Papers* 34 (1980): 53–70.

Loyal Legion of the United States, Ohio Commandery. *Sketches of War History, 1861–1865: Papers Prepared for the State of Ohio Commandery of the Military Order of the Loyal Legion of the United States, 1888–1890.* Vol. 3. Edited by Robert Hunter. Cincinnati: Robert Clarke, 1890.

Lucas, Marion B. "Camp Nelson, Kentucky, During the Civil War: Cradle of Liberty or Refugee Death Camp? *Filson Club History Quarterly* 63 (Oct. 1989): 439–52.

———. "Kentucky Blacks: The Transition from Slavery to Freedom." *Register of the Kentucky Historical Society* 91 (Autumn 1993): 403–19.

Lucas, Scott. "'Indignities, Wrongs, and Outrages': Military and Guerrilla Incursions on Kentucky's Civil War Home Front." *Filson Club History Quarterly* 73 (Oct. 1999): 355–76.

Luckett, William W. "Bedford Forrest in the Battle of Brice's Cross Roads." *Tennessee Historical Quarterly* 15 (June 1956): 99–110.

Lufkin, Charles L. "'Not Heard from Since April 12, 1864': The Thirteenth

Tennessee Cavalry, U.S.A." *Tennessee Historical Quarterly* 45 (Summer 1986): 133–51.

———. "Secession and Coercion in Tennessee, the Spring of 1861." *Tennessee Historical Quarterly* 50 (Summer 1991): 98–109.

Mackin, Sister Aloysius, O.P. "Wartime Scenes from Convent Windows: St. Cecilia, 1860 Through 1865." *Tennessee Historical Quarterly* 39 (Winter 1980): 401–22.

Madden, David. "Unionist Resistance to Confederate Occupation: The Bridge Burners of East Tennessee." *East Tennessee Historical Society's Publications* 52–53 (1980–81): 22–39.

Mallinson, David. "Forrest's Memphis Raid, August 21, 1864." *Blue & Gray* 2 (Aug.–Sept. 1984): 7–11.

Maness, Lonnie E. "The Fort Pillow Massacre: Fact or Fiction." *Tennessee Historical Quarterly* 45 (Winter 1986): 287–315.

———. "A Ruse that Worked: The Capture of Union City in 1864." *West Tennessee Historical Society Papers* 30 (1976): 91–103.

———. "Strategic Victories or Tactical Defeats? Nathan Bedford Forest at Brice's Crossroads, Harrisburg, and the Memphis Raid." *Journal of Confederate History* 2 (Summer 1988): 177–205.

Mangum, William Preston, II. "Disaster at Woodburn Farm: R. A. Alexander and the Confederate Guerrilla Raids of 1864–1865." *Filson Club History Quarterly* 70 (Apr. 1996): 143–85.

Martin, James B. "Black Flag Over the Bluegrass: Guerrilla Warfare in Kentucky, 1863–1865." *Register of the Kentucky Historical Society* 81 (Autumn 1988): 352–75.

Maslowski, Peter. "From Reconciliation to Reconstruction: Lincoln, Johnson, and Tennessee, Part II." *Tennessee Historical Quarterly* 42 (Winter 1983): 343–61.

McBride, Robert M. "'Northern, Military, Corrupt, and Transitory': Augustus E. Alden, Nashville's Carpetbagger Mayor." *Tennessee Historical Quarterly* 37 (Spring 1978): 63–67.

McBride, W. Stephen. "Civil War Material Culture and Camp Life in Central Kentucky: Archaeological Investigations at Camp Nelson." In *Look to the Earth: Historical Archaeology and the American Civil War,* edited by Clarence R. Geier Jr. and Susan S. Winter, 130–57. Knoxville: Univ. of Tennessee Press, 1994.

McBride, W. Stephen, Susan C. Andrews, and Sean P. Coughlin. "'For the Convenience and Comfort of the Soldiers and Employees at the Depot': Archaeology of the Owens' House/Post Office Complex, Camp Nelson, Kentucky." In *Archaeological Perspectives on the American Civil War,* edited by Clarence R. Geier and Stephen R. Potter, 99–124. Gainesville: Univ. Press of Florida, 2000.

McClain, Iris Hopkins. "A Note on Stewart County." *Tennessee Historical Quarterly* 37 (Spring 1978): 89–90.

McDaniel, Anthonette L. "'Just Watch Us Make Things Hum': Chattanooga,

Adolph S. Ochs, and the Memorialization of the Civil War." *East Tennessee Historical Society's Publications* 61 (1989): 3–15.

McDonough, James Lee. "The Battle of Franklin Tennessee, November 30, 1864." *Blue & Gray* 1 (Aug.–Sept. 1984): 18–33.

———. "Tennessee and the Civil War." *Tennessee Historical Quarterly* 54 (Fall 1995): 190–200.

———. "West Point Classmates—Eleven Years Later: Some Observations on the Spring Hill-Franklin Campaign." *Tennessee Historical Quarterly* 28 (Summer 1969): 186–96.

McGehee, C. Stuart. "E. O. Tade, Freedmen's Education, and the Failure of Reconstruction in Tennessee." *Tennessee Historical Quarterly* 43 (Winter 1984): 376–89.

———. "Military Origins of the New South: The Army of the Cumberland and Chattanooga's Freedmen." *Civil War History* 34 (Dec. 1988): 323–43.

———. "'The Property and Faith of the City': Secession in Chattanooga." *East Tennessee Historical Society's Publications* 60 (1988): 23–38.

McKenzie, Robert Tracy. "Civil War and Socioeconomic Change in the Upper South: The Survival of Local Agricultural Elites in Tennessee, 1850–1870." *Tennessee Historical Quarterly* 52 (Fall 1993): 170–84.

McKinney, Gordon B. "The Mountain Republican Party—Army." *Tennessee Historical Quarterly* 32 (Summer 1973): 124–39.

McMurray, W. J. "Causes of Failure at Spring Hill." *Confederate Veteran* 12 (Aug. 1904): 395–96.

McQuaid, John, and L. H. Mangum. "Cleburne's Final Charge." *Civil War Times Illustrated* 36 (Feb. 1998): 22, 24, 68–69.

McRae, James S. "David G. Cooke Joins the United States Colored Troops." *Tennessee Historical Quarterly* 64 (Fall 2005): 179–85.

Merrill, W. E. "Block-Houses for Railroad Defense in the Department of the Cumberland." In *Sketches of War History, 1861–1865: Papers Prepared for the State of Ohio Commandery of the Military Order of the Loyal Legion of the United States, 1888–1890,* vol. 3, by Loyal Legion of the United States, Ohio Commandery, edited by Robert Hunter, 389–421. Cincinnati: Robert Clarke, 1890.

Minnich, J. W. "The Affair at May's Ferry, Tenn." *Confederate Veteran* 33 (Feb. 1925): 55–56.

———. "At Bean's Station, Tenn." *Confederate Veteran* 36 (June 1928): 18–19.

Miscamble, Wilson D. "Andrew Johnson and the Election of William G. ('Parson') Brownlow as Governor of Tennessee." *Tennessee Historical Quarterly* 17 (Fall 1978): 308–20.

Mitchell, Enoch, editor. "Letters of a Confederate Surgeon in the Army of Tennessee to His Wife." *Tennessee Historical Quarterly* 5 (June 1946): 142–81.

M'Neilly, J. M. "A Roundabout Way Home." *Confederate Veteran* 28 (June

1920): 210–11.

Montgomery, James R. "The Nomenclature of the Upper Tennessee River." *East Tennessee Historical Society's Publications* 51 (1979): 151–62.

Moon, Anna Mary, editor. "A Southern Woman, in 1897, Remembers the Civil War." *East Tennessee Historical Society's Publications* 21 (1949): 111–15.

Moore, Kenneth Bancroft. "Fort Pillow, Forrest, and the United States Colored Troops in 1864." *Tennessee Historical Quarterly* 54 (Summer 1995): 112–23.

Morris, Roy, Jr. "Fort Pillow: Massacre or Madness?" *America's Civil War* 13 (Nov. 2000): 26–32.

———. "Old Cerro Gordo and the Battle of Blue Springs. " *Civil War Times Illustrated* 26 (Mar. 1987): 46–53.

Morris, Wentworth. "The Davie Home and the Register of the Federal Military Prison at Clarksville." *Tennessee Historical Quarterly* 8 (Sept. 1949): 248–51.

Myers, Marshall, and Charles Proppes, editors. "'I Don't Fear Nothing in the Shape of Man': The Civil War and Texas Border Letters of Edward Francis, United States Colored Troops." *Register of the Kentucky Historical Society* 101 (2003): 457–78.

Ney, Virgil. "Guerrilla War and Modern Strategy." *Orbis* 2 (Spring 1958): 66–82.

Nollan, Richard. "The Civil War Letters of William J. Armstrong, M.D., March 1863–September 1864." *West Tennessee Historical Society Papers* 60 (2007): 20–34.

Norris, Herbert S., and James R. Long. "The Road to Redemption." *Civil War Times* 26 (Aug. 1997): 32–38, 55–57.

O'Daniel, Patrick W. "Loyalty a Requisite: Trade and the Oath of Allegiance in the Mid-South in 1865," *West Tennessee Historical Society Papers* 60 (2007): 35–46.

Orr, Mary T. "John Overton and Traveler's Rest." *Tennessee Historical Quarterly* 15 (Sept. 1956): 216–23.

Osborn, George C. "Writings of a Confederate Prisoner of War." *Tennessee Historical Quarterly* 10 (Mar. 1951): 74- 90, and 10 (June 1951): 161–84.

Parks, Joseph H. "A Confederate Trade Center under Federal Occupation: Memphis, 1862 to 1865." *Journal of Southern History* 7 (Aug. 1941): 289–314.

———. "Memphis Under Military Rule, 1862 to 1865." *East Tennessee Historical Society's Publications* 14 (1942): 31–58.

Partin, Robert. "The Civil War in East Tennessee as Reported by a Confederate Railroad Bridge Builder." *Tennessee Historical Quarterly* 22 (Sept. 1963): 238–58.

———. "The 'Momentous Events' of the Civil War as Reported by a Confederate Private-Sergeant." *Tennessee Historical Quarterly* 18 (Mar. 1959): 69–86.

———. "The Wartime Experiences of Margaret McCalla: Confederate Refugee from East Tennessee." *Tennessee Historical Quarterly* 24 (Apr. 1965): 39–53.

Pearson, Alden B., Jr. "A Middle-Class, Border-State Family During the Civil War." *Civil War History* 22 (Dec. 1976): 218–336.

Perry, George Graham, III. "A Bend in the River: An Investigation of Black Agency, Autonomy, and Resistance in Memphis, Tennessee (1846–1866)." *West Tennessee Historical Society Papers* 62 (2009): 44–69.

Phillips, Paul David. "White Reaction to the Freedmen's Bureau in Tennessee." *Tennessee Historical Quarterly* 25 (Spring 1966): 50–62.

Poe, Orlando M. "Personal Recollections of the Occupation of East Tennessee and the Defense of Knoxville." In *War Papers: Michigan Military Order of the Loyal Legion of the United States,* vol. 1, paper 8, by Michigan Commandery. Detroit: Winn and Hammond, 1893.

Poulter, Keith, et al. "Irregular Warfare, 1861–1865." *North & South* 11 (June 2009): 17–29.

Queener, Verton M. "The East Tennessee Republicans as a Minority Party, 1870–1896." *East Tennessee Historical Society's Publications* 15 (1943): 49–73.

Quenzel, Carrol H. "A Billy Yank's Impressions of the South." *Tennessee Historical Quarterly* 12 (June 1953): 99–105.

Ramage, James A. "Recent Historiography of Guerrilla Warfare in the Civil War—A Review Essay." *Register of the Kentucky Historical Society* 103 (Summer 2005): 517–42.

Rayner, Juan Timoleon. "An Eye-Witness Account of Forrest's Raid on Memphis." *West Tennessee Historical society Papers* 12 (1958): 134–37.

Rhea, William L. "Storming Bull's Gap." *Confederate Veteran* 25 (June 1917): 302.

Rhyne, J. Michael. "'We Are Mobed & Beat': Regulator Violence Against Free Black Households in Kentucky's Bluegrass Region, 1865–1867." *Ohio Valley History* 2 (2002): 30–42.

Richardson, Joe M. "Fisk University: The First Critical Years." *Tennessee Historical Quarterly* 29 (Spring 1970): 24–41.

———. "The Memphis Race Riot and Its Aftermath." *Tennessee Historical Quarterly* 24 (Spring 1965): 63–69.

Riley, Harris D., Jr. "A Gallant Adopted Son of Tennessee—General John C. Carter, C.S.A." *Tennessee Historical Quarterly* 48 (Winter 1989): 195–209.

Riley, Mark B. "Edgefield: A Study of an Early Nashville Suburb." *Tennessee Historical Quarterly* 37 (Summer 1978): 133–54.

Riley, Susan B. "The Southern Literary Magazine of the Mid-Nineteenth Century." *Tennessee Historical Quarterly* 23 (Sept. 1964): 221–36.

Roberson, B. L. "The Courthouse Burnin'est General." *Tennessee Historical*

Quarterly 23 (Dec. 1964): 372–78.

Robertson, James I., Jr. "The Human Battle of Franklin." *Tennessee Historical Quarterly* 24 (Summer 1965): 20–30.

Robison, Dan M. "The Carter House: Focus of the Battle of Franklin." *Tennessee Historical Quarterly* 22 (Mar. 1963): 3–21.

Roth, David E. "Lt. Colonel William Shy, C.S.A." *Blue & Gray* 2 (Aug.–Sept. 1984): 12–17.

———. "The Mysteries of Spring Hill, Tennessee." *Blue & Gray* 2 (Oct.–Nov. 1984): 13–38.

Rule, D. H. "Sultana: A Case for Sabotage—'The result of no accident, but of fiendish design.'" *North & South* 5 (Dec. 2001): 76–87.

Rule, William. "The Loyalists of Tennessee in the Late War." In *Sketches of War History, 1861–1865: Papers Prepared for the State of Ohio Commandery of the Military Order of the Loyal Legion of the United States, 1888–1890*, vol. 2, by Loyal Legion of the United States, Ohio Commandery, 180–204. Cincinnati: Robert Clarke, 1888.

Sanders, Stuart W. "Quantrill's Last Ride." *America's Civil War* 12 (Mar. 1999): 6, 42–48.

Sartrace, Nicholas F., II. "America's Worst Maritime Disaster: The Ill-fated Sidewheeler Sultana." *Sea History* 92 (Spring 2000): 33–35.

Sasson, Diane. "The Self-Inventions of Laura Carter Holloway." *Tennessee Historical Quarterly* 67 (Fall 2008): 178–207.

Schmit, Steven J. "New Hope for Fort Negley." *North-South Trader* 7 (May–June 1980): 20–21, 40.

Schofield, Levi T. "The Retreat from Pulaski to Nashville." In *Sketches of War History, 1861–1865: Papers Prepared for the State of Ohio Commandery of the Military Order of the Loyal Legion of the United States, 1888–1890*, vol. 2, by Loyal Legion of the United States, Ohio Commandery, 121–52. Cincinnati: Robert Clarke, 1888.

"Selections from Documents in the Museum of the Confederacy Collections: In the Field and on the Town with the Washington Artillery." *Civil War Regiments: A Journal of the American Civil War* 5, no. 1: 92–149.

Severance, Benjamin H. "Loyalty's Political Vanguard: The Union League of Maryville, Tennessee, 1867–1869." *Journal of East Tennessee History* 71 (1999): 26–46.

———. "Tennessee's 'Fighting Joe': The Civil War Experience of General Joseph A. Cooper." *Tennessee Historical Quarterly* 64 (Fall 2005): 197–215.

Shaffer, Duane E. "Storming Fort Sanders." *Military History* 22 (Nov. 2005): 46–52.

Shockley, Garry C. "The Union Legal Response to Hood's Invasion of Tennessee." *Tennessee Historical Quarterly* 66 (Spring 2007): 20–37.

Siburt, James T. "Colonel John M. Hughs: Brigade Commander and Confederate Guerrilla." *Tennessee Historical Quarterly* 51 (Summer 1992):

87–95.

Skipper, Elvie Eagleton, and Ruth Grove, editors. "'Stray Thoughts': The Civil War Diary of Ethie M. Foute Eagleton, Part II." *East Tennessee Historical Society's Publications* 41 (1969): 116–28.

Smith, Daniel P. *Company K First Alabama Regiment, or Three Years in the Confederate Service.* Prattville, Ala.: By the Survivors, 1885.

Smith, Dwight L. "Impressment, Occupation, War's End, and Emancipation: Samuel E. Tillman's Account of Seesaw Tennessee." *Tennessee Historical Quarterly* 49 (Fall 1990): 177–87.

Smith, John David. "E. Merton Coulter, the 'Dunning School,' and *The Civil War and Readjustment in Kentucky.*" *Register of the Kentucky Historical Society* 86 (Winter 1988): 52–69.

Smith, Marion O. "The C. S. Nitre and Mining Bureau of East Tennessee." *East Tennessee Historical Society's Publications* 61 (1989): 29–47.

Smith, Timothy B. "Civil War Battlefield Preservation in Tennessee: A Nashville National Military Park Case Study." *Tennessee Historical Quarterly* 64 (Fall 2005): 236–47.

Smith, W. A., and Wallace Milam, editors. "The Death of John Hunt Morgan: A Memoir of James M. Fry." *Tennessee Historical Quarterly* 19 (Mar. 1960): 54–63.

Speizer, Matt. "The Ticket's Other Half: How and Why Andrew Johnson Received the 1864 Vice Presidential Nomination." *Tennessee Historical Quarterly* 65 (Spring 2006): 42–69.

Spevack, Edmund. "The *Report* (1865) and *Narrative* (1866) of Charles Christopher Follen." *Tennessee Historical Quarterly* 56 (Summer 1997): 112–43.

Sprague, Stuart Seely. "Slavery's Death Knell: Mourners and Revelers." *Filson Club History Quarterly* 65 (Oct. 1991): 441–73.

Storie, Melanie Greer. "'Heroic Courage and Unfaltering Devotion': A Gathering of East Tennessee Veterans." *Tennessee Historical Quarterly* 69 (Summer 2009): 174–97.

Strasser, William. "'A Terrible Calamity Has Befallen Us': Unionist Women in Civil War East Tennessee." *Journal of East Tennessee History* 71 (1999): 69–91.

Sutherland, Daniel. "The Savage War." *North & South* 11 (Aug. 2009): 68–76.

Swift, Lester L., editor. "Letters from a Sailor on a Tinclad." *Civil War History* 7 (Mar. 1961): 48–62.

Sword, Wiley. "The Desperation of the Hour." *Blue & Gray Magazine* 11 (Dec. 1993): 15–50.

———. "The Other Stonewall: The Short Life and Brilliant Career of Patrick Cleburne." *Civil War Times Illustrated* 36 (Feb. 1998): 36–44.

Taylor, Lenette S. "Uncle Sam's Landlord: Quartering the Union Army in Nashville in the Summer of 1863." *Tennessee Historical Quarterly* 61

(Winter 2002): 241–65.

Thomas, Ronald C. "The Founding of a Happy Town: Martin, Tennessee." *West Tennessee Historical Society Papers* 27 (1973): 5–17.

Townes, A. Jane. "Was Shelbyville Really a Union Town in a Confederate County?" *Tennessee Historical Quarterly* 69 (Summer 2009): 130–51.

Trimble, Sarah Ripley, editor. "Behind the Lines in Middle Tennessee, 1863–1865: The Journal of Bettie Ridley Blackmore." *Tennessee Historical Quarterly* 12 (Mar. 1953): 48–80.

Trudeau, Noah Andre. "'Kill the Last Damn One of Them': The Fort Pillow Massacre." In *With My Face to the Enemy: Perspectives on the Civil War,* edited by Robert Cowley, 382–94. New York: Berkley Books, 2001.

Tucker, David M. "Black Politics in Memphis, 1865–1875." *West Tennessee Historical Society Papers* 26 (1972): 13–19.

Turner, Martha L. "The Cause of the Union in East Tennessee." *Tennessee Historical Quarterly* 40 (Winter 1981): 366–80.

Valentine, L. L. "Sue Mundy of Kentucky, Part I." *Register of the Kentucky Historical Society* 62 (July 1964): 175–205.

———. "Sue Mundy of Kentucky, Part II." *Register of the Kentucky Historical Society* 62 (Oct. 1964): 278–306.

Vandiver, Frank. "General Hood as Logistician." *Military Affairs* 16 (Spring 1952): 1–11.

Waldrep, Christopher. "Rank-and-File Voters and the Coming of the Civil War: Caldwell County, Kentucky, as Test Case." *Civil War History* 35 (Mar. 1989): 59–72.

Walker, Cam. "Corinth: The Story of a Contraband Camp." *Civil War History* 20 (Mar. 1974): 5–22.

Wall, Lillian T., and Robert M. McBride, editors. "'An Extraordinary Perseverance': The Journal of Capt. Thomas J. Taylor, C.S.A." *Tennessee Historical Quarterly* 31 (Winter 1972): 328–59.

Wallenstein, Peter. "Which Side Are You On? The Social Origins of White Union Troops from Civil War Tennessee." *Journal of East Tennessee History* 63 (1991): 72–103.

Wasmer, Robert A. "Partisan Warfare in Monroe County, Tennessee, During the Civil War: The Murder of Joseph M. Divine." *Tennessee Historical Quarterly* 68 (Spring 2009): 67–97.

Webb, Ross A. "'The Past Is Never Dead, It's Not Even Past': Benjamin P. Runkle and the Freedmen's Bureau in Kentucky, 1866–1870." *Register of the Kentucky Historical Society* 84 (Autumn 1986): 343–60.

———. "A Yankee from Dixie: Benjamin Helm Bristow." *Civil War History* 10 (Mar. 1964): 80–94.

Weller, Jac. "The Logistics of Nathan Bedford Forrest." In *Military Analysis of the Civil War: An Anthology,* by the editors of *Military Affairs,* 170–

78. Millwood, N.Y.: KTO Press, 1977.

———. "Nathan Bedford Forrest: An Analysis of Untutored Military Genius." *Tennessee Historical Quarterly* 18 (Sept. 1959): 213–51.

Wenner, Joan. "The gunboat *Undine* traded sides during an 1864 raid by Nathan B. Forest along the Tennessee River." *America's Civil War,* Sept. 2004, 14, 16, 72.

Wilkie, Robert, "Hybrid Warfare: Something Old, Not Something New." *Air and Space Power Journal* 23 (Winter 2009): 13–17.

Wilkin, Mary, editor. "Some Papers of the American Cotton Planters' Association, 1865–1866." *Tennessee Historical Quarterly* 7 (Dec. 1948): 335–61.

Williams, Edward F., III. "The Johnsonville Raid and Nathan Bedford Forrest State Park." *Tennessee Historical Quarterly* 28 (Fall 1969): 225–51.

Williams, Kenneth H., and James Russell Harris, compilers. "Kentucky in 1860: A Statistical Overview." *Register of the Kentucky Historical Society* 103 (Autumn 2005): 743–69.

Williamson, J. C., editor. "The Civil War Diary of John Coffee Williamson." *Tennessee Historical Quarterly* 15 (Mar. 1956): 61–74.

Wills, W. Ridley, II. "Black-White Relationships on the Belle Meade Plantation." *Tennessee Historical Quarterly* 50 (Spring 1991): 17–32.

Wilson, Charles Reagan. "Bishop Thomas Frank Gailor: Celebrant of Southern Tradition." *Tennessee Historical Quarterly* 38 (Fall 1979): 322–31.

Wingfield, Marshall. "Tipton County Tennessee." *West Tennessee Historical Society Papers* 3 (1949): 5–26.

Woodbury, Mrs. Harry. "A Note on Shelby County." *Tennessee Historical Quarterly* 38 (Spring 1979): 79–82.

Yager, Wilson M. "The Sultana Disaster." *Tennessee Historical Quarterly* 25 (Fall 1976): 306–25.

Yonkers, Charles E. "The Civil War Transformation of George W. Smith: How a Western Kentucky Farmer Evolved from Unionist Whig to Pro-Southern Democrat." *Register of the Kentucky Historical Society* 103 (Autumn 2005): 661–90.

Young, J. P. "Hood's Failure at Spring Hill." *Confederate Veteran* 16 (Jan. 1908): 25–41.

Zebley, Kathleen R. "Unconditional Unionist: Samuel Mayes Arnell and Reconstruction in Tennessee." *Tennessee Historical Quarterly* 53 (Winter 1994): 245–59.

Newspapers

Clarksville (Tenn.) 83rd Illinoisan

Clarksville (Tenn.) Gazette
Clarksville (Tenn.) Weekly Chronicle
Covington *Kentucky Post*
Frankfort (Ky.) State Journal
Frederick (Md.) Examiner
Louisville Daily Journal
Maysville (Ky.) Bulletin
Middletown (Md.) Valley Register
Nashville Retrospect
Nashville Times
New York Herald
New York Tribune
Paducah Federal Union
Washington, D.C. National Tribune

Unpublished Material

Cabaniness, Jim R., transcriber. "Civil War Journal and Letters of Serg. Washington Ives, Fourth Florida C.S.A." Unpublished typescript. 1987.

Carter, Rosalie. "Captain Tod Carter: Confederate States Army." Unpublished study. Nov. 30, 1978.

Daniel, John S., Jr. "Special Warfare in Middle Tennessee and Surrounding Areas, 1861–1862." Master's thesis, Univ. of Tennessee, 1971.

Elliott, William Young, compiler. "'Most Lovely Lizzie': Love Letters of a Young Confederate Soldier." Unpublished typescript. Huntsville, Ala., 1958.

Gildrie, Richard, Phillip Kemmerly, and Thomas H. Winn. "Clarksville, Tennessee, in the Civil War: A Chronology." Typescript. Clarksville, Tenn., Sept. 1984.

Johnson, John F. "Triune in the Civil War." Typescript. Tennessee State Library and Archives, Nashville, n.d.

Map of United States Military Rail Roads, Showing the Rail Roads operated during the War from 1862–1866 as Military Lines, under the direction of Bvt. Brig. Gen. D. C. McCallum, Director and General Manager, 1866. Lithopress of J. Bien, New York, 1865.

McClain, Iris Hopkins. "A History of Houston County." Typescript. Columbia, Tenn., 1966.

Peterson, Gloria. "Administrative History, Fort Donelson National Military Park, Dover, Tennessee." Report prepared for the National Park Service, Division of History, Office of Archeology and Historic Preservation. Washington, D.C., June 30, 1968.

Tennessee Historical Society. The Battle of Nashville 1864: One Hundred and Fortieth Anniversary Symposium. Nashville, Dec. 10–11, 1864.

Wipfli, Ralph, and Steven Metz. "Coin of the Realm: U.S. Counterinsurgency Strategy." Colloquium brief, U.S. Army War College and Twenty-First Century Defense Initiative of the Brookings Institution. Carlisle Barracks, Pa., Oct. 22, 2007.

Index

513

INDEX

railroads, Union, 41, 73, 116, 117, 258, 348; Confederate raids on, 122, 159–60, **161**, 168–69, 177–78, 186–87, 199, 268–69, 270, 271–72, 300, 313, 316, 317, 351; defending, 86, **87**, 88–92, 94, 118, 119, 140, 197, 222, 373, 374; Sherman's control of, 116, 117, 186, 203, 211; as supply routes, 89, 91–92; in Tennessee, 387
Ramage, James, 160, 165
Ramsay, George D., 105
Ramsey, James G. M., 40, 46, 47, 67
Randall, James R., 146
Randolph, George, 10
Rankin, James E., 240
Richford, James Wylie, 81, 342
rearguard actions, Confederate, 157, 160, 174–75, 183, 189, 190, 197, 241, 271, 330, 334
rebels, 392–93. *See also* Confederacy, the; Confederate Army (CSA); secessionists
reconciliation, xiii, 355, 389, 398–99, 402
reconstruction, 116, 148, 387, 391–92; early, xiii–xiv, xv, 399; in East Tennessee, 9, 66; infrastructure for, 88, 125, 260; in Kentucky, 378, 384; in Tennessee, 13–19, 25, 98, 201–2, 204–5, 224, 355, 367–82. *See also* amnesty, Lincoln's proclamation of; restoration; stabilization
recruiting, Confederate, 179; by Forrest, 188, 191, 366, 367; in Kentucky, 137, 283, 361; by Lyon, 194, 244, 250, 366; in Tennessee, 104–6, 156, 316
recruiting, Union, 41, 222; of former Confederate soldiers, 84, 88; in Kentucky, 104, 257. *See also* blacks, Union recruitment of; draft, Union
Redd, Thomas M., 247
Red Hill, fighting at, 338
Red River expedition, Louisiana, 127
reenlistments: Confederate, 82; Union, 60, 62, 68, 75, 84–85, 86, 105
refugees: black, 215, 259–60; in Tennessee, 105, 300, 306, 308, 375
regionalism, 37, 68
Reid, Hugh T., 126
Reilly, James W., 294
Reindeer (Union gunboat), 312
reinforcements: Confederate, 302; Union, 99, 100, 305, 310, 315, 320
religious activities, 81, 84

Rembert Edward J., 1
Rentschler, Gottfried, 55, 60
Republican party, 157, 256. *See also* Radical Republicans
resistance, 9, 37, 38; southern, 8, 17, 41, 72, 391; in Tennessee, 202, 216
restoration, 396–402; of peace, 377–78, 389; of trade, 30, 377–78, 384; of U.S. citizenship, U.S., 102, 395. *See also* civil government, restoration of; peace, return of; reconstruction; Union, restoration of
reunionification. *See* Union, restoration of
Reynolds, Daniel Harris, 72
Rice, T. W., 311
Richards, Marie, 391–92
Richardson, Robert V., 384
Richie, W. T., xi–xii
Richmond, Lewis, 33–34
Richmond, Virginia, 121, 157, 180; fall of, 308, 358, 368, 369
Ridley, Bromfield, 311
Riggs, Bob, gang of, 356
Ripley, William Young, xi, xii
rivers, 219, 351; army-navy cooperation on, xiv, 1–2; defending, 118, 143; strategic importance of, 116, 117–18; as supply routes, 89, 92, 96; transportation on, 9, 26. *See also* Cumberland River; Mississippi River; Ohio River; Tennessee River
Roberts, Albert, 384
Roberts, Thad, 354
Robertson, George, 22
Robinson, Armstead L., 12
Robinson, James F., 20
Roddey, Philip D., 76, 178, 185, 224, 271, 273, 278, 336, 338; raids by, 197, 207
Rogersville, Tennessee, 63
Rosecrans, Fortress, 94, 315, 373
Rosecrans, William "Old Rosy", 18, 19, 225, 351, 369; in East Tennessee, 33, 34, 35, 38; at Nashville, 309, 318–19
Rosenberger, Randolph, 285
Ross, Lawrence S., 315
Rousseau, Lovell H., 96–98, 118–19, 125, 201–2, 203, 204, 225; at Battle of Nashville, 301–2, 322; counterguerrilla operations, 137, 138, 167–68, 176, 178, 187, 188, 359; at Murfreesboro, 314, 315
Rucker, Edmund W., 311, 330
Ruger, Thomas, 290